arya

DGP

The Hindustan Times
Medallist in Journalism

Prof. R.S. Dhillon's

LATEST PROBABLE ESSAYS

- **135 Full-fledged Essays with Synopsis, Aid to Vocabulary and Points to Remember**
  On Scientific Topics, Educational Topics, Social Topics, Quotation Topics, Reflective Topics, Economic Issues, Political & Current Topics
- **And Exclusive Sections on**
  Guided Composition-20 Topics, Latest Material on G.K. & Current Topics for Hundreds of Essays

Prof. R.S. Dhillon
M.A., P.G. Dip. in Journalism (Bombay)
Formerly Head, Department of English,
Aggarwal Postgraduate College, Faridabad

Recipient of:
'H.R. Gokhale Medal in Journalism',
'The Hindustan Times Medal in Journalism',
The Federation of Educational Publishers in India
'Distinguished Author' Award.

arya

ARYA PUBLISHING COMPANY
Village Johron, Trilokpur Road, Kala Amb 173 030, Distt. Sirmour (HP)
Delhi Office: 1569/30, Naiwala Street, Karol Bagh, New Delhi 110 005 (India)

arya

Earlier Editions of this book were published by **Dhillon Group of Publications**.

Published by:
Dr Vipin Gupta
ARYA PUBLISHING COMPANY
Village Johron, Trilokpur Road, Kala Amb, Distt. Sirmour (HP)

Delhi Office:
1569/30, Naiwala Street
Karol Bagh, New Delhi 110 005 (India)
Ph.: 011-41067632
E-mail: info@aryapublishing.com
Website: www.aryapublishing.com

ISBN–978-81–8296–722-9

First Edition : 1998
Ninteenth Edition : 2018
Reprint : 2019, 22
Reprint : 2023

Price: ₹ 550.00

Typeset & Designed at
Laser Tech Prints

Printed at:
Goyal Offset Works (P) Ltd.
Kundli, Haryana

LATEST

PROBABLE ESSAYS

Essay Writing is an art, not entirely creative, though not without the potential to satisfy the creative urges present in the intellectual. It is indeed a happy blend of intellect and creativity.

Some Novel Features

- *Judicious selection of topics*
- *Coverage of a wide variety of topics*
- *Synopsis i.e. gist of the entire essay given in a few lines*
- *Logical development of the theme*
- *A plethora of facts and figures to add power and punch to essays*
- *Objective and unbiased presentation*
- *Aid to Vocabulary—meanings given of all difficult words so that the reader has not to repeatedly refer to the dictionary or go to the Google.*
- *Points to Remember—should prove very handy for rapid revision.*
- *Guided Composition: An absolutely new section has been incorporated. It has 20 topics. The gist of the topic has been provided in approximately 150 words. They have to be developed into full-fledged essays in 800-1000 words. It should be a great learning experience.*
- *Latest Material on G.K. and Current Topics—This section is aimed at helping the reader refresh his knowledge of basic facts and inform him of the latest developments in all fields, to facilitate him to make use of the same in writing of Essays and to enable him to write essays an hundreds of additional topics.*
- *Quotable Quotes—These quotations, if used judiciously, add lustre, charm and credibility to Essays.*

PREFACE
Extracts from the Previous Editions

★

We have refused to move even an inch on the often trodden and beaten track. It needs hard labour and earnest effort to lay a new pitch, that too, a good solid one with even bounce. Not the one to fight shy on these counts, we have literally tried to open new vistas in our endeavour to provide a different genre of a book on essay writing.

★

Encouraged, No, Bowled Over, Yes. The nice sounding words, the well-reasoned appreciative letters received from members of the teaching community and hardworking career conscious students have delighted us. The previous editions of our book 'Latest Probable Essays', have withstood the test of time and won your trust. We could not have asked for more. The laurels, however, have added to our sense of responsibility.

PREFACE
to the Current Edition

The entire book has been rewritten, making judicious selection of the topics. Some topics from our earlier editions had to make way for fresh entrants—the topics which are currently in vogue. We could ill afford to ignore the developments in all arenas, in all continents, even in space and as such they have made their way into the present edition. All the essays have been written in an objective manner and relevant information and latest data have been incorporated.

It is hoped that the present revised edition will be well-received by both the teachers and the students and fulfil our basic objective of presenting a still better version of our, by now, fairly popular book—Latest Probable Essays.

—R. S. Dhillon

CONTENTS

Section A : (Pages 1-678)
Section B : (Pages 679-792)

Quotation Topics

Reflective Topics

Economic Issues

Political & Current Topics

GUIDED COMPOSITION—A GREAT LEARNING EXPERIENCE : List of the Essay is given in approximately 150 words. Full-fledged Essays to be developed in 800-1000 words.

THE ART AND SCIENCE OF ESSAY WRITING

Essay writing is both an art and a science. While it can satisfy the creative urge of a good writer, it also needs discipline of the mind. It is indeed a happy blend of intellect and creativity. It takes skill to organise the matter methodically. The following points may be kept in mind while writing an essay.

Format of an Essay

Introduction: The opening paragraph should introduce the topic and provide the necessary background.

Body of the Essay: All points should be properly developed. Arguments in support of and against the topic may be given in different paragraphs. Long paragraphs should be avoided.

Conclusion: Issues highlighted and arguments put forth in the body of the essay should be rounded off nicely. The conclusion should in essence sum up the whole essay.

Ingredients of an Impressive Essay

Planning: Before starting to write the essay, note down all points, facts and figures. A good building needs a proper sketch. Similarly, a good essay needs to be properly planned. Make a proper plan and execute it well.

Simple Language: Simple language is the hallmark of a good essay. Appropriate words should be used. Short sentences make for pleasant reading. The chances of committing grammatical errors are also reduced if one avoids long sentences. Slangs and colloquial language should be avoided.

Facts and Figures: Facts and figures add punch and lend weight to the arguments. Only correct and relevant facts should be incorporated in the essay. Extreme views must be avoided. Views expressed should be unbiased and unprejudiced.

Coherence and Clarity: All the issues raised and arguments given for and against thereof should be logical. Continuity must be maintained. Haphazard approach should be avoided. Precision and clarity must be ensured.

Different Types of Essays

(*i*) *Descriptive Essays* require precise knowledge on the part of the writer. Essays on Scientific, Educational, Political, Economic and Current topics should contain relevant facts and figures. For example, describing a historical monument would entail providing information about its geographical location, the year of its construction, the person who got it built, the details pertaining to its design and architectural beauty or its weaknesses, and most importantly, the story or the legend behind its construction.

(*ii*) *Biographical Essays* require knowledge of the major events in the life of the person the account of whose life is being given. In addition to that, the essay should mention the qualities or character of the 'hero', his achievements, his struggles and his principles.

(*iii*) *Narrative Essays* can be presented in the form of a story. Chronological arrangement of events is the distinctive feature of such essays. Also, the narration should be made as interesting as possible by making use of episodes which fit in the context. For example, the narration of the first day at college should make a mention of some funny incident. A journey by train or aeroplane should include some exciting experiences.

(*iv*) *Reflective Essays* require deep thinking on the part of the writer. These essays are abstract in nature and demand imagination and capacity to express ideas in a concrete manner.

(*v*) *Idiomatic Essays* need elaboration of the idiom, its relevance in everyday life, advantages that will accrue if the wisdom contained in the idiom is practised, limitations in its application, etc. Examples to illustrate the usefulness of the idiom should be quoted. While writing an idiomatic essay, one should have a clear understanding of the meaning of the idiom, otherwise the whole essay will go haywire.

Essay 1

SCIENCE HAS BENEFITED US, BUT HAS IT CIVILISED US?

SYNOPSIS

The primitive man wondered at the many facets of nature and held it in great reverence. The great advancements made in science have shrunk the world and have provided great comforts and conveniences to mankind. Many diseases have been eliminated and sufferings of man, considerably reduced. However, urbanisation and industrialisation have harmed the flora and fauna. Atomic energy, if used for peaceful purposes, can work wonders, but if used for destructive purposes, may annihilate all living creatures. Science has empowered man, but he must learn to use it for the good of humanity.

To the primitive man, the earth was like a *platter*[1]. He dared not venture to places unknown to him, lest he should fall off the edges. The sun, the moon and the stars amazed him. These heavenly bodies were held in great *reverence*[2]. He was helpless and at the mercy of Nature. Hence, he worshipped its forces. The invention of wheel and the discovery of fire were remarkable achievements of the primitive man.

The *advent*[3] of science has *altered*[4] the life of man. With his intellect, man has proved his superiority over all the other beings in Nature. Man ventured out into the sea and discovered new lands. He discovered that the earth is round and it revolves around the sun. He understood the law of gravitation. Subsequently, he invented the telephone. This invention shrank the world and man felt well-connected with far off places. Aeroplanes, trains, cars, buses and two-wheelers became his modes of transportation.

With the advancement of science, man invented objects which eased his work, provided him comfort and *recreation*[5]. It is only with the help of science that man has been able to conquer not only this earth but space also. The successful landing of man on the moon in 1969 was 'a small step for man, but a giant leap for mankind'.

The advancement in medical science has reduced human suffering to a great extent. Continuous research and experiments have led to one breakthrough after another and the life-threatening diseases of the past, namely, malaria, tuberculosis, small pox, etc., are no longer incurable. Their pathogens and causes have been identified and lines of treatment, worked out. Epidemics like cholera and plague have been *eradicated*[6] from the face of the earth. Today, the human body can be operated upon to remove cancerous tumours and to rectify any malady that may be affecting normal life. Research and development vis-á-vis drugs and antibiotics has brought relief from a plethora of ailments afflicting human lives. This has not only lowered the mortality rate but has also increased life expectancy.

With the technological advancements in space research, artificial satellites have been launched to augment communication. These satellites have helped in broadcasting, communication, meteorology and many other sectors. The invention of mobile phones, Internet, fax and e-mail have further shrunk the size of the globe.

Technological innovations such as the Bluetooth wireless service have revolutionised communication. Wireless technology undoubtedly has contributed to the trend towards remote teleworking. Working from home has become a viable option.

Agriculture too, has benefited from scientific advances. Improved methods of irrigation, better quality seeds and use of fertilisers have increased crop yield. New hybrid seeds and drought-resistant seeds have also helped to increase the yield. New tools and equipments, tractors and harvesters have benefited the farmers in different ways. Science has enabled man to identify the diseases affecting crops and to find out remedies.

Atomic energy when harnessed by man for peaceful purposes, yields remarkable results. Isotopes of some radioactive materials are used to cure diseases. Atomic energy is used to run reactors to produce electricity. It has proved to be a *viable*[7] alternative to the fossil fuels. Some isotopes are also used to sterilise crops and vegetables to keep them free from diseases. Carbon-14 is used by archaeologists to find the exact age of an organic fossil.

The *multifarious*[8] changes brought about by the advancement in science and technology have indeed proved to be a boon to human life. However, the flip side of this seems nothing short of a bane for, science has arguably de-humanised man. The readily available medical assistance has led to non-dependence on kith and kin, sounding the death-knell for human ties. Some medicos overcharge patients and *unscrupulously*[9] prescribe medicines and tests that are not required. The space and rocket sciences have increased offensives and atrocities, and aided militancy and extremism. Knowledge of means and methods of enhancing agricultural yield has promoted misuse of hazardous chemicals in crops. The *burgeoning*[10] of motorised vehicles has not only clogged the pathways but also poisoned the air that is inhaled, thus endangering the *flora and fauna*[11] in addition to posing a threat to human survival.

Better healthcare has led to a boom in human population that obviously consumes much more and thereby depletes earth's resources; exerts so much pressure on earth as to cause earthquakes and tsunamis; and tampers with Nature so much as to let loose Nature's fury in the form of cyclones, blizzards and hurricanes, etc.

So, when man ignores humanity and brutally pursues materialism, can he be called civilised? Well, civilisation pertains to advancement in social development; and science, *irrefutably*[12], has brought social change and development in human life.

With the arms and ammunitions available the world over, the earth can be annihilated altogether a hundred times. Still the earth along with all its living beings and non living things exists and is intact. Isn't this enough evidence to prove that Science has civilised mankind? Experiences and experiments have taught us that the philosophy of co-existence has no alternative.

Only about a century ago, the means of information and communication were not that developed. People in one region of the world or even within the same country did not know about the famines, floods and other disasters taking place in another region. But now, with the help of science, if people suffer anywhere on the earth, help reaches there immediately. Food supplies, medicines and other relief measures reach there in no time and all efforts are made to *mitigate*[13] their sufferings. This has become possible because science has revolutionised human life and has also made man more civilised.

Science of course, may not be able to change the basic nature of man. Man has always aspired for *pelf*[14] and power. Science cannot be held responsible for this. Science has aided the spread of knowledge. The print and electronic media have helped man to *disseminate*[15] knowledge. Science has made man aware of all the developments around the world. It has definitely provided him the tools. How he makes use of science and knowledge is up to him. Whether he uses a fork to eat or hurt his tongue with it, is purely his choice. Science has definitely led man on the path of civilisation. To what extent, man is civilised—only time will tell.

Aid to Vocabulary

1. *Platter* — a large flat plate
2. *Reverence* — feeling of high respect
3. *Advent* — arrival
4. *Altered* — changed

5. *Recreation* — amusement
6. *Eradicated* — got rid of, removed
7. *Viable* — able to succeed in operation
8. *Multifarious* — many and various
9. *Unscrupulously* — dishonestly
10. *Burgeoning* — growing rapidly
11. *Flora and fauna* — vegetation and wildlife
12. *Irrefutably* — (it) cannot be denied
13. *Mitigate* — to make something less severe, violent or painful
14. *Pelf* — wealth
15. *Disseminate* — to spread (ideas, beliefs) widely

Points to Remember

1. Primitive man held Nature in great reverence.
2. Various discoveries and inventions have altered man's life.
3. Modes of recreation were found out and conquest of the moon accomplished (1969).
4. Science has helped in the eradication and prevention of various diseases.
5. Artificial satellites have helped in communication and other sectors.
6. Bluetooth wireless service has revolutionised communication system.
7. Agriculture has benefited from scientific advances.
8. Atomic energy benefits man, when harnessed for peaceful purposes.
9. Man, by misusing science, has brought about unfavourable conditions on the earth.
10. Science may not be able to change the basic nature of man but it has revolutionised human life and also made us more civilised.

GUIDED COMPOSITION

Develop the following paragraph into a full-fledged essay in 800-1000 words. The gist of the topic is provided in approximately 180 words for your help:

BIOTERRORISM : THE BANE OF TECHNOLOGICAL ADVANCE

The impressive strides made in the field of science and technology has made us proud. It has also definitely helped us in improving the quality of our lives. Faster cars, super computers, mobile phones, cure for most diseases - all these have helped us. But the improvement in technology is almost like a double-edged weapon. The same technology that can cure deadly diseases can also create antigens that can cause diseases. In fact, biological weapons can be as threatening as nuclear weapons. Perhaps until 9/11 no one really took the threat seriously. Unleashing a strain of anthrax, small pox or plague can be as devastating as detonating a nuclear bomb and it is all the more easy. Moreover, some of these viruses have the capacity to wipe out human beings alone without causing any damage to the infrastructure around and this will definitely increase the stakes. Several attempts have been initiated to curb the menace. The US has launched Project Bio Shield to develop and purchase drugs and vaccines to combat bioterrorism. Firms like Anacor and DynPort are developing effective medications against anthrax. We, in India should also be alert and embark upon, prevent and control the danger of bioterrorism. *(180 words)*

Essay 2

SCIENCE—A BLESSING OR A CURSE?

SYNOPSIS

Everything in the universe has its uses and abuses. The same axiom applies to Science. Science has revolutionised human existence. It has made man's life more comfortable. Electricity is one of the greatest wonders of modern science. The growth of fast modes of transport and communication has transformed the world into a global village. In the field of agriculture, science has helped to increase the crop production and improve its quality. Science has enabled man to diagnose and treat many dangerous diseases. Information technology and computers have revolutionised our lifestyles. But, its misuse in many cases, has turned the boon of science into the bane of humanity. Science has posed a threat to the very existence of mankind by making it possible to produce all sorts of weapons—nuclear, biological, chemical, etc. Cyber crime is the latest addition to the list of crimes. Misapplication of science has led mankind on the path of destruction. We should use science to avail ourselves of its blessings and not misuse it to make it a curse.

Science has *revolutionised*[1] human existence. Much of the progress that mankind has made in different fields right from the stone age to the modern day is due to the advancement made in the field of science. Not only material progress but also the mental outlook of man has been influenced by the same. It has made man's life very comfortable. Agriculture, business, transport, communication and medicine, to name a few, are all highly indebted to the wonders science has produced. We have become more advanced socially and culturally. This is so because the world has undergone a tremendous change due to the rapid strides made in the field of science and technology.

With the discovery of the fire and subsequently the wheel—the era of modern science began. Electricity is one of the greatest wonders of modern science. It is a phenomenal source of energy. It can run any type of machinery. With the help of electricity, we can light our rooms, run trams and trains, and draw water for irrigation.

The discovery and development of a large number of powerful energy sources—coal, petroleum, natural gas, electricity, etc., have facilitated the growth of fast modes of transport and communication, which in turn have changed the world into a *global village*[2]. Science has given man numerous modes of transport and travel—cars, trains, aeroplanes, ships, etc. Man has even reached the moon.

Fast modes of transport are of great utility for sending foodgrains to victims of famine or medical help to eradicate epidemics across the globe. At the disposal of miscreants, they aid crime by transporting to distant places in a matter of hours, agents and weapons of mass destruction.

Science has benefited agriculture too. The food production level and food quality have improved greatly. Soil analysis, hybrid varieties of crops, fertilisers, pesticides, advanced tools and machinery, improved irrigation and harvesting methods, etc., have all contributed to the increase in the production of crops.

Today, we have stationed in outer space meteorological satellites for sending data and pictures to earth stations and helping agricultural scientists find and analyse soil patterns. Satellites also help them *trace*[3] the progress of rains, winds and even *locusts*[4] that endanger crops. Satellites can even forewarn about natural *calamities*[5] like hurricanes which cause heavy damage.

Science has enabled man to *diagnose*[6] and treat many dangerous diseases. Open-heart surgeries, organ transplants, etc., have all become possible. A number of killer diseases are now curable. Diseases such as smallpox, polio, plague, malaria, etc., have almost been eradicated. Hidden diseases in the body can be diagnosed easily with the help of X-rays. Scientists have succeeded in *cloning*[7] animals. The methods of diagnosis, prevention and treatment have developed fast. As a result of tremendous progress in medical science, the average life expectancy of human beings has increased.

Man, with the help of science, has been able to increase longevity, arrest to a considerable extent the gradual decay of human body, and control the spread of *lethal*[8] diseases by making extraordinary *life-prolonging*[9] drugs and medicines. Diseases like tuberculosis and many kinds of cancer which were considered fatal, a few decades ago, are no longer incurable.

One of the biggest achievements of science happens to be in the field of entertainment. Leisure management industry, with television shows, music concerts and films, is emerging as the largest and the most important industry in the twenty-first century. Satellite television has made it possible for millions of people to watch sporting and entertainment events taking place in different parts of the world, simultaneously.

Information technology and computers have revolutionised our lifestyles.

Automation in banks and railway stations has provided relief to the public and staff alike. Ticketing and reservation have become more efficient and convenient. In medical diagnosis, computers are used to locate and investigate accurately and precisely any abnormality or disease. The Internet has some very useful applications in our day-to-day life. Mobile phones are the outcome of advanced information technology.

However, there is a flip side to the wonders of science. It is said, science is a good servant but a bad master. As a servant it makes our life comfortable. But, as a master, science is capable of causing extensive destruction and wiping out entire mankind. It cannot be denied that the boon in many cases, has turned out to be the bane. There are innumerable examples which prove that science, a blessing, has been turned into a curse by man.

Sir Alfred Nobel experimented with *dynamite*[10] to clear huge mountains but modern man uses it to kill his fellowmen. The destructive potential of atomic energy was witnessed in August 1945, when the United States dropped atom bombs on the two Japanese cities of Hiroshima and Nagasaki. Those who survived the nuclear bombing suffered its aftermath. It is a highly disturbing fact that much of the national income of a developing country is spent on acquiring the latest weapons, bombs and missiles. Guns, revolvers, tanks, fighter planes, explosives, nuclear bombs, etc., were invented to develop a strong security system so as to protect the innocent masses, but their misuse is now crushing humanity. Apart from nuclear weapons, man has also started stockpiling biological and chemical weapons. These weapons are lethal.

Biotechnology is a great boon for fighting diseases, but along with medicines, dangerous biological weapons have also been developed. Germs are deliberately released into the air to spread diseases. Anthrax envelopes are used for spreading terrorism.

The negative effects of excessive use of fertilisers to increase yield, and of pesticides to ward off pests, are now evident. Soil salinity has increased. Traces of DDT are found in plants. Humans consume the same produce and ingest the toxins along, leading to various health complications.

Establishment and expansion of factories has resulted in all-round pollution. Motor vehicles emit a lot of poisonous substances into the atmosphere. This has led to the *depletion*[11] of the ozone layer and has resulted in global warming.

Television, a good source of entertainment, education and information, has its negative effects too. There are many programmes which promote violence and vulgarity, and teenagers are more interested in watching these programmes. Exposure to aggressiveness and violence at an early age may lead youngsters to commit shocking crimes. Sometimes, even people of mature age learn and apply different methods of committing crimes from TV serials and movies.

The power of the Internet is also being abused through unhealthy practices such as displaying *pornographic*[12] material or spreading malicious content to ruin someone's reputation. Lots of people spend their time in chat rooms for *obscene*[13] interactions. The Internet is increasingly being misused for spamming, hacking, phishing, defaming and other illegal activities.

Science has two faces—good and bad. It depends on us which face of science we want to let emerge. If we use the gifts of science in a positive manner with positive intention and in the positive direction, it will benefit mankind, but if we misuse it, the same will prove to be pervasively harmful. To save the world from destruction, we should use the gifts of science ethically and judiciously.

Aid to Vocabulary

1. *Revolutionised* — completely changed
2. *Global village* — the world as a single village
3. *Trace* — find out
4. *Locusts* — large insects that live in hot countries and fly in very large groups, destroying all the plants and crops of an area
5. *Calamities* — an event that causes great harm or damage, a disaster
6. *Diagnose* — to identify a disease
7. *Cloning* — the process of producing an organism artificially from the cell of a single ancestor
8. *Lethal* — causing or able to cause death
9. *Life-prolonging* — extending the span of life
10. *Dynamite* — explosive material
11. *Depletion* — reduce in quantity
12. *Pornographic* — showing of naked people or sexual acts
13. *Obscene* — indecent

Points to Remember

1. Science has revolutionised human existence.
2. Electricity is one of the greatest wonders of science.
3. The fast modes of transport and communication have changed the world into a global village.

4. Science is a help in the agricultural field also.
5. We have scores of meteorological satellites in space.
6. Science has enabled man to diagnose and treat many dangerous diseases.
7. Information technology and computers have revolutionised our lifestyles.
8. Science—a blessing, in many cases, has been turned into a curse by man.
9. Weapons pose a danger to mankind.
10. The world is facing the problem of all-round pollution.
11. Negative effects of television and the Internet can be seen everywhere.
12. Science should be used for peaceful purposes and positive developments.

THIS PILL LIGHTS UP TUMOURS, HELPS SPOT CANCER

Scientists have developed a new pill that can improve cancer screening by lighting up tumours and help doctors better distinguish between cancerous and benign growths.

The pill contains an imaging agent that selectively binds to cancer cells or blood vessels that are unique to tumours.

Once attached to its target, the dye fluoresces under near infrared light. Although at this wavelength, fluorescent tumours can only be detected 1 to 2 centimetres deep, pairing the technique with ultrasound in the same instrument should be able to detect most cancers. Testing in mice showed that with the proper formulation, a considerable proportion—50 to 60%—of the agent gets absorbed into the bloodstream. It also binds specifically to cancer cells with little background noise in the image. The fluorescent signal from the tumour is far stronger than the signal from the surrounding tissue.

Essay 3

ATOMIC ENERGY: ITS PEACEFUL USE AND APPLICATION IN INDIA

SYNOPSIS

A conference was organised by the United Nations on August 8, 1955 to discuss the future uses of atomic energy. Atomic energy has the potential to produce creative forces which may bring about tremendous change in our society. By the use of atomic energy, we can explore difficult regions. It can be used in the field of agriculture. It can also be used in the field of crime detection. In October, 2008, India signed and sealed a nuclear deal with the USA. The deal will not only help to generate nuclear or atomic power, but will also benefit trade in high-technology areas. It brightens up the employment opportunities in the country. The future of mankind largely depends on the handling of atomic energy. It should not be used for destructive purposes. The proper utilisation of atomic energy promises benefits of great proportions for humanity.

A conference was organised by the United Nations on August 8, 1955 to discuss the future uses of atomic energy. On this occasion, the eminent scientist Dr Homi J. Bhabha had said, "major wars should ultimately become impossible and the area of peaceful existence should eventually cover the globe." He also said, "I venture to predict that a method will be found for liberating fusion energy in a controlled manner within the next two decades. When that happens, the energy problem of the world will truly have been solved for ever for the fuel will be as plentiful as the heavy hydrogen in the oceans."

Atomic energy is regarded as one of the important sources of *inexhaustible*[1] energy. Atomic energy has the potential to produce creative forces which may bring about tremendous change in our society. Atomic energy has been successfully used to create passages for the flow of water in rocky regions, to divert the courses of rivers, to sail ships and operate *submarines*[2] and to act as power fuel in a number of other ways.

It is very likely that our conventional sources of energy, namely coal, petroleum and natural gas will be exhausted completely during the next one hundred years. The ever-increasing requirement of energy in India, thanks to its swelling population, has created a crisis. However, energy crisis, is not confined to India alone. The developed countries like the USA, Russia, Germany, Japan, etc., too, are facing this problem. There is a direct and close relation between the availability of energy and the growth of a country. So, the only desirable option is to use atomic energy for peaceful purposes directed towards economic advancement.

The peaceful use of atomic energy *ensures*[3] great benefits to humanity. By the use of it, we can *explore*[4] difficult regions which lie deep down in the rivers, lakes and oceans and discover the hidden treasure, i.e. minerals. Not only this, space journey is also greatly facilitated by the use of atomic energy. Through this, we are able to explore distant heavenly bodies. The radioactive particles are being employed to *eradicate*[5] diseases like cancer from the face of earth. To treat thyroid cancer iodine-131 is mostly used. Cobalt 60 from gamma rays is used for sterilisation of many medical products. It is cheaper and effective. A disposable syringe is one such example.

Atomic energy can also be used in the field of agriculture. It can protect the crops from harmful insects. By using radio-isotopes which are a by-product of nuclear fission, the growth of flies can be controlled. It can also be useful in the preservation of various food items. Isotopes hydrology technique can be used to measure and trace ground water resources. Radio active isotopes help in detecting pollution. Those are also helpful in determining the age of rocks and minerals.

One of the most important uses of nuclear energy is in the field of crime detection. It helps us to detect 'finger prints' and it is also used to get the quantitative measurements of the trace elements. These are regarded as indisputable proof in crime detection and cannot be challenged in the court of law. Evidently, atomic energy will dominate the sphere of technological development in our society. Thus, peaceful use of atomic energy may change the course of evolution of mankind.

Today, nuclear energy is the only viable option to generate adequate power for supplementing the ever-increasing need of our society. India is the only country which has not signed the Non-Proliferation Treaty (NPT) and yet has been able to get the waiver from the NSG (National Suppliers Group).

India's legal right to conduct nuclear tests has been fully preserved and the country has not made any *commitment*[6] in this regard to gain waiver from the NSG to participate in nuclear commerce. As the NSG waiver opens the gates for nuclear trade with India, the nuclear power generation scenario in the country is set to change completely in the forthcoming years, with both foreign investment and technology coming India's way.

At present, India has 20 nuclear reactors in operation generating 4,780 MW, while seven other plants are under construction and are expected to generate an additional 5,300 MW. India's nuclear power industry is undergoing rapid expansion with plans to increase nuclear power output to 64,000 MW by 2032*. Approximately 16 per cent of the world's electricity is produced by 439 nuclear power reactors . The use of nuclear energy helps not only to reduce the greenhouse gas emissions but also to save the cost of transport and extraction.

In October 2008, India signed and sealed a nuclear deal with the United States. The deal will not only help to generate nuclear or atomic power, but also will benefit trade in high-technology areas like pharma, semi-conductors, precision engineering, defence equipment, advanced and speciality chemicals, electronics, sensors, environmental technology, space, automation and robotics. The nuclear deal also brightens up employment opportunities in the country. It will not only increase the demand for nuclear engineers but also for mechanical, civil and electronic engineers.

India is looking for an alternative to fulfil its energy requirements. Due to the high cost and limited supply of fossil fuel, India will have to utilise nuclear energy as an alternative energy source. Some applications of the nuclear industry, for instance, fission energy, fusion energy, radioactive waste management, environmental applications, medical applications, etc., hold the promise of *exponential*[7] growth in related career avenues. These are the areas where intense research is going on and a considerable shortage of manpower also exists.

All these developments suggest that India may potentially become a major nuclear equipment supplier to the whole world in a decade or so. The multinationals of France, the US and Japan want to manufacture nuclear equipments in India to meet not just Indian but also global demand.

The determination of the future of mankind largely depends on the handling of atomic energy. If utilised properly, it will be an immense source of power and will serve humanity well. Our policy makers should be responsible enough to ensure its peaceful usage for the larger benefit of mankind.

Aid to Vocabulary

1. *Inexhaustible* — that cannot be exhausted or used up
2. *Submarines* — warships capable of operating underwater
3. *Ensures* — makes certain

*As per India 2014

4. *Explore* — travel through in order to learn about it
5. *Eradicate* — root out, destroy completely
6. *Commitment* — an engagement or obligation that restricts freedom of action
7. *Exponential* — of or increasing by extraordinary proportions

Points to Remember

1. A conference was organised by the United Nations on August 8, 1955 to discuss the future uses of atomic energy.
2. Atomic energy is regarded as one of the important sources of inexhaustible energy.
3. The peaceful use of atomic energy promises great benefits to humanity.
4. Atomic energy can be used in agriculture.
5. It can be used in the field of crime detection.
6. By establishing more nuclear reactors, currently under construction, India can generate an additional 5,300 MW energy, which is a great leap forward from the present 4,780 MW.
7. In October 2008, India signed and sealed a nuclear deal with the United States.
8. The Nuclear deal also benefits trade in high technology areas.
9. The Nuclear deal brightens up the employment opportunities in the country.
10. The future of mankind largely depends on the handling of atomic energy.

NUCLEAR AND ATOMIC ENERGY

Nuclear Power Generation (2010-11 to 2016-17)

Year	Gross Generation (MUs)	Capacity Factor (%)	Availability Factor (%)
2016-17 (Upto September-2016)	18988	78	80
2015-16	37456	75	77
2014-15	37835	82	88
2013-14	35333	83	88
2012-13	32863	80	90
2011-12	32455	79	91
2010-11	26472	71	89

WHAT IS ATOM?

The word 'atom' has been derived from the Greek word 'a-tomio' which means 'uncutable' or 'non-divisible'. The atomic theory of matter was first proposed on a firm scientific basis by John Dalton, a British school teacher in 1808. According to Dalton's atomic theory, all matter, whether an element, a compound, or a mixture is composed of all particles called atoms.

Essay 4

SCIENCE AND WAR

SYNOPSIS

If science is a blessing to mankind, it is also a vehicle of war. Nuclear weapons have now become a reality after the Chinese had first invented gunpowder. Nuclear war started with the bombing of Nagasaki and Hiroshima during the Second World War. Lakhs of people died. The Gulf War II shattered Iraq economically. Modern wars are no longer confined to the battlefield. Major cities or whole nations are targetted. Developing countries like India and Pakistan would have already become developed nations had they not spent crores of rupees towards the accumulation of weapons. There are military stations and spy satellites in space which pose a threat to mankind. Man should use nuclear energy for beneficial purposes rather than for killing fellow human beings.

Science is a blessing to mankind. Man has been able to provide himself with all the basic comforts. He has turned the world into a *global village*[1]. All this has come to be only because of science. But, of late, man has started misusing science. Science has become the medium for the manufacture of destructive nuclear weapons. The entire mankind will be wiped out if a nuclear war happens. However, science is not to blame for this. Man should use science for the progress of mankind.

Science has been made an active associate of war since the Chinese first invented gunpowder. Initially, it was used in firecrackers. That was a harmless use, but soon man began to misuse gunpowder for destructive purposes.

Man has applied science to manufacture weapons of mass destruction. Many people lost their lives because of the two major wars, World War I and World War II in the twentieth century than would have been killed since the time of known history. Over twenty million people including innocent men, women and children were killed in the First World War (1914-18) and more than thrice that number lost their lives during the Second World War (1939-1945).

With the bombing of Hiroshima and Nagasaki (in Japan) in August 1945, World War II came to an end. Property worth millions of rupees was destroyed. But it was the loss of numerous lives as well as the *aftermath*[2] which shook the whole world.

The Americans had used Uranium 235 on Hiroshima and Plutonium on Nagasaki. The people who survived, suffered from *mutation*[3] caused by the radiation from these radioactive elements. The descendants of those affected by the radiation carry genetically inherited traces of mutations to this day.

The Gulf War II (Iraq attacked by America) left Iraq shell-shocked. Airports, hospitals, schools, irrigation systems, transport links, etc., were severely affected and the economy was completely devastated. The main purpose behind the war was to *unearth*[4] 'Weapons of Mass Destruction.'

Today, the nuclear powers like the USA and Russia have enough nuclear weapons to destroy the entire world over a hundred times. More countries are likely to join the nuclear power club in the near future.

Modern wars are fought with scientific weapons like tanks, guns, bombs, missiles, aeroplanes and rockets. Wars have extended from land to sea, and then from sea to air.

Man does not spare a thought while using weapons for killing his own fellow-beings. This is because of the lack of humanitarian values. He has become a remorseless slave of machines. His attitude towards his fellow-beings has become purely mechanical. So devoid of emotions is he, that he has become insensitive towards the softer and finer aspects of life.

Modern wars are more deadly and destructive than ancient ones were. In ancient times, war was confined to a battlefield, but today even public places, schools, hospitals, etc., are not spared. Loss of life and property is tremendous. A country with a small population but adequate *armament*[5] can threaten another country with a large population but inadequate weaponry.

Developing countries like India and Pakistan have invested crores of rupees in buying and manufacturing nuclear weapons. Had this amount been used for economic development, they would have, probably, already become developed nations. Wars destroy life and property on both sides. What is achieved is little compared to all that is lost in a war. Many innocent people lose their lives. All nations should unite and co-operate to do away with nuclear weapons. They should realise the essence of universal brotherhood. They should consider themselves the citizens of one world, not of different nations.

The spy satellites, the nuclear aircrafts, the bombers and the orbiting military stations set up in space by Russia, China and the USA pose a grave danger to mankind. They enable these nations to keep an eye on the secret military preparations of one another. The next world war, it is said, would be fought in space. The *havoc*[6] to be wreaked on mankind in such an eventuality can well be imagined.

Man can however choose to use weapons for peaceful purposes. Commando operations using sophisticated weapons can rescue hostages within minutes. Advanced weapons may prove to be saviours of mankind if used judiciously. There are a number of instances, where weapons have been used to save innocent people from the evil designs of anti-social elements.

Man has used nuclear and thermonuclear energy to make weapons of mass destruction. However, nuclear energy may be put to several peaceful uses such as applications of radiation technology in the fields of agriculture, industry and medicine. Nuclear energy is also used in laser technology and desalination of water.

With increasing population, there will be a corresponding increase in the demand for transport services, industries, etc., and in consequence, the natural resources like petroleum, coal, etc., will one day be exhausted. Nuclear energy will be the alternative in such a scenario. Thus, nuclear or atomic energy if used for peaceful purposes can prove to be a boon to mankind. A kitchen knife can be used for cutting vegetables as well as for stabbing a person. Man should use atomic energy only for beneficial purposes and never for killing his fellow beings.

Aid to Vocabulary

1. *Global village* — the world as one community
2. *Aftermath* — consequences or after-effects
3. *Mutation* — a change in form or structure
4. *Unearth* — to find out by searching
5. *Armament* — weapons like guns, tanks, etc.
6. *Havoc* — widespread damage or disorder

Points to Remember

1. Science has many advantages but it can also be a potential curse to mankind.
2. The Chinese first invented the gunpowder.
3. Thousands of people lost their lives in the Nagasaki and Hiroshima bombings.
4. The Gulf War II shattered Iraq economically.
5. Man's attitude towards his fellow beings has become mechanical.
6. Developing countries spend much money in accumulating nuclear weapons.
7. Military stations in space pose a threat to mankind.
8. Nuclear energy can be used for beneficial purposes.

Essay 5

INFORMATION TECHNOLOGY: A SILENT REVOLUTION IN INDIA

SYNOPSIS

Information Technology (IT) has revolutionised the world in the fields of healthcare, education, entertainment, etc. IT is an integrated technology which integrates the software and the hardware. With the technical advancement of the hardware, the software has improved and vice versa. India is forging ahead to make itself an IT superpower. It is emerging as a major hub for software development and e-commerce. A number of institutes offer courses in advanced computer education. The importance of the Internet has been recognised. The government of India has made its public services available online. Information Technology is prone to abuse. A farsighted government would enable India to become an IT superpower.

The electronic media has *ushered in*[1] a revolution—the Information Technology (IT) revolution. It has shrunk the world to such an extent that it could be called a 'global village'. No achievement of science has brought about such a transformation as IT has. It has opened up an infinite number of new avenues in the fields of healthcare, education, entertainment, communication, commerce and agriculture.

Information Technology is an integrated technology which integrates computer, magnetic storage media, television, telecommunication, industries and various types of software to operate all these. The computer age is our new reality. The computer has *revolutionised*[2] every sphere of our life. Computers are used in schools and colleges, hospitals, transport and communication sector, banking and finance, etc. Computers have taken up key roles in all fields of activity including agriculture, weather forecast, scientific research, designing, banking and financial institutions, space research and technology, communication and media, medicine, aviation, railways, traffic control, language learning, literature and entertainment.

The software technology has seen a spurt of development and firms like Apple, Google and Microsoft have established themselves as market leaders, pioneering the IT revolution the world over. It has helped us to work efficiently and accurately. Software in tandem with hardware acts as the medium through which communication and *dissemination*[3] of information are carried out.

India is forging ahead to become a software superpower. A National Task Force on Information Technology and Software Development was formed in May, 1998. This task force recognised the potential of IT and recommended a few reforms which would allow India to join the information superhighway. It recommended the transformation of every STD/ISD booth in the country into an 'information kiosk'. This would enable every citizen to have access to information when provided with an Internet connection and e-mail facility. The task force also recognised the need to switch over to local languages. Microsoft has launched its software packages in most of the major Indian languages. The task force also suggested the need to computerise all the Central and state government departments and make the staff in these departments computer-literate.

Indian cities like Hyderabad, Bengaluru and Gurgaon are turning out to be the hubs of global software development. All the major global players in this field have set up their offices in these cities. The Indian software exports run into billions of dollars.

The Andhra Pradesh government pioneered an *ambitious*[4] programme of e-governance to make the government transparent and accountable. The Government of India, today, through its National e-Governance plan (NeGP)makes available all its basic services to the common man. The NeGP is a multi-stakeholder programme which primarily focuses on making critical public services available and promoting rural entrepreneurship. The objective of NeGP is to transform traditional processes and service delivery mechanisms and create an environment that is citizen-centric, while making interaction with the Government easier, effective and transparent.

Recognising[5] the need for computer literacy in India, efforts are on to provide computer education in all the schools. This also includes schools in rural areas. Internet, Intranet and Extranet are being evolved to carry mail, *augment*[6] finance and banking, and facilitate other multimedia communications at minimal cost. Many institutes have come up across India which offer courses in various software applications. Some have global tie-ups with IT giants abroad, e.g., NIIT with Microsoft and Jetking with ICS learning systems, which is the world leader in distance education. APTECH has a tie-up with Indira Gandhi National Open University (IGNOU) to provide computer education to the candidates and award the degree of BCA.

The interconnection of computers worldwide, i.e. the Internet, has revolutionised the concept as well as the conduct of business. Visual and audio access to offices worldwide through the network has given rise to virtual offices. One can have easy access to information via the Internet. With the click of a Mouse, a person can browse through a multitude of sites available on the Internet. Internet surfing has become one of the latest passions of the Indian youth. Multimedia has contributed to making it more colourful, true-to-life and exciting. Most of the newspapers have Internet editions which can be accessed by a large number of readers. The All India Radio made its news broadcasts more accessible, when it went live on the Internet on February 25, 1998.

The importance of the Internet as an all-pervasive medium of the future has been well recognised everywhere. A very important indicator is the number of businessmen jumping on to the e-commerce bandwagon and embarking on Internet-oriented business ventures. E-commerce is gaining popularity in India as it allows trade at low costs and offers enterprises a chance to enter the global market at the right time. E-commerce helps in various aspects of business including identifying the customer, advertising, handling orders, taxes, shipping, payment processing, etc. Internet is at the centre of a new and unique phase that has redefined the concepts of marketing, promotion, advertisement and sale.

The New Telecommunication Policy, 1999 (NTP 1999) helped to further liberalise India's telecommunications sector. The Information Technology Act, 2000 was instituted to provide a legal framework to facilitate electronic commerce and transactions. This Act also aims at recognising electronic contracts, prevention of computer crimes, electronic filing/documentation, digital signature, etc. To integrate technology into the learning environment, the Department of Information Technology has formulated two programmes. These are *Vidya Vahini* and *Gyan Vahini*. The former provides connectivity to schools across the country and the latter, IT infrastructure at all the higher learning institutions in the country. An ambitious project V-cop is in the pipeline to connect the police stations through an all-India network. The software FACT provides fingerprint statistics with a centrally located *server*[7] at the National Crime Records Bureau.

There has been a considerable shift in the learning *paradigm*[8] due to the introduction of technology and newer methods of imparting education. New technologies are being gradually integrated into the learning environment. Networking and the Internet are being used as cost-effective tools for providing better learning opportunities for students, faculty development, supporting professional development, increasing productivity of members of the learning community and improving the efficiency of educational institutions, and administration.

India is a multilingual country with 22 constitutionally recognised languages and 11 scripts. To address the problem of digital divide and pave the way towards 'Digital Unite and Knowledge for all', significant achievements have been made in language computing. Among the most important ones that have been made available in public domain are: Text to Speech (TTS) systems integrated with screen readers for 6 Indian languages; Monolingual Search Engines (Sandhan) for tourism domain for 5 Indian languages; Optical Character Recognition System for 6 languages; and English-Indian Languages (9 language pairs) and Indian Indian-languages (8 language pairs) machine translation facility.

The Information Technology Industry in India provides employment to a significant number of its tertiary sector workforce. India's outsourcing industry is expected to increase to US$ 225 billion by 2020. The most prominent IT hub is Bengaluru. It is popularly known as the Silicon Valley of India and contributes around 33 per cent of Indian IT exports. The other centres are Chennai, Hyderabad, Coimbatore, Kolkata, Kochi, Pune, Mumbai, Ahmedabad and NCR (National Capital Region). Chennai is the second largest exporter of software after Bengaluru. It houses the largest cluster of Indian Software Companies such as TCS, Infosys, Wipro, CTS, Patni, L&T, etc. The IT industry has enhanced India's credibility as a business and investment destination and put India on the global map.

India has emerged the world's largest sourcing destination for the IT industry, accounting for approximately 67 per cent of the US$ 124-130 billion market. The industry employs about 10 million workforce. More importantly, the industry has led the economic transformation of the country and altered the perception of India in the global economy. India's cost competitiveness in providing IT services, which is approximately 3-4 times cheaper than the US, continues to be the mainstay of its 'Unique Selling Proposition' (USP) in the global sourcing market. However, India is also gaining prominence in terms of intellectual capital with several global IT firms setting up their innovation centres in India.

The IT industry has also created significant demand in the Indian education sector, especially for engineering and computer science. The Indian IT and ITeS industry is divided into four major segments – IT services, Business Process Management (BPM), software products and engineering services, and hardware.

The IT-BPM sector which is currently valued at US$ 143 billion is expected to grow at a Compound Annual Growth Rate (CAGR) of 8.3 per cent year-on-year basis. The sector is expected to contribute 9.5 per cent of India's Gross Domestic Product (GDP) and more than 45 per cent in total services export in the next few years.

Indian IT service offerings have evolved from application, development and maintenance to emerge as full service players providing testing services, infrastructure services, consulting and system integration.

The National Policy on Electronics (NPE) 2012 was approved in 2012 with the vision to create a globally competitive Electronic System Design and Manufacturing (ESDM) industry to meet the country's needs and serve the international market. It has been renamed as Department of Electronics and Information Technology (DeitY). The department is expected to create an indigenous manufacturing eco-system for electronics in the country. It will foster the manufacturing of indigenously designed and manufactured chips creating a more cyber secure eco-system in the country. It will enable India to tap the great economic potential that this knowledge sector offers. The increased development and manufacturing in the sector will lead to greater economic growth through more manufacturing and consequently greater employment in the sector.

Like any other technology, Information Technology also is prone to abuse. With the help of this technology, criminals are expanding their horizons to enter the electronic space. Technology is being misused for committing financial frauds, hacking, sending threats and vulgar or malicious messages, undertaking or promoting anti-national activities, software piracy, pornography, disclosure of confidential information, and so on. Computer-related crimes are on the rise. To check all such crimes, the police has established a separate network of IT experts and developed specialised software to keep track of the new breed of educated criminals.

A far-sighted government can catapult India into becoming an IT superpower. Indian firms like Infosys and Wipro are considered to be among the best in the business. The draft National Policy on Information Technology 2011, unveiled on October 7, 2011 envisaged taking the overall revenue generation in the sector from $89 billion in 2011 to $300 billion by 2020 besides creating an additional one crore jobs. The policy looked into providing fiscal and other incentives to attract investment in the sector. It called for setting up of centres of excellence in the institutions of higher learning so as to produce at least 3000 PhDs in specialised areas of this sector by 2020.

The future of the IT industry in India is certainly bright with the kind of resilience it has shown over the years that were ridden with financial downturns.

Aid to Vocabulary

1. *Ushered in* — brought in
2. *Revolutionised* — changed
3. *Dissemination* — the act of spreading
4. *Ambitious* — actively seeking success
5. *Recognising* — realising
6. *Augment* — to increase or make greater
7. *Server* — computer program that controls and provides information to several computers linked to one another
8. *Paradigm* — example or pattern

Points to Remember

1. The revolution of IT has shrunk the world to a 'global village'.
2. It has brought efficiency and accuracy in our work.
3. The latter half of the 20th century brought about a revolution in the field of telecommunications.
4. Cities like hyderabad, Bengaluru and Gurgaon are turning out to be the hubs of global software development.
5. Many computer institutions have global tie-ups with IT giants like Microsoft, ICS, etc.
6. The importance of the internet has been recognised in India.
7. The Information Technology Act was passed in 2000. The *Vidya Vahini* and *Gyan Vahini* programmes were formulated by the department of information Technology.
8. Effect of the introduction of technology in the field of education is greatly felt.
9. Information technology is also being misused.
10. With a visionary government, India can become an IT superpower in the years to come.

DOMESTIC IT-ITES PERFORMANCE

Though the IT-ITES (IT Enabled Services) sector is export driven, the size of the domestic market is also significant. In domestic market, the IT Services is the fastest growing segment (14.4 per cent) followed by domestic software products (13.8 per cent) and BPM (12.4 per cent).

IT-ITES Employment Scenario

The IT-ITES sector has become one of the key sectors for the Indian economy because of its economic impact. This sector is the biggest employment generator and has spawned the mushrooming of several ancillary industries such as transportation, real estate and catering, security, housekeeping, etc. Direct employment in the IT services and BPO/ITeS segment is estimated to grow by over 7 per cent. Indirect job creation is estimated at 9.5 million.

Essay 6

THE INTERNET—ITS USE AND MISUSE

SYNOPSIS

The Internet has been the most outstanding innovation in the field of communication in the history of mankind. In 1989, an English scientist Tim Berners-Lee invented the Web. The Internet constitutes a gamut of services and resources. Through the internet one can connect to anyone in any part of the world. Internet is helpful to students, researchers, job-seekers, businessmen, etc. Now we can get any information with just a click of the Mouse. We can book tickets, shop, apply for jobs, pay fees, etc. There are certain disadvantages of the Internet also. Another person can hack into your personal information and misuse it for withdrawing money from your bank account or use your credit card number, etc., illegally. Through the Internet, a virus may also attack a computer and disrupt its functioning. We need to be trained and educated such that optimal benefits of the Internet could be drawn.

The last twenty years have witnessed a tremendous growth in the field of Information Technology. It has revolutionised every aspect of modern life, be it communication, entertainment, travelling, banking or business. The Internet has been the most outstanding innovation in the field of communication in the history of mankind. In 1989, an English scientist Tim Berners-Lee invented the 'Web'. On August 6, 1991, CERN, a pan-European organisation, publicised the new World Wide Web project. Today, the Internet has become the most powerful tool for people throughout the world.

The Internet consists of a *gamut*[1] of services and resources. Some people still think that e-mail is the only *constituent*[2] of the Internet. The fact is, the Internet spans an expansive worldwide web with millions of websites, including social networking forums and search engines, that provide instant link to an ever increasing resource pool on almost everything imaginable. It has also become the best business tool. The Internet enables one to communicate and share resources with anyone in any part of the world.

The foremost empowering outcome of the Internet has always been communication. With the help of the Internet, we can now communicate in a fraction of a second with a person who may be sitting anywhere in the world. Today, computer literate individuals can avail themselves of the various facilities afforded by the e-mail service which includes chatting for hours with their loved ones. Presently, with the help of a number of messenger services, it has become very easy to establish a kind of global friendship wherein one can share one's thoughts and also explore different cultures. The Internet is a virtual treasure house of information. Any kind of information under the sun is available on the Internet. Earlier searching for a piece of information was a very time consuming process. Now, the search engines like Google and Yahoo are at our service and we can find any information within minutes. Many research scholars choose the Internet as one of the sources for their research. Even teachers have started giving such assignments to their students that require research on the Internet. Some tech-savvy ministers have begun to use popular social networking and micro-blogging sites like *Twitter* to post their views on issues of social and political importance. This exercise brings them closer to the common man on a one-on-one interactive forum, though virtually.

Entertainment is another popular reason why many people prefer to surf the Internet. They download games, music and movies; visit chat rooms; or they may just explore the worldwide web. Chat rooms are virtual meeting places where one can talk to different people from different parts of the world. If one wants to plan a holiday, one need not go to Travel Agents or Airports or Railway Stations to get the schedules. One just needs to log on to the Internet and get all the details about flight or train schedules, availability of seats, weather conditions of the place, sites worth seeing, etc.

Online banking, job search, movie ticket booking, shopping, air ticketing, railway and hotel reservations, etc., are some of the many services now available on the Internet. If we need to get any information about our bank account, we just have to log on to the website of our bank, enter our bank account number and password and we will get the information we want. Through sites like *Matrimony.com, Shaadi.com*, etc., people can even search for their life partner on the Internet. All application forms for various educational courses, are now made available on websites; students need not stand in long queues to buy the forms. The Internet helps them in paying the fees too. Most of the government departments have already gone online and the rest are in the process of doing so. e-courts have been introduced to speed up the processes and reduce the number of pending cases. Many Entrance Examinations have begun to provide online option for examinees.

If one uses the Internet with all the available facilities, one may have to face its disadvantages also. In using the internet often without taking precautions, we may be playing with fire, as our personal information such as name, address, bank account number, credit card number, photographs, etc., may be hacked or *accessed*[3] by others and they may misuse it. There have been *instances*[4] where unauthorised persons have been able to take away all the money from bank accounts by hacking and using the information available online. Spamming is another term related to the disadvantages of the Internet. Spamming pertains to sending unwanted e-mails in bulk which serves no purpose and needlessly clogs the entire system. These activities can be very frustrating for any user. Various unscrupulous businesses have emerged on the e-commerce domain. Many people have also been duped online.

The Internet is also prone to virus threats. Virus is a programme which *disrupts*[5] the normal functioning of computer systems. Computers connected to the Internet are more vulnerable to virus attacks and they can crash the hard disk of the computer. Excessive use of the Internet, particularly by the younger generation results in various health problems. Young people spend their leisure time surfing the Internet and get addicted to it which in turn gives rise to many health problems like *carpal tunnel syndrome*[6], obesity, migraine, spondylitis, problems related to the eyes, and so on. The Internet is also responsible for moral degradation of the society. This is a very serious issue concerning the Internet. Children are exposed to inappropriate content at a very young age. There are thousands of pornographic sites on the Internet that can be *detrimental*[7] especially to the development of growing children. The youngsters are exposed to the numerous social networking sites via Internet. They spend much of their time glued to the computer chatting, browsing, etc. Those who are emotionally sensitive very often fall to cyber-bullying and develop a variety of psychological problems.

The Internet has become an integral part of modern life. It has indeed accommodated the world in a chat room. Nothing seems to be far as long as we have the Internet. But to safeguard ourselves against its pitfalls, we need to be more careful while using it. we need to be trained and educated such that its optimal benefits could be drawn. We should equip our computer systems with latest anti-virus software to avoid virus threats. we should be extra cautious and must never ignore precautionary steps while e-shopping, e-banking, etc. We should use the Internet with all the possible safety measures so that it can prove to be a blessing for the society.

Aid to Vocabulary

1. *Gamut* — the complete range of a particular kind of thing
2. *Constituent* — one of the parts of something that combine to form the whole
3. *Accessed* — entered illegally
4. *Instances* — particular examples or cases of something
5. *Disrupts* — makes it difficult for something to continue in a normal way
6. *Carpal tunnel syndrome* — a medical condition in which pain is caused in wrist, hand and fingers
7. *Detrimental* — harmful, damaging

Points to Remember

1. The Internet constitutes a gamut of services and resources.
2. An English scientist Tim Berners-Lee invented the Web in 1989.
3. The Internet enables one to communicate with anyone in any part of the world.
4. With the help of the Internet, we can get any information within minutes.
5. Many services like banking, job search, ticket-booking, hotel reservation, shopping, etc., are now provided on the Internet.
6. If one uses the Internet, one may have to face its disadvantages also.
7. Computers connected to the internet are prone to virus attacks, which can end up crashing the hard disk.
8. Information made available online can be hacked or accessed, and misused.
9. We need to be trained and educated such that optimal benefits of the Internet could be drawn.

INDIA NOW HAS THE SECOND LARGEST NUMBER OF INTERNET USERS IN THE WORLD!

— By Ritu Singh

With the growing internet penetration, India has emerged to become the second largest market for internet globally. With 333 million internet users, India has also outdone the United States to become the second biggest Internet market in the world, while China with 721 million internet users continues to lead the pack. Apart from being world's no. 2 internet market, India also surpassed the US to become the second-largest smartphone market in the globe, according to The State of Broadband 2016 report.

Issued annually, this report is a unique global survey of broadband network access and affordability which also says that just six nations — including China and India — together account for 55% of the total global population still offline, because of the sheer size of their populations. The report further observes that while internet access is approaching saturation in richer nations, connectivity is still not advancing fast enough in poorer parts of the world.

These are the other key findings of the report:

- Globally, an estimated 3.9 billion people are not using the internet.
- The Republic of Korea continues to have the world's highest household internet penetration, with 98.8% of homes connected; Qatar (96%) and United Arab Emirates (95%) rank second and third, respectively.
- In total, there are now 91 economies where over 50% of the population is online, up from 79 in 2015. Whereas in 2014 the top ten countries for Internet use were all located in Europe, 2016 saw Bahrain (ranked 7th) and Japan (ranked 9th) join the group.
- The lowest levels of internet usage are found in sub-Saharan Africa, with less than 3% of the population using the Internet in a number of countries including Chad (2.7%), Sierra Leone (2.5%), Niger (2.2%), Somalia (1.8%) and Eritrea (1.1%).

The figures definitely reveal a 'digital divide' but the State of Broadband 2016 is optimistic about the potential of mobile broadband, with 165 countries now having deployed 4G high-speed mobile networks. The commission also notes that future growth is likely to be driven by markets such as India and Indonesia. It argues that if today's near-universal basic mobile phone access could be converted to high-speed mobile broadband access, mobile phones could serve as a major accelerator of development, driving rapid progress towards the UN Sustainable Development Goals.

Essay 7

ADVANCES IN BIOTECHNOLOGY

SYNOPSIS

Advancements in biotechnology have helped man unravel many mysteries of nature. Science has aided man in developing several drugs to relieve human sufferings. Biotechnology has helped in the increase of agricultural produce and production of genetically modified food grains. Several new techniques have been evolved to eradicate diseases. But, in this attempt, man has subjected animals to inhuman treatment. Cloning of animals could lead to the creation of 'designer babies'. India's biotechnological advancements have made possible the creation of cloned buffaloes at Karnal (Haryana). Science should be used for human welfare.

Though man held Nature in awe, he always wished to *unravel*[1] its mysteries. With the advancements in science and technology, man aspired to control Nature and its workings. And, in this attempt, he succeeded in developing improved seeds for high yield in agriculture to feed the teeming millions. Test-tube babies for childless couples, high milk-yielding cows through artificial insemination, plastic surgery and face-lifting methods to defy ageing and remain young, are all attempts to race against Nature. The programme of selective breeding of humans, to produce 'super humans' may be a future possibility in this race.

Biotechnology has helped man realise many of his dreams. Biotechnology may be defined as the practical usage of the advancements made in biosciences for industrial purposes. The ruling by the US Supreme Court in 1980 that a live human-made micro-organism is patentable has led to incredible development in the field of biotechnology. Biotechnology calls for application of engineering and technological principles to life sciences. The discovery of polio vaccine, penicillin, pasteurisation of milk, attempts to eradicate smallpox and malaria have been the earlier breakthroughs in biotechnology. Through the ages, this branch of science has attained sophistication and drugs have been evolved to relieve the sufferings of mankind.

Biotechnologists have been successful in increasing crop yield. Over the years, the growth-rate of population in many parts of the globe has been a matter of grave concern, mainly because of poverty and food shortage. Development of hybrid seeds, through genetic engineering and tissue culture, has helped in increasing the agricultural yield. Areas, which receive less rainfall, have been identified and drought-resistant trees, developed, which could thrive in such adverse conditions and impart greenery to the location. 'Babul' and 'acacia' are planted in India in the areas which are dry. The Pusa Institute in Delhi has developed mango saplings, which can even be grown at home in large pots. They start yielding mangoes when they reach a height of 10-15 feet. In the Philippines, a gene from a rice of African origin has been introduced to the native crop to make it resistant to fungal diseases. Thus, with biotechnology an *unprecedented*[2] green revolution is on the anvil.

Another messianic endeavour of the biotechnologists pertains to relieving the sufferings of human beings. The open-heart surgery and bypass surgery were some of the earlier attempts to treat a heart patient. Now, by chelation techniques, developed by Kuala Lumpur's Mohd. Ebrahim, heart patients could avoid undergoing heart surgery. American researchers have been successful in developing a vaccine against group B streptococcus. This could save the life of infants, if administered to expectant mothers. Many, who aspired for motherhood despite the fact that it would not come naturally for them, have been able to realise their dream, thanks to different interventions and solutions enabled by biotechnology. Biotechnology has, thus helped in relieving human sufferings to a considerable extent.

Genetic engineering is the process of extracting genes bearing a specific hereditary trait from one organism and artificially inserting them into a completely different organism. This is also a component of biotechnology. There are several possible benefits from such genetic engineering. It can be used to enhance the nutritional value of food. For example, scientists are reported to be working on iron and vitamin fortified rice.

Such crops could be developed as would be resistant to pests and give higher yields, or survive extreme weather conditions. Even edible vaccines could be provided through this system. Genetically modified foods are also being produced. The two main genetically modified crops are soya and corn followed by cotton, canola and potato. Genetically Modified (GM) ingredients are turning up in animal feeds and foodstuffs being traded, processed, mass produced, sold and consumed, the world over. Biotechnology has been successful in the production of several vital substances like insulin and growth hormones interferons. Recombinant DNA techniques can be used for producing monoclonal antibodies which will be helpful in medical diagnosis. Bacteria that can biologically remove toxic chemicals and oil spills have been created. New developments in the field of biotechnology and genetic engineering have made possible the total cure of several hereditary diseases.

However, in man's attempts to conquer diseases, animals have been subjected to inhuman treatment and often, have been sacrificed. Xenotransplanting or the practice of transplanting animal organs or tissues in humans is an inhuman practice, which might soon become a reality. It has been proven that humans do not respond with the same exactness to a similar experiment as animals do. The spread of mad cow disease, or the fowl flu and AIDS from apes to man are some of the diseases that occurred because man tampered with Nature. Scientists in America are trying to work out a way to relieve the suffering of the patients of Parkinson's disease by injecting cells from pigs to their brains. But, the fear of transmission of pig viruses to humans persists.

Many ethical questions have been raised in the fields of molecular biology and genetic engineering. Hence, all genetically modified food are required to be marketed with appropriate as well as extensive safety assessment. Early in 1997, British scientists at the Roslin Institute, Scotland, created the world's first clone of an adult animal. It was a scientific breakthrough that provided a huge *impetus*[3] to the work on ageing, genetics and medicine.

In the year 2009-10, the biotechnology industry grew at a rate of 40%. Though the growth was achieved mainly through leadership in biogenerics and contract manufacturing, research leading to innovative product development did not lag behind. The social impact of such growth is evident from India assuming a dominant place in vaccine exports, diagnostics, transgenics (BtCotton) and a number of biotherapeutics.

The government has to invest US$ 5 billion to develop human capital, infrastructure and research initiatives if it is to realise the dream of growing the sector into a US$ 100 billion industry by 2025. Biopharma is the largest sector contributing about 64 per cent of the total revenue followed by bioservices (18 per cent), bioagri (14 per cent), bioindustry (3 per cent), and bioinformatics contributing (1 per cent). The high demand for different biotech products has also opened up scope for the foreign companies to set up base in India.

As of now, 63 Post Graduate teaching programmes in various areas of biotechnology namely General Biotechnology, Agricultural Biotechnology, Animal Sciences, Medical Sciences, Marine Sciences, Neurosciences, Industrial Biotechnology, Molecular and Human Genetics,

Environmental Biotechnology and Pharmaceutical Biotechnology, MTech Biochemical Engineering and Biotechnology, in addition to seven Post Graduate diploma in bio-safety and regulations, animal cell culture, etc., are being supported all over the country.

In India, though biotechnology has not made giant strides, it has not lagged behind either. The National Botanical Research Institute in Lucknow has been working to develop a disease-resistant variety of cotton. The Pusa Institute in Delhi has developed several types of seeds for crops and vegetables. But biotechnology has posed a threat to the country's biodiversity. Global companies are trying to patent those products that have been our legacy. The battle for patent of turmeric was won by us. But, the American MNCs are vying for the patent of neem and basmati rice. This has become a challenge that India must face with determination. India came up with a breakthrough in cloning when dairy scientists in Karnal (Haryana) developed several identical buffalo calves from a single embryo. Scientists are planning to clone a female and a male panda in order to save them from extinction. Sooam Biotech scientists have cloned many canines till date.

To prevent pathogenesis of viruses and bacteria there are at present 70 licensed vaccines. The pharmaceutical industry has specialised new drugs to fight against the new micro-organisms.

The Department of Biotechnology has launched the project 'Human Genome—The Indian Initiative'. The project deals with the mapping of all the genes present in man. It would, then, be possible to alter and remove defective genes in an individual. India is fast catching up with international standards of biotechnology. Biotechnology has also opened up new career opportunities. In India, along with IT, biotechnology is the most vibrant sector. Indian pharmaceutical companies are making rapid strides. The pharmaceutical industry has specialised new drugs to fight against the new micro-organisms.

Biotechnology has been able to combat a number of diseases. Its contribution in the field of agriculture is *unparalleled*[4]. Efforts are on to control the body's biological clock. A number of diseases—genetic or those caused by external sources—have been eliminated. Efforts should be made by man so as not to tamper with Nature. Biotechnology should be used for the betterment of the society by eradicating diseases and nurturing the flora and fauna. Only then can man claim to be superior to the other creatures on the earth.

Aid to Vocabulary

1. *Unravel* — solve, make clear
2. *Unprecedented* — not recorded before
3. *Impetus* — boost
4. *Unparalleled* — unequalled

Points to Remember

1. Man wanted to unravel nature's mysteries.
2. Biotechnology has helped him realise many of his dreams.
3. It helped in modifying as well as increasing agricultural produce.
4. Biotechnology has helped in relieving human sufferings.
5. It is used for enhancing nutritional value of foods.
6. Genetically modified crops are being produced with new developments in the field of biotechnology.
7. Diseases like fowl flu and AIDS occurred because man tampered with Nature.
8. Biotechnology has not made giant strides in India but it has not lagged behind either.
9. It should be used for the betterment of the society.

Essay 8

SCIENTIFIC RESEARCH IN INDIA

SYNOPSIS

The long period from the ancient India to the modern India shows that scientific research is not a new phenomenon in the country. Major advances have been made in the fields of agriculture, floriculture, Horticulture and animal husbandry. Medical research has led to the eradication of several diseases. Space research has made rapid progress. ONGC has made immense contribution in the fields of oil and natural gas exploration. CSIR has made outstanding contribution to industrial growth in the country. ISRO has taken the Indian space programme to great heights.

Science has made unprecedented progress in the modern age. However, scientific research has been a continuous process since the ancient times, when research work in various fields was done all over the world including India. There were a number of people in ancient India who contributed a lot towards the advancement of science. Charaka and Sushruta made invaluable contributions in the science of Ayurveda and plastic surgery, while Aryabhatta excelled in astronomy. India also boasts of a number of modern scientists like Acharya J.C. Bose, Srinivasa Ramanujan, C. V. Raman, S. Chandrashekhar, Dr. Homi Bhabha, Dr. Vikram Sarabhai, Dr. Hargobind Khurana and Venkataraman Ramakrishnan—several among them are Nobel laureates.

In India, today, the advancement in science and technology has made its contribution towards every aspect of human life. It includes medicine, agriculture, industry, space research, defence research, transport, poultry farming, fisheries, animal husbandry and nuclear energy. The Government of India has set up various organisations to *promote*[1] research and development in these fields. These are the Council of Scientific and Industrial Research (CSIR), the Indian Council of Medical Research (ICMR) and the Indian Council of Agriculture Research (ICAR), to promote research and development in industry, medicine and agriculture, respectively. The departments of Electronics, Space, Atomic Energy, Ocean Development, the Defence Research and Development Organisation (DRDO), the Ministry of Non-Conventional Energy Sources, the Ministry of Science and Technology, and the Ministry of Environment and Forests also have their own research and development facilities.

In 1958, the Indian Parliament passed the Scientific Policy Research Resolution (SPRR), aimed at promoting scientific research in pure, applied and educational fields. In 1983, the Technology Policy Statement (TPS) was enforced to promote *indigenous*[2] technology. It is aimed at ensuring the adaptation of international technological breakthroughs, keeping in mind the availability of resources and national priorities.

With the success of the Green Revolution in 1967-68, India's scientific research got a boost. Under the quality seed programme, India made a small beginning with a few thousand quintals of improved seeds in the 60's. Soil and water conservation measures helped in increasing agricultural yield. *Horticulture*[3] crops cover a wide range of crops, viz. fruits, vegetables, tuber crops, flowers, medicinal and aromatic plants, mushrooms, plantation crops and spices among others. While India is the second largest producer of fruits in the world, it is the largest producer of fruits like mango, banana, papaya, sapota, and pomegranate. In terms of productivity of grapes, India ranks first in the world. India occupies the second position in the production of brinjal, cabbage, cauliflower and onion and third in potato and tomato production in the world. Vegetables that are produced in abundance include potato, tomato, brinjal, okra, cucurbits, etc. Efforts are being made to bring mushroom cultivation on scientific lines leading to higher productivity and better quality. Floriculture is another sphere which has received attention after liberalisation. Orchids, tuberose and a number of hybrid flowers are cultivated for export. These are now considered to have an immense potential in the field of making perfumes also. Using the technique of tissue culture and genetic engineering, plants like brinjal, tomato, mustard, grapes, chrysanthemum and sesame have been developed. A large number of agricultural universities and research institutes have come up across India.

Animal husbandry and dairy development have played an important role in supplementing the income of households in the rural sector. Scientific research has helped in developing indigenous breeds of cattle, which are immune to animal diseases and are sturdy. Scientific research in this direction has helped the landless, small and marginal farmers. The development of Embryo Transfer Technology (ETT) has given an opportunity to introduce selective breeding approaches. Biotechnology has improved the nutritional quality of animal, bird, fish and plant products. Research in fisheries has helped in the high yield of prawns for export. At Karnal (Haryana), dairy scientists have developed a technique for producing several identical buffalo calves from a single embryo. It is India's answer to Dolly (the sheep), the world's first cloned mammal.

In the field of medical research, India has been able to bring about effective disease control methods. The polio vaccine has been used effectively to *eradicate*[4] childhood disabilities. Tests like mammography and tomography have enabled doctors to detect cancer at an early stage. We have also been able to eradicate smallpox from India. The multi-drug therapy has enabled us to control the spread of leprosy in India. Indigenous AIDS diagnostics, the ELISA system, has been developed to detect the HIV virus in patients. Under Indo-US Vaccine Action Programme, progress has been made under some of the projects undertaken in the area of viral hepatitis C and B, cholera, typhoid, E.coli diarrhoea, polio and tuberculosis. In 2000, for the first time in the world, scientists at AIIMS (All India Institute of Medical Sciences), New Delhi developed the genetically engineered clone of the hepatitis E virus. This will help to pave the way for development of a vaccine. It will also make it possible to identify a drug which can inhibit this virus.

The Indian Space Research Organisation (ISRO) and the Department of Space (DoS) have taken our space programme to great heights. Remote sensing has enabled us to predict the yield of major crops like wheat, rice, cotton, mulberry, etc., at the national level. It is able to forecast weather, floods, cyclones and droughts, which helps us to take adequate protective and relief measures beforehand. Telecommunication has also touched new heights. The Government is planning to connect the country with a National Information Highway (NIH). Cellular phones, radio paging, voice mail, fax, e-mail, electronic data interchange, etc., have brought about a revolution in the field of telecommunication.

Over the years, India has established two major space systems viz., Indian National Satellite (INSAT) system for communication, television broadcasting and meteorological services, and Indian Remote Sensing (IRS) satellites system for natural resources monitoring and management. ISRO has developed and operationalised two satellite launch vehicles, Polar Satellite Launch Vehicle (PSLV) and Geosynchronous Satellite Launch Vehicle (GSLV), to place IRS and INSAT satellites, respectively, in the required orbits.

The PSLV began carrying foreign payloads from the year 1991 with PSLV-C9 launching as many as 10 satellites into orbit in 2008 and PSLV-C20 that blasted off on February 25, 2013 launching 7 in just 4 minutes. In 2008, PSLV-C11 launched India's indigenously developed *Chandrayan-1* on its moon mission.

India prides itself on a state-of-the-art missile programme that safeguards its strategic interests and made a proud entry into the elite Inter Continental Ballistic Missile (ICBM) Club when it test fired its 5000 km range surface-to-surface missile Agni V on April 19, 2012. INS Kochi is the second vessel in the INS Kolkata series of stealth guided missile which has been commissioned into the Indian Navy on 30 September 2015. India's BrahMos supersonic land-attack cruise missile is to be carried by Sukhoi-30 fighter planes from mid-2016. The missile was successfully test fired on December 19, 2015. ISRO PSLV C34 is the new satellite launched by ISRO on June 22, 2016, carrying a record of 20 satellites in a single mission including the Cartosat-2 series satellite and 19 other satellites. India has become the 5th country among all who have their own GPS system. ISRO have launched 7th satellite for the purpose of GPS navigation, named as Navik.

The Defence Research and Development Organisation (DRDO) has come up with a new indigenously produced Advanced Air Defence (AAD) interceptor missile, Ashwin. The missile was tested on the newly named Abdul Kalam Island located in the Balashore district off the Odisha coast. This was the 12th test in the series to develop interceptor missiles. India's achievements in space technology and research show that our scientists and engineers are at par with those in advanced countries. Whenever a challenge is thrown to them, they are prepared to accept it and come out with their best for the nation.

The Oil and Natural Gas Corporation (ONGC) is involved in the exploration of oil and natural gas, and their production and sale. Natural gas is an important fuel for industry. The Fourth Five Year Plan gave an *impetus*[5] to the fields of offshore exploration, production, refining and marketing activities. In 1965, the Engineers India Ltd. (EIL) was set up to provide engineering expertise and technical services to petroleum refineries, oil and gas pipelines, petrochemical industries, and other industrial projects.

Research organisations like the Bhabha Atomic Research Centre (BARC) and the Department of Atomic Energy (DAE) co-ordinate the work on nuclear power generation. India has *harnessed*[6] atomic energy for peaceful purposes, using its own reserves of uranium and thorium. New areas like Nalgonda district of Andhra Pradesh, and Kerala have been identified as the areas with deposits of uranium. Production of radio-isotopes for use in medicine, agriculture and industry has been carried out with success. India has perfected a state-of-the-art combined process technology for the commercial production of titanium. This was once the monopoly of the countries like Japan, the USA, China and the UK.

The CSIR has contributed to the promotion of industrial development. It provides technical expertise for the upgradation of existing technologies and evolving new indigenous technologies to meet the needs of the industry. Technology transfers in areas like drugs, agro-chemicals, chemicals, food processing, petroleum refining, etc., have been carried out by the CSIR. In the area of drugs and pharmaceuticals, it has made India self-reliant. The CSIR laboratories offer solutions to the problems faced by the Indian industries. The scientific research by the CSIR covers a wide area from electronics to rural housing.

The Department of Ocean Development was created in 1981 for promoting ocean development activities in the country. It succeeded in collecting metallic modules from the ocean bed, which only a few advanced countries can boast of. Ocean exploration gives access to a vast source of metals, which have accumulated over millions of years. The Antarctic Exploration and Polar Science programme was initiated in 1981. India set up a modern and indigenously built station *Maitri*, in the Schirmacher Oasis at Antarctica in 1989. The station is linked with India through the electronic mail network making it possible to transmit online data from and to various laboratories in the country.

In January 2010, a unique ocean information service, viz., Indian Ocean Forecasting System (INDOFOS) was launched by INCOIS (Indian National Centre for Ocean Information Service), Hyderabad by integrating existing forecasts of ocean wave and the surface and subsurface parameters of the Indian Ocean. The system, provides forecast on wave heights, wave direction, sea surface temperature (SST), surface currents, mixed layer depth (MLD) and depth of 20°C isotherm up to 5-7 days in advance. This system has been operational since January 2010. The beneficiaries of INDOFOS are: traditional and mechanised fishermen, the maritime boards, Indian Navy, Coast Guard, shipping companies and oil and natural gas industries, energy industries and academia.

This gives us an insight into the extent of scientific research undertaken in India. Research carried out in various departments have made a great impact in different areas. Scientific research and investigation has turned impossible things into possible. It has lent greater impetus to the momentum of India's emergence as a world power.

Aid to Vocabulary

1. *Promote* — to help the progress of something
2. *Indigenous* — originating or existing naturally in an environment
3. *Horticulture* — the art, study or practice of growing flowers, fruits and vegetables
4. *Eradicate* — remove
5. *impetus* — stimulus or boost
6. *Harnessed* — to use the strength of something in order to achieve something

Points to Remember

1. Scientific research is not new in India.
2. In India, today, the advancement in science and technology has made its contribution towards the betterment of every aspect of life.
3. Horticulture research has helped India to become one of the largest producers of fruits and vegetables in the world.
4. Scientific research has helped in developing indigenous breeds of cattle, which are immune to animal diseases and are sturdy.
5. In the field of medical research, India has been able to bring about effective disease control methods.
6. The Indian Space Research Organisation and the department of space have taken our space programme to great heights.
7. The Oil and Natural Gas Corporation is involved in the exploration of oil and natural gas and their production and sale.
8. Scientific researches in various fields have lent greater impetus to the momentum in India's emergence as a world power.

SOME IMPORTANT SCIENTIFIC RESEARCH INSTITUTES

- Central Institute of Medicinal and Aromatic Plants, (CSIR), Lucknow (Uttar Pradesh)
- Central Food Technological and Research Institute, Mysore (Karnataka)
- Indian Institute of Petroleum (ISIR), Dehradun, (Uttarakhand)
- Central Drug Research Institute (CSIR), Lucknow (Uttar Pradesh)
- Bose Research Institute, Kolkata (West Bengal)
- Central Glass and Ceramic Research Institute, New Delhi (Delhi)
- Central Institute of Fisheries Technology, Ernakulam (Kerala)
- Central Jute Technological Research Institute, Kolkata (West Bengal)
- Central Mining Research Station, Dhanbad (Jharkhand)
- Central Rice Research Institute, Cuttack (Odisha)
- Centre for Cellular and Molecular Biology, Hyderabad (Andhra Pradesh)
- Council of Scientific and Industrial Research, New Delhi (Delhi)
- National Dairy Research Institute, Karnal (Haryana)
- National Environmental Engineering Research Institute, Nagpur (Maharashtra)

AUTONOMOUS INSTITUTIONS

- National Institute of Immunology (NII), New Delhi
- National Centre for Cell Sciences (NCCS), Pune
- Centre for DNA Fingerprinting and Diagnostics (CDFD), Hyderabad
- National Brain Research Centre (NBRC), Manesar
- Institute of Life Sciences (ILS), Bhubaneshwar
- National Institute of Biomedical Genomics (NIBMG), Kalyani
- Regional Centre for Biotechnology (RCB), Gurgaon
- Institute of Stem Cell Science and Regenerative Medicine (InStem), Bangalore
- National Agri-Food Biotechnology Centre (NABI), Mohali
- Centre of Innovative and Applied Biotechnology (CIAB), Mohali
- National Institute of Animal Biotechnology (NIAB), Hyderabad
- Translational Health Science and Technology Institute (THSTI), Gurgaon
- National Institute of Plant Genome Research (NIPGR), Delhi
- Rajiv Gandhi Centre for Biotechnology (RGCB), Thiruvananthapuram, Kerala
- Institute of Bioresources and Sustainable Development (IBSD), Imphal & Sikkim

Essay 9

SPACE PROGRAMMES OF INDIA

SYNOPSIS

Since Independence in 1947, India has made an impressive array of achievements in the scientific and technological fields. The Indian Space Research Organisation (ISRO), the Space Commission and the Department of Space together are in charge of India's space programmes. Space programmes are proving beneficial in the fields of communication, broadcasting, meteorology, disaster management, search and rescue operations, agriculture, irrigation and forest services. India has a launch infrastructure at Sriharikota. Indian space programme is closely linked with industries and educational institutions. India is the fourteenth nation to send a man to space.

India is the seventh largest country in terms of area in the world and the second largest in terms of population. Since independence in 1947, India has made an impressive *array*[1] of achievements in the scientific and technological fields. Special mention in this respect must be made of the arena of space. In spite of being a developing economy with its attendant problems, India has developed space technology and applied it for various beneficial purposes.

The foundation of space research in India was laid with the establishment of the Indian Space Research Organisation (ISRO) in 1969. Space research activities were provided additional *fillip*[2] with the formation of the Space Commission and the Department of Space by the Government of India. Space programmes are today proving beneficial in the areas of communication, broadcasting, *meteorology*[3], disaster management and resources. ISRO's maiden attempt at developing a satellite launch vehicle was a failure in 1979. However, success followed with the developmental flight of SLV-3 in 1983 and its achievement in sending back more than 2,000 pictures.

The years 1987 and 1988 proved disappointing for space programmes because the launch of Augmented Satellite Launch Vehicle (ASLV) in these two years came to a premature end. However, in May 1992, ISRO launched the ASLV-3 and its successor in May 1994. India successfully launched PSLV-C1 in 1997. After that PSLV-C2, GSLV-D1, PSLV-C5, GSLV-D2, GSLV FO1, PSLV-C6, PSLV-C7, PSLV-C8, PSLV-C9, PSLV-C10 were also launched by ISRO successfully. On October 22,

2008, India successfully launched PSLV–C11-Chandrayaan I. The moon mission marked a new chapter in the history of Indian Space Programme. After that India successfully launched PSLV–C12 and PSLV-C14.

On July 12, 2010, PSLV-C15 (carrying three satellites and one student satellite) was launched successfully by ISRO. With this successful launch, India reached a 'critical constellation' of 10 active remote sensing satellites in space, which gives it a clear edge in its region for monitoring movements across borders.

On April 20, 2011, PSLV-C16 launched satellites which will send images for applications covering agriculture, environment, forestry, etc. On July 15, 2011, PSLV-C17 launched communication satellite GSAT-12 which will augment the availability of transponders for various communication services, including tele-medicine and tele-education. On October 12, 2011, PSLV-C18 carried Indo-French tropical weather satellite Megha-Tropiques, SRMSAT, Jugnu and VesselSat satellites. The Indian National Satellite (INSAT) system is one of the largest domestic communication satellite systems in the Asia-Pacific region. The INSAT range of satellites launched by the Geo-synchronous Launch Vehicle GSLV, serve many important sectors of the Indian economy like Telecommunication Sector, Mobile Satellite Service, Television Broadcasting and Redistribution, Telemedicine, Meteorological Service, Cyclone Monitoring, etc.

Today, India has the largest constellation of Remote Sensing Satellites which provide services both at the national and global levels. From the Indian Remote Sensing (IRS) satellites, launched using the Polar Satellite Launch Vehicle PSLV, data is available in a variety of *spatial*[4] resolutions. ISRO blasted-off PSLV-C21 on September 9, 2012 as its 100th mission and PSLV-C20 on February 25, 2013 as its 103rd. On November 5, 2013 onboard the PSLV-C25, the Mars Orbiter Mission or 'Mangalyaan' was launched. On September 24, 2014, the Mars Orbiter Mission (MOM) was successfully placed into Mars atmosphere. Chandrayaan-2 which would be a follow-on mission to Chandrayaan-I with an Orbiter, Lander and Rover. Chandrayaan-2, is designed to collect samples of lunar soil and conduct *in situ* studies of chemical and mineralogical content present in the lunar soil.

ISRO successfully positioned GSAT-6, the communication satellite on August 27, 2015. It is the 25th Geostationary Communication Satellite of India built by ISRO and it is the 12th in GSAT series. On September 28, 2015, ASTROSAT, India's first observation satellite was launched into orbit, for the study of distant celestial bodies. NASA and ISRO have set the target of 2021 to put their collaborative earth observation satellite

NISAR in orbit. Isro PSLV C34 satellite was launched by ISRO on June 22, 2016. It carried a record of 20 Satellites in a single mission including the cartos at-2 series satellite and 19 other satellites. An elaborate launch infrastructure exists at Sriharikota Island, 100 km from Chennai on the East Coast of India. Full-fledged facilities of satellite integration, assembly and launch exist there. Sriharikota also houses a Telemetry and Tracking and Command network for tracking satellites and monitoring them.

India has a vibrant space science programme covering astronomy, astrophysics, planetary and space science, earth science and theoretical physics. The Indian Space Programme since its inception has been cooperative with Indian industries. ISRO has an active programme to interact with academic and research institutions all over the country for the benefit of our space programme. In this regard, the Sponsored Research Programme (RESPOND) is an important component of DOS. Under RESPOND, DOS supports research and educational activities in universities, colleges, the Indian Institutes of Technology and other research institutions.

From the very beginning, ISRO has had a very good record of international cooperation. It has a Memorandum of Understanding with 25 countries/space agencies. A UN-sponsored Centre for Space Science and Technology Education (CSSTE) was set up in India; it has trained more than 400 personnel of the Asia-Pacific region. ISRO also provides training in space applications to personnel of developing countries through its Sharing of Experience in Space (SHARES) programme.

In 1984, India became the fourteenth nation to send a man to space. Squadron Leader Rakesh Sharma along with two Russian Cosmonauts, visited space. In 1997, Dr. Kalpana Chawla became the first Indian-American woman to visit space. According to the NASA, Kalpana was one among more than 2000 applicants for a civilian scientist's position. Her academic *accomplishments*[5], physical fitness and experience as a pilot made her a natural choice. In 2000, Chawla was selected for her second flight to space. Her second flight was a moment of joy for all Indians. Her return was eagerly awaited. On February 1, 2003 unfortunately, when the spaceship was just 16 minutes away from earth, it exploded. This explosion killed all the crew members including Chawla. Sunita Williams, an Indian-American astronaut of the NASA, became the first woman to stay for a record 195 days in space.

In addition to developing spacecraft and launch vehicle technologies indigenously, India has also been successful in the application of satellite technology to benefit its national economy. At the same time, India has also been sharing space-based information with the international community and providing commercial space services globally.

Aid to Vocabulary

1. *Array* — impressive display
2. *Fillip* — stimulus or incentive
3. *Meteorology* — study of motions and phenomena of atmosphere
4. *Spatial* — of space
5. *Accomplishments* — successful completion of something

Points to Remember

1. Since Independence, India has made an impressive array of achievements in the scientific and technological fields.
2. The foundation of space research in India was laid with the establishment of the Indian Space Research Organisation (ISRO) in 1969.
3. India has successfully launched many satellites.
4. The Indian National Satellite (INSAT) system is one of the largest domestic communication satellite systems in the Asia-Pacific region.
5. The INSAT system serves many important sectors of the Indian economy.
6. India has a vibrant space science programme covering astronomy, astrophysics, planetary and space science, earth science and theoretical physics.
7. In addition to developing spacecraft and launch vehicle technologies indigenously, India has also been successful in the application of satellite technology to benefit its national economy.

ISRO LAUNCHES FIRST 'SWADESHI' SHUTTLE

The Indian Space Research Organisation (ISRO) on May 23, 2016, successfully launched its maiden "swadeshi" space shuttle with the winged Reusable Launch Vehicle Technology Demonstrator (RLV-TD) from Sriharikota in Andhra Pradesh, fulfilling its mission objectives in the first crucial test to make space travel easier and cheaper in future.

RISE & SHINE FOR ISRO'S 20-IN-1

In one go, the Indian Space Reserach Organisation (ISRO) on June 22, 2016 launched 20 satellites — earth observation satellite (Cartosat-2 series), two student satellites from Indian universities and 17 of four foreign countries. In 2008, ISRO launched 10 satellites in a single rocket. On April 28, 2008, PSLV-C9 launched a remote sensing satellite (IMS-1) and eight nanosatellites.

Russia holds the world record for placing the most number of satellites in a single launch. Its Dnepr rocket launched 37 satellites in 2014.

ISRO's feat: 20 satellites in 26 minutes

Creating a record, India, on June 22, 2016, at Sriharikota, successfully launched 20 satellites, including 17 foreign and its earth observation satellite, in a single mission in 26 minutes in a crucial step to become a key player in the multi-billion dollar space launch market.

In a precision launch, Indian Space Research Organisation (ISRO) workhorse Polar Satellite Launch Vehicle (PSLV-C34) took off in clear skies from the second launch pad of Satish Dhawan Space Centre at Sriharikota, about 110 km from Chennai, at 9.26 am and placed the new generation earth observation satellite (Cartosat-2 Series) and 19 others in the designated polar Sun Synchronous Orbit (SSO) 26 minutes later.

Thirteen of the satellites were from the US, including the 12 earth-imaging Dove satellites, from Planet Labs organisation, each of which weighed just 4.7 kg, and a 110 kg earth imaging satellite called SkySat Gen-2 made by a Google-owned company. There were two Canadian satellites and one each from Germany and Indonesia. Launching 20 satellites in a single payload was like "allowing birds to fly in space", a beaming ISRO Chairman Kiran Kumar said, adding, "PSLVC-34 has done its job."

The Feat

The mission put India right after Russia's single mission launch of 33 satellites in 2014 and Nasa's 29 in 2013	Cost of the mission is 10 times less than that of other space agencies

Essay **10**

HUMAN CLONING: AN ETERNAL MORAL DILEMMA

SYNOPSIS

The claim of producing a human clone has raised questions in the minds of theologians, scientists, physicians and legal experts. Cloning is a technique for producing a genetic twin of a living cell. The first mammal to be cloned was Dolly, the sheep. Cloning can produce stem cells which could be used for therapeutic purposes by implanting in the body. Reproductive cloning would also assist sterile couples to have offspring. The opponents of human cloning disapprove of the creation of a stock of human organs through cloning. Ethically, they are critical of how society will look upon a cloned individual. In India, there is no law to stop human cloning. The society is wary of human cloning in spite of the claims of its therapeutic and reproductive utilities. If legally permitted, it could tear the social fabric apart.

The claim in 2002-03 of a human cloning company Clonaid to have produced a human clone, has once again given rise to an eternal moral *dilemma*[1]. The issues of ethics and the process of human cloning have come to the forefront. *Theologians*[2], scientists, physicians and legal experts have expressed *scepticism*[3] and opposition to this claim. But the supporters of cloning have put forward the humanitarian and medical utilities of the use of cloning. Cloning is banned in most countries of the world.

Cloning is a technique for producing a genetic twin of a living thing, an organism that starts life with the same genes as its parent. Scientifically speaking, human cloning is achieved by using the technique of nuclear *transplantation*[4]. In this process, an egg devoid of its nucleus gains a full set of genes or chromosomes from the cells of an adult and behaves as if it has been fertilised. The adult cell may be any cell of the adult body except the reproductive cell. The reason for this is that the reproductive cell contains only half the set of chromosomes. This so called fertilised egg is implanted into the womb of a woman, where it ultimately develops into a human embryo. This is, delivered later on, as an identical replica or clone of the adult.

The concept of cloning is not new. It originated in 1953 when James Watson pointed out to Francis Crick how four nucleic acids could pair to form the self-copying code of a DNA molecule. This concept has been used for many years to clone plants, frogs, toads, etc. The prospects of cloning a human being, however, turned bright with the birth of Dolly. Dolly, was the first cloned mammal, a cloned sheep delivered at the Roslin Institute, Edinburgh, Scotland in February, 1996. However, the claims made by a research company, Advanced Cell Technology (ACT), saw repercussions throughout the world. ACT claimed during the last week of November, 2001 to have cloned the first human embryo. The latest claim of cloning a human embryo has been put forward by Clonaid. This company claims to be the first human cloning company. Founded in February, 1997 by Rael, a spiritual leader, its main goal was to produce a human clone. On December 26, 2002 the birth of the first ever human clone, that of a girl named Eve was announced by the Raelians. However, the veracity of their claim has not been ascertained.

Dolly's creation in 1997 was welcomed as a scientific breakthrough. In Japan, researchers have produced 26 generations of cloned mice from a single ancestor. They have so far produced 598 mice that are genetic copies of one mouse. No human clone has ever been born till date. In 2008, researcher's created five human embryos by Somatic Cell Nuclear Transfers (SCMT) . From a donor a somatic cell was transplanted in a host egg cell. The embryo was developed till the blastocyst stage, studied and then destroyed. However, human cloning has not been seen in the same light. The world is still wondering whether the clone of Eve is real or a publicity stunt, but the news of her birth has renewed the debate over the ethics of cloning. A few scientists have called the clone 'time-delayed genetically-identical twin' of the donor rather than his or her replica. The reason for this is their belief that it is not possible to transfer the memory and personality of the donor to the newly-cloned. This is because the environmental factors and random events are bound to be different during the development of a cloned individual. Moreover, researchers have now put forward the hypothesis that the genetic contribution to looks, height, complexion are also affected by environmental factors.

There are proponents as well as opponents of human cloning. Those who are in favour of human cloning claim that it can be used both for *therapeutic*[5] and reproductive purposes. Therapeutic cloning uses the early stage cloned embryos to take out special cells called embryonic stem cells. These stem cells have the potential to develop into any other type of cell in the body, e.g., the cells of the liver, pancreas, skin, blood, heart muscle, brain, etc. These stem cells can be implanted into the body to treat various diseases like diabetes, Parkinson's, Alzheimer's, heart diseases, cancer, especially blood cancer and *autoimmune*[6] disorders. Therapeutic cloning will also be of great help in case of organ transplantation. Often, when a person needs organ transplantation, there are high chances of organ rejection because of *incompatibility*[7]. Therapeutic cloning will enable the person to have a hundred per cent genetically identical organ. This organ would be fully compatible and hence would not be rejected.

Reproductive cloning is a form of assisted or artificial reproduction. This process can give life to an identical copy of the original cell donor. The infertile couples can, therefore, have a child of their own genetic make-up. One can also raise an identical child at least in terms of genetic make-up after the unfortunate death of their child by cloning the dead. Scientists are already talking of 'designer babies'. The use of cloning techniques makes it theoretically possible to genetically engineer children. Genes that offer benefits such as height or intelligence could be incorporated into an embryo. Defective genes that trigger a disease or disability could be disarmed.

The opponents of human cloning include people from all sections of society. They are of the view that the use of the terms like 'therapeutic cloning' and 'reproductive cloning' yields only confusion and merely depicts the intention of their ultimate use. They believe that all forms of human cloning are unnecessary and immoral and have raised many ethical, religious, social, legal and biological issues. Lawmakers in the USA say that human beings should not be cloned to stock a medical junkyard of spare parts for experimentation. Yet others fear that clones may be treated as mere commodities or objects and might not be treated as unique individuals. A black market for cloned embryos may also come up where issueless couples could buy the clone of an embryo. Dr. Rudolf Jaenisch, a biology professor at the Massachusetts Institute of Technology, believes that many cloned animals have subtle brain defects or other problems. This means little in animals but could be devastating in a human being.

Further, the ethics of cloning has been questioned. Would a cloned child be accepted in any society where heredity and racial prejudices still influence ethical standards? The physical and psychological welfare of the cloned child cannot be guaranteed. The child might suffer from a loss of identity or freedom. Cloning may encourage parents to compare their cloned child to the adult from whom it was cloned, which means, they may value their cloned children according to how well they are able to meet the expectations instead of loving them as they are. This will affect the quality of parenting and family life. This will also impart a sense of diminished individuality and personal autonomy in a cloned individual besides disturbing their psychology.

While research and debate on cloning has reached advanced stages in some countries, India is yet to wake up to the challenge. If a researcher or infertility expert were to decide to clone a human body today, no law in India could stop him. Cloning technology finds no mention in any law book. At best, legal experts are of the opinion that the general criminal law can be invoked against such practices, but the provisions are inadequate to contain the menace in its entirety.

The list of ethical, moral, social, legal and biological issues is no doubt expanding day by day. Human cloning still looks unnecessary and immoral and is going to raise troubling questions in the future as well. The *protagonists*[8] of human cloning could come out with any number of compulsive factors supporting it, from being a godsend for sterile couples to the *panacea*[9] for all sorts of diseases. But mankind has been a witness to gross misuse of scientific discoveries, foremost among which would be the *proliferation*[10] of weapons of mass destruction and the spectre of germ and chemical warfare. Human cloning threatens to tear apart the basic fabric of the society. We can carry on stem cell research without human cloned embryos.

Aid to Vocabulary

1. *Dilemma* — state of indecision between alternatives, difficult situation
2. *Theologians* — those who study religion
3. *Scepticism* — unwillingness to believe things
4. *Transplantation* — transfer (living tissue or organ) and implant in another part of the body or in another (human or animal) body
5. *Therapeutic* — curative branch of medicine concerned with treatment of diseases
6. *Autoimmune* — caused by the production of antibodies against substance naturally present
7. *Incompatibility* — inability to live, work, together in harmony
8. *Protagonists* — advocates of action
9. *Panacea* — universal remedy
10. *Proliferation* — rapid increase in numbers

Points to Remember

1. Claims of human clone being produced gave rise to moral dilemma.
2. Clone is a group of cells or organisms produced asexually from one stock or ancestor.
3. The concept of cloning originated in 1953 and in 2002, the birth of the first ever human clone was claimed.
4. Controversy is going on over the issue of human cloning.
5. Human cloning can be used both for therapeutic and reproductive purposes.
6. Some believe that human cloning is unnecessary and immoral.
7. Ethical questions have been raised about cloning.
8. India has no law regarding cloning.
9. Human cloning may tear apart the social fabric.

Essay 11

THE EDUCATION SYSTEM IN INDIA

SYNOPSIS

India has a glorious tradition of education. India's ancient universities were considered as reservoirs of knowledge. The present educational system has been inherited from the British. Education is all round development of a child. The student is judged on the basis of his/her performance in the annual examination. Securing admission in a college is a difficult task. Besides reservation and capitation fee, competition is tough, seats are limited and cut off percentage is high. Co-relation of education with employment gives a poor picture because college degree does not guarantee a job. Our educational system must correspond to the needs of industry and business. There is a lack of emphasis on vocational courses. The educational system has undergone little change since the 19th century. In order to overcome the flaws in the existing system, radical reforms need to be implemented.

The foundation of every State is the education of its youth. The instability of India could, perhaps, be attributed to the millions of educated, yet unemployed people, the country abounds in. The education system gives degrees but does not guarantee employment. The education system in India is *hackneyed*[1] and it mainly lays stress on theoretical knowledge. Apparently it requires a serious revamping exercise. In a nutshell, some radical changes must be introduced in order to tune it to the needs of the modern society. India has a glorious tradition of education. During the ancient times, Indian educational centres and universities were the temples of knowledge. India's ancient universities of Nalanda, Taxila, Pataliputra and Ujjaini were considered as the reservoirs of knowledge, and they beckoned students from many foreign countries to India. Indian education was respected around the world for its high quality, syllabi and learning. However, the glory of the past did not transcend into the future. Successive foreign invasions destroyed the country's economy, educational system and polity.

The present education system of India was inherited from the British and the education imparted under it, is predominantly theoretical. The British evolved a system of learning aimed at producing 'Brown Sahebs' and clerks in large numbers. It was Lord McCaulay's System of Education. It was supposed to perpetuate loyalty to the British educational and political institutions.

'Educational system in India has become ineffective and it needs a complete overhauling' is what almost all educationists seem to agree upon but before we proceed any further, it is imperative to know exactly what education means. Education has been defined by different thinkers in many different ways but if we draw *inferences*[2] from them, we can conclude safely that education means the all round development of a child inculcating in him/her all the human values that need to be kept intact in order to let the society progress as well as it can. Education must bring out the *inherent*[3] virtues of the child and at the same time it must eliminate the vices that may be latent in him/her; it must instill in him/her patriotism, discipline, obedience and self-respect and it must prepare the child for future so that he/she can lead a responsible life.

As per Merriam-Webster's dictionary, 'Education is a process of training aimed at developing the knowledge, skill and character of the youngsters by formal schooling, training or teaching'.

With the various flaws in the inherited education system in India, the number of universities and colleges has, increased manifold since Independence. The number of Universities has increased 34 times from 20 in 1950 to 677 in 2014, whereas, the number of colleges registered an increase of 74 times with just 500 in 1950 has grown to 37,204, as on March 31, 2013.

The pressure of the education system is taking its toll on the toddlers who, barely out of their infancy, are made to identify fruits, vegetables, animals, alphabets, numerals, etc., to qualify for admission in kindergarten. Parents seeking admission of their children are interviewed to assess their educational background and financial capability. However, the Supreme Court has now ordered that there will be no interviews for *toddlers*[4] and their parents for nursery admissions. But in the educational system, there still exists the predominance of textual knowledge. Students do not learn the practical application of knowledge. Maulana Abul Kalam Azad, the first Education Minister of free India had once observed that "there is no adjustment between the system of our education and the needs of our life." Indeed, the curricula adhered to by the system find little or no application, in the practical life of the people.

The examination-oriented system judges the student on the basis of his/her performance in the annual examination held at the end of every session. The marks mania drives every teacher and every parent to expect the very best from every student, (90 per cent or above). Parental and peer pressure to secure good percentage for entering into prestigious colleges and courses, hinders the proper development of the child.

Getting admission in a good college is a *herculean*[5] task. Applicants are many, but seats, few. Colleges offer limited seats for various courses, and hence, cut off percentage for admission is *invariably*[6] high. Some colleges have a sports or extra-curricular activities quota but this is used mainly to secure back-door entry for favoured candidates. Colleges have reservation of seats for various special categories, like Scheduled Castes, Scheduled Tribes, etc., in accordance with government directives. Applicants belonging to such categories are able to secure admission at comparatively low percentages. Capitation fee is charged by colleges in a *clandestine*[7] manner which very often sidelines the meritorious students. Dealing with the menace of capitation fees, the Supreme Court on August 14, 2003, ruled that no professional institution can charge capitation fees from students seeking admission. This ruling has affected the engineering, medical, architecture and management colleges mainly in Maharashtra, Tamil Nadu and Karnataka. The court also said that private, unaided or minority institutions imparting technical or medical education could decide their own fee structure which must be scrutinised by a committee headed by a retired High Court judge in each state.

Though the university regulations require each student to have 75 per cent attendance, the fact is that nobody observes this regulation. Reports of mass absenteeism appear in most universities as soon as teaching commences. It is often seen that the students not attending classes in the college opt to go for private tuitions or coaching. Students attend coaching classes for each and every subject. This is the latest trend going on among students. Some of the teachers who *shirk*[8] their duty in school/ college only to make extra money through private coaching are also responsible for this kind of degradation in the education system. Children of well-to-do families can afford to go for tuitions but the plight of the poor children is very sad. Education is not properly imparted in schools, colleges and universities and as a result, the bright students who are poor are the worst affected.

The present education system needs to be reformed so that all children get proper education. The bitter reality is that an average youngster who merely concentrates on the prescribed course has a bleak future as the university degree does not assure him of a *lucrative*[9] job. There is a lack of emphasis on vocational education. A modest attempt in favour of vocationalisation was launched by the UGC about a decade ago and it did achieve some degree of success. But it has been very limited.

The shortcomings in the present education system can be attributed to the fact that only a few changes have been made in the system that fails to suit the needs of the changing times. The same regimen of three-hour examinations and emphasis on *rote*[10] learning has continued. Ideally, the education system should have been overhauled after Independence. But Indian academics failed to carry out curriculum or examination reforms in the radical sense. Though some intellectuals did help in improving books on certain subjects, the *overarching*[11] colonial legacy of the classroom, text and examination remained unaltered.

The education system as of today is in dire need of reform. The few attempts so far to reform the education system have done but little. Many commissions were constituted to look into the flaws of the existing system. The Mudaliar Commission, the Kothari Commission and the Radhakrishnan Commission recommended thorough reforms in the existing system. According to the recommendations, a student's performance was to be judged on the basis of periodical tests and overall performance. Imparting of practical training to students to enhance their skills and improve their chances of employment was also recommended.

A school examination system which is designed to cut stress and bring India on par with international educational standards came into its own in 2011 when following the directions of the Human Resource Development Ministry, the Central Board of Secondary Education (CBSE) decided to give grades to Class X students commencing from the 2010 board examinations and then 2011 onwards, the examinations became optional. However, the CBSE has decided to reintroduce class X Board examinations from 2018—which will be compulsory for all students.

In another innovative step, the Open Text Based Assessment (OTBA) for class IX was introduced in March 2014 as an additional section within the main question paper with an extra time of 30 minutes allotted for the same.

All-India Council for Technical Education (AICTE) has begun to conduct a common admission test for MBA. The Ministry of HRD* has begun a single all-India entrance examination for admission to UG** Programmes in engineering to avoid multiplicity of examinations and reduce the stress level among students. The Medical Council of India (MCI) has provided for admission to any medical course on the basis of an all-India level examination. A Common Teachers' Eligibility Test (CTET) has been

*HRD: Human Resource Development
**UG: Under Graduate

introduced by the HRD Ministry, to be cleared by aspiring teachers with a minimum of 60 per cent marks to be eligible to teach upto class VIII in any government or private (recognised) school. An all-India Common Law Admission Test (CLAT) has also been introduced.

The scope of formal education should be broadened by giving a place to community work, sports, crafts and fine arts in the main curriculum. The aim should be holistic development of the personality, instead of sharpening analytical and literary minds in isolation. This would help in tapping the various talents of the students.

Unlike that of the ancient time, Education today is not for knowledge sake; its aim today is to find a job of one's own choice and draw a handsome amount of salary, so as to lead a comfortable and convenient life. And here lies the drawback of our system. Our education system appears to be giving the impression that the ultimate aim of education is to pass examinations with good marks. It fails to instil the responsibility in students, towards society and humanity that is part and parcel of true development. Another striking drawback of our education system is that it does not prepare the student with the skills that are to be tested in any profession as well as in one's life. Situation today in India is very funny. There are job vacancies but suitable candidates for those jobs are few. On the other hand, lakhs of unemployed people run helter and skelter in search of jobs but to their deep dismay, find none.

Education system should be planned keeping the requirements of industry and business in mind. It is necessary to discourage the culture of taking up graduation course at the college level just for the sake of it. Following Gandhiji's method of 'learning by doing', vocational education should be introduced in universities. The number of vocational courses in the colleges should be increased so as to be able to provide jobs to the youth. The flaws in the existing educational system need to be removed, and corrupt practices, curbed. The required changes should be brought about to make the system more effective and development-oriented.

It is encouraging to see that much of the recommended reforms and new concepts are being incorporated in the educational institutions of all kinds. A lot more still needs to be done.

Aid to Vocabulary

1. *Hackneyed* — become dull with overuse
2. *Inferences* — conclusions

3. *Inherent* — ingrained
4. *Toddlers* — children who have only recently learnt to walk
5. *Herculean* — requiring great strength or effort
6. *Invariably* — always, at all times, without varying
7. *Clandestine* — done secretly, covert
8. *Shirk* — avoid duty or responsibility
9. *Lucrative* — producing much money, profitable
10. *Rote* — learn by repeating without understanding the meaning
11. *Overarching* — covering a wide range of topics, interests, activities, etc.

POINTS TO REMEMBER

1. In ancient times, Indian education was respected around the world for its high quality, syllabi and learning.
2. The present educational system is a British legacy.
3. The number of universities and colleges in India is increasing.
4. Students learn their lessons by rote in the examination-oriented system.
5. Securing admission in a good school or college is a herculean task today.
6. The standard of teaching is deteriorating day by day.
7. College degree does not assure employment.
8. There is a need to reform the existing educational system.

NO. OF PVT., STATE AND CENTRAL UNIVERSITIES AND COLLEGES			
2011-12	**University Level Institutions**	**Colleges**	**Diploma Granting Institutions**
Central	152	669	NL
State	316	13,024	3,207
Private	191	19,930	9,541
Total	**659**	**33,623**	**12,748**
NO. OF UNIVERSITIES AND COLLEGES			
Year	**Student Enrolment (In Million)**	**Number of Universities**	**Number of Colleges**
1970-71	2	103	3,604
1980-81	2.8	133	4,722
1990-91	4.9	190	7,346
2000-01	8.4	256	12.806
2006-07	16.6	387	24,170
2011-12	25.9	659	33,693

Source: Twelfth Five-Year Plan

ANSWER TO INDIA'S TRANSFORMATION LIES IN ITS EDUCATION SYSTEM: JAVADEKAR

Union HRD Minister Prakash Javadekar on October 18, 2016 said the answer to country's sustainable transformation lies in its education system, as he underscored how India was once prosperous in the past due to universities like Nalanda, Takshila and Vikramshila. "I always say India had 25% of the world GDP and 35% of world trade for centuries together. Today, we are not even 1% of world trade. We are lagging behind as far as GDP is concerned," he said. "And therefore, how nation can sustainably transform is the real thing. The answer lies in our education system," he said.

Javadekar was speaking through a video link at an international conclave on higher education organised in Gandhinagar as a part of pre-Vibrant Gujarat Investors' Summit. Javadekar said that had there been a ranking system in the past, universities like Nalanda, Takshila, Vikramshila would have ranked number 1, 2 and 3 in the world.

"Indian universities were the best. The world's talent used to come here to learn. So I believe that only those countries can prosper which have the best of universities," he said, stressing the need to improve higher education in the country. For making higher education better, he said, we first need to improve "the learning outcomes of primary and secondary education".

"In primary education, we have to inculcate and promote inquisitiveness in a student, because that is the foundation for any new innovation. Unless you promote inquisitiveness, there will be no new thoughts and people won't be able to inculcate innovative attitude," he said. "But at the higher learning centres, a government's duty is to provide atmosphere for research, innovation and improvement of quality," he further said.

Source: Press Trust of India

Essay 12

REFORMS NEEDED IN INDIAN EDUCATIONAL SYSTEM

SYNOPSIS

The Article 21A of our Constitution lays down that, the state shall provide free and compulsory education to all children of the age of six to fourteen years. The Government of India has introduced 'Sarva Shiksha Abhiyan' to cover the entire country. According to UNESCO's report, India's ranking in the fight against illiteracy is very low. Poor infrastructure, shortage of well-qualified teachers, obsolete teaching methods etc., are responsible for this grim picture. From elementary school level to college level, the quality of teaching needs to be upgraded. UGC has directed all universities and colleges in India to have an internal quality assurance cell to improve the quality of higher education. The government has taken some important steps in the Eleventh Five Year Plan towards this end. Semester system and gradation system are some of the important methods taken to improve the standard of our educational system.

The word 'education' implies human progress. The 86th Amendment to our Constitution adds a new Article 21A, which says : "The state shall provide free and compulsory education to all children of the age of six to fourteen years in such manner as the state may, by law, *determine*[1]." This makes the right to education a fundamental right for children in this age group. A new fundamental duty is added making it mandatory for all parents to send their children to school when they are six to fourteen years of age. But, the real picture is quite different.

Our government has launched a national programme, 'Sarva Shiksha Abhiyan (SSA),' which aims to cover the entire country to provide useful and relevant elementary education for all children between six to fourteen year age group. The goal of this programme was to bridge all gender and social category gaps at primary stage by 2007 and at elementary education level by 2010. But, the overall scene is not encouraging. UNESCO's Global Monitoring Report *evaluates*[2] 127 countries in all and places India on the bottom rank of 15 countries with a low 'Education for All' development index. Moreover, India's ranking in the fight against illiteracy has slipped from 100 to 105.

In spite of providing free and compulsory education, the educational backwardness of India even after 65 years of independence is quite alarming. If we observe, we would find that there are two possible causes of this backwardness. First, is the direct cost of schooling, which imposes a substantial burden on poor families and the second is the low quality of teaching, which reduces the child's interest in education.

The schools are really in a bad state in India, especially those run by government. Poor infrastructure, shortage of teachers, unimaginative syllabus, poor teaching methods, all contribute to the sorry state of Indian education. It is also a fact that there is an acute shortage of qualified teachers nationwide, especially in rural areas. The ability and skills of the teachers are a matter of concern. A study by National University of Educational Planning & Administration (UNEPA) shows that almost half of 47 lakh elementary school teachers in India have not studied beyond class XII. Only one-third of those teachers, who teach classes I to VIII, are graduates.

Elementary school is generally viewed as a training ground for young minds. But unfortunately, because of unqualified and untrained teachers, children do not get this basic training properly. These teachers are unable to understand the peculiar needs of young children. They do not know that children's needs, interests and responses may differ and they have to deal with every young child differently. For this, we need qualified and trained teachers. All those teachers, who are recruited to teach in elementary schools should receive training—both before they start teaching and on a regular basis throughout their career. In some states, it is compulsory for candidates to undergo a teachers' training programme, but the rule is not as rigorously implemented as it ought to be.

Today, secondary education is regarded as a preparatory ground for university education. The board examinations demand cramming to analysis and application. They lay stress on content by neglecting the in-depth understanding of the subject. A single examination evaluating system, a *redundant*[3] syllabus unable to inspire the students are some of the main problems of secondary education in India.

After passing out of school, students are pushed into horrible experience of seeking admission into colleges. There is no uniformity of procedure, here various considerations other than the intelligence of the students play an important role. The worst victim of the whole system are the unfortunate students, who are caught in a situation of complete chaos and confusion. Here also, the main aim of the student is to pass the university examination. For this, they are completely dependent on private tuition provided by college teachers as the classes are not taken regularly by the respective teachers.

In the coaching classes, teachers only teach the answers to the probable questions from the examination point of view. So, the students are completely unaware of total knowledge of the subject matter. This partial knowledge of a subject cannot help student in any way, except to pass the examination. Naturally, such individuals cannot contribute to the development of our society. Again in our country, there is a wide gap between education and its marketability. Our faulty education system cannot groom the students to get the appropriate jobs.

The University Grants Commission (UGC) has directed all universities and colleges in India to have an internal quality assurance cell to improve the quality of higher education. This decision was taken under the UGC Act, 1956. This is the first step for the introduction of mandatory *accreditation*[4] for universities and for colleges under the Eleventh Plan.

By creating these mandatory cells, the UGC aims to provide an internal mechanism to improve the quality of education in the institutes of higher learning. UGC provided financial incentive of rupees five lakh to universities and rupees two lakh to colleges to set up this cell. The cell has a full-time director to look into the quality aspects of education. It is helped by an advisory body headed by the chairman of the institution. The cell helps to develop and apply quality *parameters*[5] for various academic and administrative activities. It maintains institutional data and solicits feedback from students on quality issues. It also prepares annual quality assurance report to be submitted to UGC and NAAC (National Assessment and Accreditation Council), which is also available for public viewing.

Another target of reforms is the examination system. Most educationists agree that India's universities need to update their evaluation procedures. Annual examinations have become irrelevant for testing knowledge. Replacing this with continuous assessment has also been suggested by the experts. The *semester*[6] system and continuous assessment and evaluation system have been introduced in all central universities.

The important measures, which are required to be taken, should be started from primary-level. Primary level education should be more creative, interesting and practical. At the secondary and higher secondary level, a pattern of common evaluation system or gradation system may be introduced. From the academic year 2010-11, Class X students are being handed their results based on internal examinations and a 'continuous and comprehensive evaluation' of such qualities as physical education and speaking skills. Students can, if they wish for an examination to test their skills, but this is voluntary. However, the CBSE has decided to reintroduce compulsory 10th class Board examinations from 2018.

Proper education is regarded as a necessity for overall development of society. So, it is the duty of our government to introduce a scientific modern education system, which can eliminate all the evils from our society.

Aid to Vocabulary

1. *Determine* — find out or establish precisely
2. *Evaluate* — to find the value or amount of
3. *Redundant* — superfluous, not needed
4. *Accreditation* — recognise officially
5. *Parameters* — a rule or limit that controls what something is
6. *Semester* — a half-year course or term in universities

Points to Remember

1. According to the Constitution, the State shall provide free and compulsory education to all children of the age of six to fourteen years.
2. The Government of India has taken up 'Sarva Shiksha Abhiyan' to cover the entire country.
3. The overall school system is in shambles.
4. Modern education system must be replaced with a more interactive system.
5. A single examination evaluating system and a redundant syllabus fail to inspire the students at school level.
6. College education is unable to groom the students to get the appropriate jobs.
7. UGC has directed all universities and colleges in India to have an internal quality assurance cell to improve the quality of higher education.
8. Government has taken some important steps in the Eleventh Five Year Plan to improve the quality of teaching.
9. Semester system and gradation system are some of the important measures taken to improve the quality of education in our country.

"Education does not mean simply cramming up of books and passing certain examinations. As a matter of fact, a good system of education has the least number of books as it lays greater stress on practical training. The primary aim of any system of education should be to mould the character of students so as to help them face life with courage and determination. The basic education has to be adopted as the foundation on which the whole system of education is built in the country...."

—Pt. Jawaharlal Nehru

WE CAN LEAD IN HIGHER EDUCATION: PRESIDENT

Expressing hope that India will again lead the world in higher education, President Pranab Mukherjee on October 3, 2016 said excellence in higher education was the hallmark of India for 1,700 years, from 6th century BC to 11th century AD.

Mukherjee said from the glory of Taxilla to the collapse of Nalanda, India led in higher education and attracted students from across the globe.

Mukherjee expressed concern over higher education institutions in India failing to make a mark globally.

He said 736 universities and over 36,000 colleges have failed to feature among the best institutions in the global rankings for best 200 institutions.

He, however, added that the situation has changed somewhat from last year, when two institutions, including IIT Delhi, found place among the top ranking institutions of the world.

"I am confident that in the coming years, more institutions will find a place in the world's top ranked institutions. Because this is our field," he said.

"It pains me now that every year, 6,000 students leave India for higher education abroad in the US, Australia and European countries," he said.

Essay 13

ARE EXAMINATIONS NECESSARY?

SYNOPSIS

Examinations are conducted for evaluating the students' knowledge. The present system of education ignores students' individual skills and intelligence. Even then, parents and teachers judge students' potential through examinations. The Indian system of education is based on the pattern set up by the British. Nothing much is taught beyond the syllabus and only examinations are used to evaluate the progress or grade of a student. Various commissions, which were set up to improve this system, recommended practical training and periodical tests. Cheating, leaking of question papers and other corrupt practices, that have cropped up in the examination system should be checked. The aim of education should be to equip the student with the necessary skills and intelligence to face the tough battle of life.

Examinations are aimed at judging the students' knowledge within a specific time frame. They enable the teachers to get a feedback or to know how well the students have understood the subject. A good result, besides encouraging the students, makes the teacher as well as the parents happy. The effort of the teacher is rewarded when students pass an examination with good marks. Thus, a teacher's *dedication*[1] towards the profession of teaching is also judged through examinations. Parents take pride in their children when they perform well in the examinations.

Education is supposed to be knowledge oriented but now-a-days students don't learn to acquire knowledge, rather they study only with a view to pass or score good marks in tests. The teachers themselves teach students with the objective that the students have to pass the examination. Students take their studies seriously only when it is time for them to appear in the examinations. Examinations make them work hard because every student wants to score good marks. Examinations help the teachers and the parents in analysing the amount of labour put in by the students in gaining knowledge.

However, there are certain flaws in the examination system. The system of education in India is based on the pattern set up by the British. The knowledge imparted is restricted to the curriculum framed. Students are taught according to the prescribed syllabus and little beyond. When a student is unable to grasp a particular subject, he seeks private tuitions or enrols himself in a coaching institute.

Students *tend*[2] to learn their subjects by heart, without applying their mind. As such, *cramming*[3] enables many students to pass examinations though, they retain little of what they crammed. Most students anticipate examinations with anxiety. They, at a very young age, begin to feel the tension and stress of examinations.

Class XII is meant to be the culmination of years of preparatory learning to decide on vocation choices, but Class XII for a vast-majority of students ends up being a stressful journey into the unknown. The Boards, the competitive tests, the three hours allotted to shape a life—it has become a system that focuses on pointing out the inadequacies rather than highlighting the abilities of students. Inspite of scoring good marks in examination, students fail to get admission in their desired course and/or college.

Examinations are just the first in a series of tests that initiate students into a fiercely competitive world. But the importance attached to them is unreasonably high. During the examination period and till the result is declared, not only the students but also their parents remain tense. It is regarded as nothing less than a do-or-die situation.

Students do not get enough time for games and are unable to pursue their hobbies due to the burden of examinations. This affects their health adversely. Failure in examination lowers the *self-esteem*[4] of the students and generates a negative self-image in their mind. Today, some schools utilise the services of psychologists and counsellors to help the students cope with the pressure of examinations.

Dr. Rajesh Sagar, professor of psychiatry at AIIMS, acknowledges the hazards of high pressure education and says he is seeing more and more child patients in his day to day practice. He says parental expectation to perform coupled with a student's own expectation from himself/herself is taking toll on his/her health, especially in college admission season. Cut throat competition, dearth of avenues, a premium of high performance all harm the child's psychological health.

The anxiety of not being able to score well enough to get into a good college is causing many psychological disorders in children. Some children even commit suicide after failing in the Board Examinations.

The emphasis on marks scored is not the only factor creating stress in the examinees. Students are disillusioned with the examination system because corrupt practices have become a common affair. Leakage of question papers, copying and cheating in the examination halls, and bribing the authorities to tamper with and alter the marks, all undermine the credibility of the examination system. The prevailing education system does little to equip students with skills and training that may enhance their career prospects.

In order to overcome the shortcomings present in our educational system, many Education Commissions were set up from time to time to suggest changes in the pattern. Acting on their suggestions, the Central Board of Secondary Education (CBSE) and other State Boards of Secondary Education decided to introduce a separate stream of *vocational*[5] education. According to educational experts, ongoing evaluation is more effective than board examinations. To evaluate a student's performance continuously during the whole year, periodic tests may be held regularly. This could make the examination system more acceptable and practical.

The aim of education should be to build the students' character and personality. It should widen their *sphere*[6] of knowledge. The educational system should not only be theoretical and academic but should also equip the students with the necessary skills and intelligence to face the tough battle of life.

Students should not be encouraged to learn by *rote*[7]. projects and term papers may add soul and substance to the students' knowledge base. When History, Geography and Mathematics are reduced to mere digits on a marksheet, they cease to inspire or give joy.

The method of teaching as well as of assessing needs to be overhauled. It should be designed to ensure a healthy, inspiring and joyful process of learning for the students. Students require a less burdensome and a stress-free learning experience which is enjoyable and refreshing.

Nevertheless, the system of examination, that has been operational for decades, cannot be changed overnight. It will take considerable time and effort to change the system. While this *transition*[8] takes place, the unfair practices like cheating in the examination hall and leakage of question papers should be checked. It must also be seen that the answer sheets of students are properly assessed by the teachers, so that fair evaluation takes place. These measures will build the credibility of our education system and we may, then, be able to strengthen the knowledge base of our manpower that can take the nation to greater heights.

Aid to Vocabulary

1. *Dedication* — devotion
2. *Tend* — be inclined, directed to
3. *Cramming* — learning by heart
4. *Self-esteem* — good opinion of one's own character and abilities
5. *Vocational* — of or relating to qualifications and preparation needed for a particular job
6. *Sphere* — range of interest
7. *Rote* — the process of learning something by repeated study rather than by understanding
8. *Transition* — the process or a period of change from one state or condition to another

Points to Remember

1. Examinations are tests for evaluating the students' performance.
2. Examinations make the students work hard.
3. There are certain flaws in the examination system.
4. Students and their parents feel the tension of examinations.
5. Students getting low percentage of marks suffer hardships.
6. In order to overcome the shortcomings in our educational system, education commissions were set up from time to time, to suggest reforms.
7. The aim of education should be to equip the students with the necessary skills and intelligence to face life.
8. The system of examinations cannot be changed overnight.

APTITUDE TEST

In a move to help students choose realistic career goals and tackle parental pressure, the Centre is planning an aptitude test for class 11 and 12.

The HRD ministry, sources said, is ready to set up a National Testing Service (NTS), a body that will conduct a test similar to Scholastic Aptitude Test (SAT) which would include questions on numerical, verbal and diagrammatic reasoning.

Initially, the test will be conducted for class 11 and 12 students and later will be introduced for those in class 9 and 10, sources said.

On the lines of US-based Educational Testing Service (ETS), the largest educational testing and assessment organisation that conducts various tests like GRE and TOEFL in US and abroad, the government will set up the NTS that will develop and conduct the aptitude test for students from 2017-18 academic session. Sources in the ministry said all stakeholders including various higher education institutions (IITs and NITs), regulatory bodies (CBSE and AICTE) and educationists will be consulted to set up NTS.

Essay
14

EDUCATING THE GIRL CHILD

SYNOPSIS

The hypocrisy of the Indian male has led to large scale female illiteracy in the country. As per Census 2001, the female literacy rate was 53.67 per cent. As per Census 2011 the female literacy rate is 65 per cent. The discrimination between sons and daughters in a family is responsible for female illiteracy. Parents feel that educating the girl child is waste of money because she has to remain within the confines of her home. In India, states like Kerala have worked on increasing female literacy. Andhra Pradesh and Tamil Nadu have also worked towards women empowerment which has led to low population growth. The Government should work with the NGOs towards achieving total female literacy. Apart from education, vocational training should also be imparted to them. This would raise their standard of living and help in social reforms.

According to Hindu *mythology*[1], the deity of learning is Goddess Saraswati (a female), but there are cases aplenty where women were forbidden from receiving education. This reflects the *hypocrisy*[2] prevalent among the Indian men.

In the early Vedic age, families were patrilineal and the birth of sons was eagerly awaited. But at the same time, daughters born into a family were taken good care of and their education was never neglected. However, in the later Vedic age, the daughters began to be considered as a social burden. The girls of only the upper classes enjoyed the privilege of receiving education. In the medieval period, the situation worsened as girls were virtually deprived of education. In the nineteenth century, Raja rammohan Roy worked for the emancipation of women and the process of educating the girl child was put back on track.

According to United Nation's consensus, over the half of the population of the world is that of women, yet they do two third of the world's work, earn one-tenth of the world's income and own less than one-hundredth of the world's property.

In India, the statistics on female literacy rate are dismal. The overall literacy rate increased from 18.3% in 1951 to 64.84% in 2001. The female literacy rate increased from 8.86% in 1951 to 53.67% in 2001. As per Census 2011, the overall literacy rate has gone up to 74.04% from 64.84%. For males it has risen to 82.14% from 75.26% and for females to 65.46% from 53.67%. The percentage of girls enrolled at the primary level of education is slightly more than that of those enrolled at the upper primary level.

This difference in the respective male and female literacy rates owes its origin to the traditional practice of discrimination that has been the norm since very early. Female foeticide and infanticide are practices that *manifest*[3] the preference for the male child. A female child, if spared life, is considered to be worthy only for subordination to the male and is brought up accordingly in the Indian family system. The girls are denied medical care, education and most childhood privileges and are kept subjugated. Such gender bias is attributed to the popular notion of people that girls should be confined within the walls of the house. Boys, on the other hand, are educated because they would grow up to provide for their family and support their parents in their old age.

In many lower middle class families, parents deem it unreasonable to first spend for the education of the girl child and later give a lump sum as dowry. It is widely believed that if a girl is well educated, it becomes difficult to find a suitable match for her. So, they prefer to keep her illiterate. Socio-economic problems of drug addiction and alcoholism in the family and severe monetary constraints result in large female dropouts at the upper primary level. Female illiteracy has made women *vulnerable*[4] to exploitation when forced to work to supplement the family income, at half the wages that their male counterparts earn for the same work.

The literacy rates among women are *abysmally*[5] low in some states. This has crippled the State machinery as none of the development schemes is able to penetrate the lower strata of society. Social evils like child-marriage and child labour, and high population growth accompanied by high mortality rate in these states, are the result of illiteracy among women.

It has been rightly said, "if you educate a man you educate a person, but if you educate a woman you educate a family." It can be noticed in those states, where female literacy is not neglected, have recorded low population growth. In the rest of the states, the condition of women is pathetic. Illiteracy has forced them to be dependent upon their parents and, later on, to be controlled by their husbands. Marriage at a young age, followed by the birth of a number of children, leads to maternal and infant mortality. At only a few places in such states, the females are aware of the various contraceptive methods available in the country.

Women are exploited when they work in the unorganised sector and also at home. Being uneducated herself, the mother is unable to teach her children or give them proper guidance. Child labour is prevalent among the illiterate class mainly because the mother is unable to guide her children and protect them from this *menace*[6]. These are but some of the ill-effects of female illiteracy.

To *ameliorate*[7] the lot of women, therefore, it is imperative to educate them. The Government and the Non-Governmental Organisations should work together to achieve total female literacy. This could be a stepping-stone towards the rapid development of the country. The Government had, as a step in this direction, declared the year 2001 as the Year of Women Empowerment. In the rural sector, apart from education, vocational training should also be imparted to the womenfolk. The trained women could later set up small scale industries on a co-operative basis and earn their livelihood. Co-operatives like AMUL and SEWA in Gujarat are some of the success stories, which have resulted because of women empowerment. Women working in such co-operatives help themselves and also contribute to the national economy. Women from rural areas can set up small scale industries like manufacturing perfumes, incense sticks, papads, pickles and handicrafts and nurturing plants in nurseries. It can help them raise their standard of living as well as the per capita income of the nation.

Education creates awareness which could lead to the decline in child-marriage, child labour and other social evils. Social reforms can only be achieved if the girl child in every family is educated. As Swami Vivekananda said, "Educate your women first and leave them to themselves, then they will tell you what reforms are needed."

Indifference towards the education of a girl child derives inspiration from the belief that she can go astray in the company of outsiders around her which would bring dishonour to the family. The rising graph of crime against women, the adverse mindset of the society and mind boggling incidents taking place frequently in educational institutions too are responsible, to a far extent, for this situation. Steps to curb all these should immediately be taken to instil confidence among women and their parents.

Parents should not create a gender bias among their children. Every child born into this world is the responsibility of the parents and hence it is prudent to limit the size of one's family. More children would mean less attention on each child which could prove *detrimental*[8] to the development of the family. However, the situation is slowly changing now. Girls are getting better education facilities and are aspiring to become independent. They are found to be more determined and committed towards education and they outdo boys in various examinations. Girls are also more responsible and sincere in their work. They show *diligence*[9], coupled with higher maturity levels than boys. Educated girls are known to support their parents in their old age even as their brothers fail to do so. They are also making inroads in the male-dominated/professions gradually and are able to walk beside the men rather than behind them. They are breaking every *glass ceiling*[10] and conquering all male *bastions*[11].

Educated women can even put an end to the *dowry* system if they stand up against it. Parents should be enlightened about the fact that the money they wish to preserve for their daughter's dowry could be utilised for her education which would grant her independence. Young men and women should be encouraged to say no to dowry and to consider education as the eligibility criterion for marriage. Thus, education of the girl child would mean the *emancipation*[12] of women and the social development of the nation. The nation can no more afford to ignore the needs of the girl child or discriminate against her or happily *relegate*[13] her existence to the stereotyped role of a wife, mother or sister. She needs to be recognised as the 'woman of the future' and a productive citizen of the country entitled to all the fruits of social and economic progress on an equal footing with her male counterpart.

Aid to Vocabulary

1. *Mythology* — the study of myths describing the legendary deeds of God and imaginary persons
2. *Hypocrisy* — concealment of one's true character
3. *Manifest* — make clear
4. *Vulnerable* — capable of being hurt
5. *Abysmally* — very badly
6. *Menace* — a thing or person that threatens to harm somebody
7. *Ameliorate* — make better
8. *Detrimental* — harmful
9. *Diligence* — capacity for hard work
10. *Glass ceiling* — unfair prohibition
11. *Bastions* — exclusive domains
12. *Emancipation* — freedom from social, political or moral restraint
13. *Relegate* — to put in a lower or less important position, rank, etc.

Points to Remember

1. In the early vedic age, the daughters were taken good care of and their education was never neglected. However, the situation changed drastically in later ages.
2. As per Census 2011, the statistics on female literacy rate are dismal. It is much lower than the male literacy rate. The male literacy rate is 82.14% while the female literacy rate is 65.46%.
3. In some rural areas, it is believed that if a girl is well educated then it becomes difficult to find a match for her.
4. Social evils like child-marriage and child labour are some of the outcomes of illiteracy among women.
5. The Government and the Non-Governmental Organisations should work together to achieve total female literacy.
6. Education of the girl child would mean emancipation of women and consequently social development of the nation.

WOMEN EMPOWERMENT SCHEMES

- National Programme for Education of Girls at Elementary Level (NPEGEL) scheme addresses obstacles to girls' education through village – level women's groups and community groups that follow up on girls' enrolment, attendance and achievement, and recommend village specific action.
- Kasturba Gandhi Balika Vidyalaya (KGBV) scheme provides for setting up of residential upper primary schools with 75 percent seats for SC/ST/OBC and minority communities and 25 percent for girls from BPL (below poverty line) families.
- Centrally sponsored scheme for setting up of girls' hostels for Senior and Higher Secondary Schools provides 100 seats in each of the 3500 educationally backward blocks.
- Mahila Samakhya Scheme through Mahila Sanghas or Women's forums, enables women to meet, reflect, ask, articulate and make informed choices. These sanghas, through various programmes, work to bring a change in the rural women's outlook and increase awareness on gender parity and education.
- The government of National Capital Territory of Delhi has initiated an ambitious LADLI scheme for enhancing the social status of the girl child through financial assistance (upto two girls in a family) for education, leading to self-reliance and protection from discrimination and deprivation.
- The centrally sponsored scheme National Scheme of Incentive to Girls for Secondary Education (NSIGSE) was launched in May 2008 with the objective to establish an enabling environment to reduce the drop-outs and to promote the enrolment of girl children belonging mainly to SC/ST communities in secondary schools.
- The Sarva Shiksha Abhiyan (SSA) is being implemented to achieve the goals of universal access and retention, bridging of gender and social gaps in enrolment levels and enhancement of learning levels of all children.
- Mahila Samakhya (MS), which has a special focus on the Educationally Backward Blocks (EBBs) is a unique, process-oriented programme which has demonstrated ways of empowering rural poor and marginalised women. It has promoted their effective participation in the public domain and in educational and learning processes.

Essay
15

IS SEX EDUCATION NECESSARY IN SCHOOLS?

SYNOPSIS

The issue pertaining to introduction of sex education in Indian schools is very important. A survey shows that 53 per cent of children are sexually abused. Discussing sex is still considered a taboo in India. Parents feel embarrassed to talk openly with their children in this regard. Due to ignorance about sex-related facts, the youth fall victim to AIDS and other sexually transmitted diseases. Many NGOs are trying to create awareness about AIDS. Sex education can help people to make informed choices regarding health and sexuality. It is high time sex education was introduced in schools for the benefit of the youth of the country.

The issue pertaining to introduction of sex education in Indian schools is very important. Recommendations of the National Curriculum Framework 2005 focus on cultivating a proper understanding of sex-related issues with special emphasis on teenage pregnancies, drug addiction and adolescent sex education. A survey sponsored by the Ministry of Women and Child Development, Government of India, was carried out by the NGO*, 'Prayas' in association with UNICEF**. It depicted that more than 53 per cent of children in India were sexually abused. In half of these cases, the persons who committed the crime, were found to be in a position of authority and responsible for the protection of children. A majority of the children did not report for fear of reprisal. A report, released in 2013, by the Asian Centre for Human Rights (ACHR) based on National Crime Records Bureau (NCRB) figures reveals a total of 48,338 reported cases of child rape between 2001 and 2011.

Sex education has become a debatable issue. Many people feel that such *delicate*[1] issues should be left to the discretion of parents. Parents themselves feel *embarrassed*[2] to talk openly with their children in this regard. Discussing sex is still a *taboo*[3] in Indian society. It is believed that educating our children about sex can break down the pre-existing notions of modesty and tear apart the moral fabric of our society. But with the alarming increase in the instances of AIDS, unwanted/unplanned/unwed

*NGO – Non-Governmental Organisation
**UNICEF – United Nations International Children's Emergency Fund

pregnancies and other diseases related to sex, it has become imperative that sex education be given due importance in schools and colleges.

Physical and mental changes in children start appearing with puberty. Sexual development begins much earlier than that. Many children find it strange or difficult to cope with the changes. They grow up with curiosity stamped on their minds. So, it is very important to impart sex education. It makes growing children aware of the various changes taking place in their bodies and prepares them for responsible adulthood.

Surveys indicate that on an average, every urban student watches television and/or *youtube* for two hours daily. Explicit sex scenes shown on some foreign television channels, the vulgar scenes shown in Indian cinema, Internet pornography and indecent video albums, etc., have more negative than positive *impact*[4] on them. Such visuals *stimulate*[5] the youngsters sexually, whereupon, in the absence of sound knowledge about sex, they commit mistakes which result in unwanted pregnancies, HIV-positive cases and other sexually transmitted diseases (STDs). In India, 15 percent of the HIV/AIDS patients are actually children under 15 years of age. Sex education can help people make informed choices regarding health and sexuality.

Teaching children about sex in classrooms would encourage them to view it as a natural, normal and healthy part of life. If children and youngsters learn about sex in a scientific and objective way, they would be more careful before indulging in the same. At least they would be careful enough to take *precautions*[6] so as to avoid pregnancies and diseases. Because of lack of sex education, India and most Asian and African countries have higher incidence of HIV/AIDS victims. Even instances of unwanted pregnancies are reportedly much higher in such countries as compared to those in the developed world.

Parents, in India, normally hide their affection towards each other, in front of their children. The children grow up believing that love is taboo and it is indecent to display one's affection in public. Parents need to understand the psyche of their children. The love they display for their children, by giving gifts, sharing and caring for them, should also be shown for each other by behaving like perfectly normal friends. In addition, parents should talk with their children more often to give them a feeling of security in the family. This will encourage the children to talk about their problems freely and parents will get to play a positive role in helping their children out of their complexes, if any. Interaction with the friends of their children may also help in giving an insight into the minds of the younger lot.

There has been a rise in incidents of physical abuse of children. According to a study undertaken by the World Health Organisation (WHO), over 50 per cent of children faced one or more forms of sexual abuse. Children fall victim to the advances of predators who often turn out to be members of their family. They keep silent and live with the *trauma*[7] throughout their lives.

Modern society is faced with a big challenge as far as sexual abuse in children is concerned. We now live in nuclear families, where both the parents are working. The end result is that most of our children are sent to crèches unless there is adequate family support in the form of relatives or grand parents. It is now imperative to educate our little children as early as possible about the evil touch. Once we as mothers or fathers make them understand that they should report unwanted advances at home, they will feel stronger and happier knowing that they will be protected and not punished for something they were ignorant about. Sex education imparted to the adolescents can supply them with the tools to report and resist abusive behaviour, and will provide them with a forum for expressing their fears and feelings honestly and openly. In a world which witnesses all kinds of exploitation, children are the most *vulnerable*[8] lot. They need not only to be protected and taught the difference between good touch and bad touch but also to be educated regarding various forms of child abuse.

Many psychologists have argued that sex education has the potential to liberate us from socially organised sexual oppression. In addition, it helps adolescents come to terms with their sexual identities and orientations and to overcome feelings of guilt and shame. During the period of *adolescence*[9], one begins to see the world in a mature way and to develop one's own opinion. Therefore, optimum support, guidance and acceptance is necessary to save adolescents from going astray.

Many NGOs have introduced training programmes on AIDS and HIV awareness. They should be encouraged, and schools and colleges should co-operate with them to create greater awareness among the growing children.

School life remains an *integral*[10] part of every child's development. Along with the academic subjects, sex education should be imparted too. Trained teachers, psychologists and medical consultants should deal with the subject. While imparting sex education, boys and girls should be divided into two groups (one of boys and the other of girls) and they should be taught separately. Lady teachers should teach the girls and male teachers should teach the boys. This way, the children will not feel embarrassed. They will freely clarify their doubts and queries. Proper care should be taken to develop the contents of the subject. These should be decided by experts, doctors and psychologists. It is high time sex education was introduced in the educational curriculum. Sex education in schools would help to *dispel*[11] many of the myths prevalent among school children. It will promote liberal thinking among the youth and also ensure a safer and healthier lifestyle.

Aid to Vocabulary

1. *Delicate* — requiring careful handling
2. *Embarrassed* — ashamed or self-conscious
3. *Taboo* — a cultural or religious custom that forbids people to talk about or do certain things
4. *Impact* — a strong impression or effect
5. *Stimulate* — to encourage or make one excited
6. *Precautions* — safety measures
7. *Trauma* — emotional shock
8. *Vulnerable* — that can be hurt or harmed easily
9. *Adolescence* — the stage when a person grows from a child into an adult
10. *Integral* — essential
11. *Dispel* — to make something go away

Points to Remember

1. Introduction of sex education in schools is an important issue.
2. Sex is still considered a taboo in Indian society.
3. Due to ignorance of sex-related facts, the youth easily fall victim to AIDS and other sexually transmitted diseases (STDs).
4. A WHO study shows that over 50 percent of children faced one or more forms of sexual abuse.
5. Little children need to be educated about good touch and bad touch by the parents so that they are not subjected to child abuse.
6. Sex education can help people to make informed choices regarding health and sexuality.
7. It is high time sex education was introduced in schools for the benefit of the youth of the country.

SEX EDUCATION: AWARENESS PROGRAMMES PLANNED*

According to the Family Planning Association of India (FPAI), Dharwad, unit office-bearers Hemal Desai and Shubhendu Akalwadi, will launch programmes to create awareness among adolescents and youth through comprehensive sexuality education in high schools and colleges. In India, there are 2.1 million HIV-infected people and among them 50 per cent are youth. Every year, 4.4 million girls seek abortion services and among them, 50 per cent are unsafe abortions, 10 per cent women become pregnant at an adolescent age adding to the increasing maternal mortality and 30 per cent girls are sexually abused.

New Project

To help prevent this trend, the FPAI has taken up a new project. "By the youths for the youths," and youth will be given education on advocating comprehensive sexuality education and sexual reproductive health rights.

This project was launched in 2001 and the Education Department was roped in to educate students and every year, 2,000 students are being counselled. Now, the youths, who are trained by the FPAI, will approach students of classes 8, 9 and 10, PU I and II year and hold discussions with them. The FPAI will expand this programme to 3,000 adolescents and youths by planning various youth activities. The entire programme has been divided into eight components, of which four will be held jointly for boys and girls.

Orientation Programmes

Orientation programmes for teachers and sensitisation programme for parents would also be held. Suman Patil said that this programme would be held at five colleges in Dharwad, five in Dharwad Rural, five in Hubballi and Hubballi Rural, Kalghatgi and Navalgund.

**Source:* The Hindu

Essay 16

THE VALUE OF GAMES AND SPORTS

Synopsis

Games and sports keep one physically and mentally fit. People in general stay away from sports. Sports keep one away from diseases relating to heart, obesity, mental stress and sleeplessness. They instil in the player a spirit of self-confidence, self-reliance, discipline, justice, fair play and patriotism. Games provide us with recreation and enjoyment. Games are very essential for students but they are neglected in schools. Even parents do not have high opinion about games and they want their children to devote more time to studies. Although games and sports contribute hugely to good health, it remains ignored in India. India lacks funds, and proper training facilities are not provided to the players. Some sports bring rich dividends to sportsmen. The government has formulated a New National Sports Policy. Effective measures should be taken to popularise and to encourage participation in games and sports.

We all are familiar with the maxim, 'Health is wealth'. According to the World Health Organisation, 'Health is a state of complete physical, mental, social as well as spiritual well-being of an individual and not merely the absence of disease.' Academics serve the purpose of nourishing the mind. But a healthy mind resides in a healthy body. One can develop and maintain a healthy body by actively participating in games and sports.

Recreation, particularly sports, is still a *farthing*[1] for the people of India, for they believe more in earning money and amassing wealth for the future generation. Games and sports, therefore, remain neglected from their day to day lives. They, in fact, consider them as unnecessary and as mere wastage of time. The moment a child opens his/her mouth to express a desire to go to play, the parents or the elders snub him/her with the *refrain*[2] that their examination is at hand or he/she had not done well in the previous examination. This mindset is, to a considerable extent responsible for the *reluctance*[3] of children towards sports and games. The one who has not played any game in his/her childhood can hardly develop an interest for the same in the latter part of his/her life. This *vicious cycle*[4] continues. But things have begun to change for the better.

Games keep our body alert, active, youthful and energetic. They *instil*[5] in us a spirit of adventure. Games increase the circulation of blood, *boost*[6] *metabolism*[7], burn *calories*[8] and improve the respiratory and digestive system. A healthy person can work hard cheerfully for a long period of time, and can face dangers boldly. Games also instil in the players the spirit of self-reliance, self-confidence, justice, and fair play. They enable them to cultivate virtues like discipline, honesty, integrity, loyalty and patriotism.

While playing games, various muscles of the body get exercised and one need not join a gymnasium for this purpose. *Brisk*[9] walking, running, cycling, skipping, swimming and yoga are common activities to keep oneself fit. They also tone up the body of both the young and the old. Mild exercises are beneficial for patients recovering from heart attack and those who suffer from obesity, diabetes, blood pressure, etc. Exercise invigorates the mind and the body and helps to keep one fit.

Games are an excellent means of recreation. Soccer, cricket, lawn tennis and wrestling are watched by millions of fans all over the world. When we watch and play games, we forget all our worries and anxieties. They enable us to divert our mind from negative thoughts.

A sportsperson develops team spirit, learns to adjust with other person's shortcomings, and respects and follows the rules of the game he/she plays. Sportspersons display punctuality, *diplomacy*[10] and self-discipline. Sports build in us the character to face the challenges of life and not be deterred by failures, they are but the stepping stones to success. Such an approach would help one reorganise one's skill after any setback and work harder with renewed vigour to achieve one's goal.

Games generate a feeling of sportsmanship and broaden one's outlook. They are very essential for students. In our schools, however, games and sports are not given much importance. A period of half an hour or forty-five minutes once or twice a week is all that is given to sports or games. Children find it difficult to pursue a sport of their liking in the *specified*[11] period. Some schools cannot afford funds for sports equipment while most schools do not have a playground. Many schools do not employ any physical instructor to guide the children in various sports. Even parents want their children to complete their home assignments after school hours rather than go outdoors to play games. They fail to realise that games make children strong, both mentally and physically. Many school children become *obese*[12] due to lack of participation in games. Obesity puts them in the high risk category of *contracting*[13] diseases like diabetes, heart ailments, etc. The education system needs to be reformed, to ensure that equal importance is given to sports and games.

There is hardly anyone in the present era who is unfamiliar with the advantages of playing games yet the majority of the adult population in India never opts for playing games,; it is the students or the children who are found to be playing different sorts of games; they too go to play against the will of their respective parents. Fortunately, with the advent of IPL cricket followed gradually by similar *leagues*[14] in other sports like football, hockey, tennis, wrestling, kabaddi, etc., that have all been seen to bring in good money for the players, sports as a means of livelihood is beginning to find favour with quite a few people. Games and sports not only strengthen the bones and muscles of the body, but also accelerate blood circulation raising the rate of metabolism and respiration. In short, games and sports are an integral part of life and those who tend to ignore this compromise their health.

The apathy of the general public and authorities for sports and games is evident from our country's poor performance in international sports events. In Beijing Olympics, India's best-ever performance of winning one gold and two bronze medals was lauded as a 'historic breakthrough' for the country. India then followed it up with a tally of six medals at the London Olympics. However, it is grossly disappointing to see that even players from small countries like South Korea, Romania, etc., are able to win a far larger number of medals. India is far behind other countries in a number of games. Moreover, in the absence of funds and facilities, the players are unable to utilise their talent and energy in a productive manner. For example, hockey is mostly played on grass courts in India even as the entire world has adopted the astro-turf. There is also a lack of training of international standard. The players lack *motivation*[15] to excel in the absence of awards and incentives. They are unaware of the diet they should follow to keep themselves fit. Cricket is the only game which is given importance. But *accusations*[16] of match-fixing, faulty selection procedures and misappropriation of funds have dented the image of cricket in India.

Sports no doubt have plenty of advantages but they also have drawbacks. Some sportsmen fracture or lose their limbs, or get permanently disabled while playing games. Many students take too much interest in games and ignore their studies. The unprecedented flow of money into some sports, mainly cricket, has given rise to corrupt practices like rigged elections and match-fixing. The Government formulated a National Sports Policy in 2001. It promotes the popularity of sports among public at large. It aims at the development of *infrastructure*[17] and the provision of better coaching facilities. The National Welfare Fund for sportspersons was set up in March 1982 with a view to assist outstanding sportspersons of yesteryears, who had brought glory to the country in sports but are living in neglect and want. The scheme was reviewed in July 2009 to provide for lumpsum ex-gratia assistance to outstanding sportspersons of yesteryears.

Seventy per cent of our population lives in villages. To popularise games and to tap hidden talent in rural areas, the Rural Sports Programme was launched in 1970-71. The scheme has been revised. Grants to Sports have been increased. Sports scholarships are given to talented boys and girls. Following years of encouragement, some rural sports like Kabaddi, Archery and Wrestling have made a foray into the international arena today and medal hauls have been made in the Asiad, the Commonwealth Games and even in the Olympics.

Sports and games being an effective means of ensuring general good health, measures should be taken to ensure people's active participation in games. The Government should evolve a long-term national sports policy. Children should be informed about the advantages of playing games. They should be made to play games regularly. Training facilities for various games should be introduced. The existing training facilities should be upgraded and expanded. The selection of players for national and international games should be fair. For this, Government has already introduced a scheme related to talent search and training. Under this Scheme, assistance is provided to promising sportspersons for training and training-cum-competitions in India and abroad, and for purchase of equipment and availing of scientific support. Support staff such as coaches, sports scientists, doctors, masseurs, etc., are also encouraged as well as assisted for undergoing specialised training, for attending seminar/conferences and major international sports events, and for appearing in qualifying examinations. This scheme is implemented through Sports Authority of India (SAI). The Ministry of Youth Affairs and Sports implements various schemes as incentives to sportspersons to take up sports. Various awards like Rajiv Gandhi Khel Ratna Award, Arjuna Awards, Dhyanchand Award, Dronacharya Award, Maulana Abul Kalam Azad Trophy, Rashtriya Khel Protsahan Award, etc., are conferred to recognise spectacular and outstanding performances of the sportspersons. All these schemes are introduced to encourage and motivate sportspersons for higher achievements and to inspire the younger generation to take up sports as a career.

It is a foregone conclusion that if *maximal*[18] participation in sports and games is ensured, it will improve the overall health of the nation and its citizens.

Aid to Vocabulary

1. *Farthing* — a thing of little value
2. *Refrain* — a statement or comment that is often repeated
3. *Reluctance* — disinclination
4. *Vicious cycle* — harmful cycle of cause and effect
5. *Instil* — implant gradually
6. *Boost* — increase
7. *Metabolism* — chemical processes in plants or animals that change food, minerals, etc., into living matter and produce energy
8. *Calories* — units of the energy-producing value of food
9. *Brisk* — quick
10. *Diplomacy* — tact or skill of dealing with others amicably
11. *Specified* — stated
12. *Obese* — very fat
13. *Contracting* — catching, developing
14. *Leagues* — groups of sports teams that compete over a period of time for championship
15. *Motivation* — stimulation
16. *Accusations* — statements accusing a person of a fault, wrong doing or crime
17. *Infrastructure* — the basic structures and facilities necessary for a country or an organisation to function efficiently, eg., buildings, equipments, etc.
18. *Maximal* — greatest possible

Points to Remember

1. Games and sports keep one fit physically as well as mentally.
2. They help us to fight against various diseases.
3. They provide us with recreation and enjoyment.
4. Games and sports are very essential for students.
5. They are neglected in schools.
6. Our players do not perform well at the international meets.
7. Indian players lack funds and proper training facilities.
8. The Rural Sports Programme was launched in 1970-71.
9. The National Sports Policy, 2001 has been formulated. It aims at the development of infrastructure and provision of better coaching facilities.
10. The Government should evolve a long-term sports policy to ensure maximal participation in sports.

SPORTS

Sports and games have always been as an integral component in all round development of human personality. Apart from being means of entertainment and physical fitness, sports have also played a great role in generation of spirit of healthy competition and bonding within the community. Achievements in sports have always been a source of national pride and prestige.

However, unlike in the past, the modern sports have become highly competitive. The use of modern equipments, infrastructure and advanced scientific support has changed the scenario of sports at international level. Keeping in line with the growing demands for advanced equipments, infrastructure and scientific support, Government of India has taken a number of initiatives.

National Sports Policy 2001

National Sports Policy, 2001 envisages mainly broad basing and promotion of excellence in sports. The salient features of the National Sports Policy 2001 are: (i) broad basing of sports and achievement of excellence; (ii) up-gradation and development of infrastructure; (iii) support to National Sports Federations and other appropriate bodies; (iv) strengthening of scientific and coaching support to sports; (v) incentives to promote sports; (vi) enhanced participation of women, scheduled tribes and rural youth; (vii) Involvement of corporate sector in sports promotion; and (viii) promotion of sports mindedness among the public at large.

Essay **17**

THE FUTURE OF ENGLISH IN INDIA

SYNOPSIS

English is one of the most widely spoken languages across the world. In India, it was first introduced by Lord William Bentinck, the Governor-General of India (1828-35). It was supported by many eminent personalities and social reformers. English has made an invaluable contribution towards the unification of the country. It has become an integral part of every section of society, be it government, media or education. It is taught in public as well as government schools. The young generation passionately speaks HINGLISH — an amalgam of Hindi and English. English is a must for Indians aspiring for higher education or seeking better job opportunities. It is the mode of communication in urban society. Some people of Hindi speaking areas in India are against the usage of English. English is considered as a passport to a secure future.

English is one of the most widely spoken languages. It is probably the only language which is spoken in all the continents of the world. It is indeed the *lingua franca*[1] of the modern times. Most educated Indians are well versed in the language. It is extensively used in Government offices, by the media—both electronic and print, in educational institutions of higher learning and in the legal world. It is also used for social interaction and in the business spheres.

In India, English was first introduced by Governor-General William Bentinck(1828-35) in the nineteenth century. It was supported by many eminent personalities and social reformers including Raja Rammohan Roy. In pre-Independence era, Indian leaders used English for spreading thc message of national struggle. Through the medium of English, they could speak about the Indian struggle for freedom to an international audience.

Some people from the Hindi-speaking areas are against the usage of English language primarily because it is viewed as a symbol of British imperialism. English-speaking Indians have been accused of being west-oriented. The English-speaking Indians are rightly criticised, in some cases, for building up an image of being more modern, educated and cultured. Some of them may in reality be narrow-minded, communal and conservative. However, the importance of English is undeniable.

English has made an *invaluable*[2] contribution towards the unification of the country. Although India is a *multi-lingual*[3] country having 22 official languages, English remains an associate official language. It is widely used in communication. English acts as the link-language in our country. It is easy to find people who know English in every part of the country. Thus, a south Indian can communicate easily with a north Indian, if both of them are well-versed in English. Most educated Indians today are bilingual.

The present generation has ushered in a peculiar language known as HINGLISH which is an amalgam of English and Hindi. It is very difficult, if not impossible, to state for sure whether it has raised the standard, glory and beauty of the language or has marred it but one thing can safely be said that the language, thus, has been popularised more, for all and sundry feel elevated, speaking the Queen's language, even if in an impure version.

In the media also, English has an important place. English newspapers are published and read in almost all Indian states. There are several popular English news channels on Television as well. Entertainment channels namely FOX, HBO, MGM, ZCafe and the informative ones like Discovery, National Geographic and History Channel, all of which are in English, enjoy a wide viewership in India.

India is the third largest 'English books' producing country after the USA and the UK. Creative writing in English has been an integral part of the Indian literary tradition for many years. Writers like Bankim Chandra Chatterjee, Raja Rammohan Roy, Toru Dutt, Michael Madhusudan Dutt, Sarojini Naidu, etc., wrote in English. Today also Indian writers have successfully used the language to create rich literature. Indo-Anglican literature is now well-developed and internationally recognised. Vikram Seth, Arundhati Roy, Jhumpa Lahiri, Anita Desai, Upamanyu Chatterjee, Arvind Adiga, Amitav Ghosh, Chetan Bhagat, Jeet Thayil, etc., are some of the important names in this field.

In the education system of India, English is the *premier*[4] language. Most of the public schools and colleges prefer to have English as their medium of instruction. It is taught in public as well as in government schools. English is an international language. If we want to remain in touch with the outside world, we will have to retain English. English is a must for the Indians aspiring for higher education or seeking better job opportunities abroad. English is an important working language of the United Nations. Many Indians who have excellent communication skills are working in international agencies under the United Nations. Indians like Shashi Tharoor are acknowledged for their commendable speeches and debates at international forums.

Almost 73% of people in India speak English. English is important for every field of knowledge. All research and other literature in science and technology, space study, nuclear technology, medicine, engineering, etc., is published in English for a wider reach. It is found that those who go to English medium schools have a high percentage of intercaste marriages, as opposed to those who study in regional medium. It is also found that higher numbers of those educated in English migrate from their own state. Thus, English not only overcomes caste rigidities, but also helps in the migration of skilled manpower, both of which are good for the nation.

English is used for correspondence between different departments of the Union and the state governments, between the Centre and the states, as well as between any two states. Most of the business houses in the country use English language. Most public sector enterprises prepare their reports and carry out their day-to-day work in English. All formal and informal communication in the corporate sector is done mainly in English. With the increased use of computers in small and large offices, English language has got a further boost.

After Independence, the states of our country were reorganised on the basis of the language spoken in a particular region and Hindi was declared as the national language. But the imposition of Hindi as national language was opposed tooth and nail by the southern states of India. These states were assured by Pt. Jawaharlal Nehru, the first Prime Minister of free India, that Hindi would not be imposed on them. On the other hand, some people of the Hindi-speaking areas in India are against the usage of English. But we cannot ignore the importance and utility of the language in binding the people of different states of India. The growth of English is higher in non-Hindi-speaking states, mostly the southern states which account for over 60 per cent of the students enrolled in English medium schools. English medium also accounts for over 90 per cent of the enrolment in the North-Eastern states. The importance of English has been further established by the Muslim Madarsa Board soliciting government help to set-up English medium schools.

The English language has taken deep roots in the country. It has acquired its own identity and character. English plays an important part in maintaining professional relationship between India and foreign investors, who *flock*[5] to India. The *upsurge*[6] of multinational companies and BPOs (Business Process Outsourcing) in India is due to this proficiency of Indians in English.

India is all set to give a boost[7] to education. The allocation of funds for education has increased considerably across the different Five Year Plans. The English and Foreign Languages University (EFLU), Hyderabad, an institution of higher learning, is an autonomous organisation, which undertakes teacher education programme to enhance the professional competence of teachers of English. The EFLU also implements two schemes of the Government of India through English Language Teaching Institutes (ELTI) and District Centres for English, to bring about substantial improvements in the standard of teaching and learning in the country for which grants are given by EFLU to various state governments.

All said and done, the fact is that English language has a very bright future in our country and the Centre and states can ill afford to neglect its study. Most state governments have introduced the study of English language at the primary school stage itself so that children can pick up the language at the initial stage of their learning process and acquire good command of it. English plays a key role in various spheres and has virtually become a global passport to a secure future. It may, sooner or later, be declared as the national language of India.

Aid to Vocabulary

1. *Lingua franca* — common language spoken by people of different languages
2. *Invaluable* — precious
3. *Multi-lingual* — consisting of many languages
4. *Premier* — first in importance and position
5. *Flock* — to go or gather together in great numbers
6. *Upsurge* — growth
7. *Boost* — help or encourage someone or something to increase its value and importance

Points to Remember

1. English is one of the most widely spoken languages.
2. In India, English was first introduced by Governor-General Lord William Bentinck in the nineteenth century.
3. English acts as the link language in our society.
4. India is the third largest English book producing country after the USA and the UK.
5. English is a must for higher education and foreign jobs.
6. With the increased use of computers in small and large offices, English

language has got a further boost.

7. Some people of the Hindi-speaking areas of India are against the usage of English.
8. The upsurge of MNCs and BPOs in our country is due to the proficiency of Indians in the use of the English language.
9. The EFLU is an autonomous organisation which undertakes teacher education programme, and implements two schemes of the Government of India to bring about substantial improvements in the standard of teaching and learning.
10. English is considered as a passport to a secure future.

Essay 18

NEW CAREERS IN THE 21ST CENTURY

Synopsis

Everyone plans for his/her career and chooses it according to his/her ability and inclination. In ancient India, professions were hereditary. The British brought along with them western education. Later, careers in engineering, medicine, law, teaching and computers became important. New careers have opened up in the fields of wildlife, biotechnology, corporate law, sports, medicine, insurance, medical transcription, environmental science, disaster management, waste management, event management, etc. Conventional occupations are still in demand. More and more avenues in careers are opening up everyday.

Everyone plans for his/her career and chooses a course of study in keeping with his/her inclination and ability. In ancient India, the professions or vocation were hereditary and the son would necessarily follow his father's footsteps. Every social class was assigned a duty or service to the society and every generation carried on performing that duty without any discontent or opposition. The topmost class in the social hierarchy, the Brahmanas, they were engaged in performing the religious duties. They were also involved in the *propagation*[1] of education among the various classes excluding the Shudras, they were at the lowest *stratum*[2] of the society and did only menial jobs. The Kshatriyas engaged themselves in learning martial arts and warfare and were the protectors of the nation. They mostly formed the kingly class. The Vaishyas were engaged in trade and commerce and formed the business community.

The influence of western education ushered in by the British that changed this hierarchy. There were only two distinct classes of people—one comprising of those who were educated in English and the other consisting of those who were not. The former occupied the clerical posts in the British government. After Independence, people *yearned*[3] for careers as doctors, engineers and lawyers. Some of them also joined the field of teaching, civil services, etc. The 21st century saw the *boom*[4] in the IT industry. Careers in IT, whether at home or outside India, witnessed great demand. Many Indians left India and went to foreign countries as software professionals.

However, in today's changing world, there is a boom in new careers which were unheard of before. These are as varied as those in the field of wildlife, biotechnology, corporate law, journalism and mass communication, sports, medicine, insurance, *BPOs*[5] and *KPOs*[6], and many more. For those who have keen interest in nature and wildlife, there are career prospects in the Indian Forest Service as well as in other agencies that work voluntarily for the welfare of animals. Another option, for science students, pertains to the field of biotechnology. It is one of the fastest growing professional domains today. It finds application in every aspect of daily life and every industry from chemical, *pharmaceutical*[7] and textile industries to genetics and agriculture. In the field of medicine, also, biotechnology can help provide cures for genetically-inherited diseases. Careers as researcher, lecturer, reader, professor, etc., in academic institutions are also in great demand.

Corporate law is another career option for law graduates. The job profile of the corporate or business lawyer pertains to providing assistance vis-à-vis the tie-ups of foreign firms with Indian collaborators. This career came to the forefront in 1991 with the *liberalisation*[8] of Indian economy and boomed in the late nineties. Today with more and more economic liberalisation, the scope of corporate lawyers is widening. This kind of legal practice is most suitable to women. Traditionally, law has been associated with verbal battles in the courtroom; corporate law is, in a way, a blending of law and business *acumen*[9].

Journalism and mass communication offers a range of good career prospects. Many universities offer a postgraduate degree in this field and some offer a bachelor's degree too. It has got in its ambit a wide range of subjects like advertising, public relations, print journalism, radio and television journalism, etc. A person can specialise in any one of these subjects. Jobs in this field include reporting, anchoring (both TV and radio), editing, copywriting, designing, public relations, etc.

Insurance is another sector which has promising career prospects. The General Insurance Corporation and the Life Insurance Corporation along with many private insurance companies have opened up avenues for careers. So, for those seeking a career in finance and business, the insurance industry offers the best of both worlds. It is a growing industry with a challenging job profile.

Medical science is one field which offers a whole range of career options today with unprecedented increase in areas of specialisation. In medical science, the specialists and super-specialists in various areas of specialisation are in great demand not only in India, but also all over the world. However, aquiring a degree in Medicine is an extremely arduous task, starting from the pre-medical examination that is a tough nut to crack. The career of a doctor involves total focus, dedication, willingness to put in hard work and above all, absolute commitment. Apart from MBBS (Allopathy), one can opt for BAMS (Ayurveda), BHMS (Homoeopathy), BNYS (Naturopathy), etc.

Medical transcription is a relatively novel concept in India. In this profession, the use of high-speed telecom, satellite linkages and the internet have enabled Indians to enter the healthcare sector of developed countries by transcribing their medical records. Healthcare is a rapidly growing industry, and the demand for quality documentation is increasing. This career is open to graduates with a science background, who have good command over English and are willing to work at odd hours. There are about 200 MT units in India employing between 5,000 and 8,000 people and generating revenues in the range of $25-50 million every year. There is enormous potential for expansion in this sector. The opening of health insurance companies would also increase the demand for medical transcriptionists.

BPO (Business Process Outsourcing) Centres popularly known as Call Centres offer tremendous opportunities for employment. BPOs involve engineering services, financial research, payroll and accounting, insurance claims processing, technical support for R&D operations, chip-design, tele-marketing, etc. India, with over 250 million English speakers and a pool of 15 million college graduates forms the back office to the world through BPOs.

The KPO (Knowledge Process Outsourcing) industry offers immense potential for outsourcing. Several online jobs are available on the internet. One can work as content writer, graphic designer, web designer, on-line tutor and so on. Content writing is a very vast field which employs specialised professionals like, academic, technical, resume, grant proposal, business plan and essay writers. The list is quite inexhaustible. Indians who have charmed the world with their intellectual gifts form the backbone of these KPOs.

Learning languages has its own charm. Proficiency in foreign languages like French, German, Russian, Japanese, Spanish, Italian, Chinese and Arabic opens opportunities to work in the diplomatic services as interpreters, translators and tourist guides.

Nanotechnology is the combined application of science, engineering as well as technology with a view to develop in the nano range novel materials and devices pertaining to various fields. It studies the structure and behaviour of materials at atomic or molecular level. Nanotechnology is expected to usher in the next industrial revolution. It will have wide applications in biotechnology, and in pharmaceutical, medical, agricultural, textiles, food and beverage, and environmental industries. It is a research-oriented discipline. National research organisations and certain universities offer facilities for research.

Some other professions which have begun to see a growth in demand are those related to environmental science, disaster management, waste management, event management and retail management. Agriculture is one of the oldest occupations of the world and employs more than half the population of the world. Some job profiles in this sector include research, opportunities in agro-business sector and agro-industry sector, services in agriculture corporations and banking sector, job opportunities in estates and tea gardens, agricultural engineering and agricultural management.

However, the conventional careers such as teaching, engineering, medicine and law continue to remain at the top in the list of professions that are much sought after. Computers have opened up numerous career opportunities in our country as well as in foreign destinations. A sizeable proportion of the computer professionals in the USA is of Indians.

With the emergence of more and more fields of study, the career options would gradually widen. After completing school or college education, students in times to come would have a wide variety of careers to choose from. However, one should select one's career according to one's aptitude and inclination. Parents and teachers should provide necessary guidance in this respect.

AID TO VOCABULARY

1. *Propagation* — spreading
2. *Stratum* — a class in a society
3. *Yearn* — to desire something very strongly
4. *Boom* — a sudden increase in trade and economic activity
5. *BPO* — Business Process Outsourcing
6. *KPO* — Knowledge Process Outsourcing
7. *Pharmaceutical* — use or sale of medical drugs
8. *Liberalisation* — to give more freedom
9. *Acumen* — keen insight

Points to Remember

1. In ancient India, career was generally hereditary and a son would necessarily follow his father's footsteps.
2. The British rulers introduced western education.
3. today, new careers are booming.
4. New careers are as varied as wild life, biotechnology, corporate law, journalism and mass communication, sports, medicine, insurance, BPOs, KPOs, etc.
5. Other careers are environmental science, disaster management, waste management, careers in the agricultural sector, etc.
6. Conventional careers—teaching, engineering, medicine, law, etc., continue to be in demand.
7. One must select his/her career according to his/her aptitude and inclination.

SOME EMERGING CAREERS	
1. Fashion Design	8. Hotel Management
2. Medical Transcription	9. Advertising
3. Retail Management	10. Tourism Management
4. Hospital Management	11. Radio Jockeying
5. Software Engineering	12. TV Presentation/Journalism
6. Call Centre	13. Investment Banking
7. Animation/Graphics	14. Fashion Photography

Essay
19 DISTANCE EDUCATION

SYNOPSIS

India has a large number of colleges but the formal system of education has failed to reach the masses. Distance education is a concept that aims to democratise higher education and make it accessible to all those who are interested in it. The IGNOU was set up in 1985 to bring all correspondence educational institutes under a single umbrella, or central university. There are other open universities at the state level as well as the national level. At the national level, IGNOU caters to the needs of those students who do not find a place in the conventional system. With the use of technology, IGNOU has also brought about innovations in the overall educational system. There is a need for allocation of more funds.

India witnessed a 30-fold increase in the number of universities and colleges which grew from 30 and 695 in 1950 to 659 and 33,623 in 2011-12 respectively as per the Twelfth Five Year Plan. Regrettably, though, education is available to only 5-6 per cent of the youngsters in the age group of 17-23 years. The need for higher education increased with time but the facilities, equipment and space failed to keep pace with the growing demand. As a result, the option that was explored was to allow students to appear for their Degree examinations as private candidates. The need of continual education to upgrade the competence of in-service personnel, also, posed formidable challenges.

The term 'distance education' includes a range of teaching and learning strategies, such as *correspondence education*[1], home study, independent study, external studies, virtual classroom, e-conference or teaching at a distance. The idea is to democratise higher education and make it easily accessible to all those who are interested in it. It provides high quality information to all regardless of age, region or formal qualifications. It also offers need-based academic programmes by giving professional and vocational orientation to courses. It provides options to study according to one's pace, place and convenience. Through Distance Education, even the employed can continue their studies and acquire degrees, to further enhance their career prospects.

The first university to set up a school of correspondence courses and continual education was the University of Delhi, in 1962. The UGC

(University Grants Commission) had recommended the setting up of the Delhi University Distance Education Department. Having been satisfied with this, it gave permission to the Punjab University, Patiala, to set up a Directorate of Correspondence Courses in 1968. By 1993, there were over 40 such institutions.

After the United Kingdom Open University (UKOU) started functioning in 1971, Indian educationists also thought of bringing all correspondence institutions under a single umbrella or central university. The concept of an 'open' university would be an openness to ideas and operations. It would prepare its curricula from all existing universities in the country and abroad. The method of imparting education would be multi-media integration using not only postal communication (as in correspondence education) but also radio and television programmes, and group or individual guidance. Setting up of a network of regional offices, with some resources being made available from the existing colleges and universities, was thought to be an essential feature of this system.

The Andhra Pradesh Open University, now known as B.R. Ambedkar Open University was the first state level open university to be inaugurated in 1982. Other state level universities are the Kota Open University established in 1987 in Rajasthan and the Yashwant Rao Chawan Maharashtra Open University. At the national level, the Indira Gandhi National Open University was set up in 1985. The main objectives of the University was promoting and developing distance education in India and setting and maintaining standards in distance education.

The Distance Education Council (DEC) was established under statute 28 of the IGNOU Act, 1985. DEC has launched many initiatives for determination of standards in the system and provides financial, academic and technical support to the 13 State Open Universities and over 200 Directorates attached to conventional Univeristies and Private/ *Autonomous*[2] Institutes, referred to as Distance Education Institutions (DEIs). It is the general duty of the DEC to take all such steps as are necessary for the promotion of the Open University/Distance Education System, its coordinated development, and the determination of its standards. DEC also strives to develop a network of open universities/ distance education institutions in the country in consultation with the State Governments, universities, and other concerned agencies; to identify priority areas in which distance education programmes should be organised; and to provide such support as may be considered necessary for organising such programmes, etc.

IGNOU has emerged as the largest open university in the Commonwealth countries and has study centres in the Middle East, South-east Asia and Ethiopia. The University has a large number of short-term and long-term programmes (courses) leading to certificates, diplomas and degrees. The methodology of instruction is a combination of self-instructional written material, audio-visual material aids, counselling sessions, *teleconferences*[3], distance learning facilitators, practicals and project work and an exclusive educational TV channel—Gyan Darshan (launched in 2001). The evaluation system is a two-tier one. There is a set of questions and assignments relating to the subject matter which has to be answered by the student over a period of time. The Term End Examination is held twice a year and a student has more than one opportunity to sit for the examination (twice in some cases to ten in others). IGNOU has 60 regional centres, 7 sub-regional centres and 1298 study centres all over the country.

The open universities have taken steps to streamline the courses. Changes are evident in the areas of restructuring the degree programmes providing them flexibility and modularity, reforms in examinations, vocationalisation of education, and extension of education.

The National Institute of Open Schooling (NIOS) was established with a vision of sustainable inclusive learning with universal and flexible access to quality school education and skill development. From a small project of the CBSE for out-of-school population and second-chance learners, it has grown today to be the largest open school of the world and has been hailed as a mega open school. It is not only a National Board with the authority to examine and certify learners but also a National Resource Organisation for Open Schooling. The Institute develops curriculum, prepares its own self-learning material and produces its own audio/video material and multi-media packages for the learners registered with it. It accredits conventional schools and agencies to provide student support services to its enrolled learners. It conducts two public examinations in a year as well as On-Demand Examination throughout the year to benefit the learners. It also functions as a publishing house and brings out several publications every year. The Institute conducts researches in Open Schooling and also organises training and capacity building activities for Open and Distance Learning functionaries.

With the advent of technology and its wider implications, distance education would better be known as 'open flexible education'. Quite a few business schools including foreign educational institutions have introduced online courses through the Internet. Even examinations can be taken online. IGNOU has its own television channel *Gyan Darshan* and FM Radio channel *Gyan Vani*. IGNOU also runs its courses on the Internet and maintains an online library called *e-gyankosh*. Students can take their course lessons and can download information through the Internet.

However, in spite of the strengths of distance education such as *convergence*[4], flexibility (of place, pace and age), cost effectiveness and continuous learning, there are certain shortcomings, primary among them being the lack of *credibility*[5] of distance education in the eyes of the people. However, the spread of distance education in India is gradually gaining momentum. More and more funds need to be allocated to enhance resources and greater awareness about the quality and credibility of distance education needs to be created among people.

Aid to Vocabulary

1. *Correspondence education* — instructing and conducting courses by post
2. *Autonomous* — self-governing, independent
3. *Teleconferences* — it is the electronic means which can bring together three or four people in two or more locations
4. *Convergence* — meeting at a point
5. *Credibility* — property of being believable or convincing

Points to Remember

1. The need for higher education is increasing but the demand is not fulfilled.
2. Distance education includes a range of teaching and learning strategies.
3. The concept of an 'open' university envisages an openness to ideas and operations.
4. There are many state-level open universities.
5. The national-level open university, IGNOU, has emerged as the largest open university in the Commonwealth countries.
6. At the school-level, the National Institute of Open Schooling (NIOS) formerly National Open School (NOS), was set up as an autonomous body.
7. Many business schools including foreign educational institutions have introduced online courses on the Internet.
8. It is necessary to develop the credibility of distance education.

INDIRA GANDHI NATIONAL OPEN UNIVERSITY (IGNOU)

It was established by an Act of Parliament in 1985 to provide access to quality education to all segments of the society. It offers high-quality, innovative and need-based programmes at different levels, to all those who require them; and reaches out to the disadvantaged by offering programmes in all parts of the country and through its centres abroad at affordable costs. IGNOU has been steadily expanding opportunities for life-long higher education and democratising education by making it inclusive. IGNOU offers academic support to students through a three tier network. It comprises of headquarters at New Delhi, 67 regional centres and 2,726 study centres spread across the country. IGNOU has established 21 special study centres (11 in jail; seven in rural remote areas; two in minority-Economically and Educationally Backward Blocks [EEBB] and one in slum area).

Essay
20

THE ROLE OF PRIVATE UNIVERSITIES IN HIGHER EDUCATION

SYNOPSIS

A large number of private universities have been established to fulfil the emerging needs of higher education. Central universities and state universities alone cannot fulfil this need. In 1995, the Government of India passed the Private Universities Establishment and Regulation Bill. The needs and demands of every individual student are catered to in a private university. These private universities have to operate without government aid. Private universities are more like business houses than educational centres. They treat the students on par with their foreign counterparts. The government universities can survive even if they do not meet the expectations of the students, but the same is not true in the case of private universities. The syllabus of the private universities is job-oriented and market-driven. Private universities not only help students but also give a boost to our economy.

The impact of globalisation as well as India's policy of economic liberalisation is visible in every sphere of our society. Our education sector is no exception. While there is regular increase in the number of students, the seats in colleges and universities do not increase proportionately. The students are the victims in this situation. The number of seats available in colleges and universities falls way short of the number of students seeking admission.

All India Council for Technical Education (AICTE) was set up in November 1945 as a national level Apex Advisory Body to conduct a survey on the facilities on technical education and to promote development in the country in a coordinated and integrated manner. The purview of AICTE (the Council) covers programmes of technical education including training and research in Engineering & Technology, Architecture & Town Planning, Management, Pharmacy, Applied Arts and Crafts, Hotel Management and Catering Technology, etc., at different levels.

Thus, it seems that there is a wide array of higher educational services dispensed through governmental universities. But when we consider the *demographic*[1] factors, the inadequacy of educational institutions at the higher level is revealed. A huge number of students are unable to secure admission in the state-run universities. Therefore, the Government of India passed the Private Universities Establishment and Regulation Bill in 1995 to encourage the setting up of private universities. The Ministry of HRD set up a core group of six members, drawn from the private sector, who gave their views and recommendations with regard to the involvement of private institutions in higher studies.

The aforesaid core group recommended that the main emphasis should be on maintaining the high quality of education. Urgent steps should be taken to protect the system from degradation. Research in universities should be encouraged and supported; provided and steps should be taken to ensure its high quality. Efforts should be made to *delve*[2] into India's ancient *corpus*[3] of knowledge and to relate it to contemporary reality. Open university system should be developed further. A modern customisation of the rural university or the Gurukul System should be consolidated and developed on the lines of Mahatma Gandhi's revolutionary ideas on education. The Government has suggested to the private institutions to follow all these guidelines.

The private universities have to operate without government aid. They should, therefore, be given the *flexibility*[4] to raise resources. The legal and administrative framework regarding the operation, investment, etc., of private sector organisations, should be simplified. Rules and regulations should be such that foreign students are also attracted to study in India. Not only students, but the foreign educational institutions and universities may also be facilitated to come to India and operate their extension campuses in India. Foreign institutions attract not only native students, but foreign students as well. Apart from promoting global interaction, this helps improve the economy.

Private universities, particularly when they collaborate with foreign institutions, not only fulfil the desire for higher studies of the students, but also place the students on par with their foreign counterparts. Students get the opportunity to become competent and skilled like the students studying in reputed universities abroad. Private institutions need to develop their professional manpower with a view to keep themselves right on the *cutting edge*[5], globally. Some such universities in India have invested heavily in courses which are of contemporary significance.

Some private universities are sadly run more like business houses than educational centres. They cash in on the students' need for higher education. They produce graduates and postgraduates in large numbers but fail to place them in the workforce. This is rather unfortunate. It is the duty of the private institutions to safeguard the interests of the students. The effort and time of the students and the monetary investment of their parents should not go waste. It is, however, true that the government universities can survive even if they do not meet the expectations of the students, but the same is not true in the case of private universities.

Private universities run on the fees collected from the students. The expenditure of running a private university is very high. Thus, it is necessary for them to keep their courses so attractive and job-oriented that there is great lure among the students to seek admission in them. But its flip side is that often students with low calibre and achievement get admission in these institutions only because their parents can afford to pay hefty fees. This is counter productive to quality and healthy competition and hence, not desirable for any academic institution.

In the recent past, a large number of private universities have been established in most of the states of our country. The crucial question is whether we should allow private universities in such large numbers. The answer is in the affirmative, if we think about the limited seats available for a particular course in a State-run university. The present State-run universities fall short of enough seats for students who seriously want to *pursue*[6] higher studies. Such void can be filled only by private universities. However, in State-run universities, students have to pay only a moderate fee while in private universities, the fee structure is usually very high. Only children of rich families can get admission in these institutions.

It is a fact that the increasing educational needs can be met only by private universities. Many of them are not only multi-disciplinary institutions, but also centres of excellence. Therefore, they should be permitted to offer courses in any discipline. They must adopt a market-driven approach in developing their syllabi. They should modify their old courses and introduce new courses without harming the interests of the students. By adopting modern and need-based programmes, these private universities not only help the students but also *boost*[7] economic growth. A country's socio-economic development is directly linked with its education system. The nation cannot ignore private educational institutions, as they cater to a large number of students. Efforts should be made to encourage good private universities to grow and contribute to the enormous task of building a highly skilled and professional manpower. One can readily acknowledge that having a large number of good private universities will make our higher education more modern, competitive and job oriented and hence, will boost economic growth. So private universities can be beneficial both for the students and the nation.

Aid to Vocabulary

1. *Demographic* — of the study of the statistics of birth, death, disease, etc., of people
2. *Delve* — search energetically, research
3. *Corpus* — collection of texts, writings, etc.
4. *Flexibility* — ability to bend without breaking, being adaptable
5. *Cutting edge* — an edge that cuts, the most significant factor
6. *Pursue* — continue or proceed along
7. *Boost* — promote, increase or assist

Points to Remember

1. The seats available in state universities are not adequate. To fulfil the demand, a large number of private universities have been established.
2. The technical education system in our country offers different courses.
3. The Government of India passed the private universities Establishment and Regulation Bill in 1995.
4. Private universities have to follow the guidelines stipulated by the Government of India.
5. The private universities have to operate without government aid.
6. Private universities place the students on par with their foreign counterparts of reputed universities.
7. Some private universities are run more like business houses than educational centres.
8. The expenditure of running a private university is very high. Thus, students have to pay hefty fees.
9. Now, it is felt that increasing educational needs can only be met by private universities which also boost our economy.

NO AUTONOMOUS COLLEGES IN PRIVATE SECTOR IN KERALA

Kerala State education minister Prof. C Raveendranath said that the government will not sanction autonomous colleges in the private sector.

Speaking after inaugurating the celebrations to mark the attainment of NAAC accreditation with A-grade by the Calicut University on October 15, 2016 the minister said that the varsities in the state would be allowed 100 percent autonomy in academic affairs.

He reiterated that the government will not sanction new self financing colleges, private universities and autonomous colleges in the private sector. The minister called upon the universities to take up socially- relevant research.

"A lot of research work in private universities is aimed at just getting patents and to make profits out of it. Instead the varsities should focus on research projects which can be of benefit to the society," he said.

Source: The Times of India

Essay
21

STUDYING ABROAD

SYNOPSIS

A large number of Indian students go abroad to pursue higher education. The United States of America, England and Australia are the countries which attract a large proportion of Indian students. They offer high quality education in various fields. Students interested in studying abroad have to undergo some mandatory tests in order to meet the preliminary entry requirements. Being a costly affair, it must be planned meticulously. The embassies of various countries help the students in gathering necessary information. Entry into any university abroad helps the candidates to acquaint themselves with different cultures. The reason for the exodus of students is that the educational system in India is outdated. To remove corruption in the education system of India, steps recommended for reform should be taken immediately. The system should be revamped to accommodate practical aspects in academic pursuits.

In the ancient times, foreign students came to India to gain knowledge at the universities of Taxila and Nalanda. These centres were considered the *citadels*[1] of learning. With the passage of time, the Indian universities have lost their appeal. Most of the Indian universities lack proper *infrastructure*[2], good administration, dedicated academicians and sincere students. This has prompted many youngsters to *vie*[3] for foreign universities. Acquiring a degree from abroad grants distinction to, and enhances the job prospects of the person.

The United States of America, England and Australia are the three major countries which *beckon*[4] Indian students. However, the racial attacks on Indian students in Australia, the UK and the USA, have dampened the spirit of those wanting to study in those countries. New Zealand, Germany, Singapore and Canada are the other countries which are *thronged*[5] by Indian students seeking educational degrees. The education system of the United States of America has maintained a very high standard. It has been an extension of the American dream of attaining excellence through hard work and labour, to usher in prosperity and opportunity for all its citizens. The ample allocation of State funds has helped the US establish a very sound academic infrastructure. The education system in Great Britain is around 600 years old. The universities of Oxford, Cambridge and Aberdeen were established in the 14th and the 15th centuries. They offer high quality education along with extending personal care. Australia is one country where the education system has been scientifically planned. It has 35 internationally reputed universities. Canada is also preferred by several students worldwide because the Canadian government has worked towards building a low-cost and efficient education system. Though an expensive proposition in itself, studying abroad could help a person enhance his/her knowledge amidst a much wider interactive field, and gain access to the culture of various countries, in addition to granting a globally accepted qualification.

The universities abroad offer high quality education in the fields of arts, pure and applied sciences, computer science, engineering, architecture, medicine, nursing, tourism, hotel management, commercial pilot training and management. The academic programme awards degrees for bachelor's, master's and doctoral courses, and diplomas in certain fields. Students interested in studying abroad are required to appear for TOEFL, GMAT, IELTS, GRE and SAT tests, depending upon the courses they wish to pursue. TOEFL or the Test of English as a Foreign Language is meant to check the proficiency of the aspiring candidates in written English and comprehension. Those who want to pursue teaching or research are supposed to appear for TSE or the Test of Spoken English. GMAT or the Graduate Management Admission Test is essential for a person aiming for an MBA degree in the USA or Canada. The test checks the proficiency of the students in Mathematics, Data Sufficiency, Reasoning, Comprehension, Sentence Correction, and it also includes two 30-minute Essays. IELTS or the International English Language Testing System assesses all the four language skills: listening, reading, writing and speaking, conforming to the international standards of language assessment. IELTS is recognised by universities and employers in a large number of countries including Australia, Canada, New Zealand, the UK and the USA. GRE or the Graduate Record Examination helps the candidate in getting admission to postgraduate programmes in technical areas. SAT or the Scholastic Aptitude Test, it tests candidates in Comprehension, Mathematics and Verbal Ability. This test has to be undertaken by students interested in pursuing undergraduate studies in the USA.

A three-day education fair 'Education India' is held every year at Pragati Maidan, New Delhi. It provides a unified forum for students, working professionals in the field of education and educational publishers. Over 250 renowned Indian and foreign institutes and private bodies from nearly

30 countries participate in the fair. The exhibitors represent international universities, colleges, business schools, recruitment consultants and international education councils. Innovative products and technologies are created for the classroom and beyond, are also demonstrated by certain companies that manufacture such products. Indian students and parents are provided with the opportunity to interact with 50 leading universities and educational institutes from India and overseas, and acquire first-hand information and counselling. This event is attended by both Indian and foreign *dignitaries*[6]. Such fairs are very useful for students interested in foreign education.

Since applying for a course in a foreign university is a time-consuming and costly affair, students must plan the process *meticulously*[7]. The application fees being high, one has to make a limited and informed choice of universities. Applications should be made only for those courses which the candidate *ardently*[8] wants to pursue and in those universities which offer those courses. In England, the applications are made through a computerised national system known as the Universities and Colleges Admission Service (UCAS). This helps the candidates in avoiding submission of multiple applications. A single UCAS form allows them to make 6 choices in terms of preferred universities and courses. Care should be taken to ensure that the university is accredited by the Council of Post-secondary Accreditation (COPA). COPA also gives an idea about the ratings of various universities which helps the candidate in taking a decision. Admission offers are received only after the assessment of the candidates' merits and the marks obtained in various tests. Application for a student visa should be made well in advance as it takes a lot of time. The procedure, right from planning the trip, and procuring the application form to obtaining of visa, could take more than a year; hence, it should be planned well ahead of time. The British Council Centres and embassies of various countries in India help students in collecting information regarding the universities in their respective countries.

The expenses to be incurred as fees for the whole year in abroad vary from university to university. So, an aspirant should have a fairly sound financial background. Student scholarships are offered by selected universities which help the student in meeting the fee requirement partly. Most of the students get hostel accommodation, while the rest secure campus accommodation. The campus atmosphere is *conducive*[9] not only to the pursuit of academic studies but also to the overall development of the student. He/She is exposed to the influence of various cultures which helps in experiencing and knowing the unique aspects of different cultures. Students can earn their pocket expenses by doing part-time jobs at libraries, retail stores, eating joints or restaurants. Apart from academics, students may also actively participate in various debates, sports or symposia held in the campus.

Studying abroad is costly but aspirants believe that once they are able to get admission in a foreign university, lifelong benefits follow. After completing their academic pursuits, they wish to continue living in the foreign land. In India, emphasis is laid on the theoretical aspects rather than on the practical applications of the course. Many of the subjects taught in the Indian universities have little practical significance in life. Even after having gone through the grind, when the students venture into the job market, they are often frustrated. They are confronted with *nepotism*[10] and partisanship which favour less competent candidates for jobs. The system of reservation also lets less meritorious students get jobs. This leads to the *exodus*[11] of many brilliant students to the West because the traits of hard work and intelligence are much valued there. Extraordinarily intelligent and persevering professionals are known to migrate to the West in search of better opportunities and due recognition.

The Government of India should rise to the challenge and address the issue. The educational system should be transparent and robust enough to be able to do justice to the requirements of students including the meritorious ones. Save for the premier institutes like the IITs, IIMs, AIIMS, IISc (Bangalore), TIFR and a few others, not many can be considered on par with the prestigious universities and institutes in the developed countries. The school curricula should be *revamped*[12] to accommodate the applied aspects of education. The system should also lay emphasis on the 'quality' of education so that our degrees and diplomas find acceptance outside the country as well.

After the completion of courses abroad, many students get lucrative job offers there. They do not want to return to India. This has led to a brain drain from our country.

As per the data collected under All India Survey on Higher Education (AISHE) report, 2014 — over 189 thousand Indian students were enrolled in higher education institutions abroad. This population accounts for 4.7% of the total internationally mobile students worldwide and is the second largest source of foreign students after China (17.3%). At the same time, India's gross outbound enrolment ratio is of 0.11%, which is quite low compared with many other Asian countries, such as China (0.6%), Japan (0.5%), Malaysia (1.9%), the Republic of Korea (3.6%), and Sri Lanka (1.0%). Indian foreign students are dispersed over 50 countries of the world.

Corruption, although a universal phenomena, is rampant in India in general and in the education system of India in particular. This gives birth to nepotism, favouritism, casteism, bribery and so forth, that *restrains*[13] students with merit from rising. As a step ahead in the direction of a progressive and prosperous India, corruption, should be eradicated completely and every step recommended by educationists to revamp the education system in India should be implemented.

The Government, the university administration and the academicians must be made accountable to the students at large if we want to make the education system more effective. If targeted measures are undertaken, Indian educational system could also attract a much larger number of foreign students, and students from our country would, perhaps, not need to go abroad for higher studies.

Aid to Vocabulary

1. *Citadels* — forts or strong places
2. *Infrastructure* — the system which supports the functions of an organisation
3. *Vie* — to compete eagerly with somebody or something
4. *Beckon* — call
5. *Thronged* — visited by multitudes
6. *Dignitaries* — renowned persons or persons holding high office
7. *Meticulously* — carefully, with attention to detail
8. *Ardently* — full of enthusiasm or passion
9. *Conducive* — contributing or helping
10. *Nepotism* — favouritism to relatives in conferring offices
11. *Exodus* — departure in large numbers
12. *Revamped* — revised
13. *Restrains* — prevents, stops

Points to Remember

1. The present state of Indian universities makes students opt for education in foreign shores.
2. The United States of America, England and Australia beckon many Indian students.
3. Students have to qualify some mandatory tests to study abroad.
4. There are different courses offered by various universities.
5. The lifestyle of Western countries attracts the students.
6. The Government must take necessary steps to arrest the 'brain-drain' in education.

INDIANS LOOKING WEST

Most preferred Courses, States

- California, New York, Texas
- 37.5% take admission in engineering courses and 31.4% in maths
- Telugus constitute majority of these students

Admission Business

- US Hyderabad consulate processed highest number of student visas in India
- An estimated 1000 educational consultancies and agents operate in Hyderabad and towns like Guntur, Vizag

Since 2012, the trend has remained unabated

Year	F1 Visas issued	Indian students in US
2010	26,845	103,895
2011	24,706	100,270
2012	37,964	96,754
2013	36,141	102, 673
2014	56,653	132,888

5 nations account for half of foreign students in US

Country	Students in US	%
China	304,040	31.2%
India	132,888	13.6%
South Korea	63,710	6.5%
Saudi Arabia	59,945	6.1%
Canada	27,240	2.8%
Rest of the world	387,103	39.8%

Essay
22

STUDENTS AND POLITICS

SYNOPSIS

Politics, as commonly perceived, means active participation in political meetings and movements which is not beneficial for students. Students took active part in the Freedom Movement of India. It was the demand of the time and circumstances. To keep themselves abreast of the political situation, students should read newspapers and magazines besides watching news channels. To acquire leadership qualities, they should take part in debates on the burning social, political and economic issues. They may take part in oration and other related competitions or discussions if they wish to eventually seek a political career. They may also take part in students' union activities but such unions should not function under or for any political party.

Politics is the art and science of government. It encompasses all activities related to acquiring and retaining power in a government or influencing the actions and policies of governance. However, politics, as understood commonly, means active participation in political movements, taking out processions, organising political meetings, shouting political slogans, *condemning*[1] one party or approving another. many students, today, are found indulging in such activities. Some even become members of political parties.

While it is true that our future leaders will emerge from amongst the Youth of today, their *indulgence*[2] in politics at the cost of studies is certainly not desirable. Education should be their primary aim. They should *equip*[3] themselves with knowledge and skills of some profession rather than wasting time in politics. Their duty is to gain knowledge, develop their personality and pursue a career so as to be able to contribute to their country's progress.

Having said that, it must be borne in mind that politics per se is an academic discipline and a student of politics or political science participating in political activities will only gain hands-on experience of this discipline. So, what is undesirable, is all and sundry engaging in political activities merely for fun and without any serious aspiration for learning the art.

Students suffer immensely if they go astray. If they miss their classes and take part in meetings and rallies, they lag behind in their studies. Being immature and inexperienced, they end up losing valuable time and regret the same at a later stage.

The pre-independence era was different. Students took an active part in politics during the freedom movement. It was the demand of the time and circumstances. Political parties used students to support and further their cause. After every *agitation*[4], many students were put behind bars. India gained independence after a long struggle which saw an active participation of students in large numbers.

Times have changed and the goals of the nation are, basically, of an economic nature now. India needs development in every field and requires a robust manpower. So, students need to acquire professional skills in all fields. Politics demands time and energy which students cannot afford to spare. Besides attending classes, a student needs to study at home for at least 3 to 4 hours a day. If a student takes part in politics, he/she will have less time for studies. Moreover, students do not have the maturity to understand politics. Taking part in political activities at such a tender age may harm them. If one has an aptitude for politics, one should better wait till attaining the minimum qualification of a Bachelor's degree.

Even for those who aspire for a political career, indulging in political activities during studentship does more harm than good. Many political parties exploit students for their own selfish ends. They ditch the young students once their ends are served. They sow the seeds of discontent and unrest among the students. They encourage holding of strikes, pickets and processions. Such strikes and agitations affect the academic career of the students. They do not derive any real benefit from such agitations. So, they should tread cautiously and be wary of political parties with vested interests.

The university elections, over the years, have gained huge importance for national parties have started taking active interest in these elections by fielding their candidates. Many a time, these elections turn ugly with incidents of violence. The colleges and the universities become battlefields with rival groups of students attacking one another. Local politicians incite and abet innocent youth to use violent methods to achieve their ends. The real cause of education takes a beating and the students' career gets derailed. That is why students are advised to stay away from politics.

The flipside of the coin here, is that, students being the future of the nation, must be aware of the democratic set up and values of the country. Participation in politics enables them to have hands on experience of problems the country is reeling under. This knowledge subsequently enables them to find solutions to those problems, which in turn goes a long way in making them responsible citizen of the country in future. Thus, not only the contemplating power of the students is enhanced but also their mind is channelised towards strengthening of the nation leading to national integration.

There are also certain other advantages of students' participation in politics. One develops fine qualities of public speaking. This is learnt in the college forum itself. After such a beginning, one can go on to become a noted orator in future. In a democratic country like India, it is very useful if students know about day-to-day politics. One overcomes shyness and gradually sheds inhibitions if one takes to the debating platform.

However, viewing the *pros and cons*[5] carefully, it is advisable that students should not take active part in politics. Their primary concern should be studies. Apart from studies, they should read newspapers and magazines and watch news channels to keep themselves abreast of the national and international political trends and developments. Acquiring the qualities of public speaking is possible in many other ways, too. Every institution or university organises debates, regularly. They should participate in debates on the burning social, economic and political problems faced by the country. Debates and declamation contests are often arranged for students to give them a chance to learn the art of *oratory*[6]. If a student has a clear bent of mind for this art, he/she can master the art of public speaking and can become a good orator.

Students must avoid becoming workers of any political party. In our country, many political parties follow a 'catch them young' policy. They overtake college elections and induce the candidates to contest under their banner. Soon, the students are absorbed as the workers of the political party. But that is not the right time for students to join politics. Politics demands maturity that can be attained on the back of a strong foundation of education.

Students can acquire some sort of training in democratic and political processes from the students' unions. They can air their grievances, queries and concerns as well as seek solutions to their problems through them. They should, however, ensure that members, patrons and office bearers of these unions are chosen amongst the genuine students and not from those who enrol themselves in colleges only with the purpose of contesting elections and gaining access to one or the other political party.

Students are the country's hope and the architects of its future. If they are well educated, they become better citizens. They should be aware of the affairs of the country. They should keenly watch the activities of politicians but not take part in active politics before acquiring sound political knowledge and also learning about political ideologies. It will help them to become enlightened citizens which is a prerequisite for the success of democracy.

Aid to Vocabulary

1. *Condemning* — blaming, disapproving
2. *Indulgence* — doing what one finds interest or pleasure in
3. *Equip* — furnish, provide
4. *Agitation* — commotion, disturbance
5. *Pros and Cons* — advantages and disadvantages
6. *Oratory* — the art of public speaking

Points to Remember

1. Studies should be the primary objective of students.
2. They should not take part in politics.
3. Students took active part in politics during the freedom struggle.
4. Politics demands a lot of time and energy.
5. Political parties exploit students.
6. One may develop leadership qualities if one participates in politics.
7. Students with political ambitions should read newspapers and take part in debates.
8. Students' unions should not be influenced by political parties.
9. Students are the country's hope and architects of its future.

HP GOVERNOR ACHARYA DEVVRAT AGAINST STUDENT POLITICS

Himachal Pradesh governor Acharya Devvrat expressed his concern over student politics. He said political activity at university level is uncalled for. He said universities were centres of higher learning and human development, but unfortunately political activities in such institutions pollute the educational environment.

Presiding over the 27th annual court meeting of HPU in Shimla on September 26, 2016 Devvrat said universities were institutions of intellectuals and should give an impression of wisdom and learning. He said any educational institution could attain new heights, provided one and all associated with it show strong willpower, work honestly and share responsibility and accountability.

Referring to the student politics, frequent agitations and protest demonstrations on the campus, he said responsible people should think about the problem and come forward to resolve it for the benefit of the institution.

"It was our responsibility to give right direction to the youth and their constructive suggestions should be taken as well to improve the overall atmosphere of the educational institutions," he said. He said in an era of cut-throat competition, there was a need to introspect and analyse work. Plans should be made at the department level, Devvrat added.

While speaking at the 47th foundation day of Himachal Pradesh University in July, 2016 Himachal Pradesh C.M. Virbhadra Singh had expressed his displeasure on the frequent agitations of students on university campus. Virbhadra Singh had even asked the students involved in protest demonstrations to leave the university and join politics. He said education should be not be connected or linked to any ideology.

Source: The Times of India

Essay **23**

RIGHT TO EDUCATION
—An Opportunity and a Challenge

SYNOPSIS

Education means an all round development of the individual. The system of education introduced by the British in our country was inadequate to cater to the nation's needs. After independence, India has been trying to restructure its education system. The Right to Education Act, implemented on April 1, 2010 is a giant leap towards universalisation of education in our country. According to this law, the state shall provide free and compulsory education to all children of six to fourteen years of age. Today, the state is seen as the chief provider of education. The Right to Education is recognised as a human right by the United Nations. Many Western and Asian countries have adopted this as a law. In our country, the implementation of RTE Act faces massive hurdles in terms of manpower, logistics and finances. The report on elementary education in India gives a bleak picture. Our government must launch a massive awareness campaign, so that parents can take advantage of this law.

Education is a continuous process which helps to prepare an individual to play his/her role as an *enlightened*[1] member of the society. It means an all round development of the person. Education enables people to acquire a greater control over their destiny. Education is a foundation for a bright future. When a person is educated, he is likely to be more aware of his own rights. A country ruled by foreign rulers is usually deprived of a proper education system. Our country is no exception. The system of education, introduced by the British government in India was aimed at producing a large number of clerks. After Independence, India has been trying to restructure its education system to suit the needs of technological and industrial development of our country. Several commissions under the chairmanship of well-known educationists have been set up from time to time to review and suggest policies and action plans for improvement.

The Right to Free and Compulsory Education Act is a giant leap towards universalisation of education in India. The Supreme Court's historic Unnikrishnan Judgement in 1993, gave all children up to 14 years of age a Fundamental Right to Education. The court contended that the Fundamental Right to Life (Article 21) of the Constitution should be read in 'harmonious construction' with the Directive principle in Article 45 to provide free and compulsory education to children of 0-14 years. However, Article 21A, introduced under the 86th Constitutional Amendment Act, 2002, limited the scope of the Fundamental Right to Education to 6-14 year-olds, not recognising the importance of early years. Article 21A of the Constitution says: "The State shall provide free and compulsory education to all children of the age of six to fourteen years in such manner as the State may, by law, determine." It is globally accepted that the early years are the most critical years for lifelong development. India cannot afford to deprive its youngest 16-crore population of a right to nutrition, health and early childhood education, as *enshrined*[2] in the Convention of the Rights of Children, to which India is a signatory. On August 27, 2015 the law commission recommended to the government that children should be provided free and compulsory education from the age of 3 and not from 6 to 14 years as provided under the right to education, stating that 90 percent of the brain develops before the age of five.

After the Fundamental Right to Education bill was framed in December 2002, the successive governments in subsequent years made several attempts to pass it in the Parliament in order to enact it into a law. The law finally came into effect on April 1, 2010, when India took the historic step of granting all children 6-14 years of age the right to free and compulsory education—a revolution that was to put nearly one crore children in school at a budget of ₹1,71,484 crore over a period of five years.

Today, the State is seen as the chief provider of education. From April 1, 2010, it became *incumbent*[3] upon the State to provide children in the age group of 6 to 14 years not just free schooling but quality education as well. No child is to be detained or, expelled and there will be no board examination till class VIII. 25 per cent reservation for poor children even in private and minority schools and one teacher for every 30 students is the prescribed norm. No direct (school fees) or indirect cost (uniforms, textbooks, mid-day meals, transportation) need be borne by the child or parents to obtain elementary education. Schools have to constitute School Management Committees (SMCs) comprising local officials, parents, guardians and teachers. The SMCs are to monitor utilisation of government grants, the infrastructure in schools including the number of classrooms, barrier free access for the physically challenged, sanitary conditions and safe drinking water. RTE mandates the inclusion of 50 per cent women and parents of children from disadvantaged groups in SMCs.

India is a late *entrant*[4] to the group of countries that have legislated for compulsory education. The Right to Education is recognised as a human right by the United Nations. Most countries in the West had enacted laws, making elementary education a responsibility of the state. UK was one of the last countries in Europe in 1870 to make it the State's responsibility to provide compulsory education. It was after this, that Gopal Krishna Gokhale in 1911, urged the Imperial Legislative Assembly to grant the Indian people the Right to Education.

In the Asian region, Japan, China, South Korea, Malaysia and Mauritius have similar laws. The duration of Compulsory Education however varies. In its immediate neighbourhood, India becomes the first with such a law.

The implementation of RTE Act faces massive hurdles in terms of manpower, logistics and finance. There is an acute shortage of qualified teachers across government schools, mostly in rural India. To improve the quality of learning, it is critical that the government make clear budgetary provisions for training teachers. States need to recruit and deploy teachers at a 30:1 ratio, establish neighbourhood schools within three years and train all teachers. These require massive sums of money. The human resource development ministry has estimated a *requirement*[5] of about ₹ 34,000 crore every year for a period of five years.

The 2008-09 District Information System for Education report on elementary education in India painted a bleak picture. Of the 1.29 million government and private schools covered, over 60 per cent did not have electricity, 46.4 per cent did not have toilets for girls and almost 50 per cent did not have boundary walls to ensure the safety of students.

Launched in March 2009, Rashtriya Madhyamik Shiksha Abhiyan scheme with the objective of enhancing access to secondary education and improving its quality, envisages to achieve an enrolment rate of 100 per cent by providing a secondary school within a reasonable distance of any habitation by 2017. The other objectives include improving the quality of education, removing gender, socio-economic and disability barriers, providing universal access to secondary level education by 2017 and achieving universal retention by 2020. The Central government shared 75 per cent and state governments, 25 per cent of the project expenditure in the Eleventh Five Year Plan. The sharing pattern is 50:50 for the Twelfth Plan.

The majority of poor parents are not aware that education is now the right of their child. The government needs to launch a massive awareness campaign so that parents become aware of the Act and can take advantage of it. *Implementation*[6], obviously holds the key to its success. And that clearly will be the government's biggest challenge. Former Prime Minister Dr. Manmohan Singh had said, "I want every Indian child, girl and boy, to be touched by the light of education". It is important for the country that we nurture our children and young people with the right to education so that India's future as a strong and prosperous country be secure. The government must prioritise social inclusion, and address the concerns of the Scheduled Tribes, Scheduled Castes, Other Backward Classes, Minorities and Women in order to make the RTE a living reality.

Aid to Vocabulary

1. *Enlightened* — having or showing a good understanding of how people should be treated
2. *Enshrined* — remembered and protected (someone or something that is valuable, admired, etc.)
3. *Incumbent* — pressing
4. *Entrant* — a person who enters or joins
5. *Requirement* — something that is needed or that must be done
6. *Implementation* — make (something) active or effective

Points to Remember

1. The system of education introduced by the British was not properly systematised.
2. After Independence, several commissions were set up. It was in December 2002, that the Fundamental Right to Education was framed.
3. Right to Education Act was finally implemented on April 1, 2010. According to this law, the state shall provide free and compulsory education to all children of the age of six to fourteen years.
4. The Right to Education is recognised as a human right by the United Nations.
5. India is a late entrant to the group of countries that have legislated for compulsory education.
6. The implementation of RTE Act faces massive hurdles in terms of manpower, logistics and finance.
7. This Act has not recognised the importance of early years, i.e. 0-6 years of education.
8. Our government needs to launch a massive awareness campaign for the RTE Act.

SARVA SHIKSHA ABHIYAN (SSA)

Sarva Shiksha Abhiyan (SSA) is a flagship programme started by the government of India in 2002 for universalising elementary education. It is mandated by the 86th amendment of the constitution of India, making education free and compulsory for children of 6-14 years age group a fundamental right. It is a time bound programme

Some of the objectives/features of SSA

- To Provide Education to all children.
- All children should complete primary schooling.
- All children should complete elementary education.
- To provide quality education.
- To construct schools within the radius of 1 km.
- To bridge social, religious and gender gaps with the help of the community for the management of schools.
- It is a joint venture among the central, state and local government.

For the successful implementation of SSA, many schemes like Lok Jumbish Project, Mid Day Meal Scheme, Operation Black Board etc., were started.

MIDDAY MEAL SCHEME (MMS)

Midday Meal Scheme was implemented by the Government of India so that the goal of Universal Elementary Education (UEE) could be achieved. The main aim of MMS is enrolment, attendance and retention of children and to provide nutrition to them. Free midday meals are provided to the children. Many NGO's like Askaya Patra, Nandi Foundation, etc., are doing the needful.

HALF OF 43 MILLION 6-14-YEAR-OLD WHO DON'T ATTEND SCHOOL LIVE IN THREE STATES

While over 27% of children aged 6 to 14 in Bihar are not attending school just under 6% in Lakshadweep keep away from classes.

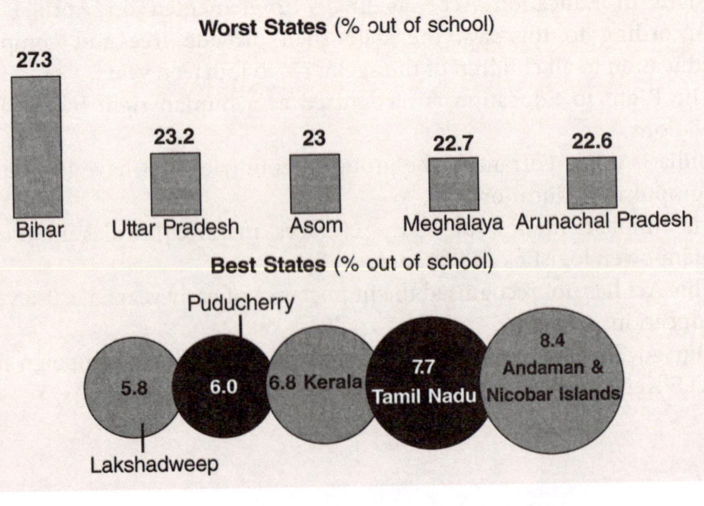

In fact, Bihar, Uttar Pradesh and Rajasthan account for almost half of those not attending school.

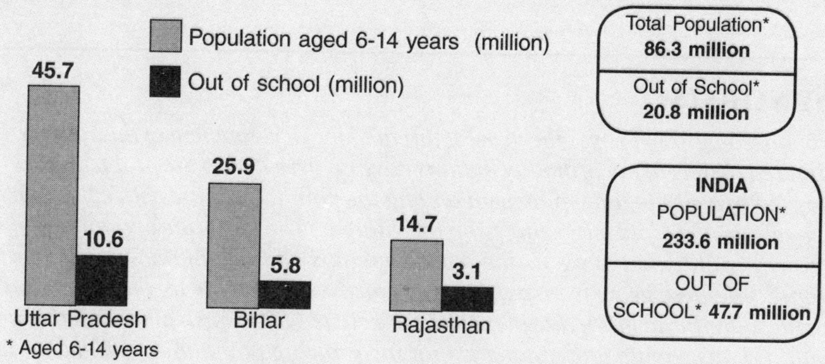

Source: Census 2011

Essay

24

POPULATION EXPLOSION

SYNOPSIS

Population growth poses the gravest threat to the development of the country. Bigoted beliefs of the orthodox Indians have contributed to the problem. This has led to a rise in unemployment among the youth. The cities have become the refuge of people migrating from the villages. The high rate of population growth could soon make us the most populous country in the world. This unprecedented growth in population can be attributed to the immense strides that India has made in the field of science. The most important thing that Indians should understand is that the growing population will make it impossible for the administration to meet basic needs such as food, clothing and shelter. By educating people about the benefits of having a smaller family, we will be able to check population growth. Kerala is an excellent example of this. The Non-Governmental Organisations should work with the government to achieve this aim.

India is the second most populous country in the world. A developing nation by economic status, India cannot afford any increase in her population. India accounts for only 2.4 per cent of the world's land area but it is inhabited by 16.7 per cent of the world's population.

The country's population which was 345 million at the time of independence grew up to 1,028 million with a population density of 325 per sq. km., as of March 1, 2001 (Census 2001). Every decade registered a continuous growth until Census 2011, which recorded a decline in decadal growth, i.e., for the first time since Independence, India added fewer people to its population in the decade (2001-11) than in the previous one. According to the official data, India saw a decline in the population growth rate over the decade 2001-2011. The country's decadal growth rate came down from 21.54% in 1991-2001 to 17.64% in 2001-2011. The average annual exponential growth rate decreased from 1.97 in 2001 to 1.64 in 2011.

While decadal population growth rates have consistently been declining since the 1960's, the absolute addition in each decade was always higher than in the previous decade. That has now changed. India added 181 million people to its population between 2001 and 2011 against 182 million in the preceding decade. However, even 181 million equals the total population of Brazil, the world's fifth most populous country.

Male population rose by 17.2% to 624 million and female by 18.1% to 568 million. According to the Census 2011, Uttar Pradesh is the most populous state in the country, followed by Maharashtra, Bihar, West Bengal and Andhra Pradesh. Population density has risen by 17.5% from 325 to 382 per sq. km. India became the second country in the world after China to cross the one billion population mark. If the current trend remains unchanged, India would become the most populous country on the earth with 17.2 per cent of world's population by 2050.

The most important cause of the uncontrolled growth of population is illiteracy. According to the 2001 Census, the literacy rate in our country was about 65 per cent. As per the Census 2011, the literacy rate has gone up to 74 per cent from 65 per cent. Illiteracy is the root cause of the slow pace of success of the family planning movement. The uneducated people believe that more children means more hands to add to the family income. They fail to realise that it also means more children to feed and clothe. Early marriage of girls results in early motherhood and more children. The lack of proper sex-education also accounts for this misery. Education leads to awareness. This, in turn, checks population growth.

Poverty is another cause of the rise of population. About 28 per cent (estimates vary) of the population in India lives below the poverty line. A large number of children are born among the poorer sections of the society. We see hundreds of children in the slum areas living in extreme poverty. Illiteracy and poverty go hand in hand.

The desire for a male child has created many problems. Many couples refuse to adopt family planning measures till they have a male child. This leads to the *queuing*[1] up of female children. This has led to an alarming increase in female infanticide cases resulting in the falling sex ratio.

Another cause of population explosion is a sharp increase in the birth rate coupled with a relative decline in the death rate mainly as a result of better health facilities in the country. The Economic Survey 2013-14 shows the ratio of birth rate to death rate as 21.6:7.0. There are several factors that have brought down the death rate. These are *elimination*[2] of famines, control of *epidemics*[3], successful treatment of deadly diseases like malaria, tuberculosis, etc. As a result, the life expectancy of Indians has risen considerably. The good news is that today we are in a position to fight many diseases which were at one time considered to be life threatening. But the flipside is that the nation is burdened with overpopulation due to the advances in medical sciences.*Infiltration*[4] is another cause of the rise of population. This takes place in mainly in the North-Eastern states of India.

Overpopulation gives rise to various problems. Food production in the country is low as compared to the growth of population. The number of unemployed persons has increased to an alarming level. This has resulted in the migration of people from villages to cities and towns in search of work. The poor take shelter in slums and live in cities in very unhygienic conditions. Slums lack the basic amenities of potable water, healthcare and sanitation.

Our resources are limited. The non-renewable resources of energy are exhaustible. These resources namely coal, petroleum, wood, etc., may get exhausted very soon if the population goes on increasing rapidly. The water table has gone down. At some places, the hope of getting water at even 200 feet below the ground level is *feeble*[5]. Overpopulation has also led to increasing levels of pollution. Pollution causes *chronic*[6] diseases.

Trees are cut down to meet the rising need of space for the growing population. This poses a threat to our environment. There is an acute shortage of space in the crowded cities. People are forced to live by the roadside in small huts made of plastic cover and *husk*[7]. Children do not get admission in schools easily. It has also become difficult for students to get admission in good colleges and universities.

A significant drop in the population growth of India's most backward states is driving the sharpest ever decline in the country's population growth rates. For the last 30 years, India's eight most backward states—Uttar Pradesh, Uttarakhand, Bihar, Jharkhand, Madhya Pradesh, Chhattisgarh, Rajasthan and Odisha—had grown at a constant rate, increasing their populations by a fourth every ten years. For the first time, growth rates have sharply dropped in these states. In fact, population growth has dropped faster in these eight states than in the better off states.

This contributed to an all-India population growth rate of less than 18% over the last decade (2001-2011). India's growth rate declined by almost four percentage points as compared to the previous decade, the sharpest decline ever in any decade.

Overall, fertility is declining. Not only is the rate of growth of the population of children under the age of six dropping, the absolute numbers too have dropped considerably.

Among the major states, Bihar's 0-6 age group population is close to 18% of its total, indicating that Bihar's fertility is probably still higher than the rest of the country.

Uttar Pradesh remains the most populous state (199.5 million) followed by Maharashtra (112 million). In population, these two states put together surpass the United States, the world's third most populous country after China and India. Growth rates have, however, declined in all of the six most populous states—Uttar Pradesh, Maharashtra, Bihar, West Bengal, Madhya Pradesh and Tamil Nadu. Nagaland and Kerala are the slowest growing states. For the last 20 years, Kerala has been growing at the pace of the developed world, and grew less than 5% over the last decade. With Maharashtra's growth rate declining to 16%, the average annual growth rate is now less than 2% in all of the southern states.

Census 2011 marks a milestone of sorts considering the population grew at the lowest ever rate in a decade, except between 1911 and 1921. The other gains include a rise of 9.21 percentage points in literacy (6.9 per cent increase for male and 11.8 per cent increase for female literacy) and a gain of seven points in the overall sex ratio — up from 933 females per 1,000 males in 2001 to 940 now. Also, the majority of the states identified as gender critical have shown improved sex ratios, Jammu and Kashmir, Gujarat and Bihar being the only ones where declines were noticed.

People's *intolerance*[8] for the girl child, however, continues with the child sex ratio dipping alarmingly by 13 points to settle at 914 (against 927 girls per 1,000 boys between 0 and 6 years in 2001) — the lowest since 1961. Haryana, Punjab, Delhi and Chandigarh lead this dubious club, with 830, 846, 866 and 867 child sex ratio, respectively. Dadra and Nagar Haveli, which had the highest child sex ratio of 979 in 2001, posted the steepest decline of 55 points to settle at 924. The Indian government has taken several steps to ensure that population growth retards to targetted levels. The Family Planning programme was brought into effect in 1951; it was later renamed as the Family Welfare programme. Couples were encouraged to go in for Planned Parenthood. The slogan "*Hum do hamare do* (Two children per couple) was widely publicised. It yielded good results. Today, couples having a single child, especially a girl child, are granted free education and financial support for their child.

Steps should be undertaken by the Government to make India a fully literate State. Family planning programmes should be undertaken more effectively. The Government should provide incentives to citizens who adopt the small family norm. The non-governmental organisations should work with the Government to check population explosion.

AID TO VOCABULARY

1. *Queuing* — lining up
2. *Elimination* — to get rid of
3. *Epidemics* — diseases spreading rapidly among many people in a place

4. *Infiltration* — crossing over illegally into a bordering country
5. *Feeble* — not effective, weak
6. *Chronic* — lasting for a long time
7. *Husk* — the dry outer covering of some fruits or seeds
8. *Intolerance* — inability to accept

Points to Remember

1. India is passing through the phase of population explosion.
2. Overpopulation has caused serious problems in every sphere.
3. Poverty, illiteracy, high birth rate, low death rate, etc., are the various causes of overpopulation.
4. Food production is low, compared to the growth of population.
5. Our limited resources may get exhausted one day if population explosion is not checked.
6. Cutting down of trees poses a threat to the environment.
7. According to Census-2011, growth rate declined sharply during 2001-2011 as compared to the previous decade (1991-2001) in India's eight most backward states.
8. Majority of the states identified as gender critical have shown improved sex ratio except Jammu and Kashmir, Gujarat and Bihar.
9. Effective steps should be undertaken by the Government to check population growth.

POPULATION GROWTH 1950-2014

Computing the number of births and deaths registered in the year under consideration with the figure given by the census, once a decade, the population of the country is recorded every year. The total population in India was last recorded at 1238.9 million people in 2014 from 359.0 million in 1950, changing 245 per cent during the last 50 years and more. Population in India averaged 744.18 million from 1950 until 2014, reaching an all time high of 1238.89 million in 2014.

Population in India is reported by the Ministry of Statistics and Programme Implementation (MOSPI).

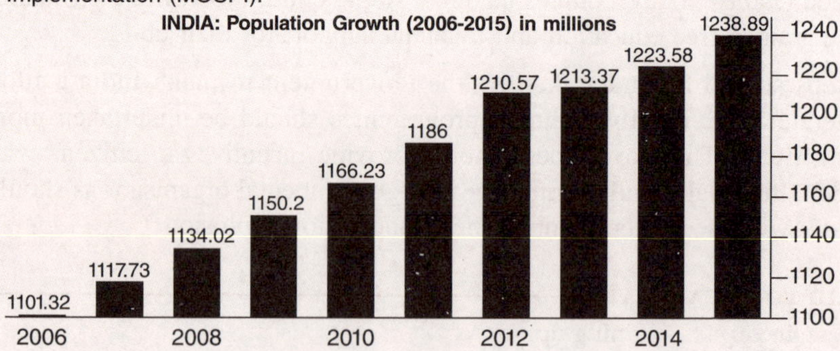

Source: www.tradingeconomics.com

STABILISING POPULATION

Birth of a Nation

Humanity has expanded exponentially over the past 15 years, with a billion people added since 1999. In 2015, the world's population became 7.3 billion, and is expected to be 9.7 in 2050 and 11.2 billion in 2100, estimates the United Nations.

In India, 26 million babies — the populations of Sweden, Norway, Denmark and Finland combined — are born every year. 350 million people were added to India's population in a decade, compared to China's rise by 210 million in the same period.

Things on Track

India's Total Fertility Rate (TFR) is steadily declining, from 2.6 in 2008 to 2.3 in 2013, just 0.2 points away from the replacement population target of 2.1, after which the population begins to decline. West Bengal has India's lowest fertility of 1.6, with Maharashtra, Kerala, Tamil Nadu, Karnataka, Andhra Pradesh, J & K, Punjab, Delhi and Himachal Pradesh all recording TFR below 2.

"If this continues, India may achieve its demographic transition and reach replacement levels by 2022," said Dr. P Arokisamy of International Institute for Population Sciences, Mumbai. Incentivised and coerced female sterilisation camps continue in pockets but these are an anomaly now. The way ahead is ensuring women have access to standardised care.

The Highest and Lowest Female Fertility Rates

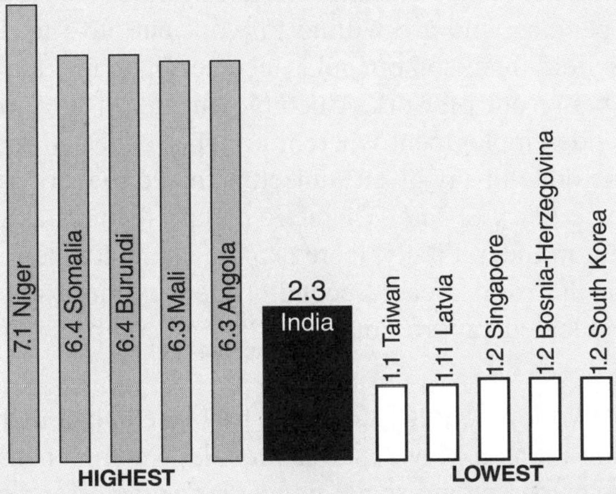

Looking Ahead

The health ministry has identified around 100 districts for micro-planning to achieve targeted TFR of 2.1.

- TFR in 23 districts of the country is above 4
- The 23 districts are in UP, Bihar, Rajasthan and MP
- Asom and MP have shown immense progress in bringing down fertility rate
- In 123 districts in 7 states, TFR is between 3 and 3.9
- India has a TFR target of 2.1

TFR is the average number of children expected to be born per woman during her entire span of reproductive period. Around 24 states have achieved a TFR of 2.3.

Essay 25

UNEMPLOYMENT IN INDIA

Synopsis

Unemployment means the state of being without paid work. It leads to wasting of valuable human resource. India is a developing country. The size of employment in any country depends considerably on the level of development. The socio-economic consequences of unemployment are dangerous. It leads to poverty, backwardness, and crime. The high rate of unemployment can be attributed to many factors, viz., population growth, outmoded and unproductive education system, lack of vocational education, etc. The Government has launched various schemes to provide employment to the unemployed. Other measures, like emphasis on self-employment and vocational education can also be effective in solving the problem of unemployment in India.

Unemployment is a situation characterised by the existence of those able-bodied persons who are willing to work but have to do without a job that may yield them some regular income. In simple terms, it means the state of being out of work. Unemployment can be further defined in terms of underemployment wherein a highly educated individual, for example a doctorate in any given subject, is forced to work as a clerk due to some strange quirk of fate. There are certain features associated with unemployment in India. Firstly, there is more unemployment in the urban areas than in the rural areas. Secondly, there is more unemployment among the educated (approximately 12%) as compared to the others (3.8%).

The World of Work report 2012 released by United Nations International Labour Organisation on May 22, 2012 provides a comprehensive analysis of recent labour market and social trends; it also assesses risks of social unrest and makes employment projections for the next five years. The report emphasises that if policy instruments are not carefully designed, they could *exacerbate*[1] the employment situation and aggravate further equity concerns, with potentially long-lasting adverse consequences for both the economy and the society. This report calls for a carefully designed policy approach that takes into consideration the urgent need to create quality jobs while at the same time laying the ground for a more productive, fairer economy and labour market. So far, the majority of the unemployed labour force has been illiterate or semi-literate.

Analysts in the Planning Commission are of the considered view that unemployment among the educated classes is bound to rise rapidly in the near future. The Government needs to take effective measures to generate employment opportunities, otherwise the educated unemployed would be the single largest casualty in the new millennium.

India is a developing economy. The nature of unemployment here sharply differs from that which prevails in industrially advanced countries. In India, there is the prevalence of chronic underemployment or disguised unemployment in the rural sector. Disguised unemployment is defined as the lack of enough work. The individual concerned is apparently employed, but is actually a small time worker earning low wages. Agriculture which is the principal occupation in the countryside is, a seasonal occupation. It is called seasonal occupation because the farmers are unoccupied for nearly five months in a year.

Unemployment amounts to a waste of manpower. The socio-economic fallout of unemployment is dangerous. It leads to poverty, slow rate of economic growth and a general restlessness in the society. It tends to lead the *disgruntled*[2] youth astray and thus threatens the peace, prosperity and stability of the country. When the youth does not find gainful employment, it is inclined to drift into unlawful money-making channels that are neither beneficial for them nor helpful to the country.

The education system in India has lost its relevance, because it still follows the pattern laid down by Lord Macaulay, which was intended to produce only 'babus' or clerks to serve the British. There is a lack of emphasis on vocational education. Corruption is prevalent in the recruitment process. *Nepotism*[3] and bribery favour the less competent and undeserving jobseekers. The old and primitive system of agriculture is also responsible for unemployment and underemployment. The farmers have small land holdings. Agriculture is a seasonal activity and does not engage the farmers full-time, all through the year. There is inadequate attention towards labour-intensive industries. Reforms in the education system as well as the agricultural and unorganised sectors are imperative to absorb the youth of India in gainful employment.

In the aftermath of the global financial crisis of 2008, it was the *National Rural Employment Guarantee Act* (NREGA)—renamed *Mahatma Gandhi National Rural Employment Guarantee Act* (MGNREGA) in 2009-10—passed by the Government of India that saved many people from starvation, especially in the rural areas. Other major schemes to supplement the wage employment and to provide alternative avenues for poor are *Swarna Jayanti Gram Swarojgar Yojana* (SGSY)—restructured as *National Rural Livelihood Mission* (NRLM) in 2009-10—and *Swarna Jayanti Shahari Rozgar Yojana* (SSRY), launched by the Government of India. Another scheme to empower women is *Mahila Kisan Sashaktikaran Pariyojana* (MKSP) launched as a sub component of NRLM.

India's population is rising at 1.2 per cent while jobs are growing at a slower rate. To provide employment to 12.8 million young people who enter the labour force every year remains a challenge, specially when a majority of the workforce comprises of dropouts from schools. Around 200 million children enter primary schools but only 20 million finish class 12. These youth are not employable as they have neither education nor skills. To make them employable, they should be given vocational training. On July 15, 2015, the government of India launched the National Mission for skill Development to realise the vision of a skilled India.

If there were jobs in tribal areas and in other backward rural areas, a lot of problems that India is facing today in terms of *insurgencies*[4] would disappear. More village enterprises are needed to generate jobs; and to encourage investment, better infrastructure is needed.

It is important to have jobs in the villages in order to stem the flow of migration into cities. With around 500 million people already living in 70 big cities, greater urbanisation in the future will lead to a precarious situation. To prevent the growth of slums under these circumstances will be a challenge.

The manufacturing sector is the biggest employer of semi-skilled and skilled labour. The organised or industrial sector jobs have, however, not been growing and have been more or less *stagnant*[5] in the past few years. The current rate of unemployment in India is 8 per cent which means there are 41 million registered job-seekers. There could be many more jobless people who are not registered and are *disguisedly*[6] unemployed.

It is the informal sector or the unorganised small and medium-scale enterprises that have been absorbing 92 per cent of the labour force. Yet, they are the ones that are most *vulnerable*[7] to getting hit by any global crisis, and their employees end up getting fired without any notice or compensation.

The government of India has launched schemes to provide financial assistance, insurance and other support to SMEs (Small and Medium Enterprises) and ARI (Agricultural and Rural Industry) so that more and more job-seekers could be absorbed by them.

The unemployment issue must be tackled with utmost care. Emphasis on vocational training and job-oriented school *curricula*[8] is the need of the hour for making India gain in the employment quotient. A young, healthy, trained and disciplined labour force will be the biggest asset to India for achieving a high rate of growth.

To help the youth build their career, the Directorate General of Employment and Training (DGE&T) has evolved various training programmes. A new "Skill Development Initiative" has been taken for imparting short-term vocational training with an outlay of ₹ 550 crore to one million persons over a period of five years. The National Employment Service (NES) with a network of 956 Employment Exchanges provides employment assistance to job seekers including special groups like handicapped, ex-servicemen, scheduled castes and scheduled tribes, women, etc., through placement against jobs notified by employers.

Under the Employment Exchanges (Compulsory Notification of Vacancies), Act, 1959, it is obligatory for all establishments in public sector, and such of those non-agricultural establishments in private sector which employ 25 or more workers, to notify their vacancies (with certain exemptions) to Employment Exchanges and supply periodic information as prescribed in the Act and the rules framed thereunder.

In addition, University Employment Information and guidance bureaus are functioning in 82 universities. A special scheme operates in 22 select districts to motivate and guide job seekers to take up self-employment. 'Coaching-cum-Guidance Centers for Scheduled Castes and Scheduled Tribes' provide to job-seekers registration guidance, pre-submission guidance, confidence building training, pre-recruitment training and special coaching in typing and shorthand. In addition, these centres also impart to SC/ST job-seekers computer training through outsourcing.

India can become a dominant world power and a reverse brain-drain may take place if Non-Resident Indians (NRIs) and industrial houses invest in job-creating enterprises. A beginning has already been made in this direction. The index of a fully employed work force is the availability of jobs according to qualifications and skills, and the security of *commensurate*[9] pay. In such a scenario, the number of jobs should be greater than the number of job seekers.

The future of the country lies in the hands of the youth. Their betterment would be *tantamount*[10] to the betterment of the country as a whole.

Aid to Vocabulary

1. *Exacerbate* — to make worse
2. *Disgruntled* — unhappy and annoyed
3. *Nepotism* — the practice among people with power or influence of favouring their own relatives
4. *Insurgencies* — rebellious activities inside the nation
5. *Stagnant* — dull, sluggish, motionless
6. *Disguised* — unrecogniseable, misrepresenting
7. *Vulnerable* — that may get harmed
8. *Curricula* — course of study
9. *Commensurate* — proportionate
10. *Tantamount* — equivalent

Points to Remember

1. Unemployment means the state of being out of work.
2. Agriculture, the principal occupation of many is actually a seasonal occupation.
3. Unemployment is more prominent in urban areas than in rural areas.
4. The socio-economic consequences of unemployment are dangerous.
5. There is a lack of emphasis on vocational education.
6. The present scenario for job-seekers is very grim.
7. Various programmes have been undertaken by the government to reduce unemployment.
8. Measures should be taken to reduce seasonal unemployment.
9. A multi-dimensional strategy must be adopted to reduce the problem of unemployment.
10. The government of India has launched schemes to generate more employment.

WORLD'S LARGEST EMPLOYERS

Employer	Country	2015	2010
United States Department of Defence	United States	3.2 million	3.2 million
People's Liberation Army	China	2.3 million	2.3 million
Walmart	United States	2.1 million	2.1 million
McDonald's	United States	1.9 million	1.7 million
National Health Service	United Kingdom	1.7 million	1.4 million
China National Petroleum Corporation	China	1.6 million	1.7 million
State Grid Corporation of China	China	1.5 million	1.6 million
Indian Railways	India	1.4 million	1.4 million
Indian Armed Forces	India	1.3 million	–

JOBLESS GROWTH CANNOT BE CALLED DEVELOPMENT

Unemployment is not only the problem of the jobless individual but the problem of the nation as a whole. Since labour cannot be stored, it is the biggest wastage of human resources.

Due to the rise of population in India, nearly 12 million people enter the job market every year and the gap between newly generated jobs and jobseekers leads to the surge in unemployment. Albeit unemployment has remained a big problem since Independence. The number of unemployed has reached 160 million at present. India has 65 per cent of its population below the age of 35 years. This population is directly affected by the situation of employment in the country. As modern techniques and mechanisation, along with automation, are applied, the demand for labour force has further depleted. There are 437 million jobs in the unorganised sector, including the agricultural sector. There is no potential to generate more jobs in the agricultural sector. It is only the manufacturing sector that has a job-generation potential. However, in the last so many decades, only 12 per cent of the population is dependent on the manufacturing sector and job generation has slowly stagnated. There are only 28 million people dependent on the manufacturing sector, whereas in a country like China, this number is 64 million.

Investment is the critical factor for the generation of new jobs, where India is more dependent on foreign investment. That is why a number of concessions are offered to foreign investors.

In the "Make in India" Conference held in February, 2016 at Mumbai, it was announced that the manufacturing sector's contribution in the GDP of India would become 25 per cent by 2022. It is just 16 per cent at present and 100 million new jobs would be generated. These expectations can only be realised if adequate investment is made. The escalating imports of consumer goods are hampering job generation in India. Small-scale units are generating four times more jobs, with 25 per cent of investment as compared to the large units. However, these units are highly affected by foreign imports.

The enhancing of the industrial base by prudent economic policies should be the goal. China has 34 per cent of workers engaged in the manufacturing sector. Similarly, India should give a big push on the front of investment, either domestic or foreign, to shift the underemployed agricultural population towards full employment in the industrial sector. MGNREGA should provide more jobs but only productive jobs can be the basis for sustainable development.

Essay 26

ILLITERACY IN INDIA

SYNOPSIS

Illiteracy is a major social problem in India. Illiteracy is the state of being unable to read or write. A country's progress depends much on literacy, about 26 per cent of the population of India is illiterate. The rate of illiteracy is highest among the agricultural labourers and the poor. The Constitution has made elementary education a Fundamental Right for children between the age of 6-14 years. Majority of the villages in India still do not have a primary school. Even today, single teacher schools exist in many parts of India. The Government has been taking steps to remove illiteracy for years. The people as well as the NGOs should assist the Government to carry out its policies more effectively.

Illiteracy is a major social problem in India. The Government of India considers a person who has attained the age of seven years and does not know how to read or write in any language illiterate. A country's progress depends much on literacy. Illiteracy is a curse on mankind particularly in the advanced age of the 21st century. An illiterate person is unaware of the modern developments—both national and international and continues to live a rudimentary life.

India is home to one in every three illiterate persons in the world. About 26 per cent of the population of India is illiterate though, over the decades, literacy rates have shown improvement. The total literacy rate in 1951 was only 18.33 per cent. It rose to 52.21 per cent in 1991 and 64.84 per cent in 2001. Census 2001 projected, male literacy rate as 75.26 per cent and female literacy rate as 53.67 per cent. As per Census 2011, literacy rate has gone up to 74.04 per cent. For males it has risen to 82 per cent and for females to 65 per cent. Kerala remains the most literate state with 94% literacy, Lakshadweep ranks second at 86.66%. The state of Bihar ranks the last with a literacy rate of 61.8%.

The rate of illiteracy is highest among agricultural labourers. The main cause of illiteracy is poverty. Poor parents cannot afford to send their children to schools. They produce more children, thinking that more working hands will add to the family income. These children work in both organised and unorganised sectors. There is a high *incidence*[1] of school dropouts in the rural areas. Effective steps should be undertaken to lower the dropout rate.

Providing education was the responsibility of the state government until after the 46th Constitutional Amendment of 1976, the Central Government undertook the larger responsibility of monitoring educational policies and programmes. The most notable of these are the National Policy on Education (NPE), 1986 and the Programme of Action (POA), 1986 later updated in 1992. These policies brought about uniformity in education and made adult education programmes a mass movement. They laid special emphasis on education of girls, establishment of schools like *Navodaya Vidyalayas* (NV) and *Kasturba Gandhi Balika Vidyalayas* (KGBV) in each district, encouraging sports, etc.

The scheme of *Sarva Shiksha Abhiyan* (SSA) launched in 2001 covers the entire country. It aims at *imparting*[2] quality elementary education to all children in the age group of 6-14 years. It seeks to open new schools in areas which do not have schooling facilities. It seeks to strengthen the existing *school infrastructure*[3] and provide additional teachers. It also seeks to provide computer education in rural areas to *bridge*[4] the digital divide. The Education Guarantee Scheme (EGS) providing a primary school for at least 25 out-of-school children within a distance of 1 km; Alternative and Innovative Education (AIE) providing intervention for very deprived children like street kids, child labourers and adolescent girls; National Programme for Education of Girls at Elementary Level (NPEGEL) to address obstacles to girls' education at the micro level; and the National Programme of Nutritional Support to Primary Education (NP-NSPE) popularly called the *Midday Meal Scheme*, are the important components of SSA. The National Institute of Open Schooling (NIOS) facilitates education, skill upgrading and training through open and distance learning while *Jan Sikshan Sansthans* offer vocational training to tap the potential of school drop-outs. National Means-cum-Merit Scholarship launched in 2008-09 arrests drop-out rate at class VIII and encourages meritorious students from weaker sections to complete their education up to the senior secondary level. An HRD survey shows that the annual dropout rate is 4.7% in primary schools and 3.13% in the upper primary section.

Children and youth are the *assets*[5] of a nation. They are the citizens of tomorrow. It is unfortunate that illiterate youth form a major part of the youth population in the world. Statistics show that 40 per cent of our population consists of the youth. If they remain illiterate, their future as well as that of the nation will remain bleak.

The Right to free and compulsory Education (RTE) Act under Article 21A of the Constitution of India became operative on April 1, 2010 as India took the historic step of providing its citizens the right to free and compulsory education—a revolution that will put nearly one crore children in school and involve a budget of ₹ 1,71,484 crore over five years. From April 1, 2010, it became *incumbent*[6] upon the State to provide children in the age group of 6 to 14 years not just free schooling but quality education as well. Schools running in tents or making students sit under trees are no longer allowed. Stringent rules have been set up to ensure that the Act is well implemented. Children not attending school are located and the student-teacher ratio has been restricted to 30:1 (for classes I to V) and 35:1 (for classes VI to VIII).

As per the RTE Act, 25% of seats in all the private elementary schools should be set aside for the EWS (economically weaker section) students. The latest review of the RTE Act is indeed heartening. A report by National University of Educational Planning and Administration (NUEPA) states that the number of school buildings have increased considerably between 2003 and 2014. As many as 1.98 lakh primary schools have been opened and nearly 95% of them have buildings.

The National Literacy Mission (NLM) was launched in 1988. It aimed at imparting *functional*[7] literacy to illiterates in the age-group of 15-35 years, its principal *strategy*[8] being the Total Literacy Campaign. The National Literacy Mission is one of the three important instruments to eradicate illiteracy. The other two are universalisation of elementary education and non-formal education.

In the context of the overall policy of the government aimed at empowerment of women, and in recognition of the fact that literacy is a prerequisite for socio-economic development, the National Literacy Mission has been recast as SAAKSHAR BHARAT with prime focus on female literacy. The flagship programme of the government is covering all adults though its primary focus is on women. Not only has the scheme been relieved of the shortcomings noted in its *preceding*[9] editions, but also, several new features have been added to it. Basic literacy, post literacy and continuing education programmes now form a *continuum*[10], rather than sequential segments. The principal target of the mission is to impart functional literacy to 70 million adults in the age group of 15 years and beyond. In the year 2010-11, out of the total outlay of ₹1300 crore for Adult Education, an amount of ₹1167 crore was allocated for SAAKSHAR BHARAT. The programme was initially rolled out in 167 districts in 19 states, to cover 3.83 crore non-literates in over 80,000 Gram Panchayats under this scheme and also to establish 81,007 Adult

Education Centres, one each in a Gram Panchayat. It further covered 49.86 lakh non-literates in over 11,996 Gram Panchayats and established 11,996 Adult Education Centres one in each Gram Panchayat. It is still expanding.

Literacy is essential for *sustained*[11] productivity. Illiterate farmers and workers fail to make proper use of the modern technologies both in the agricultural and in the industrial sectors. Literate people think more *rationally*[12] than the illiterates. They have better employment opportunities as compared to the illiterate. They can make informed choices and take intelligent decisions which can have a telling effect on the quality of their lives.

On July 15, 2015 the Government of India launched the ' Skill India' Programme aimed at preventing the youth among the marginalised sections of the society from taking to extremism. The 'Skill India' programme is being conducted under the aegis of the Pradhan Mantri Kaushal Vikas Yojana (PMKVY) and the National Mission for Skill Development (NMSD).

Illiteracy is a national problem. Effective steps should be taken to eradicate it. Though the Government has taken serious steps in this direction, it will take some time to get more tangible results. The people as well as the Non-Governmental Organisations (NGOs) should also collectively assist the Government in carrying out its plans. This will speed up the economic and social development in our country.

Aid to Vocabulary

1. *Incidence* — the extent to which something happens or has an effect
2. *Imparting* — giving
3. *School infrastructure* — the basic facilities necessary for a school to function efficiently
4. *Bridge* — to reduce the distance, to provide a way to
5. *Assets* — valuable property
6. *Incumbent* — a matter of duty
7. *Functional* — practical and useful
8. *Strategy* — a plan designed for a particular purpose
9. *Preceding* — appearing before
10. *Continuum* — continuous structure
11. *Sustained* — that can be kept going or maintained
12. *Rationally* — sensibly, logically, judiciously

Points to Remember

1. Illiteracy is a major social problem in India.
2. About 26 per cent of the population of India is illiterate. The literacy rate in India is 74 per cent (Census 2011).
3. The rate of illiteracy is highest among agricultural labourers.
4. The Central Government monitors educational policies and programmes.
5. The National Literacy Mission was launched in 1988.
6. Literacy Mission is one of the three important instruments to eradicate illiteracy. The other two are universalisation of elementary education and non-formal education.
7. The RTE has made elementary education a fundamental right for children in the age group of 6-14 years.
8. The latest review of the RTE Act is indeed heartening.

> The RTE needs to be amended to grant children the right to education from the age of three rather than six according to the Law commission. This observation was made with the view of making the government take cognizance of the fact that 80% of the brain develops before the age of five. So, the child's ability to absorb new ideas and concepts reaches a peak during this period. Related areas such as malnutrition, disease, poverty, social exclusion and the abuse of kids were also highlighted by the Law commission. The idea was backed by international conventions and treatises.

THE LITERACY RATES OF THE STATES AND UNION TERRITORIES OF INDIA

Rank	India/State/Union Territory	Literacy Rate (%)—2011 Census	Literacy Rate (%)—2001 Census	Decadal Difference (%)
	India	74.04	64.83	9.21
1	Kerala	93.91	90.86	3.14
2	Lakshadweep	92.28	86.66	5.62
2	Mizoram	91.58	88.80	2.78
3	Tripura	87.75	73.19	13.56
4	Goa	87.40	82.01	5.39
5	Daman & Diu	87.07	78.18	8.89
6	Puducherry	86.55	81.24	5.31
7	Chandigarh	86.43	81.94	4.49
8	Delhi	86.34	81.67	4.67
9	Andaman & Nicobar Islands	86.27	81.30	4.97
10	Himachal Pradesh	83.78	76.48	7.30
11	Maharashtra	82.91	76.88	6.03
12	Sikkim	82.20	68.81	13.39
13	Tamil Nadu	80.33	73.45	6.88
14	Nagaland	80.11	66.59	13.52
15	Manipur	79.85	69.93	9.92
16	Uttarakhand	79.63	71.62	8.01

17	Gujarat	79.31	69.14	10.17
18	Dadra & Nagar Haveli	77.65	57.63	20.02
19	West Bengal	77.08	68.64	8.44
20	Punjab	76.68	69.65	7.03
21	Haryana	76.64	67.91	8.73
22	Karnataka	75.60	66.64	8.96
23	Meghalaya	75.48	62.56	12.92
24	Odisha	73.45	63.08	10.37
25	Asom	73.18	63.25	9.93
26	Chhattisgarh	71.04	64.66	6.38
27	Madhya Pradesh	70.63	63.74	6.89
28	Uttar Pradesh	69.72	56.27	13.45
29	Jammu & Kashmir	68.74	55.52	13.22
30	Jharkhand	67.63	53.56	14.07
31	Rajasthan	67.06	60.41	6.65
32	Arunachal Pradesh	66.95	54.34	12.61
33	Bihar	63.82	47.00	16.82

The list does not include the newly created states of Telangana and residual Andhra Pradesh in 2014. A Times of India report quoted the literacy rates of the separate states as: Telangana—66.5% and Andhra Pradesh—91.1%.

LITERACY RATE UP, BUT SO IS ILLITERACY

Population Rising But Enrolment Not Keeping Pace

The overall literacy rate in the country has gone up to 74.4%, but the drop in the illiteracy rate has not matched the increase in population.

Between 2001 and 2011, the population above the age of 7 grew by 18.65 crore but the decrease in the number of illiterates is just 3.11 crore.

A 2015 UNESCO report said that in terms of absolute numbers, India — with 28.7 crore illiterates — was the country with the largest number of adults without basic literacy skills in 2010-11 compared to 2000-01 when it had 30.4 illiterates.

The fact that illiteracy is not being tackled is evident from the enrolment rates in primary and upper primary schools. Over 12 years (2000-01 to 2013-14), the number of children who enrolled in primary schools increased by just 1.86 crore, and at the upper primary level by just over 2 crore. The population during this period, however, increased by more than 18 crore.

Going by 2011 Census data, most states, barring a few like Nagaland, have recorded an increase in population but the enrolment rate does not mirror that. The country also seems to be having a problem with retaining people in schools and colleges. An average of 326 out of 1,000 students in rural areas are dropping out, while the same is 383 per 1, 000 in urban areas,. the National Sample Survey Organisation's (NSSO) last survey reveals. This data counts people up to the age of 29.

UNESCO has put the number of out-of-school (OOS) children at 17 lakh in India. A survey commissioned by the Centre put the number for 2014 at 61 lakh, with SC and ST children making up 79.03% (39.73 lakh) of these.

Essay
27

CHILD LABOUR

SYNOPSIS

Children in India are looked upon as gifts of God yet, they suffer from malnutrition, poverty, disease, exploitation through labour, and so on. Child labour is often perpetrated by the parents for greater family income. According to various estimates, the number of child labourers in India ranges from 45 million to 60 million. Children are forced to work due to poverty, over-population and illiteracy. Thanks to constitutional provisions, child labour is absent in the organised sector but is very much prevalent in other sectors and often in hazardous conditions. Awareness of the plight of the children needs to be created among everyone. Special schools have been set up to provide non-formal vocational education to child labourers.

Children are looked upon by Indians as gifts of God and they constitute about 36 per cent of the Indian population. However, it is a national shame that a considerable number of them perennially suffer from malnutrition, poverty, disease, cruel exploitation through forced labour and worst of all, illiteracy. Large sums of money are allocated and spent every year in India and at international seminars and conferences that focus on the plight of children, but many of them continue to lead a miserable life.

The worst and the most widespread form of misery suffered by children in India is exploitation through child labour. The economically backward classes believe that more hands bring in more resources. Thus, they produce, on an average, four to five or more children who remain illiterate; and several of them eventually go *delinquent*[1]. In this way, exploitation of child labour is *perpetrated*[2] under the active encouragement of the parents themselves.

According to an ILO (International Labour Organisation) report—'Accelerating Action Against Child Labour'—there are 215 million children employed as child labourers worldwide of which 115 million are working in hazardous occupations. The condition is worse in the developing countries of Asia and Latin America. According to 'Child Labour Facts and Figures: An Analysis of census 2001' made by International Labour Organisation (ILO), the share of workers aged 5-14 years and 5-17 years in the total workforce of the country was projected at 3.15 per cent and 7.05 per cent respectively.

As per a US report released on October 4, 2011, Asian nations – India, Bangladesh and the Philippines – lead the world in the number of products (130 kinds of goods) made by child workers. The annual report is titled 'Findings on the Worst Forms of Child Labour'. It focuses on the hazardous work performed by children. A list of goods produced by child labour, issued alongside the report, higlighted the degree to which youngsters in developing nations were forced to work, rather than sent to school, for little or no wages. The list was topped by India, with its children, being employed to make as many as 20 products, including bidis, bricks, fireworks, footwear, glass bangles, incense, locks, matches, carpets, silk fabric and thread, and footballs. India also topped a separate list of products made by forced or *indentured*[3] child labour.

Studies find that the root cause of child labour is poverty. Poverty is also responsible for the lack of education, poor healthcare and limited alternative employment. Poor children in India, in both rural and urban areas, are compelled to work when they ought to be in school laying the foundation of their careers. Poverty, illiteracy and social backwardness of parents, an unproductive education system and other compelling factors force them to carry a heavy burden on their frail and tender shoulders.

The government of India is committed to ensuring that the children of India are not exploited in any way. The Directive Principles of State Policy, as well as the Fundamental Rights embody these principles most effectively. Legal action can be taken if these rules are not observed stringently. General development programmes as also project based action may be brought into force according to the circumstance of the area in question.

The Child Labour (Prohibition and Regulation) Act bans employment of children below the age of 14 in about 16 hazardous occupations and 65 processes. These include building and construction works, production of hosiery goods, carpet weaving, brick kilns, working as domestic servant or even in the tea-shops, road-side eateries, etc. In September 2008, one more occupation and 8 more processes were included in the list of prohibited areas for child labourers. These are—food processing, timber handling, mechanical lumbering, working near the furnace, i.e., being exposed to extreme heat or coolness, merchandised fishing, slate stone mixing, pencil industries, etc. On June 7, 2010 the Technical Advisory Industry on child labour added two more occupations to the banned list, namely the caring of elephants and working in a circus.

According to the National Commission for Enterprises in Unorganised Sector, the potential child labour pool in the country remains high at 45.2 million children. NGOs estimate that the number of child labourers *cumulates*[4] to 60 million, which is 6% of the total population of India. However, a National Family Health Survey report claims that 15% of children in India remain in employment.

Of the total child labourers, about 87 per cent are in the rural areas working in farms, plantations, fisheries and cottage industries. Primary education is free and compulsory but children do not go to school as they have to work for family income. This deprives them of the opportunity to attend school or to acquire the type of human *capital*[5] which may allow them to have a fair chance in the labour market. Child labour, as it is unskilled, fails to form a competent labour force for the future of the country. Another effect of this is that there is an abundant supply of child labourers, which reduces the bargaining power of all workers. The long hours of work in unhygienic and hazardous conditions on the one hand and the lack of proper nutrition and healthcare on the other have disastrous effects on the health of children. The employer is however, only concerned with his own profit. He employs children since they are docile, are willing to do monotonous jobs and are cheap labour. Besides, they are also more trustworthy and do not form trade unions.

However, efforts are being made to increase awareness among people and to eradicate the evil of child exploitation. The world has set an aim to eliminate the practice of child labour by 2016. The boycott of products which employ child labour in their process industry, by the western countries, has led the various developing nations to ban child labour. In 1995, Indian carpet manufacturers, exporters and NGOs created a brand known as 'Rugmark' which certifies that no child was involved in the manufacture of the carpets sold under the brand.

The problem of child labour is a complex developmental issue. The root cause of the problem is poverty. If poverty is eradicated, the need for child labour will automatically decline. Children are forced to work when they should be actually sent to school and as such are deprived of the fruits of education. These deprived children grow up as under-privileged parents and repeat what their parents did. Thus a *vicious cycle*[6] of *destitution*[7] is formed and the demon of child labour is reborn generation after generation. To tackle the problem, the Government must strike at the root of the cause, i.e. poverty.

Child labour can be checked by reducing poverty in rural areas, offering income opportunities and improving general health. The Government of India expanded the National Child Labour Project across the country during the 11th Five Year Plan. The scheme, under which children withdrawn from work are sent to special schools where they are provided with bridge education, vocational training, midday meal, stipend, health-care facilities etc., is operating in 250 child labour endemic districts across 20 states. Government had initiated the National Child Labour Project (NCLP) Scheme in 1988 to rehabilitate working children in 12 labour endemic districts of the country. More than 10,000 special schools have been sanctioned with enrolment of approximately 5 lakh children. At present, there are 8020 NCLP schools being run in the country with an enrolment of about 4 lakh children, and 6.47 lakh working children have already been main streamed to regular education under the NCLP Scheme. Kerala has managed to virtually eliminate child labour from its agriculture sector. The child labourers and their families benefit from various schemes of different Ministries in the government like Women and Child Development, Human Resources Development, Rural Development, Urban Housing, Rural Poverty Alleviation and the Panchayati Raj Institutions. The Railways have also been requested to ensure that there is no trafficking of children for work.

However, banning of all employment opportunities for children would be an insensible and *unfeasible*[8] move. In many poor families, it is imperative for children to work. A distinction must be made between forced labour and employment in a family-based cottage industry like pottery or knitting, where the children can work in their spare time after school. These children come from a social stratum where their families cannot afford even the basic necessities of life. As a result, they beg, indulge in petty crimes and sometimes even act as drug peddlers. If child labour is evil, then allowing the child to get into undesirable activities is an even bigger evil. The solution is not slapping a blanket ban on child labour but ensuring a conducive atmosphere where employers do not exploit children and happily allow them to spend some hours at school too. Mr. Lalu Prasad Yadav, former Chief Minister of Bihar, had introduced for shepherds *Charwaha Vidyalayas*, where they could study while tending to their flock. This novel model could well be utilised in customised version for child labour employed in various labour-intensive industries.

Vocational and technical education can be imparted right from the primary stage so that poor students can earn and learn simultaneously. Education would make them aware of their plight and they would gradually be able to choose other ways of earning their livelihood rather than be vulnerable to exploitation. Employers will not be able to exploit children and youth if they are skilled. People in general, including the youth, can help the government in carrying out measures to check or eliminate child labour. Reportage of unlawful exploitation, if one comes across such an instance, can rescue many child labourers. A new model based on international cooperation, that is between the US-Department of Labour and the Indian Government has come into force in ten districts of the states of Bihar, Jharkhand, Odisha, Gujarat and Madhya Pradesh. The project was launched on July 31, 2010 in Bhubaneshwar, the capital of Odisha. Two such projects are also being implemented in Karnataka (funded by the Government of Italy) and in Andhra Pradesh (funded by the DFID or the Department For International Development). There is a close link between child labour and youth employment outcomes. Child labourers, more often than not, continue in their work through adolescence. Alternatively, they are likely to take up similar or related occupation. Globally, almost 40 percent of employed adolescents are in hazardous work. Promoting decent work opportunities for employable youth is a major developmental goal across countries. The way forward is a coherent policy approach towards eradicating child labour and overcoming the youth decent work deficit in a comprehensive and integrated manner.

The task of eliminating child labour will require committed citizens in every neighbourhood to join hands. A methodical, sympathetic and sincere approach by every stakeholder in the society is necessary if we want to banish this evil practice for good.

Aid to Vocabulary

1. *Delinquent* — young person who takes to illegal or immoral acts
2. *Perpetrated* — committed
3. *Indentured* — bonded, contractual
4. *Cumulates* — adds to
5. *Capital* — resource
6. *Vicious cycle* — self-perpetuating, harmful sequence of cause and effect
7. *Destitution* — deprivation, lack of food, shelter, etc.
8. *Unfeasible* — not practicable

Points to Remember

1. Children are looked upon by Indians as gifts of God but a large section of them are forced to work at an early age.
2. There are between 45 to 65 million child workers in our country, according to various estimates.
3. The root cause of child labour is poverty.
4. The unskilled child labour matures into an incompetent labour force which is detrimental for the future of the country.
5. The Government runs the national child labour Project scheme across the country to rehabilitate child labourers.
6. The need of the hour is vocational and technical education from the primary stage of education.
7. A methodical sympathetic and sincere approach is necessary in our society if we want to banish this evil practice completely.

ERADICATING CHILD LABOUR

The Indian Government has been for years following a comprehensive policy to rehabilitate children working in hazardous occupations and processes. Employment of children in homes, dhabas, restaurants, hotels, motels, tea-shops, resorts, spas or other recreational centres has also been included in the list of prohibited occupations.

NO CHILD'S PLAY

- There are 215 million child labourers worldwide of which 115 million work in hazardous occupations, says a 2010 ILO report
- The 2011 census says that there are 12.7 million child labourers in India, the highest for any country
- The National Commission for Enterprises in Unorganised Sector says that the potential child labour pool in India remains high at 45.2 million children
- NGOs estimate the number of child labourers cumulates to 60 million or 6% of the total population of India

Adolescents in Hazardous Work Constitute the Majority of Employed Adolescents in Many Countries

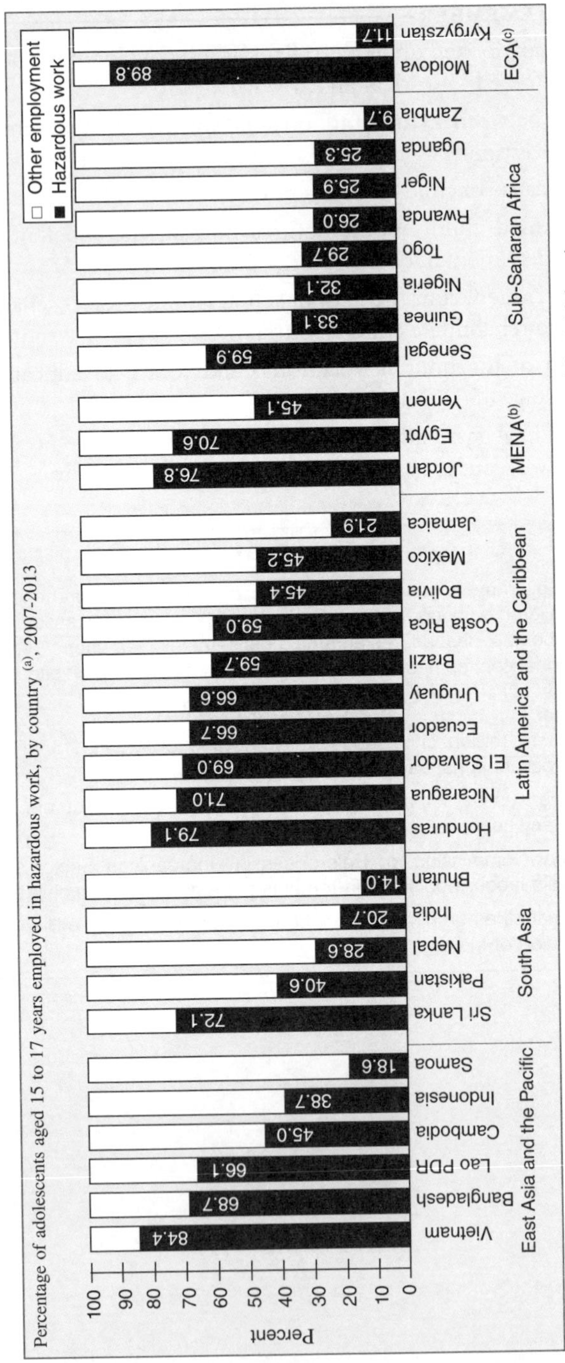

Notes: (a) Countries selected on the basis of data availability. (b) MENA-Middle East and North Africa region. (c) ECA-Eastern Europe and Central Asia region.

Source: Calculations based on national household surveys

Essay
28

CHILD ABUSE

Synopsis

Child Abuse is defined as 'the violent treatment of a child by another person, usually the caregiver. It is recognised as a major social problem. there are a number of forms of child abuse as 'physical', 'sexual', 'emotional', 'substance' and 'neglect'. Physical abuse is extremely dangerous to the child and may cause permanent disabilities. A study shows that more than 53 per cent of Indian children were sexually abused and majority of victims did not dare to report the abuse. Emotional abuse is seriously detrimental to or impairs the child's psychological and physical health. The study shows that 32.1 per cent children have tasted one or the other alcoholic substance. 'Neglect' is also thought of as a dangerous kind of abuse. Girl child neglect is also found to be quite prevalent. The consequences of child abuse and neglect may be devastating. The psychological and physical effects may last a lifetime.

Child Abuse is defined as 'the violent treatment of a child by another person, usually the caregiver'. It includes physical, sexual, emotional abuse and neglect. Child abuse is prevalent in almost every culture across the world and has been a problem for as long as there has been recorded history. The term 'Child Abuse' is also known as Child maltreatment.

Although the extent of child abuse is difficult to measure, it is recognised as a major social problem. It is present in all income, racial, religious and ethnic groups, whether in urban or rural areas. It is, however, more common in some groups, especially those below the poverty line.

There are a number of forms of child abuse as physical abuse, sexual abuse, emotional abuse, etc. Physical abuse can be classified as any attempt to harm a child, where the caregiver is conscious of the risk. Physical abuse is extremely dangerous to the child and can cause permanent physical and mental disabilities. Unexplained bruises, broken bones or burn marks on a child may be signs of physical abuse. In a study, nearly one-half of the children (48.7 per cent) in India, were reported to have been beaten up by family members. While interpreting data on physical abuse, one needs to keep in view the Indian scenario in which beating, mostly slapping is generally resorted for disciplining children.

A large number of children are of school going age, who reported receiving corporal punishment in schools. This physical punishment whether at home or in school, does not work effectively. It is much better to choose a punishment that fits the action, for example, if a child has a fight over TV, take away TV privileges.

Sexual abuse refers to any sexual behaviour between a child and an adult or an older, bigger, or more powerful person, for that person's sexual gratification. Sexual abuse ranges from unwanted kisses to inappropriate touching to sexual intercourse. A survey carried out by 'Prayas', one of the biggest NGOs in the country, in association with UNICEF, depicted that more than 53 per cent of children in India were sexually abused and majority of victims (73 per cent) did not dare to report the abuse. Children are forced and threatened not to tell anyone of the encounters because of the social *humiliation*[1] of being involved in sexual abuse. Three out of every ten young adults admit that sexual abuse has been inflicted on them by close relatives. Boys are as much sexually abused as girls are. out of 69 per cent physically- abused children in 13 sample states, 54.68 per cent were boys.

Emotional abuse refers to a chronic attitude or behaviour directed towards a child, or the creation of an emotional environment, which is seriously *detrimental*[2] to or impairs the child's psychological and physical development. This type of abusive behaviour can bring down an individual's feeling of self-worth and self-esteem. It leaves victims feeling inadequately helpless or worthless. The result of emotional abuse is often that the child either runs away or withdraws socially.

Substance abuse in children is also shown to be alarmingly high. The study shows that 32.1 per cent children have tasted any one of the substances like alcohol, bhang, ganja, charas, heroin, smack, brown sugar, etc. The prevalence of substance abuse is distinctly lower among females than among males.

Neglect is often thought of as the most dangerous kind of abuse. Neglect refers to any serious omission or commission by a person, which *jeopardises*[3] or impairs the child's psychological, intellectual or physical development. Neglect includes anything from leaving children alone for long periods of time, to not giving them proper health care and not giving them enough to eat. This type of neglect is directly related to poverty. This is because those living in abject poverty have to work hard to get the basic *commodities*[4], so parents or guardians cannot always spend time with their children. Not giving enough time to children is also present in modern day lifestyle where both parents are working and they do not have the time to spend with their children.

Girl child neglect is also found to be quite prevalent. Out of those girls having brothers, 48.4 per cent cases reported parents taking side of their brothers. One-third of the girls, who have brothers, reported that their parents gave more love and attention to their brothers. 48.4 per cent of girls wished they were boys. In 83 per cent of cases, parents were the abusers.

The consequences of child abuse and neglect may be devastating and far-reaching. Physical injuries can range from bruises, scrapes and burns to brain damage, permanent disabilities and in some cases even death. The psychological effects of abuse and neglect may last a lifetime and it may include a lowered sense of self-worth. Study shows that abusing directly affects the child's performance in schools.

In severe cases, abuse may result in psychiatric disorders, like depression, excessive anxiety or dissociative identity disorder, as well as an increased risk of suicide. Behavioural problems often develop after abuse, including violence and juvenile delinquency.

It is a matter of great shame that an evil like child abuse does have an existence in our society. It is illegal to abuse any child physically, emotionally, sexually or through neglect. It is also not good for a person not to report if he suspects child abuse.

The study, conducted by Prayas Institute of Juvenile justice in collaboration with the Ministry of Women and Child Development, Government of India, supported by UNICEF, reveals shocking facts about the insidious growth of child abuse in the society and calls for immediate action on the part of the government coupled with a social awakening through a proactive partnership between the government and NGOs and the masses at large.

The *gravity*[5] of the situation demands that the issue of child abuse must be placed high on the national agenda. Ministry of Women and Child Development has taken measures such as enabling legislation to establish the National and State Commission for Protection of Rights of the Child, the Integrated Child Protection Scheme, etc. These, however, are not enough. The government, civil society and communities need to complement each other and work towards creating a protective environment for children.

Aid to Vocabulary

1. *Humiliation* — to feel ashamed or stupid and lose the respect of other people
2. *Detrimental* — harmful, damaging
3. *Jeopardises* — to risk harming or destroying something or somebody, endanger
4. *Commodities* — products or raw materials that can be bought and sold
5. *Gravity* — a very serious state, quality or condition

Points to Remember

1. Child Abuse is defined as the violent treatment of a child by another person usually the caregiver.
2. It includes physical, sexual, emotional abuse and neglect.
3. Physical abuse can be classified as any attempt or harm done to a child, where caregiver is conscious of the risk.
4. A study shows that more than 53 per cent children in India have been sexually abused.
5. Emotional abuse is seriously detrimental to or impairs the child's psychological and physical development.
6. Neglect refers to any serious omission or commission by a person which jeopardizes the child's psychological or physical development.
7. The consequences of child abuse and neglect can be devastating. Behavioural problems often develop after abuse, including violence and juvenile delinquency.
8. Child abuse is a social problem and needs an immediate action on the part of government, NGOs and masses at large.

Essay **29**

DRUG ADDICTION

SYNOPSIS

In a fast-changing society, man has become prone to stress and depression. This has led people to committing suicide or has driven them to drugs. Drugs help them temporarily to relieve tensions, induce excitement and boost self-confidence. But they prove harmful in the long run. Repeated use of a particular drug has a profound effect on the brain. Drug abusers are prone to the harmful effects of drugs and also to diseases like AIDS. Most of the drug victims today are teenagers or unemployed youth facing some trauma or the other. They are generally pulled into this vortex by friends. Parents in such cases need to be supportive and understanding. The Government on its part has tried to curb this menace. The society should also feel responsible towards these victims. One should adopt a matter-of-fact fail approach while dealing with drug addicts. The family and non-governmental organisations can help to de-addict and rehabilitate the drug addicts.

Bertrand Russell in *The Conquest of Happiness* said that the sole reason of unhappiness finding refuge in the heart of man is the *unhindered*[1] growth of "self-centred passions". These passions are more often materialistic. And in the pursuit of materialistic passions man becomes alienated from society. Failure in his pursuit often leads him to discontentment and dejection and he finds himself a misfit in this world. In the modern world, none is unaffected by stress. The stress to outdo the others in the rat race of consumerism often leads one to depression. Even children are not spared from this. They are pressurised to fare better than their classmates in examinations and other co-curricular activities. So man, right from childhood, has to bear the brunt of being born in the fast-paced society.

A section of the youth, unable to cope with the high expectations of their loved ones, or to seek temporary escape from the *rigours*[2] of life, opts to either end their lives or experiment with drugs. The illusive and momentary escape and mental relaxation provided by the initial intake of drugs, encourages people to indulge in them more often. Their body then gradually, becomes totally dependent on drugs and cannot survive without the daily dose. With regular intake, the amount required to produce the effect also increases. This physical and mental dependence on drugs is called drug addiction.

Drug abuse is both an individual and a social problem. While people of all ages and at all places are exposed to drug abuse, the most *susceptible*[3] among them are the youth. It has attained the proportions of almost an epidemic among the youth. It is mostly introduced to an unsuspecting person by his/her friends and it has usually been observed that once addicted to drugs, a person initiates others into the same. Some youngsters take drugs because they want others to believe that they are bold and mature, and old enough to take drugs. Some get addicted because they are poked fun at, if they do not use drugs regularly. And some take drugs just to seek company or to break boredom. In addition to these, other factors that lead to drug addiction are — lack of parental care and supervision, lack of moral and religious education, media and pop culture, broken homes, hatred for any authority, etc. One seeks refuge in drugs to relieve tension, ease depression and shed inhibition, but the period of *ecstasy*[4] being short-lived one tends to increase the dose and frequency of drug intake. The intensity of addiction to a drug varies from person to person . It depends on the genes, the mental health, family and social environment of an individual. The major factors that influence the extent of dependency on drugs include - traumatic experiences, family history of addiction, depression, panic disorders and the method of administration. Injecting or smoking a drug is doubly dangerous to the brain. Even in cases where drugs are taken under medical supervision, the withdrawal symptoms can be tortuous, unless it is monitored closely by the concerned doctor.

Drugs, broadly speaking, are chemical compounds which when consumed alter the way the body functions. Drugs are prescribed by physicians to cure diseases and sometimes to enhance physical and mental capacities. But, *psychotropic*[5] drugs involve the risk of the patients' becoming dependent on them. They are classified into four groups. *Tranquillisers* (also known as depressants) like *calmpose* induce a feeling of calmness, relaxation and drowsiness. *Opiate* such as opium and heroin are physically addictive. They are used as intoxicants to relieve pain. *Stimulants* like cocaine produce feelings of excitement, increase self-confidence and flow of ideas. *Hallucinogens* can alter a person's thoughts, feelings and perception. Lysergic Acid Diethylamide (LSD), marijuana, cannabis, etc., are different hallucinogens which are all very addictive in nature.

Repeated use of a particular drug is bound to have a profound effect on the functions of the brain, the dopamine levels in the brain are increased causing a feeling of relaxation coupled with pleasure. It is impossible to obtain normalcy without the regular and continuous use of these drugs. Even drugs used for medicinal purposes such as inhalants, Xanax, Vicodin (or speed) etc., are used with caution,so that the patient does not develop over-dependence on any.

The profile of a majority of drug addicts is the same. They start off during teenage years by smoking cigarettes and eventually graduate into drugs like opium and smack. The first experience with drugs is not very pleasant, but the kick or ecstasy it provides to the brain makes the user dependent on it. The myth that the use of drugs provides great peace and tranquillity has caused many people to fall prey to this habit. Indeed, drugs have multi-dimensional adverse effects on the human body and mind. People addicted to opium tend to lose weight, and fertility, and they may develop a total disinterest in work. Heroin addicts suffer from muscle cramps, vomiting, diarrhoea, shivering and perspiration, if they are unable to have their daily dose. LSD can cause severe damage to the central nervous system. Drug abusers, being careless, run the risk of contracting diseases like AIDS by using contaminated needles. Failure in getting their regular dose of drugs because of shortage of money, can also make them resort to crime and murder. Drugs can reduce *cognitive*[6] operations making it difficult for the youth to develop a *functional*[7] set of values and ideals. Reduced cognitive operations lead to poor academic performance and a decline in self-esteem. A drug addict in due course gets alienated from the mainstream of the family, neighbourhood and society in general.

Our country has been confronting the problem of an increased trafficking in drugs. The northern region has become the hub of growers, suppliers and couriers. Cultivation of poppy and extraction of opium is legal in U.P., Rajasthan and Madhya Pradesh for medicinal purposes, but a large part of it finds its way into illegal trade. Drug trafficking is also patronised by some politicians and bureaucrats for the purpose of serving their vested interests. The amount of money involved in trafficking has made the narcotics mafia so strong that they enjoy a *dubious*[8] *nexus*[9] with dishonest politicians and hence the law- enforcing departments often find it difficult to prosecute the criminals.

Most of the drugs available in India are smuggled through Afghanistan and Pakistan. The Government of India has enforced *stringent*[10] laws to curb the menace of drug trafficking. The Narcotic Drugs and Psychotropic Substances Act of 1985 has made drug offences non-bailable. The Narcotics Control Bureau has on several occasions intercepted huge hauls of drugs. The Government should allow the cultivation of drug-yielding crops for medicinal purposes only under *surveillance*[11] so as to stop its diversion into illegal trade. Article 47 of the Constitution *enjoins*[12] the State to *endeavour*[13] to bring about *prohibition*[14] of consumption, except for medicinal purposes, of intoxicating drinks and drugs which are injurious to health.

For the total recovery of the addict, psychological treatment along with medical treatment through individual counselling, group therapy, re-education and yoga is of immense help. The planning of treatment must focus on self-exposure and self-help. Unless an individual wishes to get rid of this habit, and has a strong will power, it is really difficult for him to give it up. Awareness campaigns may also be used to serve the purpose. The media, the NGOs, self-help groups and other governmental and non-governmental agencies can play an influential role to educate people about drug abuse.

We just cannot blame the youth for going astray. They find hypocrisy everywhere. They see the wide gulf between the great values taught in the classrooms and the outside world of elders that promotes the sub-culture of corruption, greed, deceit and subtle violence. They cannot reconcile with these two extremes. The family, being the basic unit of the society, should be a role model for the children. There should be regular counselling sessions in schools and colleges to guide students to cope with stress on the campus, and later, in their life after their academic pursuits are completed. The federation of Indian NGOs for Drug Abuse Prevention (FINGODAP) was launched by the Society for Promotion of Youth and Masses (SPYM), New Delhi in 1995. FINGODAP is a registered national apex body of five hundred NGOs working in the area of drug demand reduction and prevention of AIDS. The aim of this organisation is to implement effectively the programme for drug demand reduction. The NGOs give counselling and treatments to several drug abusers and restore their shattered lives. The family, friends and relatives of the drug abusers should effectively contribute towards their rehabilitation. It can be most shocking for parents to discover that their wards are victims of drug abuse. Instead of reacting with panic and confusion, they should adopt a matter-of-fact approach. It is important to be supportive and understanding mainly because such a problem crops up during the difficult period of adolescence. It is applicable in case of not only the parents, but also other related people such as teachers, coaches, peers etc.

Aid to Vocabulary

1. *Unhindered* — unchecked
2. *Rigours* — severe conditions
3. *Susceptible* — prone to
4. *Ecstasy* — state of strong feeling
5. *Psychotropic* — acting on the mind
6. *Cognitive* — involving conscious mental activities
7. *Functional* — workable
8. *Dubious* — doubtful
9. *Nexus* — network
10. *Stringent* — strict
11. *Surveillance* — close watch on suspicious person or action
12. *Enjoins* — to instructs
13. *Endeavour* — to try
14. *Prohibition* — banning

Points to Remember

1. Growth of 'self-centred passions' has led people to depression.
2. Drug abuse is both an individual and social problem.
3. Drugs are mostly introduced to a person by his friends.
4. The intensity of addiction to a drug varies from person to person.
5. Drugs provide temporary relief from stress but produce harmful effects in later life.
6. Repeated use of a particular drug is bound to have a profound effect on the functions of the brain.
7. India has been confronted with the problem of increased trafficking in drugs.
8. The Government has to make more stringent laws to deal with this menace.
9. Parents should be role models for their children, they should be supportive.
10. NGOs should also help in eradicating this menace.

5% OF ADULT POPULATION USED DRUGS IN 2014

Around 5% of adult population, or 250 million people, aged between 15 and 64, used one drug in 2014 across the world.

In 2014, there were around 2 lakh deaths reported due to drugs.

Around 12 million people inject drugs with 14% of these living with HIV.

A global survey of over 1 lakh Internet users (three quarters of whom had taken illegal drugs) in 50 countries in 2014 suggests proportion of drug users purchasing drugs via Net had risen from 1.2% in 2000 to 25.3% in 2014.

Drug users purchasing drugs via Net	
Year	**% of Total**
2000	1.2
2009	4.9
2013	16.4
2014	25.3

In Afghanistan, total value of illicit opiate economy was $ 2.8 billion in 2014– equivalent to 13% of the country's GDP

Iran reported largest opiate seizures worldwide in 2014, accounting for 75% of global opium seizures, 61% of global morphine seizures and 17% of global heroin seizures.

Essay 30

THE TICKING AIDS TIME BOMB

Synopsis

The spread of the dreaded disease AIDS has threatened the existence of man. It is supposed to have spread by the cross-species transmission of virus. India is also in the grip of the AIDS menace. It is known to spread to healthy people through sexual contact with an AIDS victim. Exchange or sharing of contaminated needles or syringes, transfer of virus from mother to child in pre-natal and post-natal stages or transfusion of contaminated blood can also cause AIDS. Several prejudices and myths accompany the disease. AIDS is a later stage of the infection. The AIDS virus destroys the immune system of the human body. As no effective cure has been found, the Government, the NGOs and other agencies should work towards its prevention. People should also do away with their prejudice and work towards the welfare of the AIDS victims.

The *acronym*[1] AIDS spells a *holocaust*[2], threatening the existence of human beings in a big way. AIDS or Acquired Immune Deficiency Syndrome is caused by a group of related *retroviruses*[3] known as HIV (Human Immuno-deficiency Virus). It was first conclusively identified in 1981. According to the researchers at the University of Albama in Birmingham, the AIDS virus spread by the cross-species transmission of virus from chimpanzees to people in Africa. The chimps have been presumed to be the carriers of this dreaded disease for thousands of years, without being susceptible to it. It infected humans in the 1940's or early 50's when someone in the west equatorial Africa is supposed to have contracted the virus after consuming the animal as food. However, French biophysicists have claimed that the US army had released the virus as part of an experiment on gene manipulation of pathogens, conducted on prisoners. The first case of AIDS was reported in the USA in 1981. Since then, people in more than 175 countries have contracted the dreaded disease.

The disease is said to spread to a healthy person through sexual contact with an AIDS-infected person because the HIV virus is present in sexual fluids, saliva and blood. This accounts for both homosexual and heterosexual contacts. In fact, through various researches, it has been found that deep kissing where saliva is exchanged can infect the partner.

On June 5, 1981, a case study on an unusual cluster of pneumonia cases among gay men in the US alerted the world to AIDS. Soon, HIV/AIDS became a global *pandemic*[4]. By the end of 2010, 34 million people globally were living with HIV and 30 million had died of it. All in less than three decades.

In India, the first case of AIDS was reported in 1986 from Chennai. Since then, there has been an increase in the number of HIV infections over the years. In July 2003, India with the world's second highest population had at least 4 million HIV positive people. HIV sentinel surveillance data showed Maharashtra as the most affected state followed by Tamil Nadu, Andhra Pradesh, Karnataka and Manipur. In the year 2000, the prevalence of HIV in all parts of the country highlighted the spread of infection from urban to rural and from high-risk behaviour groups to the general population. 80% of the infections were contracted through sexual transmission, 8% through prenatal transmission, 6% through injecting drug among users and 4% through blood transfusion. Sex workers are supposed to be the biggest carriers of this disease. Truck drivers plying on national highways and other casual visitors visiting red-light areas carry the HIV virus and in turn transmit it to their families. Another group under high risk is of transgenders.

On the brighter side, HIV infections have fallen by nearly 56 per cent between 2006 and 2010. India overshot treatment targets for 2012—with 4.48 lakh HIV positive patients on the life saving anti-retroviral therapy, as against the target of 3.4 lakh. Emerging nations such as India, China, Indonesia and Brazil are leading the fight against AIDS. Sixty countries have *stabilised*[5] infection, including India and South Africa, which are home to the largest number of people with HIV. The number of new HIV infections in south and south-east Asia dropped by more than 40 per cent between 2006 and 2010. In India also, the number of new infections have dropped significantly. Beside, the estimated number of people living with HIV (PLHIV) has decreased from 24.1 lakhs in 2000 to 20.9 lakhs in 2011. The theme of "Getting to Zero" adopted by UNAIDS for the period 2011-2015 clearly reflected optimism regarding global response to HIV.

The year 2007 had particularly been a good year for India, with the data backed by UNAIDS halving India's HIV-infected population from 5.2 million in 2006 to 2.5 million. The sharp drop in the India's numbers led the United Nations to slash its global estimates from nearly 40 million to 33 million in its 2007 AIDS Epidemic Update. Still, India is the third worst-affected country with HIV after South Africa (5.5 million) and Nigeria (2.9 million).

The National AIDS Control Programme, NACP, started in 1992 has, in its III phase, the overall goal of halting and reversing the epidemic in India. This phase has, therefore, placed the highest priority on preventive efforts by integrating prevention with care, support and treatment through a four-pronged strategy—(1) Preventing new infections with targeted interventions; (2) Providing greater care, support and treatment; (3) Strengthening the resources at the district, state and national levels; and (4) Strengthening the nationwide Strategic Information Management System.

Wider access to Anti Retroviral Therapy (ART) has resulted in decline of the number of people dying due to AIDS-related causes. In subsequent phases of the National Aids Control programme (NACP) from (1999-2007), efforts were made not only to increase awareness through the media, but also to involve NGO's and encourage the formation of networks for People having HIV (PLHIV). In the 4th phase of the NACP programme (2012-2017), efforts were made to reduce new infections and further step up measures to overcome this bane. The link worker scheme was set up to prevent the spread of AIDS in the high risk groups of the rural areas of India. In 2013-2014 the condom Social Marketing scheme was successfully implemented in the 15 states of India. Blood transfusion was monitored more closely. It was to be ensured that the social stigma attached to AIDS got removed.

In 2001, no one had access to the AIDS treatment. Now, 86 per cent of drugs to poor people are given in India. Within 10 years of setting the goal of providing treatment to all, 6.6 million people were on anti-retroviral therapy at the end of 2010, a nearly 22-fold increase since 2001.

On the flip side, AIDS has long been a *taboo*[6] because of its association with sex. No doubt, unprotected sex with an infected person is a major cause of the disease but there are other factors too, like being infected through the use of *hypodermic*[7] needles or syringes. An AIDS-infected mother can transmit the disease to her child during the *pre-natal*[8] stage. In the *post-natal*[9] stage, it can pass to the infant through the mother's milk. These are the only known sources of contracting the AIDS virus. The disease cannot spread through casual contact with an AIDS patient, like sharing his linen and utensils, shaking hands, hugging, coughing, sneezing or by sharing the swimming pool. Lady Diana, the late Princess of Wales, in an attempt to bust the myth to the media and public, had once taken off her gloves and shaken hands with an AIDS victim.

As a matter of fact, AIDS is a later stage of infection of the Human Immuno-deficiency Virus (HIV). It can take around 7-10 years to develop other infections through HIV. The virus destroys the immune system of the body. The victim suffers from severe weight-loss and weakness due to persistent diarrhoea, pneumonia, fever, non-recovery from wounds, etc., and finally dies. Although scientific research has come a long way since the virus was first identified in 1981, no effective cure for the dreaded disease has been found till date. The drug zidovudine, is known to delay the progression of AIDS. A combination of powerful drugs that can make life easier and longer for a person living with HIV/AIDS is now available.

Since AIDS affects the young adults more, the country's economy is destabilised due to decreased labour force, increased public expenditure and a reduced taxable population. However, there is hope if the disease is detected in its early stages.

The best safeguard against the dreaded disease is precaution. A person may be infected by having sexual contact with an AIDS victim, by using unsterilised syringes, or through blood transfusion. Maintaining high moral values could reduce the occurrence of AIDS in the country.

The Government of India addresses HIV/AIDS epidemic, not only as a health problem, but also as a developmental issue, which *impinges*[10] on various economic and special sectors of governmental and non-governmental activity. The government has sought international assistance to face the challenge. Rehabilitation of such patients through community involvement is being planned. Many Non-Governmental Organisations are involved in the AIDS prevention campaigns and are helping the government in its endeavour.

The Government should create greater awareness and *disseminate*[11] vital information to combat AIDS. Since the spread of AIDS can be effectively stopped by taking preventive measures, awareness is the key to containing and eventually eliminating it. China has made it compulsory for people with AIDS to marry each other as per a 2003 legislation on marriage and population. There have been good public service given through television advertisements that have helped to some extent to remove the stigma attached to AIDS. Other forms of media too must be used for spreading awareness about AIDS. Organising AIDS awareness campaigns at *brothels*[12] to protect the sex workers and their clients could help in controlling AIDS. They should be informed about the precautionary measures required against the spread of the disease and the consequences of being affected. Literary pullouts, brochures, pamphlets, mainly in the vernacular languages, should be distributed along with newspapers in all states which would help in creating awareness among all. What is needed for combating AIDS is a concerted and vigorous national campaign, and not just an occasional statement or conference resolution.

Victims of aids are ill-treated through ostracism, rejection, discrimination and avoidance. As a result, most people avoid getting themselves HIV tested or even getting treatment. The net result is that a manageable illness is converted into a death sentence even as the environment is perpetuating the spread of the disease.

Since AIDS is a fatal disease for which no cure is known, we must first of all guard ourselves against contracting the disease. The people who are already suffering from AIDS should be accepted and taken care of without any *misgivings*[13] and *prejudice*[14]. They may have contracted the disease because of ignorance and the rest of the society does not have the right to *ostracise*[15] them. Movies like *Phir Milenge* and *My Brother Nikhil* have beautifully dealt with the problems of AIDS and of the treatment the patient gets from the society after it is discovered that he/she is HIV positive. Even ad campaigns on the issue have been very effective in sending out strong messages on prevention and breaking the myths surrounding the spread of the disease.

Aid to Vocabulary

1. *Acronym* — word formed from the initial letters of other words
2. *Holocaust* — loss of many lives
3. *Retroviruses* — any group of RNA viruses which insert a DNA copy of their genome into the host cell in order to replicate e.g. HIV that causes AIDS
4. *Pandemic* — disease spreading over a whole country or the world
5. *Stabilised* — firmly fixed not easily changed
6. *Taboo* — prohibition by social custom or general consent
7. *Hypodermic* — injected beneath the skin
8. *Pre-natal* — before birth
9. *Post-natal* — after birth
10. *Impinge* — to have a negative effect
11. *Disseminate* — spread
12. *Brothels* — house where men pay to have sex with prostitutes
13. *Misgivings* — particular feeling of doubt or fear
14. *Prejudice* — preconceived opinion
15. *Ostracise* — to exclude from society

Points to Remember

1. AIDS, the dreaded disease, is said to have been contracted from chimpanzees by the people of Africa.
2. In India, the first case of AIDS was reported in 1986 from chennai.
3. The HIV virus passes from person to person through blood transfusion, unsafe sex, injecting of drugs using infected syringes/needles and from infected mother to her unborn child.
4. Many preventive measures can be taken to avoid the disease.
5. The Government should work with NGOs to achieve success in spreading awareness among the masses.
6. Irrational beliefs associated with AIDS should be done away with.
7. AIDS affects the young adults more; this can lead to the destabilisation of the country's economy

GLOBAL FUNDING DIPS BY 90%, MAY CRIPPLE WAR ON AIDS

International funds for India's National AIDS Control Programme have dried up severely, posing a serious threat of surge in new HIV cases. Estimates show a reduction of almost 90% in funding from various multilateral, bilateral and philanthropic donor organisations over the last three years.

While many multilateral organisations, including World Health Organisation (WHO) and several UN agencies such as UNICEF and United Nations Development Programme (UNDP), have either drastically scaled down or diverted funds from India's HIV control programme to other countries, natural and even philanthropic donor organisations like Bill & Melinda Gates Foundation, Clinton Health Access Initiative and World Vision have slashed funding to the national programme.

Instead of financing AIDS control programme, many of the organisations, mainly the bilateral and philanthropic donors, have shifted focus to management of other diseases such as tuberculosis and family planning, sources said.

Source: The Times of India

BIG BATTLE		
India has the third largest population of HIV infected people in the world		
• 0.27% Adult HIV prevalance • 20, 88,638 People living with HIV/AIDS • 1,45,446 HIV/AIDS-infected children • 1,16,459 New infections • 1,47,729 AIDS-related death	• India has demonstrated an overall reduction of 57% in the annual new HIV infections among adult population • India is facing drastic cut in funding of HIV programme by organisation including WHO, UNDP and UNICEF.	• Bilateral and global philanthropic organisations such as Bill & Melinda Gates Foundation have shifted focus to other disease management such as tuberculosis and family planning.

Essay 31

SHOULD SMOKING BE BANNED?

SYNOPSIS

In the present society, cigarette smoking is glamourised. More and more people, especially the youth is getting addicted to smoking. But the harmful effects of smoking cannot be denied. Scientific researches and various studies have been conducted to find out the ill-effects of smoking on human health. It has been proved that smoking can be fatal since it causes several deadly diseases. Therefore, there should be some restriction on smoking. But in a liberated society, people talk about their individual freedom and right to live their life according to their wishes. In that case, the right of the non-smoker to get a pollution-free environment should be taken care of. A total ban on smoking is not easy and perhaps not possible. It has however been banned in public places.

Many surveys, studies and scientific researches have proved that smoking is injurious to health. Smoke is unhealthy and suffocating. It pollutes the environment. There are two types of smokers—active and passive. The person who smokes is active and others who are near him and inhale the smoke are passive smokers. Both are equally affected by the ill- effects of smoking. Smokers and non-smokers meet at many places like offices, buses, hotels, etc. So, considering the ill-effects of passive smoking on health and environment, smoking has been banned in public places. A person who wants to smoke may do so at places or zones where it is permitted.

In the present society, movies and television programmes have glamorised cigarette smoking. More and more young boys and girls are attracted to it. Even the 'statutory warning' on the cigarette packets does not stop them. The young generation considers smoking as a mark of sophistication and thinks that those who smoke are smart, *suave*[1] and modern and also have an intellectual streak in them.

Smoking is undoubtedly an unhealthy practice. Those who smoke suffer from several health problems. A chain-smoker is the worst sufferer. Cigarettes contain 4,000 types of chemicals out of which 43 are *carcinogenic*[2]. The carbon monoxide concentration in cigarette smoke is greater than 20,000 ppm. This is diluted to 400-500 ppm during inhalation. It displaces oxygen from haemoglobin and the result is the *impairment*[3] of the central nervous system. It may also cause *cardiac*[4] and pulmonary diseases (related to lungs). These may eventually lead to heart-attacks. Cigarettes also contain ammonia and other hydrocarbons which could cause asthma, other respiratory infections and lung cancer. The dust particles in it may cause irritation of the eyes, cancer, and *emphysema*[5]. Its nicotine content is highly addictive and reaches the brain immediately. It *constricts*[6] the blood vessels, raises the blood pressure and gives the central nervous system a minor *jolt*[7]. It can lead to reproductive disorders in the long run.

The interesting part is that smoking or the usage of tobacco can be easily overcome compared to any form of addiction. According to the report of the Tobacco Control in India (2004) more than 8 lakh tobacco related deaths occur in our country every year. India is the second largest consumer of tobacco in the world after China. The GYTS (The Global Youth Tobacco Survey) concluded that about 15% children in the age group of 13–15 years are addicted. It says that 47.8 per cent men and 2013 per cent women consume tobacco in India.

Some important data are found in 'A Nationally Representative Case-Control Study of Smoking and Death in India', the most exhaustive study of smoking published in the 'New England Journal of Medicine'. This research was done by a team from India, Canada and the UK and was supported by the World Health Organisation. According to this study, India is in the midst of a catastrophic epidemic of deaths due to smoking. While the study found no safe levels of smoking, cigarettes were found to be more dangerous than *bidis*.

There are 120 million smokers in India. The study also found that among men, about 61% of those who smoke would die at the age of 30-69 compared with 41% of otherwise similar non-smokers. Among women, 62% of those who smoke will die within 30-69 years of age compared with only 36% of non-smokers. Smokers in India start at a later age than those in Europe or America and smoke less, but in India smokers die not only from lung diseases and cancer but also from tuberculosis and heart-attacks.

It is very alarming that tobacco use among young women has risen rapidly in India, with 9.7% girls between the ages of 13 and 15 years using some form of tobacco as compared to 3.1% adult women. According to WHO, 14.1% children between the ages of 13 and 15 start smoking in India or use some form of tobacco. The tobacco epidemic has shifted to the developing world, where 80% of the over 8 million annual tobacco-related deaths are feared to occur by 2030.

Scientists have discovered that smoking has a far more damaging effect on women's health than men's. The harmful effects of smoking can kill women eight years earlier than men. Scientists claim that smoking can cut 11 years off a woman's average life expectancy. And in case of a man, it is just 3 years off. They even added that women are more *susceptible*[8] to the commonest form of lung cancer, adenocarcinoma. If a pregnant woman smokes, it is harmful not only to her own health but also to the expected baby.

It is an alarming fact that nearly 700 million children worldwide live in the home of a smoker. Passive smoking increases the risk of bronchitis, pneumonia, middle-ear infection, cardiovascular impairment, asthma and behavioural problems in children. A US study found deficiencies in reading and reasoning skills among children even at low levels of smoke exposure.

The single best way for giving one's own family a smoke-free environment is to quit smoking. Quitting requires planning and a strong will. Today, effective support systems like *psychotherapeutic*[9] interventions along with *pharmacotherapy*[10] and nicotine replacement therapy are available to make the quitting process easier. Smoking affects both the active and the passive smokers. When we keep all the adverse consequences of smoking a policy to ban smoking in public places is justifiable. A blanket ban on smoking may upset the state *exchequer*[11]. The sale of cigarettes would stop with such a ban and the government would lose revenue from excise duties. The tobacco industry would face closure. Millions of people working in these industries would be rendered jobless.

But if the government cares for the health of its citizens, it should rise above the economic considerations and find a way out. The government of India has banned smoking at least in public places. It has also strictly instructed that children below 18 years of age should not be employed in tobacco industries. They are not allowed to buy or consume tobacco. In the workplaces, there should be an arrangement for separate smoking zones for smokers.

Aid to Vocabulary

1. *Suave* — confident, elegant and polite
2. *Carcinogenic* — any substance that produces cancer
3. *Impairment* — damage or make something weaker
4. *Cardiac* — relating to heart
5. *Emphysema* — enlargement of the air vessels of the lungs
6. *Constricts* — makes tighter, smaller and narrower
7. *Jolt* — disturb, push or shake from their original or normal position
8. *Susceptible* — easily harmed by something
9. *Psychotherapeutic* — working on the mind, using counselling for the purpose of curing a person

10. *Pharmaco therapy* — usage of medicines to cure tobacco addiction
11. *Exchequer* — treasury or revenue department

Points to Remember

1. Smoking affects both active and passive smokers.
2. In the present society, TV and movies have glamourised cigarette smoking.
3. Cancer, damage to nervous system, cardiac diseases, asthma, lung cancer, etc., can be caused by smoking.
4. India is in the midst of a catastrophic epidemic of deaths due to smoking.
5. India is the second largest consumer of tobacco in the world after China.
6. Smoking affects women more adversely than men.
7. Passive smoking causes many health and behavioural problems in children.
8. If one wants to quit smoking, it requires planning and strong intention.
9. Keeping the interests of both smokers and non-smokers in mind, there should be a ban on smoking in public places.
10. In the workplaces, there should be an arrangement for separate smoking zones for smokers.

BIDI SMOKING AND PUBLIC HEALTH

India is among the world's largest tobacco consuming societies. Tobacco usage in India is also contrary to world trends since chewing tobacco and the bidi are the dominant forms of tobacco consumption, whereas internationally the cigarette is the most prominent form of tobacco use. About 19% of tobacco consumption in India is in the form of cigarettes, while 53% is smoked as bidis, the rest is used mainly in smokeless form. Bidis tend to be smoked by lower economic classes and have a level of social acceptance in different cultures.

Available evidence indicates that tobacco consumption is the single most preventable cause of disease and death. It also imposes very high socio-economic costs on the society. Government of India has enacted "The Cigarettes and other Tobacco Products (Prohibition of Advertisement and Regulation of Trade and Commerce, Production Supply and Distribution) Act 2003", with a view of protecting public health by prohibiting smoking in public places, banning advertisement of tobacco products, banning sale of tobacco to minors and within 100 yards radius of educational institutions, prescribing pictorial health warnings etc.

There are a number of studies, reports and reviews on cigarette use and its harmful effects. Similar studies on other tobacco forms, including bidi are very few. The bidi monograph bridges a very important gap in the area of public health as it provides a comprehensive review on impact of bidi consumption. The compilation of scientific studies on bidis provides a plethora of information on the consumption patterns and associated usage risks. Since the problem of bidi usage is unique to South Asia, the monograph would be extremely useful for public health managers both in India and neighbouring countries, to promote effective initiatives for curbing bidi usage. The monograph has been prepared by the Healis-Sekhsaria Institute of Public Health, Navi Mumbai, in collaboration with the Centres for Disease Control and Prevention, Office on Smoking & Health, USA and with active support from Government of India and the World Health Organisation.

Source: Naresh Dayal (Health & FW Secretary, Government of India)

Essay 32

THE EFFECTS OF RAGGING

Synopsis

Ragging is the action of teasing, criticising or nagging a person. It is generally committed by the senior students in educational institutions. Ragging often takes place in hostels. There are a few senior students in every hostel who project of themselves as rowdies. They indulge in severe ragging and no one dares to confront them. Ragging originated in the west. The new students were subjected to simple teasing and mock interviews. Today, it has degenerated into torture of the innocent. The new students who resist and complain to authorities are tortured the most. Ragging has some positive effects, but it should be discouraged. Effective steps need to be taken to deal with this problem.

The exact meaning of the word 'ragging' is 'teasing' or 'playing rough jokes on'. The main *objective*[1] of ragging is to 'break the ice' between the senior students and the new entrants in an academic institution. By means of an interaction, they get to know one another which fosters brotherhood and bonhomie among them. But in practice, it is nothing short of torture and abuse of the newcomers in the educational institutions.

Ragging pertains to any disorderly conduct whether spoken or written or by an act which causes *annoyance*[2], hardship or psychological harm to a student. It is generally *wreaked*[3] by 'senior' students upon the first year students.

Ragging generally takes place in colleges and hostels. There are many tales of torture and humiliation that are associated with ragging. The new students know that they are in for a series of practical jokes at the hands of the senior students. Once they fall into the *clutches*[4] of the latter, they do not find a way to escape. There are a few senior students in every hostel who do not take interest in studies and indulge in ragging, bullying, etc. They project themselves as rowdies. No one dares to confront them.

Ragging originated in the western countries. Initially, it was confined to European Universities where the seniors would simply play practical jokes on the freshers. Soon this practice spread all over the world. Today, it has spread in the Indian society too. Young students enrolled in Indian universities are *plagued*[5] by ragging. At the start of every academic session, the media airs the news of suicides by new entrants, who could no longer bear the disgrace, *ignominy*[6] and dishonour *inflicted*[7] on them by their seniors. Ragging has caused intense fear among students, shattered their trust in humanity and marred their ability to make sound judgement about the people (seniors) around them.

Some people feel that ragging is a socio-cultural problem. The truth is that in some cases, ragging has occasionally ended in fighting, serious injuries, and even deaths, leading to the tragic end of some brilliant careers.

Senior students tease the new students about their looks and manners. The tall and the short, the fat and the lean, all become easy targets. Those wearing glasses, get their glasses snatched away and are made to read without them. Some are made to bow before the senior students and are forced to greet them with folded hands. Very often the eatables brought by the new students are eaten by the seniors in the former's presence.

Ragging is a sort of mock interview of the new entrants. The senior students take the position of interviewers, while the new students become the interviewees. Sometimes, they are asked indecent questions and forced to make obscene gestures or perform crude acts.

A new student who resists becomes a target of harassment. He may be falsely accused of stealing a thing or things from a senior and hence may be put on a mock-trial. During the trial, he might be forced to admit his guilt. If he does not admit his guilt, he is pressurised through physical threats and humiliation. After the trial, the accused could be asked to polish the shoes of senior students. He could be asked to wash their clothes even. If the new student complains to the warden or any other authority, he becomes a target of regular harassment. Ragging, at times, takes such an ugly turn that it may result in grievous physical impairment of the victim.

Ragging has some positive effects too on the new students. Those who endure it, get *emboldened*[8]. They become courageous. They get used to facing hardships in life. They learn to face unpleasant situations boldly. Many a time, it is seen that the juniors and the seniors become very good friends after the ragging period gets over. However, the positive effects of ragging are few and the negative effects far outweigh them.

In the beginning, 'ragging' was an *amusing*[9] practice. It is sad that it has *degenerated*[10] into a social evil. It has become a synonym for 'torture'. The problem is that ragging is not only a socio-legal concern but it has a psychological basis too. The perpetrators, themselves struggling against personality disorders, end up leaving psychological scars on their victims too.

Ragging in India commonly involves serious abuses and clear violation of human rights. The Supreme Court has taken a strong stand to curb ragging. Ragging has been declared a criminal offence. The Supreme Court of India has defined it as "any disorderly conduct whether by words spoken or written or by an act which adversely affects the physique or psyche of a fresher or a junior student is an act of ragging." If through ragging, the norms of decency and morals are violated, or one's body gets injured, or if any wrongful restraint or criminal intimidation is involved in it, then it becomes a legal offence.

India's first and only registered anti-ragging NGO, Society Against Violence in Education (SAVE) has claimed that ragging is widely and dangerously prevalent in engineering and other professional institutions, mainly in the hostels.

For such cases, there are certain punishments prescribed in UGC's anti-ragging guidelines which include a fine upto rupees twenty-five thousand, cancellation of admission, withholding of scholarship, *debarring*[11] from appearing at examinations, expulsion from hostel, and suspension or rustication from the institution for a period of one to four semesters. Even the institutions wherein ragging is prevalent could be punished by withdrawing of *affiliation*[12] and other privileges, debarring from awarding any degree, and withholding grants.

The real picture was revealed by a report of an NGO, CURE (Coalition of Uprooting Ragging from Education). Between July 2003 and June 2008, there were cases of 28 deaths, 10 attempted suicides, 14 students leaving colleges and a large number facing threats and humiliation. Only 54 per cent cases sought police intervention.

The most affected areas are West Bengal (with 30 cases), Uttar Pradesh (with 27 cases) and Andhra Pradesh (with 25 cases). The Raghavan Committee made a report on this social evil. The Supreme Court accepted its report and directed educational institutions at the very minimum to expel the guilty. It also allowed institutions to register police cases against the accused. The Court wanted that, "the punishment should be exemplary and justifiably harsh to stop the recurrence of ugly incidents." It deterred many but did not stop ragging altogether.

Most authorities have tackled the problem with an iron hand. However, more effective steps need to be taken to deal with this evil. Institutes should arrange counselling session for freshers so that they can speak their mind. Anti-ragging cells should also be established. A fresher party should be organised by the institute itself within two weeks of the start of the academic session so that the junior and senior students can easily mingle and interact with one another. Several institutions have employed these measures but a hundred percent prohibition is far from done. Presently, there are only four state legislations in India that prohibit ragging. These are:

1. The Prohibition of Ragging Act,l 1996. (Applicable in the state of Tamil Nadu)
2. The Kerala Prohibition of Ragging Act, 1998.
3. The Maharashtra Prohibition of Ragging 1999.
4. The Prohibition of Ragging in Education Institutes Act, 2000. (Applicable to the state of West Bengal).

In the other states and union territories in India, ragging is banned only through circulars and administrative orders.

Aid to Vocabulary

1. *Objective* — aim, purpose
2. *Annoyance* — harassment, irritation
3. *Wreaked* — gave play to any harmful act
4. *Clutches* — power of control
5. *Plagued* — be under constant worry or distress
6. *Ignominy* — public shame or disgrace
7. *Inflicted* — imposed
8. *Emboldened* — gained courage or confidence
9. *Amusing* — funny and enjoyable
10. *Degenerated* — lost moral qualities
11. *Debarring* — officially preventing or excluding
12. *Affiliation* — connection with a larger organisation

Points to Remember

1. Ragging scares many students in colleges and hostels.
2. Senior students who project themselves as rowdies, torture the new entrants.
3. Ragging originated in the western countries.
4. Ragging is not just a socio-legal problem but also has a psychological basis.
5. Ragging is a sort of mock-interview of the new students by the senior students.

6. The new entrants who resist and complain to the authorities become a target of regular harassment.
7. Ragging has some positive effects too. However, the positive effects are few and negative effects far outweigh them.
8. There are certain punishments prescribed for ragging in UGC's anti-ragging guidelines.
9. The Supreme Court accepted the Raghavan Committee report and directed the institutions to take necessary steps to root out this evil.
10. Effective steps need to be taken to deal with this problem.
11. In India, there are several legislations concerning ragging.

SAY NO TO RAGGING	
What is Ragging? Any Act Resulting in : • Mental/physical sexual abuse • Verbal abuse • Indecent behaviour • Criminal intimidation/wrongful restraint • Undermining human dignity • Financial exploitation/extortion • Use of force *Each of the above is a criminal offence*	**A Student Indulging in Ragging can be :** • Expelled from the institution • Banned from the mess/hostel • Denied scholarship • Debarred from examinations • Denied admission to any institution • Prosecuted for criminal action • Prosecuted by police on the basis of FIR filed by the Institution.

WHAT COLLEGES & OTHER INSTITUTIONS MUST ENSURE

- Include in their Prospectus guidelines to prevent ragging and factual information on ragging, if any.
- Obtain undertaking from each student not to indulge in or abet ragging.
- Form Anti-Ragging Committees.
- Form Anti-Ragging Squads.
- Conduct orientation programmes for freshers.
- Enquire into each incident of ragging.
- Take strict disciplinary action against students indulging in ragging.
- File F.I.R. with local police where victims are dissatisfied with action taken.
- Ensure access to mobile phones and public phones in hostels to enable timely communication.
- Publicise telephone numbers of all important functionaries (Heads of Institutions, Faculty Members, Hostel Wardens and District Authorities).
- Encourage complaints or information (oral or written), and protect confidentiality of the source.
- Constitute Monitoring Cells.

Essay
33 GENERATION GAP

SYNOPSIS

The communication gap between the successive generations can be traced back in the world history. The new generation accused Queen Elizabeth II of being remorseless on the death of Princess Diana. The growing consumerism has caused the drifting away of the parents from their children. The youth are a dejected lot and such a state of mind makes them rebel against parental authority. Parents fail to treat them as individuals and interfere with their life. Children have their own identities which parents ought to respect. They must encourage and support their children. Egotism and persistence should be shed for the sake of the family unity. Children should also reciprocate with love and affection. They should uphold the moral values of the society. Discord among the members of the family should be resolved through talks.

Generation gap refers to the distancing of people of successive generations with respect to communication, behaviour, thinking, etc. It pertains to a rift in the relationship between children and parents, the young and the old. It is a conflict between two ideologies. When a young person and an old person cannot understand each other's viewpoint, it is said to be the case of generation gap. This gap is widening at an alarming rate and destroying the social fabric all over the world. Our country is also getting *entangled*[1] in similar problems between parents and children of a family. This has resulted in the *mushrooming*[2] of several old-age centres in India, which take senior citizens, *bereft*[3] of their childrens' love, into their fold. Children, on the other hand, unable to communicate with or air their views before their parents, take advice from their friends, who are as inexperienced as they themselves are.

The *decadence*[4] of the joint family system has given rise to the nuclear family system. Grandparents, who occupied the apex in the hierarchy of the traditional family system, find themselves neglected. Their children, no longer look up to them for advice and their grandchildren do not respect them.

High standards of living and increasing *consumerism*[5] have forced parents to venture out in search of new avenues to provide for the family. This has led to the distancing of parents from their children. Children are provided with material comforts which are mistakenly believed to substitute for parental love and affection. In the hour of need, children are unable to find their parents beside them. Parents feel that providing their children with all the luxuries of life would help them gain respect and affection from them. The two generations,in a *futile*[6] attempt to hold on to the family tradition, have started *drifting*[7] away from each other.

The youth, all through the ages, have remained *vivacious*[8], bubbling with life and zest. They wish to gain name, fame and *affluence*[9] in a short span of time. But the harsh realities of life lead them to frustration. Right from infancy, children are put through the *rigours*[10] of life, when they are required to undergo tests for admission to nursery classes. As they grow up, they are expected to outdo their classmates both in the academic and the co-curricular fields. Pressurised into pursuing a career of the choice of their parents, they soon feel dejected. This dejection often makes them rebel against parental authority.

Parents, perhaps justifiably on their part, feel that in this fast changing, self-centred and hypocritical world, it is their duty to safeguard their children from going astray. So right from childhood, children are instructed to do only the good things in life. Everything is explained to a child in terms of its being either good or bad. Roaming around with friends till the early hours of the morning and dancing the night away at a discotheque are considered to be 'against our culture'. Parents tend to believe that being young, their children always need to be guided. This creates a rift in the family as the youngsters feel that they are not treated as grown up individuals but as immature children, liable to go astray at every step.

The media plays an important role in creating, as well as in bridging, the rift between the two generations. Movies of the sixties and the seventies portrayed the mother as kind, yielding and *naive*[11], while the father was ruthless, unloving and orthodox. Parents were unwilling to accept change or the fact that their children had their individualities. The parents usually clung to age-old traditions while the children never questioned their authority. The children grew up in *awe*[12] of their parents and never raised any objections against them. The parents of the eighties, though modern, could not wholly give up the cultural tradition handed down by their parents. The older generation was reluctant to change their ways and wanted their children to maintain respectability in society. The younger generation was portrayed as rebellious. However, the movies of the recent times show parents having evolved from their shell and having woken up to the needs of the children. At the same time, there are some serials on television which portray and, in a way, perpetuate generation gap and the inability of the generations to reach an understanding.

Parents need to understand the fact that their children are individuals with their own identities and that no two people are alike. People have to change, adapt and adjust, with the changing times. It is wrong on the part of parents to cling on to orthodox beliefs and impose them on their children. Some parents have the tendency to push their children into those fields which remained untraversed, though coveted, by them. Such impositions could land them in a course or a career not suitable to their temperament or interest, which may lead them into frustration and turn them into rebels. Parents have the moral obligation of protecting their children from becoming *wayward*[13].

According to an Arabic saying, 'when the shoes of the father fit the feet of his son, the former should treat the latter as his friend.' Parents should befriend their children and provide them with love, support, security and encouragement. Parents ought to keep in mind the fact that children of the new generation have to be respected in order to get respect from them. To avoid conflicts, issues like keeping the room tidy, going out to late night parties and watching television, should be settled out with the children during their childhood. They should be taught about the need for cleanliness and discipline right from childhood rather than in their youth. In this way, they would grow up as responsible youngsters.

Children, on their part, should always listen to their parents and if they find something objectionable, should talk it over with their parents. Parents never want to hinder their children's progress. It is important for the youngsters to uphold the moral values of their families. The young generation should *empathise*[14] with their parents because sooner or later they would also enter into parenthood. Talking things out is the best way to resolve the differences within a family. Although the influence of the western culture is creating a lot of problems related to generation gap, its effect is still limited in our country due to the influence of our social and family traditions.

Generation gap is a negative phenomenon. The society can gain a lot if generation gap is bridged. Older people should understand that the youth are more emotional and enthusiastic, and hence they need to be motivated instead of being criticised. On the other hand, the younger generation should show more willingness to accept the advice of the older people which is for their own good. The two generations should understand each other and collaborate rather than contest. As it is evident from the discussion above that generation gap symbolises a *conflict*[15] between two generations, it becomes *imperative*[16] that certain corrective measures are taken to overcome this *malaise*[17]. That the two generations concerned can't ever stay in peace is a *myth*[18] which has to be busted. It should be maintained that they are not competitors; rather, they are complementary to each other. To foster a harmonious relationship *egotism*[19] will have to be shed first and then one should open heartedly listen to another in order to reach an amicable and desired solution. Resolution of conflict and installation of peace are bound to add to their happiness and hence improve the quality of life.

Family is the basic unit of a society. Parents should respect their children as individuals and children should also *reciprocate*[20] with respect and affection. It is the obligation of the new generation to uphold the sanctity of the institution of family and refrain from indulging in immoral activities. Familial discord should be resolved amicably, within the confines of the home rather than be taken to the court of law. In this way, parents would be able to win the love and trust of their children and the children would also be able to look up to them. None would be burdened with the guilt of not supporting the other in the hour of need. In this way, the generation gap would certainly be narrowed, if not bridged.

Aid to Vocabulary

1. *Entangled* — twisted or mixed
2. *Mushrooming* — developing quickly
3. *Bereft* — deprived of, without
4. *Decadence* — decline
5. *Consumerism* — the state of the society being driven by needs and wants of materialistic things
6. *Futile* — worthless
7. *Drifting* — being carried away
8. *Vivacious* — lively
9. *Affluence* — wealth
10. *Rigours* — severity or strictness
11. *Naive* — simple
12. *Awe* — fear mingled with respect
13. *Wayward* — turning away from what is proper
14. *Empathise* — understanding another person's feelings
15. *Conflict* — rift
16. *Imperative* — necessary, obligatory
17. *Malaise* — condition that harms a group, society, etc.

18. *Myth* — impossible, hard to believe
19. *Egotism* — conceit, belief in the superiority of self
20. *Reciprocate* — to give something in return

Points to Remember

1. The generation gap between successive generations can be traced from the past to the present age.
2. In a nuclear family, children are provided with material comforts, but they are unable to find their parents beside them in the hour of need.
3. Today, the young people wish to gain name, fame and money in a short span of time.
4. Parents feel that being young their children always need to be guided.
5. At times, the media plays an important role in creating and perpetuating generation gap.
6. Parents should befriend their children and youngsters must uphold the moral values of their family.
7. Familial discord should be resolved within the confines of the home.

Essay 34

TRADITION AND MODERNITY

SYNOPSIS

Every age witnesses a tussle between tradition and modernity. The new generation regards tradition as obsolete and regressive while the older generation views modernity as something that corrupts the new generation. The present generation does not share time with the older generation. In the course of time, slow but steady changes take place. The traditional relationship shared between the parents and the children is changing. Primitive man held Nature in awe but in the modern day, industrialisation has come to cause environmental pollution. Generally, relationships are based on selfish grounds. Earlier, the spirit of enquiry used to be suppressed and also condemned as being rebellious. People have become more health conscious. Tradition should be guided by reason. It has, however, been realised that neither tradition nor modernity can survive in isolation. Hence, it would be unwise of the warring generations to disregard either.

Every age witnesses a tussle between tradition and modernity. The successive generation of every age has denounced tradition as *obsolete*[1] and *regressive*[2]. Therefore, tradition has come to be considered unnecessary to the needs and the *ethos*[3] of the modern times. On the other hand, the older generation of every age criticises as well as condemns modernity. From the traditional to the modern, society undergoes a radical change. The social change affects the individual's personal as well as social life. Change in every respect, be it social values, institutions, individual relations or economic pursuits, can well be seen in the modern society.

Life is like a stream that runs its course through various *terrain*[4] or different situations that keep changing in a *span*[5] . Human relationships too undergo considerable changes. When a child is born into a family, it is bonded with several relations. As it grows up, the existing bonds are *fostered*[6] into new ones. A young sapling given enough sunlight, nutrition and water grows into a healthy tree. Similarly, sacred beliefs and attitudes, are *nurtured*[7], modified or adapted to suit the modern times. Science and technology also keep registering radical changes. Thus, we can say that with the passage of time, the texture of life undergoes a total transformation.

Children of the previous generation in their leisure hours sat with their parents and grandparents sharing their views and experience; and learning thereby etiquettes and manners. With the rapid growth of science and technology, TV, Internet and mobile phones have begun to consume most of their time preventing them from *imbibing*[8] moral values. The new generation prefers to play games on mobile phones or to chat on social sites like whatsapp, Skype, twitter etc. Spending quality time with parents or grandparents thus has become an unnecessary and unwanted part of their life.

The traditionalists find modernity unacceptable and harmful to the new generation. They disapprove of the undesirable changes that happen to crop up in human relationships. The traditional joint family system has given way to the nuclear family system. In the joint family, the older generation was looked after well and the younger generation was also cared for. The family led a harmonious life. In the nuclear family system, where the majority has both the parents working, children grow up bereft of parental love. Creches and childcare homes do not provide for a *conducive*[9] environment with regard to healthy development of the children. The children in such situations may get adversely affected and they may grow up to become complex adolescents with psychological problems.

The traditional relationship shared between parents and children was one of awe, reverence and blind faith. The older generation occupied an exalted position in the hierarchy of the traditional joint family system. The younger generation obeyed the elders and never questioned them. In the nuclear family system, the parents tend to be overbearing as they are anxious to safeguard their children in the fast-changing, self-centred and *hypocritical*[10] world. This creates a rift in the family; and the two generations, in a futile attempt to hold on to the family tradition, start drifting away from each other.

Primitive man held nature in awe because he was unable to understand its mysteries. His earliest inventions and discoveries, the wheel and fire, laid the foundation of science and technology. However, with industrialisation, science and technology made such rapid strides as to wreak havoc on human life. Harmful *effluents*[11] emitted by the industries of the modern age have polluted the land, water and air. Drinking water has become the source of recurring epidemics. Atmospheric pollution is responsible for several respiratory diseases. Noise pollution is creating severe nervous problems for people. It is making them more irritable and less tolerant. Adulteration of food and usage of dyes and preservatives in foodstuffs are known to cause diseases like dropsy and cancer. Primitive man respected nature and never tampered with it. But the modern man being driven by *unbridled*[12] industrialisation, has created an ecological imbalance in the environment.

The belief in the theory of *Vasudhaiva Kutumbhakam* (the universe is one family) or universal brotherhood has given way to the modern theory of materialism and consumerism that only propagates *avarice*[13]. Human relationships are based on selfish grounds. They are cultivated and developed with the sole purpose of taking advantage of the other. People are becoming increasingly egoistic and self-centred. Few are ready to help the needy on simple, humane or *compassionate*[14] grounds. Man, in order to show his superiority, exploits the weak. Financial considerations have become a guiding factor in all human relationships. Moral values have died a painful death. The means do not matter anymore for the modern consumerist, only the end matters. Man is ready to stoop to the meanest level to make monetary gains.

In the olden times, the spirit of enquiry used to be suppressed and also condemned as being rebellious. Anything new was considered suspicious and viewed as a threat to tradition. The modern world thrives on the quest of knowledge—inventions, discoveries, research and innovation. Change is the order of the day. Hence, change in human relations is also inevitable. The older generation should understand the fact that their children, who are born into the modern world, are individuals with their own identities. They have to keep pace with the changing times. Parents should not cling on to orthodox beliefs or impose them on their children. Instead, they should befriend their children and provide them with unconditional love, support, security and encouragement. Besides, they should try their best to mould themselves to the modern day requirements.

The quest for knowledge has taken man far. Science has enabled man to cure ailments and eradicate dreaded diseases, to predict the weather and take safety precautions ailments and, to increase food production and feed the teeming millions. If science and technology has led to pollution, the former has also made possible inventions and discoveries that can control as well as curb the latter.

Since life has become more stressful and people suffer from lifestyle diseases, they have become more conscious about their health.

Indifference and apathy towards food have become things of the past. Intake of green vegetables and fruits has grown manifold even as the consumption of fast foods is on a rising *trajectory*[15]. Such a lifestyle burns a hole in one's pocket and compels one to keep others – even one's own parents – at bay.

It has, however, been realised that neither tradition nor modernity can survive on their own. Comparative studies on modernisation in the new states have shown that contrary to stereotyped beliefs, old traditions are not completely displaced by modernisation. In India, caste associations, which are otherwise typical symbols of tradition, have increasingly been found to serve the ends of political modernisation.

Thus, tradition and modernity as *heuristic*[16] concepts are easy to formulate but to separate them at substantive level is rather difficult. Individually, neither of them is adequate to meet the needs of the society. At any given period of history, it has been the balanced combination of the two which has truly served the society.

The positive aspect about all this is that people today are seeking the best of both worlds—the traditional as well as the modern. In fact many of today's youth are seeking the age old traditional methods of yoga, ayurveda, etc., to relieve stress and strain. Urban India is reporting a number of intercaste marriages. So, casteism is being roundly rejected by the educated youth.

Modern values are being inculcated in the youth through the medium of cinema, television and especially the internet. The Internet has taken over the world in a big way. The most interesting synthesis of the traditional and the modern can be found in the virtual world of the Internet. Virtual *poojas* can be performed, religious places can be visited, prayers and devotional music can be listened to, ancient texts can be read; all at the click of a mouse. Simultaneously, the latest songs, movies, videos, or even books are all at your beck and call. Social media like *Twitter* and *Facebook* have made forays into private lives of individuals. Professional networks like *Linkedin* make it easy for people to acquire jobs and make career moves. People of all ages be they traditional or modern are benefited. It is left to us to surf through this magical jungle and locate what we want.

Tradition is the foundation of progress. The world has witnessed how literature and scientific progress of the early civilisations have served as the stepping stone for advancement in modern times. Thus, it could be said that tradition and modernity go hand in hand; which means, with the changing times, new sense and sensibilities get incorporated in culture and tradition. Modernity and tradition are inter-dependent as it is only on the foundation of the latter that the former has found its form.

AID TO VOCABULARY

1. *Obsolete* — no more of use
2. *Regressive* — moving backwards to less developed state
3. *Ethos* — guiding beliefs
4. *Terrain* — area with particular physical feature
5. *Span* — period of time
6. *Fostered* — developed
7. *Nurtured* — developed
8. *Imbibing* — absorbing or learning
9. *Conducive* — having the quality of promoting
10. *Hypocritical* — insincere, pretentious
11. *Effluents* — industrial discharge
12. *Unbridled* — uncontrolled
13. *Avarice* — greed for wealth
14. *Compassionate* — merciful
15. *Trajectory* — path (of a moving object) under the given forces
16. *Heuristic* — serving to discover by trial and error

POINTS TO REMEMBER

1. Every age witnesses a tussle between tradition and modernity.
2. The traditionalists find modernity unacceptable and the new generation finds tradition obsolete.
3. The older and the younger generations are drifting away from each other.
4. Rapid industrialisation has polluted the environment and created an ecological imbalance.
5. Relationships between men are based on selfish grounds and people are becoming extremely egoistic and self-centred.
6. Tradition should be guided by reason.
7. It has been realised that neither tradition nor modernity can survive in isolation.
8. Today people are making the best of both worlds—the traditional as well as the modern.
9. Modern youth are seeking yoga, ayurveda and other traditional methods to relieve stress and strain.
10. The virtual world of the Internet has a unique combination of both the traditional and the modern.

CULTURAL PRECONDITIONS FOR DEVELOPMENT

Tradition and Modernity Reconsidered in the Light of Post-modernism

—Dawa Norbu

Successful industrialisation and modernisation have taken place in societies which have had traditionally high literate cultures. At any rate such traditions propagated and promoted high literate cultures which have made the tasks of modernisation much easier.

The natural history of industrial development suggests certain pre-conditions for primary development such as cultural adaptability, political stability, organisational discipline, work culture etc., and certain other prerequisites for modernisation such as literacy, rationality, entrepreneurship, innovation and so on.

While the non-dogmatic and open-ended character of a tradition does ease the problems of modernisation, especially in the initial stages, the same tradition must be able to maintain social order. Political stability is one of the basic conditions for sustained development. Such a stability stems from shared value system emanating usually from religion in most traditional societies.

Since modernisation is essentially a vocational civilisation, it presupposes discipline and work culture. Freedom may be one of the blessings of a modern society; yet paradoxically discipline is required in any modern setting, school, college, university, office, factory, mines and plantations all of which operate on the basis of routinisation and regulation.

Essay 35

THE INSTITUTION OF MARRIAGE

SYNOPSIS

Marriage is an institution which admits men and women to family life. In India, marriage is considered very sacred. It is said that marriages are made in heaven and celebrated on earth. While the concept of marriage remains the same across the globe, the way of solemnising it differs extensively. Marriage among the Hindus has a religious sanctity. Marriage among the Muslims is more of a social contract rather than being a religious scenario. The Christians clearly recognise the need and necessity of marriage. The key to a successful marriage is love, understanding, mutual respect, trust, commitment and togetherness. Problems are bound to surface in a marriage since two individuals having different personalities arrive at a decision to begin a new conjugal life. Many people argue that love marriages offer more independence and freedom as compared to arranged marriages. It is highly debatable. People have started condemning the institution of marriage. Live-in relationship is a choice in place of marriage in modern society. But this practice is considered sacrilegious to our culture by a large section of the society. Let us hope that future generations would respect the sanctity of marriage.

Marriage is an institution which admits men and women to family life. It is believed to be a stable relationship in which a man and a woman are socially permitted to have children implying the right to sexual relations. In India, marriage is considered very *sacred*[1]. It is said that marriages are made in heaven and celebrated on earth. Marriage is a special bond shared between two souls, who tie the wedding knot pledging to remain companions for a lifetime. It is a physical, mental and spiritual union of two souls. It also plays a crucial role in transmitting the culture and civilisation from one generation to the other, through the legitimate procreation process. The institution of marriage is beneficial to the society as a whole, because it is the foundation of the family, which in turn is the fundamental building block of the society.

While the concept of marriage remains the same across the globe, the way of solemnising it differs extensively. Different laws and terms of agreement have been formulated in different parts of the world to legalise the ceremony; even the rituals performed during the ceremony are different in various parts of the globe. In India, marriages are celebrated like religious festivals. A number of rituals and customs are performed before and after the wedding. Every religion has different customs for marriage.

Marriage, apart from being a legalised union of two people, has a huge social significance. This is primarily because, in India, marriage is and has always been the union of the families of two individuals.

Marriage among Hindus has a religious *sanctity*[2]. Once a marriage is solemnised, it is difficult to break matrimonial bonds. Marriage and children are considered essential for the repayment of parental debt by way of continuation of race, which is the religious duty of every Hindu. Marriage among the Muslims is both a social as well as a religious contract, which is legalised after *Nikah*. But it is considered more of a social institution than a religious institution. The Christians clearly recognise the need and necessity of marriage. Christian marriages take place for having good family life and for maintaining family relations and ties as well as for enjoying the benefits of mutual cooperation which family life is bound to bring with it.

Life, according to the Vedas, is divided into 4 parts; namely *Brahmacharya*[3], *Grahasthya*[4], *Vanprastha*[5] and *Sanyasa*[6]. Since, marriage is a union of two different souls in order to continue the race, it is extremely sacred but to the *dismay*[7] and disappointment of many, this despite several attempts to *preserve*[8] its sanctity, has almost lost its worth. Marriage today has become a *ploy*[9] to satisfy one's greed and make a fortune through dowry. As per the constitution of India, the Hindus are restricted to *monogamy*[10] whereas their Muslim counterparts can lawfully adopt *polygamy*[11] if they so desire.

Earlier it was said that marriage is a bond which takes place, between two families and not between two individuals. But in modern society, this concept is fading fast. In modern western society, marriage is the concern of the would-be-spouses. It is of no concern to the kinship group. The married couples, immediately after marriage, or a little later, establish their new household. But in India, the situation is quite different. Here, after the wedding, the bride comes to her in-laws' house and has to accept or adopt the new house as her own 'real' home. In metropolitan cities, the scene is changing as both men and women are working professionals. usually, the modern couples after their marriage, prefer to live separately—away from their parents so as to be free from any interference.

The key to a successful marriage is love, understanding, mutual respect, trust, commitment and togetherness. While many couples are able to explore and discover all the key ingredients in their marital relationships, others find one element or more lacking in their bond. This is the reason why a number of couples face adverse consequences, like divorce. Lack of trust, disrespect, hate and jealousy, misunderstanding contribute to the deterioration of the bond.

Life is not a bed of roses and things often do not work as smoothly as we want them to. Marriage is no exception. Problems in marriage are bound to arise because two individuals invariably having two different personalities, choices and opinions come together for life. To avert clashes, people often change their ways, make compromises, or negotiate on the issues but they do arise, at times, situations when they cannot help but, just stand stubbornly and let things fall apart. Because of immature attitude and serious lack of tolerance and patience, many people fail to keep the spark of married life alive and their relationship gradually decays.

There are a number of problems a couple might face, right from *conjugal*[12] problems to those pertaining to in-laws and even financial troubles. Some couples face communication gap. They do not talk to each other and fail to make their view points clear which leads to misunderstanding and clashes. Conflict with in-laws is also a major problem a couple may face. Many face problems related to money and they quarrel blaming each other for the lack of financial stability. Marital problems tend to rise after the initial phase of marriage, often due to family *obligations*[13] especially raising children, caring for elderly parents and the like.

Many people argue that love marriages offer more independence and freedom as compared to arranged marriages. Knowing one's spouse before marriage allows partners to have better respect and understanding for each other's needs and desires. This way, they are better adjusted in the marriage when they finally take their wedding vows. But not all love marriages have a happy ending. There is a world of difference between meeting or courting someone and living with that person. In a love marriage, two persons meet and get to know each other, but not each and every trait of their personalities comes to the fore until after they start living together i.e., post marriage. After marriage, all their objectionable personality traits come to the forefront, and what *ensues*[14] is a clash of personality.

Marriage, as an institution, is now coming under heavy *strain*[15]. In many cases, people do not think of marrying due to personal as well as other reasons. A decade ago, urban India was a different landscape altogether. People married for various reasons—for love, to unite two families, for social security, for convenience, for children or purely for physical pleasure. But in 21st century India, 'urban singles' seem to have attained all of these. They have social security in the form of well-paid jobs, hectic social lives and plenty of friends. These 'singles' do not believe in the institution of marriage. They believe that one can get a pet dog or cat if one wants companionship. Friends can provide companionship. One can go for a *live-in relationship*[16] for companionship. People who believe in live-in relationships argue that in this relationship, one can get to know each and everything about one's partner. If the two persons are convinced that they are *compatible*[17] with each other, they can enter into a serious relationship or marriage and if they are not, they can part ways. These people cite reports on the rate of divorce getting higher to assert that. Live-in relationship avoid divorce as in such a relationship, people are not bound to live together all their lives.

The Supreme Court's observations on pre-marital sex and live-in relationships are progressive and egalitarian, and reflect the winds of change in the corridors of the higher judiciary. The apex court gave a new interpretation to live-in-relationship when it said that living together is part of the individual's right to life, guaranteed under Article 21 of the Constitution. There is nothing wrong—legally or otherwise—if two adults want to live together. The apex court has even declared that children born out of such a relationship are legitimate. However, the main drawback with regard to such relationships pertains to women and children lacking the security which a marriage would have otherwise guaranteed.

All the alternatives discovered so far in lieu of traditional marriage, be it live-in relationship, love-marriage, or life of a bachelor/spinster, lack durability, sanctity and social consensus. They scarcely *cater to*[18] every human need. Hence, despite its negative by products like domestic violence, dowry system, child marriage, bride-burning, marital rape etc., traditional marriage is the best option. Its negative fallouts, with some grains of wisdom can well be *eradicated*[19].

Live-in relationship at best is *sacrilegious*[20] to Indian culture. Marriage gives stability and security, particularly to women and children, which a live-in relationship cannot. Critics dubbing live-in relationship as a threat to social norms and cultural ethos are perhaps, guided by the fact that India is widely known as a country with strong moral values and traditional integrity. A live-in relationship may look attractive to some but it usually lacks the accountability, marriages ensure. There is no doubt that there are misunderstandings, disputes, disagreements, etc., in married life but these are of a nature that can be talked on and worked out between two mature individuals. Not everyone can live all their life alone. At the end of the day, everyone needs someone for company. Everybody feels good to love and be loved. Marriage holds two people together for life.

The institution of marriage is changing with our changing social values. New values replace the old ones. Let us hope that the future generations will respect the sanctity of the institution of marriage and not be *lured*[21] by western culture.

Aid to Vocabulary

1. *Sacred* — connected with God, considered to be holy
2. *Sanctity* — the state of being holy
3. *Brahmacharya* — bachelorhood
4. *Grahasthya* — active married and family life
5. *Vanaprastha* — handing over to the next generation all household responsibilities
6. *Sanyasa* — renunciation of worldly life
7. *Dismay* — despair
8. *Preserve* — to keep (something) from harm or loss
9. *Ploy* — a clever trick
10. *Monogamy* — the state or practice of being married to only one person at a time
11. *Polygamy* — the state or practice of being married to more than one person at the same time
12. *Conjugal* — relationship between a married couple
13. *Obligations* — moral duties
14. *Ensues* — follows as a result
15. *Strain* — pressure on someone because of too much to do or manage
16. *Live-in relationship* — a relationship wherein a couple lives in a shared household without having got married
17. *Compatible* — able to exist together, tolerant
18. *Cater to* — serve
19. *Eradicated* — rooted out, eliminated
20. *Sacrilegious* — violating sacredness
21. *Lured* — attracted, fell for

Points to Remember

1. Marriage is an institution which admits men and women to family life.
2. It is believed that marriage is a special bond shared between two souls.
3. While the concept of marriage remains the same across the globe, the way of solemnising it differs extensively.
4. In India, apart from being a legalised way of uniting two people, it has a huge social significance.
5. Marriage among Hindus has a religious sanctity while among Muslims it is a social institution rather than being a religious institution.
6. The key to a successful marriage is love, understanding, mutual respect, trust, commitment and togetherness.
7. Problems in marriage are bound to surface since two individuals of different personalities meet.
8. Marriage, as an institution, is now coming under heavy strain.
9. Live-in-relationship is now legalised.
10. No other relationship can give assurance and security as marriage does.
11. Let us hope that the future generations will respect the sanctity of the institution of marriage.

The Supreme Court has set certain guidelines for determining the nature of a live-in relationship for the protection of women under the Domestic Violence (DV), Act. Duration of the relationship, shared household, pooling resources, sexual relationship, having children, socialising in public are some of the factors to be taken into consideration.

The duration of relationship was defined by section 2(F) of the DV Act as a "reasonable period of time to maintain and continue a relationship, which may vary from case to case depending upon the situation."

The verdict was delivered by Justices K.S. Radhakrishnan and Pinaki Chandra Ghose in a case where a woman applied for maintenance after the end of a live-in relationship with a man.

Essay 36

THE JOINT FAMILY SYSTEM

SYNOPSIS

The ancient system of joint family has given way to the nuclear family system. Lack of residential space, escalating prices, high cost of living, incompatibility of the members and a host of other factors have contributed to the disintegration of the joint family system. The senior citizens of the society enjoyed great respect in the joint families. At present, they are known to spend their old age bereft of the love of their children. The children too had a good time; and were well cared for, in the midst of their kith and kin. But in the nuclear families, where both the parents pursue their careers, the children feel rudderless. In a joint family, the grandparents catered to the emotional and spiritual needs of the children. There is a need for both, the older and the newer generations, to understand each other. The growing unrest among the youth can be dealt with by the guidance of the elders. We must understand the needs of our elders and take care of them. Financial constraints and interference of the elderly in family matters mostly are responsible for the creation of the gulf between the young and the old. Seeing the positive and negative aspects of both the family systems, the new generation is to make its choice.

In India, the joint family system has been prevalent since ancient times. In the *patriarchal*[1] family, a male member was the head of the family. His wife, sons, daughters-in-law and grandchildren constituted a joint family. The house would be on a *sprawling*[2] *landscape*[3] and could accommodate all. The head of the family would feel proud of his *teeming progeny*[4]. The day, the photographer was called to take the snaps of the whole family, was one of the proudest moments of his life. However, with time, the joint family system disintegrated, giving rise to the nuclear family system.

The nuclear family consists of a man, his wife and their children. This change has come because of the migration of people to the cities in search of jobs. The Industrial Revolution brought with it a phenomenal increase in job opportunities in and around major industrialised cities and towns. This forced men and women to move out of their family home and away from parents. Parents accepted, though with a great degree of sadness, that their children have to move away for the sake of their career and start a new life away from them. The emergence of the nuclear family was viewed as a dilution in relations between the parents and the adult children. But as the nuclear family became the order of the day, parents or older generations had to accept the reality.

In the cities, because of lack of living space, it becomes necessary to keep the family small. People find it difficult to accommodate their own parents in their homes. *Escalating*[5] prices and the high cost of living in the cities are also the reasons for the disintegration of the joint family. The newly-wed bride in a family is said to cause *discord*[6] in a joint family. It is generally believed that mother-in-law and daughter-in-law do not get along well in any household. The mother-in-law may put certain restrictions on the newly-wed bride, which might displease the latter. This could make the son and the daughter-in-law walk out of the house. By setting up another home, the daughter-in-law could have privacy in her own life and lead her life as she may like.

The media too is responsible for the disintegration of the joint family. It often portrays the mother-in-law as a threat to the well-being of the young bride. In some movies, she is shown to *instigate*[7] her son against the young bride. She nurses a grudge against her daughter-in-law for not bringing enough dowry and constantly harasses her. On television too, many of the serials and advertisements portray the elders as having a *tyrannical*[8] hold on their family, thus, curbing the growth and development of the family. Newspapers also report about the gruesome acts committed in some families. The onslaught of the foreign media has made the younger generation aware of the western liberal views. The young crave for independence, privacy and non-interference from elders. The dual influence of the domestic and the foreign media has made the young girls develop a 'phobia' for mothers-in-law. They, therefore, find it difficult to adjust with the senior lady of the household.

In earlier times, the older members of the family enjoyed great respect. The younger generation went up to them for advice. The older generation whiled away their time in the company of their counterparts or amused themselves with the pranks of their grandchildren. In the wake of urbanisation, lack of accommodation in the cities and economic crunch, the social status of the older generation has suffered. The communication gap between the older and the newer generations has widened a great deal. At a seminar, organised by the Institute of Human Behaviour and Allied Sciences in New Delhi, it was pointed out that over 40 per cent of the elderly in the capital had no caretakers. The statistics could be considered as a reflection on the state of society across India. The capital has witnessed the rising crime graph of murders of senior citizens. A number of old-age homes in India have come up in the last few years. Senior citizens are known to spend their old age *bereft*[9] of the love of their children. The most severely isolated and lonely are the people over seventy-five years of age, particularly women who are widowed and living alone. One out of eight senior citizens said that no one cared whether they were alive or not. A study undertaken by the NGO 'Help Age India' painted a grim picture of the lives of senior citizens. Children want their parents' property but they do not want to take the responsibility of looking after their ageing parents.

Everything changed with the passage of time yet, in the joint family system, not only the younger generation stayed in control but also the other members were kept in check—a watchful eye always restrained them from going astray. This must not sound as if the children were in chains. They, on the contrary, enjoyed the most in the company of their cousins and other relatives. There was somebody always there to look after them and cater to their needs. Now-a-days, due to dearth of time, the office-going parents can't afford to be with their little children when they come back from school; the maid servants do take good care of them but there is no touch of love or affection that children crave for. This leads them to feel neglected and in order to fill the *void*[10] in their life they tend to go astray. In case of emergency these older folk used to come to their rescue.

It may be argued that in the nuclear family, the mother is able to look after the needs of her children well. She is able to take care of their personal needs in a much better way than she could in a joint family. The family earns, spends and saves money for itself. Parents plan for the welfare of their children by investing money for their future. They keep money aside for their own requirements. As the parents are close to their children, in the absence of other kin, they are, able to understand each other better. The parents are able to put them in a better school and invest in their careers. In the joint family system, children do not get individual attention. The womenfolk are always busy with the household chores, so they never find time to attend to their children. The children are not educated much, as the trend is to join the family occupation. There are many restrictions on the womenfolk who are not allowed to venture out of doors. The joint family system is seen by many as one of chaos and disharmony because of the size of the family.

However the fact is that in cities, due to financial crunch, both the parents pursue a career of their own. This leaves the children *rudderless*[11]. They have no one to seek advice from or to discuss their grievances with. In the joint family system, they could approach their uncles and aunts or even their grandparents for advice. Today, we see infants being enrolled in creches. During their formative years, children are bereft of the company of their family. Overcrowded, poorly ventilated buildings and apathetic staff of the creches are known to have a negative influence on the well-being of the children. They grow up alienated from their own family. This is where the joint family system scores over the nuclear family system. The grandparents take care of the children well, catering to their emotional and physical needs. The time spent by the children with their grandparents is beneficial for their emotional and social development. It helps to develop a sense of responsibility towards their kin. It can become a training ground for the next generations to learn and develop attributes and skills of living in harmony with other citizens in society. If our family life is based on tolerance, love and warmth, it will be reflected positively in society at large.

The elders in the family should not cling to the age-old traditions, where the children never questioned their authority and grew up in awe of them. With education and growing awareness, children today are getting influenced by the western liberal views and they have begun to question the traditions handed down to them. Parents should understand that the children of the modern era *prize*[12] their individuality and hence they should be given a free hand to assert their identities. They should be advised only when necessary otherwise they regard it as interference. The children, on their part, should be able to convince their parents very politely about their perhaps unusual approach to life. They should pay heed to the advice of their parents who are elderly and experienced. Being parents, they would always have concern for the betterment of their children. Parents should talk it over with their children, if they find anything objectionable. The young generation should *empathise*[13] with their parents because sooner or later, they would themselves approach parenthood.

A growing unrest has been witnessed in the society. It is because the youth are being misled. With growing consumerism, the youth crave for name, fame and *affluence*[14]. In the nuclear family with working parents, the youth appear neglected and receive no guidance from their parents, which makes them turn to friends for advice. Many a time, friends are known to misguide the youth. In the joint family system, the grandparents are there to guide the young ones. Being old and experienced, they are able to provide solutions to their problems. The older generation, because of its experience and maturity, is an asset to the society and hence, should be revered rather than ignored. We must appreciate the true worth of our elders. We ought to understand their needs and take care of them. It is always one's privilege to be able to serve one's parents, and one should do this earnestly and respectfully. We are what we are because of the dedication with which they brought us up. Our lawmakers have enacted legislation to ensure that children take care of their parents. Experts have stressed the need of creating more old-age homes for the increasing number of senior citizens who become homeless because of the apathy of their children.

In most of the cases of apathy of children, it has been found that financial constrains and unwarranted interference by the older folk are responsible for their separation. Elders, therefore, should restrict themselves from interfering in family matters; they should not, in other words, expect something more than enough from the next generation. They should learn to *forgo*[15], *forbear*[16] and forgive. Anger and *retaliation*[17] only make matters worse. They should not try to *pry*[18] into the lives of other members unless those things call for their attention.

The media should also try to work for the restoration of harmony between senior citizens and the youth. The *stereotype*[19] of the 'evil' mother-in-law should give way to a caring and loving kind. The younger generation, which is depicted in the media as adamant and unyielding, should also give way to an affectionately understanding one. Serial makers and film makers should take up the moral responsibility of depicting the relationship between the two generations as a *compatible*[20] one. It, however, depends upon the two generations what they wish to imbibe from the media and how.

Both the nuclear and the joint family systems have their strengths and limitations. After analysing the various aspects of both the systems, the onus is on the new generation to make the right choice.

Aid to Vocabulary

1. *Patriarchal* — a society where the eldest male of the family is considered to be the head of the family
2. *Sprawling* — spread out
3. *Landscape* — an extensive natural area
4. *Teeming progeny* — great number of descendents or children
5. *Escalating* — increasing
6. *Discord* — disagreement, opposition of views
7. *Instigate* — to incite to do something evil
8. *Tyrannical* — severely oppressive
9. *Bereft* — deprived
10. *Void* — empty space
11. *Rudderless* — unguided
12. *Prize* — view highly
13. *Empathise* — to understand another person's feelings
14. *Affluence* — wealth
15. *Forgo* — relinquish
16. *Forbear* — hold back, abstain from
17. *Retaliation* — attack in return
18. *Pry* — interfere or inquire

19. *Stereotype* — standard type or widely accepted type of person
20. *Compatible* — capable of existing together

Points to Remember

1. The reasons for the disintegration of the joint family system are lack of living space, high cost of living, and lack of understanding between the younger and older generations.
2. The media is also partly responsible for the disintegration of the joint family system.
3. Senior citizens are neglected by their children.
4. In a nuclear family, the mother can look after her children very well.
5. In a joint family, the grandparents take care of the children well, catering to their emotional and physical needs.
6. The need for parents and children is to change their attitude towards each other.
7. The older generation is an asset to the society and hence should be revered.
8. The media should act responsibly and contribute to the restoration of harmony between the two generations.

A joint family is more than living together*

A joint family is on a disintegrating path ever since society graduated into an age of technological advance, changing gender roles and better employment opportunities. Interdependence on each other in large families seems to have been replaced by independent living and self-sufficient attitude.

Living together under one roof which was once about shared values and harmonious co-existence, today raises questions on adjustment and compromise. Couples post weddings settle down away from their in-laws and relatives to avoid what they now call an 'intrusion' into their conjugal space that decades back did not mean the same.

It is often perceived that the percentage of couples that come to discuss their marriages on the brink of dissolution to psychologists and doctors seems to be more from nuclear than joint families. The reason being, as Dr Kamal Khurana, marriage counsellor points out, "Couples part of joint families have seniors and elders to confide in as opposed to the ones coming from a single unit who find aid in us." As a note of caution he adds, "It is important that elders in family respect the autonomy of the couple and not impose dictates that may impede the relationship. Dictatorship and mentorship are two separate things and should never be mixed."

To believe that familial ties are unbreakable in cases where members are living together too can be bit of a misnomer. Every social structure dissolves and takes a new shape. Families entering new systems indicate a sign of thinking and evolving culture. Explaining this emerging phenomenon, actor and film maker Sudeshna Roy feels, "Little condominiums are the new face of joint families wherein every family living in independent housing estates/flats contribute in the well-being of extended families."

Staying away or close, the spirit of togetherness in a family should remain alive, forever!

**Source* : The Times of India

Essay 37

CARING FOR THE SENIOR CITIZENS

SYNOPSIS

Medical science has helped in raising the life expectancy of man. In India, the population of senior citizens is around 90 million. With the disintegration of the joint family system, in many cases the elderly have found themselves to be a neglected lot. As the providers of the family, they were duly respected but after retirement many of them receive no respect from their children. The younger generation, due to its own constraints, often feels helpless and is unable to provide for their parents. The lonely senior citizens become vulnerable to violence. People should plan their future and save money for their life after retirement. They should respect the individualism of their children. The Government and many NGOs are working for their cause. We should empathise with them and do our bit for their welfare.

Medical science has made possible combating a number of diseases afflicting mankind. It has helped in eradicating dreaded diseases and has promoted healthcare for all. This has resulted in the lowering of infant mortality rate as well as in the increase of *life expectancy*[1] of man. Consequently, we now have the phenomenon of "population ageing". The significant rise in the number of senior citizens and the need for proper healthcare and privileges for them are matters of great concern and challenge before the nations all over the world. The United Nations had designated the year 1998 as the 'International Year of Older Persons'.

Man being, by nature and necessity, a social animal lives in society to satisfy his needs. To *banish*[2] him from participating actively in the celebrations of life, therefore, is an inhuman act which must not be allowed to take confinement of a hard-core terrorist or a criminal accused of any solitary crime, is somehow justifiable but excluding from social interaction is not acceptable. An ordinary man/woman who has laid down all his/ her golden years in the service and building of the nation invites, *scathing*[3] criticism. The offence of considering the elderly people of the family as unnecessary liability in the lurch can never be forgiven—neither in this world nor in the world beyond. The present generation eagerly grabs the fruits of civilisation but shirks the responsibility to look after the tree that produced them, can we call it modernity?

In the last five decades of the twentieth century, life expectancy increased by 20 years to the present average of 66 years. During the same period, the ratio of the world population of citizens over 60 years of age changed from 1 among 13 to 1 among 10. In Europe, the ratio is 1 among 5. The current global population of senior citizens is over 600 million, of which 360 million, around 60 per cent, reside in the developing countries. By 2020, the world is expected to have around 1 billion senior citizens. In India, life expectancy of an average citizen was just 23 years in 1901, which could add a mere 9 years till 1951 to become 32 years. In 1981, the average national life expectancy reached 52 years, which went up to 64.4 years in 2010. A comprehensive Global Strategy and Action Plan on Ageing and Health (2016-2020) and a related resolution were adopted in May 2016 by the World Health Assembly. The aim of the strategy is that every country should commit to action on healthy ageing. It suggests the development of age-friendly environments and the alignment of health systems to the needs of older population.

India, and spread to all has been considered one of the worst places to grow old; its position among 96 countries is 71 in the global age watch index. So far as the health care of the elderly is concerned, it stands at the lowest. An average 60 year old in India is expected to live 12.6 years in good health. Almost one in two elderly in India don't have any relations to count on while two in five don't feel safe walking alone at night; one in three is not satisfied with freedom of choice in life while 30% are unhappy with the transport system. The study reveals that it is the health status of the older population that is mainly responsible for these conclusions to be drawn. Aren't these figures mind-boggling? Eager to figure in the list of super powers of the world, India is yet to chalk out some concrete plans to look after its older folk in a befitting manner!

In the joint family system, the older members of the family enjoyed great respect. The younger generation sought their advice, permission and blessings before *embarking on*[4] any endeavour. The elders felt good seeing their children's kids and their activities. Since the financial matters were handled mainly by the seniors, they did not have to face any humiliation at the hands of their children. However, with urbanisation, the joint family system disintegrated to be replaced by the nuclear family system. Lack of accommodation in the towns and cities, financial crunch faced by the new generation, emergence of the career-oriented woman and *callousness*[5] towards the older generation of the family have collectively contributed to the relegation of the social status of the senior citizens. The communication gap, which was perhaps non-existent between the older and the newer generations, has widened a great deal and neither seems to understand the other.

Want of privacy and desire for non-interference in their personal lives have made many younger members move out of the lives of the elders, leaving them lonely and neglected. It seems, the saying 'old is gold' stands true only for material objects. People throng auction houses and furniture galleries to buy antique *objets d'art*[6] and furniture but fail to respect and show reverence towards the older citizens. During their tenure as the earning-head of the family, they commanded respect and awe from the other members of the family. As long as they were providers, their dependants looked to them for the *gratification*[7] of their needs. After their retirement, when they hope to bask in the glory of their professional achievements, they are shocked at the lack of respect and gratitude shown by their children. In this materialistic world the emotional bond between the parents and the children seems to have *slackened*[8], giving way to *individualism*[9] among the children. Their perception of 'home' as a safe *haven*[10] is shattered before their very eyes.

In India, boys were once reared to be the future providers of the family and the supporters of the parents during old age. However, it is usually witnessed that the daughters-in-law and the mothers-in-law do not share the same vibes any longer. This leads to a major rift in the family. With new arrivals in the family, the accommodation seems insufficient to support and provide privacy to the members. The older generation in its attempt to keep the family together, keeps offering advices which are often ignored. Due to continuous interference in their lives, the younger generation develops a grudge against the elders and is forced to leave them. Some children have the *audacity*[11] to *usurp*[12] the property and wealth of their parents and put them in old age homes in which they *languish*[13] for the rest of their lives. Abandoned by their own loved ones, they wait for state funds to provide them with the basic necessities of life. The life of those, who are resigned in their own homes, their children having left them, is not bereft of dangers. They remain vulnerable to violence and, very often, even unattended to natural deaths.

A study undertaken by the NGO *Help Age India* has painted a grim picture as far as the lives of senior citizens are concerned. Of late, cases of neglect and abuse faced by the elderly have seen a steep rise. The survey has thrown up some startling facts—one out of eight old people said that no one cared for them. At least 13 per cent felt trapped within their own homes and 21 per cent revealed they were more or less alone or socialised with very few people. Among the most isolated and lonely are people over 75, particularly older women, who are widowed and are living alone. In Delhi, *Help Age* India received 300 complaints, in a month, of ill-treatment, including those from parents whose children had already taken away their property. Experts have stressed the need for creating more old age homes given the increasing number of senior citizens who has become homeless because of the apathy of their children. Currently, 11 per cent of India's elderly either live alone or with those who are not relatives. By 2025, it is estimated that 25 per cent of those over 60 and 40 per cent of those over 75 are likely to be living alone.

The parents, on their part, should also understand the psyche of the new generation. Faced by stiff competition in the race for survival, growing consumerism and escalating prices, the younger lot faces a great deal of pressure which was not felt by the earlier generations. The joint family system could provide for the whole extended family, even though it had only a few earning members; for if means were scarce, so were wants. In the present consumerist society it requires both the parents to provide for their family. Even if they feel the urge to provide for their ageing parents, they find themselves left with little after tending to the needs of their nuclear family. It would, therefore, be *prudent*[14] of a couple to save money which could provide them with financial security for life after retirement. The old people after their retirement should not depend entirely on their children. There are various types of post-retirement occupations available and these people should engage themselves in those occupations. This way, they can be financially independent and will not be a burden on their children. The government should make laws relating to the social security of senior citizens. In a country like India, around 90 per cent of the working class comes from the unorganised sector and they have no facility of any kind, whatsoever, to provide social security after retirement. They are totally dependent on their children. Only proper laws can ensure that the senior citizens are socially secure.

At a seminar, organised by the Institute of Human Behaviour and Allied Sciences in New Delhi, it was pointed out that 40 per cent of the elderly especially in the capital have no caretakers. In Delhi, violence against the elderly people is increasing. Delhi Police maintains a list of senior citizens who live unattended and monitors their condition. A National Policy for Older Persons to provide financial security, healthcare, shelter and protection against abuse and exploitation was approved by the Union Cabinet in January 1999. Senior citizens also get concessions in rail and air travel and income tax. In order to benefit the elderly, living below the poverty line, the *Annapurna* scheme was launched. The elderly, residing in the rural areas, would receive a free supply of 10kg of foodgrains every month.

The Health Ministry runs the National Programme for the Health Care of the Elderly (NPHCE). This programme has been rolled out in 100 districts of 21 states. It is 'designed to be preventive, curative and rehabilitative for the elderly'. Under this programme, district hospitals were aided to start a 10-bedded geriatric ward. Eight regional 30-bedded geriatric centres have been set up in places like AIIMS New Delhi, PGI Chandigarh, Government Medical College in Jaipur and Madras Medical College. In the sub-centres, male health workers are trained to make domiciliary visits to the elderly in areas under their jurisdiction. Non-Governmental Organisations like *Agewell Foundation* and *Help Age India* work to mitigate the plight of the senior citizens. They raise funds through donations and sale of souvenirs like cards, calendars, etc., for those who are bereft of the love of their own children. Though such homes provide them with the basic necessities of life, the emotional support of their children is absent.

It is indeed unfortunate that Indian society is getting engrossed with increasing westernisation more and more apathetic towards its elderly. Our senior citizens are no more under the protective umbrella of Indian values. We must accept our mistake and work on the problem from this *vantage*[15] point to *redeem*[16] ourselves. The youngsters who belong to the working class should be made to contribute a part of their income to the State. Let us at least adopt some of the good aspects of western culture. Senior citizens, there, are placed under the care of the government. They are a much happier lot compared to their Indian counterparts.

The Indian society must eliminate the trauma faced by the senior citizens. The children should *empathise*[17] with their parents; they too would one day grow old and helpless. History repeats itself and the wounds inflicted on one's parents could backfire upon oneself. The grandchildren usually remain witness to the atrocities committed by their parents on their grandparents and could replay them on their own parents. The elderly are an asset to the community for their experience and maturity and hence, should be valued and respected. Schools and colleges should organise trips to old-age homes so that children realise their responsibility towards the senior citizens of the country in general, and their own parents in particular. A group of students could adopt a senior citizen and provide him/her with emotional security. Offering a seat to an elderly person in a crowded bus or sharing the load of a bag of an elderly person are a few ways by which we can show them that we care for them. They devoted their wonderful years to nurture the future citizens of India and hence, we owe them unconditional love and affection. We have to abide by our social responsibility towards the protection of our senior citizens and we have got to strive towards its fulfilment.

Aid to Vocabulary

1. *Life expectancy* — the number of years that a person is likely to live, as projected by statistical probability
2. *Banish* — exclude, drive out
3. *Scathing* — very harsh or severe
4. *embarking on* — starting
5. *callousness* — indifference
6. *Objets d'art* — object of art or any valuable article
7. *Gratification* — satisfaction
8. *Slackened* — become inactive
9. *Individualism* — social theory favouring free action of individuals
10. *Haven* — shelter, a place of refuge
11. *Audacity* — an act of daring or of showing no respect
12. *Usurp* — take forcefully
13. *Languish* — to live through a period of suffering and unhappy circumstances
14. *Prudent* — wise
15. *Vantage* — of advantage
16. *Redeem* — make amends for one's mistake
17. *empathise* — to understand another person's feelings

Points to Remember

1. Science has helped to increase life expectancy of man which has increased the number of senior citizens in the world who remain without love and care.
2. Disintegration of the joint family system in India has led to the neglect of the senior citizens of the country.
3. The youth in order to assert their individualism, ignore the existence of their parents.
4. Parents should save money for themselves rather than be dependent and they should let their children lead their own lives.
5. The Government and the NGOs should work together towards the cause of the senior citizens.
6. The society should also work for this cause. Children should have empathy for their parents.

GROWING OLD

The population over the age of 60 years has tripled in the last 50 years in India.

Proportion of older people increases (%)

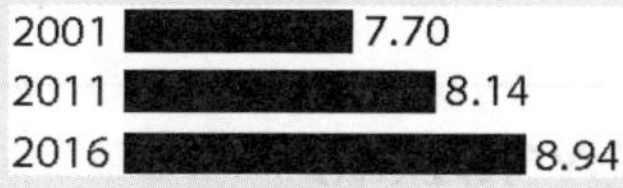

- According to 2001 Census, there were 75.93 million Indians above the age of 60 years. Census 2011 declared it to be 96.30 million.
- The projections for the next censuses till the year 2051 are 133.32 million (2021), 178.59 million (2031), 236.01 million (2041) and 300.96 million (2051).
- By 2050, the number of Indians (aged above 80) is to increase more than six times to nearly 5.14 crore.
- 20 per cent of this category (aged above 80) in India suffer from Alzheimer's.

Essay 38

SOCIAL REFORMS IN INDIA

Synopsis

The history of the Indian civilisation dates back to the third millennium BC. The basic elements of the social structure based on caste system were laid down in the Vedas. Castes in India were governed by normative conduct. In the medieval period, the series of Muslim invasions led to a religious upheaval. A number of socio-religious leaders emerged to instil social and religious spirit into the people through the Bhakti Movement. It played an important role in removing the rigidities of the caste system. Sufism also helped to infuse the ideals of solidarity and brotherhood between Hindus and Muslims. Under the colonial rule, the caste system got reinforced. There was an emergence of the intellectual Indian who worked towards social and religious reforms. Independent India inherited an archaic social structure. Social revolution was required to integrate the fragmented society. The Constitution provided the right to equality to all citizens. Land reforms were carried out. Social reforms helped to evolve and regenerate our country.

The history of the Indian civilisation dates back to the third millennium BC. Agriculture became the primary occupation of the inhabitants. It provided a stable social order. The basic elements of the social structure, based on caste system, were laid down in the Vedas. The *Dharma shastras* were written which formed the basis of the conduct of the classes. While *Dharma* meant the pursuit of a collective goal, *Swadharma* meant the pursuit of individual occupation, assigned to one's caste, with devotion. In the post-Vedic age, the *Brahmins* conducted the rituals and the *Kshatriyas* defended the territory. The *Vaishyas* were entrusted with business transactions, while the *Sudras* toiled in the field and remained in *servitude*[1] to the other three. The land belonged to the villagers and the chieftains who collected one-sixth of the agricultural produce as revenue as per the *Dharma shastras*. The panchayats looked into the work of the villages and mediated between the ruler and the subjects.

Castes in India were governed by *normative*[2] conduct. One's caste was determined by one's birth. It remained unchanged throughout one's lifetime. Violation of the caste rules could lead to lowering of the status of the individual. Through the practice of *hypergamy*[3], an upward mobility of a girl from a lower caste was possible within the caste structure. The society was basically patriarchal with traces of matriarchy in some regions of the south and the North-East. In the four-tier social structure, only the upper three castes were allowed to participate in the affairs of the State. The caste unity and village self-rule declined in due course due to internal and external factors.

In the medieval period, the rise of Islam and a series of Muslim invasions changed the course of Indian history. It led to a religious upheaval. A number of socio-religious reformers emerged to instil social and religious spirit into the Indian consciousness through the Bhakti Movement. The forerunner of the Hindu revivalist movement was Shankaracharya. The Bhakti Movement emerged in the south in the 6th-8th century AD and in the north in the 14th-17th century AD. The movement played an important part in *tempering*[4] the rigidities of the caste system. Among the chief exponents of the movement were Ramananda, Chaitanya, Kabir and Guru Nanak Dev. They preached the ideology of *Bhakti* (Devotion) to God. Ramananda eliminated the caste barriers among his followers and used Hindi to preach his gospel of love and devotion. Chaitanya Mahaprabhu preached universal love and brotherhood and disregarded ritualism and casteism. Kabir preached 'to foster a spirit of unity' between Hindus and Muslims. Guru Nanak Dev, the founder of Sikhism, was opposed to all distinctions between people on the basis of caste or religion.

The Bhakti Movement helped in transforming the society by eliminating the caste distinctions among Hindus. Sufism also extended its influence over the society. The Sufi saints worked for humanity at large, transcending all religious and communal distinctions. The movement had a social, political and cultural influence on the people. Sufism helped to end the Hindu-Muslim rivalry and infused the ideals of *solidarity*[5] and brotherhood between the two religions.

The British period was marked by an attempt to infuse into Indians colonial culture and ideology. Modern English education was imparted to the Indians to educate and train them to occupy the lower ranks in the administrative structure. This led to the emergence of the intellectual Indian, who eventually worked for social and religious reforms that led to a mass awakening and caused the regeneration of Indian society.

Social reform became an integral part of religious reform in India and this was equally true of Brahmo samaj, Prarthana Samaj, Arya Samaj, Rama Krishna Mission and Theosophical Society in Hinduism as of other movmements among Muslims, Parsees and Sikhs. The social reform movements have aimed at uprooting social evils. Raja Rammohan Roy was the *harbinger*[6] of the social reforms movement in India. In 1829, he launched a reform movement known as Brahmo Samaj which worked for the evolution of a casteless society. He also worked for the abolition of *sati, polygamy* and *untouchability*. The need to elevate the status of women was felt by Raja Rammohan Roy and Iswarchandra Vidyasagar. Vidyasagar dug up old Sanskrit references and proved that Vedic texts sanctioned widow remarriage. His efforts were rewarded when the Hindu Widows Remarriage Act (1856) legalised marriage of widows. Vidyasagar also worked for the cause of girls' education and was associated with no less than thirty-five girls schools in Bengal. In Bombay (now Mumbai), the students of Elphinstone Institute became the spearhead of the movement for women's education and founded the Students, Literary and Scientific society.

Slavery in India was akin to *indentured*[7] or bonded-labour. Generations were enslaved through indentures or agreements of service in lieu of money lent on interest that would compound to amounts that was never payable. In northern India, slaves generally served as domestic servants while in South India, slaves were mostly employed in cultivation. In 1843, slavery was declared illegal in India and all existing slaves were emancipated without any compensation to the slave-owners.

Amongst other social evils still existing in India society, superstition, under the garb of which a number of criminal offences are committed, is one which needs to be addressed at once. Women, who dare to break the norms of the society, particularly in rural areas, are burnt alive on the false accusation of practising witchcraft. To win favour of or to appease the Gods and Goddess(es), tender–aged children are sacrificed, young girls are forced into prostitution, and so on and so forth. Bereft of any scientific base, superstitions *sprout*[8] in fearful minds and take their toll on the poor and the downtrodden. Scarcely has anything been done to eliminate this evil from the society. It is high time our educationists and thinkers paid a serious attention to this vice which is gradually acquiring *elephantine*[9] proportions. As a corrective measure, *slaughtering*[10] of animals, unmindful of any belief or ritual prevalent in any religion, sect or caste, should be banned altogether; and children should be trained to think, act and behave scientifically so that they grow up as responsible adults and refrain from being party to this *heinous*[11] crime.

The history of social reform movement and its course in the 20th century is marked by the coming into existence of a number of social organisations both at the national and provincial levels. The Indian National Social Conference, Bombay Social Reform Association, Mrs. Annie Besant's Hindu Association, All-India Anti-Untouchability League (later known as Harijan Sevak Sangh), All India Depressed Classes Federation, Satya

Shodhak Samaj in Maharashtra and Shri Narayana Dharma Paripalana Sabha in Kerala, Arya Samaj, Dev Samaj, Ramkrishna Mission, Theosophical Society, etc., are some of the main organisations which acted against social evils. The caste system was largely criticised by Jyotiba Phule and Narayana Guru.

Though many social evils like drinking, beggary, etc., caught the attention of the social reformers in the 20th century, the condition of women and the depressed classes received greater attention. This was because of the dynamic leadership of Mahatma Gandhi and also due to the politicisation of the problems of the depressed classes.

India became a Sovereign Democratic Republic in 1950 with the framing and adoption of the Constitution. The Preamble to the Constitution, the Fundamental Rights and the Directive Principles of State Policy were framed in accordance with the principle of social justice. Democracy was chosen for India because it would help in furthering the cause of social revolution. It promotes the liberal democratic ideals of adult suffrage, liberties for individuals and groups, a competing party system, an independent judiciary and elected representatives in the legislative houses.

Land reforms were carried out to break the old feudal socio-economic structure of rural India. These reforms were intended for the modernisation of agriculture. The Green Revolution increased the agricultural yield, especially of the major cereal crops, making India self-sufficient in foodgrains.

In spite of all efforts made by great men of the past and the present to rid Indian society of its social evils, they continue to persist even after more than six decades of independence. Dowry deaths, female foeticide and infanticide, and other crimes against women are fairly common in our society. The real challenge is that the people differ in theory and practice. They condemn social evils in public but they follow and promote them in private.

Though some of the social reforms have failed to percolate among the masses, they have helped our country to evolve and regenerate. The pace of social reforms should increase so that we may in near future become a casteless and classless society, where all members may get full opportunity for growth, progress and prosperity.

Aid to Vocabulary

1. *Servitude* — slavery
2. *Normative* — based on established norms

3. *Hypergamy* — marriage to a person of superior caste or class
4. *Tempering* — making less severe
5. *Solidarity* — holding together
6. *Harbinger* — forerunner
7. *Indentured* — bound in agreement
8. *Sprout* — bloom
9. *Elephantine* — very large like an elephant
10. *Slaughtering* — killing of animals for their meat, etc.
11. *Heinous* — very bad or evil

Points to Remember

1. The caste system was structured by the Vedas.
2. In the medieval period, the Bhakti Movement and Sufism preached the ideals of universal love and brotherhood.
3. Under the colonial rule the caste system got reinforced.
4. Practice of sati, untouchability, slavery, polygamy, etc., were the main issues of social reforms.
5. In the twentieth century, the condition of women and the depressed classes received greater attention.
6. India became a Sovereign Democratic Republic in 1950.
7. Since Independence, many important steps have been taken for social reforms.

CONSTITUTIONAL MECHANISM FOR UPLIFT OF SCHEDULED CASTES AND SCHEDULED TRIBES

The deep concern of the framers of the Constitution for the uplift of the Scheduled Castes and Scheduled Tribes and Other Backward Classes is reflected in the elaborate constitutional mechanism set-up for their uplift. Article 17 abolishes Untouchability. Article 46 requires the State 'to promote with special care the educational and economic interests of the weaker sections of the people, and, in particular, of the Scheduled Castes and the Scheduled Tribes, and to protect them from social injustice and all forms of exploitation. Article 335 provides that the claims of the members of the Scheduled Castes and the Scheduled Tribes shall be taken into consideration, consistently with the maintenance of efficiency of administration, in the making of appointments to services and posts in connection with the affairs of the Union or of a State. Article 15(4) refers to the special provisions for their advancement. Article 16(4A) speaks of "reservation in matters of promotion to any class or classes of posts in the services under the State in favour of SCs/STs, which are not adequately represented in the services under the State.' Article 338 provides for a National Commission for the Scheduled Castes and Scheduled Tribes with duties to investigate and monitor all matters relating to safeguards provided for them, to inquire into specific complaints and to participate and advise on the planning process of their socio-economic development etc. Article 330 and Article 332 of the Constitution respectively provide for reservation of seats in favour of the Scheduled Castes and the Scheduled Tribes in the House of the People and in the legislative assemblies of the States. Under Part IX relating to the Panchayats and Part IXA of the Constitution relating to the Municipalities, reservation for Scheduled Castes and Scheduled Tribes in local bodies has been envisaged and provided.

Essay
39

HUMAN RIGHTS IN INDIA

SYNOPSIS

'Rights', according to the New Webster's Dictionary, constitute a just claim or title. The legal basis of the modern concept of human rights is the slogan, "Liberty, Equality and Fraternity", of the French Revolution. Almost all the rights envisaged in the Universal Declaration of Human Rights are enshrined in the Indian Constitution. The poor suffer atrocities at the hands of the rich in general and the police in particular. Despite civilisational advancements and frequent alarms raise by Amnesty International, human rights violations are taking place in India. Women are subjected to various harassments. The Supreme Court has interpreted some existing laws in favour of women. There is a need to make the police accountable to the public. Transparency in the functioning of the bureaucracy is needed to lend credibility to the system.

Rights, according to the *New Webster's Dictionary*, constitute a just claim or title, whether legal, *prescriptive*[1] or moral. 'Rights', according to the *Longman Dictionary of Contemporary English*, are the political, social and other advantages to which one has a just claim, morally or legally. Oscar Wilde defines 'right' as a reasonable claim to freedom in exercising certain activities. According to H.J. Laski, 'rights' are those conditions of social life without which no man can seek, in general, to be himself at his best. Bosanquet says that a 'right' is a reasonable claim recognised by the society and enforced by the state. Thus, the idea of the basic rights of human beings has been *postulated*[2] differently by different thinkers, political theorists and philosophers during the last few centuries.

The legal base of the modern concept of human rights is the slogan, "Liberty, Equality and Fraternity", of the French Revolution. The Universal Declaration of Human Rights adopted on December 10, 1948 declares, "All human beings are born free and equal in dignity and rights. They are endowed with reason and conscience and should act towards one another in a spirit of brotherhood". December 10 is observed as Human Rights Day every year. Almost all the rights envisaged in the Universal Declaration are *enshrined*[3] in the Indian Constitution, either as 'Fundamental Rights' or as 'Directive Principles of State Policy'.

Fundamental Rights offer to all citizens individually and collectively those basic freedoms and those conditions of life which alone can make life significant. Such rights are considered essential for the moral and material upliftment of the people. The Directive Principles of State Policy instruct the State to provide to all citizens, men and women equally, an adequate means of livelihood, just and human conditions of work, a decent standard of living, full enjoyment of leisure, and social and cultural opportunities. The Preamble to the Constitution mentions the essential individual rights as "freedom of thought, expression, belief, faith and worship".

To guarantee certain rights to each individual would be meaningless unless all inequality is banished from the social structure and each individual is assured of equality of status and opportunity for the realisation of one's potential. While in theory, human rights are guaranteed to all the citizens, in reality only a few reap the benefits of these rights. If viewed carefully, human rights seem to be limited to the exercise of Universal Adult Franchise.

Even after more than six decades of Independence, land reforms have not been implemented throughout the country and peasants still suffer under tenancy laws. Not all the children of the country are receiving primary education. Unemployment has continued to be a major problem, for the youth.

The undertrials in India face punishment even before they are actually convicted. They spend more time behind bars than conviction for a petty crime would warrant. According to a survey conducted in June 2003, for the Tihar Jail's 10,013 undertrials, legal punishment for their offence was far less than the number of years they had already spent behind bars waiting for court verdict on their case. The ratio of undertrials to convicts was roughly 83:17. There were 412 inmates at the Tihar who had been granted bail, but were still languishing in jail because of their inability to furnish surety amounts.

Although Human Rights violation is a universal phenomena rampantly prevalent in war zones, terrorist-affected areas and oppressive societies, it is very much common in India. The mighty seem to be in dictating terms to the downtrodden. On flimsy pretexts and petty allegations, the weak are arrested and compelled to suffer either starvation or third degree torture in police custody. Food served in asylums or in most of the government run schools are far below the standard. Considered incapable of contributing to the family income, the elderly people in many a family are either treated like dirt or ruthlessly *banished*[4] from the house to live in *peril*[5] and *penury*[6]. Women, particularly in their in-laws' home, and children in some households, are no exception to this rule. Criminalising, *ignorant*[7] tribals for hunting a protected animal or for having committed any other petty crime is another abuse of human rights in the country. Might is supposed to prevail; justice being there in name only. Customs or laws, relatives or friends, NGO's or the UNO — none seems to come to the rescue of the victims.

Despite civilisational advancements and frequent alarms raised by organisations like Amnesty International, abuse of human rights by governments as well as political killings has been increasing. Amnesty International reported several instances of human rights abuse in various countries of Asia, Africa and Latin America. Amnesty International, at the same time, acknowledges that anti-nationalist and *secessionist*[8] groups are increasingly adopting violent means to challenge the power of governments and such groups, in India, have committed numerous human rights violations, in many states including Jammu & Kashmir, Punjab and Andhra Pradesh. Therefore, the police and the paramilitary forces have had to deal with the terrorists in a tough manner so as to contain the killings of innocent civilians and restore normalcy in the states.

Women constitute another vulnerable section of the society whose rights are violated. The Fundamental Rights and the Directive Principles of State Policy in the Constitution give due status to women in the social structure of the society. The Government from time to time initiates various Acts for the *amelioration*[9] of the plight of women. Yet they are subjected to physical assaults, molestations and brutal murders. Women in India are still harassed and subjected to torture by their in-laws for dowry. In January 1992, the National Commission for Women was set up to safeguard women's rights. The same year, the 73rd and the 74th Constitutional Amendments provided for 33 per cent reservation of seats for women at various levels of Panchayati Raj bodies and Municipalities. The Judiciary has also interpreted some existing laws in favour of women. In the Shah Bano case, the Supreme Court reinterpreted the Muslim Sharia and compelled the father to provide maintenance to his child. In the Mary Roy case, the Court ruled that daughters have equal inheritance rights as sons to property in Christian families. In November 1995, the Court gave the widow and the daughter of a deceased, equal right to inherit property left behind by deceased person. In 1998, it made sexual harassment at workplace a separate offence. In February 1999, the Court ruled that a mother has an equal right with the father to act as the guardian of a minor child. The mass media and the socio-economic reforms have played a *pro-active*[10] role in the empowerment of women.

The record of human rights violation in India is not as bad as brought out by Amnesty International, when compared to other countries of Asia and Africa; yet, a lot of work is needed in certain areas. In all cases of custodial deaths and physical assaults, there should be mandatory enquiries. Besides this, some remedial measures at micro and macro levels should be taken on a priority basis. These may include insulation of the police against political control, improvement in the supervision of investigation, prompt execution of arrests, time-bound completion of enquiries and adequate punishment to the guilty. The Government has made some efforts to put an end to the violation of human rights by the police. A number of police commissions, including the Punjab Police Commission (1961-62), the U.P. Police Commission (1970-71), the Shah Commission and the National Police Commission have been constituted to look into the human rights issues relating to police actions and they all have stressed the need to make the police accountable to the public.

The constitution of the National Human Rights Commission is a *landmark*[11] initiative taken with a view to safeguard human rights. Some human rights groups, however, are sceptical about it. What is needed is a constitutional commission with active members appointed by a proper *collegium*[12] and having investigative and prosecutional powers over all violations. The commission should end discrimination and promote socio-economic justice for all.

Corruption is rampant in every department of the Government. Even the Judiciary is not free from corruption. Institutions that are supposed to uphold the rule of law—the police and other agencies of the law enforcement machinery—are the worst violators of laws. The situation is getting desperate and there is an urgent need for developing a culture of respect for human rights among law enforcement officials. This is the minimum requirement for preserving and perpetuating the rule of law, without which a democratic State cannot sustain itself for long.

For tackling the problem of human rights violations in a democratic set-up successfully, the police must function in a transparent manner. The police should involve the representatives of the public in setting priorities in different areas. Transparency in the functioning of bureaucracy is needed to lend credibility to the system. Human rights are the *inalienable*[13] rights of man, the protection of which is the primary responsibility of the State. Sustained empowerment of the people will help to develop a full-fledged culture of protection of human rights in India. Human rights, justice, constitutional empowerment and development of democracy are intertwined. They complement one another and reinforce good governance.

Aid to Vocabulary

1. *Prescriptive* — established by custom
2. *Postulated* — suggested as true
3. *Enshrined* — preserved
4. *Banished* — forced to leave
5. *Peril* — danger, risk
6. *Penury* — extreme poverty
7. *Ignorant* — unaware, lacking knowledge
8. *Secessionist* — separatist
9. *Amelioration* — to make better
10. *Pro-active* — controlling a situation by making things happen
11. *Landmark* — a turning point
12. *Collegium* — an inner circle of an organisation, with authority divided almost equally among its members
13. *Inalienable* — that cannot be taken away

Points to Remember

1. 'Right' means a just claim, morally or legally.
2. The legal base of the modern concept of human rights is the slogan, "Liberty, Equality and Fraternity".
3. Fundamental Rights offer to all citizens those basic freedoms and conditions of life which alone can make life significant.
4. In theory, human rights are guaranteed to all citizens but in reality only a few reap the benefits of these rights.
5. Despite civilisational advancements, abuse of human rights as well as political killings has been rising.
6. Women constitute the most vulnerable section of society.
7. The Government from time to time initiates various Acts for the amelioration of the plight of women.
8. The constitution of National Human Rights Commission is a landmark move with a view to safeguard human rights.

> The advanced countries in the West claim that they champion human rights. They take advantage of their financial and economic status to project a clean image. The developing and under-developed countries are often blamed for Human Rights violations. At times, baseless allegations are made about Human Rights violations in India especially in areas hit by insurgency.
>
> It is wrong to put the blame squarely on the shoulders of the poor countries. We must all accept responsibility for the violation of important Human Rights such as the right to survival and to freedom of expression.

Essay 40

STATUS OF WOMEN IN INDIA

SYNOPSIS

Women in ancient India were held in high esteem. But with the passage of time, their status deteriorated. Polygamy, dowry, sati and female infanticide came into practice. Sati was banned in 1829 by Lord William Bentinck, the Governor General of India. At present, rape, dowry deaths, female foeticide, etc., have become a common affair. Certain laws have been passed by the government for the safety and empowerment of women. 33% seats are reserved for women in the Panchayati Raj system. Women must come forward and fight against exploitation and stake a claim for their rights. A nation's progress and prosperity can be judged by the way it treats its womenfolk. Men must recognise and accept the fact that women are equal partners in life.

Women in ancient India were held in high *esteem*[1]. The position of a woman in the *Vedas* and the *Upanishads* was associated with that of a mother (*maata*) or goddess (*devi*). In the *Manusmriti*, woman was considered as a precious being to be protected first by her father, then by her husband, and finally, by her son. With the passage of time, the status of women got lowered. Muscle and money power dominated the society. Since men fought the wars, and ran the enterprises of industrial production, they considered themselves superior to women.

In the early Vedic age, girls were looked after with care. They were given the facilities of education. Remarriage of widows was permitted. But in the later Vedic period, daughters were regarded as a source of misery. The practice of *polygamy*[2] *deteriorated*[3] the status of women. Women in the later civilizations were not allowed to go to schools. In the medieval period, the practice of *purdah, dowry* and *sati* became common. Sati and polygamy were glorified. It was thought that the role of the womenfolk was confined to home. Their main duty was to cook food, clean utensils, wash clothes and attend to all other menial jobs for the family. Thus, women were deprived of their rightful place in society and their exploitation went on unabated for centuries. The inhuman practice of *sati,* where the wife burn herself alive on the *funeral pyre*[4] of her husbanded, continued for centuries. Raja Rammohan Roy fought against this evil practice, and it was finally abolished by Governor General Lord William Bentinck in 1829.

With the advancement of medical science, the malpractice of *female foeticide*[5] is being witnessed on a large scale today. The resultant drop in the number of females has led to a skewed female-male ratio. As per the Census 2011, the sex ratio is 940 females to 1000 males. According to 2001 Census, the female population was 498.7 million. Women represented 48.2 percent of the country's population. As per Census 2011, the female population has risen by 18.1 per cent to 586 million. However, their ratio with the male population remains skewed. Prenatal sex selection is driven by deep-rooted cultural norms that favour sons and consider girls inferior. Daughters are considered as a burden by some as they require dowry for their marriage. And those who fail to get a hefty dowry with them are often subjected to torture and domestic violence.

Dowry deaths have become common. The better educated and employed a groom is, the higher is the demand of dowry. The birth of a girl child is, therefore, not welcomed. In many parts of India, women are viewed as an economic liability, despite contributing in several ways to our society and economy. For the same reason, many girls are married off as early as possible. Early marriages lead to teenage pregnancies which pose a health risk and often prove fatal to both the mother and the child.

According to the National Family Health Survey-3, 37 per cent married women have experienced physical and sexual violence at the hands of their husbands. Almost 46 per cent of women aged 18-29 years got married before the legal minimum age of 18 years. Most of these are deprived of basic education. According to Census 2011, literacy rate for males is 82 per cent, while for females it is 65 per cent.

Rape, sexual harassment, molestation, eve-teasing, forced prostitution domestic violence, etc., are a common affair today. The crime graph against women is increasing at an alarming rate. Many women suffer online abuse. A new UN report reveals that almost three quarters of women online are exposed to some form of cyber violence worldwide. The report combating online violence against women and girls, 'A worldwide wake up call' states that only 35 per cent women in India reported their victimisation while the large majority 46.7 per cent did not, and 18.3 per cent were not even aware that they were victimised.

The condition of an Indian widow is quite *deplorable*[6]. Many get banished to widow homes; those who don't are condemned to a life of misery. The woman's contribution towards home as a housewife is not recognised. Sexual harassment at workplaces is also a common affair. Women were *subjugated*[7] in the past and their subjugation continues even today. In a patriarchal society like that of India, women have no voice or say. Their wishes and wants do not matter. Women who have still managed to break the glass ceiling are few and far between.

It is a shame that even after nearly seven decades of Independence, women are still exploited. The 73rd and 74th constitutional amendments have provided 33 per cent reservation for women in the Panchayati Raj system. The Union Cabinet has approved a proposal to reserve 50 per cent seats in Panchayats and urban local bodies for women. These quotas are far from being met.

Women have now started demanding their rights. They want to work side by side with men and contribute towards the social, economic and political development of the society. Swami Vivekananda's remark is *ponderable*[8] in this regard—"It is impossible to think about the welfare of the world unless the condition of women is improved. It is impossible for a bird to fly with only one wing."

Women themselves should come forward and unite in their march towards improving their status. They should draw inspiration from empowered women like Indira Gandhi, the first woman Prime Minister of India; Vijayalakshmi Pandit, the first woman President of the UN General Assembly; Kiran Bedi, India's first woman IPS Officer; Kalpana Chawla, the first Indian-American woman astronaut; Pratibha Devisingh Patil, the first woman President of India; J. Manjula, the first-director general of Defence Research and Development Organisation (DRDO), and many others. Some of the great women of the pre-Independence period were Rani Laxmi Bai of Jhansi, Chand Bibi, Ahilya Bai and Razia Sultan.

The modern woman is independent and self-sufficient. She is called the superwoman as she manages all fronts deftly and single-handedly. Women are now fiercely ambitious and are proving their *mettle*[9] not only on the home front, but also in their respective careers. Women have monopolised nursing in hospitals and nursing homes. Women's contribution in politics and social services cannot be denied.

Many programmes aimed at welfare of women have been *implemented*[10] under the Five Year Plans. In 1985, a separate Department of Women and Child Development was set up. The major programmes of this department include Support to Training-cum-Employment Programme (STEP) for women, Mahila Kosh, Women's Development Corporation, etc. The Supreme Court has given a landmark ruling that a mother has the right to act as the guardian of her minor child. It has also made sexual harassment at workplace an offence.

The Indian Constitution has *bestowed*[11] equal rights on women. They enjoy all social, political and economic rights. At workplace, discrimination of women on the basis of their gender has stopped to a large extent and they are earning equal wages as men. Many NGO's are playing an important role by helping women fight against the injustices.

Women in India have come of age in all spheres of life. They are enrolling in universities and colleges in large numbers. They are entering into all kinds of professions like engineering, medicine, politics, media, teaching, etc. A nation's progress and prosperity can be judged by the way it treats its womenfolk. In order to improve the status of women in India, the evils of illiteracy, dowry, ignorance, domestic violence, sexual abuse and pre-natal sex determination will have to be eradicated. Women ought to be given their rightful place in Indian society.

Men must recognise and accept the fact that women are their equal partners in life. No society will ever prosper as a whole as long as half of it is constantly treated as somehow inferior.

Aid to Vocabulary

1. *Esteem* — high regard
2. *Polygamy* — the practice of having more than one spouse at the same time
3. *Deteriorated* — made worse in condition
4. *Funeral pyre* — large pile of wood on which a dead body is burnt
5. *Female foeticide* — killing of a female foetus i.e., baby girl before birth
6. *Deplorable* — that which should be condemned
7. *Subjugated* — under control and obedience
8. *Ponderable* — having appreciable weight
9. *Mettle* — strength of spirit
10. *Implemented* — carried into effect
11. *Bestowed* — given (something) as a gift or honour

Points to Remember

1. Women enjoyed a respectable status during early Vedic times.
2. In the medieval ages, a woman was not supposed to step out of home.
3. Sati was banned in 1829.
4. The female population ratio with male population remains skewed.
5. Crime against women is increasing at an alarming rate.
6. Women are still exploited even after nearly seven decades of Independence.
7. Women have now come forward and have started demanding their rights.
8. They should unite in their march towards improving their status.
9. The Indian Constitution has bestowed equal rights on women.
10. Men must realise that women are equal partners in life.

COUNTRIES WITH THE MOST WOMEN		COUNTRIES WITH THE MOST MEN	
Martinique	118.3	United Arab Emirates	274.0
Latvia	118.0	Qatar	265.5
Lithuania	117.2	Oman	197.0
Curacao	116.8	Bahrain	163.0
Guadeloupe	116.2	Saudi Arabia	130.1
Ukraine	115.9	India	107.6

Women per 100 men in 2015

Men per 100 women in 2015

DRAMATIC DECLINE IN UNDER-AGE MARRIAGE OF GIRLS

Signalling a strong wave of women empowerment, indicators for female health, literacy, financial means and age of marriage over the past decade show positive upswings, the findings of the fourth national family health survey (NFHS-4) 2015-16 reveal. Findings of the survey depict a dramatic decline in under age marriage with women found to be marrying late even though the trend for men seems to be the reverse.

The latest survey shows a marked improvement in literacy rate of women. In around 11 out of 13 states, literacy rate of women have gone up over the past decade. While Goa tops the list with 89% literate women in the age group of 15-49 years, Sikkim is a close competitor with 86.6%. In Bihar, the female literacy rate jumped from 37% in the 2005-06 survey to 49.6%. The literacy percentage increased in Karnataka, Tamil Nadu and West Bengal.

FAIR GROWTH

Literacy rate (% of women who are literate in 15-49 age group)			(% of women in 20-24 age group who are married before 18 years)		
State	NFHS-4 (2015-16)	NFHS-3 (2005-06)	State	NFHS-3 (2015-16)	NFSH-3 (2005-06)
Bihar	49.6	37.0	Bihar	39.1	60.3
Goa	89.0	83.6	Goa	9.8	11.7
Haryana	75.4	60.4	Haryana	18.5	39.8
Karnataka	71.7	59.7	Karnataka	23.2	41.2
Madhya Pradesh	59.4	44.4	Madhya Pradesh	30.0	53.0
Tamil Nadu	79.4	69.4	Tamil Nadu	15.7	21.5
Uttarakhand	76.5	64.7	Uttarakhand	13.9	22.6
West Bengal	71.0	58.8	West Bengal	40.7	53.3

Source: National Family Health Survey-4, 2015-16

Essay

41 CRIME AGAINST WOMEN

SYNOPSIS

The woman in today's world has created a distinct place for herself. In ancient India, women were respected. In the medieval age, the position of women deteriorated. Soon after, with the spread of western education, women started gaining importance. However, in recent times, different crimes against women such as female foeticide, dowry death, molestation, eve-teasing, rape and domestic violence have been on the rise. The reason for this is that man in the patriarchal society of India, is unable to accept that woman can earn more, be more influential and enjoy greater social prestige than him. Society, police, court, all look down upon the woman who has been raped, and they traumatise her rather than empathise with her. In many cases, they hold her responsible and make no genuine effort to secure justice for her. Hence, the current scenario necessitates a social reawakening to make all sections of society realise that women are as invaluable as men.

Woman in today's world has created a distinct place for herself. In India, women were respected even in ancient times. The Vedas and the epics have upheld the equality of men and women. During the medieval period, the position of women deteriorated. The dowry system, sati and purdah system downgraded woman. The British brought along with them western education. This led to the *empowerment*[1] of women. After Independence, sadly, crimes against women have taken varied forms. These include *female foeticide*[2], or *infanticide*[3], dowry death, eve-teasing, molestation, abuse at workplace, domestic violence and rape.

Softer by nature and weaker by *brawn*[4], a woman is always *vulnerable*[5] – anywhere and everywhere. Owing to patriarchal system of family in India the mindset of male members of the society has not undergone change with regard to the liberty of women with passage of time. A woman excelling her male counterpart is regarded as an *aberration*[6] and is resented for encroaching on his domain. Greed for material by way of dowry to become rich overnight is another factor leading to this pass. Measures to *eradicate*[7] crime against women have time and again been suggested, recommended and implemented by many but all of them failed to hit the target. To achieve 100% success in controlling the menace, though remains an impossibility, everyone should contribute, in whatever way they can, to improve the situation.

The World Health Organisation has prepared a 'World Report on Violence and Health' (WRVH). Even in a developed society like the USA the statistics on the women-victims of violence are alarming. Nearly 22 per cent of women in the USA have reportedly been physically assaulted by an intimate partner or beaten at least once. In a national survey, 14.8 per cent of women over 17 years of age reported having been raped at least once in their lifetime. About 45,000 to 50,000 women and children are trafficked annually to the USA. The National Crime Records Bureau (NCRB) registers a case of cruelty by husbands and relatives every 9 minutes. The crime graph against women has been going up every year.

In ancient times, Indian women enjoyed a high and respectable position in the society. In the Rig Veda, we find references of great scholarly women. In the Brahminic age, their position began to decline and they were relegated into the background. Gradually, they were forced to live life without individuality and identity. They had to face evil practices, viz., sati, child marriage, ban on widow remarriage, etc. Atrocities on women have their roots, to some extent, in their weaker social position. Women are perceived as the weaker sex, dependent on men economically, socially and otherwise. If she is uneducated and unskilled, a woman seldom has any choice other than bearing the cruelty of her oppressors.

Violence against women has the *tacit*[8] approval of society all over the world. Crimes against women stem from the fact that men, even today, cannot accept them as their equal. They are not ready to accept the fact that women can earn more money, respect and social eminence than them and are breaking every *glass ceiling*[9] with the passage of time. The term *rape* is defined as forceful sexual assault on a woman against her will. However, there are quite a few obstacles in delivering justice to the victim. First of all, while registering an *FIR*[10], the woman finds herself in an awkward situation. She has to give an account of the incident and this becomes emotionally and psychologically traumatic for her.

Then there is the question of evidence gathering. Not only rural women, but also most urban women are unaware of the need for medical examination of rape victims within 24 hours of the incident. Failing this, the case is bound to fall through for lack of evidence. It is in reality the *stigma*[11] attached to a rape victim that stops her from reporting the crime or causes her to delay in reporting the crime. One of the major obstacles to justice in rape cases is the poor quality of police investigation. The reason behind this ranges from gender bias to corruption. The general apathy as well as inefficiency of the police is also, to a great extent, responsible for it. When the case comes up for hearing, the victim has to face several humiliating questions in the court. Her past record and conduct is invariably discussed. Thus, the judgement tends to become biased against women.

In 2011, National Crime Records Bureau released reports which show that rape is India's fastest growing crime and has increased by 873.3% since 1971. Delhi retained its tag of the country's rape capital, topping the list of 35 major cities in the country reporting the highest number of rape cases (414) in 2010. Mumbai was next with 194 cases, followed by Pune (91), Jabalpur, Bhopal and Jaipur.

Crimes have continuously increased during 2010-2014 with 2,13,585 cases reported in 2010, which increased to 2,28,649 cases in 2011, which further increased to 2,44,270 cases in 2012 and 3,09,546 cases in 2013. In 2014, a total of 3,37,922 such cases were reported. Uttar Pradesh with 16.8% share of country's women population has reported nearly 11.4% of total crimes committed against women at all India level, by reporting 38, 467 cases.

Activists believe that the tide of growing rape cases is not being diligently handled by the investigating agencies. This could in fact be contributing to increasing incidence of rape. The process of reportage, apprehension, trial and conviction is seem to be weak. Several women's organisations have been demanding changes in rape laws to widen its umbrella and incorporate stringent punishment. In most verdicts, the accused is usually let off for lack of evidence. Hence, the fear of law does not come as a potent force that can deter a man from committing such a shameful crime.

We have to begin by changing our perception of woman as a domesticated being without a voice. If we want to make society safer for women then our approach has to be multi-dimensional. We have to tackle the issue of women's liberation from the social, legal and procedural points of view.

From the social point of view, we need to change our attitude towards women. Our society *ostracises*[12] a woman who has gone through the *trauma*[13] of rape. A woman who has been raped is always the topic of discussion. She does not get respect or love from the family members and friends. As a result of which she feels emotionally drained and sometimes ends her life. The victim should be dealt with special care and given love and affection. Legally also there are shortcomings which need to be addressed. The legal provisions for the offence of rape in India provide a number of loopholes for the culprits. To attain success in such investigations, the police have to work in close cooperation with social groups. Interaction at all levels of society is necessary to prevent the rapist from escaping conviction. The police must also build an image of a trustworthy force, so that people can readily seek their help rather than fight shy of them.

Indian laws hand down up to 10 years of imprisonment for various sexual offences, including rape. But the system is such that even this sentence is rarely awarded. The reason for this is attributed to the fact that investigations can at best be termed as *shoddy*[14] and then there are procedural delays. Though the maximum pronounceable punishment for rape is life term, it is rarely handed down. The legal provisions and enactments incorporated in the Indian Penal Code (IPC) following the recommendations of Justice Verma Committee added *stringency*[15] to the rape laws. The maximum penalty sentenced is 7 to 10 years of life imprisonment. Most of us agree that nothing short of a death penalty should be handed down for such heinous crimes, but legal experts warn that rapists may, in such a case, resort to murder after rape to avoid being caught.

Delhi, the capital of our country, has been given the epithet—"the rape capital of India". Unfortunately, this is true. In fact many rape cases are not reported in the name of family honour, police apathy or lack of medical evidence. Rape is also quite common in villages and urban areas due to caste wars, honour, family feuds and repressive attitudes. It is ironical that the local Panchayats advise the victim to marry her rapist to avoid social trauma.

Apart from rape, women suffer from various other forms of crimes and abuse. Domestic violence where a woman is subjected to cruel and inhuman treatment is common in India. According to the National Family Health Survey, nearly two in five (37 per cent) married women have experienced physical and sexual violence at the hands of their husbands. Although the proportion of girls married off in the 15 to 19 year age group has declined from 56 per cent in 1971 to about 27 per cent in 2006, it still means that over 1.5 crore girls are married early, and 16 per cent girls of this age group, that is about 2.4 lakh women already become mothers or are pregnant, according to the National Family & Health Survey–3. Dowry related violence and abuse are quite common and sometimes even murder is committed. Women are sometimes harassed in offices, public places, during travel, etc. Unfortunately, most of these cases go unnoticed as the victims are too scared to complain while others around them are too *callous*[16] about it to raise a voice.

Financial empowerment of women not only enhances their security, but also instils confidence in them. Domestication of women has turned them into house maids (now referred to with the *euphemism* [17] 'home maker') and child-bearing machines. Women have to attain the freedom to get educated, pursue a profession and have control over their income. The Government needs to take necessary steps to start more women's colleges and institutions with job-oriented courses so that women become more self-reliant and thereby escape exploitation.

The Indian government has taken some important steps to bring about changes in the social condition of women. Hindu Code Bill (1956), Hindu Succession Act, Anti Dowry Act (1961), Equal Payment of Remuneration Act (1976), Right to Divorce, etc., are some laws which provide them social security. It is a confounding fact that despite sufficient legal safeguards, violence against Indian women has only increased.

Adding new laws have seldom solved social problems. We need a social awakening which has to be brought about by the people themselves. The entire mindset of Indian society in general has to undergo a drastic change so as to eradicate this scourge. Social reformers should devote some time to educate people and make them aware that it is inhuman to ostracise a rape-victim. They should teach people to accept a woman in her *multifarious*[18] roles, both inside and outside her home. The media should also play a proactive role in changing the discriminatory mindset of society and in spreading awareness about the laws. The police should be sensitised so as to be ready to cooperate. One is given to believe that in future, crimes against women would decrease greatly and would finally disappear. It is important to understand that a woman is a man's partner, matching strides with him and that she deserves equal power and respect.

The Domestic Violence Act has come as a positive and progressive step towards a more egalitarian and modern society. It promises to give women—wives, mothers, mothers-in-law, sisters, daughters and even adopted daughters—protection against physical, verbal and sexual abuse and the right to freedom—the freedom to exercise her will.

Aid to Vocabulary

1. *Empowerment* — giving power to
2. *Female foeticide* — killing of female foetus
3. *Female infanticide* — killing of female infants

4. *Brawn* — muscular strength
5. *Vulnerable* — prone to be attacked
6. *Aberration* — deviation from the standard
7. *Eradicate* — to remove
8. *Tacit* — that is suggested indirectly or understood rather than said in words
9. *Glass ceiling* — unfair system of barring women from power
10. *FIR* — first information report
11. *Stigma* — mark of shame or disgrace
12. *Ostracise* — exclude from society
13. *Trauma* — emotional shock
14. *Shoddy* — poorly done
15. *Stringency* — strictness, severity
16. *Callous* — indifferent, apathetic
17. *Euphemism* — mild word to replace an offensive one.
18. *Multifarious* — having great variety

Points to Remember

1. Woman in today's world has created a distinct place for herself.
2. Violence against women has the tacit approval of society the world over.
3. In most cases, the police do not properly investigate the case of a rape victim.
4. We need to change our attitude towards a rape victim.
5. In most cases, the accused are let off for lack of evidence.
6. Domestic violence is common in India.
7. Financial empowerment of women enhances their security and instils confidence in them.
8. Social awakening is required for eliminating crimes against women.

Essay 42

EMERGENCE OF THE CAREER-ORIENTED WOMAN

SYNOPSIS

In ancient India, women commanded respect but in the medieval period the practice of child marriage and dowry system led to the lowering of the status of women. The modern Indian woman takes up a career to share the responsibility of the family with her husband. Education has led to the spread of awareness among women and now they feel the need to assert themselves. Gender bias creates problems for women at the workplace. The career-oriented women strive to realise the objective of balancing family and career. The modern man acknowledges that it is imperative to share responsibilities at the homefront and he also respects female colleagues. However, perverse men dare to indulge in sexual harassment at the workplace. With the cooperation of family and society, women have been able to make their mark in all walks of life. The Indian women look poised to command respect from their male counterparts soon enough.

The status of women pertains to the position of women as individuals in the social structure, defined by her *designated*[1] rights and obligations. The traditional role of the Indian woman was of a typical housewife who was literally confined to the four walls of her home. The ancient scriptures, like the *Ramayana* and the *Mahabharata*, reveal that women in ancient India commanded a great deal of respect from men. Manu in the first century BC felt that the Indian woman should remain dependent on her father before marriage, on her husband after marriage and finally on her son. In the medieval period, parents gave their daughters away in marriage at a very early age. This practice gave rise to the system of child marriage which led to the lowering of the status of women. The dowry system also became prevalent during this period. Indian women, through centuries thereafter, remained subjugated and oppressed because the society believed in clinging on to orthodox beliefs formulated in ancient India. In the 20th century, the women in India awakened to the need to *redeem*[2] their status and work to improve their position in society.

Until around 6th or 7th decade of the preceding century, girls were not permitted by parents who harboured different *apprehensions*[3], to step out of the house. Among them, the most prominent one was that it would be quite difficult, if not impossible, to find a suitable match for an educated girl. Secondly, a girl was supposed to be the property meant for some other family into which she would eventually be married, and so there was seen no sense in investing money in their education. To add fuel to the fire, the customs and traditions too forced the parents to *confine*[4] girls within the precincts of the house; it was against the family honour to let them go out for any reason. The fear of their being kidnapped, eve-teased, molested or even raped was yet another reason, the girls were restrained from going to school or college. Last but not the least important reason behind this notion was that the male members of the family thought that she would demand her share of paternal property if she were allowed to get education. All the above factors constituted to *retain*[5] them uneducated until the government of India *prioritised*[6] girls education and launched various schemes to empower women.

The Indian society was based on the joint family system, wherein the income generally was low but was enough for the *sustenance*[7] of the family. The 20th century ushered in industrialisation in India. This led to the exodus of families to the cities and resulted in the disintegration of the joint family system. Lack of accommodation in urban areas forced the families to adopt the nuclear family system. The cost of living in the cities was always high. The responsibility of running the household fell solely on the husband. He had nobody to look to and hence asked his better half to share the responsibility of the family. Equations in today's world are thus changing and women are actively seeking employment and pursuing very challenging careers. Today, the idea of woman being the weaker or inferior sex or the belief that a woman is useful only for home making and producing babies is redundant. Today, women are a force to reckon with in all types of professions ranging from hotel business to merchant navy and defence forces.

In the nuclear families, parents, being aware of the demands of the changing times, treat their sons and daughters alike. Daughters are given the right to educate themselves and further their career prospects. Education has led to awareness among women about their rights and privileges which had been, hitherto, denied to them. The influence of the media, both domestic and foreign, has helped them in attaining liberal views. They have acknowledged the rapid strides made by women in the advanced countries. The success of women *entrepreneurs*[8] of the West has influenced the Indian women and they have increasingly felt the need to question their subjugation. Education, coupled with liberal views and the avid support of parents, has helped women gain a new identity in the male-dominated society.

The modern Indian women have felt the need to *assert*[9] themselves. The occupation of home-making or housekeeping has not been given due credit or appreciation. Once grown up, children take up their own responsibilities and mothers find it difficult to spend their spare time. Economic independence has got its own advantages. It enables women to contribute towards the family income, spruce up their homes and indulge in buying gifts for their families. As wives shoulder the responsibility of the household, husbands need to turn to them for advice. This helps in boosting their self-esteem. By being assertive, women of the present times command respect from their husbands as well as from their male counterparts at the workplace. But the picture is quite different at times. The age-old belief of male superiority creates various problems for women. Gender bias becomes an obstacle at the recruitment stage itself. The belief that women are less efficient than men leads to the injustice of unequal remuneration for the same job. Moreover, women colleagues seldom lend support to one another. They, more often than not, pursue success at the cost of one another. All these factors inevitably put a much greater strain on women than what men experience.

Women used to be totally involved in their household work, children and home. Now they are equally concerned about their careers and are making inroads in those fields which were considered to be male domains. Even young girls, as compared to boys of the same age, have proved to be more responsible and committed towards their work. The women of today have dual responsibilities—towards work as well as family. As both are equally demanding, the modern day husbands help them in realignment of the traditional Indian structure of division of labour. Men now help shoulder responsibilities at the home front. The latest *gadgets*[10] help women in managing the household chores and take some pressure off their shoulders. It has been noticed that children of working mothers grow up as responsible individuals because of the awareness of the dual responsibilities borne by their mothers. The *indispensable*[11] support of their husbands and children enable women to balance family and career. Women have become successful in their endeavour because of their inherent managerial skills which, till a few decades ago, were displayed only at home.

The family usually helps and encourages the emergence of the career-oriented woman. It is at their workplace that women often face gender *discrimination*[12] at the hands of their colleagues or bosses. Many a time, women face sexual harassment at their workplace. A number of such *infamous*[13] cases have been reported in the media. This exposes the fact that sexual harassment meted out to women at the workplace, which was earlier thought to be a western phenomenon, is prevalent in India too. It also exposes the *perverse*[14] nature of a few *incorrigible*[15] men, who dare to indulge in such activities, unmindful of public *ignominy*[16]. On the other hand, if a woman is promoted on merit, her success is viewed as a favour given to her by her boss. It puts great psychological pressure on the woman. *Male chauvinism*[17] has made the emergence of career-oriented women unacceptable to men at large. But, with the co-operation of family as well as society women have been able to make their mark in all walks of life. A fundamental change is required in the attitudes of the employers, policy makers, family members and other relatives and the public at large. India now has legal provisions to protect women from sexual harassment at the workplace.

Young women are ambitious. They take good advantage of the opportunities offered to them because, for girls, freedom is hard to come by even in 21st century India. Girls are generally hardworking and sincere as compared to boys. They know that they can only make hay while the sun shines for they will eventually have to get married. Once married, these flowers in most cases start wilting. The job then becomes a necessary evil. They cannot give it up of their own free will. The double role is thrust upon them. They have to learn to grapple with it regardless of ill-health, pregnancy, menopause, etc.

Not only the work pressure in offices, but also, problems in family life, create tensions for working women. A nuclear family leaves its children rudderless. They have no one to seek advice from or discuss their grievances with, as both the parents are busy with their respective jobs. This often leads to serious problems for the lonely child. Working women have to tackle such *unwarranted*[18] problems that keep raising their ugly head at their home front.

The society claims that women have become career-oriented and have found their individuality. But, in some cases, these so-called career-oriented women harbour deep into their hearts, some dark secrets which are, heartrending and force humanity to think whether women have indeed got their due.

For instance, many women, especially from the state of Kerala are sent to foreign countries such as Saudi Arabia, Dubai, etc., to work as nurses or even as maids. Their employers take advantage of these lonely females, confiscate their passports, abuse them sexually and refuse to let them go. All the while their families in India happen to be enjoying the income earned with blood and tears.

The statistical Annexe of the 2015 HDR presents the 2014 HDI (values and ranks) for 188 countries and UN-recognised territories, along with the IHDI for 151 countries, the GDI for 161 counties, the GII for 155 countries, and the MPI for 101 countries. India's HDI value for 2014 is 0.609 - which put the country in the medium human development category—positioning it at 130 out of 188 countries and territories. Between 1980 and 2014, India's HDI value increased from 0.362 to 0.609, an increase of 68.1% or an average annual increase of about 1.54 percent. India has a GII value of 0.563, ranking it 130 out of 155 countries in the 2014 index. In India, 12.2% of parliamentary seats are held by women, and 27.0% of adult women have reached at least the secondary level of education compared to 56.6% of their male counter parts.

In the new millennium, Indian women are poised to command respect from their male counterparts. By being bold and assertive, women have gained credibility and have achieved a respectable position in the social structure of India. The *altruistic*[19] and sacrificing mothers have given way to *resolute*[20] mothers. They are poised to realise the dual objective of self-sustenance as well as providing for the family with *panache*[21]. Indian women have evolved and have eventually emerged as successful career-oriented women.

Aid to Vocabulary

1. *Designated* — specified
2. *Redeem* — restore
3. *Apprehensions* — doubts that something bad will happen
4. *Confine* — to limit
5. *Retain* — to keep intact
6. *Prioritised* — declared most important of all things to do
7. *Sustenance* — survival, keep alive
8. *Entrepreneurs* — persons who make plans for business or a piece of work and get that going
9. *Assert* — to affirm positively
10. *Gadgets* — small tools or devices for personal use
11. *Indispensable* — essential
12. *Discrimination* — treating one differently or as inferior
13. *Infamous* — notorious
14. *Perverse* — (a mentality of) inappropriate sexual desires
15. *Incorrigible* — who cannot be corrected
16. *Ignominy* — disgrace
17. *Male chauvinism* — the phenomenon of men being prejudiced against, or inconsiderate of, women

18. *Unwarranted* — not justified
19. *Altruistic* — nature of helping others without any selfish motive
20. *Resolute* — determined
21. *Panache* — lots of energy and style

POINTS TO REMEMBER

1. In ancient times, women were respected but, in later ages, there was a lowering of the status of women.
2. In a nuclear family, husband and wife share the responsibilities of the family.
3. Education, liberal views and the support of parents have helped women.
4. The modern Indian women have felt the need to assert themselves.
5. A gender bias creates problems at the workplace for a woman.
6. The husbands and the children have also helped in the emergence of the career-oriented women.
7. Women face sexual harassment at the workplace yet they have been able to make their mark as professionals.
8. In the new millennium, women have evolved and emerged as successful career oriented women.

There have been many women achievers in India—Indira Gandhi, the first woman Prime Minister of India; Vijayalakshmi Pandit, the first woman President of the UN General Assembly; Pratibha Patil, the first woman President of India; Kiran Bedi, the first woman IPS officer, who was awarded the Magsaysay Award; Kalpana Chawla, the first Indian-American astronaut and first Indian woman in space; and Sunita Williams, Person of Indian Origin and American astronaut—she holds the records for longest single space flight by a woman, and total spacewalks by a woman.

Women have achieved much in sports as well as in the entertainment industry. One can never forget the year 1994 when three Indian beauties —Sushmita Sen (Miss Universe), Aishwarya Rai (Miss World) and Dia Mirza (Miss Earth). took the world by storm. Sportstars like Sania Mirza, Saina Nehwal, Mary Kom, P.V.Sindhu, Sakshi Malik and Dipa Karmakar and many others are the pride of the nation in view of their sporting excellence. But all these accolades seem worthless when one thinks of the plight of the ordinary woman.

WOMEN-HEADS OF STATE/GOVERNMENT

Name	Country	Years	Post
Sheikh Hasina Wazed	Bangladesh	2009-till date	Prime Minister
Michelle Bachelet	Chile	2014-till date	President
Kolinda Grabar Kitarovic	Croatia	2015-till date	President
Angela Merkel	Germany	2005-till date	Chancellor
Ellen Johnson Sirleaf	Liberia	2006-till date	President
Dalia Grybauskaite	Lithuania	2009-till date	President
Ameenah Gurib-Fakim	Mauritius	2015-till date	President
Bidhya Devi Bhandari	Nepal	2015-till date	President

WOMEN-HEADS OF STATE/GOVERNMENT			
Name	**Country**	**Years**	**Post**
Beata Szydlo	Poland	2015-till date	Prime Minister
Park Geun-hye	South Korea	2013-till date	President
Sirimavo Bandaranaike	Sri Lanka	1960-65 1970-77 1994-2000	Prime Minister
Indira Gandhi	India	1966-77 1980-84	Prime Minister
Golda Meir	Israel	1969-74	Prime Minister
Margaret Thatcher	United Kingdom	1979-90	Prime Minister
Dame Eugenia Charles	Dominica	1980-95	Prime Minister
Gro Harlem Brundtland	Norway	1981-81 1986-89 1990-96	Prime Minister
Milka Planinc	Yugoslavia	1982-86	Prime Minister
Corazon Aquino	Philippines	1986-92	President
Benazir Bhutto	Pakistan	1988-90 1993-96	Prime Minister
Violeta Chamorro	Nicaragua	1990-97	President
Khaleda Zia	Bangladesh	1991-96 2001-06	Prime Minister
Mireya Moscoso	Panama	1999-2004	President
Helen Clark	New Zealand	1999-2008	Prime Minister
Gloria Macapagal-Arroyo	Philippines	2004-10	President
Luisa Diogo	Mozambique	2004-10	Prime Minister
Yulia Tymoshenko	Ukraine	2005-2005 2007-10	Prime Minister
Portia Simpson-Miller	Jamaica	2006-07 2012-2016	Prime Minister
Cristina Fernandez de Kirchner	Argentina	2007-2015	President
Jadranka Kosor	Croatia	2009-11	Prime Minister
Johanna Siguroardottir	Iceland	2009-13	Prime Minister
Julia Gillard	Australia	2010-13	Prime Minister
Kamla Persad-Bissessar	Trinidad & Tobago	2010-2015	Prime Minister
Laura Chinchilla	Costa Rica	2010-14	President
Helle Thorning-Schmidt	Denmark	2011-2015	Prime Minister
Yingluck Shinawatra	Thailand	2011-14	Prime Minister
Dilma Rousseff	Brazil	2011-2016	President

Essay 43

THE DOWRY SYSTEM IN INDIA

SYNOPSIS

The dowry system is a monstrous curse on our society. It is as old as the institution of marriage itself. In an era, where science, technology and industry have made rapid progress and mankind claims to be more civilised, dowry regrettably, has become a part and parcel of marriage. The dowry system is the root cause of female infanticide and female foeticide. Marriages based on dowry are unhappy marriages. The instances of dowry deaths are on the rise in spite of the laws enacted by the government. Many social reformers have tried to eradicate this evil practice, but in vain. Girls should become financially independent to make dowry redundant. The youth should come forward to fight this evil.

Dowry system is a monstrous curse on our society. It reflects and perpetuates man's superiority over woman. It *scorns*[1] the idea that men and women are equal. It has reduced the social status of women. The Dowry Prohibition Act passed in 1961 has not made any difference. Law has proved to be a failure. The dowry system is a cancer which can destroy the very *fabric*[2] of our society.

The dowry system is as old as the institution of marriage itself. Apart from India, it has a long history of prevalence in Europe, South Asia, Africa and other parts of the world. In ancient times, parents used to give gifts to their daughter at the time of her marriage. These gifts were given as tokens of love and affection. Many Indian kings gave as dowry to their daughters part of their kingdom along with other gifts like elephants, jewellery, etc. Some kings considered the birth of a princess a burden, though. They *resorted*[3] to *female infanticide*[4]. Female infanticide is another social evil directly connected with the system of dowry.

There was no demand for dowry during the ancient and medieval times. As a girl did not inherit the property of her parents, she was given gifts to *compensate*[5] for this loss. The groom's party never questioned or demanded dowry. But that what was a voluntary practice very soon become obligatory owing entirely to the growing materialism in the society. Today, dowry is both expected and demanded. Parents virtually auction their son for marriage. Boys carry a price *tag*[6] depending on their professional or educational status. There are 'rates' fixed for IAS, IPS,

PCS, IES officers and qualified engineers and doctors. Till some decades ago, the dowry system was not customary in some of the communities in India but today it has become so. In an *era*[7] where science, technology and industry have made rapid progress and mankind claims to be more civilised, it is regrettable that dowry has become a *part and parcel*[8] of marriage.

Marriage no longer remains a pious bond of two souls; it has turned into an unfathomable well from where any amount of wealth and prosperity could be drawn by the groom and his family. Surprisingly, women if they belong to the groom's side, outdo men in demanding dowry as well as torturing the bride if she fails to meet their demands.

The items generally demanded in dowry are land, cash, ornaments, clothes, furniture, refrigerator, music system, television, car, motorcycle, scooter, etc. Besides these, the parents of the bride are supposed to offer dinner and gifts to the family and relatives of the groom every time they visit the former's place.

If the girl brings less than the expected dowry, it leads to an unhappy married life and even to divorce. In extreme cases, the groom and his parents *torture*[9] the bride and even kill her. At times, she commits suicide to put an end to her wretched life. Some brides are *pestered*[10] to keep on procuring one thing or the other from their parents till long after their wedding. The more they get, the more the in-laws demand. In spite of the laws enacted by the government against dowry, the cases of dowry deaths are on the rise. Hundreds of deaths and bride-burnings are reported every year in our country and there are many more that are not reported at all.

The number of cases related to bride burning has been on the rise. In 2005, as many as 6,787 dowry death cases were reported. This rose to 7,618 in 2006 and 8,093 in 2007. National Crime Records Bureau had reported 75,930 incidents of torture and cruelty against women in matrimonial homes in 2007. According to them, there were 1948 convictions and 3,876 acquittals in dowry cases in the year 2008. Incidents of dowry deaths (8,172) during the year 2008 had increased by 14.4 per cent over the 1998 level. Indian police handles over 2,500 bride-burning deaths annually.

Two sections of the Indian Penal Code have been used to nab those implicated in cases of dowry, section 498A (cruelty by husband and relatives) and section 304B (dowry death).

According to the 'Crime in India' report, a total of 1,74,395 persons were arrested under section 498A in 2009, out of which 41,351 were women and 23,374 people were arrested under section 304 B out of which 5,182 were women. On November 23, 2010, the Supreme Court ordered all trial courts in India to add murder charges under Section 302 to Section 304B of Indian Penal Code (IPC) against the accused in every dowry death case.

On the flip side, there have been many a case of filing of false suit by the bride or her family. In several such cases, the groom's folks were found to be innocent and they had been implicated only to extract money from them. It has become quite easy for some to file a suit against the groom and his family; and get to acquire a large chunk of his wealth as maintenance.

Because of this evil practice of dowry, we Indians have become an object of ridicule in the eyes of other nations. Social reformers like Mahatma Gandhi, Swami Dayanand Saraswati and others tried to *eradicate*[11] this evil. Unfortunately, this practice has become even more rampant today.

A number of girls in India remain unmarried simply because their parents are poor and cannot *afford*[12] a substantial dowry. Some parents sell off their property to get their daughters married. This makes many of them *bankrupt*[13]. There has been an increase in female foeticide cases because many parents want to avoid the eventuality of having to pay dowry. While a male child is prized for he would go on to earn his bread as well as get a hefty dowry, the girl child is considered a curse for she would erode the family fortune through her dowry.

When dowry becomes a precondition of marriage, the husband and wife can never lead a happy life. Such marriages are bound to end in tensions, quarrels, divorces, etc. Children born to such parents grow up harbouring complexes throughout their lives—an effect of the disagreements that they happen to have witnessed within the family.

Several women organisations have come into being to check this malpractice. They hold seminars, rallies and demonstrations to *mobilise*[14] public opinion against its prevalence. Young boys and girls have been taking *oath*[15] to marry without dowry. But a lot more needs to be done.

Awareness and education can help to *curb*[16] this evil practice. Young boys and girls should not agree on dowry under the pressure of their parents. Educational institutions should canvass against the dowry system. More *stringent*[17] laws should be strictly enforced to check this malpractice. Young women themselves should come forward and lead the movement. They need not feel weak or helpless. They should try to become economically independent and refuse categorically, proposals which demand dowry. Inter-caste marriages should be encouraged. The prospective grooms too should come forward to play an active role for bringing about a social change in this regard. The media, both print and *electronic media*[18], should contribute to making people aware of the negative effects of dowry.

If the dowry system is to be abolished altogether, the mindsets of both men and women ought to undergo a stark change; otherwise, whatsoever be the laws or customs, the situation will never improve. Steps taken by the government are laudable but to succeed, it would require the mass appeal; Though everyone seems to be agreeing to the proposition of 'no dowry' on the face of it, few want the practice eliminated for it serves them as a quick road to prosperity.

Man and woman are the two wheels that run the vehicle of life. Life can never be a smooth ride if one of its wheels is mistreated. So, man and woman should be taken as equals and should be allowed to enjoy equal rights for the progress of the nation.

Aid to Vocabulary

1. *Scorns* — rejects
2. *Fabric* — basic structure
3. *Resorted* — turned for aid
4. *Female infanticide* — killing of a female child soon after birth
5. *Compensate* — to make up for
6. *Tag* — label to show price, address, etc.
7. *Era* — period
8. *Part and parcel* — an essential part
9. *Torture* — severe physical or mental pain
10. *Pestered* — troubled or annoyed
11. *Eradicate* — remove, get rid of
12. *Afford* — manage to provide
13. *Bankrupt* — unable to pay debts
14. *Mobilise* — prepare for active service
15. *Oath* — promise, pledge
16. *Curb* — check, restrain
17. *Stringent* — strict and precise
18. *Electronic media* — television, Internet, etc.

Points to Remember

1. The dowry system has lowered the status of women.
2. The dowry system is as old as the institution of marriage itself.
3. Some parents virtually auction their sons for marriage.
4. Cash, land and things of everyday use are demanded in dowry.

5. The bride who brings insufficient dowry is made to suffer.
6. Because of this malpractice, we have become the object of ridicule in the eyes of other nations.
7. A number of girls in India remain unmarried as they cannot afford dowry.
8. Several women organisations have come up to check this problem.
9. Awareness and education can help curb this evil practice.
10. Man and woman are the two wheels of life and must be equal for a smooth ride.

Essay
44

CORRUPTION IN PUBLIC LIFE

SYNOPSIS

Corruption is a widespread phenomenon in today's public life. Incorruptible officers and public figures have become a microscopic minority. Bribery, money laundering, incentives, fees for services rendered and scams have become a way of life. Corruption at high levels of political leadership percolates downwards, first, into the entire bureaucratic system and then amongst the civilians. The government can tackle corruption only if serious efforts are made to improve the socio-economic conditions of the people. Factors responsible for corruption are mainly two—payment of money to earn a job, and the rapacious demands by the political executive. Proper utilisation of funds is necessary in the sectors of health, education and infrastructure. The Supreme Court has denied any mercy to the culprit of corruption. However, the urgent need of the hour is to adopt a zero tolerance attitude towards corruption.

The word, 'corruption' means the moral degradation of a person who gives undue favours to someone in exchange for *monetary*[1] or other considerations. It could also be nepotism i.e., *favouritism*[2] shown towards one's relatives or friends at the cost of deserving applicants. Corruption is a *widespread*[3] *phenomenon*[4] in today's public life.

This is not a modern phenomenon. History proves that it was prevalent in the political and civic life of even the mauryas. The great political statesman, Chanakya or Kautilya has discussed corruption in his popular book *Arthashastra.* The only difference is that, due to the *immense*[5] development of the media, corruption is getting increasingly *exposed*[6] and investigated today.

It has become *rampant*[7] in almost all walks of a common man's life. One faces corruption right from one's birth to death, for there is corruption in hospitals, educational institutions, offices, government departments and even in crematoriums and graveyards.

Corruption pertains to lack of integrity. This could be lack of intellectual integrity, financial integrity or moral integrity. The World Bank defines corruption as the use of public office for private gain. According to Transparency International, an NGO based in Berlin, India ranked 76 among 168 countries in Corruption Perception Index (CPI) of 2015. The least corrupt countries are Denmark, Finland and Sweden and the most corrupt countries are Afghanistan; North Korea and Somalia. From the ranking, it is obvious that India is one of the most corrupt countries of the world.

In India, there are innumerable cases of *graft*[8] that come into notice from time to time. In recent years, various scandals and cases of corruption such as the Fairfax, Adarsh Scam, 2G Spectrum Scam, Haryana Teachers Recruitment Scam, Vyapam Scam, etc., have come to the fore Corruption in defence deals is certainly very alarming for a country. The media reported that there were kickbacks even in the procurement of coffins for the Kargil war heroes. The year 2012 was rocked by the Tatra trucks scam while the Augusta Westland choppers deal scam that began to break in February 2013, threatened to reach unprecedented proportions.

Bribery is the most common form of corruption in India. Government functionaries rarely do a job without taking bribes in some way or the other. some departments like the Income Tax, Customs and Excise, CPWD, Municipalities, etc., are the most infamous in this regard.

Educational institutions such as schools and colleges have also been affected by the cancer of corruption. *Reputed*[9] and big schools in most of the cities are alleged to be charging big amounts of money for the admission of students. There are also reports of certain medical, engineering and management institutions taking donations or capitation fee for the admission of students. This is not all. Tampering with the marksheets of students, manipulating the results of examinations, all form a part of corruption. This can ruin the career and the future of *deserving*[10] students.

Corruption is more *pronounced*[11] in politics. It is an open secret that every candidate spends lakhs of rupees to contest an election for the membership of Legislative Assembly or Parliament. Once elected, he is tempted to retrieve the amount spent by any means, fair or foul. This leads to *enormous*[12] corruption.

Corruption is also widespread in trade and commerce. Unscrupulous traders indulge in corrupt practices like black-marketing, *adulteration*[13], etc., to cheat the customers. big business houses and multinationals amass a lot of black money by indulging in unfair practices. In short, there is no sphere of activity which is free from corruption.

The existence of too many controls, rules and regulations, restrictions, permits and licences is also responsible for the growth of corruption. In this process, those persons who are at the helm of affairs make a lot of money. It is not India alone which has been badly affected by it. Corruption is a global phenomenon. Every country is facing this problem.

Factors responsible for corruption, according to a former Director of the CBI, are at least two: Firstly, the public servant pays a huge sum of money to a minister to earn his job. Every recruit, therefore, sets about the task of recovering his investment the moment he completes his training and is given independent charge to exercise authority in public interest. Secondly, the public servants's *rapacious*[14] demand for an exorbitant sum of money (quota) on his table exerts pressure on his subordinates to collect more and more in bribes. Meeting that huge target is a hard task that drives many of the lowly government officials to indulge in questionable practices.

The best way to deal with this *menace*[15] is to eradicate it from its roots. Rules and regulations must be simplified so that they are easily understandable to the common man. Only persons of high moral character and proven integrity should be chosen for a government job. All citizens should be educated so that they are well aware of their rights and duties. They should be bold enough to assert their rights. The best way to fight this problem is to develop a vigilance machinery within one's own country. This is possible only when there is *wholehearted*[16] support and cooperation of the people of the country.

Kudos to the three member bench of the Supreme Court which firmly believes that a corrupt public servant, despite given ample opportunity, would never ever reform himself and he, therefore, deserves no sympathy or mercy. This may look stern or out of tune with the philosophy that *penology*[17] is blind without the *leavening*[18] effect of mercy and opportunity for the criminal to lead a new life. But severity of punishment to act as a *deterrent*[19] is what the country needs in this hour of crisis. It is a pity that 1.2 billion Indians are not only willing to put up with corruption but are also a party to it because no citizen, for lack of time, wants to wait for the services which he is entitled to under the law.

Indian society is witnessing a wave against corruption as has never been seen in the past. The movement led by Anna Hazare, demanding an *ombudsman*[20] to judge graft cases against anyone in public office, got tremendous public support. Anna Hazare's fast led to political calculations that eventually saw the Lokpal Bill introduced in the Parliament. The Jan Lokpal Bill is an Indian draft anti-corruption bill that provides for the Jan Lokpal, an independent body similar to the Election Commission with the power to prosecute politicians and bureaucrats without prior government permission. The Lokpal Bill is not the only law we have on corruption. After the Bofors scam, we had the Prevention of Corruption Act (PCA) of 1988. There was an earlier one since 1947. The 1988 PCA consolidated with 1947 PCA, 1952 Criminal Law Amendment Act and some sections of IPC. Corruption has grown in Independent India in spite of all these laws. The real problem in our society is that people have been accused, but have not been convicted. For sure, the Jan Lokpal Bill by itself, is not likely to root out the endemic and entrenched problem of corruption. Nevertheless, it marks a significant beginning and represents an important milestone in people's fight against corruption.

Aid to Vocabulary

1. *Monetary* — related to money
2. *Favouritism* — showing favour or inclination
3. *Widespread* — widely distributed or disseminated
4. *Phenomenon* — a fact or occurrence
5. *Immense* — huge, very large
6. Exposed — display publicly and indecently
7. *Rampant* — unchecked, abundant
8. *Graft* — misuse of power for personal gain
9. *Reputed* — famous, well known
10. *Deserving* — meritorious
11. *Pronounced* — proclaimed, declared
12. *Enormous* — massive
13. *Adulteration* — making a substance impure by adding other things
14. *Rapacious* — avaricious, greedy
15. *Menace* — a threat, a dangerous person or thing, a nuisance, etc.
16. *Wholehearted* — with full heart and sincerity, without any doubt
17. *Penology* — scientific study of punishment and prison management
18. *Leaving* — making less serious for severe
19. *Deterrent* — barrier, check
20. *Ombudsman* — official appointed to investigate complaints against public authorities

Points to Remember

1. The term, 'corruption' means the moral degradation of a person who bestows undue favours on some.
2. Corruption is not a modern phenomenon. It is rampant in almost all walks of life—right from one's birth to death.
3. Corruption has become a global phenomenon. It is prevalent everywhere, be it politics, educational institutions, trade or commerce, etc.
4. There are many factors that cause corruption.
5. It could affect the overall progress of the country. The best way to deal with this problem is to eradicate it from its roots.
6. The best way to fight this disease is to develop a vigilance machinery within one's own country. For this, wholehearted support and cooperation of the people is a must.
7. The movement led by Anna Hazare to curb corruption in public life got tremendous public support and led the passage of the Lokpal Bill.

Essay
45

CASTEISM IN MODERN INDIA

SYNOPSIS

The concept of caste originated in ancient India. In the Vedic Age, there were four castes in India—Brahmin, Kshatriya, Vaishya and Sudra—constituted on the basis of vocation. Because of its divided gentry, India could not put up a united resistance against the Turks and the Mughals and later the British, as a result. They succeeded in making India their colony. In modern India, the caste system is more pronounced in the rural areas. Casteism is used as a tool to attract the voters especially in the rural areas. The Mandal Commission recommended reservations on the basis of caste. (Unlike other social evils, casteism is ratified by a sizeable number of people in Indian society.) Casteism has led to conflicts in many parts of India. Casteism is being overtaken by regionalism, nationalism, religion and western thought, though it has not yet disappeared.

The concept of caste, that is a social class based on family origin, rank or wealth, originated in ancient India. In the later Vedic Age, the concept of *chaturvarna*, i.e. the four castes, became rigid. The four castes—*Brahmins* (priests), *Kshatriyas* (warriors), *Vaishyas* (business class) and *Sudras* (menial workers) were initially constituted on the basis of *vocations*[1]. But later on, this became hereditary and was a tool used by the socially *affluent*[2] classes to subjugate the masses and *perpetuate*[3] the system of *hierarchy*[4]. In modern India also, the caste system plays a predominant role in most aspects of life.

The role of the caste system may not be as much visible in the urban areas as it is in the rural areas. City life has changed our outlook on many matters. Social mingling, professional interaction and education have, to a great extent, removed from our minds the rigidity of caste. Inter-caste marriages and inter-mingling of different castes in various aspects of life has increased to a great extent.

However, the same cannot be said of rural India. In most villages of India, marriages as well as social mingling outside one's caste are socially forbidden. The conflict between the landholding classes, which invariably belong to higher castes, and the landless labourers is a continuous one in many states of India. This conflict is so *grave*[5] that even today an inter-caste marriage can lead to a bloody *carnage*[6].

The Indian Constitution does not recognise the caste system. It treats every human being as equal. The Constitution has made separate provisions for the amelioration of the woes and advancement of all 'backward classes'. The Constitution does not define 'backward classes'. The report of the first Backward Classes Commission was not satisfactory. The second Backward Classes Commission was headed by Mr. B.P. Mandal and was popularly known as the Mandal Commission. The report of the Mandal Commission recommended 27 per cent job reservation for Other Backward Classes in 1990. This was in addition to the 22.5 per cent reservation already provided for the Scheduled Castes (15 per cent) and Scheduled Tribes (7.5 per cent). This led to the outbreak of violent protests by the non-reserved castes and classes all over the country. Some students, belonging to the upper castes, even attempted to burn themselves alive. Thus, Mandalism redefined the worldview of Indian democracy, opening up possibilities to demolish the hierarchy of caste and yet *Polarising*[7] the society. The Supreme Court upheld OBC quota in Central educational institutions clearing the way for reservation of 27 per cent seats for backward castes. The total reservation guaranteed, as of now, is 49.5 per cent.

Casteism is one of the greatest evils which plague our society. It increases the social rift. It has compartmentalised our political system. Now, most of the castes have their own political leader or political party who serve only their needs. In some states, caste politics creates large-scale violence during elections.

Unlike other social evils such as dowry system, bride burning, marital rape, domestic violence, eve-teasing, child marriage, child abuse, child labour, etc., casteism is the order of the day, *ratified*[8] by a sizeable number of people in Indian society. Instead of hanging one's head low in shame, instead of eating a humble pie on the atrocities committed in the name of caste, people, on the contrary, take pride in asserting that they belong to a particular caste. Other social evils, at least outwardly invite scathing criticism but casteism seems to be perpetuated by all; no leader, NGO or the Government appears to be serious to *eradicate*[9] this menace which takes, through caste wars, a heavy toll on human lives every year.

The conflict between the land owners and the landless labourers takes the form of class conflict in many parts of India. Reservation has brought the oppressed class into the mainstream. They are now educated and aware. Being a major vote bank, the Dalits have entered politics in a big way. The rise of BSP especially in Uttar Pradesh and its impact on national politics is an example of the rising influence of the Dalits. Similarly, some sections among the OBC's have gained major foothold in many important states of India. Casteism lends *hypocrisy*[10]to Indian democracy. Castes seem to be gradually dying, but casteism is only getting stronger. From the politician aspiring to represent a constituency to the NRI seeking a bride, caste plays a prominent role.

Caste, however, is not an overwhelming feature of Indian behaviour. Caste affiliations may be strong enough to bring leaders of one caste together to the forefront. But this would not be sufficient to ensure political power for the party in the election. Again, an NRI with urban roots is unlikely to be comfortable with a marriage alliance in his/her own caste if the match hails from rural areas. This, however, does not indicate that Indians have moved away from narrow loyalties. The growing regional identity has only strengthened caste ties.

Education and westernisation has *mitigated*[11], to some extent, the rigidity of caste in India. The westernised Indians form an increasingly close-knit group that shares a common lifestyle and taste. They are often reluctant to mingle socially with the non-westernised Indians. Indeed, they look down upon the latter. They would not consider caste when deciding whom to marry but, would definitely prefer a westernised Indian. None of this suggests that caste has disappeared or is even likely to disappear in the near future. However, casteism has not been and can never be the ideology of change.

Many efforts had been made, before and after Independence, to rid India of the caste system. Our great leaders like Mahatma Gandhi and Dr B.R. Ambedkar fought all their lives against this evil. But as long as there is no national awakening against casteism, the caste-related carnages in some parts of India will remain a dark reality.

Casteism rears its ugly head once in a while, competing for the rest of the time, with regionalism, nationalism, religion and western thought but, for sure, it no longer has the influence it once had. The onus now lies on the youth of India to make their motherland a casteless society.

AID TO VOCABULARY

1. *Vocations* — careers or occupations
2. *Affluent* — wealthy
3. *Perpetuate* — to make something (a bad situation, a belief, etc.) continue for a long time
4. *Hierarchy* — organisation with grades or classes ranked one above another
5. *Grave* — serious
6. *Carnage* — violent killing of a large number of people
7. *Polarising* — dividing, splitting into two

8. *Ratified* — justified
9. *Eradicate* — root out
10. *Hypocrisy* — pretence
11. *Mitigated* — made less severe

Points to Remember

1. The caste system in ancient India was based on chaturvarna.
2. Urban life has changed the role of caste.
3. In rural India, casteism is maintained more strictly.
4. Political parties use casteism for securing their vote bank.
5. Introduction of the Mandal commission generated strong protests from students belonging to the upper castes.
6. Casteism lends hypocrisy to Indian democracy.
7. Besides casteism, religion and regional identity also plays an important role in our society.
8. Education and westernisation have mitigated the rigidity of caste to some extent.
9. Casteism rears its ugly head at times.
10. The onus is on the youth to make their country a casteless society.

CASTEISM—AN UNFINISHED NATIONAL AGENDA

Scheduled Castes and Scheduled Tribes have been, for centuries, the most neglected, marginalised and exploited people. The scourge of untouchability was a blot on the Indian civilisation. Despite the constitutional declaration of its abolition under Article 17 of the Constitution, it persists in many subtle and not so subtle ways. It has been an unmitigated tale of prejudice, discrimination and exploitation. At stake, in the ultimate analysis, is the very integrity and survival of Indian society. Without transforming vertical inequality in society into horizontal equality, democracy will have no meaning. If the law is not in favour of disadvantaged, they will never achieve true equality of opportunity and freedom of choice. The nation's unity will be at risk. In some form or the other, overt or covert, in many subtle ways, the prejudice against these weaker sections persists. This is perhaps because of the mindset of certain sections of the society. Indeed to refer to the Scheduled Castes and Scheduled Tribes and other backward classes as mere 'sections of society' is a grave misuse of words. They together constitute the vast and not merely a section.

Essay 46

THE ROLE OF RELIGION IN OUR LIFE

SYNOPSIS

Indian society is a religion-dominated society. The Constitution of India grants its citizens complete freedom to follow and spread the religion. Religion has been defined differently by different sociologists. According to Comte, "religion involves consensus and agreement between groups." Durkheim suggests that, "in worshipping God, men are in fact worshipping the society." In our country, one of the important features of religion is religious tolerance. Religion advocates universality and it is an agency of social control. It is regarded as the ultimate source of social cohesion. It shapes economic, political and domestic institutions. It has facilitated certain welfare services to humanity. Religion has contributed greatly to the growth of literature, art and music. According to Marx, "religion is the opium of the masses." It has also resulted in wars, devastation, communalism and genocides.

Indian society is a religion-dominated society. The influence of religion over the masses is very strong in the country. Here, everything is done in the name of religion. Even misdeeds are committed in the name of religion. Both in the rural and the urban areas, people believe in religion and worship gods and goddesses. There are different sects of a particular religion, each of which *preaches*[1] its own faith and ideology without creating any obstacle to others.

Religion has been defined differently by different sociologists. According to MacIver and Page, "Religion, as we understand the term, implies a relationship not merely between man and man, but also between man and some higher power. Hence, it normally invokes a sanction which may be called *suprasocial*[2], whether it be primitive ghost fear, the present wrath of God, the penalties of an afterlife or of torture in hell, or merely the sense of being out of tune with the infinite when its supposed laws are disobeyed." Religion, according to Ogburn, "is attitude towards superhuman powers." According to Arnold W. Green, "it is a system of beliefs and symbolic practices and objects governed by faith rather than by knowledge, which relates man to the unseen supernatural realm beyond the known and beyond the controllable."

The fundamental rights enshrined in the Constitution of India grant complete freedom to their citizens to follow and propagate the religion of their own choice. Religion, therefore, is what we assume. Relics and rituals recommended in the *scriptures*[3] cannot guide our actions, for, several of them more to be futile and more often than not, end up thwarting the progress of an individual. To a butcher, the principle of non-violence does not hold, for killing innocent animals earns him his bread and butter. The practice of violence, thus, cannot render a butcher *irreligious*[4].

Sociologists believe that religion has played an important role in the formation of societies. It provides the unifying principles to every society. According to Comte, religion involves consensus and agreement between groups, and between individuals. "It contains within itself intellectual aspect, dogma and love." It addresses itself simultaneously to intelligence, emotion and will.

Emile Durkheim argues that all societies divide the world into two categories: the sacred and the non-sacred. He believes that sacred things must be symbols, which represent something. To understand the role of religion in society, the relationship between sacred symbols and the things which they represent must be established. The '*totem*' is a symbol; it is the sign by which each clan distinguishes itself from all others. Durkheim argues that if the "totem" is at once the symbol of god and of the society, is that not because god and the society are one and the same? Thus, he suggests that in worshipping god, men are in fact worshipping society. Society is the real object of religious *veneration*[5]. Durkheim argues that social life is impossible without the shared values and moral beliefs which form the 'collective conscience'. In their absence, there would be no social order, social control, social solidarity or cooperation. In short, there would be no society. Durkheim's ideas remain influential, though they are not without criticism. His views on religion are more relevant to small, non-literate societies, where there is a close integration of culture and social institutions and where members share a common belief and value system. They are less relevant to modern societies, which have many subcultures, social and ethnic groups, specialised organisations and a range of *divergent*[6] religious beliefs, practices and institutions.

Religion has been in existence in human society from time immemorial. Religious practices, beliefs and rituals have a great impact on our life. Religion has a positive, *elevating*[7] and socialising impact on the society. But there is hardly a phase of human activity on which religion does not have its impact. Religion also has certain indirect effects which are by and large dysfunctional. Care must be taken to negate those effects by inculcating tolerance in the society.

Religion has continued to be a part of us for its goodness. One important feature of religion in our country is religious tolerance. It is left to the will of the people to accept or follow any particular religion. More often than not, people following different religions co-exist in harmony. Religions always talk about the betterment of humanity. Religions advocate universality, i.e., brotherhood and upliftment of all, rather than one particular community.

Religion is an agency of social control. It disciplines human behaviour. Cooperative involvement in rituals and ceremonies gives to the society the character of a *collective*[8]. It provides the model for right livelihood, for it specifies what action may be performed and how. It restrains one from doing what may not be right. The belief in inner voice and the law of *Karma* has its impact on human action. Human action is always guided by these principles.

Man is an emotional creature. In times of his sufferings, religion serves to soothe his nerves. Faith in God consoles him and sustains his interest in life. He interprets a misfortune as the '*Will of God*' or a divine test of his resilience and thereby endures his misery.

Religion is regarded as the ultimate source of social *cohesion*[9]. There are many religious values which bring about social cohesion. It is religion that asks man to renounce evil activities and requires him to impose limitations upon his wants and desires. One of the most important functions of religion is discipline. It is religion alone which mitigates barbaric anarchy and teaches reverence and obedience.

Besides this, religion shapes economic, political and domestic institutions. Religious rites are performed on many occasions such as birth, initiation, marriage, sickness, death and so on; and they are intimately concerned with family and kinship interests and with political institutions. Religion is regarded as the central element in the life of a civilisation.

Religion facilitates certain welfare services for humanity. The religious scriptures are great literary works; they are chroniclers of history and storehouses of knowledge. Religion nurtures an inclination for charity among people. Believers have opened many charitable institutions like hospitals, rest houses and temples to help the needy.

Religion has contributed greatly to the growth of literature, art and music. In our country, both in Hindu and Muslim religions, a vast literature has grown to give different interpretations to the religious scriptures. Sometimes, religious themes are sources of inspiration for some artists' finest paintings. 'Praises' of God has led to the creation of some of the world's finest music and dance forms.

Thus, religion is the supremely integrating and unifying force in human society. But certain thinkers have presented a different perspective on religion. To Karl Marx, religion is an illusion which eases the pain produced by exploitation and oppression. In his words, 'Religion is the sigh of the oppressed creature, the sentiment of a heartless world and the soul of soulless conditions. It is the opium of the masses.' Religion acts as opium to dull the pain produced by oppression. It is simply a misguided attempt to make life more bearable.

Hinduism has precious treasures to offer to the world. But the Brahmins chose to impose the negative aspects of it, such as casteism, the sati system, etc., upon Hindu society; which were soon ridden with blind superstitions.

So, the cleansing was undertaken by great reformers like Raja Rammohan Roy, Mahatma Gandhi, Ishwar Chandra Vidyasagar, Swami Dayanand Saraswati, Vinoba Bhave and a host of others. Religious leaders like Shankaracharya, Rama Krishna Paramhansa, Swami Sivananda, etc., attempted to bring out the positive aspects of religion. Swami Vivekananda reached the shores of America to proclaim the greatness of India at the World Conference of Religions in Chicago in 1893.

Even today, endeavours are under way in various quarters to repackage and present the various forms of our ancient treasure such as yoga, ayurveda, the scriptures, etc., to the masses, so that, the current generations is not deprived of their benefits.

Religion has resulted in wars, devastating communalism and *genocides*[10]. Europe in the sixteenth and seventeenth centuries, witnessed great unrest due to religious conflicts. The wars between the Christians and the Muslims in Europe resulted in the death of thousands of people. In India religious *antagonism*[11] persisted despite the *Bhakti* movement. Prevalence of communal disharmony in our country had brought about its partition. Communal sensibility persists even today in a section of the society. The need of the hour is to employ religion as the agent of national integration.

Religion and religious practices serve to elevate our sensibility. For example, all religions teach us not only to love God, but also our fellowmen. To forgive and forget is the dictum of all saints. However, it is easy to preach but hard to practise especially in today's times where man kills man for the sake of self-preservation. Terrorism would have never spread its tentacles, had we exercised tolerance and love towards our fellowmen. Religion has much to offer but it depends on us how we interpret it and how much of it we learn or follow.

Aid to Vocabulary

1. *Preaches* — teaches, advocates and spreads
2. *Suprasocial* — transcending social limits

3. *Scriptures* — sacred writings
4. *Irreligious* — one who does not practice religion
5. *Veneration* — showing deep respect
6. *Divergent* — different
7. *Elevating* — raising to a higher position
8. *Collective* — a cooperative enterprise
9. *Cohesion* — the act or condition of sticking together
10. *Genocides* — the mass exterminations of human beings, especially of a particular race or group
11. *Antagonism* — a strong feeling of dislike or hatred

Points to Remember

1. In our society, the hold of religion over the masses is very strong.
2. Sociologists have defined religion differently.
3. Comte and Durkheim's views are very significant in this respect.
4. Religions always speak about religious tolerance and betterment of humanity.
5. Religion is an agency of social control.
6. Religion is regarded as the ultimate source of social cohesion.
7. Religion shapes economic, political and domestic institutions.
8. It has contributed greatly to the growth of our literature, art and music.
9. Karl Marx thinks religion is an illusion which eases the pain produced by exploitation and oppression.
10. Religion has resulted in wars, devastation, communalism and genocide.

GUIDED COMPOSITION

Develop the following paragraph into a full-fledged essay in 800-1000 words. The gist of the topic is provided in approximately 162 words for your help:

WE HAVE ENOUGH RELIGION TO MAKE US HATE, BUT NOT ENOUGH TO MAKE US LOVE ONE ANOTHER

The reason behind the acts of violence and hatred, in the name of religion, is that 'we have just enough religion to make us hate, but not enough to make us love one another.' Since the dawn of human civilisation, man has fought bloody battles on religious issues. Religion, however, in such cases was only an outward excuse. The real reason being, desire to have power over other lands and possess riches. Even today, religious issues are utilised for material gain and power. Thus, it is not religion that is responsible for the unrest in the world, rather it is man's greed and his limited perception of religion. People indulge in violence and destruction because of religion, little realising that all religions teach the lesson of love, affection and brotherhood. People magnify the difference between one religion and another instead of realising that each religion is only a different means towards one God. Innocent people are killed in religious conflicts, when every religion considers taking life as an unforgivable sin. Thus, people have imbibed just enough reason to hate and fight and not enough to form a bond of universal love. *(162 words)*

Essay 47

SECULARISM IN INDIA

SYNOPSIS

India is a secular country. She has no state religion. All religions and their followers are equal in the eyes of law. Despite onslaughts, secularism has thrived in the country. The Constitution grants freedom of faith, worship and religion. It allows one to practise and propagate the same. India is the second most populated country in the world. She is the melting pot of various races and religions. Hinduism, Islam, Christianity, Sikhism, Buddhism, Jainism and Zoroastrianism are the major religions in India. There is unity in spite of the diversity. But communal acts like the demolition of Babri Masjid, Mumbai blasts, blood bath in Gujarat, etc., have posed a threat to secularism. Dirty politics, poverty, illiteracy, economic backwardness, orthodox beliefs, etc., are the main causes of communal disharmony in India. These should be checked. Communal violence showed a rising trend this year. The State should promote tolerance, social justice, economic welfare and equality among all the citizens. This would help us to create a harmonious nation.

India is a secular country. People of different religions, cultures, castes, sects and creeds live in India. There is no official religion of India. Every citizen has the freedom to practise the religion of his choice without any interference from the State. That India is a secular country is clearly stated in the Preamble to the Constitution of India. The word 'Secularism' was *incorporated*[1] in the Preamble under the 42nd Amendment in 1976. Articles 25 to 30 provide for the freedom of religion and protection of cultural and educational rights of the minorities. The Constitution grants freedom of faith, worship and religion.

Though India is a Hindu-majority nation, its spirit and soul is secular. Despite several disputes and contradictions; onslaughts by foreign intruders; and multifarious styles, languages, dresses, festivals, beliefs, customs, traditions of its people; India through the centuries has remained disintegrated; the basic structure of secularism, could not be broken. In today's world of unrest and upheavals, terrorism and other socio-economic problems, India remains unflinchingly firm. Attempts to destroy its secular fabric have always been thwarted.

The Indian culture has equal respect and tolerance for all religions. One can witness temples, mosques, gurudwaras and churches situated close to one another. People of different communities, cultures and religions live together as one family. There is no favour from the state towards any particular religion or its followers. All religions and their followers are equal in the eyes of law. There is complete religious freedom.

The concept of secularism is western in origin. It emerged as a result of the struggle between the church and the state. It was intended to separate the church from politics. The Indian concept of secularism is based on *Sarva Dharma Samabhava*, i.e., equal status for all religions. Secularism forms three fundamental rights in Part III of the Constitution, viz., the Right to Equality, the Right to Freedom of Religion and the Cultural and Educational Right. The logic behind constitutional guarantee of religious practices is to promote secularism. Secularism is also an integral part of our legal system.

India is a vast country with the second largest population in the world. India's population has crossed the one billion mark. India is the *melting pot*[2] of various races and religions. Some of the religions and faiths were born in this land while others were brought in by the successive political and cultural invasions. Over a period of time, these got *assimilated*[3] in the country. Hinduism, Islam, Christianity, Sikhism, Buddhism, Jainism and Zoroastrianism are among the major religions in India.

Hinduism is the oldest religion of India and accounts for over 80 per cent of the total population of India. Muslims constitute about 13 per cent of the total population; Christians 2.3 per cent, Sikhs 2 per cent and Jains half a per cent. Buddhists form less than three quarters of one per cent of India's population. Parsees in India are few in number and most of them live in the Mumbai region. There is unity amongst the Indians in spite of the diversities. Secularism is the *essence*[4] of Indian democracy. It reflects the Indian tradition of religious tolerance, co-operation and mutual respect for one another.

Since ancient times, we have had the concept of 'Vasudhaiva Kutumbakam' or the whole world is a family. Our secularism has its roots in the principle of universal brotherhood which *propagates*[5] the message of peace and harmony. It is one of the high values of humanism that constitute Indian philosophy.

But there are certain events which show that all communities have not always lived in peace all over the country. The communal riots between Hindus and Muslims are a *legacy*[6] of the British who followed the policy of 'divide and rule.' that culminated in the partition of India. The

Partition was followed by large-scale migration of population. Thereafter, Hindu-Muslim riots have broken out several times on either side of the border, causing great loss of human life and property.

The massacre of Sikhs in 1984 after the assassination of the then Prime Minister, Indira Gandhi, the *demolition*[7] of the Babri Masjid in December 1992, the Godhra *carnage*[8] and the subsequent riots in 2002, etc., reveal the chinks in the secular armour of India. There have been instances of attacks on religious places of worship and various incidents of communal flare ups. Many a time, a misunderstanding over a small matter has also led to communal tensions. But these riots could not spell the end of communal harmony. Life does return to normal and the two warring communities do, eventually, live in peace. There is no ill-will between the communities. By and large, they have been living together and sharing each other's feelings. Secularism can be strengthened further, only by *instilling*[9] feelings of brotherhood and friendliness among the people of India.

Political parties are often responsible for communal riots. All politicians ought to commit themselves to national unity and securalism. On the contrary, most of them play the communal card to their advantage. Communalism serves their vested interests. They often try to *rake up*[10] some communal issues in different parts of the country. It helps them to *tarnish*[11] the image of other political parties and make their own position safe, and prospects secure, in a particular area. They use different communities as their vote banks. Lack of education and enlightenment, poverty, existence of orthodox beliefs and narrow-minded elements are the main causes of communal disharmony in India.

The poor, illiterate and backward classes get easily influenced by *fundamentalists*[12] and reactionary communal forces. Again, failure of the social reform movements in the post-Independence era has led to the *fragmentation*[13] of the society on the basis of caste, creed, religion, etc. In an ideal, well-established, modern polity, religion should have no connection with politics.

Communalism is a great obstacle in the path of secularism. Communalism should be *weeded out*[14] from the society by all means. *Eradication*[15] of poverty and illiteracy, fair distribution of national wealth, removal of unemployment, etc., can ensure lasting peace. To *evolve*[16] into a secular state, a secular mind has to be developed. People belonging to different religions should live in perfect harmony. No political party should be permitted to contest elections by stirring up the emotions of people of a particular religion, caste or sect. The mass media should present *unbiased*[17] information only. The people will have to accept the fact that India's unity lies in harmonising its rich diversity. The State should promote tolerance, social justice, economic welfare and equality among all the citizens. This would help us to strengthen the secular fabric in India.

Aid to Vocabulary

1. *Incorporated* — included
2. *Melting pot* — a place where large number of people; ideas, etc. are mixed together
3. *Assimilated* — absorbed
4. *Essence* — most important quality
5. *Propagates* — spreads an idea, knowledge, etc., widely
6. *Legacy* — a thing passed on to people from earlier events
7. *Demolition* — pulling or knocking down a building
8. *Carnage* — the killing of many people
9. *Instilling* — making someone feel in a particular way over a period of time
10. *Rake up* — to talk about something unpleasant that happened in the past and that people would like to forget.
11. *Tarnish* — to spoil or sully (reputation, image, etc.)
12. *Fundamentalists* — the strict followers of the basic teachings of a particular religion
13. *Fragmentation* — breaking into parts
14. *Weeded out* — got rid of
15. *Eradication* — elimination, complete removal
16. *Evolve* — to develop naturally and gradually
17. *Unbiased* — impartial, not favouring a side or aspect at the expense of another

Points to Remember

1. India has no State religion.
2. All religions and their followers are equal in the eyes of law.
3. The concept of secularism is western in origin.
4. There is no ill-will between different communities in India.
5. There is unity in spite of the diversity in religion.
6. Repeated communal riots have posed a threat to secularism in India.
7. Political parties are often responsible for communal riots.
8. Communalism should be weeded out from the society by all means.

8,000 CHRISTIANS ATTACKED IN 2015

In the history of post independence India, 2015 was by far the worst year for the country's Christians, says a report released by the Catholic Secular Forum (CSF).

Statistics compiled by the forum, which has been documenting religious persecution of Christians for decades, show that there have been at least 365 major cases where community members and their institutions have been attacked for practising and spreading their faith.

"There were 120 attacks in 2014. The attacks have more than tripled in one year." Retired Karnataka High Court Judge MF Saldanha who helped compile the report said, "India moving up to number 17 in the global Christian persecution index put out by Open Doors, an international watchdog."

Eight Christians were killed and at least 8,000 were attacked or severely harassed by fundamentalist forces in different parts of the country in 2015.

Of the 8,000 victims, 4,000 were women and 2,000 were children, the report says. Madhya Pradesh, Karnataka, Tamil Nadu, Andhra Pradesh and Chhattisgarh once again topped the charts (see table).

Pegging the blame on Hindutva groups, the CSF report says, "There has been a very marked rise in attacks on the minorities".

The report also says that only those cases which were reported to the police have been documented. Alleging that a majority of incidents go unreported, the report says that "victims are often too scared to complain"; and that "there were some shocking cases of persecution that were left out because the victims were forced to compromise with their attackers by the police and the political establishment."

The CSF's 2013 report, which counted 4,000 offences against Christians in India, was used by Indian Christian groups in California to lobby for minority protection as one of the terms of reference for India-US talks.

Attacks on Community Members from 2012-2016 in States Where Anti-Christian Violence has been a Regular Feature

States	2012	2013	2014	2015
Karnataka	67	43	14	16
Madhya Pradesh	28	11	23	29
Tamil Nadu	25	10	5	12
Andhra Pradesh (AP & Telangana)	20	25	6	26
Chhattisgarh	20	13	19	21

Source: Catholic Secular Forum

Essay 48

INDIAN SOCIETY AT A CROSSROAD

Synopsis

Historical evidence has proved beyond doubt that Indian civilisation in ancient times was highly developed and technically more advanced than other contemporary civilisations in the rest of the world. The modern youth, under the influence of Western culture, have drifted away from familial ties. Initially, the deterioration was attributed to Western influence and foreign media; but, ironically, the Indian mass media has degenerated further than its foreign counterparts. There is a rise in juvenile offences; even the youth have taken to plunging themselves into unproductive habits. This has exposed them to indiscipline which in turn has contributed towards the spread of unrest in the society. Terrorism is patronised by some nations to meet its personal ends. Women, children and senior citizens in the country have been subjected to abuse and maltreatment. The country has been bogged down by corruption, nepotism and red-tapism. But the age of materialism has helped people break away from the age-old yoke of casteism. Western culture should not be viewed as an alternative to our own culture but only as a supplement.

Historical evidence has proved beyond doubt that Indian civilisation was highly developed and technically more advanced than other contemporary civilisations in the rest of the world, even before the advent of the Aryans. The Greeks, Huns, Turks, Afghans, Mughals and the others not only left an impact on our culture but also were themselves influenced by it. But the real dilemma started with the arrival of the British who came to rule over India with the primary objective of economic exploitation. The educated Indians were impressed by the British and hence, they adopted their lifestyle. This resulted in a cultural clash between the Indian and the Western ways of life, which continues to this day. Indians are traditionally a simple, hardworking peace-loving people. But the influence of Western culture is believed to have caused moral degeneration among them. It is also said to have given rise to a palpable *discontent*[1] and restlessness among the youth. Evidently, our culture and civilisation is under threat of being influenced by the powerful impact of Western values.

The modern youth under the influence of Western culture have drifted away from familial ties. They crave for independence, privacy and space. As a result, the traditional joint family system has given way to the nuclear family system. The generation gap between two successive generations has widened and they have started drifting away from each other. There has been a rapid rise in population and consumerism has come to drive the *populace*[2]. Unemployment is increasing rapidly as a result of which there is a simmering discontent in every sphere especially among the youth. The cost of living in cities has increased manifold as a result of which the husband is no longer the sole breadwinner; it has become imperative that the wife earns to share the responsibility of the household.

One of the major causes of the deterioration of Indian culture is the spread of Western culture through the media. With a large number of foreign satellite channels beaming programmes for the Asian countries, Indians are generously exposed to the Western culture. These channels propagate violence, vulgarity and *promiscuity*[3] in the name of entertainment and for the purpose of gaining wide viewership. Only a few programmes accord priority to the spread of knowledge and education. Aping the western media culture, without *discretion*[4], has led to the degeneration of the Indian mass media.

Indian film industry, which used to produce movies with social messages and providing wholesome and clean entertainment, now resorts to copying Hollywood movies and producing their Indianised versions for the Indian audience. In fact, the majority of the films made in India today are based on violence, gang-wars and smuggling, or else are woven around college romance and other *amorous*[5] themes.

The negative influence of the mass media has been witnessed across the country. *Juvenile*[6] offences are on the rise, and universities and colleges have become training grounds for crimes and gang fights. Students indulge in drug abuse and premarital sex as a result of which there has been a rapid rise in teenage pregnancies, AIDS and other sexually transmitted diseases. Most of the modern youth do not have any concern for morality or respect for Indian traditional values.

According to an estimate, 55 per cent of the suicides committed in India are by people below the age of 30 years. Unable to cope with or live up to the expectations of their loved ones, the youth end their lives. *Nepotism*[7] and corruption are the other ailments of our society which disillusion people, especially the youth. The wave of frauds and scams at the highest political and bureaucratic levels have exposed the hollowness of our entire system. The acquisition of a degree does not guarantee them jobs. Recommendation by some higher-up, or bribery, enables incompetent people to secure jobs which causes frustration among the meritorious youth.

The *deplorable*[8] condition of the youth has made them vulnerable to exploitation by politicians and antisocial elements. The *disgruntled*[9] youth thus contribute towards the spread of unrest in the society. Communal disharmony has been on the rise in the whole country. Several committees and commissions have been set up to enquire into the various incidents of violence and communal tensions. They have reported that the growing nexus between politicians and criminals is the reason behind the incidents of communal violence.

Irrespective[10] of religion, caste, or creed; people in general lived in peace in the previous era. Since the advent of terrorism, mindless killing of innocent people got the sanction of some religious fanatics and even some *rogue*[11] nations. They train and manufacture terrorists to *annihilate*[12] their adversaries. In order to inject validity into their act of violence, the terrorist groups give a religious colour to it and call it a crusade – a war to save one's own religion. The most heart-rending fact about it is that these agents of terror make no *discrimination*[13] whatsoever among children, women and elderly; they kill one and all.

Women, children and senior citizens are three of the most vulnerable sections of Indian society. A woman's contribution towards home-making is invariably ignored at home, while at the workplace, she is often subjected to sexual harassment. Various factors have contributed towards the increase in the number of incidents of eve-teasing, molestation and physical assaults on women. Minors have also been subjected to molestation and abuse. In most cases, it has been found, that persons known to the children have been the perpetrators of such assaults. The senior citizens, especially those who, thanks to their own family are *condemned*[14] to reside alone have been fatally attacked in many parts of the country.

The country has made rapid strides in every field but it has been bogged down by corruption, nepotism, *red-tapism*[15] and bribery. The politicians mobilise public support on caste and communal lines. All this has often resulted in fractured verdicts by the masses. This phenomenon has had an adverse effect on the quality of governance.

Every generation has passed through a transitional phase. Change is always on. However, what has happened in the last thirty years is that the pace of change has increased. When a country treads on the path of development, traditional thinking gives way to progressive thinking, with which the old generation finds difficult to adjust.

We have to accept that with the spread of education, the traditional values will have to change. The modern educated Indian is more liberated, better off financially, has a healthy outlook on life and understands the world better. The educated Indian woman does not want to remain confined to the four walls of the house only to bear and rear children. She has entered all professional fields in a remarkable way. Over 100 women are members of parliament and about the same number occupy ministerial positions in the union and state governments.

Sex education is being imparted in many educational institutions. The Supreme Court of India has put a stamp of legitimacy on couples who live together even without having got married. However, women empowerment in India has a long way to go. The condition of uneducated women in rural parts of the country has not improved significantly. child labour, child abuse, rapes and dowry deaths are fairly common.

India has contributed a large number of highly qualified scientists, doctors, engineers and financial wizards to the developed world. Indian business houses and industrialists have acquired many firms abroad. Indian names find prominent places among the richest business magnates of the world.

With liberalisation, foreign companies have entered the Indian market which has led to better employment opportunities and availability of high quality products. We should view. Western culture with *discernment*[15] and adopt only what is good in it. It does not differentiate between the two genders, rather shows respect towards the fair sex. The role played by foreign TV channels in increasing our awareness about the world around us, cannot be overlooked.

In general, the Western world has progressed a lot and this has made us look up to them as our ideals. However, we can only hope that our country, right now at a crossroads, will choose a 'middle path' which would be paved with the dual bricks of traditional Indian values and modern Western virtues. Western culture should not be viewed as an alternative to our own culture but only as a supplement.

We should learn to imbibe the best out of all cultures and assimilate it into the global society we live in. The Western world has a lot to offer in terms of cleanliness and responsibility towards the community as a whole. These countries boast of clean streets, pollution free environs, traffic discipline—things which were quite unheard of until recently in our country. As a matter of fact, it would not be impossible to achieve such ends with the active cooperation of the general public.

We Indians are extremely adept at preserving social values; and, even today, in spite of all the Western influence Indians are extremely family oriented. The family acts as a buffer during times of stress and strain, easily pulling us through difficult situations. Westerners value our ethical and moral values. They come here in quest of peace. We should strive to preserve these values and add to them the Western virtues of public commitment, professionalism, transparency in administration, etc. Gandhiji's words show us the right path to follow—"I do not want my house to be closed by walls on all sides and windows to be stuffed. Rather, I want all the cultures to blow freely through my house. But I do not want to be swept off my feet by any of them."

Aid to Vocabulary

1. *Discontent* — dissatisfaction
2. *Populace* — the people living in a country
3. *Promiscuity* — the state of being indiscriminate especially in sex
4. *Discretion* — the ability to make sound judgement
5. *Amorous* — openly showing or feeling love
6. *Juvenile* — of minors, young, youthful
7. *Nepotism* — unfair practice of favouritism shown to relatives by a person in power or office
8. *Deplorable* — miserable
9. *Disgruntled* — discontented
10. *Irrespective* — regardless of
11. *Rogue* — different from, and harmful to, others
12. *Annihilate* — to destroy completely
13. *Discrimination* — distinction
14. *Condemned* — doomed, punished
15. *Red-tapism* — the state of following rigid or excessive procedures causing delay or inaction especially in public offices
16. *Discernment* — the ability to make good judgement

Points to Remember

1. Ancient Indian civilisation was more developed than other contemporary civilisations in the rest of the world.
2. The modern youth have drifted away from familial ties.
3. The deterioration of the Indian society has been attributed to the Western influence and the foreign media.
4. Our film industry has also deteriorated.
5. There has been a rise in juvenile offences.
6. The deplorable condition of the youth has made them vulnerable to exploitation by politicians and anti-social elements.
7. Women, children and senior citizens are three of the most vulnerable sections of the society.
8. The modern Indian men and women are more liberated, better off financially and have a healthy outlook on life.
9. We should adopt the features of Western culture with discernment.

Essay
49

SUPERSTITIONS

SYNOPSIS

Superstition is irrational fear of the unknown and mysterious which gives rise to peculiar beliefs and actions. It is a worldwide phenomenon. It has come down to us from ancient times. Superstitions originated when man was helpless before nature. The element of fear and lack of scientific knowledge gave rise to superstitions. They are more deep-rooted in India than in most other countries. Some superstitions pertain to ill-luck and danger while others, to luck and happiness. Superstitions sometimes lead to horrifying crimes like child sacrifices and burning of women who are believed to be witches. One should follow a belief only if it has a logical and a scientific reasoning behind it.

Superstition is the irrational fear of what is unknown and mysterious. It is the belief that a certain event brings good or bad luck which cannot be explained by reason or science. In short, superstition means blind belief. Superstition is a worldwide phenomenon. People in every country believe in and practise one or the other superstition.

Superstitions have come down to us from ancient times. Primitive people were ignorant of the wonders of science. They were at the mercy of the forces of nature. They did not understand the causes of physical changes taking place around them. They respected and worshipped the forces of nature like the sun, the moon, fire, wind, water, storms, etc. They believed that diseases were caused by the *wrath*[1] of gods as well as evil spirits. They tried to satisfy the gods with offerings, prayers, sacrifices, etc. They tried to *ward off*[2] evil spirits by offering sacrifices. Sacrifice of birds and animals to please the gods and goddesses and to *atone*[3] for one's sins is a common practice. Thus, it is fear which gave rise to superstitions.

Encyclopedia Britannica classifies superstitions into three categories—religious, cultural and personal. Most of the religious superstitions originate as a set of peripheral beliefs often closely associated with particular religious practices. Fear of omens, foretelling future, being wary of an evil eye are a part of our culture. Beliefs that wearing a particular colour or writing with a particular pen will bring good luck are examples of personal superstitions.

There are certain common superstitions which are shared by all the people in the world. Belief in spirits, ghosts and witches; the belief that the cries of certain birds like owls and ravens and the mewing of cats are *ominous*[4] are superstitions believed in by people all over the globe. It is also a common superstition that when comets are seen, they *portend*[5] the death of great men.

People in the West still regard '13' as an unlucky number because at the Last Supper, Lord Jesus dined with his twelve disciples and was subsequently *crucified*[6]. Salt was spilled on the table on which they dined and, therefore, even now spilling of salt is considered as unlucky. They consider Friday as an *inauspicious*[7] day to start a new work for the crucifixion was carried out on a Friday. They also believe that going under a ladder brings ill-luck.

India is home to a number of superstitions. If a black cat crosses one's path, or, if someone sneezes, interrupts or calls while one is going out—they are all considered to be bad omens. The hooting of an owl and the howling of a dog are considered to be signs of death or danger. Chickenpox is considered to be the manifestation of the anger of a goddess. So, the goddess is *appeased*[8] with offerings. To ward off evil spirits, people, hang an earthen pot with an ugly face painted on it on the *facade*[9] of their house. Owners of new vehicles hang women's *braids*[10] at the back of their vehicles to ward off the evil eye. The sight of a peacock before the start of a journey is thought to bring good luck. The fall of a lizard on one's body is supposed to bring bad luck. Three lizards moving towards someone signifies his/her marriage whereas four of them approaching someone symbolizes death. Sweeping the floor at night, looking into a broken mirror, trimming nails, hair or beard on Tuesday, Thursday or Saturday, plucking leaves or flowers from a plant at night are supposed to yield bad luck. Banyan and peepal trees are believed to be the haven of ghosts, spirits, witches, etc. Lemon and chilli totem, and a mother *apparitions*[11], putting a kohl mark on her baby's forehead are some of the superstitions of warding off an evil eye.

Certain hours and days are considered inauspicious. People consult astrologers and priests to know the auspicious hours and days to start their work, projects or journey. Likewise, the time and date of marriage, inauguration, foundation-laying ceremonies, etc., are fixed according to the advice of astrologers and the position of the planets and stars.

Some superstitions are supposed to bring good luck or happiness. People believe that meeting a Shudra on one's way for some work brings success. If one finds a horse-shoe and brings it home it could bring luck to the finder and the family.

Superstitions can sometimes lead to horrifying crimes. Child sacrifices have been made to please gods. Women, who were suspected of practising witchcraft were tied and burnt alive. Joan of Arc was burnt to death because she was regarded by the Englishmen as a witch.

Experiments are on to find out whether man has a soul, which leaves him when he dies. People are said to have confronted ghosts and apparitions. But it remains to be proved whether ghosts do exist, and possess the power they are supposed to have, or not. In some cases, there are scientific reasons behind the superstition. For example, dogs are very sensitive to changes around them. They become restless before the onset of a natural calamity and hence, they wail to inform their masters of the approaching danger. In South India, people apply sandalwood paste on their foreheads for good fortune. There is also a scientific reasoning behind it. Sandalwood keeps the forehead cool.

The common matters or actions of day-to-day life should not be looked at with a superstitious angle. There is nothing wrong in sneezing. One can sneeze at any time of the day. So, if it happens when one is about to go out, one should not take it as a bad omen. Similarly, when one goes out, it is very natural to ask where he is going. A black cat crossing one's path near one's home means that one should check one's kitchen instead of worrying about what may happen in the future.

The world today is governed by science. Science has made life easy and man has advanced a lot. Superstitions have no application in today's life. So, there is no point in continuing with the superstitions that were passed on to us by our ancestors. We should follow only those ones which have a scientific and logical basis. A person believing in superstitions is always *haunted*[12] by unknown fears and anxieties and never gains self-confidence. Education and social awareness can wipe out superstitions to some extent. Parents should not encourage any kind of blind beliefs and superstitious practices at home. A scientific outlook and temper should be cultivated to do away with superstitions.

Aid to Vocabulary

1. *Wrath* — great anger
2. *Ward off* — prevent
3. *Atone* — to compensate
4. *Ominous* — unlucky, fateful
5. *Portend* — warn
6. *Crucified* — killed after being fastened with nails to a cross
7. *Inauspicious* — not lucky

8. *Appeased* — satisfied or pleased
9. *Facade* — the front of a building
10. *Braids* — threads of silk or cotton used for hair, etc.
11. *Apparition* — an image of a person who is dead
12. *Haunted* — frequented

Points to Remember

1. Superstition means blind belief.
2. Superstitions have come down to us from our ancestors.
3. The people of the west, who are more advanced than us, also believe in superstitions.
4. Superstitions are more deep-rooted in India than in any other country.
5. Some superstitions are supposed to bring good luck and happiness.
6. Superstitions can sometimes lead to horrifying crimes.
7. There are certain superstitions that have scientific reasoning behind them.
8. The common matters or actions of day-to-day life should not be influenced by superstitious beliefs.
9. Education as well as scientific outlook can help to wipe away superstitions.

IN THE GRIP OF SUPERSTITION

One of the most important aspects in uplifting quality of life in rural areas is addressing the evil of superstition. Many individuals have lost their life in brutal murders that took place on the suspicion that they were sorcerers and practitioners of black magic.

Fear is the main source of superstition, and also one of the main sources of cruelty, in the opinion of Bertrand Russell, a famous British philosopher and logician. "Yes, if this fear is conquered, there will hardly be any scope for superstition."

"The government should take up programmes in rural areas deploying cultural troupes to scientifically explain the reasons behind some of the unexplained phenomena."

Essay 50

OUR CULTURAL HERITAGE

SYNOPSIS

A safe and secure society is needed for the blossoming of arts and sciences. India has a rich cultural heritage. Though it has been subjected to a series of cultural invasions, it has retained its originality and traditional character even after absorbing the best of the external influences. India is home to one of the earliest civilisations of the world—the Indus Valley Civilisation. Tolerance of all faiths is a part of our cultural heritage. Co-existence of many religions seemingly different from one another contribute to the enrichment of our culture. The Indian paintings and sculptures have left their mark on different civilisations. Our ancestors excelled not only in philosophy but also in science. The Indian literary heritage is among the oldest in the world. Indian music and dance have made their mark on the cultural scenario. It encompasses a large body of poetry, drama and works on various arts and sciences written in many Indian languages. India should not fall prey to the ill-effects of western culture.

For thinking minds to blossom, for arts and sciences to develop, a primary condition, is a safe and secure society. A rich culture is impossible in a community of *nomads*[1] where people struggle for life. India has got all the gifts of nature. Nature yielded enough food and man did not have to toil very hard for meeting the basic needs.

Before we proceed further, let us understand what culture is. Culture is the storehouse of symbols, ideas and material products associated with a social system. In India, great civilisations and cultures have flourished from time immemorial. The diversity of India is tremendous. It is a land of many languages. It is home to many *ethnic*[2] groups. But there are certain common links which act as threads and effect unity among diversity. India has many great traditions.

Cultural heritage stands for things that have been passed on from earlier generations to the present generation. Of special significance are the works of literature, music and art in all its forms and shades. India has a rich cultural heritage. It is a healthy blend of various cultures.

The Indus Valley Civilisation is among the oldest (being about 6,000 years old) and the most developed civilisations of the world. The people were fairly advanced and had access to public baths, neat and clean houses, good towns with wide roads and other facilities. They even had a script which closely resembles those of the Dravidian languages.

The Vedas are the earliest documents of the human mind that the world possesses. The Vedas give us abundant information. There are four Vedas: *Rig, Yajur, Sama and Atharva*. In them, we find freshness, simplicity and charm and an effort to understand the mysteries of the world.

Ancient Indian epics, namely the *Ramayana* and the *Mahabharata* hold the *eternal*[3] lesson of victory of good over evil. The *Bhagvad Gita* is a book full of philosophical principles. Lord Buddha (563-483 B.C.) preached that perfect happiness could be gained if one exercised control over one's passions. Hinduism has a large number of gods and goddesses, besides the ten *incarnations*[4] of Lord Vishnu. It allows its followers to worship God in any form they like.

Guru Nanak Dev (1469-1539), the founder of Sikhism laid supreme stress on true faith, simplicity and purity of life and religious tolerance. Hinduism, Buddhism, Jainism, Christianity and Islam are among the major religions followed in India. Traditionally, tolerance of all faiths is a part of our cultural heritage. India is a secular country and the State treats all religions equally.

The four major religions of India—Hinduism, Islam, Christianity and Sikhism—co-exist without coming in the way of one another; rather complementing one another. While the main thrust of Hinduism is on the preservation of truth and non-violence, Islam emphasises honesty. Muslims are supposed to be people of high integrity who would never accept undue money from any malafide source; infact, attachment with one's own money is considered a sin in Islam. Christianity preaches forgiveness even to the 'Killer' whereas Sikhism lays emphasis on purity, of love and universality and on spreading the message of fraternity and brotherhood.

Indian paintings and sculpture left a deep impact on different civilisations. Rock caves in Hoshangabad, Mirzapur and Bhimbetka are witness to the paintings of primitive men. The paintings of the Ajanta caves are a rare piece of work. Many painters emerged during the British colonial rule. Amrita Shergill, Jamini Roy and Rabindranath Tagore were the *pioneers*[5] of modern painting. The Ashoka pillar, the Sanchi stupa, the temples at Konark, Khajuraho and Mahabalipuram are unique works of Indian sculpture. Jama Masjid, Red fort, Taj Mahal and Humayun's Tomb show a blend of Indian and Mughal architecture. All these marvels were created during the Mughal period of Indian History.

Astrology and astronomy were quite popular in ancient India. Aryabhatta precisely calculated the time of solar eclipse more than two thousand years ago. The concept of 'Zero' was invented in India. Indian scientists/ scientists of Indian origin like C.V. Raman, Subramanian Chandrashekhar, Hargobind Khorana and Venkataraman Ramakrishnan have won Nobel prizes for their contributions in the field of science.

Music is one of the oldest forms of expression of human thoughts and emotions. Indian music is based on the concept of *ragas* and *talas*. There are two major schools of classical music—the Carnatic and the Hindustani. Indian musicians like Bhimsen Joshi, M.S. Subhalakshmi, Kishori Amonkar, Pt. Jasraj, Ustad Amjad Ali Khan, Ustad Bismillah Khan, Ustad Zakir Hussain, Pt. Ravi Shankar and others have popularised our music in India and abroad.

Dance in India has an unbroken tradition of over 2000 years. Its themes are derived from mythology, legends and classical literature. There are two main forms of dance in India. These are folk dance and classical dance. The Indian style of dance is based on *rasa, bhava* and *abhinaya*. They are not just the movement of legs and arms, but of the whole body. Most of the classical dances were conceived and *nurtured*[6] in the temples. They attained their full *stature*[7] there. Classical dance forms are based on ancient dance discipline. Most of the Indian classical dance styles are depicted on the walls and pillars of famous Indian temples. There are five main classical dance forms namely, Bharatanatyam, Kathakali, Manipuri, Kathak and Odissi. Other prominent dances are Kuchipudi and Mohiniattam. Some well-known classical dancers are Sanjukta Panigrahi, Sonal Man singh, Birju Maharaj, Gopi Krishna, Guru Bipin Sinha, Javeri Sisters, Kelucharan Mahapatra, etc.

India has a rich literary heritage which includes regional literature. Regional literature in fact, has often contributed to the *fostering*[8] of a national identity and a national culture. India has always been a linguistically diverse community. Even in the ancient times, there was no common language which was spoken by all Indians.

Sanskrit was the language of the elite whereas Prakrit and Ardha Magadhi were commonly spoken by the masses. During the Mughal rule, Persian took the place of Sanskrit as the court language while Urdu and Hindustani were the languages of the common masses in North India. However, the Dravidian languages continued to flourish in the south.

Kalidasa's *Abhijnanam Shakuntalam* and *Meghdutam*, Vishakhadatta's *Mrichchhakatikam,* and Jaideva's *Geet Govindam* are rated very highly for their literary excellence. The period from mid-14th century to mid-17th century was dominated by the *Bhakti Kavyas* or devotional poetry. Kabir, Surdas and Tulsidas were famous poets of this era. The modern period of Hindi was ushered in by Bhartendu Harishchandra. Poets like Maithili Sharan Gupt, Jayashankar Prasad, Sumitra Nandan Pant, Surya Kant Tripathi 'Nirala', Munshi Premchand and Mahadevi Verma have made rich contribution to modern Hindi Literature. India has produced a number of literary marvels in English as well. These were Toru Dutt, Nissim Ezekiel, Sarojini Naidu, Michael Madhusudan Dutt, to name a few. Rabindranath Tagore won the Nobel prize for his collection of poems 'Geetanjali'.

It is true that India has a rich cultural heritage and that Indians have excelled in different spheres. However, it should also be acknowledged that we have inherited some negative aspects of our culture as well. Division of society on the basis of division of labour gave birth to the caste system. The caste system created a gulf among people leading to disunity and conflicts in the society. Child marriage, sati, untouchability, dowry, female infanticide and many other social evils were subsequently born in the Indian society. The widows in many parts of our country were condemned to a life of misery.

The philosophical thoughts of Raja Rammohan Roy, Dayanand Saraswati, Ramakrishna Paramahansa Dev, Swami Vivekananda, Rabindranath Tagore, Mahatma Gandhi and Jawaharlal Nehru have contributed a lot to eliminate the negative elements from Indian culture. Since independence, Indians have been keen on promoting their sense of national identity and cultural unity.

Culture is dynamic, cross currents of other cultures always influence the culture of a country. It is more so in the present day world, where boundaries virtually have ceased to exist. Let us keep our windows and doors open to other cultures and to their healthy influence, but we should stand steady and not be swept off our feet against its onslaught.

Aid to Vocabulary

1. *Nomads* — members of tribes that wander around
2. *Ethnic* — having a common national or cultural tradition
3. *Eternal* — existing always
4. *Incarnations* — living human forms
5. *Pioneers* — persons who were the first to study and develop a particular area of knowledge etc.
6. *Nurtured* — brought up with care

7. *Stature* — level of respect commanded
8. *Fostering* — encouraging, developing

Points to Remember

1. India has a rich and unique cultural heritage.
2. The Indus Valley civilisation is one of the earliest civilisations of the world.
3. Tolerance of all faiths is part of our cultural heritage.
4. India has a heritage of unique works of sculpture and painting.
5. The concept of 'Zero' originated in India.
6. Indian music is based on ragas and talas and Indian dance is based on rasa, bhava and abhinaya.
7. The Indian literary heritage is one of the oldest in the world.
8. Our culture also has its negative aspects in caste system, dowry, etc.
9. We should assimilate only the good points of western culture.

Essay

51

UNITY IN DIVERSITY

SYNOPSIS

India has absorbed different faiths, cults, beliefs, sects, religions, languages, manners, lifestyles, etc. Unity and synthesis are the charateristics of Indian culture. People of different cultures, and religions live together in India. True to the spirit of secularism, India makes no discrimination on the basis of caste, creed or sex. All religious festivals are celebrated together by people of different religious affiliations. India is a secular nation. It is clearly stated in the Preamble to our Constitution. When the British ruled India, people from different cultures, religions and regions of the country came together to oppose them. Such cohesion is conspicuous in times of crisis. Today certain anti-national forces are trying to disrupt the unity of the country. We should bury our differences and work unitedly against these evil forces.

India is a big country. Her civilisation is around 6000 years old. She has given birth to many important cultures and religions of the world. She has also accepted within her folds different cultures of the world. People of many races have come to India and settled here. She has absorbed different faiths, cults, beliefs, sects, religions, languages, manners, lifestyles, etc. Unity and synthesis are the characteristics of Indian culture.

India's fundamental unity rests upon her *peculiar*[1] diversity of culture. There is no single character or aspect that can be defined as culture. It is expressed through different kinds of language, literature, religion, philosophy, customs, traditions, beliefs, art and architecture. India has achieved cultural unity by fusion of many cultures. She has *assimilated*[2] the good qualities from all cultures. Various cultural groups co-exist in perfect harmony in India. this has made Indian society a multi-cultural society.

In India, people of different religions live together. Hence, she has a multi-religious society. Besides Hinduism, other religions like Christianity, Islam, Sikhism, Buddhism and Jainism have a large following in India. According to Census 2011, Hinduism is practised by 79.8 per cent of the people, there are 14.2 per cent Muslims, 2.3 per cent Christians, 1.7 per cent Sikhs, 0.7 per cent Buddhists and 0.4 per cent Jains. The rest of the people follow other religions.

Unlike many gulf and Arabian countries where Islam is the state religion because the majority of their population follows Islam, India *opted*[3] for secularism instead of being a Hindu country despite having almost 80 per cent Hindus in the country and she, therefore, makes no discrimination whatsoever in the name of faith, caste, creed, sect, religion or sex; she is sovereign, democratic and secular in her true spirit, mind and soul because the cultural heritage that she possesses is the *conglomeration*[4] of different religious, faiths and beliefs. Its unnecessary to add here that this unity is obvious in the way the Indians live in peace and harmony *encompassing*[5] one and all.

India is famous for the *fervour*[6] with which her people celebrate religious festivals. Hindu festivals like Diwali, Dussehra, Holi, etc., are celebrated all over the world. Muslims celebrate Eid. Christians celebrate Easter and Christmas. Sikhs celebrate Guru Nanak Jayanti. Buddha Purnima and Mahavira Jayanti are celebrated by the Buddhists and the Jains respectively. During these festivals all people exchange greetings, forgetting their religious *affiliations*[7]. That India is a secular nation is clearly stated in the Preamble to our Constitution.

We find a heartening streak of emotional unity in our country. The very name of our country India brings us emotionally close. We may be in any part of the world but we will always be called Indians, no matter what religion we follow and what region we belong to. India's diversity has always been recognised as a source of its strength. When the British ruled India, women and men from different cultural, religious and regional backgrounds came together to oppose them. India's freedom movement had thousands of people of different backgrounds taking part in it. In his book 'The Discovery of India' Jawaharlal Nehru says that Indian unity is not something imposed from outside but rather it is something *ingrained*[8] in the people. Commendable tolerance of beliefs, customs, rites and rituals, is practised here and every variety, appreciated and encouraged.

Independent India inherited a conservative community which followed the rigidities of the caste system and had diverse religions. The Indian Constitution gave paramount importance to secularism in order that society was free from any discrimination. It declared that there would be no state religion in India. The State would neither establish a religion of its own nor confer any special patronage upon any particular religion. The Indian concept of secularism is founded on its traditional principle as *Sarva Dharma Samabhava*.

The Indian civilisation has always been based on religious and moral values. Herein lies its unity and strength. In all parts of the country, cultural unity, as well as the unity of way of life transcends the vast diversity in faiths and beliefs—at times bordering on superstition, magic, charms and other practices. One may travel from one part of the country to any other, one will invariably recognise a common, familiar trait in some aspect of life which will make one feel at home. This is because Indian culture has preserved its fundamental character through the ages. We have experienced revolutionary economic and political changes in recent times yet our past remains very much with us. Our rich cultural heritage, as it passed from one generation to another, has only got nurtured and renewed.

Indian culture has remained alive and dynamic because it has always been tolerant of different cultures. It imbibed the good qualities of other cultures and constantly upgraded itself. Influence of various cultures has made it rich and vibrant. Significant contributions have been made to it by the Dravidians, Aryans, Greeks, Persians, Arabs, Mughals and Europeans. The Persian and western influences on our art, literature, painting and dress have now become an integral part of our own culture.

Despite diverse languages, cultures, dresses, beliefs, religions, sects, caste and backgrounds, the people of India live and work in perfect harmony to uplift the nation to a higher level. Our togetherness, indicative of our strong bond is unparalleled when any untoward incident takes place in the country. The entire nation *condemns*[9] that and protests in *unison*[10]. Against one such pathetic incident of intolerance, many *litterateurs*[11] of India surrendered their awards and titles conferred on them in recognition of their works of art.

At times, we have witnessed conflicts and disturbances. Certain anti-national and external forces try to *disrupt*[12] the unity of the country by inciting communal feelings and sentiments. The demolition of Babri Masjid, Mumbai blasts, 1984 riots, Gujarat riots of 2002, blasts in the capital of the country, terror attack in Mumbai, etc., resulted in the loss of thousands of lives. The militancy problem in Jammu and Kashmir and *insurgency*[13] in the North-east have further weakened the secular fabric of India. Terrorism should not be allowed to raise its ugly head or destroy our basic unity. We can overcome these problems if we bury our differences and work unitedly for the unity and integrity of the country.

In recent times, there has been a cultural awakening of the educated youth who have become aware of the beauty of our art forms and crafts. They have started taking interest in educating themselves about their rich cultural traditions. The government has also started organising big cultural events to promote national integration. It has set up four regional cultural centres in different parts of the country. Now National Youth Festivals are celebrated from 8th to 12th January every year. This is a major activity under the programme of National Integration Camp (NIC). The idea behind this Youth Festival is to organise a gathering of the youth so that the concept of National Integration, and spirit of communal harmony, brotherhood, courage and adventure may be propagated. It is an effort from the government to strengthen the common bond of unity that ties the people together in spite of the diversity in their religions and beliefs.

The heart of India is one. We have inherited a common and rich culture. We should *strive*[14] to achieve and maintain the ideal state of common brotherhood. We should all *carry the torch*[15] for unity irrespective of our different faiths and creeds.

Aid to Vocabulary

1. *Peculiar* — strange or unusual
2. *Assimilated* — to fully understand an idea or some information
3. *Opted* — chose
4. *Conglomeration* — collection of heterogenous elements
5. *Encompassing* — to embracing
6. *Fervour* — enthusiasm, passion
7. *Affiliations* — connections with a religion or political party
8. *Ingrained* — rooted deeply
9. *Condemns* — to reproaches
10. *Unison* — agreement, concord
11. *Litterateurs* — men of letters
12. *Disrupt* — interrupt continuity of something
13. *Insurgency* — rebellion
14. *Strive* — to try hard to achieve something
15. *Carry the torch* — crusade

Points to Remember

1. Unity and synthesis are the characteristics of Indian culture.
2. India has achieved cultural unity by fusion of many cultures.
3. Customs, traditions and beliefs associated with all religions promote tolerance and brotherhood.
4. The Constitution declares that there would be no State religion in India.
5. Our rich cultural heritage has passed from one generation to another.
6. Indian culture has remained alive and dynamic.
7. India's diversity has always been recognised as a source of its strength.
8. India's freedom movement had thousands of people of different backgrounds taking part in it.
9. At times, we face regional and religious conflicts.
10. We should strive to achieve and maintain the ideal state of common brotherhood.

Essay

52 NATIONAL INTEGRATION

SYNOPSIS

India is the land where the followers of different religions have co-existed peacefully. The British gained control over us because we were divided by narrow considerations. The Revolt of 1857, though unsuccessful, was able to give a jolt to the British. They realised that Indians, if united, would overpower them. So, they adopted the policy of 'Divide and Rule', which culminated in the partition of India in 1947. Political integration of the country was engineered by Sardar Patel. Emotional integration was facilitated through the Constitution of India. Communal forces are still at play so as to disintegrate the country. We should emerge from the narrow walls that separate us and must build a united India.

India is a land, where followers of different religions co-exist in harmony. India has demonstrated to the world its unique capacity for accepting and embracing people of every religion into its fold. And that precisely is the reason why India has emerged *unscathed*[1] through every crisis and has made history to reach the present age. The subject of 'National Integration', is debated in every school and college and has become a national topic. But we should *delve*[2] into the history of India to find the reasons for our present plight.

In 1757, the British annexed Bengal after defeating Siraj-ud-Daula, the *Nawab* of Bengal, at the Battle of Plassey. Then, started the *tyrannical*[3] rule of the British which lasted for about 200 years. In fact, the British could easily conquer India because the Indians were divided amongst themselves by narrow considerations. Soon the exploitation of the Indians began. The opposition to all these at one stage culminated in the Revolt of 1857 in which the Indians fought unitedly against the British. The Revolt, however, was unsuccessful in shaking off the yoke of British rule. But one concrete picture emerged from the revolt—that the Indians were not communal and different communities could fight unitedly against the foreign rule. The British felt threatened. In an attempt to create disharmony amongst the Indians, they *propounded*[4] the policy of 'Divide and Rule'. This sowed the seeds of distrust and intolerance among Indians which eventually resulted in the partition of India in 1947.

The joy of gaining Independence was overshadowed by the partition of India and the *carnage*[5] that it set off.

Because of these events, the Indians became acutely aware of the significance of national integration. Integration, at the very outset, was political in nature. The integration of the princely states with the Indian Union was successfully engineered by Sardar Vallabh Bhai Patel. The next step towards integration was emotional in nature as it provided for a continual process of social engineering encompassing every aspect of Indian society—and it was done by means of the Constitution.

The Constitution of India aids in the unifying process by declaring India as a Secular Democracy. The citizens of India have been given the freedom to practise any religion or culture. This is a giant step to ensure national integration in this multireligious, multicultural and multilinguistic country. Though there have been efforts to introduce Hindi as the national language, Hindi has not been imposed on states that do not want to use it. Through the medium of cinema, radio and television we are being taught to pride ourselves on our unity in diversity and to keep it alive and kicking.

Apart from religious and emotional integration, the government has also taken steps to ensure economic integration to some extent. A certain percentage of seats in the employment, education and administrative sectors have been reserved for the underprivileged sections of the society so as to integrate them into the mainstream.

Sardar Patel's legacy of political integration has been seriously undermined in the twenty-first century. More and more states are being carved out as a result of ongoing people's agitations often stoked by politicians with vested interests. After Jharkhand, Chhattisgarh and Uttarakhand, now Telangana has been created. Gorkhaland and Bodoland will probably be the next—it is only a matter of time. However, the heartening fact is that the intention is not to secede from the Indian Union. It is only an appeal to the Parliament for exclusive attention.

National integration is always a difficult end to achieve in a country which is as multi-ethnic, multicultural and multilingual as India. Apart from these, India also has a sizeable population that is not literate. The growing influences of communalism, casteism, *linguistic chauvinism*[6] and other such divisive tendencies are threatening the integrity of the nation. Casteism has become one of the major policy determinants in India. The 'Mandalisation' of Indian politics opened up avenues for a number of leaders who are opportunistic and narrow-minded. Political parties are formed and elections are fought on the basis of caste affiliations. Needless to say, this is a major threat to the integrity of India.

Communalism is also alarmingly on the rise. Divisive elements within the society including several political leaders are playing communal cards to maximise their gains while the country suffers the consequences. The Ayodhya issue was a major blow to the secular credentials of India. The bomb blasts and the ensuing riots in Mumbai happened as a fallout of the Ayodhya incident. In 2002, the ugly face of communalism was witnessed again when Godhra massacre and the resultant Gujarat riots happened. Thousands were killed and massive internal displacements took place. Such incidents seriously hamper all attempts towards national integration. Jammu and Kashmir and various states in the North-East especially Nagaland are also facing serious crisis. Pakistan is actively *sponsoring*[7] terrorist activities in Kashmir with the intention of wresting control of the region by proxy war. However, India has successfully repulsed these attacks. In the North-East, there are several insurgent groups involved in terrorist activities calling for secession from the Indian Union. The ominous fallout in Asom, triggered by a doctored *inflammatory*[8] MMS was one of the several other flare-ups in the past. The armed naxal groups active in Andhra Pradesh, Bihar, Jharkhand, West Bengal, Madhya Pradesh and Chhattisgarh are also a threat to national unity.

The country cannot afford to give in to the demands of the *secessionist*[9] groups. The militants, on their part, resort to killing innocent civilians to pressurise the government. The successive governments that have come at the Centre have failed to meet the requirements of the people. They have failed to understand and analyse the problems of the natives of a region in turmoil. This is perhaps the reason for the growing unrest across the country. The country has test-fired bombs and missiles, that could be used for defence in case of external threat. But, the threat of disintegration within the country is yet to be resolved. The intolerance among the disgruntled sections of the Indian population is only growing.

The Nagaland Peace Accord signed on August 3, 2015 by the government of India with NSCN (IM) the largest of the Naga insurgent groups in the presence of other Naga Leaders is an attempt to silence India's longest running insurgency in the North-East. Infiltration from Bangladesh that was cause for some instability in the country was tackled with the swapping of adversely-held boundary enclaves between India and Bangladesh under the Land Boundary Agreement on June 6, 2015 which also demarcates the international border between the two countries clearly. However, there are several groups active in the country that unleash violence from time to time to draw attention to their various demands.

There is a dire need for emotional integration in the country. People should emerge from the narrow walls that divide them. Even after more than six decades of Independence, if we continue to fight amongst ourselves, we would hardly be able to fight a foreign aggression, if it were to happen. The British could rule over us only by *capitalising*[10] our many internal differences. We should realise the threat and wake up to the cause of national integration. We must emerge from the *realms*[11] of intolerance and indifference. We have to prove to the world that India can remain united, being an *amalgamation*[12] of diverse cultures, traditions and faiths.

AID TO VOCABULARY

1. *Unscathed* — uninjured, unharmed
2. *Delve* — to search deeply
3. *Tyrannical* — cruel and unjust
4. *Propounded* — put forward
5. *Carnage* — massacre
6. *Linguistic chauvinism* — considering one's own language superior to those of others
7. *Sponsoring* — backing, patronising
8. *Inflammatory* — provoking strong reactions
9. *Secessionist* — seeking withdrawal (from Union of India)
10. *Capitalising* — using to one's advantage
11. *Realms* — regions
12. *Amalgamation* — combination

POINTS TO REMEMBER

1. India is a land of harmony that has been struck from time to time by agents of disharmony.
2. Intolerance was brought about by the 'Divide and Rule' policy of the British.
3. National integration is a difficult end to achieve in India.
4. Communal riots occur in different parts of India.
5. The Government should scrutinise the problems and take necessary steps to restore harmony.
6. Emotional integration is the need of the hour.

Essay 53

INDIAN FESTIVALS

SYNOPSIS

A festival is a celebration of life. Festivals bring peace and joy to the masses. They break the monotony of life. Indian festivals are numerous. They are of three types—national, religious and seasonal. The first type of festivals, i.e., national festivals are celebrated with great patriotic fervour. The second type of festivals depict the religious association of the people. The third one marks the change of seasons. The people celebrate their faith or seasonal change with gaiety and enthusiasm. The national festivals include Republic Day, Independence Day, Gandhi Jayanti, etc. The religious festivals of India include Guru Parav, Holi, Lohri, Buddha Purnima, Mahavir Jayanti, Dussehra, Diwali, Janmastami, Chhath, Navaratri, Eid, Christmas, Hanukkah, Nauroz etc. The seasonal festivals include Bihu, Baisakhi, Onam, Pongal, Basant Panchami, Makar Sankranti etc. Festivals may also have a negative influence on the society if not observed in the true spirit. Festivals should be celebrated with simplicity. They should be celebrated to promote national integration and communal harmony.

Elimination of monotony and infusion of joy mark almost all the festivals celebrated across the world. All in general and children in particular are *enthused*[1] *enormously*[2] in these celebrations. They look forward to festivals with curiosity and excitement for it offers them an opportunity to do something new. They wear new dresses, decorate their houses and surroundings and celebrate festivals with much *fanfare*[3].

A festival is a celebration of life. It is a celebration, entertainment or series of performances of a certain kind, often held periodically. Festivals break the *monotony*[4] of life. They bring peace and joy to the masses. All nations have their religious and cultural festivals.

Indian festivals are numerous. They are as varied as the people themselves. They are harmonious, rich, and colourful. They can be divided into three broad categories—national or political, religious and seasonal. Most Indian festivals have their origin either in religion or in myths and legends of popular faiths. Some are connected with the memory of very respectable men and events. They are intended to keep alive the memory of those events and personalities, and hence, they inspire people to follow their examples. Then there are festivals which are associated with the seasons of the year.

National festivals, namely the Republic Day, the Independence Day, Gandhi Jayanti, etc., are celebrated with great patriotic zeal. These days have been declared as national holidays and are celebrated in all parts of the country with a lot of enthusiasm and fervour . The capital, New Delhi, is the seat of national celebrations on such occasions. It witnesses one of the most majestic parades on the Republic Day. Apart from the Armed Forces, school children from across the country also participate actively in this parade. The states of India exhibit on *tableaux*[5] their distinctive features, resources and recent achievements. The parade is also an occasion to display India's military strength, and a number of arms, ammunitions, tanks and fighter aircrafts. On Gandhi Jayanti, leaders and people from different walks of life pay their homage to the Father of the Nation. On the Independence Day, the Prime Minister of the country unfurls the national flag and addresses the nation from the ramparts of the historic Red Fort.

The religious festivals of India include Durga Pooja, Dussehra, Diwali, Janmastami, Shivratri, Guru Parav, Ram Navami, Holi, Chhath, Navaratri, Eid-ul-zuha, Eid-ul-fitr, Christmas, Buddha Purnima, Mahavir Jayanti, Nauroz (a festival of the Parsees) and Hanukkah (a festival of the Jews).

Diwali is the most prominent of the Hindu festivals. It is the festival of lights. On this day, the Hindus celebrate the return of Lord Rama to Ayodhya after his victory over the demon king, Ravana. The houses are cleaned and whitewashed for the festival. On this day, people from all walks of life wear new clothes, light up their homes, and worship goddess Lakshmi. Businessmen start their new accounts. A variety of sweets are prepared, *relished*[6] and gifted to one another. Crackers are burst and the children as well as the youth enjoy them.

Ram Navami is celebrated as the birthday of Lord Rama. Janmastami is celebrated as the birthday of Lord Krishna. Durga Pooja is celebrated in Bengal, Assam, Odisha and some other parts of India, with great pomp and show. Goddess Durga is worshipped for nine days. On the tenth day, Vijayadashmi, the statue of the goddess is immersed in a water body. In Northern India, Dussehra is observed on the Vijayadashmi day, celebrating the victory of good over evil, of Rama over Ravana. In Maharashtra, Lord Ganesha is worshipped with great pomp and show during the ten-day long Ganesha Chaturthi festival.

Holi is celebrated at the end of the winter season. 'Raaslila', a cultural dance of Manipur is staged during this festival. The dance is dedicated to Lord Krishna and the *gopis*[7]. Holi is a festival of colours. People shower colour on one another. Holi is celebrated in honour of Prahlad, Lord Vishnu's protege whom the Lord saved, when his father and the Lord's *antagonist*[8], Hiranyakashipu, schemed to burn him on a pyre. It celebrates the victory of good over evil.

Chhath is celebrated mainly in Bihar and also in other parts of India. Sun-god is worshipped at sunset and again on the following sunrise with fruits, etc., as *arghya* (offering).

Eid is celebrated to mark the end of Ramzan. It was during the month of Ramzan that the Holy Quran was revealed to Prophet Mohammed. The Muslims fast during the month of Ramzan. At the end of the month, Eid is celebrated with feasts.

Guru nanak Dev's birthday is celebrated by the sikhs and members of other communities. On this occasion, religious *congregations*[9] are attended, lamps are lit and crackers are burst. The days of *martyrdom*[10] of Guru Arjun Dev and Guru Teg Bahadur are also of special significance to the community. These days are observed as days of peace and harmony, and langar sewa (serving of free food) is organised on a very large scale on these days. Buddhists and Jains celebrate their religious festivals Buddha Purnima and Mahavir Jayanti, respectively, with great devotion.

Christmas is the most important festival of the Christians. It is celebrated as the birthday of Lord Jesus Christ on 25th December. The Christmas tree is decorated with artificial stars, lights, toys, etc., on this day. Cakes and puddings are served. Children are dressed in new clothes. A person disguised as Santa Claus distributes sweets among children. Prayers are offered in churches.

Jews celebrate their festivals in a similar fashion as those of Christians. They go to the *synagogue*[11] to pray before the Almighty. The Jews in Kerala celebrate Hanukkah, the birthday of the Greek god Zeus, with great religious fervour. The Parsees celebrate Nauroz during August-September each year. It is the beginning of their new year.

The seasonal festivals are celebrated in different ways all over the country. Bihu is celebrated with great *fervour*[12] in Asom. Baisakhi is celebrated as a mark of harvesting the wheat crops in Punjab. Onam is celebrated in Kerala as a harvest festival. Pongal is also a similar festival celebrated in Tamil Nadu. Basant Panchami is celebrated throughout North India and West Bengal. It marks the end of the winter season. Seasonal changes mark a new beginning. Happiness fills the heart of the people during these festivals.

Since every festival in India has a political, religious or mythological[13] background, children get ample opportunity to learn from them. When they celebrate a national festival, they learn about the freedom movement of India and thus, *patriotism*[14] is infused in them. So is the case with celebrating a religious festival. Most of them celebrate the victory of good over evil. Thus, the lesson learnt is that the truth prevails ultimately. Again, when they celebrate a festival which marks the advent/end of a season, they learn the name of a Hindi month. Festivals, thus, help them to know about their motherland as well as Nature more explicitly.

Festivals may also have a negative influence on our society if we do not celebrate them in the right spirit. The bursting of crackers during Diwali pollutes the atmosphere severely. Gambling disturbs public as well as family life. During Holi, drunkards engage in *brawls*[15] in the streets. Temples are decorated with expenditures running into millions of rupees that could be better utilised in feeding the hungry or for the economic development of the country.

Colour is the essential theme of Holi. But it must neither be sprayed on people who resent it nor be used to settle scores with opponents. The bursting of crackers should be reduced to a minimum. Festivals should be celebrated with simplicity and in a peaceful manner. People belonging to other communities should be invited during religious festivals. This will help in promoting national integration and communal harmony.

AID TO VOCABULARY

1. *Enthused* — to entertain, to make happy
2. *Enormously* — greatly
3. *Fanfare* — lot of excitement and activity
4. *Monotony* — constant and boring, dull and never changing or varying
5. *Tableaux* — picturesque presentation
6. *Relished* — savoured , enjoyed
7. *Gopis* — milkwomen with whom Lord Krishna spent time in his native place
8. *Antagonist* — adversary, enemy
9. *Congregations* — groups of people who gather in a religious place
10. *Martyrdom* — the state of being a martyr. *Martyr*: a person who is put to death for refusing to give up a belief or faith
11. *Synagogue* — a building where Jews meet for religious worship and teaching
12. *Fervour* — passion
13. *Mythological* — related to religion

14. *Patriotism* — love for the nation
15. *Brawls* — rough or noisy fights in a public place

Points to Remember

1. Festivals break the monotony of life.
2. Indian festivals are of three types—national, religious and seasonal.
3. The major national festivals of India are the Republic day, the Independence day and Gandhi Jayanti.
4. The religious festivals of India include Durga Pooja, Dussehra, Diwali, Ram Navami, Guru Parav, Chhath, Eid, Christmas, etc.
5. The seasonal festivals include Bihu, Baisakhi, Onam, Pongal, Makar Sakranti, Basant Panchami, etc.
6. Festivals may have a negative influence on the society if not celebrated in the right spirit.
7. Festivals should be celebrated to promote national integration and communal harmony.

Essay 54

RURAL DEVELOPMENT IN INDIA

SYNOPSIS

It is often said that India lives in its villages. The rural areas are characterised by prevalence of large-scale poverty and absence of social reforms. After Independence, the issue of rural empowerment was ignored. The Community Development Programme, which was launched in 1952, had failed and subsequently Panchayati Raj Institutions were set up. Ineffective implementation of rural development programmes led to several socio-economic disabilities like illiteracy, child labour, exploitation of women, etc. There is a mismatch between the country's growth and resources allocated for rural development. The Panchayati Raj Institutions were given constitutional status in December 1992. The need was felt to empower the rural folk for the effective democratisation of the country. Several schemes were introduced for the welfare of the villagers. IRDP was conceived to provide self-employment opportunities to the rural poor. Land reforms were undertaken. The budgets proposed several new schemes to strengthen rural infrastructure. The rural sector badly needs infrastructural development. The government should take necessary steps to achieve the objectives of rural development. According to UNDP, the widening income inequalities must be curbed.

It is often said that India lives in its villages. The rural areas are characterised by large-scale poverty, low levels of productivity, lack of adequate basic services and social reforms. The United Nations Development Programme (UNDP) report, has ranked India at 135 among 187 countries of the world in terms of successful implementation of social reforms. The report exposes lack of literacy, primary education and women's participation in politics, apart from high infant mortality ratio and high population growth rate in the rural sector. The reason attributed to India's failure in achieving the desired objectives pertains to the lack of appropriate orientation of her rural development programmes. Lack of *infrastructure*[1] as well as basic services have led to the *exodus*[2] of rural population from villages to cities. Several policies were formulated to *ameliorate*[3] the plight of the masses but they failed to *percolate*[4] among them and alleviate their misery.

Mahatma Gandhi desired to establish in independent India panchayats, which would function as democratic 'little republics' for the self-sustenance of the rural areas. He had said "Indian independence must begin at the bottom. ... Panchayats having full powers—every village has to be self-sustained and capable of managing its own affairs." However, after Independence, the issue of rural empowerment was ignored. In 1952, the Community Development Programme was launched to seek people's participation as well as their involvement in the task of rural reconstruction but it failed in its mission. Absence of a governing body at the village level to coordinate with the state vis-à-vis implementation of the development programmes was one of the major reasons why things did not work out as per expectations. An urgent need for delegation of power to the rural sector was felt. The states favoured the setting up of Panchayati Raj Institutions (PRIs) and by 1960, many states had adopted Panchayati Raj.

In the early 70's, the slogan of Garibi Hatao was used as an election plank to target the sentiments of the poor. Despite the fact that the massive support of the poor had helped the *ruling elite*[5] in gaining power, the government went in for centralisation of powers riding on a misplaced notion that a strong Centre would be able to effectively carry out rural development and create the desired impact. The Panchayati Raj Institutions, consequently, suffered from inadequate financial resources. This led to the decline of the Panchayati Raj as the panchayats were unsuccessful in their endeavour to work "as agents of change or agencies of development."

As of now, the country stands divided between the two sections – the rich Indians and the poor Indians. The former enjoy all luxuries of life, whereas the latter are not destined to satisfy even the bare minimum needs of food, clothing and housing. One section is shining and spending excessively, even *squandering*[6], whereas the other is starving.

As per the findings of Boston Consulting Group in its study, "Global Wealth: Winning the Growth Game", 928 Indian ultra high net worth houses (with wealth over $100 million) were holding 20 per cent of the country's wealth in 2014. Their share is likely to go up to 24 per cent in 2019. About 95 Indians, with a combined worth of $295 billion, have appeared in the Forbes' List of Billionaires of 2015. They own approximately 10 percent of the country's GDP.

Ineffective implementation of measures for rural development has led to several socio-economic disabilities like illiteracy, child labour, exploitation of women, poor housing, lack of primary healthcare facilities, poor sanitation, unavailability of *potable*[7] water and poor income generation from fragmented land holdings. The exodus of rural folk to the cities has led to the *burgeoning*[8] of urban population and the *mushrooming*[9] of slums. According to a World Bank report, one in every six persons living in abject poverty across the world is an Indian. India's economic growth rate, of late, has been in the range of 6% to 9%. But, the poor have largely continued to remain unaffected by this indicative prosperity.

There is a mismatch between the economy's growth and resources allocated for rural development. The GDP from 1980-81 to 2014-2015 has increased 17 times. However, the rural development expenditure in this period rose merely 3.6 times. There was only a marginal rise in the rural development expenditure, from 7 per cent in the pre-reform decade to 8 per cent in the post-globalised era. In the first half of FY 2016, government expenditure witnessed a quick rise in two key social sectors – health and especially agriculture and rural development – both in real terms and as a share of GDP. The benefits of this policy have concentrated among the urban elite, while the rural masses as well as the urban slum dwellers continue to wallow in poverty. The agricultural sector is paying the price for urban development in terms of continual shrinkage of the cultivable area.

To empower the rural folk for the effective functioning of development programmes, the Ministry of Rural Development, renamed the Ministry of Rural Areas and Employment is operating major programmes for rural development under Mahatma Gandhi National Rural Employment Guarantee Act (MGNREGA), National Rural Livelihoods Mission (NRLM), Indira Awas Yojana (IAY), Pradhan Mantri Gram Sadak Yojana (PMGSY), National Social Assistance Pragramme (NSAP), Integrated Watershed Management Programme (IWMP), National Land Records Modernisation Programme (NLRMP), National Rural Drinking Water Programme (NRDWP) and others. A new Department of Rural Employment and Poverty Alleviation has been formed to provide employment in the rural sector with a view that gainful employment of both the unemployed and the underemployed could eradicate rural poverty. The programme of Development of Women and Children in Rural Areas (DWCRA) is aimed at income generation for women, and intended to help them realise economic self-reliance. The Department has also launched self-employment programmes—one of them being Integrated Rural Development Programme (IRDP)—in addition to facilitating land reforms, rural housing, provision of drinking water and sanitation facilities.

The old *agrarian*[10] structure with its genesis in the feudal system thwarted the development policies intended for the rural sector. The old feudal system, which formed the basis of the socio-economic structure of rural India, hampered the modernisation of agriculture, as well as, agricultural productivity and led to the exploitation of the masses. Hence, land reforms remained one of the major policies for rural and economic development. Eventually, land reforms helped to replace the feudal system with an egalitarian social structure.

The scheme of Sarva Shiksha Abhiyan (SSA), a national flagship programme launched in 2001 has been implemented in all districts of our country. The aim of SSa is to provide useful and relevant elementary education for all children in the 6-14 age group. It focuses on elementary education of satisfactory quality with emphasis on education for life. Education Guarantee Scheme and Alternative and Innovative Education (EGS and AIE) are important components of SSA to bring out-of-school children in the fold of Elementary Education.

Most of the marginal farmers have taken to dairying and have become a part of the White Revolution in India. Dairy development has helped the country's programme of rural development. Amul in Gujarat is the success story of cooperative dairying, which enabled a large number of villagers in Gujarat to raise their standards of living through economic growth.

Rural Banks have been established "to fulfil the aims of institutionalising the credit structure and enhancing its area and coverage." These are intended to save the rural population from banking with the moneylenders. Funds are allocated at low rates of interest to rural *entrepreneurs*[11] to start small-scale industries.

The government has launched the Bharat Nirman Project—a time-bound action plan for the development of rural infrastructure. Under this project, initiatives are being undertaken in the areas of irrigation, roads, rural housing, rural water supply, rural electrification and rural telecommunication connectivity. The *Annapurna scheme, Jawahar Rozgar Yojana, Gram Samridhi Yojana, Swarn Jayanti Gram Swarozgar Yojana*, etc., are the important schemes pertaining to employment generation and poverty alleviation in rural areas. *Swarnajayanti Gram Swarozgar Yojana* (SGSY) is aimed at providing self-employment opportunities to the rural poor below poverty line. The national scheme for Training of Rural Youth for Self-Employment (TRYSEM) equips the rural youth, in the age group of 18-35 years, with necessary skills and technical know-how so as to enable them to take up self-employment in agriculture and allied sectors, industries, services and business activities. Assistance under the SGSY to individual *Swarozgaries* or Self Help Groups is given by the government in the form of Revolving Funds Assistance and Capital Subsidy linked to credit by the banks. The National Rural Employment Guarantee Act was brought into force in 200 most backward districts with the objective of providing 100 days of guaranteed unskilled wage employment to each rural household. During 2009-10, it was rechristened as Mahatama Gandhi National Rural Employment Guarantee Act. In the first year of its implementation (2006-07) in 200 districts, 2.10 crore households were employed and 90.5 crore persondays were generated. The average wage per person per day in the FY 2013-14 was ₹ 132.59 which is double the average rate paid in FY 2006-07. The notified wage at present varies from a minimum of ₹ 153 in Meghalaya to ₹ 236 in Haryana.

The rural sector badly needs infrastructural development in the shape of roads, power supply, education and health facilities so that its productivity and purchasing power may be augmented. It can act as a comparable alternative to its urban counterpart and can be relied upon in the time of financial instability, economic uncertainty and global recession.

As India lives in villages, sincere efforts must be undertaken by our national leaders for the decentralisation of power. Short-sightedness, lack of understanding and negligence have already led to the poor condition of the rural population. During elections politicians invariably bring up the issues of rural development and poverty alleviation. They even lure the rural electorate through free distribution of articles like laptops, bicycles, TVs and even sarees, flouting stringent laws enforced by the Election Commission to prohibit such acts. But little is done once they come to power.

Rural Development will help in solving many of the problems faced in the urban sector, namely, overpopulation, sanitation, health, etc., as it will discourage the rural population from moving to urban areas in search of jobs and better facilities in life. The government must take necessary steps to achieve the objectives of rural development.

According to the United Nations Development Programme in 2014, investments in social security, jobs and laws that protect vulnerable populations are to be prioritised so that the widening income inequalities may be curbed. To this end, the state needs to redefine its role and enlarge its sphere of participation with an assurance of efficient and ethical governance.

Aid to Vocabulary

1. *Infrastructure* — the system which supports the operation of an organisation
2. *Exodus* — departure of many persons
3. *Ameliorate* — to make better
4. *Percolate* — spread through
5. *Ruling elite* — those who are elected to rule
6. *Squandering* — splurging, wasting
7. *Potable* — drinkable
8. *Burgeoning* — increasing
9. *Mushrooming* — spreading
10. *Agrarian* — agriculture-based
11. *Entrepreneurs* — persons who undertake a business or enterprise

Points to Remember

1. It is often said that India lives in its villages.
2. Though Panchayati Raj was not favoured initially, it came to be adopted by many states by 1960.
3. The bureaucracy, political system and lack of funds led to the decline of the Panchayati Raj.
4. This led to several socio-economic disabilities like illiteracy, child labour, exploitation of women, poor housing, lack of primary healthcare facilities, lack of sanitation and potable water.
5. Remedial measures for development, employment, land reforms, etc., are being taken.
6. Introduction of National Literacy Mission, White Revolution, establishment of Rural Banks are important measures for rural development.
7. Rural development must be accorded top priority.

Essay
55

DROUGHTS IN INDIA

SYNOPSIS

Owing entirely to its devastating effect on the poorest, drought stands apart from other natural calamities. India is a fertile country with numerous rivers. But it has experienced droughts throughout history. Even in the 21st century, some states in India face severe droughts. Droughts lead to loss not only of crops but also of human life and livestock. About 56 per cent of water supply for irrigation depends on rainfall and the rest on rivers. Deforestation and receding ground water levels have also created problems. The river linking policy should be put into operation to prevent further droughts. Also, in spite of having surplus foodgrains, political bickerings prevent the proper supply and distribution of food stock. The Government should focus its attention on long-term planning to solve the problem of drought.

Amongst *innumerable*[1] natural calamities like flood, tsunami, landslide, earthquake, eruption of a volcano, etc., drought, stands apart, for it causes death slowly but surely; like a sweet poison. Criminal apathy of the ruling political party, deforestation at an alarming rate unmindful of its devastating effects, non-judicious utilisation of water resources available in the country, over dependence on rain for agricultural purposes, non popularisation of rain harvesting techniques, wastage of water at a large scale, etc., are some of the reasons attributed to its occurrence year after year. Needless to add, corrective measures are imperative to *ameliorate*[2] the condition of the common man in general and of the farmers in particular.

India, in spite of being a country with number of rivers, has often experienced severe *droughts*[3]. Millions of people have died in India due to drought and subsequent famines. The causes of recurrent droughts need to be studied in detail. Even after more than six decades of Independence, our country is not free from droughts.

In 1955, droughts occurred in Rajasthan, Bihar, Odisha and Tamil Nadu. After that, in Kalahandi (Odisha) in the 1980's and Bolangir (Odisha) in 2000, severe droughts hit the lives of people. Rajasthan has seen 39 droughts in the past 46 years. In 2002-2003, the fifth consecutive drought affected 41,000 villages in 32 districts of Rajasthan. The number of direct victims is estimated to be about 4 crore people and over five crore cattle. The standing crop covered only 40 per cent of the 75 lakh hectares of cultivated land. This led to a direct fall of ₹ 7,000 crore in Rajasthan's rural income.

In pure human terms, the misery of the fifth consecutive drought was distressing. The villagers were so *emaciated*[4] that they could not earn their full daily wages at the relief sites. This could well be a picture of any other Indian state in a year to come. Although the government undertakes extensive relief measures for providing food and work to the victims of drought, there ought to be some permanent solution to prevent the occurrence of droughts.

One of the main reasons for drought-related famine and suffering is the over-dependence of agriculture on annual rainfall. About 4,000 cubic billion metres of rain which is about 75 per cent of the total rain, falls during the 70 to 90 days of the monsoon. The land water resources in the country are limited. This is because of the fact that India's landmass of 329 million hectares accounts for only 2.4 per cent of the earth's land area while its population accounts for 16.7 per cent of the world population. Thus the water-carrying and maintaining capacity of the land is decreasing every year.

Deforestation[5] is one of the major reasons for the drought-prone areas retaining lesser and lesser amount of water. The village tanks get silted up leading to a further reduction in water supply for irrigation. The government does not have a well developed rain harvesting plan. Inter-state disputes over sharing of rivers water never get resolved. The controversy over the Kaveri river water sharing, between Tamil Nadu and Karnataka, is a glaring example. There are no plans to *decongest*[6] densely populated areas, which results in the boring of too many tubewells and lowering of the level of underground water.

Deforestation on a large scale has polluted the environment too. This has generated more heat and has led to the melting down of glaciers. Reversing this process would entail uprooting people from their homes and rehabilitating them somewhere else. This is a highly controversial issue as the experience in the ongoing Sardar Sarovar Dam Project or river Narmada shows. The politicians do not show interest in small and medium irrigation projects. The focus is only on the large and extensive projects. Local solutions are not given due importance. This leads to regional disparities. The result is that irrigation can be assured for only 44 per cent of India's agriculture. India lacks a proper plan and well thought-out strategy to develop measures that will help to prevent droughts. Our agricultural methods are often primitive and non-scientific. The government, more often than not, resorts to stopgap arrangements. While countries with very limited water resources are successfully implementing drought-control measures, we even with a large number of rivers and other water systems continue to face the problem of droughts every year.

For a country so rich in river resources, the permanent solution for famine is easy the linking of all rivers. Such a scheme was conceived in the late fifties by the then Irrigation and Power Minister K.L. Rao. A committee headed by M.N. Dastoor made two proposals. One, connecting all the Himalayan rivers under the 'Garland Canal Scheme'; the other, the 'Peninsular Canal Scheme' connecting the 17 southern rivers. The project would be able to deliver water for irrigation of an additional 25 million hectares of land. A further 10 million hectares were to benefit from increased use of groundwater and generation of 34 million KW of power while reducing floods and droughts. The ambitious plan failed to take off. A similar plan has now again been drawn to link the major rivers of the country.

In spite of all the planning the question of implementation of these plans remains a big problem. No state is willing to announce that it has surplus water. As a result, many parts of the country continue to suffer from water shortage. As 56 per cent of cultivation is dependent on rain, groundwater continues to be drawn up indiscriminately for the rest. This leads to a sharp drop of 3 to 5 per cent in the water level every year. In some areas, all the three levels of soil stand exhausted. The government agencies and the NGOs working in this field need to focus more on sustainable developmental measures. Improved watershed management, construction of dams, effective rain-harvesting techniques, afforestation and spreading awareness regarding water conservation are steps that could be initiated for avoiding droughts.

There was a record production of 257.13 million tonnes of foodgrains in 2012-13. The government of India sanctioned a pilot scheme for 'National Project for Repair, Renovation & Restoration (RRR) of water bodies directly linked to Agriculture'. The government approved this scheme for the improvement of the overall agricultural conditions in our country. The National Food Security Act (NFSA) is being implemented in all the drought affected areas.

It is a real shame that though there is a large surplus of foodgrains in India and it exports foodgrains to 30 countries, there is not adequate food supply for a section of its own population. The reason for this is the political *bickerings*[7] among the different political parties and gross mismanagement at the administrative level. Drought has become an annual phenomenon and millions of words are written and spoken on it all the time. It is high time our leaders woke up to the reality of the sufferings of the common man. The political leaders need to shed their desire to please the vote banks. They need to focus their attention on long-term rather than short-term planning in order to *eradicate*[8] the problem of drought in India.

Aid to Vocabulary

1. *Innumerable* — countless
2. *Ameliorate* — improve
3. *Droughts* — prolonged dry weather, absence of rain
4. *Emaciated* — thin and feeble
5. *Deforestation* — process of removing forests
6. *Decongest* — clearing of abnormal accumulation of population
7. *Bickerings* — quarrels
8. *Eradicate* — get rid of

Points to Remember

1. India, though a land of rivers, has often experienced droughts.
2. The effect of droughts in Rajasthan in 2002-03 was severe.
3. Over-dependence of our agriculture on rainfall is one of the causes of drought.
4. Deforestation is another reason for drought.
5. India lacks a proper plan and strategy to prevent droughts.
6. Solution would be implementing 'linking of all rivers' policy.
7. Water-level is receding every year.
8. In order to eradicate the problem of drought, the political leaders need to focus their attention on long-term planning.

CHINESE DAMS GIVE NORTH-EAST JITTERS

Beijing's Plan To Build 32 Dams On Tibetan Rivers Could Hit Asom, Arunachal Pradesh

Officials in the country's north-east region, particularly Arunachal Pradesh and Asom, have more furrows on their forehead than ever before.

Their worries have multiplied ever since China announced that it would build a dam across Xiabuqu, tributary of the mighty Tsangpo river that flows southwards into Arunachal as the Siang and then joins the Brahmaputra.

The consequences of the proposed dam are yet to be determined, but speculations abound over China's plans to harness water from rivers that pass its territory before entering India. Such a move would deliver a veritable blow to millions dependant on the rivers for sustenance on this side of the border.

China's Dam Diplomacy

- Two on Indus at Jiele and Sanbo, both dam and Storage
- One on Sutlej in Zhanada country, dam and storage
- Eight on Tsangpo, of which 540 MW Zangmu dam commissioned
- Thirty-two Tsangpo tributaries dammed/to be dammed by China

India's Counter

- Seventy-six dams planned on the Brahmaputra in Arunchal and Asom but only one has been constructed so far.

Source: Press Trust of India

Essay 56

POISON IN EVERY SIP: WATER POLLUTION

SYNOPSIS

Water is one of the most common and yet the most vital substances that are readily available all around us. Water is essential for the existence of life. The importance of pure drinking water cannot be overstated. The United Nation's evaluation of global water for citizens ranked India 120th among 122 countries. Surveys have found bottled water to contain a high concentration of pesticides. This could lead to cancer, damage of liver and kidney, neurological and reproductive disorders. Pesticides are most difficult to remove. They along with industrial effluents pollute surface water. The groundwater has also become polluted. Children are affected to a far greater extent than adults. It is hoped that authorities will take the necessary precautions and adopt the latest techniques of water purification.

Water is one of the most common sources of our survival and at the same time most vital substance that is readily available all around us. Two-thirds of the earth's surface is covered with water and it is also present below the surface of the earth. Water is essential for the existence of life. Water constitutes 70 per cent of our body weight while it constitutes 90 per cent of our blood. It is essential for irrigating our crops as well as for our daily activities. It is also needed in factories and power plants.

As water forms such an important part of our life, the importance of pure drinking water cannot be overstated. It is *imperative*[1] that the water gushing out of the kitchen tap be clean and be suitable for drinking. The Municipal Corporation of Delhi itself admits that 12 per cent of the drinking water supplied in the capital is contaminated. Forget about tap water, a survey in the capital city of India, Delhi, has shattered all illusions about purity of bottled water in the country. The use of various brands of bottled mineral water is common not only among the foreigners but also among local residents. The survey found that bottled water contains a high concentration of *pesticides*[2]. Now it seems that purity, or rather the impurity of drinking water is just a matter of degree. Some people happen to drink more polluted water as compared to others. But no one in the city seems to be getting anything close to pure drinking water. The same is found to be the case with all the towns and cities across India.

The first United Nations' Global Water Evaluation Survey ranked India at 120th among 122 nations in the world in terms of quality of water for citizens. Finland topped the list as the country with the best quality of drinking water. The World Water Development Report—*Water for People, Water for Life*—was released on March 5, 2003. This report stated that 50 per cent of the population of developing countries was exposed to polluted water resources.

The Asian rivers are the most polluted in the world. They have three times as many bacteria from human waste as the global average. These rivers have 20 times more lead than those of industrialised countries. The report said that the global water crisis will reach unprecedented levels in the years to come. About two million tonnes of waste are dumped every day into water channels. The report, based on latest data from the ministry of urban development (2013), Census 2011 and pollution control board, estimates that 75-80% of water pollution is from domestic sewage flowing into water bodies including rivers. Contamination of water has almost doubled in recent years. This leads to various water borne diseases like cholera, dysentery, jaundice and diarrhoea, etc.

An assessment by Water Aid, an international organisation working for water sanitation and hygiene stated that 80% India's surface water is polluted. A survey conducted by the Centre for Science and Environment (CSE) revealed that 'safe' bottled water could cause *cirrhosis*[3] or cancer. This survey was held in metropolitan cities and the chemicals that were found to be present in dangerous levels were chlorpyrrifos and lindane. Both these chemicals affect the central nervous system. The side-effects are nausea, cramps, blurred vision and allergic *rhinitis*[4].

Water pollution is one of the most serious problems created by urbanisation. It affects not only the individual living species but the entire ecosystem. A National Lake Assessment found that almost 20% of the nation's lakes had high levels of nitrogen and phosphorus. Nitrogen in excess poses a serious risk to infants.

The drinking water supply of Delhi presents a dismal picture. The river Yamuna is the main source of drinking water for the people of Delhi. Unfortunately, it is highly polluted. The Delhi Jal Board supplies water to the households. It is believed that only 18 out of the 33 tests prescribed by the Bureau of Indian Standards (BIS) for drinking water are carried out. The tests for the presence of mercury, cadmium, selenium, arsenic, lead, zinc, ionic detergents, mineral oil and pesticides are not conducted. In 1996, an Indo-Dutch study of the Yamuna river was conducted which found the presence of pesticides like DDT, aldrin, dieldrin heptachlor and

BHC in the water supplied as drinking water. The Indian Toxicological Research Institute in Lucknow had also found pesticide *residue*[5] in almost all essential commodities of life. It also found that the people of Delhi had the world's highest levels of DDT accumulated in their body fat.

Cancer, liver and kidney damage and *neurological*[6] and reproductive disorders are just a few of the fatal and *chronic*[7] health conditions that are caused directly by the consumption of pesticide-ridden water. In Kerala, studies have directly linked the use of pesticide Endosulfan to cancer of the reproductive organs.

According to experts, pesticides are the most difficult to remove as they enter surface and groundwater as runoff from crops. They even pollute freshwater bodies like rivers, lakes and estuaries. Higher concentration of nitrates has a detrimental effect on human and animal health. According to the World Health Organisation (WHO), the safe concentration level of nitrates in drinking water is 10 milligram/litre of water. Nitrates are water-soluble and hence are *leached*[8] away with groundwater, leading to accumulation in drinking water.

To add to the pesticide load in water, there are industrial *effluents*[9] that are being dumped into the rivers. These originate from the paper and sugar industries, distilleries, glass, nickel and chromium plants along the riversides. The concept of water purity has changed from focus on solid residue and natural pollutants to pesticides and industrial effluents in the wake of modernisation and development.

The condition of the groundwater is no better. Pollution has trickled through the troubled waters of the Yamuna. A study conducted by the Guru Gobind Singh Indraprastha University revealed that the concentration of arsenic, mercury, nitrates, sulphates and dissolved salts in the capital's groundwater exceeds permissible limits. The entire rural belt of Delhi's unauthorised colonies and slum *bastis*[10], which is home to several lakhs of the population, receive untreated groundwater.

The government has, till date, spent millions to clean up the Yamuna but the problem persists mainly because most sewage facilities are malfunctioning. Moreover, the river water remains stagnant for nearly nine months which makes matters worse.

The government has already taken steps in course of the Five Year Plans to rebuild or repair the sewage systems and the drains. The Yamuna Action Plan was implemented in 1993 by the National River Conservation Directorate (NRCD) of the Ministry of Environment and

Forests with aid from The Japan Bank for International Cooperation. In 2007, the government set up plans to repair sewage lines with the vision of improving water quality to 90%.

However, in 2009 the Union government was forced to admit that the Ganga Action Plan (GAP) and the Yamuna Action Plan (YAP) had been failures in spite of drowning ₹ 1,700 crore in them. Investigations revealed that the plans had failed due to the adoption of the Thames model which involved the usage of a centralised sewage treatment system. Lack of enough power supply as well as funds had led to the failure.

In August 2009, the Delhi Jal Board introduced a new plan to clean up the 22 km stretch of the Yamuna in Delhi by constructing interceptor sewers costing nearly ₹ 1,800 crore. Under Jawaharlal Nehru National Urban Renewal Mission (JNNURM) project of Ministry of Urban Development (MoUD), DJB is implementing an interceptor sewer project costing ₹ 1,357.71 crore to intercept sewage flowing into river Yamuna. The timeframe for completion of YAP-III scheme is December, 2018.

If this is the quality of water in the capital city of India, one can imagine what must be the case with other cities and towns of the country. As for most rural parts of the country, people have no choice. They are condemned to drink the untreated water. The most alarming fact with regard to pesticide and effluent pollution of water pertains to young children getting the worst hit. Children do not have a fully developed *immune*[11] system to help them fight off the effects of toxins. Most people are said to receive up to 12 per cent of their lifetime dose of toxic chemicals in the first year of their life.

The quality of water is deteriorating every day and testing of water samples substantiates the presence of high levels of pollutants such as residual pesticides, heavy metals and organic matter like hydrocarbons, microbial and bacterial content, etc. It is only hoped that the authorities will adopt the latest techniques of water purification and ensure safe drinking water for every citizen of the country.

Aid to Vocabulary

1. *Imperative* — important
2. *Pesticides* — chemical substances for destroying pests especially insects
3. *Cirrhosis* — chronic disease of liver
4. *Rhinitis* — inflammation (swelling) of nose
5. *Residue* — remainder, leftover
6. *Neurological* — relating to the nervous system

7. *Chronic* — lingering, long-lasting
8. *Leached* — percolated through some material
9. *Effluents* — liquid waste flowing from industries
10. *Bastis* — (Hindi) overcrowded settlements with poor living conditions
11. *Immune* — body's natural resistance

Points to Remember

1. Water is one of the most common and yet the most vital substances that are readily available all around us.
2. Bottled water is contaminated with high concentration levels of pesticides. People of the city receive polluted water.
3. United Nations' Global Water Evaluation Survey ranked India at 120th among 122 nations in the world.
4. Asian rivers are the most polluted in the world.
5. Pesticides cause cirrhosis, cancer and also affect the central nervous system.
6. The Yamuna river, the main source of water in Delhi, is polluted with pesticides and industrial effluents.
7. Cancer, liver and kidney damage, neurological and reproductive disorders are the effects of consuming pesticide-ridden water.
8. Industrial effluents dumped into rivers cause severe water pollution.
9. Groundwater is not free from pollution either.
10. The most alarming fact with regard to polluted water pertains to its effect on children as their immune systems are not fully developed to fight off the effects of toxins.

A team of researchers led by Prof. Tim Walsh of Cardiff University in the UK has discovered new strains of antibiotic-resistant bacteria in water samples taken from Delhi. The European Union funded study claims that the bacteria, also called the water bug (super bug) are not confined to hospitals and are also found in the wider environment. The study was done after the discovery that most patients found carrying the bacteria had spent time in the hospitals in India.

The researchers named the bacteria, NDM-1. Certain species of the bacteria, which cause dysentery and cholera, are untreatable. NDM-1 makes bacteria highly resistant to almost all antibiotics. Experts say that there are no new drugs on the horizon to tackle it. The Indian Health Ministry says that the findings are not backed by clinical and epidemiological evidence. While the Cardiff University researchers insist that it is a matter of public health and more environmental studies are needed in cities in India, Pakistan and Bangladesh, the Health Ministry has questioned their motives. The implication is that since India is emerging as a destination of medical tourism, the western medical fraternity perhaps sees a potential loss of business. Such studies deter foreigners from visiting India.

Essay

57

GLOBAL WARMING

Synopsis

The term 'Global Warming' refers to an average increase in the earth's temperature which in turn causes changes in the climate. Warming takes place due to the increasing levels of greenhouse gases. Human activities add to the levels of these gases. Since the Industrial Revolution, the amount of carbon dioxide in the atmosphere has gone up by 40 per cent. The rise in sea level is also a major cause of concern. Global warming poses a great threat to the flora and fauna of the earth. It also poses a significant threat to public health. The United Nations Framework Convention on Climate Change (UNFCCC) was formed in 1992. The Conference of Parties (196 nations as of now) has been meeting annually since 1995 to tackle climate change. The Kyoto Protocol (1997) asked for 5% emission cuts by 2012. Developed countries agreed on greenhouse gas limits at the COP 15, Copenhagen. COP 21 at Paris made a climate deal to cap global warming at 1.5 °C. By the efficient use of energy, plantation of trees and adopting a clean approach for the environment, we can help prevent global warming.

The term 'Global Warming' refers to an average increase in the earth's temperature, which in turn causes changes in the climate. Warming takes place because the amount of greenhouse gases in the atmosphere is rapidly increasing due to human activities. Greenhouse gases accumulate in the atmosphere covering it like a blanket, *trapping*[1] heat waves *radiating*[2] off the earth. These heat waves feed back into air, land and sea, changing weather patterns.

The most prevalent greenhouse gases are carbon dioxide, methane and nitrous oxide. Other atmospheric gases like oxygen and nitrogen do not have this effect. Carbon dioxide and methane are released into the atmosphere when solid waste, fossil fuels, plastics, wood and wood products are burnt. Human activities add to the levels of these gases, causing severe problems.

The earth goes through warm and cold periods, but the increase in carbon dioxide levels over the past 200 years is due to industrialisation. Since the Industrial Revolution, the amount of carbon dioxide in the atmosphere has gone up by 40 per cent. Eleven of the past twelve years rank among the 12 warmest years since 1850. In 2014 some cities in United States recorded the warmest summers. A report by the World Meteorological Organisation released on July 3, 2014 stated that deaths from heat had increased by more than 2000 percent over the previous decade.

Melting of polar ice in the Arctic and Antarctica region, coupled with melting ice sheets and glaciers across Greenland, North America, South America, Europe and Asia is expected to raise sea levels. The sea levels are expected to rise between 18 to 59 centimetres by the end of the century, and if the melting of ice at the poles continues it could add between 10 to 20 centimetres. There has been a reduction in Arctic sea ice. In the year 2012, the smallest amount of ice cover was recorded. Only 25 glaciers bigger than 25 acres are now found in Montana's glaciers. Researcher bill Fraser has noted the decline of the adilie penguins, foxes and alipine plants because they have moved to cooler areas farther North or higher. There has been a considerable change in the ecosystem. Scientists claim that carbon dioxide level in the atmosphere is the highest now in 650,000 years. The worldwide consumption of fossil fuels (petrol, diesel, coal) has increased drastically. The world now burns at least five billion tons of fossil fuels each year. Deforestation has reduced the absorption of carbon dioxide by trees.

There is an excess of carbon dioxide in the atmosphere not only because of high current emissions, but also because of accumulated emissions from the past. The developed world—home to 15 per cent of the world's population, emits 45 per cent of the greenhouse gases. For example, the US emits about 20 tonnes of carbon dioxide per person—25 times more than India's 0.8 tonnes. Scientists say that to avoid a catastrophe, global warming needs to be limited to no more than 2°C above pre-industrial levels.

The rise in sea level is a major cause of concern. A large number of cities located in coastal areas, like Mumbai, Kolkata, Tokyo, New York, London, Sau Paulo and island nations like Maldives may get *submerged*[3]. There would be acute scarcity of fresh water, if Quelccaya Ice Cap in Peru continues to melt at the current rate. It will be gone by 2100, leaving thousands of people who rely on it for drinking water and electricity helpless. In 2014, the World Meteorological Organisation has reported that the sea level rises 12 inches (3 millimetres) per year on an average worldwide.

Global warming poses a great threat to the *flora and fauna*[4] of the earth. A large number of species may become extinct. About 20 to 30 per cent of species assessed so far are likely to become extinct if global average warming exceeds by1.5°–2.5°C. Deserts may expand and rising temperature may add to the intensity and frequency of dusty storms. Floods and droughts may become more common. Snowfall and rain have already increased across the world. All this will immensely affect the quality of agricultural land, ultimately causing adverse effect on agricultural produce.

Moreover, climate change is posing a significant threat to public health —more so in the poor and developing countries. Studies have shown that global warming is influencing the geographical distribution and incidence of diseases, especially those transmitted by mosquitoes, such as malaria and dengue.

The growing concern over increasing global temperature has led different countries to draw out a plan of action to avert the situation. Various nations of the world, called the Conference Parties (CoP), The United Nations Framework Convention on Climate Change (UNFCCC) was adopted at the Earth Summit in Rio de Janeiro in 1992. It was a treaty signed by 192 countries. It did not set any binding targets for countries for cutting emissions, but only called for stabilising carbon emissions. The COP or Conference of Parties comprising 196 nations as of how, has met annually since 1995, and reviewed the progress made. A protocol was adopted on December 11, 1997 in Kyoto (Japan). Under this protocol, 39 industrialised countries committed themselves to reduce their emissions by 5.2 per cent of the 1990 levels, by 2012.

The Copenhagen Summit 2009 was the first global agreement of the 21st century to control global warming — the gravest challenge to humanity. 192 member nations of the UN signed a legally binding agreement setting targets and deadlines for managing emission of greenhouse gases. But a comprehensive agreement was not possible. The developed world wanted a new treaty, with fewer responsibilities. The emerging economies, on the other hand, saw all these as bedrock principles.

World leaders from 193 countries signed a new global climate regime, called the Cancun Agreement on December 11, 2010. After a week of heated talks between negotiations, the politicians began to steer the climate talks at Cancun. The negotiators had, as their job required, stuck to their respective positions. The politicians, as the end result of the Cancun Agreement showed, were instead looking for a compromise face-saver and not a permanent resolution for the problem.

The US wanted a slow start. It did not want to be compared to other rich countries and said it would take a measly target for 2020 claiming it was only beginning on the path of having a green economy and could not jump start to deep emission cuts. It also demanded that other emerging economies, such as India and China, too should take strong actions because their emissions would otherwise rise in the future. The Kyoto Protocol, on reducing greenhouse gases, was to expire in 2012 but was extended to 2020 at the Doha Summit, 2012.

The climate conferences in Warsaw (2013) and Lima (2014) decided that all countries would put forward their proposed emissions reduction targets for the 2015 agreement as "Intended nationally determined contributions" in advance of the Paris conference.

A landmark climate agreement aimed at slowing down global warming was signed in Paris with key players like India, US and China approving the final draft of a "historic" measure to save the planet from a catastrophe. The Paris agreement will legally bind the world in keeping the planet's warming "well below" two degree Celsius with an endeavour to limit it to 1.5 degrees, the level scientists say is needed to avert the worst effects of global warming.

The pact also commits $100 billion a year from 2020 to help developing countries cope with the problem. Besides, it will make it binding for nations to open their books every five years for scrutiny on their contribution to the global effort to cut greenhouse gas emissions.

As humanity strives to achieve better living standards for all, there is an increase in fuel consumption, industrial production and other such activities that cause emissions. So, in the present technological and political climate, economic growth means higher emissions. conversely, cuts in emissions would mean lower growth. This problem leads to the controversy about who should cut emissions, by how much, and how?

We can help prevent global warming in numerous ways. Efficient use of energy, plantation of trees, adopting a clean approach for the environment are the different ways to help prevent global warming. The modern environment movement started with fighting against polluting factories, power plants, oil spills, sewage and toxic dumps. Every individual should be aware of the importance of protecting the environment. With effective co-operation between citizens and government officials only, we may be able to slow down the effects of global warming.

Aid to Vocabulary

1. *Trapping* — not allowing to escape, will holding
2. *Radiating* — moving in a specified direction from a source

3. *Submerge* — place beneath the surface of water or some other liquid
4. *Flora and Fauna* — all the plants and animals that live in a particular area, time, period or environment

Points to Remember

1. The term 'Global Warming' refers to an average increase in the earth's temperature, which in turn causes change in the climate.
2. The most prevalent greenhouse gases are carbon dioxide, methane and nitrous oxide.
3. There is an excess of carbon dioxide in the atmosphere because of current high current emissions and accumulated emissions from the past.
4. The rise in sea level is a major cause of concern.
5. Global warming is a great threat to the flora and fauna of the earth.
6. Climate change poses a significant threat to public health.
7. To control the alarming situation, the Conference of Parties adopted the United Nations Framework Convention on Climate Change (UNFCCC) in 1992.
8. As per the Kyoto protocol, 39 industrialised countries committed themselves to reduce their emissions by 5.2 per cent of 1990 levels by 2012, which was later extended to 2020.
9. At the Copenhagen Summit-2009, a comprehensive agreement to control global warming acceptable to all countries could not be formulated.
10. The Paris climate deal aims to cap global warming at 1.5 °C.

THE INTERNATIONAL CONVENTIONS

1. UN Framework Convention on Climate Change (UNFCCC). New York, 09-05-92; Convention on Biological diversity (CBD), Rio-de-Janeiro.
2. Cartegena Protocol on Biosafety under CBD (29-01-2000).
3. Kyoto Protocol to the UNFCCC (Kyoto, 11-12-1997); Amendment to Annex-B of the Kyoto Protocol to the UNFCCC (Nairobi, 17-11-2006).
4. Convention on the Law of the Non-Navigational Uses of International Water courses (New York, 21-05-1997).
5. Rotterdam Convention on the Prior Informed consent Procedure for Certain Hazardous Chemicals and Pesticides in International Trade (Rotterdam, 10-09-1998).
6. Stockholm Convention on Persistent Organic Pollutants (Stockholm, 22-05-2001).
7. International Tropical timber Agreement, 2006 (Geneva, 27-01-2006).
8. UN convention on the Law of the Sea (Montego Bay, 10-12-1982).
9. UN Convention on the Law of the Sea (10-12-1982 relating to the Conservation and Management of Straddling Fish Stocks and Highly Migratory Fish Stocks (New York, 04-08-1995).

LEADING POLLUTERS			
WORLD'S TOP GREENHOUSE GAS EMITTERS		TOP PER CAPITA EMITTERS	
Country	**Percentage share**	**Country**	**Tonnes of emission per capita**
Others	27.33	US	19.86
China	25.26	Russia	16.22
US	14.40	Japan	10.54
EU	10.16	Iran	9.36
India	6.96	EU	8.77
Russia	5.36	China	8.13
Japan	3.11	Mexico	5.99
Brazil	2.34	Brazil	5.10
Indonesia	1.76		
Mexico	1.67		
Iran	1.65		

India ranked 120th with emissions of 2.44 tonnes/capita
Source: World Research Institute

GLOBAL STUDY SOUNDS AN ALARM

Was conducted by climate advisors to the govts in US, UK, China

India may be hotter by 8ºC, lose $200 billion per year

Effect: Temperature likely to cross 50º Celsius mark by the turn of the century

By 2050...

- India will face acute water crisis in summer
- Drought probability will also rise
- Food production is likely to go down

HEAT WAVE

- Temperature would rise 5 degrees Celsius if the global rise is 2 degrees Celsius and up to 7-8 degrees if global increase is 4 degrees Celsius

MORE FLOODS

- Ganga could flood six times more frequently
- Chances of floods in Kolkata will increase by 1,000 times with sea level rising by one metre

WORST AFFECTED STATES IN INDIA

Rajasthan, Punjab, Haryana, Chandigarh, Delhi, Bihar and Uttar Pradesh

HOW IS GLOBAL WARMING TACKLED

- Focus, in tackling global warming, is on slashing greenhouse gas (GHG) emissions
- Nations responsible for 90%+ global emissions have declared their targets
- EU will cut its emissions by 40% from 1990 levels, by 2030
- US will cut by 26% to 28%, from 2005 levels, by 2025
- China says emissions will peak by 2030, and reduce thereafter

Essay

58

WILDLIFE CONSERVATION

SYNOPSIS

India is a country with a rich variety of flora and fauna. India's astounding bio-diversity is largely due to its unique topography. Wildlife is an inseparable part of our natural treasure. Deforestation, mining, etc., are responsible for the loss of natural habitat of animals. Unregulated hunting, toxic chemicals, climate change, overexploitation of resources, etc., pose a threat to the wildlife. There has been a growing awareness of the necessity for wildlife conservation. India has been a part of many national and international conventions to protect the wildlife. In 1983, the Government of India adopted a National Wildlife Plan to provide a strategy as well as a programme for wildlife conservation. Wildlife is also an indispensable part of our national income. Wildlife safari provides a boost to our tourism industry.

India is a country with a rich variety of flora and fauna. India's astounding bio-diversity is largely due to its unique *topography*[1] that offers a wide range of climatic zones across the length and breadth of the country. From the steaming tropical wet evergreen jungles of the Ghats in the Indian Peninsula to the alpine forests of the Himalayas, India offers an amazing range of biological and ecological diversity. The main wildlife zones in India are the Deccan Peninsula, the Indian coasts, the Western Ghats, the Gangetic plain, the Northeastern Region, the Himalayas, Semi Arid zones, the Indian Deserts, and the Indian Islands. The climate and vegetation of these areas range from the tropical to the temperate and the arctic, and is home to tigers, snow leopards, elephants, antelopes, deer, bears, jackals, hyena, wild buffalo, etc.

Wildlife is an inseparable part of our natural treasure. But, India is continuously losing this heritage due to deforestation and excessive poaching. There are several threats to wildlife. Loss of natural habitat is responsible for the rise in the number of endangered species. Each year fewer natural wildlife habitat areas remain due to excessive deforestation and urbanisation. Cutting trees for farms and towns, *lumbering*[2], mining and building dams all are responsible for the loss of natural habitat of the animals.

Unregulated hunting and poaching cause a major threat to wildlife.

Poaching is the illegal hunting, killing or capturing of animals. Animal products, such as hide, ivory, horn, teeth and bones are sold to dealers, who make clothes, jewellery and other materials from them. Hunting for sport is also practised in various countries. All forms of hunting and poaching have led to the extinction of many species.

Pesticides and toxic chemicals, which are deliberately spread to make the environment toxic are also a major threat to the wildlife. Some pesticides and chemicals, such as Polychlorinated Biphenyls (PCBs) are found in the environment. Wildlife is also exposed to many forms of petroleum by-products, such as crude oil and fuel oil. Chemical compound such as *antifreeze*[3] (ethylene glycol) and metals, such as mercury and cadmium, also pose a grave threat to the wildlife.

Climate change and natural disasters also put wildlife in danger. Animals, birds and small insects are all under threat as their specific habitats alter. However, some are able to adapt to their new habitat, but those who are not able to adapt, perish. Natural disasters such as floods, earthquakes, volcanoes, storms, forest fires, etc., all are responsible for the dwindling number of wild animals.

Environmental pollution and overexploitation of resources also pose a threat to the wildlife. Acid rain is produced due to the burning of high-sulphur coals in electrical power plants. Acidification can *sterilise*[4] water bodies, which lead to the killing of aquatic animals. Nowadays, oil spills have devastating effects on marine animals. Overexploitation of resources, such as over-fishing have also been a major cause behind the *extermination*[5] of many species.

There has been a growing awareness of the necessity for conservation and preservation of India's wildlife. Wildlife is an essential and integral part of nature. The wild animals, birds and insects all help to maintain a balance in the *ecosystem*[6]. To prevent the extinction of species, conservation efforts have been initiated. The Constitution of India entails the subject of forest and wildlife in the Concurrent List. The Federal Ministry acts as a guiding light dealing with policies and planning on wildlife conservation while the State Forest Departments have been vested with the responsibility of the implementation of national policies and plans. In 1983, the Government of India adopted a National Wildlife Plan to provide a strategy as well as a programme for wildlife conservation. The 1983, action plan was revised and a new plan (2002-2016) has been adopted.

The Indian Board of Wildlife, headed by the Prime Minister, is the apex advisory body overseeing and guiding the implementation of various schemes for wildlife conservation. It was constituted on December 7, 2001. The Animal Welfare Division became a part of the Ministry of Environment and Forests in July 2002. The main task of the division is to implement effectively the various provisions of the Prevention of Cruelty to Animals (PCA) Act, 1960. Some of the important rules framed under the Act include, Performing Animals (Registration) Rules, 2001; Transport of Animal Rules, 1978 and 2001; Prevention of Cruelty (Slaughter Houses) Rules, 2001; Animal Birth Control (Dogs) Rules, 2001 and Breeding of and Experiments on Animals (Control and Supervision Rules) 1998. The Wildlife Crime Control Bureau was constituted in 2006 through the amendment to the Wildlife (Protection) Act 1972. The powers and functions of the bureau are defined under Section 382 of the Act.

The Central Zoo Authority (CZA) has evolved a national policy on wildlife conservation mainly through breeding of *endangered*[7] species. Zoos in India are regulated as per the provisions of the Wildlife (Protection) Act 1972 and are guided by the National Zoo Policy, 1998. The Zoological Survey of India (ZSI), with its headquarters in Kolkata and 16 regional stations, is responsible for surveying the faunal resources of India. Possessing a tremendous diversity of climate and physical conditions, India has a great variety of fauna numbering over 90,000 species. The Protected Area Network in India includes 99 National Parks, 515 Wildlife Sanctuaries, 43 Conservation Reserves and 4 Community Reserves*.

The Government of India has launched many schemes to protect the wildlife. The centrally sponsored scheme, 'Project Tiger', was launched in April 1973 with the objective "to ensure maintenance of the viable population of Tigers in India for scientific, economic, aesthetic, cultural and ecological values, and to preserve for all times, areas of biological importance as a national heritage for the benefit, education and enjoyment of the people." This international effort was led by Guy Mountfort of World Wide Fund for Nature (WWF). The estimated number of tigers in India is 1411. The findings of this estimation/assessment are *benchmarks*[8] for future tiger conservation strategy. An area of 29284.76 square kilometres has been notified by 15 tiger states as core or critical tiger habitat.

Another important scheme, namely, 'Project Elephant', was launched in February 1992 to assist states housing free ranging populations of wild elephants to ensure long-term survival of identified viable populations of elephants in their natural habitats. The total number of Elephant Reserves in the country till 2009 was 27.

India is a part of some major international conventions related to wildlife conservation. The first is Convention on International Trade in Endangered Species (CITES). The Government of India signed the convention on July 20, 1976. The second is the Coalition Against Wildlife Trafficking (CAWT). It is not a legal entity, but a partnership among organisations to end illegal animal trafficking. Third is the International Whaling Commission (IWC). India has been a member of IWC since 1981 and has played an active role in bringing about a *moratorium*[9] on commercial whaling.

The wildlife is also an indispensible part of our national income. From the tourist's point of view, our wildlife is a great attraction. Many tourists from within India and abroad travel to wildlife sanctuaries and national parks to a have a glimpse of these wild animals. Wildlife Safari is also very popular in India. These wildlife safaris provide adventure and excitement to all and sundry. People get to see these animals in their natural habitat, where they are protected and nurtured. The government should come up with better

executed schemes to protect the wildlife. The authorities concerned along with the common man should work together to protect the wildlife and to maintain a balance in our ecosystem.

Aid to Vocabulary

1. *Topography* — the physical features of an area of land
2. *Lumbering* — process of cutting down trees to make wooden boards
3. *Antifreeze* — a chemical added to the water in the vehicles to stop it from freezing
4. *Sterilise* — clean and free of germs
5. *Extermination* — to kill
6. *Ecosystem* — everything that exists in a particular environment
7. *Endangered* — a type of animal or plant that has become rare and could die out completely
8. *Benchmarks* — something that can be used as a standard to judge the quality or level of other things
9. *Moratorium* — a temporary stopping of an activity

Points to Remember

1. Wildlife is an inseparable part of our natural treasure.
2. There are several threats to wildlife.

3. Lumbering, unregulated poaching, toxic chemicals, climate change, natural disasters, environmental pollution, etc., pose a threat to wildlife.
4. There has been a growing awareness of the necessity of conservation of wildlife.
5. India is a part of many national and international conventions to protect the wildlife.
6. Wildlife also supports our tourism industry and is an indispensable part of our national income.

SOME IMPORTANT WILDLIFE SANCTUARIES IN INDIA		
1.	Dachigam Wildlife Sanctuary	Jammu & Kashmir
2.	Corbett National Park	Uttarakhand
3.	Sunderbans Wildlife Sanctuary	West Bengal
4.	Kaziranga National Park	Asom
5.	Ranthambore National Park	Rajasthan
6.	Periyar Wildlife Sanctuary	Kerala
7.	Keoladeo Ghana Bird Sanctuary	Rajasthan

Essay 59

GLOBALISATION AND ITS IMPACT ON SOCIETY

SYNOPSIS

The end of the 20th century witnessed a worldwide transformation in the social, cultural, political, economic as well as ethical spheres of life. Consequently, an ideological conflict, which witnesses consumerism and materialism at with a logger heads non-violent, non-exploitative world order, has come to the fore. Some major problems stemming from this conflict pertain to rejection of traditions by the younger generation, degradation of environment and poverty. The concept of oneness of all countries, or globalisation which wipes out the differences between industrialised and developing countries, is seen as a remedy for these problems. However, globalisation is not panning out the way it was expected to. We should sit and ponder, what kind of society to choose, a society guided by the market forces or one based on enterprise, sharing and caring.

The last two decades of the 20th century witnessed a worldwide transformation that continues to have an impact even today. This is a *multidimensional*[1] transformation that encompasses different aspects of our life. Social, cultural, political, economic as well as ethical changes are taking place. The transition from traditional to modern, national to global, old to new, is the order of the day. Now the choice is between *consumerism*[2] and *materialism*[3] on one side and non-violent and non-exploitative socio-economic order on the other.

One aspect of change in society is the influence of Western civilisation through globalisation. Other changes include degradation of environment, rapid erosion of values and cynicism with regard to institutions. Another unfortunate development is the alienation of the younger generation which is manifest in their rejection of tradition and loss of faith in the social, political and cultural norms. Other problems relate to insecurity, disparities between and within nations, poverty amidst plenty and other phenomena such as international terrorism. The world is getting increasingly interdependent. Rapid technological changes have resulted in instant communication. Today, this vast world of ours is a global village owing to advancement in science and technology. Apparently, the process of global integration bodes well for humanity.

Globalisation is the process by which a national economy moves towards a single borderless world economy with open markets. It is the expansion of markets for goods, services, capital and labour beyond national boundaries.

The concept of globalisation emerges from the aspiration of various nations of the world to come together as one uniform world order. The distances as well as differences, both physical and mental, have to be reduced to a bare minimum. The ways and means of communication need to be advanced even more to enable people to be in constant touch, and to live as one global family.

Towards the end of the 20th century, the world had become somewhat unipolar, and globalisation was seen as the way to bring numerous benefits to the developing nations. The yawning gaps and disparities between the industrialised world and the third world countries had reduced to a certain extent. This was achieved through the adoption of reformed models of economic management.

However, we continue to observe consumption disparities even in the 21st century. In the globalised world, 20 per cent of the world's richest people account for 86 per cent of total private consumption expenditure. The poorest 20 per cent account for only 1.3 per cent consumption. The richest five per cent consume 45 per cent of all meat and fish while the poorest five per cent consume 0.5 per cent. In energy consumption, the richest five per cent consume 55 per cent while the poorest five per cent are left with hardly any. The gap between the rich and the poor is growing at a fast rate. Thus, questions are being raised as to whether globalisation can provide solutions to the world's complex socio-economic problems.

Joseph Stiglitz, winner of the Nobel Prize for Economics in 2001 made certain observations in his celebrated book 'Globalisation and its Discontents'. He commented that the Western countries acting through the International Monetary Fund and the World Trade Organisation have failed. They have mismanaged the process of privatisation, liberalisation and stabilisation. In addition to this, he also opined that by following their advice many third world countries are actually worse off now than they were before. Stiglitz also says, "Globalisation today is not working, it is not working for many of the world's poor. It is not working for much of the environment. It is not working for the stability of the global economy".

After Independence, India adopted a policy of planned economy. But unfortunately, the country failed to achieve the desired result for which it was pursued. So under the leadership of the then Prime Minister

Indira Gandhi the seeds of liberalisation of the economy were sown. Our economy slowly proceeded towards globalisation by opening up to foreign investment and competition. Finally, the policy adopted by the succeeding Prime Minister Rajiv Gandhi and his successor P.V. Narasimha Rao helped to open up our economy to globalisation. The New Economic Policy announced by P.V. Narasimha Rao in July 1991 aimed at making the Indian economy competitive and much better-integrated with the world economy.

We Indians are also gradually converting ourselves into global citizens by acquiring the skills and the knowledge required to compete at the world stage. Our youth who account for nearly 50% of the population are acquiring enviable communication skills in English which is the global language. Our IITs and IIMs are churning out masterminds. Evidently, India is living up to the reputation of being a storehouse of knowledge.

The developed countries with expanding economies need more man-power which the developing countries are able to provide. It means the youth of a developing country are better placed to find employment and the country as a whole stands to attain economic progress. First it was the BPO's (Business Process Outsourcing) or the Call Centers setting their stops in India and now it is the KPO's (Knowledge Process Outsourcing). By the year 2020, IT and IT-enabled sectors alone will require 3 million additional hands. India enjoys a distinct advantage.

A host of multinational companies (MNCs) have made a foray into Indian commerce space, thus opening a world of opportunities for the employable youth of the country. Globalisation has benefited Indian society considerably, indeed.

However, on the flip side of the coin, the adverse impact of globalisation is prominently felt in the developing and underdeveloped countries of the third world. Critics of globalisation term this process as 'neocolonialism'. Third world societies are feeling the heat because liberalised economic policies as well as decentralisation process which are being unleashed in these States are not backed up with adequate social security measures. As the human development standards in these countries are very low, there is a lack of conducive social and economic environment required for proper implementation of globalisation policies. Liberal free market economy, which is considered to be the solution for underdevelopment and poverty by many, has not lived up to its expectations.

If one were to provide a solution to the present-day discontentment, rising inequalities, prevailing social tensions and psychological *dysfunctions*[4], then the search for an alternative world view becomes absolutely necessary. It has been well recognised that no valid socio-economic *paradigm*[5] can be formulated unless man's relationship with the world is properly understood. The new world view offers a new paradigm for building a socio-economic system free from exploitation and also for resolving the dilemma which mankind is presently faced with. This paradigm has universal applicability and addresses mankind as a whole. It requires attitudinal changes with regard to the relationship between human society and the ecosystem, the consumption levels and the growth rates with consequent changes in the value system.

Our choice is between a society having high affluenced but a tormented soul and a non-exploitative society caring for its members, like a family; one having social tensions, psychological dysfunctions, rising inequalities, violence and hatred all around and one having a reasonable standard of living with peace and harmony and a socio-economic order free from the ills of consumerism and materialism. We could either choose a world which functions as per the rules of the market forces—devoid of any emotional bonds—or we could choose a world full of fraternity with everyone enterprising, sharing and caring akin to a family.

The creation of this alternative paradigm is not really easy. Over the past five decades, the world has seen several models and paradigms which failed to provide concrete results. What we really need is a globalised economy placed in a humane context. The policies should be introduced in such a way that the weaker sections of the society and their interests are sufficiently protected by adequate social security measures. Because along with a vibrant economy, the developing world needs to improve health care, literacy rates, education, and a host of pressing social welfare standards in order to reap the rewards of globalisation.

Aid to Vocabulary

1. *Multidimensional* — having more than one side to it
2. *Consumerism* — the culture of purchasing goods and services and not being interested in spiritualism
3. *Materialism* — tendency to prefer material possessions and physical comfort to spiritual values
4. *Dysfunctions* — abnormality or impairment of function
5. *Paradigm* — example or pattern or model

Points to Remember

1. Last two decades of the 20th century witnessed a worldwide crisis.
2. Through globalisation, the influence of the western civilisation is felt.

3. Concept of globalisation indicates the desire to be a part of one uniform world order.
4. The disparities between the rich and the poor are growing fast.
5. The adverse impact of globalisation is being felt in the developing and underdeveloped countries.
6. The effects of globalisation are not good for poor sections of society.
7. No valid socio-economic paradigm can be built unless man's relationship with the world is properly understood.
8. Globalised economy must be placed in a humane context.

Essay 60

THE ROLE OF THE MEDIA

Synopsis

The media today, has become an important means of communication and has made its presence felt. The print media still enjoys a large readership. At times, its reputation does get maligned, but it works to restore its credibility. The audio-visual media that provides 'infotainment' also enjoys a considerable viewership. So, it becomes the moral responsibility of the media to be unbiased. Cinema, which caters to the largest number of viewers, is one medium which is basically meant for entertainment. The Internet, fax and e-mail have enabled people to transmit and receive the latest information. The media has quite a large following and coverage; therefore, it should act in a responsible way.

The media, an important means of communication, is a vast source of information and entertainment for people across the world. The impression it leaves upon the human mind, the views and ideas it may end up propagating, do indeed affect the people's lifestyles and their way of thinking.

The mass media today *encompasses*[1] newspapers, books, radio, television, cinema, Internet, e-mail, fax, etc. Although the use of Internet and e-mail is a somewhat recent *phenomenon*[2], the other forms of media have coexisted for many decades. In the Indian context, an attempt is being made to synthesis the traditional and folk forms of communication on the one hand and the modern print and audio-visual media including satellite communication on the other. Even though the audio-visual media scores over the print media, the latter still holds its ground. The media has the ability to penetrate the remotest corners of the earth and make its presence felt. The intense coverage of the devastating tsunami in Japan (March 11, 2011), and earthquake in Nepal (April 25, 2015), for instance, demonstrates the extensive reach of the electronic media. The media coverage of the Gulf War of 1991, the terrorist strikes in the USA on September 11, 2001 and the heinous massacre of school children in Pesawar, Pakistan (December 16, 2014) are other such examples.

The print media enjoys vast readership. The advent of the audio-visual media has never threatened its popularity. Some of the journalists, in fact, enjoy great fan-following and are respected and idolised for their work. Indians have won the Nobel Prize, the Booker Prize and other accolades in the *literary*[3] world. Some people mistakenly believe that banning of books like *'The Satanic Verses'* by Salman Rushdie or *'lajja'* by Taslima Nasreen may *throttle*[4] the freedom of expression.

The acts of the notorious and dreaded *paparazzi*[5] have maligned the reputation of the media. It is, perhaps, the reader's wish to gain access to the private lives of the rich and the famous which drives the paparazzi to literally chase them. Another criticism pertains to some newspapers that allegedly indulge in yellow journalism simply because a piece of sensational news sells like hot cake. But, at the end of the day, the print media will have to understand its power and reach. As it makes a great impact on its readers, it should act responsibly and concentrate on giving only the true picture rather than a distorted or *biased*[6] one.

The audio and the audio-visual media includes radio, television, theatre, drama, etc. The audio visual media scores over the print media because it takes the viewer to the place of action and caters to the needs of the illiterate people as well. Developing countries like India can rely on the media for mass communication. Broadcasting started in India in 1927 with privately owned transmitters at Mumbai (Bombay) and Calcutta (Kolkata). The first news bulletin went on air on July 23, 1927 in erstwhile Bombay. With the advent of television and subsequently the digitalised channels, people thought that the days of radio were numbered. Setting up private FM stations in the cities, radio reinvented itself and it now draws many listeners. It is, in fact, the rage today.

The media can be used for disseminating information in addition to imparting education to the masses. The media can generate public involvement through advocating issues and transferring knowledge, skills and techniques to the people. Awareness about the various rural development programmes could be spread by means of the media. Lack of awareness about various government schemes is to be blamed, to a certain extent, for hindering the national development process. The media should be used for infotainment, i.e., for both information and entertainment. As the media enjoys a wide reach, it should not distort news nor present a biased picture before the audience. At the same time, the media needs to work freely to do its job well. It is for this reason that in India, the Prasar Bharti Bill was introduced to grant *autonomy*[7] of the media. The Constitution of India guarantees freedom of expression but it should not be misused. The people in the media should feel responsible towards their audience. Only then can the media uphold its core values. A code of ethics has been formed for the media persons and journalists.

It provides the rules to be followed by the media persons while working. The Press Council of India was set up under Act 37 of 1978 to safeguard the freedom of the press and to work towards improving the standard of newspapers and news agencies.

The Films Division was set up in 1948 to revive the production of newsreels and documentary films. Cinema too has a deep influence on people. The audience tends to follow the *mannerisms*[8] of the film heroes and the heroines. So, actors should not portray on screen, anything which could have a negative influence on the audience. Jackie Chan, the famous actor, portrays himself as a *teetotaller*[9] and non-smoker on screen. This is because, he is aware of his responsibility as an icon of the media. In India, at present, cinema is going through a phase of *eroticism*[10]. Therefore, the content and treatment ought to be handled responsibly so as to avoid ruffling feathers. The Censor Board should intervene only in extreme cases.

With the advent of the Internet and e-mail, the world has really shrunk. Any person with a computer can have access to information at various websites. All major newspapers, magazines, satellite channels have their sites on the Internet. A person who, for some reason is not able to go through a newspaper or watch television, can gain access to the latest information by *browsing*[11] through their respective sites. With the help of fax and e-mail, messages can reach the receiver instantly in any corner of the globe. All these inventions have shrunk the globe to such an extent that the world can now be called 'a global village'.

The foreign electronic media has also made its entry in India. The CNN, STAR TV and the BBC World Service have become a part and parcel of daily viewing in all urban centres. Their shows have found their way into Indian living rooms though it had not been a case of smooth sailing initially. Controversies had erupted from time to time and many Indian newspapers and magazines had sought court protection to stop the foreign print media from entering the country.

The media today enjoys a wider coverage as well as a wider viewership than perhaps a decade ago. It has survived and has held its own to this day. Some stray incidents may have tainted the image of the media but it has constantly worked to restore its credibility. Today, we are observing the emergence of a new phenomenon—trial by the media. In the famous Jessica Lal murder case, Priyadarshini Matoo rape and murder case, Ruchika Girhotra–SPS Rathore case, Anna Hazare's 12-day fast for Jan Lokpal Bill and the heinous Nirbhaya gang rape case, the media played the role of the 'watch dog' of democracy. The extensive coverage of public outcry pressurises the authorities so that they could not avoid swinging into action. It was the proactive role of the media that brought the guilty to book, in some of these cases; and in the Nirbhaya case, it effected new legislation and enforced greater stringency in the existing rape laws.

Another raging phenomenon today is Net Activism or the act of generating public outcry on the social media i.e., the social networking sites such as Facebook, Twitter, etc. Anybody using the Internet can post a statement, opinion or visual that is likely to go viral, garnering 'likes' that may multiply by the thousands in an instant. Atrocities and offences that would normally go unnoticed are now captured on smartphones and uploaded on these sites. Within no time, these become media headlines jolting the lawmakers and custodians of law out of their stupor, and forcing them to act.

When the political class of India found itself at the receiving end of Internet activism, it ingeniously introduced in the IT-Act, the draconian section 66A which drastically curtailed the freedom of expression of the Indian citizen by criminalising 'offensive" or "annoying" posts. Several arrests were made invoking the ignominious law until a landmark judgement by the Supreme Court struck it down and upheld the freedom of speech guaranteed under Article 19(1) (A) of the Constitution of India.

Aid to Vocabulary

1. *Encompasses* — includes
2. *Phenomenon* — occurrence
3. *Literary* — dealing with literature
4. *Throttle* — obstruct
5. *Paparazzi* — journalists or photographers who chase famous people to get their interesting stories or photographs
6. *Biased* — influenced
7. *Autonomy* — right of self-governance
8. *Mannerisms* — the peculiar ways of behaviour that have become a habit
9. *Teetotaller* — one who never drinks alcohol
10. *Eroticism* — the quality arousing lust
11. *Browsing* — going through information here and there

POINTS TO REMEMBER

1. The media has the ability to penetrate the remotest parts of the earth and make its presence felt.
2. The media can be used for disseminating information as well as for imparting education to the masses.
3. In urban sectors, media is generally used for infotainment, i.e., for providing both information and entertainment.
4. The Press Council of India was set up under Act 37 of 1978 to safeguard the freedom of the Press, maintain and improve the standard of newspapers and news agencies.
5. Films Division was set up in 1948 to revive the production of newsreels and documentary films.
6. The advent of Internet and e-mail has made the world 'a global village.'
7. Today, the media enjoys a wider coverage as well as a wider viewership. As a result, a new phenomenon, trial by the media has emerged.
8. Net activism generates public outcry and forces authorities to act.
9. Section 66A of the IT Act was struck down after media uproar.

SOCIAL MEDIA

The world today is a 'global village' mainly because of the Social Media. It has created a virtual world with millions of inhabitants who interact freely cutting across vast distances with much ease.

Mark Zuckerberg co-created *Facebook* during his sophomoric days with his partners Eduardo Saverin, Dustin Moscovitz and Chris Hughes. It is the most famous social networking site with more than 600 million users world wide.

Twitter was created in 2006 by Jack Dorsey as a microblogging site which is also extremely popular with more than 190 million users the world over. A "daylong brainstorming session" held by board members of a pod casting company *Odeo* led to the birth of *Twitter*.

Handling social media has now become a skill by itself. Companies are hiring social media experts to take care of their communication and advertising needs. Ordinary people are able to advance their careers with the help of these sites. Celebrities utilise these sites to communicate directly with their fans on a day-to-day basis or otherwise. The social media has immense possibilities, some of which are yet to be explored. However, there are certain drawbacks too, just as in other forms of media. Posts made on such sites can invite both negative and positive comments. They can influence young minds and lead to psychological problems too. So it is advisable to exercise caution while expressing oneself in social media.

SEC 66A IS DEAD BUT/SOME OTHER IPC PROVISIONS STILL SCARE

Sec 5001 Defamation; Sec 505 I public mischief; Sec 506 I criminal intimidation; Sec 5091 insulting modesty; Sec 124A I sedition; Sec 295A1 Blasphemy

'WE NEED TO TOLERATE UNPOPULAR VIEWS'

Striking down Section 66A (IT Act), SC said seamless exchange of views on any subject was cardinal to democracy and argued against stifling annoying statements of citizens.

It found Section 66A offensive to free speech guaranteed under Article 19(1)(a) regulated under Article 19(2). The court said freedom of speech and expression embodied three concepts—discussion, advocacy and incitement. "Mere discussion or even advocacy of a particular cause, howsoever unpopular, is at the heart of Article 19(1)(A). It's only when such discussion or advocacy reaches the level of incitement that (restrictions in) Article 19(2) kicks in." The court faulted Section 66A for being vaguely-worded and widely-cast to catch every internet user. It accepted that "public's right to know is directly affected by Section 66A."

Writing the judgment, Justice Nariman said as citizens of a democratic country we must realise the importance of giving space to the right to dissent and air views even if they were unpopular.

Essay 61

TELEVISION AND PRESENT-DAY STUDENTS

SYNOPSIS

Television is a wonderful invention of science. It is an important medium of instruction, education and entertainment. Television has become an addiction in modern times. Students prefer watching entertainment programmes rather than informative ones. Some of these programmes contain a lot of vulgar stuff based on sex, crime and violence. They leave a bad impression upon the young minds. They lose interest in games and hobbies. Food habit of the children is by and large formed by the advertisements that appear on TV screen. Constant watching of the television affects the eyesight. Most children become obese as a result of being glued to the television. Children should be guided by the parents to lead a disciplined life.

Television, a miracle of science, was invented by J.L. Baird. It was introduced in India on an experimental basis in Delhi on September 15, 1959. This was made into a regular service in 1965. On April 1, 1976, Doordarshan was delinked from All India Radio to form an independent Directorate. There had been persistent demands for All India Radio and Doordarshan to be made into independent and unbiased bodies. The Prasar Bharati Act is a step in that direction. With the help of a TV, one can see on screen live telecasts of various events across the world while sitting in the comfort of one's own house.

Television is an important medium of *instruction*[1], education and entertainment. It is a *boon*[2] for students in a developing country like India. Educational programmes can reach out to the students living in the farthest and remotest parts of the country. Informative programmes like the University Grants Commission's (UGC) special instruction on all the subjects meant for students pursuing distance education, benefit every student. Channels like *Discovery* and *National Geographic* are the fountains of knowledge. There are several news channels, which provide information on various national and international events. Programmes featuring debate and discussion *enhance*[3] one's knowledge and reasoning skills.

Television *mobilises*[4] public opinion, which is a must for democracy. It helps to focus attention on social and political evils prevailing in the society. It popularises the government's plans and policies. Thus, students remain aware of the various events going on in the country and around the world.

In modern times, television has become an *addiction*[5]. Students remain *glued*[6] to the *idiot box*[7]. Educational programmes no longer interest them. They prefer watching films, music and serials. They fail to differentiate between good and bad programmes.

Watching TV constantly for 2-3 hours or more really harms them both mentally and physically. Most of the programmes contain a lot of *vulgar stuff*[8]. They promote sex and violence. Contract killings, murders, kidnaps, rape scenes, offering and accepting of bribes, etc., are shown in an *explicit*[9] manner. These scenes influence the impressionable minds of the children.

Increasing influence of television is being felt on school-goers. They like to have their meals with the television switched on. They forget their home work *assignments*[10]. They are not able to concentrate on studies. They lose interest in playing games and pursuing their hobbies. They prefer watching television rather than playing outdoor games. Sporting events like cricket, tennis, wrestling, etc., entertain them a lot. The regularity of life and the punctuality of work gets disturbed. Regular viewing of the television makes them lazy and affects their health.

Food habits of the young children by and large are formed by the advertisements that appear on the TV screen. These ads are prepared in such a way as to impress deeply the young minds. Instead of taking healthy home-made food, they begin to insist for food that was displayed on TV in an ad. Mostly those food stuffs lack in nutrition and are comparatively costly. Only the parents can dissuade them from falling a prey to these high sounding ads; teachers too can contribute in this endeavour.

Watching television is gradually turning into a health hazard. Constant viewing of the television causes damage to the eyes. Late night television viewing adversely affects the health. It causes indigestion and other health- related problems. Some children do not eat properly as they *indulge*[11] themselves in television-viewing, while some overeat. Today, most children are *obese*[12] because they spend more time sitting or relaxing in front of the television. *Cardiac*[13] problems are on the rise because of obesity. People these days suffer from kidney problems, diabetes, arthritis, blood pressure, depression, etc. The latest survey says that addiction to television is one of the important causes of these diseases.

Studies suggest that Television programmes portray higher levels of sexuality of teens and adults than what exists in reality. As a result, it adds up to early teenage sex. Television also does not portray the negative consequence of sex, such as unexpected teenage pregnancy or sexually transmitted diseases. The researchers recommend that this situation can be rectified by the proper guidance of parents as well as teachers.

Tender minds of the children are affected by the programmes they watch. Surveys point out that some children who get involved in crimes do get the ideas from television serials or films. There are numerous examples of children trying to imitate the dangerous stunts enacted in various television programmes or *commercials*[14]. Juvenile *delinquency*[15] is becoming a major problem in the society.

Today's children are the citizens of tomorrow. If prolonged watching of television is allowed to continue in homes, the children and youth will have knowledge only about films and related topics and little of other subjects. This will adversely affect the nation's growth and development.

However, watching television is not altogether bad. It is just like a knife which can be used for cutting fruits and vegetables and also for stabbing a person. Much depends on the choice of the viewers. Besides watching shows that provide only entertainment, students should watch more of those programmes which may help them in gaining knowledge. Excess of anything is bad. One should not be glued to the television till late hours. The time spent in watching TV can be regulated.

Young minds should not be exposed to violence. It is the duty of the parents to guide their children. Parents should also watch informative programmes with their children. They should encourage their children to play outdoor games and also to participate in co-curricular activities for better health. The concerned authorities should ensure that movies and programmes meant for adults are aired only at late-night hours. Similarly, advertisements which may harm the impressionable minds should be allowed only in late-night programmes. Watching a right mix of different programmes is desirable. Students should watch informative and knowledge-based programmes apart from other programmes like sports, dance and music that help them to relax. Some such programmes are Zed-education and programmes on Discovery Channel.

Television, till a couple of decades ago, was considered a luxury. Now it has become a part of every household, be it rich or poor. It is the most powerful medium of mass communication.

Aid to Vocabulary

1. *Instruction* — process of teaching
2. *Boon* — help, blessing
3. *Enhance* — heighten
4. *Mobilises* — generates

5. *Addiction* — strong habit
6. *Glued* — attached
7. *Idiot-box* — television
8. *Vulgar stuff* — low and mean things
9. *Explicit* — open
10. *Assignments* — works
11. *Indulge* — to allow (yourself) to have or do something as a special pleasure
12. *Obese* — very fat
13. *Cardiac* — connected with the heart
14. *Commercials* — advertisements aimed at financial profit
15. *Juvenile delinquency* — offences committed by people below age of legal responsibility

Points to Remember

1. Television is a miracle of science.
2. It is the medium of instruction, education and entertainment.
3. It mobilises public opinion.
4. Watching television has become an addiction.
5. Crime and violence are shown in an explicit manner.
6. Students lose interest in studies, games and hobbies.
7. Television is gradually turning into a health hazard.
8. Parents should guide their children on the kind of shows that they should watch.
9. The government should check the programmes and objectives of the electronic media.
10. Watching a right mix of different programmes is desirable.

CONSORTIUM FOR EDUCATIONAL COMMUNICATION VYAS CHANNEL

CEC has established and is running an exclusive 24×7 CEC-UGC Higher Education Satellite Channel of MHRD called Vyas channel. The 24×7 transmission is based on educational content produced on various undergraduate subjects to supplement the classroom teaching. The advantages of having such channel is that education can reach to large number of viewers across millions of households. The knowledge and information gap which exists due to lack of communication in remote places gets bridged to a great extent through this mode. With the mission to carry knowledge to households and students, teachers and public to bridge the knowledge and information gap and to provide the same quality of higher education to all, the channel on higher education was launched on 26th January, 2004.

The undergraduate educational programmes are being telecast on Vyas 24Hours Higher Education Channel available on DD Direct Plus, a DTH platform of Doordarshan and also on Dish TV, a private DTH operator. To ensure the reach and availability of our channel throughout the country and globally, CEC is using the powerful medium of internet and is thus webcasting the channel. The channel is also available on www.webcast.gov.in/vyaslive.

Essay **62**

INDIAN CINEMA AND THE IMAGE OF WOMEN

SYNOPSIS

When cinema was introduced in India, women were not allowed to act. In the 1930s, women started acting in films. The fifties portrayed the emergence of the bold and assertive women. The heroines of this era were immortalised for the roles they essayed. The sixties witnessed a new phase, when women were used as glamour dolls. Parallel cinema also emerged during this period. In the seventies, Hindi 'avante-garde' cinema reached its bloom period. In the eighties, many women directors, depicting real-life characters, flourished. The parallel cinema depicted women in a fair light, while the commercial cinema of the nineties failed to do so and only commodified the woman. Now many directors are making films on women's issues.

The development of the Indian film industry is as old, varied and exciting as the history of the medium itself. The image of women in Indian cinema tends to change with the changes in our society and at times it turns out to be the other way round. The first Indian silent movie was *Raja Harishchandra* directed by Dadasaheb Phalke. This film was released in 1913 with *subtitles*[1] in Hindi as well as English. In this film, the characters of Taramati and other females were played by men dressed as women because women were not allowed to act in films in those times. Other prominent film-makers of this decade were J.F. Madan, Krishna Rao Mistry, Suchet Singh, Manilal Joshi, A.M. Irani, V. Shantaram and Chandulal Shah.

The most remarkable thing about the birth of films with sound in India is that they came with a bang and quickly took the place of the silent movies. The first Indian talkie *Alam Ara* was directed by A.M. Irani and with this, women ventured into films. Zubeida, Prithvi Raj Kapoor and Yakub were the main artistes of this film. During the thirties, attempts were made to produce talkie films in different regional languages. In the latter half of the thirties, several studios had sprung up in Calcutta, Bombay, Kolhapur, Lahore, Madras and so on. In this period, a number of films depicting social injustice were made. The notable films were *Duniya Na Mane*, *Admi aur Padosi*, *Achhut Kanya*, *Karma*, *Devdas*, *Vidyapati*, *Sant Tukaram*, *Mukti*, etc. Devika Rani worked in Himanshu Rai productions and was a dominant heroine of those times. Her portrayal of the untouchable girl in *Achhut Kanya* won her many *accolades*[2]. Again, Yamuna Roy's role in *Devdas* and Kanan Devi's role in *Mukti* were greatly praised. Films like *Dahej*, *Patita*, etc., portrayed the dark side of our society. In *Patita*, the hero, being aware of the social implications of his association with the dishonourable lady, marries her and helps in the emancipation of the victim. *Mahal* was another movie, wherein the heroine chooses and proposes to the man she likes. It could thus be said that the heroines of the thirties and forties were not submissive, and thus, films made a bold statement vis-à-vis reformation of society and emancipation of women.

It was in the fifties that Hindi films found their unique style. The techniques, grammar and motifs were shaped into a formula which continued to remain unchanged over decades. The impact of neo-realism was evident in some distinguished films like *Do Bigha Zamin, Madhumati, Awara, Boot Polish, Shri 420, Jagte Raho, Mother India, Pyaasa, Kagaz Ke Phool*, etc. The 50's saw the emergence of immortal heroines like Madhubala, Sadhana, Nargis, Geeta Bali, Waheeda Rahman, Vyjayantimala, Nutan, Meena Kumari, Suraiya, Saira Banu and a host of other talented heroines. Madhubala was the *epitome*[3] of beauty and *enamoured*[4] cinemagoers through the ages. Nargis did excellent movies during her long association with the RK banner. Her association with Mehboob Khan, however, was successful in producing the all-time classic *Mother India*. The representation of the mother as a bold, *assertive*[5] woman was perhaps shown for the first time on Indian screen and was in stark contrast to the typically forlorn Indian mother. Nutan, as a *juvenile*[6] *delinquent*[7] in *Bandini* and Seema as an untouchable in *Sujata*, inspired a great deal of awe. Meena Kumari was another heroine of those times who was greatly appreciated for her acting genius. Her portrayal of a *courtesan*[8] in *Chitralekha* as well as in *Pakeeza* is immortal. Waheeda Rahman's roles in Guru Dutt's films were praised by all. K Asif's *magnum opus*[9] *Mughal-E-Azam* set a new record at the box office, wherein Madhubala played a silent lover and sufferer at the hands of a man. In *Sahib, Bibi aur Ghulam*, Meena Kumari portrayed a devoted wife to an *adulterous*[10] husband, while in *Guide*, Waheeda Rahman portrayed an ambitious woman who dumped the very person who helped her to scale heights.

The cinema of the fifties has left such a deep impact on our minds that whenever we think of an ideal mother we think of Durga Khote or Nirupa Roy while Lalita Powar stands out as the embodiment of a domineering and cruel mother-in-law. Incidentally, the 50's opened up the world market for Indian films.

After the creative heights of the fifties, the sixties proved a bit of a disappointment. It was a period of mediocre films in the Hindi Film Industry. Films were made mostly to please the distributors and to meet the demands of the box office. The sixties witnessed a new phase in terms of depiction of women in cinema. They were portrayed mainly as glamour dolls in every movie that would invariably be hero-oriented. Asha Parekh, Saira Banu, Mala Sinha, Vyjayantimala all played this type of adjunct roles. At the same time, there were a few remarkable feature films with memorable characters too.

The late fifties and sixties also witnessed the advent of parallel cinema in India with the emergence film makers like Satyajit Ray, Ritwik Ghatak, Mrinal Sen and Shyam Benegal. Satyajit Ray's classic *Pather Panchali* projected Indian cinema on to the world screen. Here, the helplessness of a woman in a starving family was portrayed to great effect. Ritwik Ghatak's *Meghe Dhaka Tara*, *Komal Gandhar* and *Subarnarekha* brought to life the sacrifice and helplessness of women in our society. Actresses like Madhabi Mukherjee and Supriya Devi portrayed these roles excellently. Mrinal Sen's *Bhuvan Shome* starring Utpal Dutt and Suhasini Mulay depicted the innocence and vulnerability of a village girl in our society. Shyam Benegal's *Ankur* showed how a woman (lead role played by Shabana Azmi) could stand up for her rights, when cornered or *provoked*[11].

The seventies further widened the gap between multi-starrer big budget films and offbeat films. The popular Hindi hits of this decade include Kamal Amrohi's *Pakeeza,* Raj Kapoor's *Bobby*, Ramesh Sippy's *Sholay*, *Zanjeer*, *Deewar*, etc. *Pakeeza* reflected the predicament of a *nautch-girl*[12] whom the male protagonist proposes to marry defying the norms and inviting the criticism from the society. With *Bobby*, teenage romance came as a breath of fresh air in Indian films.

The 'avante-garde' or new wave of Hindi cinema seemed to have reached its bloom period towards the end of the seventies with the coming-of-age of film-makers like Govind Nihalani (*Aakrosh, Ardha Satya*), Saeed Mirza (*Albert Pinto Ko Gussa Kyon aata hai*), Rabindra Dharmaraj (*Chakra*), Biplab Roy Chowdhari (*Shodh*), and a few others. The new cinema movement continued with a vigorus spirit in the following decade also. Shyam Benegal's films like *Manthan, Bhumika, Nishant* and Ketan Mehta's *Mirch Masala*, etc., portrayed the oppressed condition of women in our society. Actors like Smita Patil and Shabana Azmi portrayed these roles with great aplomb. Films like *Masoom* and *Ijaazat* reflected the agony of the wife of an unfaithful husband. *Umrao Jaan* narrated the story of a girl accidentally sold into an ancient profession of the world, the courtesan's. *Ek Chaadar Maili Si* made a statement on the peculiar situation of an Indian widow, who is forced to marry her young brother-in-law to retain her share of the family property. These films tried to highlight the reality of our society.

The eighties saw the advent of women directors and film-makers, namely, Vijaya Mehta (*Rao Saheb*), Aparna Sen (*36 Chowringhee Lane, Paroma*), Sai Paranjpe (*Chashme Baddoor, Katha, Sparsh*), Kalpana Lajmi (*Ek Pal, Rudali*), Prema Karanth (*Phaniamma),* Deepa Mehta *(Earth, Fire, Water—Elements Trilogy)* and Meera Nair (*Salaam Bombay*). The most commendable attribute of these directors is their individuality. The central theme of the films by these women directors by and large is women's rights. Directors like Mahesh Bhatt (*Sadak, Zakhm*), Madhur Bhandarkar (*Chandni Bar, Page Three, Fashion, Heroine*) and Rituparno Ghosh (*Unishe April, Dahan*) have given films that make man realise and regret the atrocities committed by him on women.

The late eighties and early nineties saw the revival of the musical love story in *Mr. India, Tezaab, Qayamat Se Qayamat Tak, Maine Pyar Kiya, Ashiqui*, etc., which were clean, musical films bereft of any vulgarity. These films gave women a fair deal of dignity. At that time, Indian cinema was facing tough competition with television and these films brought those audiences back to the theatres. However, the late nineties depicted women as a symbol of glamour and thereby degraded the image of women.

The last ten years of Indian cinema have seen entirely new categories and idioms being created within mainstream cinema. Nearly everyone tried something new with subjects, treatment, roles, language techniques and limits. Directors like Mira Nair, Kalpana Lajmi, Deepa Mehta, Meghna Gulzar, Nagesh Kukunoor, Ashutosh Gowarikar, Gautam Ghosh, Aparna Sen and Rituparno Ghosh made films on issues related to women's rights, individuality and self-reliance. Today, Indian women have created a distinct place for themselves. Many directors are highlighting this newfound *emancipation*[13] of the womenfolk.

R. Balki's *Cheeni Kum* captured the social dynamics commissioned by a woman entering into a relationship with a man of her father's age, thus reflecting the changing norms in Indian society. Sujoy Ghosh told a thrilling *Kahani* of a headstrong woman who single-handedly trails her missing husband's killer, outmaneuvering the investigating officers. Madhur Bhandarkar's *Fashion* won Priyanka Chopra a National Film Award for the portrayal of a fiercely ambitious small-town aspirant who willingly compromises with values and stoically braves hurdles in her journey to reach the top of the world of fashion. Gauri Shinde depicted the predicament of an Indian woman confounded by the language barrier in a foreign country who eventually braves all odds to master the foreign language *(English Vinglish)*. Such movies reflected the increasingly assertive voice that the new-age woman has come to find.

Cinema has played an important role in empowering women by setting their characters in a world which was much ahead of their times. Thus, in a way cinema anticipated the liberated woman of today. As did films like *Bhumika*, *Arth*, *Ankur* or *Manthan* in the bygone era, today's features films, namely *The Namesake, Heroine, Fashion, English Vinglish, Kahani, Queen* etc., make a bold statement about the Indian woman's remarkable *resilience*[14]. The *protagonist*[15] in each of these films *braves*[16] all odds to break free of the shackles of social norms, and sheds all inhibitions to exercise her will and *assert*[17] herself. Such films truly celebrate the spirit of the emancipated woman.

Besides Hindi films, those, in regional languages are also very popular in their respective regions. Most of them have a 'social' theme and they also try to offer resolutions to various problems that women of different strata of society face in their own way.

The influence of cinema has always been significant in every aspect of life. It makes an impact on human psyche. Viewers learn a number of things through this medium. Over the years, we have become more *discerning*[18] as an audience, since we are new living in a global village. We like to experience real-life stories through cinema. Cinema in these changing times ought to depict the Indian woman in her real-life situations. More movies on issues concerning women, should be made so as to educate the masses with regard to the betterment of the position of women in the present-day society.

Aid to Vocabulary

1. *Subtitles* — Translations displayed in a particular language of what is being said in a different language on-screen
2. *Accolades* — strong praise and approval
3. *Epitome* — a perfect example
4. *Enamoured* — charmed
5. *Assertive* — expressing forcefully
6. *Juvenile* — young and not legally adult
7. *Delinquent* — young people showing tendency to commit crimes
8. *Courtesan* — a prostitute whose clients are noble and socially important people
9. *Magnum opus* — a great work of art, considered the best piece of work of the person who created it

10. *Adulterous* — married person having an affair with someone other than the spouse
11. *Provoked* — incited to become angry
12. *Nautch-girl* — professional dancing girl
13. *Emancipation* — freedom from restraint
14. *Resilience* — succeeding despite setbacks
15. *Protagonist* — main character
16. *Braves* — faces or endures
17. *Assert (one self)* — insist on (one's) rights and act/speak strongly
18. *Discerning* — having or showing good judgement or insight

Points to Remember

1. In Indian cinema way back in 1913, women were not allowed to act.
2. In the thirties of the last century, women started acting in films.
3. The fifties saw the emergence of the bold and assertive woman.
4. The women of the sixties were reduced to being mere glamour dolls. Parallel cinema also emerged during this period.
5. In the seventies, the Hindi 'avante-garde' cinema reached its bloom period with actors like Smita Patil, Shabana Azmi, etc., coming to the fore.
6. In parallel cinema, many women film-makers of the eighties showed women in powerful roles.
7. The nineties saw women as a symbol of glamour, and degraded their image.
8. Today many directors are making films on women's issues.

COMMERCIAL CINEMA OFFER GREAT WOMEN CHARACTERS NOW: FILMMAKER KIRAN RAO

Filmmaker Kiran Rao feels Indian cinema has started coming up with better roles for women now. She feels it would have been impossible to make a film like 'Queen' a decade ago. The Kangana Ranaut-starrer is often hailed as one of the best films to have been made in recent times on women. It's great that in popular commercial cinema there are great women characters, and wonderful roles for women.

Kiran Rao says the film industry only scouts for talent irrespective of gender, and that is the reason why there are so many women working in Bollywood in various departments. "As we all know many women work behind the scenes who may not be directors...We have women working everywhere and there is always room for more. "The industry is welcoming, they only look at talent. We are only interested in your voice. There's no way more women are not going to be in the film industry as we go along. I firmly believe it," she further said. The fact that films can be made with more sensitivity towards the question of gender is something we believe is important to acknowledge. At the 18th Jio MAMI Mumbai International Film Festival with Star', whose co-chairperson was Kiran, two new awards were introduced, called 'best film on gender equality' and 'best Indian female filmmaker'.

The director hopes the awards will encourage more women to come in Bollywood.

Source: PTI

Essay
63

THE ROLE OF ADVERTISING

SYNOPSIS

Advertising is a form of mass communication. It pertains to numerous forms of presentation including signs, symbols, etc. It gives information, arouses interest and tries to persuade people to buy a product. Over the years, the standard of advertising has improved a lot. Advertising is dynamic and plays a crucial role in educating, informing, inspiring and motivating a layman on a number of social issues. Advertisements are also used to promote things like alcohol, tobacco, cigarette, etc., that can be injurious to health. Advertising has a bright future in India and it has the potential to help in economic development.

Advertising is a form of mass communication. It involves the process of transmission of information by the manufacturer or a seller of a product or service to modify or stimulate the behaviour of the buyer to buy a particular product. The term advertising is derived from the Latin word *'advertene'*. It means "to turn people's attention to a specified thing". Advertising pertains to numerous forms of presentation such as signs, symbols or illustrations in print media, a commercial on radio or television, poster, etc. Thus, advertising is the communication link between the seller and the buyer.

Advertising plays a major role in consumer marketing, and has enabled companies to meet communication and other marketing objectives. Typically, advertising is used to inform, persuade, remind and also enhance consumer's knowledge. It essentially reinforces their attitudes and perceptions.

The first advertising agency was set up in 1875—N. W. Ayer and sons of Philadelphia had for the first time offered to produce advertisement and also to manage the bookings of space in newspapers. The earliest advertisements in India were published in the *Bengal Gazette* or the *Calcutta General Advertiser.* The advertisements then focused on informing about sales of furniture, arrival of ships, births, deaths (obituaries), etc.

With the dawn of the 19th century, advertising acquired a different character altogether. And another decade later, it completely transformed into a tool of hard-selling, harping and even exaggerating the virtues of products and services. With the passage of time, publications and bigger organisations established their own advertising departments. Today, there are many industries which spend heavily on advertising.

Today, the world is dominated by all kinds of advertisements—economic, commercial as well as political. Advertising is a paid form of non-personal presentation of ideas, goods or services to those who need them the most and also to *persuade*[1] the same target group to act upon or make a purchase. It gives information, arouses interest and tries to obtain satisfaction of people by selling products or services to them. It appeals to the imagination of the viewers and motivates them to purchase the right product. One of the basic ingredients of today's popular culture is consumption and it is the advertising industry that makes mass consumption possible. Advertising is an important element of our culture because it reflects, and also attempts to change, our lifestyles.

The advertising message has to reach a billion people, who speak different languages, practise various religions and are scattered all across India. Advertisers can reach their audiences through television, radio, cinema, print media, outdoor advertising, sales promotion and the Internet. Advertising, which was originally an American concept, found its place in a country like India and created an *incredible*[2] awareness among the people in the past decade. During the pre-Independence era, Indian advertisements were mostly about clothes, travelling, eating, tea, etc. In the post-Independence period, the focus of advertisements shifted from luxury goods to consumer goods. In early 20th century, the advertising agencies such as Indian Advertising Agency and Calcutta Advertising Agency were started. The Advertising Agencies Association of India (AAAI) was established in 1945, to represent the interests and problems of the advertising profession.

In 1976, the first commercial air time appeared on television and in 1980, the first advertisement sponsors were entertained. The standard of advertisements has improved a lot since then and in the modern world, advertisements control our life from morning to night. They dictate the brand of tea with which we begin our day and the brand of laxative we take before going to bed at night. In everyday life, we find advertising exploring new avenues and markets and, finally, reaching those people and places that had remained untouched by its ever-expanding reach.

Advertising is *dynamic*[3]. As a mass medium, it changes with changing markets, changing lifestyles, changing methods of distribution and changing techniques of communication. It informs about a wide range of available choices and facilitates the selection process. Advertising also helps in the development of the society as it increases consumption, raises the standard of living and improves the quality of life of people. Our perception of anything and everything has been shaped by advertising. It contributes substantially to consumer education and knowledge about a product or service, and also builds confidence in consumers.

As of today, advertising plays a crucial role not only in India but all over the world in educating, informing, inspiring and motivating the layman on a number of social issues and themes. Advertisements on environment protection, healthy living, etc., contribute to the welfare of a nation. In India, advertising is performing the function of developing social conscience. Many advertisements have been prepared for social schemes and campaigns like Clean Ganga, donation of eyes, immunisation, family planning, awareness about AIDS, pollution, anti-drug addiction, etc. Advertising campaigns can uplift the tone and *tenor*[4] of communication in the society. Advertising campaigns, through mass media are given much importance as they help the masses to understand the messages and participate in developmental programmes with positive attitudes. Sometimes big advertising agencies, which are socially aware and concerned, produce these advertisements themselves for the government or social organisations on a no profit, no loss basis. As technology is changing, the advertising medium is also acquiring new dimensions. With the advent of e-commerce and the internet, today Indian advertising, in tune with global dynamics, is making giant strides in netvertisement (advertising on the Net).

Against its numerous advantages, advertising has some undesirable impacts as well. It creates the need for products which are not really required thereby affecting human values. Advertisements are also used to promote things like alcohol, tobacco, cigarette, etc., that are injurious to health. Advertising affects the young minds to a great extent, especially when entertainment is *interspersed*[5] with commercial messages. Adults may be able to develop a rational resistance to this onslaught, but children usually cannot owing to their impressionable minds. For the TV advertiser, therefore, children are a very attractive target group to be cultivated. Statistics indicate that children constitute nearly 34.75 per cent of the total population and therefore it becomes imperative from the point of view of the advertiser that they be made an important target segment for product promotions.

TV advertising targeting children is an investment for the future. By the time they grow up to become buyers, they are already oriented towards certain brands and kinds of products. Advertisements, however, are criticised for portraying women in a *derogatory*[6] manner or for commodifying them which affects children and society adversely. Advertising is seen by many as a threat to the cultural identity and self-realisation in many developing countries. It brings, to many people, alien ethical values. It may deviate from consumer demands in developing countries to areas which can inhibit development priorities. it affects and can often deform ways of life and lifestyles. Vulgarity, violence and sex must be avoided in the promotion of products. Advertising should not be allowed to compromise human values.

Overall, advertisements spread awareness about new and innovative products thereby helping in improving the living standard of people. However, one should be judicious and rational enough to assess the information provided by various advertisements and should not blindly trust them. Though advertising has its negative effects, the positive side far *outstrips*[7] the negative side. The future of advertising in India is bright. It is also expected to fulfil its social responsibility and is likely to spur economic growth in the country.

Aid to Vocabulary

1. *Persuade* — convince
2. *Incredible* — that cannot be believed
3. *Dynamic* — active
4. *Tenor* — the general character and meaning of something
5. *Interspersed* — placed here and there
6. *Derogatory* — lowering one's reputation, insulting
7. *Outstrips* — surpasses

Points to Remember

1. Advertising is a form of mass communication.
2. Advertising plays a major role in consumer marketing.
3. The first advertising agency was set up in 1875.
4. Advertising was an American concept which has found its place in India.
5. Advertising is dynamic.
6. Advertisement helps in educating, informing and inspiring people on social issues. Advertising medium is acquiring new dimensions.
7. Advertising has some undesirable effects also.
8. Advertising impacts people's ways of life and lifestyles.
9. The future of Indian advertising is bright if it fulfils its social responsibility too.

'INTRUSIVE ONLINE ADS RUINING CONSUMER EXPERIENCE IN INDIA'

Nearly half of Indian consumers who are connected on the Internet feel they are "constantly followed" by online advertising and the menace of intrusive and uncontrolled campaigns are ruining consumer experience, according to global research agency Kantar TNS. In a study titled 'Connected Life', the research agency said the findings point to the need for a major rethink for the online advertising industry in India in terms of how it should reach out to consumers.

"What would come as a shock to the industry, it has been found that nearly half (47 per cent) of India's connected consumers feel 'constantly followed' by online advertising." The menace of intrusive and uncontrolled online advertising is ruining the consumer experience in India."

In the study of over 70,000 consumers by Kantar TNS, it was also found that the connected consumers in India are fans of social media. "The top five most popular social media platforms in India are Facebook (75 per cent), YouTube (64 per cent), Twitter (34 per cent), Instagram (25 per cent) and Snapchat (19 per cent), representing alternative ways of interacting with audiences," it added. More than half (53 per cent) of the online 16-24 year olds in India say, they trust what people say online about brands more than 'official' sources such as newspapers, brands' own websites or TV advertisements. The older generation's 'influencer network' is still primarily friends and family.

Kantar TNS said developments in mobile technology are a clear driver, with the number of smartphone users across the Asia-Pacific now numbering over a billion, and increasingly powerful smartphone cameras giving connected users the opportunity to take and share photos instantly.

Source: Press Trust of India

Essay 64

THE ROLE OF YOUTH IN INDIA

SYNOPSIS

Youth is the valuable human resource of every country. The young people constitute about forty per cent of the total population of India. During the freedom struggle, the youth of our country played a significant role. There is a generation gap between the young and the old. The youth should be guided and their energies should be utilised for the progress of the nation. Today India is burdened with many social, political and economic problems. The youth can come forward and check them, and work for the betterment of the nation. Given facilities and responsibilities, youth in India can put the nation on the path of progress. The youth can also provide relief to the afflicted persons during natural calamities. By performing a constructive role, the youth can make India prosperous in every field.

The youth of every country is its valuable human resource. The young people can play an important role in various developmental activities going on in the country. The responsibility for change, progress and *innovation*[1] lies on their shoulders. Youth is the carrier of cultural identity of a country. Youth can make or *mar*[2] a society. Therefore, their energies should be directed properly.

The youth of our country played a very important role during our freedom struggle. The political leaders gave a lead to the students and they joined the struggle in large numbers. However, since the attainment of Independence, the youth have remained more or less inactive. They have stayed away from *contemporary*[3] national politics.

Considering the immense potential of the Youth, the leaders of the freedom movement did not at all hesitate to call upon them and they, in turn, exhibited their full might to change the history of India.

The potential of the Youth was manifested again in the Jay Prakash Narayan Movement in 1977 that changed the whole system and overthrew the long-standing political dispensation at the Centre. The unparalleled might that the Youth possess can alter the destiny of the country. Since those historic occasions, our youths have remained passive owing largely to the *callousness*[4] of the ruling government that has failed to engage them actively in the elimination of different problems that the country is faced with, and they, therefore, indulge in destructive activities leading to the regression of the nation.

The youth constitute about 60 per cent of the total population of India. The youth today have often been misunderstood by the elders. There has always been a struggle between tradition and modernity. The elders consider the youth to be immature and inexperienced. The widening generation gap has made them feel *alienated*[5]. The growing population has aggravated the problem of unemployment. Reservations and *nepotism*[6] have further heightened the problem. Schools and colleges do not *groom*[7] them for a bright future. All these factors have made the youth a frustrated lot.

Students constitute majority of the youth. They indulge in acts of indiscipline and rowdyism in many universities, colleges and schools. Thus, their energies and *zeal*[8] are being misused for destructive purposes. They hold rallies, stage demonstrations and resort to strikes, etc. They go to the extent of taking law into their own hands. They lack proper guidance and good leadership. They should be properly guided so that they use their energies gainfully.

The students alone cannot be blamed for this. Political leaders *exploit*[9] students' power for their own vested interests. If there is good leadership, students' power can be utilised for bringing about social, economic and political reforms in the country. The government can come out with innovative programmes to engage the youth constructively in some kind of stipend-based vocational training that can subsequently absorb them in the mainstream services.

Today India is burdened with many problems in the social and economic spheres. Corruption, increasing population, high illiteracy rate, social evils like child labour, dowry, drug addiction, etc., are some of the burning problems. The youth should take an active part in solving these problems, which have hampered the progress of the country. The power of youth can bring about drastic change in the society. This in turn will help in the fast progress of the nation.

Corruption has become rampant in the country. The common man *encounters*[10] corruption everywhere starting from politics, bureaucracy to government offices. The youth should organise themselves, form anti-corruption cells and expose the guilty. On a higher level, they could also expose the malpractices by both the politicians and the public servants. This would prevent the domination of ruling class and the powerful from indulging in corrupt practices.

The population of India has crossed the one billion mark. This has *hindered*[11] the progress of the country. Family planning programmes have not been totally accepted by the people. Youth organisations should take up the responsibility of educating the poor about the benefits of family planning. It is the duty of the youth to further the government's efforts to control population.

Illiteracy is another burning problem in our country. The youth should encourage the illiterate parents to send their children to school. They should *initiate*[12] steps to teach the illiterate people of their neighbourhood. They should teach them *elementary*[13] reading and writing. They should also educate them about hygiene and the need for cleanliness. The youth should inform the masses about the harmful effects of drinking, smoking, drug addiction and chewing tobacco.

One of the worst social problems faced by India is the evil of dowry. Hundreds of deaths, suicides and bride burnings are reported every year in our country. Many more of these cases do not come to light at all. The youth should come forward and fight against this evil practice. They should not come under the pressure of their parents to demand, give or accept dowry. The youth can also help in the removal of other social evils like child marriage, casteism, gambling, etc.

The youth should work for national integration. They should fight against communalism, casteism, regionalism, etc. Sometimes, natural calamities like earthquake, flood, cyclone, drought, etc., *afflict*[14] one part or the other of our country resulting in the loss of life and property. Students can mobilise relief to the affected people by raising funds for them and organising relief works.

The government has become conscious of the need to *tap*[15] the youth power. With the lowering of the voting age to 18 years, the youth have become politically important. The youth should cast their vote after careful consideration of the character and policies of the politicians and the respective political parties. Thus, the youth can play a *decisive*[16] role in choosing their leaders.

The first National Youth Policy was formulated and laid in the Parliament in 1988. Again a new National Youth Policy was formulated in 2003 by the Ministry of Youth Affairs and Sports to galvanise the youth to rise up to the new challenges. The age group of youth, as per this policy is 13 to 35. The new policy recognises four thrust areas viz., Youth Empowerment, Gender Justice, Inter-Sectoral Approach and Information and Research Network. The policy provides implementation mechanism through which various development programmes and activities will be undertaken for the youth with active involvement of the state governments and Union Ministries and Departments. Some of the important programmes are National Programme for Youth and Adolescent Development, National

Youth Festival, National Youth Awards, National Service Scheme, Indira Gandhi NSS* Awards, etc.

The Department of Youth Affairs and Sports is implementing a number of schemes for youth development. Our Five Year Plans have laid much *emphasis*[17] on the importance of youth in national development. The government has also introduced several schemes to increase employment opportunities for the youth.

The youth should play a responsible role for the betterment of the country. By playing a constructive role, the youth can make India prosperous in every field.

AID TO VOCABULARY

1. *Innovation* — introducing new ideas, methods, etc.
2. *Mar* — damage or spoil
3. *Contemporary* — belonging to the same time
4. *Callousness* — immaturity
5. *Alienated* — caused to feel different and not a part of a group
6. *Nepotism* — the unfair practice by a person in power of giving jobs and other favours to relatives
7. *Groom* — train a person for a particular career
8. *Zeal* — great energy or enthusiasm
9. *Exploit* — to use someone for one's own advantage or profit
10. *Encounters* — faces or meets something unpleasant
11. *Hindered* — delayed progress
12. *Initiate* — to cause to begin, to put a scheme into operation
13. *Elementary* — basic
14. *Afflict* — to cause trouble or pain or distress
15. *Tap* — to extract or obtain
16. *Decisive* — producing a definite result
17. *Emphasis* — special meaning or importance

POINTS TO REMEMBER

1. Youth constitute about forty per cent of the population of India.
2. The youth played an important role during the freedom struggle.
3. The youth today are a frustrated lot.
4. Students indulge in acts of indiscipline and rowdyism in the educational institutions.
5. India today is burdened with many problems.
6. The youth can check corruption.
7. They can help to check the increasing population.

*NSS – National Service Scheme

8. They can educate the illiterate masses and engage in such other related activities.
9. They can provide relief to victims of natural calamities.
10. They can work for national integration.
11. The government has undertaken steps for the benefit of the youth.
12. The youth can make India prosperous in every field.

NATIONAL SERVICE SCHEME

National Service Scheme (NSS) is a noble experiment in academic expansion. It inculcates the spirit of voluntary work among the students and teachers through sustained community interactions. Over the years, NSS has emerged as India's student youth movement in linking with the community. National Service Scheme, popularly known as NSS was launched in Gandhiji's Birth Centenary year-1969, in 37 universities involving 40,000 students, with primary focus on the development of personality of students through community service. Now, NSS has more than 3.2 million student volunteers on its roll spread over 208 Universities in 10,313 colleges/ institutes of higher and technical education and 7542 Secondary Schools all over the country.

Essay 65

THE ROLE OF THE INTELLECTUAL IN SOCIETY

SYNOPSIS

Among the intellectuals, teachers were held in high esteem in ancient India. The duty of philosophers is to combat dogmatism and irrational beliefs. They are known to initiate revolutions. Rousseau, Montesquieu and Voltaire encouraged people to rise against the despotic rule. The intellectuals are radical in their approach. Some revolutions were accompanied by unprecedented reigns of terror. India has followed a path of tolerance towards all faiths, but the society is bogged down by various maladies. The intellectuals are faced with the challenge of leading the masses from darkness to light. They cannot afford to evade the huge responsibility that lies ahead of them.

Since ancient India has been acknowledged worldwide as the mother of all branches of knowledge, it is no surprise that the intellectuals in general and teachers/gurus in particular have enjoyed the apex place in Indian society. In case a guru was to make his august appearance in the court of king or an emperor, the latter along with all his family members and ministers paved the way for the former's arrival and extended a warm welcome. The guidelines and recommendations of gurus were the sacred commandments for the king. No significant programme what so ever could be organised without their consent or patronage.

In the present world, the duty to *combat*[1] *dogmatism*[2] and irrational beliefs and to reconstruct man's institutions on a more rational basis has been bestowed on the intellectual. The history of mankind has been a *perennial*[3] struggle between rational and irrational forces, between knowledge and enlightenment on the one hand and ignorance, prejudice, lust for power and factionalism on the other. Plato wanted his statesmen to be men of supreme intelligence and impeccable integrity because he felt that, only such men could lighten the darker side of human nature and influence positive human thought. Plato's *Republic* has exercised tremendous influence on human thought. Both Plato and Aristotle provided supreme examples of what the intellectuals can do for their own age and for posterity. Intellectuals influence man's thoughts, direct them into the right channels and seek to establish human relations on a rational and moral basis.

The intellectuals are known to initiate revolutions. The exhaustive wars undertaken by the despotic ruler of France, Louis XIV weakened the country, which led to the growth of discontent among the masses. Later, under the rule of Louis XVI and Marie Antoinette, the plight of the people further *aggravated*[4]. There was an acute shortage of food. The nobles indulged in extravagance and the royalty showed apathy towards the plight of the masses. The writings of the French political philosophers like Jean Jacques Rousseau, Montesquieu and Voltaire, paved the way for the French Revolution (1789). Their views stimulated and inspired people to revolt against the tyrannical rule of the king and their faith in the old institution of the royalty was undermined. The French Revolution with its slogan of 'Liberty, Equality and Fraternity' ushered in a new era in history. When the intellectuals raised their voices against the wrong policies of the government, the common people felt encouraged to rise against the corrupt king and the nobles.

The evils of capitalism, ushered in by the Industrial Revolution, were voiced by Charles Dickens in his works, like *David Copperfield*, *Oliver Twist* and *Hard Times*. In 1809, the word 'socialism' was coined which was presented as an alternative to capitalism. Great thinkers, like Robert Owen, Saint-Simon and Charles Fourier wanted to replace capitalism with the socialism of their imagination. What Rousseau was to the 18th century, Karl Marx was to the 19th century. Marx and his associate, Frederick Engels, introduced the concept of socialism that was not based on sentiments, but on a thorough scientific study of the history of human society. Their joint efforts culminated in the *Communist Manifesto* which formed the basis of modern international communism. The starting point of Marxism is the Hegelian *dialectics*[5]. To state the dialectic in simple language, human progress is by means of contradiction. It is in the form of *thesis*[6], *antithesis*[7] and *synthesis*[8]. Marx developed the theory of dialectical materialism, i.e., the economic interpretation of history. The stage through which society passes are: primitive communism, feudalism, capitalism and communism. Lenin reinterpreted Marxism to suit Russian conditions. His unique contributions were the theory of revolution, organisation, party and leader. Lenin explained two stages of communism. The lower stage is called socialism where the state is under the dictatorship of the *proletariat*[9]. The second stage is communism when the State machinery completely withers away. Communism's applied form was seen only after the October Revolution of 1917 in Russia, when it became the first communist state in the world under Lenin. With the passage of time, many countries also adopted the theory of communism propounded by Marx and Lenin.

The intellectuals have been radical in their approach to the problems faced by the society. They studied the *rudiments*[10] of the social structure to *delve*[11] into its flaws and limitations. They also studied the *efficacy*[12] of holding on to the age-old traditions and myths. They were not deceived by false appearances. In England at the beginning of the previous century, Victorian complacency was shattered and a new spirit of rationality developed.

H. G. Wells, George Bernard Shaw, Bertrand Russell and Aldous Huxley provided Englishmen with fresh ideas, gave them a new insight into the contemporary situation and influenced their thought.

However, one should take note of the dictum, "Wisdom lies in hastening slowly." It is a fact which has been often ignored by the radical intellectuals. Every society follows an age-old system of customs and traditions, which embody the wisdom of ages. A sudden cleavage between tradition and modernity is known to disrupt the social order of the prevalent period. Revolutions have been accompanied by unprecedented reigns of terror as in the case of the French and the Russian revolutions. The revolutions degenerated into mindless violence. A true intellectual, therefore, does not recklessly challenge the social norms laid down by the society. Apart from having lofty ideas, an intellectual should take into account the extent to which the society is prepared for a change. Violent revolutions generally breed dictators, *tyrants*[13] and *despots*[14].

A positive contribution to the social good can be made by an intellectual only if he is honest towards his endeavour and has no *ulterior*[15] motives in the framing of his philosophy. He should not seek popularity by swimming against the tide and using technical *jargons*[16] to create the impression of being progressive. He should *eschew*[17] both dogmatism and *scepticism*[18] and engage himself in the study of the problems which directly affect the society rather than *dissipate*[19] his energies in *sterile*[20] speculations. When an intellectual becomes a pure theorist, imposing his own theories upon history and rationalising his own prejudices and pre-conceived notions, he becomes a dangerous thinker. Followers of *Fascism*[21] and *Nazism*[22] advocated war as an instrument of national policy. They justified the gruesome *extermination*[23] of the Jews and the use of brutal methods to crush opposition. They also encouraged myths and falsehood as the instruments of propaganda.

India has followed a path of tolerance towards all religions and faiths. It has always honoured intellect rather than *pelf*[24] and power. The caste system, which initially only represented the system of division of labour, went on to create a *pernicious*[25] situation in the country. The *pseudo-intellectuals*[26] occupied the apex of the social hierarchy, while the small and marginal farmers formed the base. Our national leaders felt the need to revitalise the nation on the lines of socialism, secularism, nationalism and democracy. It was felt that if these values were imbibed by the masses it would facilitate the industrial and technological revolution required for raising the standard of living of the masses. In the process of uniting against the colonial rule the Indians not only explored their ancient Indian heritage but also imbibed western thoughts and education. Raja Rammohan Roy wanted Indians to blend the wisdom of the East and the West and to modernise their outlook, shedding their old superstitions, caste prejudices and evils in the social system.

The Indian intellectuals of the past delved into the profound realities of life. They sought answers to the lingering questions on life and death and salvation of the soul. Lord Buddha and Lord Mahavira asked men to follow the path of righteousness and *renunciation*[27] for the attainment of salvation. The propounders of the 'Bhakti Movement' emphasised on devotion to a God as a means of attaining *moksha* as against the pathways of *karma* (action) or *gyan* (knowledge). The influence of Islam led to the revival of anti-caste and monotheistic ideas. The famous propounders of this movement were Ramanand, Vallabhacharya, Namdeva, Eknath, Tukaram, Ramdas, Surdas, Kabir, Chaitanyadev, etc. At the time of the British rule Raja Rammohan Roy, Iswarchandra Vidyasagar, Bankimchandra Chatterjee, Vivekananda, Rabindranath Tagore, Prem Chand, A.K. Ghalib, Muhammad Iqbal, Sarojini Naidu and many intellectuals of India penned patriotic writings. This period witnessed a cultural-ideological struggle against the *retrograde*[28] elements of traditional culture. This paved the way for Independence from the colonial rule.

As of today, every individual exercises the freedom of expression through social networking sites, namely *facebook, twitter, linkedin*, and so on. When intellectuals post their opinion on these sites, it gets instant reactions, was killed by assailants and an innocent man was lynched by a communally worked up mob, a host of Sahitya Akademi awardees returned their honour to protest against the growing intellectuals opened up a heated debate and stirred the conscience of the nation. Such is the power of the intellectual.

The contemporary intellectuals are seeking to build a new civilisation driven by science and technology and the western ideals of secularism, nationalism, parliamentary democracy and socialism. Indian society is *bogged down*[29] by various maladies and its politicians exploit the vulnerability of the masses by provoking them and arousing their passions. The intellectuals are faced with the challenge of leading the society from darkness to light, ignorance to knowledge, irrationality to rationality and from narrow-mindedness to openness. They have to instil a new outlook in the masses through their ideas and creations. The intellectuals cannot afford to evade the huge responsibility that lies on their shoulders.

AID TO VOCABULARY

1. *Combat* — to fight against
2. *Dogmatism* — assertion of dogmas or doctrines
3. *Perennial* — everlasting
4. *Aggravated* — worsened
5. *Dialectics* — A method of examining and discussing opposing ideas in order to find the truth

6. *Thesis* — A statement that someone wants to discuss and prove
7. *Antithesis* — The exact opposite of something (of a thesis)
8. *Synthesis* — A combination or blend of different things (ideas, etc.)
9. *Proletariat* — the working class or the lowest social or economic class of a society
10. *Rudiments* — elementary notions
11. *Delve* — to search deeply
12. *Efficacy* — effectiveness
13. *Tyrants* — cruel and unfair rulers with total power
14. *Despots* — cruel rulers with absolute power
15. *Ulterior* — hidden or kept secret
16. *Jargons* — the terminology used by a particular class, trade or profession
17. *Eschew* — avoid
18. *Scepticism* — doubting the truth of a doctrine or theory
19. *Dissipate* — disperse
20. *Sterile* — not producing result, unproductive
21. *Fascism* — society ruled by dictatorial authority
22. *Nazism* — absolute dictatorship like Germany under Adolf Hitler
23. *Extermination* — the act of rooting out
24. *Pelf* — money
25. *Pernicious* — destructive
26. *Pseudo-intellectuals* — those who imitate or pretend to be intellectuals but aren't
27. *Renunciation* — the act of giving up of worldly pleasures
28. *Retrograde* — moving backward
29. *Bogged down* — to prevent somebody from making progress in an activity

Points to Remember

1. The intellectuals have the duty to combat dogmatism and irrational beliefs.
2. The intellectuals are known to initiate revolutions.
3. Marxism-Leninism had a great influence over many countries.
4. A true intellectual does not recklessly challenge the social norms laid down by the society.
5. Intellectuals in India have advocated socialism, secularism, nationalism and democracy.
6. The propounders of the Bhakti movement and the social reformers of pre-independence era contributed a lot to our society.
7. India, at present, is bogged down by many maladies and looks up to intellectuals to lead it from darkness to light.

Essay
66

NON-GOVERNMENTAL ORGANISATIONS

SYNOPSIS

Non-Governmental Organisations or NGOs are voluntary organisations which work for the cause of the society. During our freedom struggle, many leaders worked for the upliftment of the underprivileged. After Independence, many NGOs associated themselves with the cause of emancipation of women. Some organisations like Mother Teresa's 'Missionaries of Charity' work for the underprivileged and for the mentally and physically challenged children. Some also work for the senior citizens and others, for stray animals. The NGOs are able to penetrate at the grassroots level. People from all walks of life should come forward to help the NGOs in their endeavour after assessing their work. Industrialists should give patronage and philanthropic help to such organisations.

Non-Governmental Organisations or NGOs, as these are popularly known as, are voluntary organisations which work for a worthy cause. As the name suggests, these organisations do not work under the government. They work independently *thriving*[1] on donations and rarely depend on government aid. The NGOs have achieved much more for the society than what the government expected of them. They have come a long way on account of their desire and determination to serve. The NGOs have been able to bring about a difference in the society. Their contribution to the society is *commendable*[2].

India has a long record of social service, social reform and voluntary agencies. Voluntary organisations were established in India during the freedom struggle to fight against British oppression and for the emancipation of the downtrodden and the underprivileged. Some were established to fight against the *atrocities*[3] committed by the Indians on their less privileged *counterparts*[4]. As early as 1828, Raja Rammohan Roy established the Brahmo Samaj to work for the evolution of a casteless society. Annie Besant founded the Theosophical Society in India which preached universal brotherhood. The Ramakrishna Mission was established by Swami Vivekananda to train the workers to work towards selfless national service. Lala Lajpat Rai formed the Servants of the People Society to work towards the upliftment of the downtrodden. NGOs emerged in India soon after Independence when Mahatma Gandhi made a plea for dissolving the Indian National Congress and transforming it into a Lok Sevak Sangh. However, this plea was rejected. But many associates and followers of Mahatma Gandhi established voluntary agencies to work closely with the governmental programmes on social and economic issues. These agencies set up handicraft and village industries, rural development programmes, credit cooperatives, educational institutions, etc.

The second stage of the growth of NGOs in India was around 1960 when many individuals noticed that the governmental programmes were inadequate to deal with the problems of the deprived sections. These groups formed grassroots level organisations that worked towards the emancipation of the poor, the landless, the tribals, the bonded labourers and many other social groups. They worked at the micro-level, had limited resources and lacked coordination.

After Independence, the *priorities*[5] of the voluntary organisations changed. Earlier, they were involved in fighting the enemy from outside, now they focused on the enemy within. Today, they work towards the *emancipation*[6] of women, upliftment of the underprivileged and for equal rights to special children. Natural calamities like flood, drought, cyclone, etc., keep affecting the lives of people. Several NGOs have helped the affected people by providing them with relief materials.

Sarojini Naidu was associated with the All India Women's Conference, which is the oldest and the most important women's organisation in India. The main aim of such organisations is to improve the condition of women. They work for the cause of those women who are battered, bruised and harassed for dowry. Such women are *persuaded*[7] by these organisations to opt for family planning and healthcare facilities. Adult literacy campaigns are also aimed at improving their lot. The cases of divorced or separated women, their rights and custody of their children, are taken up by these organisations. These organisations have worked commendably in helping women secure an honourable position for themselves in the society.

Some organisations support the cause of the underprivileged. Mother Teresa was a champion of the *downtrodden*[8]. She established the 'Missionaries of Charity.' Later, she established 'Nirmal Hriday' and 'Shishu Bhawan' for the mentally and physically challenged children. Now, many organisations such as CRY, AKANKSHA, AKSHARA have been established, to take care of such children. They also counsel the parents of the special children. This helps the parents in taking better care of their children. These voluntary bodies take the children with special needs under their care, teach them special skills and help them overcome their handicaps, thus instilling confidence among them. Help Age India, Sargam Sanstha, Smile Foundation, Give India, Lepra Society, Udaan, Deepalaya, Uday Foundation, Karmayog, Pratham are some important NGOs of India.

The Federation of Indian NGOs for Drug Abuse Prevention (FINGODAP) is the registered national apex body of more than five hundred NGOs working in the area of drug demand reduction and prevention of HIV/AIDS in partnership with Ministry of Social Justice and Empowerment and National AIDS control Organisation. It tries to implement better policies for the drug demand reduction programme.

Some voluntary organisations like dignity, Age Care India and Help Age India, have set up homes for senior citizens. During the twilight years of their life the elderly feel neglected; so they come over to old age homes and spend the rest of their lives happily in the company of people of their own age who have also been neglected by their respective families.

People for Animals (PFA), Society for Prevention of Cruelty against Animals (SPCA) and People for Ethical Treatment of Animals (PETA) are some NGOs working towards animal welfare. They set up animal shelters for stray dogs, cats and cows. They undertake sterilisation and vaccination programmes for dogs. They are doing a great service to the neglected animals by providing them food and treatment.

Since Independence, until around 1980, little was done by the Indian Government to define the role of an NGO or to recognize its importance. In 1980, through the sixth Five Year Plan, the government identified the areas in which an NGO could act. Those areas included family welfare, health for all, water management and soil conservation, environmental protection, education, etc. Under the seventh Five Year Plan, the Indian Government envisioned a more active role for NGOs. In the Eighth Five Year Plan, the importance of NGOs was further enhanced. In this way, the government is giving more funds to the NGOs. Today, India has a vigorous NGO sector. It is estimated that about 25,000 to 30,000 NGOs are active in India.

A few of the NGOs are now confronted with a credibility crisis as they have been charged with *embezzlement*[9] of funds and scandalous acts. The Council for the Advancement of People's Action and Rural Technology (CAPART) blacklisted 899 such NGOs from April 1, 1984 to July 30, 2015 while the Central Social and Welfare Board (CSWB) blacklisted 3180. The Dutch Government terminated its contract with an NGO for aiding a multi-crore water supply and sanitation project in Uttar Pradesh. The reason cited was misappropriation of funds. In Andhra Pradesh, an adoption racket was unearthed wherein NGOs bought infant girls from Lambada tribals and sold them at exorbitant prices to foreigners. These NGOs, which have been working under the guise of facilitating adoption, claim that they have helped to curb female infanticide. Such NGOs have been blacklisted and debarred from obtaining funds. The media needs to fulfil its social responsibility in this regard. It should highlight the genuine efforts of good NGOs and expose others who betray the trust of the public. The Government of India has taken steps to monitor every unit of foreign donations obtained by the NGOs through the enactment of the Foreign contribution (Management and Control) Act, 2005.

The public and the corporates, especially the philanthropists, want the government to identify the genuine NGOs. There are many NGOs which are making huge profits in the name of social service. The identification process is not so easy. It will involve deep investigations that would call for allocation of funds and work force. But once this is done and the results are made public, corporates will be more enthusiastic and forthcoming in providing funds as well as associating with the activities of the NGOs. As of now, their credibility, in general, is quite suspect.

Celebrities appear quite inclined towards associating themselves with various NGOs. This draws a lot of media attention. The concerned NGOs are able to make people aware of the work they do and getting sponsorship becomes easier.

One problem with the NGOs in India, as with NGOs everywhere in the world, has been their increasing dependence on governmental funds or on donations from external sources like the World Bank. This has resulted in a lack of flexibility on the part of NGOs in picking their missions and objectives, since many of them are expected to perform certain tasks in return for receiving funds. Some NGOs have themselves created structures that have become more bureaucratic in nature and, hence, less effective in playing a constructive role.

The success of the genuine Non-Governmental Organisations lies in the fact that they are able to make a difference at the grassroots level. This, precisely, is the area where successive governments in India have failed. The NGOs' work, therefore, is *laudable*[10]. The government should fund the NGOs solely on merit. It is very necessary for the urban middle class to wake up to the contribution made by NGOs towards the betterment of society. They should participate in the NGOs' endeavour through monetary contributions or by volunteering their services. Schools should organise trips to where such organisations have set up their base to make the students realise the reality of life and make them responsible towards the society. The rich and the affluent should be philanthropic and give patronage to any such organisation of their choice. Their *charisma*[11] would then be reflected in the organisation they support and at the same time work wonders for social welfare.

Aid to Vocabulary

1. *Thriving* — growing
2. *Commendable* — praiseworthy
3. *Atrocities* — cruelties
4. *Counterparts* — persons who serve the same purpose as another
5. *Priorities* — the state of having things in the order of importance
6. *Emancipation* — setting free from restrictions
7. *Persuaded* — urged effectively
8. *Downtrodden* — oppressed
9. *Embezzlement* — misappropriation of money towards one's own use
10. *Laudable* — praiseworthy
11. *Charisma* — power to inspire and attract others

Points to Remember

1. The contribution of NGOs to the society is commendable.
2. Voluntary organisation is not a new concept in India.
3. NGOs work mainly towards the emancipation of women, upliftment of the underprivileged and care of retarded children.
4. NGOs like 'age care India' and 'help age India' work for the helpless senior citizens.
5. Some NGOs are charged with embezzlement of funds and scandalous acts.
6. Dependence on foreign donations has resulted in a lack of flexibility on the part of the NGOs.
7. People from all walks of life should support genuine NGOs.The intellectuals are known to initiate revolutions.

THE UNEASE OVER THE NGO NOTIFICATIONS

The implications of falling under the ambit of the Lokpal Act have discomfited many non-governmental organisations. The notifications from the Department of Personnel dated June 20, 2016, and an official memo on June 24, 2016 laid down the procedures and timelines for filing returns of public servants, the definition of which in the Lokpal and Lokayukta Act includes office bearers of NGOs. Section 14 (1) of the Act includes directors, managers, secretaries and other officers of societies, trusts and associations of persons that receive more than ₹ 10 lakhs under the Foreign Contribution Regulation Act (FCRA) under its ambit. It does the same in the case the organisations wholly or partly funded by the Central government if they receive an annual grant above a limit that may be fixed by it. (This has been set at ₹ 1 crore)

Earlier, Central government employees had been asked to file their assets and liabilities under the Lokpal Act. But what the June 20, 2016 notifications did was extend this to those working in NGOs and set the deadline for submissions of their returns to a designated authority.

"As the Act was passed in Parliament and defines those who work in NGOs as public servants, the rules are the same and they are expected to follow it," said K.S. Dhatwalia, spokesperson for the Home and Personnel ministries. But the notification which makes it mandatory for senior staff of NGO's to provide details of cash, bank balances, immovable properties and loans of themselves, their spouses and dependent children has caused a deep discomfort within a section of the NGOs. But what triggered the June notifications? According to official home ministry sources, it was the large amount of funds sent from foreign donors to Christian missionaries and Islamic organisations. On March 28, 2016 the Ministry of Home Affairs (MHA) put two foreign donors — U.S. based Compassion International and South Korea's Family Federation for World Peace and Unification — under the "watch-list" after adverse reports from security agencies.

Source: The Hindu, VIJAITA SINGH

Essay 67

THE BEGGAR PROBLEM IN INDIA

SYNOPSIS

Left with no respectable alternative some people take recourse to begging in India. The beggar problem in India is a socio-economic problem. There are numerous kinds of beggars in India. The anti-begging Act of India was revised in 1959. The operation of this law is often inhumane. Our mega cities are full of beggars. The majority of them see begging as a profitable profession. Steps taken casually cannot solve the problem; taking concrete steps is the need of the hour. During religious festivals, beggars receive more alms. There are some gangs who control and exploit the beggars. This problem should be tackled at the grassroots level and all the members of the society should help in eradicating this problem. Vocational education, counselling and employment opportunities can solve this problem.

Circumstances prevalent in our society are such that people who are illiterate or poor find it enormously difficult, if not impossible, to lead their life with honesty and honour because of the unnecessary harassment by the police as well as the local gangsters. There seems to be complete *anarchy*[1], *chaos*[2] and commotion everywhere so far as the downtrodden people are concerned. If a helpless man starts a business of his own, he is tortured by the locals and the anti social elements. To add fuel to fire, the police do not come to their rescue, rather, they aggravate the problem. Like the gangsters, they too expect the poor man to grease their palm. Left with no alternative, such people die of starvation, commit suicide or resort to begging. To a vast majority of people, therefore, begging as a profession comes to them not by choice but by compulsion.

The beggar problem in India is a socio-economic problem. Poverty is the root cause of this problem. According to the United Nations Development Programme's (UNDP) Human Development Report-2015, India is ranked 130th among 188 countries. In India, substantial percentage of the people who live below the poverty line are deprived of the basic requirements of life. Associated with the problem of poverty are the problems of unemployment and social insecurity. There is no proper *enumeration*[3] of beggars in our country. The number of woman and child beggars is ever increasing. Census 1931 mentioned just 16 per cent woman beggars. The figure shot up to 49 per cent in 2001.

In India, there are numerous kinds of beggars. There are *destitute*[4] women, children, blind, crippled or lame persons, lepers, etc. *Abject*[5] poverty and helplessness force them to beg. It is common to find beggars at rubbish dumps, road sides, traffic lights, under flyovers and in railway stations. The weak, *crippled*[6] and mentally ill share the same space with children, women and able-bodied men. The line that separates beggars from the casual poor is getting thinner in our country, where one in every four persons goes to bed hungry every night and 78 million people are homeless.

Begging in our country is a crime. It was in the 1920's that begging was first declared a crime in British India. The law was updated as the Bombay Prevention of Begging Act in 1959, and was extended to eighteen states including Delhi. This law provides for the jailing up to three years in special "beggars courts" of anyone caught begging. The punishment can be extended to 10 years in case of second and repeated offences. The definition of beggars under this law includes not just beggars who seek alms, but also traditional artistes who collect alms by 'singing, dancing or by *fortune*[7] telling, etc. This criminalisation of begging is a relatively recent development in our society. Traditional societies have been much more tolerant of people who live by begging. In our society, Sadhus and Buddhist monks were respected as 'Bhikshus' and not as criminals. This practice enabled them to break away from all forms of material *bondage*[8].

The enforcement of the anti-beggar law is often inhumane. Teams of policemen armed with sticks, conduct periodic drives against beggars. They are arrested and presented before the magistrate of beggars court and the judge orders the police to send the beggars to *certified*[9] beggars home. These are really subhuman habitations. Many Non-Government Organisations (NGOs) like Chetna, Ashray Adhikar, Abhiyan, etc., are striving to improve the condition of beggars.

Legislation of the laws already in force does not bring beggars any *succour*[10] instead it adds to their miseries and makes them more disabled. *Inured*[11] to living at an open space like the traffic light junctions, footpaths, the temples etc., all their life, they find it very difficult to live within a confined space in jail when arrested and imprisoned. Moreover, the space they are forced to live in hardly corresponds to their basic needs like clean toilet and other basic things. It is, therefore, high time some concrete steps were taken to bring them back on track. No casual step or half hearted effort is going to resolve this issue.

Our mega cities are full of beggars. We can find them everywhere on the street, at every traffic signal and at every temple and tourist site.

According to a study by the Delhi School of Social Work, there has been a phenomenal increase in the number of beggars in India. There are around 60,000 beggars in Delhi, over 3,00,000 in Mumbai, nearly 75,000 in Kolkata and about 56,000 in Bengaluru and so on. Mumbai is home to the majority of beggars. According to the Maharashtra Government, they are worth ₹180 crore a year with daily income ranging between ₹20-80. A majority of beggars sees it as a profitable and *viable*[12] profession. In Delhi, more than 66 per cent beggars are able-bodied. The survey reveals that begging as a livelihood wins over casual labour. Nearly half of the adult beggars collect between ₹50 and ₹100 a day, not much less than the daily wage of a labourer. Some of them even earn between ₹100 and ₹500 a day.

In some particular seasons, begging increases in India. On the eve of different religious festivals like Eid, Durgapuja and Navaratre, the beggars get more alms. In our society, we think it is our duty to help the less fortunate, but in this way, we encourage begging which is counter productive to social and economic progress. So, instead of giving them alms, we should donate money to the genuine organisations which take care of the helpless beggars. We may also help them with food and work if we can, at our end.

There exist dangerous beggar *mafias*[13] and gangs. They abduct children, cut off their limbs and blind them so that they can evoke pity and get alms. They train the children and then employ them for begging. The government must take strict action against these criminals, because they ruin the future of the children of our society. It should also encourage beggars to earn their livelihood by other means.

Sometimes, criminals when they are released from prison are *shunned*[14] by the society and do not have any other option, but to become beggars. The government must run some programmes to rehabilitate them.

India's beggary laws are a *throwback*[15] to the centuries old European *vagrancy*[16] laws which instead of addressing the socio-economic issues make the poor responsible for their position. The anti-beggar legislation is aimed at removing the poor from the face of the cities. Eliminating the poor has never eradicated poverty. Begging is undesirable, but the solution is not as simple as banning them from public places. The nation should strive to eradicate poverty and not the poor.

India aspires to achieve world standards in every field. To achieve this goal, socio-economic measures are needed to curb the beggar problem in our country. This problem can be tackled at the grassroots level if all sections of the society — Central government, state governments,

NGOs and private organisations and individuals — contribute to it. The government should start institutions where orphans, physically handicapped and widows may find shelter and get training to work according to their mental and physical state. The beggars' home must be habitable. emphasis should be placed on vocational education so that the children of the beggars do not in turn become beggars, but can earn their livelihood. Imparting education and creating employment opportunities for these underprivileged people is the only solution. Another important aspect is counselling. Leading a respectable life is the right of every human being. Counselling the beggars on the importance of basic human traits like self-esteem or self-respect may motivate them to give up begging. Such measures should be launched on top priority if we want a beggar-free India.

AID TO VOCABULARY

1. *Anarchy* — lack of law and order
2. *Chaos* — confusion
3. *Enumeration* — naming one by one, specifying as in a list
4. *Destitute* — extremely poor
5. *Abject* — miserable, despicable
6. *Crippled* — unable to move or walk normally
7. *Fortune* — chance, luck, future, large amount of money
8. *Bondage* — physical control, slavery
9. *Certified* — officially approved
10. *Succour* — support or strength offered in times of need
11. *Inured* — less affected by something unpleasant, being used to it
12. *Viable* — capable of being done
13. *Mafia* — organised body of criminals
14. *Shunned* — avoided
15. *Throwback* — reversion to ancestral character, similar to someone or something from the past
16. *Vagrancy* — laws for vagrants (homeless wanderers)

POINTS TO REMEMBER

1. The beggar problem in India is a socio-economic problem.
2. There are different kinds of beggars in our country.
3. The anti-begging law was updated in 1959.
4. The beggars' homes are really subhuman habitations.
5. Our mega cities are full of beggars.
6. We should help the beggars by donating money to the proper organisations.
7. The government must take action against the beggar mafias.
8. Begging is the last resort of the helpless poor.
9. Providing vocational education, counselling and employment opportunities only can solve this problem.

ACCORDING TO A SURVEY CONDUCTED BY DELHI COMMISSION FOR PROTECTION OF CHILD RIGHTS '80% KIDS ARE FORCED INTO BEGGING'

Panel for child rights hints at organised racket, 56.9% child beggars have other livelihood

- 84% of child beggars living alone were involved in some or the other intoxicants of which nearly 75% were involved in substances like smack
- Most children were initiated into begging in childhood by their parents or by relatives
- Gender distribution shows that begging is more prevalent among boys
- A large number of beggars are migrants
- More than 54% migrated with their family due to poverty
- A large number of children talked of being chased or beaten by police, shopkeepers, or watchmen who did not want them to beg in their area.
- The educational status of child beggars was found to be very dismal
- Majority i.e. 402 (66.45%) were illiterate
- Only 203 (33.6%) had primary education
- Substance abuse among child beggars in Delhi revealed that 307 (50.7%) out of 605 were addicted to intoxicants
- Adults pose as parents to earn money from child beggars
- 78,000 of country's beggars are 12th passouts

CITY BEGGARS NOT SO POOR AFTER ALL

About 90 to 95 per cent beggars are not willing to accept rehabilitation

Hyderabad has 25,000 beggars and each of them earns about ₹ 500 per day — a business turnover of about ₹ 456 crore per year. Another figure thrown up was 14,000 beggars who earn ₹ 300 a day, totalling ₹ 153 crore a year. Children, on the other hand, earn more than adults.

These shocking numbers emerged from a day-long seminar on creating a beggar-free Hyderabad. As a clutch of NGOs were brought together under one umbrella to debate the issue, what became apparent is the scope of the problem.

"All of these beggars are not genuine. Most of them are criminals and have come from other states, Only 5 per cent of these beggars are real, the others are fake who are in it for the money," said Jayaprakash Bharat, who studied the beggar menace in the city and presented his statistics at the seminar. "We will create a beggar-free city," vowed Mayor Bonthu Rammohan, while addressing the seminar. "Ninety per cent of the beggars are fake. We will create a mass awareness programme about not giving alms to beggars and at the same time rehabilitate genuine ones. These fake beggars are spoiling the image of the city, and at the same time, many of them hold criminal records," the Mayor said.

The focus on fighting the menace should be about taking care of the destitute, the old and the disabled, said Madhavi, a speaker at the seminar. "If we can create an infrastructure to help these people, then the menace can be solved. And we need to rehabilitate beggars if we want to solve the problem," she added. "About 90 to 95 per cent beggars are not at all willing to accept rehabilitation in old age homes, schools, and ashrams/orphanages. There are many reasons for them for not accepting this proposal and also rejecting help from the NGOs. The main reason is that their incomes are very high," said Mr. Jayaprakash.

Source: The Hindu

Essay
68

TERRORISM

Synopsis

Terrorism has the potential to uproot the ethics of civilisation. It is the greatest enemy of our nation. With the finance and support provided by some ill-advised agents, it is now flourishing rapidly. Collecting funds is no more a tough job for them. Terrorism has acquired global dimensions. Developed nations may play an important role in uprooting terrorism. Laws alone are not sufficient to put an end to terrorism. The cooperation of the general public and psychological rehabilitation are very much required. The dignity of human life must be maintained at any cost while trying to eradicate terrorism.

The world is in the grip of terrorism. It is a scourge that affects us all. It has acquired global dimensions with the preceding decade witnessing some of the worst terrorist attacks in the world. The word, 'terrorism' was first used in France, and later popularised during the Russian Revolution.

Terrorism refers to extortion, kidnapping and killing to attract wider attention to a particular cause thereby forcing a targeted authority to concede demands of the perpetrators of terror. One of the former UN Secretary-Generals was of the view that the struggle to gain control over economic resources and political power is the main cause of terrorism.

It is also defined as a method whereby an organised group or party utterly discontented with the state machinery seeks to achieve its *parochial*[1] aims, primarily through the use of violence. Suppressed, marginalised and/or denied what they view as their basic human right, these groups unleash terror on unsuspecting civilians to make a statement. Terrorism is considered as one of the most evil forces destabilising the sense of fraternity among people. It even paralyses the economic development of a country. Since the last two decades, it has become a problem of overriding concern in Indian society.

There was a time when our dauntless freedom fighters terrorised the colonial rulers by dint of their *ideology*[2] and spirit of sacrifice. But today, the lives of innocent people are at the mercy of terrorists. Today, terrorism is pitted against the State—it has a distinct political purpose and it aims at creating fear and panic among the masses. Today's terrorists have no sense of national *integrity*[3]. They indulge in anti-social, anti-national activities and spill the blood of innocent people.

Terrorists *obtain*[4] funds from different sources. They collect money by *extortion*[5], robbery, kidnapping, etc. Smuggling arms and drugs have now become a popular method of procuring money for terrorist activities.

In India, terrorism did not even exist three decades ago. After a few regional political movements, terrorism has increased considerably. The separatist movements in various states of the country have added fuel to the fire. The anti-national elements are believed to be encouraged by some neighbouring countries that provide the former money, arms and ammunitions to further certain political agendas.

Today, terrorism has become a grave concern affecting our country's future. Terrorists are now using chemical agents (cyanides) and biological agents (anthrax) besides the *sophisticated*[6] guns and bombs. The threat of nuclear attack by terrorists is also *looming*[7] large in our country.

The nature of contemporary terrorism keeps changing with new tactics and new organisational structures being adopted. Terrorist groups try old, new and different strategies all at the same time. They are concerned only with what will work to their advantage. Mumbai terror attacks of 1993 may be the beginning of a new era of terrorism. There have been four stages of global terrorism, as of today, viz.,

(1) 1980-1990: Era of backyard struggle

(2) 1990-2001: Rise of global Jihad

(3) 2001-2007: Maturing of local Guerrilla terrorism

(4) 2008-2013: Possible start of global Guerrilla terrorism

United Nations as well as various developed and developing countries has *resolved*[8] to counter terrorism. Terrorist groups like HAMAS, AL-QAIDA, LTTE, etc. have been declared unlawful. Their funding through the *hawala** has been checked. Our government also has taken measures to check their activities. We have formed the National Security Guard (NSG) and set up various law enforcement agencies to meet the emergency situation.

Under the government's agenda to check terrorism, the (Aadhar) or Unique Identity Card (UIC) scheme for each citizen has been

---

*Hawala - an illegal Value transfer system

implemented from 2010 onwards and a zero tolerance towards terrorism, from whatever source it originates, is to be pursued. The second Administrative Reforms Commission (ARC) had recommended UIC for checking illegal migration and terrorist infiltration.

However, *repressive*[9] laws alone may not prove effective to control terrorism. To control terrorism effectively, cooperation between citizens and police is vital. Our intelligence agencies (C.B.I.**, RAW***, etc.) need to be more alert. Above all, our judicial system should be fair and speedy.

Repressive measures taken by some developed countries have helped and can further help to fight the menace of terrorism. For instance, the punitive bombing of the ISIS (Islamic State of Iran and Syria) by the UK, Russia and the US forced the terror operatives to lie low for the some time. When we are living in a global village, and enjoying the fruits of globalisation, we must fight terrorism with global cooperation too. Terrorism is a global problem, and no country can solve it in isolation. All the countries of the world should work unitedly to combat and eliminate this global menace. However, we must keep in mind that while taking anti-terrorist measures, we must preserve the dignity of human rights at all costs. Furthermore, terrorism should not be branded or associated with any religion, because all religions preach love, and want people to co-exist in peace and harmony.

Terrorism is a crime against humanity. It should be crushed with an iron hand. The forces behind it must be exposed. There are no short-cuts in the difficult task of combating terrorism. As far as possible, the authorities should analyse the cause of growing disaffection against the establishment with an open mind. Efforts must be made to motivate terrorist outfits to sit for a dialogue.

Efforts must be made to motivate terrorist outfits to sit for dialogue. Genuine problems of disgruntled groups should be taken up immediately and earnestly for finding their short-term and long-term solutions. Countries which patronise militancy should be clearly identified, declared as 'terrorist states' and *quarantined*[10] from the global community. It is imperative for all countries to come together and check this evil that is assuming unprecedented proportions.

**CBI - Central Bureau of Investigation

***RAW - The Research and Analysis Wing

Aid to Vocabulary

1. *Parochial* — narrow minded, specific to a small group or area
2. *Ideology* — a set of ideas or beliefs that form the basis of an economic or political theory or that are held by a particular group of persons
3. *Integrity* — the condition of being whole and not divided
4. *Obtain* — to get or acquire something by making an effort
5. *Extortion* — to obtain something by violence, threats, etc.
6. *Sophisticated* — highly developed
7. *Looming* — largely present everywhere
8. *Resolve* — to decide firmly
9. *Repressive* — that supresses by force
10. *Quarantined* — isolated to prevent infection

Points to Remember

1. Terrorists want to achieve certain goals by means of violence.
2. Terrorists have no caste, creed or religion.
3. Fraternity as well as human civilisation always falls victim to the hands of the terrorists.
4. They obtain funds by extortion, kidnapping, etc.
5. Anti-terrorism acts require high-handedness as well as rehabilitation.
6. Even as we undertake a crackdown on terrorism, we must safeguard human dignity and human rights at all costs.

Essay
69

CHARACTER MAKES A MAN

SYNOPSIS

Character is the aggregate of the peculiar qualities which constitute personal individuality. The scope as well as the definition of character has been undergoing changes according to the stage of civilisation in which man is placed. The words, moral and immoral, have been associated with character. Character is also linked with the customs of a particular country. The blind aping of the West has led to widespread moral corruption. It is difficult to point out a single factor which might be responsible for shaping the character of a person. Character is the index of a person's state of mind.

Character of a person, according to the New Webster's Dictionary, is the set of certain qualities exhibited by him/her. According to the Chamber's 20th Century Dictionary, *character* is the 'nature, personal appearance and the aggregate of peculiar qualities which constitute personal individuality.' According to Goethe, "Talent develops in quiet places, while character develops in the full current of human life." What *character* is and what place it has in the assessment of the personality of a man, have been matters of discussion for centuries for psychologists, educationists, religious leaders and administrators. There have been no definite conclusions as to the definition of character. The definition has undergone changes and has been *amended*[1] by different thinkers from time to time. The definition of *character*, and all that the word encompasses, also undergoes change with the stages of civilisation through which man passes.

The words moral and immoral have been associated with character. It suggests that the external acts of a person are the outcome of his basic *instincts*[2] and his character may be assessed as good or bad based on them. The external act or thinking of a person is subject not only to his instincts, but also to the existing customs and conventions of a particular society and different stages of existence of the same society. The word 'character' has, therefore, remained absolutely flexible. A particular trait of a man's character that was considered good at a particular stage may be considered bad now and what was considered bad earlier may be considered good under the prevailing circumstances.

What is considered to have no *bearing*[3] on the character of a person in the western society, these days may be considered to be *degeneration*[4] or moral degradation according to certain standards and values set in the eastern countries. The people of these countries are bound by their ancient culture and traditions and are not ready to forsake it. Character has, therefore, been *inevitably*[5] linked with the customs of a particular country. The definition of character and the place assigned to it in assessing the usefulness or uselessness of a person and his suitability for a particular profession has also been undergoing a change according to the customs and conventions prevalent in a particular country.

The colonial rule in India ended in 1947 but the citizens could not recover from the colonial hangover. Struggling to keep pace with the changing times, man has sacrificed his ideals and has become corrupt. Corruption has become so *rampant*[6] that it has taken over people from all spheres of life. *Avarice*[7] has been the major reason for corruption.

Mahatma Gandhi, Jawaharlal Nehru and Lal Bahadur Shastri were men of strong character, who never *faltered*[8] from their ideals. Character is of supreme importance in one's life. No individual can become great without having a good character. In today's times, we hardly have a politician whose reputation has not been maligned with accusations of various kinds. The unruly events in our state legislatures and the parliament is a reflection of the degeneration of the Indian society. The British Broadcasting Corporation (BBC) described the violent incident in the Uttar Pradesh Assembly as "*rowdy*[9]." The adage, "If wealth is lost, nothing is lost, if health is lost, something is lost and if character is lost, everything is lost," seems to find no takers.

To what extent and in what manner, character contributes to the making of a person depends *invariably*[10] on his individuality. A certain category of people are likely to give a very exaggerated importance to character in the shaping of an individual's life. Certain people are of the opinion that making or unmaking of character is not in the hands of a person, it owes its origin to the heredity of the person and to the environment in which he has been brought up. The psychologists of the modern times are unanimous on the point that the environment plays a very *vital*[11] role in shaping the character of a person. The place of character in the life of man and the role that character plays is, therefore, subject to a variety of reasons and it is difficult to imagine a situation where one single factor alone might have been responsible in shaping the character of a person.

There have been varied views and opinions but all agree on one common point that the character of a person is the index of the state of mind or the personality of that person. Personality in this sense means the overall *persona*[12]. Character is also the motivation that drives a person in his various dealings with others around him. The role that character has to play in the life of a person may differ from person to person. But one thing is certain that every individual has certain basic characteristics in him and those characteristics form the anchor of his suitability in a particular society and for a particular responsibility. Character is the greatest wealth that an individual possesses. Just as the face is said to be the index of the mind, the character is rightly said to be the index of a person's overall personality.

Aid to Vocabulary

1. *Amended* — changed or improved
2. *Instincts* — innate impulses
3. *Bearing* — reference
4. *Degeneration* — deterioration, degradation
5. *Inevitably* — unavoidably
6. *Rampant* — unchecked
7. *Avarice* — extreme greed for money or gain
8. *Faltered* — staggered, stumbled
9. *Rowdy* — rough and disorderly
10. *Invariably* — constantly
11. *Vital* — essential
12. *Persona* — the outward behaviour of a person that presents him as a particular type of person

Points to Remember

1. Character constitutes individual personality.
2. Moral and immoral words are associated with character.
3. Character depends on the customs prevalent in a particular society.
4. Character depends on the heredity of a person.
5. Rampant westernisation and growth of avarice have led to moral corruption in the society.
6. Character is the index of a person's overall personality.

Essay 70

COWARDS DIE SEVERAL TIMES BEFORE DEATH

SYNOPSIS

Death is an inevitable part of life. It has been the subject of study of many researchers, scientists, philosophers and thinkers. Nobody knows what happens after death. A brave man is always prepared for the unexpected. Hitler is infamous for his dictatorship but he was so brave that in the midst of enemies he thought of aggression instead of flying away. Cowards run away from all dangers. They fear death. A brave man is adventurous enough to risk his life and achieve his goals. He also faces adverse circumstances boldly. Cowards do not contribute to the society. They brood over the past and fear the future. They have a pessimistic attitude towards life. They get disheartened when confronted with adverse situations. One should remain brave and enjoy life. Only cowards die several times before death.

Man is mortal. Death touches all, the rich and the poor, the young and the old and the ruler and the ruled. Nobody knows what happens after death. One dies leaving behind everything one has. Death has been the subject of study for many researchers, scientists, philosophers and thinkers.

A brave man puts up a bold front when he faces any danger. He is always prepared for the unexpected. He can overcome any adverse situation. Cowards, on the other hand, are unable to face dangerous situations. They run away from all dangers. They fear death. Hence, it has been said that cowards die several times before death. Death is an *inevitable*[1] part of life. A brave man lives life to the full, while a coward kills his conscience several times before his actual death. This is because a coward succumbs to a *trying*[2] situation.

Human existence is full of risks and dangers. One may be exposed to danger anywhere. It may be at the workplace, at home, on road, etc. The traffic on the road has become *unruly*[3] enough to pose a threat to life. Bomb blasts have become a common affair at certain places. A brave man prepares himself to face such unexpected dangers. He is adventurous enough to risk his life to achieve his goals. A coward, on the other hand, sits and broods. He depresses himself and also those who are associated with him.

The brave are always willing to take risks. Mangal Pandey was daring enough to challenge the British rule. He was aware of the consequences, but sacrificed his life for the freedom of the country. The freedom fighters were punished *harshly*[4] by the British, but they did not give up their mission. They felt proud to be a part of the freedom struggle. It was this spirit which forced the British to leave India. Cowards lack such *initiatives*[5]. They fear punishment. They cannot contribute to the society.

A brave man *strives*[6] for success single-mindedly. No defeat can make him lose hope. One such incident is the meeting between Alexander and Porus. Porus was defeated by Alexander and brought before the latter in chains. Alexander asked him what treatment should be meted out to him as a prisoner. Porus promptly replied that he expected Alexander to treat him in the manner a king would treat another king. In such cases, a coward would lose all hope. He would not have the courage to give such answers.

Another incident that illustrates this point pertains to Adolf Hitler. He is infamous for his dictatorship but he was really brave. In the battlefield, once his commander in-chief reported that his whole army had been surrounded on all sides by the enemies. Adolf Hitler readily retorted, "Wow! Now we can attack on any side". In the midst of enemies, where anyone else would have been inclined to run way, his positive thinking led him to think of aggression. Such an unusual response could not have come from a coward. Fighting till the end, to the last drop of blood or until victory has been achieved is the spirit the brave rear in themselves with no fear at all.

A coward cannot face a crisis. He runs away from it. A brave man confronts danger boldly. In doing so, he gains self-confidence and earns respect. Bravery knows no age. One can show an act of bravery at the age of eight or eighty. Every year, the nation gives bravery awards to children who displayed great courage and saved the lives of those in danger. Such brave individuals risk their own lives for others. They, thereby, earn fame, glory and national *acclaim*[7].

The brave do not waste their time in brooding over matters. They believe in action. They live in present and bear no anxiety for the future. Their courageous attitude enables them to live life to the full. They do not worry about future. They do not get disheartened by *adverse*[8] circumstances. They enjoy life because they accept each day as it approaches.

The cowards are often unable to live in the present. They brood over the past. They remain *pessimistic*[9] about the future. Fear of the unexpected and fear of the future makes them depressed. They easily lose their self-confidence. They cannot face adverse circumstances boldly. They often blame others for their inaction. They hardly enjoy life. They always see the negative side of life. Because of this attitude, they can never do anything great in life. They are afraid of the dangers ahead and never take any risk. That is why they hardly succeed in anything they do.

Life is full of uncertainties. Dangers and difficulties are a part of life. One should be bold and courageous enough to face all the problems and difficulties of life. We should never be afraid of facing the challenges because challenges are often the best tools of empowerment. If we dream, we must have the courage to turn our dreams into reality. We should be *consistent*[10] in our efforts and *endeavours*[11]. Our courage should not be shaken by failures. On the contrary, failures should form a foundation for us to dream again. They should be the stepping stones to achieve success. One who does not accept this reality is a coward. One should not act as a coward, otherwise, he would not die once but several times before death.

Aid to Vocabulary

1. *Inevitable* — certain to happen
2. *Trying* — difficult to deal with
3. *Unruly* — not easy to control or manage
4. *Harshly* — cruelly
5. *Initiatives* — power to act before other people do
6. *Strives* — to try hard for a long time to achieve something
7. *Acclaim* — to praise publicly
8. *Adverse* — not favourable
9. *Pessimistic* — given to believe that the worst will happen
10. *Consistent* — always behaving in the same way or having the same opinions
11. *Endeavours* — attempts to do something

Points to Remember

1. Death touches all.
2. Cowards are unable to face dangerous situations.
3. Risks and dangers are a part of life.
4. Cowards do not contribute to the society.
5. A brave person strives for success single-mindedly.
6. A coward cannot face a crisis with confidence.
7. Cowards brood over the past and fear the future.
8. One should remain brave and enjoy life.
9. Challenges are the best tools of empowerment.
10. We should be consistent in our endeavours.

Essay
71

SWEET ARE THE USES OF ADVERSITY

SYNOPSIS

Adversity implies difficulties, trouble and misfortune. It tests the potential of man and brings out the best in him. It enables one to meet the challenges of life. Adversity can be turned into an advantage with little tact and wisdom. It strengthens in a man the spirit of self-confidence and willpower. One who has never tasted what is bitter does not know what is sweet. Adversity is a part of life. Great men emerged successful through the worst of adversities. Adversities reveal what the necessities of life are and what are luxuries. They give us a chance to judge our friends and foes. They bring man closer to man. They take man nearer to God. They stimulate the artistic qualities in an artist. We can achieve the desired results in adverse situations through a carefully planned approach. Adversity makes man develop as a more mature and powerful individual.

Adversity implies difficulties, troubles and misfortune. It tests the potential and resilience of man and brings out the best in him. It is a blessing in disguise. It acts as a stimulant to the earnest worker. Adversity makes one wise and enables one to meet the challenges of life. It strengthens in a man the spirit of self-confidence and willpower.

One, who is brought up in luxury, finds it difficult to face the adverse circumstances of life. He/She does not know how to *cope*[1] with them. One who has seen *ups and downs*[2] in life calmly fights against them. Sufferings bring out the best in a person.

According to a German proverb, 'one who has never tasted what is bitter, does not know what is sweet'. Adversity is a part of human existence. It makes man aware of his inborn virtues. Great men like Mahatma Gandhi, Lal Bahadur Shastri, Abraham Lincoln and others faced adversities boldly and emerged successful.

Though adversity often leads to disastrous ends, it, due to lack of a strong will power, can be turned into an advantage with a little tact and wisdom. It is rightly said that 'prosperity bakes friends and adversity tries them'. Albert Einstein once thanked those (persons) who had not extended a helping hand to him in his endeavour, for what he could do alone, he could not have done in that case. In the journey of life, wealth of a person attracts many a person with ulterior motives but as soon as adversity falls upon him, they desert him, leaving him in the lurch.

We learn a lot from our sufferings. Pain and agony are usually followed by happiness and prosperity. One should never give up one's struggle midway. One's *perseverance*[3] can lead one to success.

Adversities reveal what the necessities of life are and what are luxuries. A rich and prosperous man takes his luxuries for necessities. He can hardly distinguish between the essentials and the inessentials. A man who has gone through adversities, can easily understand the condition of the deprived. Abraham Lincoln passed through very tough times during his early life and later on became the President of the USA. Nobody did greater service to the slaves and the deprived than Lincoln did.

Adversities give us a chance to judge our friends and *foes*[4]. We come to know of their nature and *intentions*[5] during our difficulties. False friendship, based on selfish *motives*[6] is exposed during adverse times. Only true friends come to our rescue. They encourage us and support us during such difficulties.

Adversity brings man closer to man. It teaches man the great lesson of humanity. It broadens his outlook. It frees man from *vanity*[7] and *snobbery*[8]. It makes him humane. Adverse conditions make man humble and sympathetic.

Adversity stimulates the artistic qualities in an artist. Surdas, Milton and Homer wrote immortal *verses*[9] when they were blind. Rabindranath Tagore's personal tragedies made his writings more powerful. Munshi Prem Chand who has left an indelible mark on Hindi and Urdu literature had to face a lot of hardship in life. Adversity is known to bring out the creative best of people.

Adversity takes man nearer to God. When in distress, man tries to draw his strength from his faith in God. Faith gives him the power to fight the adverse circumstances in life. Taking refuge in God gives man a relief from his tiring life and fills him with renewed vigour.

Almost all human beings face adverse circumstances. The student loses his rank in the class or fails in the examination. The young sales executive may fail to effect sales. The trader may lose his interest in business. Nations face economic and political crises. Adverse circumstances are thus a part of life. But every failure leads to success. Failures are, indeed, the stepping stone to success.

We cannot expect everyone to agree with us. We usually equate disagreement with enmity in spite of knowing that intelligent people rarely agree on anything. Every individual has a perspective that is unique. So we should try to persuade the other person but should not be unhappy, if we fail. We learn from our mistakes and failures and ultimately reach our goal.

Adversity is the tool for improving our abilities. We should plan ahead for solving our problems. If our efforts fail, we must review our plans and start afresh. We must try and try until we succeed. We can take valuable suggestions and advice from others. *Resources*[10] must be properly utilised for the solution of the problem. We can achieve the desired results in adverse situations through a carefully planned approach.

Adversity makes superior men out of ordinary mortals. Suffering tests the patience and *fortitude*[11] of a person. It makes him realise his real strength. Gandhiji stoically suffered untold miseries at the hands of the British, both in South Africa and in India. The adversities did not make him sacrifice his principles rather, they made him determined and steadfast to hold them up. The more difficult the circumstance, the firmer should be the determination.

Adversity has its negative effects too. A man who does not get the fruits of his hard work may lose interest in life. He may get disheartened and disillusioned. He may become a pessimist. He may even try to commit suicide. But success and failures are a part of life. One should try and try again until one succeeds. Adversity tests our qualities and polishes our personality. Adversities last for a short time. One should remain an *optimist*[12] during one's tough times. It saves us from false notions as it is an eye-opener. Adversities make man develop himself as a more mature and powerful individual. Shakespeare was right when he said, "Sweet are the uses of adversity."

Aid to Vocabulary

1. *Cope* — manage
2. *Ups and downs* — changes of fortune
3. *Perseverance* — to continue trying though the going is tough
4. *Foes* — enemies
5. *Intentions* — that which one proposes or plans to do
6. *Motives* — a factor that induces a person to act in a particular way
7. *Vanity* — excessive pride in oneself
8. *Snobbery* — attitude or behaviour of people who think themselves to be better than others

9. *Verses* — poetry
10. *Resources* — things that give help and support when needed
11. *Fortitude* — mental strength and courage to face danger, pain, etc.
12. *Optimist* — a person who is always hopeful and expects the best in all things

Points to Remember

1. Adversity enables one to meet the challenges of life.
2. One who lives in luxury is hardly aware of the ups and downs of life.
3. Great men emerged successful through the worst of adversities.
4. Adversities reveal what the necessities of life are and what are luxuries.
5. Friendship can be judged during adversities.
6. Adversity brings man closer to man.
7. It stimulates the artistic qualities in an artist.
8. It takes man nearer to God.
9. It is the tool for improving our abilities.
10. Adversity makes superior men out of ordinary mortals.
11. Adversity makes man develop himself as a more mature and more powerful individual.

Essay

72 STRIKE WHILE THE IRON IS HOT

SYNOPSIS

To achieve success, it is essential to make an attempt at the opportune time. Everyone wishes to succeed in every endeavour he or she undertakes. Success builds confidence while failure leads to dejection. The proverb is closely associated with the occupation of a blacksmith. When the iron is red hot, it can be easily moulded into the desired shape. But if he misses the opportunity of striking the hot iron into shape, no amount of hammering would have any effect on it later. Interpreted and applied to daily human activities, it means seizing the opportunity when it presents itself. A wise person always remains alert and makes the best use of the opportunity that comes his way. The proverb can be applied to any walk of life and its efficacy can be evaluated. The sagacious strike at the right opportunity and achieve success.

Its no secret that success, brings alongwith it, name, fame and prosperity which enhance self worth, self respect and self confidence. In order to achieve success, four things according the Late Indian Prime Minister Mrs. Indira Gandhi, are indispensable – (1) farsightedness (2) discipline (3) firm determination and (4) hard labour. To make an attempt at the opportune moment can be added to the list because work done after it generally does not bear the desired fruit.

Everyone in life aspires to succeed in every endeavour he or she undertakes. Success builds confidence while failure leads to *dejection*[1]. Success is appreciated while failure brands a person as incompetent. There are several factors which go into making any venture a success. To be successful, one has to plan, make strategies and put in *concerted*[2] effort. Of course, luck also plays its part. Any effort carried out in a planned manner and with *perseverance*[3] is sure to bear fruit. One has to take stock of the situation and act when the time is appropriate.

The proverb 'strike while the iron is hot' is closely associated with the occupation of a blacksmith. He puts the iron in fire till it becomes red hot. Once the iron is red-hot, it becomes soft and he loses no time in moulding it to the desired shape. If he allows it to cool, he loses an excellent opportunity.

Interpreted and applied to daily human existence, the proverb means seizing the opportunity when it presents itself. While people who are not watchful and who let the opportunities slip by, find it extremely difficult to succeed in any endeavour; the wise always remain alert and make the best use of the opportunities that come their way. When opportunity knocks at the door, those who make the best use of it succeed, while others who do not, are left behind. Opportunities seldom repeat themselves. Therefore, an opportunity once missed is gone forever or for a long period.

When the sea is in tide, the sailors who are alert, seize the chance to set their ships on sail. Those sailors who remain anchored at land miss the opportunity, and are forced to postpone their journey till the arrival of another tide. Similarly, there is a tide in the affairs of human beings, that is, there is a certain time which is *propitious*[4] for achieving certain objectives.

This proverb can be applied to any sphere of life and its *efficacy*[5] can be evaluated. In the field of sports, those players who make the best out of the opportunities succeed in their game and make their nation feel proud of them. Players succeed by taking advantage of their opponents' weaknesses and seizing the opportunity of defeating them.

The history of the world would have taken a different course if in the Second World War, Hitler had seized the opportunity of carrying out an offensive against Britain rather than Russia. While he battled Russia, England was able to gather the support of its allies and defeat Hitler. His ambition of conquering the world was *nipped in the bud*[6] because he did not grab the opportunity when it came to him. Nadir Shah, the Persian ruler, attacked and plundered India's wealth, when India was being ruled by the weakest of the Mughal kings, Mohammad Shah Rangila. Apart from the wealth, he also took away the Peacock Throne of Shah Jahan, which was a precious *relic*[7].

India followed an *archaic*[8] pattern of society divided into castes and sub-castes. The *splintered*[9] society was never able to resist any invasion. The Aryans invaded and settled down in India and shared the religious beliefs, culture and traditions with the inhabitants of the country. In the medieval period, Turk and Muslim invasions became frequent because the country was divided into small empires which individually were not strong enough to defend themselves.

The aggressors knew the weaknesses of India and grabbed the opportunity to *plunder*[10] India's wealth. Timur Lang's invasion took place when India was under weak rulers. The Mughal dynasty was founded by Babur which restored stability in the north. The country prospered under his successors, especially Akbar. The decline of the Mughal dynasty led to the era of British rule in India. The British took advantage of the growing instability in the country to further their vested interests.

In the field of politics, too, this maxim holds good. A politician's success largely depends on his skill in winning popular support. There are certain people who are more often than not caught *slumbering*[11] when they ought to have recognised an opportunity. For having missed it, they curse their stars or they blame their misfortune for their failures. No doubt, there are times when individual alertness does not help much and success depends on mere chance. But such times are few and far between.

Sometimes it also happens that one who takes the risk gets all the success. We should be open to new challenges because facing challenges makes one more confident and courageous. Generally, those who keep their eyes and ears open to act at the right opportunity, achieve success. They join the *bandwagon*[12] of successful people, because by being *sagacious*[13], they make the best out of the opportunities that come their way.

Aid to Vocabulary

1. *Dejection* — depression of mind
2. *Concerted* — very strong
3. *Perseverance* — steadfast pursuit of an aim
4. *Propitious* — favourable
5. *Efficacy* — effectiveness
6. *Nipped in the bud* — failed before its realisation
7. *Relic* — something that is from a past time, place, culture, etc.
8. *Archaic* — old and no longer useful
9. *Splintered* — to make something break into small, sharp pieces
10. *Plunder* — to steal things from a place especially using force
11. *Slumbering* — sleeping
12. *Bandwagon* — a figurative wagon conceived as carrying a band of political leaders likely to be successful, a popular activity with growing support
13. *Sagacious* — wise

Points to Remember

1. Success gets appreciated while failure brands a person as incompetent.
2. The proverb is associated with the occupation of a blacksmith.
3. In daily human existence, it means seizing the opportunity when it presents itself.
4. This proverb can be applied to any walk of life.
5. In the field of history and politics, this maxim holds good.
6. One should be open to new challenges.
7. Those who act at the right opportunity achieve success.

Essay
73

MAN DOES NOT LIVE BY BREAD ALONE

SYNOPSIS

Apart from his basic needs—food, clothing and shelter; a man needs several other things to survive. Survival is the first and the foremost concern of all living beings. They need food for their survival and to carry out the functions of life. However, food is not the only concern of man. His superior intellect fills him with certain cravings which are equally strong and need fulfilment. He is curious by nature and has the urge to probe into inexplicable things. In his quest for knowledge, he feels the need to acquire fame and affluence. He has an innate sense of beauty and appreciates it in all its forms. Love is another instinct that binds all human beings. He begins to stagnate if he stays in the same environment for long. He finds an outlet to vent his boredom through creativity. He indulges in entertainment. Man also aspires to fulfil his spiritual needs. Hence, it can be said that man does not live by bread alone.

Apart from his basic needs – food, clothing and shelter, a man needs several other things to survive. Among them, spiritualism and an urge to know the unknown and create something new stand apart. Unlike animals, man possesses intellect which distinguishes him from species of animals. Therefore, bread, though, it is an integral part of his life, is not the only thing that enables him to lead life. He needs food for his intellect also which comes in the form of creativity, scholarship, recreation and service. To love and be loved, to respect and be respected, to be in the company of near and dear ones etc., go a long way in the shaping up of his personality.

Survival is the first and the foremost concern of all living beings. They need food for their survival and to carry out the functions of life. Inability in procuring food could threaten the existence of all living beings. Darwin suggested the theory of 'survival of the fittest' which is applicable to all living beings. Carnivorous animals like tigers, lions and cheetahs sometimes turn into man-eaters. Illegal poaching of small animals by man has led to the reduction in their number which makes bigger animals prey on man for their survival. When there is scarcity of food, many living beings are known to indulge in *cannibalism*[1] for their sustenance. Scarcity of food is known to create *havoc*[2] in the lives of both humans and animals. The devastating effect of scarcity of food, on humans, was witnessed during the Bengal Famine of 1943.

However, food is not the only concern of human beings. The primary concern of other living beings is only food, yet they are known to respond positively to human love and affection. Man is superior to all living beings because intellect has been *bestowed*[3] upon him. This faculty fills him with certain *cravings*[4] which are equally strong and need fulfilment. Non-fulfilment of these cravings leads to frustration and lack of motivation. Sometimes, it is also known to produce mental strain leading to nervous breakdown.

Man is curious by nature. He has the urge to probe into *inexplicable*[5] things. During ancient times he held nature in awe because he knew little about the occurrence of natural phenomena. In his quest for knowledge, he has discovered and invented many things that have helped him in carrying out his daily activities smoothly. His knowledge has enabled him to conquer land, ocean and space and thus unravel many a mystery of Nature. He feels the need to get recognition, adulation and admiration from the public for his successful endeavours. Success is, very often, measured in terms of material wealth possessed by a person. Hence, apart from knowledge, man also strives for fame and *affluence*[6].

Man has an *innate*[7] sense of beauty. He appreciates beauty in all its forms. Nature has given beauty to the world with its bounty of *flora and fauna*[8]. A bed of blooming flowers instils a sense of pleasure in the beholder. A bunch of flowers is presented to a patient, who is *convalescing*[9], to cheer him up. Keats had said, "A thing of beauty is a joy forever". The *aesthetic*[10] sense in man makes him *hanker after*[11] different forms of beauty.

Music concerts and dance programmes *enthral*[12] the audience because beauty in the performing arts is highly appreciated. Music is known to calm strained nerves. Drawing, sketching and painting are also known to release stress. Even ancient man expressed himself through paintings. In his quest for beauty, man created beautiful architectural wonders. In other words, his quest for beauty, made him creative.

Love is another instinct which binds two human beings. Man wishes to be loved and appreciated. A relationship between two human beings is known to sustain if it is based on mutual love and understanding. All religions preach brotherhood, love and peace. Man holds God in awe. The love of God motivates people to be generous, kind and selfless. Right from the time of his birth man is bound by various relationships.

With the passing of time, the existing relations get fostered, while new ones are also formed simultaneously. In every relationship, man expects others to reciprocate his love and understanding. Gautam Buddha, through his love, is known to have reformed the dreaded dacoit Angulimala. History supports the fact that most of the dreaded killers were those, who were deprived of parental love and affection. In the absence of love, man could create adverse conditions for both himself and the society.

Man begins to stagnate if he stays in the same environment for long. Monotonous activity leads to low morale, frustration and reduced output. Hence, he needs to find ways to overcome his boredom. He exercises his talent and skill through creativity. In his leisure, he devises means to express himself in poetry, music or hobbies like gardening, painting and sculpture. The famous painter Vincent Van Gogh lived a life of abject poverty during his lifetime but did not forsake his love for painting. Beethoven was deaf but that did not deter him from composing music. A potter and a carpenter, despite their poverty and ignorance, create objects for the use of other human beings. Even homemakers occasionally change the decor of their homes to satisfy their creative urge. Man through his creativity can moued anything to his desired shape. All this shows that man is creative by nature.

To set himself free from routine existence, man indulges in entertainment. Without any means of recreation, life would become dull and unbearable. Recreation keeps the mind and body, sound and fit. Theatre, cinema, television, sports and games provide recreation. Food satisfies the appetite, while entertainment satisfies the senses.

The entertainment media provides man a temporary escape from the rigours of life and takes him to a world of fantasy and illusion. Watching games on television or at a stadium also refreshes a tired mind and *alleviates*[13] one's *blues*[14]. Celebration and observing of various rituals during festivals are also means of escape from the daily routine of life. Festivals are occasions of *revelry*[15] exchanging gifts and greetings and getting together with friends and relatives. Old bonds are strengthened and new ones are formed during such occasions. This gives a new energy to life. Man understands the value of familial ties and needs an assurance of being loved and wanted.

Man also aspires to fulfil his spiritual needs. Physical and spiritual needs are two aspects of man's existence. Food caters to his physical needs while the spiritual aspect seeks answers to fundamental questions of his existence. Great thinkers and philosophers have pondered over the significance of life and man's existence in the universe.

Gautam Buddha realised that the source of all evils in the world is ignorance. Ignorance is dispelled only by knowledge. So knowledge is the sole means of liberation. He felt that man should follow a *pious*[16] path and lead a selfless life. Only then can he attain salvation. To get away from this materialistic world, man seeks solace through various means. Meditation, prayers and preachings of religious persons help man to fulfil his spiritual needs. only that man, who strives for excellence and perfection in every sphere of life and does not feel content with just earning his bread, truly lives. Food, undoubtedly, is the fundamental need of man yet it is certainly not the only one. Hence, it can be said that man does not live by bread (food) alone, he aspires to satisfy his many other needs also.

Aid to Vocabulary

1. *Cannibalism* — the practice of eating one's own kind
2. *Havoc* — a situation of damage, destruction or confusion
3. *Bestowed* — given
4. *Cravings* — strong desires
5. *Inexplicable* — incapable of being explained
6. *Affluence* — wealth
7. *Innate* — inborn
8. *Flora and fauna* — vegetation and wildlife
9. *Convalescing* — recovering from illness
10. *Aesthetic* — pertaining to the appreciation of the beautiful
11. *Hanker after* — strongly desire
12. *Enthral* — captivate
13. *Alleviates* — lessens
14. *Blues* — depressed mood
15. *Revelry* — noisy celebration
16. *Pious* — having a dutiful spirit of reverence for God

Points to Remember

1. Survival is the first and the foremost concern of all living beings.
2. Man's intellectual faculty fills him with other cravings.
3. In his quest for knowledge, he feels the need to acquire fame and affluence.
4. He appreciates beauty in all its forms.
5. Love is another aspect that binds two human beings.
6. Man needs an outlet to vent his boredom.
7. Man indulges in entertainment to set himself free from his routine scenario.
8. He also aspires to fulfil his spiritual needs.

GUIDED COMPOSITION

Develop the following paragraph into a full-fledged essay in 800-1000 words. The gist of the topic is provided in approximately 160 words for your help:

DIGNITY OF LABOUR

Every man who earns his living through hard work deserves to be treated with dignity. One does not become small in doing work with one's hands. There are some people, who wrongly assume that manual work is below their dignity. They like to take up white collar jobs and consider themselves superior to a person who earns his bread by the sweat of his brow. This is a totally absurd idea. Every work, intellectual or physical, has its own dignity. As long as a man does honest and sincere work, he deserves to be respected. A labourer who tills the land or pulls a cart is as worthy of regard as another who is engaged in intellectual pursuit for his living. It is indeed sad that people pay obeisance to a successful person, who has risen by exploiting others. They treat the poor manual worker or labourer with indifference and disdain. No wonder Gandhiji laid so much emphasis on manual work as an integral part of any educational system to make the youth aware of dignity of labour.

(160 words)

Essay **74**

THE PEN IS MIGHTIER THAN THE SWORD

Synopsis

Early man lived on the strength of his muscle power. The destinies of nations were shaped by wars. Later on, man realised that the use of weapons could kill a man but could not bring about a change of heart. Ideas have a much larger impact than violence. Ideas are propagated by writing. Writing has helped man to store and propagate his thoughts, beliefs and ideas. The pen has been able to unite people to stand up against tyranny and injustice. Good literature survives the test of time. The pen stands for positive and constructive efforts. It can plead for progress and social reform. It promotes cultural values. Wars, on the other hand, tend to destroy civilisation. It is the power of the pen that has, through the ages, shaped human history.

Early man lived on the strength of his muscle power. In the struggle for existence, it was the survival of the fittest. Gradually, man became civilised and progressed in various fields. The destinies of nations were shaped by wars. With time, man realised that the use of weapons could not solve all problems. Weapons could kill a man but could not bring about a change of heart or establish order in the society.

Ideas have a much larger impact than violence. Force is incapable of changing the ideas and beliefs of the people. When people are influenced by new ideas, changes occur in the society. Ideas are *propagated*[1] by writing. Brave deeds and *valour*[2] shown in the battlefield are certainly praiseworthy, but no clash of arms could achieve what great men through their writings have achieved.

The invention of the printing press by Johann Gutenberg has helped man to store and propagate his thoughts, beliefs and ideas. The printed word has become the most powerful medium of disseminating ideas and beliefs. Newspapers have become a mighty weapon. Public opinion is generally formed not by clash of arms but by the writings of great men and by newspapers. The pen has been able to unite people to stand up against tyranny and injustice.

Editors' ideas are expressed through the power of the pen. The printed word makes a permanent impact on several generations. It *moulds*[3] life according to the times. Violence can only suppress human spirit, it is the pen that can liberate it. The pen stands for positive and constructive efforts, while the sword signifies negative postures and destruction all around. The sword can force people into submission but cannot propagate an idea. The pen can solve many complex issues. The sword can only destroy. History is proof that wars have *annihilated*[4] entire human civilisations.

Writers, thinkers and artists raised the consciousness of the modern world by *wielding*[5] the power of the pen. The French Revolution of 1789 owed inspiration to the writings of Rousseau and Voltaire. Karl Marx's *Das Capital* inspired Lenin, the leader of the Russian Revolution of 1917. The *Communist Manifesto*, the combined work of Friedrich Engels and Karl Marx in 1848 formed the basis of modern international communism.

Charles Dickens (1812-70) exposed the evils of capitalism in his works like *David Copperfield, Oliver Twist* and *Hard Times*. Mahatma Gandhi's philosophy of life was based on the teachings of the *Gita*. David Thoreau's *Civil Disobedience* inspired Gandhiji for Satyagraha during the freedom struggle in India. In the Vietnam war, journalists and photographers played a key role in bringing about an end to the conflict.

India's freedom struggle was based on the supremacy of the pen over the sword. The major national newspapers, *The Hindu, The Tribune, Bengalee, Mahratta, Kesari* and *The Amrita Bazar Patrika* waged a *campaign*[6] against the British rule. The leaders were able to communicate their ideas to the people through the press. They were able to generate within them a feeling of nationalism and unity. Gandhiji himself edited two newspapers, *Navyug* and *Harijan* to mobilise the masses. The victory of our freedom movement over the British to some extent was the victory of the pen over the sword.

The victories of the sword are short-lived. Alexander's desire to conquer the world remained unfulfilled. Hitler *overran*[7] Europe but was defeated in the Second World War. the plays of Shakespeare, the poetry of Keats and Wordsworth, or the novels of Dickens still appeal to the people. In their writings, they present a graphic account of the political situation, the social conditions and the beliefs prevalent in the period they lived and wrote in.

The pen is mightier because it gives good counsel, promotes cultural values and graces of life. It thus removes the *cobwebs*[8] from society. War, on the other hand, destroys cultures and *negates*[9] the cultural values. It takes nations decades to re-build what wars destroy and to rehabilitate the countless victims of the war. There are some people who think that resort to the sword and the compulsions of war encourage some virtues like unity, *tenacity*[10], heroism, inventiveness and valour. But this is only an illusion. The pen can promote these virtues more effectively and permanently than a war can.

The sword implies the use of *brute*[11] force while the pen relies on reason and thought. The pen stands for progressive endeavour but the sword stands for regressive destruction. The pen can solve many complex problems through peaceful means. It can plead for progress and social reform. It promotes cultural values and expands knowledge.

A writer who records his noble thoughts is a teacher of humanity. The pen has a stronger influence than the sword. The written word can change a person. It can influence people for many a generation. The pen is indeed mightier than the sword. It is the power of the pen that has through the ages shaped human history.

Aid to Vocabulary

1. *Propagated* — disseminated, spread
2. *Valour* — personal courage shown in fighting
3. *Moulds* — shapes
4. *Annihilated* — destroyed completely
5. *Wielding* — having and using
6. *Campaign* — organised course of action to arouse public interest
7. *Overran* — ravaged (country) with hostile force
8. *Cobwebs* — a fine net of threads made by a spider to catch insects; stagnation, degeneration
9. *Negates* — to stop something from having any effect
10. *Tenacity* — strength and determination
11. *Brute* — beastlike, cruel

Points to Remember

1. Ideas have a much greater impact than violence.
2. The invention of the printing press has helped man to store and propagate his thoughts, beliefs and ideas.
3. The printed word moulds life according to the times. Wars have annihilated civilisations.
4. Writers, thinkers and artists raised the consciousness of the modern world through the power of the pen.
5. India's freedom struggle was based on the supremacy of the pen over the sword.
6. The victories of the sword are short-lived, but good literature survives the test of time.
7. The pen has shaped human history through the ages.

Essay 75

AMBITION IS THE GREATEST ENEMY OF PEACE

SYNOPSIS

Man is essentially an ambitious being. His acquisitiveness, pride, ambition and selfishness drives him on in his pursuit of personal gains. History has remained testimony to the fact that many wars were waged to satisfy the ambitions of the kings and emperors. History, epics, legends and literature have recorded how lofty ambitions of men have disturbed the peace of the people around them. Ambition spells doom for the man who nurtures it and also leaves behind a trail of death and destruction. All religions preach universal love and peace. Great philosophers have also preached the message of love and renunciation. International peace remains a cherished dream. For peaceful co-existence, we should take lessons from history and turn to the humanitarian and ethical values. Only then, man may hope to live in peace and harmony.

Man is essentially an ambitious and a competitive being. There has been no substantial change in man's nature during the course of his evolution. He is still barbarian at heart, ready to kill another for his own survival or simply to prove his supremacy over the other, possibly a weaker person. Man may boast of all the technological advancements that have been made in the past centuries as a result of his *ingenuity*[1], yet the fact remains that they have not made man wiser or more judicious. His lust for power is as strong as ever. Driven by an *unbridled*[2] ambition, he continues with his endeavour, unmindful of the havoc he may cause in the lives of others. It is no longer a struggle for survival, rather it is just an indulgence of his whims and fancies to fulfil his endless desires. His *acquisitiveness*[3], pride and ambition drives him on in his pursuit of personal gains.

History has remained *testimony*[4] to the fact that wars were waged by kings and emperors just to satisfy their ambitions. Alexander the Great was young and ambitious and came all the way from Greece to India. He aspired to rule over the whole world. Ashoka was also an ambitious ruler and waged wars to annex new lands. On one such expedition, he saw the trail of death and destruction of the enemy camp in the war that he had won. He was so much moved by the bloodshed that he decided to forsake war and work for the good of humanity. He realised and regretted that to fulfil his ambitions, he had unknowingly sacrificed the lives of many innocent people. Chandashoka transformed into dharmashoka. In modern times, Hitler would be remembered as the most ambitious man on earth. He believed in the superiority of the Aryan race and wanted to *exterminate*[5] the Jews from the face of the earth. The gas chambers, the torture cells and the bodies from mass graveyards *exhumed*[6] after the end of the Second World War are grim reminders of the German *holocaust*[7].

The eighteen-day Mahabharata war was fought because Duryodhana aspired to rule over India and deprive the Pandavas of their throne. According to the *Ramayana*, Queen Kaikeyi wanted to enthrone her son, Bharata as the King. This led Rama to forsake his throne for his younger brother and undertake fourteen years of exile. In *Macbeth*, though the king Duncan is killed by Macbeth to fulfil his vaulting ambition of taking over the former's empire and later suffers from the trauma of guilt. Brutus murdered Caesar in *Julius Caesar* and admitted to his countrymen that his ambition had made him do so.

History, epics, legends and literature have recorded how lofty ambitions of men have disturbed the peace of the people around them. Ambition overpowers a man and he cares little for the well-being and emotions of others. Under the powerful sway of his ambition, he goes on a *rampage*[8] caring little for the trail of sorrow he leaves behind or for the loss of men and property. Ambition always spells doom for the man who nurtures it and also leaves behind a trail of death and destruction.

All religions preach universal love and peace. But, these remain *utopian*[9] ideals, which are beyond the realm of anybody's understanding. Gautam Buddha felt that man should cast off all desires and follow the path of righteousness to achieve perfect happiness. Great philosophers and prophets have preached the message of love and *renunciation*[10], and a control over one's passions to attain salvation. The 20th century saw Mahatma Gandhi pursuing the freedom struggle on the ideals of love, tolerance and non-violence. On the eve of independence, however, he was a disillusioned man because the country was partitioned, which led to the outbreak of communal violence. His efforts of obtaining freedom through peaceful means were shattered because of the lofty ambitions of some leaders to grab power. The partition led to a carnage, in India as well as in Pakistan, which resulted in huge loss of life and property.

International peace remains a cherished dream. Global terrorism is sponsored by a few countries to fulfil their ambitions. With a view to stall the surge of communism and the influence of Russia on other countries, the USA supplied monetary and arms assistance to various countries. The move *boomeranged*[11] on it, when the US itself became a victim of terrorist attacks. Terrorist outfits devastated the World Trade Centre in New York and the Pentagon in Washington, killing thousands of people in 2001. Ambitious attempts by nations to gain supremacy in the world have resulted in nuclear arms proliferation. Nuclear tests carried out by both India and Pakistan have made the situation in the Indian subcontinent grim. For peaceful co-existence, we should take lessons from history and turn to the ethical and humanitarian doctrine of universal peace instead of nurturing the ruthless pursuit of personal ambition. Only then can man hope to live in peace and harmony.

Aid to Vocabulary

1. *Ingenuity* — the quality of being clever
2. *Unbridled* — unchecked
3. *Acquisitiveness* — keenness to acquire things
4. *Testimony* — evidence given in support of a fact
5. *Exterminate* — to root out
6. *Exhumed* — dug up after having been buried
7. *Holocaust* — vast destruction, killing large number of people
8. *Rampage* — wild and destructive run
9. *Utopian* — impractical
10. *Renunciation* — the act of giving up all desires
11. *Boomeranged* — recoiled on originator

Points to Remember

1. Man is essentially an ambitious and competitive being.
2. Many ambitious kings waged wars just to satisfy their ambitions.
3. From epic to drama, everywhere ambition has been shown as the cause of disturbances in our lives.
4. Great philosophers preached that one should cast off all the desires and follow the path of righteousness.
5. In the modern world, global terrorism is sponsored by a few countries just to further their ambitions.
6. For peaceful co-existence, we should take lessons from history and turn to humanitarian values instead of encouraging ruthless ambition.

Essay 76

WHERE THERE IS A WILL, THERE IS A WAY

Synopsis

Willpower is the greatest driving force in man. It helps him to get through all the difficulties in life. He continues his journey towards his chosen goal. The real essence of life lies in struggle. A wise man accepts the challenges of life with a calm mind. One should have a firm determination to strive and win. Many great men won success by sheer determination and oneness of purpose. One can even overcome physical disabilities and social barriers. It is this spirit which has enabled man to explore the unknown. The achievements of mankind till date are the products of strong determination and willpower. Patience, commitment to the objectives and perseverance certainly yield rich dividends.

Willpower is the greatest driving force in man. It helps him to overcome all the difficulties in life. *Willpower*[1] is the most essential ingredient of success. It enables a person to find a way to overcome the obstacles in his path and continue his journey towards his chosen goal. A man who loses heart at the sight of failure can never achieve his goal. But a man who is determined to attain his objective is not disheartened by failures. One should not lose heart in the face of *adversities*[2].

The real *essence*[3] of life lies in struggle. Determination and calmness help a person in his endeavour. They provide him inspiration to achieve success. A wise man accepts the challenges of life with a calm mind. Our ancient scriptures also advocate that one should do one's duty with determination. One should have a firm determination to strive and win. Many great men won success by sheer determination and oneness of purpose. Mahatma Gandhi fought for the blacks in South Africa. His strong willpower helped him to secure for India independence from the British rule. Martin Luther King was a civil rights leader, in the USA, who brought about *radical*[4] changes in the social setup. Nelson Mandela fought against racial discrimination in South Africa. Abraham Lincoln ended slavery in the USA. Aung San Suu Kyi took on Myanmar's *military junta* to bring democracy in the country.

Different people have different objectives in life. Goals may range from a career in administration, engineering, medicine, law, management, etc., to entrepreneurship. Men achieve success by their strong willpower.

Even the physically challenged succeed in achieving success by their strong willpower and determination. Beethoven had become deaf before he composed his famous Ninth Symphony. John Milton wrote *Paradise Lost, Paradise Regained* and *Samson Agonistes* after he became blind.

While a patient with a weak will is likely to *succumb*[5] to a critical ailment, another with the same state of illness may overcome his condition by dint of sheer determination to live. Helen Keller was both blind and deaf, but she became an educator of the blind. Louis Braille was also a blind educationist. He introduced the Braille script for the blind. Sudha Chandran has an amputated leg, but even with an artificial limb, she became a famous Bharatnatyam dancer and an actress. The Paralympics witness an array of achievements of the physically challenged sportspersons. Thus, a person of strong willpower can overcome physical disabilities in the *pursuit*[6] of his goal. He/she can overcome social barriers as well.

Man's strong desire and willpower have led to the discovery of unknown lands. He has been able to explore the depths of the ocean. It is this spirit which has enabled man to climb peaks like Mount Everest. He explored space and landed on the moon. Major breakthroughs have been made in the fields of information technology, engineering and medicine. The achievements of mankind till date are the products of strong determination and willpower, and will continue to be so.

However, some people do become victims of adverse circumstances. Their efforts are hardly rewarded with success. They become dispirited, disillusioned and disheartened. They lose the will to fight. They become pessimistic in their attitude. But they should not lose heart because success always follows failure. Night is always followed by the day, so one should not lose hope, come what may. Patience, commitment to the objectives and *perseverance*[7] certainly yield rich dividends. One should have an aim in life. One should strive hard for achieving it. Success is not restricted to a few. It can be achieved by anyone who dares to go for it. One should have a positive approach towards life. There are many who undergo despair, failure and defeat. But their determination to win and achieve takes them forward. Where there is a will, there is a way!

Aid to Vocabulary

1. *Willpower* — strong determination that allows man to do something difficult
2. *Adversities* — troubles, difficulties
3. *Essence* — that which makes a thing what it is

4. *Radical* — new, not ordinary
5. *Succumb* — be overcome by death
6. *Pursuit* — the action of looking for or trying to find something
7. *Perseverance* — continued steady effort to achieve an aim

Points to Remember

1. Willpower enables one to find a way to overcome the obstacles in one's path.
2. Determination and calmness provide inspiration for achieving success.
3. Many great men achieved success by sheer determination and oneness of purpose.
4. Different people have different objectives in life.
5. A strong willpower enables one to overcome physical disabilities and social barriers.
6. The achievements of mankind till date are the products of strong determination and willpower.
7. Patience, commitment to the objectives and perseverance certainly yield rich dividends.

Essay **77**

A THING OF BEAUTY IS A JOY FOREVER

SYNOPSIS

Beauty lies in the eye of the beholder. Beauty is a combination of qualities that delight the senses. It is an inborn instinct in human beings to appreciate beauty. Man developed an eye for beauty right from the Stone Age. Artistic creations are man's attempts to depict the joy evoked by a thing of beauty. Man cherishes the beautiful moments and things in life. Human imagination helps to revive and relive the happy moments spent in the company of beautiful things. Nature abounds in beauty. Poets and painters seek inspiration from beauty. The creations of sculptors, architects and musicians are appreciated by all. Spiritual beauty is something nobler and higher than physical beauty. The beautiful aspects of nature uplift the spirit of a pessimist. Beauty links man with eternity. A thing of beauty is a joy forever.

Although a thing of beauty may not *invariably*[1] appeal to one and all because beauty, most often, lies in the eye of the beholder; a quest for it is on since time immemorial. Different styles and fashions that are prevalent today, are the outcome of this quest for beauty. John Keats has rightly remarked in 'Hyperion' that 'The first in beauty is the first in might'.

Beauty is not skin-deep. Beauty is a combination of qualities that give pleasure to the senses. Many a writer, poet and filmmaker has portrayed the supremacy of the spiritual beauty over the physical beauty. It is an inborn *instinct*[2] in human beings to appreciate beauty. Beauty both of nature and of human form has been a powerful attraction for men and women of all times and *climes*[3].

A beautiful object fills the heart with joy and delight. The soul gets *stirred*[4] by the external view of beauty. Man has developed an eye for beauty right from the Stone Age. The earliest cave-paintings depicting animals and trees prove the caveman's love for beauty. Artistic creations are man's attempts to depict the joy inherent in beauty.

A person may see a beautiful thing for a short duration but its memory lasts for a long time. Man cherishes the beautiful moments in life. Human imagination helps to *revive*[5] and relive the happy moments spent in the company of beautiful forms and objects. A colourful butterfly seen for five minutes gives instant delight for the same period of time, but if that scene is recaptured twenty times, the joy becomes twenty-fold.

Nature abounds in beauty. The sunrise, the sunset, the moon, the stars, the rainbow and the seasons delight the senses. Beautiful sights and sounds of nature provide pleasure to man. The rivers, the forests, the green mountains, the snow-capped peaks and the flowers are beautiful objects of nature. They leave an *impression*[6] on the mind of man. Recollection of this impression becomes a constant source of joy.

Beautiful objects are a source of inspiration for poets to compose poetry. Poets are more moved by beautiful sights than people of ordinary imagination. Keats was a great lover of beauty in all its varied forms. In most of his poems Keats appreciates different forms of beauty. The dancing daffodils seen by Wordsworth during his travels left a deep mark on his mind. He composed a poem on daffodils after four years of that visit but he felt the same delight, which he had felt while seeing them and which is reflected in the poem. This proves that any aspect of beauty leaves an everlasting impact on the human heart and soul. The great Sanskrit poet Kalidas has also graphically described in his poem *Kumar Sambhav,* the beauty of the forests blooming all around with the touch of spring.

Beautiful sights influence the painter to draw upon their beauty. His paintings are a poetry of colours which depict nature as it is, on the canvas. A painter always remains in search of a source where he could find any form of beauty whether in nature or in man to adorn his canvas with everlasting charm of beauty. A human face painted by a master painter will not only show the physical structure in its exact form but also reveal the emotions of the subject. The paintings of Leonardo da Vinci, Raphael, Hogarth, Rabindranath Tagore, Nandalal Bose, M.F. Hussain and others are a feast for the eyes and the mind.

What is true of poets and painters is equally true of sculptors, architects and musicians. They derive pleasure by their creation of beauty. Their beautiful works are appreciated by all. A musician creates beauty by the harmonious blending of various notes and tunes. This harmony is a source of pleasure for the listeners. The music of Tansen, Baiju Bawra, Ustad Fayyaz Khan, Ustad Amjad Ali Khan, R.D. Burman and others has been widely appreciated and *applauded*[7]. The marvels of Michelangelo's sculpture are admired the world over.

Beauty is present everywhere, be it nature, literature, sculpture or architecture. Cement, stone, wood, etc., have no shape or beauty but when they are used artistically by the architect, they take the form of a beautiful building. A number of historical monuments all over the world are great specimens of art and beauty. Their beautiful structures attract tourists from all over the world. Taj Mahal in India, Eiffel Tower in Paris, Opera House in Australia, The Roman Colosseum, are some of the buildings which are famous for their exquisite beauty.

Spiritual beauty is something nobler and higher than physical beauty. It is related to the beauty of the spirit and the soul. Spiritual beauty touches our soul. The pleasure and joy we derive from it is *sublime*[8]. Spiritual beauty is accompanied by truth and goodness—*Satyam, Shivam, Sundaram* as expressed by a sage. We find a similar view in Keats' poetry in which he says, 'Beauty is truth, truth beauty'. Keats regards spiritual beauty as the source of true joy. Beauty according to Shelley is eternal. An object of nature may decay and man may die, yet both survive in thought, for beauty never dies.

Beautiful objects of nature also uplift the spirit of a *pessimist*[9]. People take a break from the environment of big cities and flock to hill stations. The beautiful sights of nature in the hill stations refresh the mind. They influence a person to perform his tasks more efficiently than before. Beauty of nature has a soothing effect on the mind. In one of his poems, shelley said that even death will be peaceful for him if it comes while watching the beautiful aspects of nature.

Beauty, whether physical or spiritual always gives us joy. Harmony is the defining principle for any form or thing of beauty. This harmony is the *attribute*[10] of the soul. Beauty links man with *eternity*[11]. A thing of beauty is a joy forever.

Aid to Vocabulary

1. *Invariably* — always being the same
2. *Instinct* — tendency that one is born with to behave in a certain way
3. *Climes* — regions, climates
4. *Stirred* — excited
5. *Revive* — to bring back into existence
6. *Impression* — a deep lasting effect on the mind or feelings
7. *Applauded* — praised
8. *Sublime* — most exalted kind
9. *Pessimist* — a person who expects the worst to happen
10. *Attribute* — characteristic
11. *Eternity* — a very long time that seems endless

Points to Remember

1. A thing of beauty delights the senses.
2. Artistic creations are man's attempts to depict the joy inherent in beauty.
3. A beautiful thing leaves a deep impact on the mind.
4. Nature abounds in beauty .
5. Poets and painters seek inspiration from things of beauty.
6. The creations of sculptors, architects and musicians are appreciated by all.
7. Spiritual beauty is something nobler and higher than physical beauty.
8. The beautiful aspects of nature heal the pessimist.
9. Harmony is the defining principle of beauty.

Essay

78

FAILURES ARE THE PILLARS OF SUCCESS

SYNOPSIS

Failure is an impermanent entity; Man is destined to face challenges in life. Obstacles and difficulties are bound to come in the way. But one who keeps on striving is eventually crowned with success. Success is the result of hard work, firm determination and dedication. Every failure is a stepping stone to success. A man who has not tasted failure does not know the value of success. The brave have the confidence to welcome challenges in life. The pessimist sees difficulties in every opportunity. The optimist sees opportunities in every adversity. The inventions and discoveries are the result of hard work and sustained efforts. Our freedom fighters underwent various troubles and hardships to attain freedom. Failures prepare the foundation for bigger things in life.

A common saying 'Winners never quit and quitters never win' has far-reaching implications in the context of failure and success, for success in almost all the cases embraces those who never quit; instead they proceed on and on despite many failures. Victory in the battle field embraced King Bruce in his 7th attempt, George Bush was elected the President of America after several futile attempts. History and literature are replete with such stories. Dr APJ Abdul Kalam's recommendations to the students to read failure stories instead of success stories too propound this point. Although it is said and is true too to a far extent, that nothing succeeds, like success it is more pertinent to know that failure, infact, is a non-existent entity; the moment we decide not to take any more attempt; failure takes us into its fatal claws.

Man is destined to face challenges in life. Life is not a bed of roses. Obstacles and difficulties are bound to come in the way. Everyone desires success. However, everybody does not succeed in achieving his goals. Failures are a part of our lives. But one who keeps on *striving*[1] is eventually crowned with success.

Success is the result of hard work, firm determination and dedication. Sometimes, an attempt proves to be a failure. But one need not be deterred by it. Failure is a natural phenomenon. It carries a treasure of invaluable experience. Success and failure are two *facets*[2] of the same coin.

Every failure is a stepping stone to success. Failure teaches us a lot. It reveals our weaknesses that must be overcome. It informs us about the problem areas in our work. It guides and inspires us to put in more effort. It reveals the loopholes in our planning so that we may plug them. It gives us strength to act more decisively. We come to know about our limitations. It gives us a guideline for future course of action. Failure, thus, prepares a person to go for the next *endeavour*[3] with a better chance of success.

A man who has not tasted failure does not know the value of success. He becomes too self-assured and easy going. Most great men like the famous inventor of the US, Thomas Alva Edison, achieved success only after a long battle with failures. Undeterred by setbacks, they learnt from their mistakes and renewed their efforts until success came to them.

One who has met with failure may not need to put in the same amount of labour as was invested in one's maiden attempt. One is merely required to analyse the lapses and omissions and to improve the means and methods one needs to adopt. Success without failure is seldom possible. Fortune favours the brave. And the brave are those who go ahead, overcome their failures and achieve their goal.

The brave have the confidence to welcome challenges in life. Failures should not result in *pessimism*[4]. Pessimism acts as a *stumbling*[5] block on one's way to success. The pessimist sees difficulties in every opportunity. The *optimist*[6] sees opportunities in every difficulty. Failure, thus, acts as a ray of hope that *spurs*[7]. In case of failures, one should not be *perturbed*[8] by the comments and criticism of the people.

The inventions and discoveries seen by the world have all been the result of hard work and years of *sustained*[9] effort. All the inventors and discoverers met with failures on the way, but they never gave up until success came. Life saving drugs like Penicillin are the result of enormous efforts of such people.

Nothing great has ever been achieved without consistent effort in the face of seemingly insurmountable difficulties. The freedom struggle of India is a classic example of the heroic sacrifices made by the freedom fighters, who cared neither for their own lives nor for that matter, for those of their family members. To them, what mattered most was the freedom of the country. Every setback strengthened their resolve further. Ultimately, the mighty British empire had to bow down and the Britishers had to leave India lock, stock and barrel. The same can be said of Nelson Mandela of South Africa who despite facing grave odds succeeded in freeing his nation from the white man's rule. Similarly, Aung San Suu Kyi kept up her struggle for democracy in Myanmar until the *military junta* relented.

The youth of today are restless. They expect results immediately. They need to realise that Rome was not built in a day. Success is bound to follow once we start working towards our objective. One should not be depressed or dejected when one meets failure on the way, rather, one should keep striving till success is achieved. One must consider failures as stepping stones to success.

Today, we lead a comfortable life. We have numerous facilities and conveniences *at our disposal*[10]. All these were not available in the past. They were all invented and discovered over a period of time. It was possible only through hard work and toil.

The Indian educational system needs to be modified. The foundations of knowledge should be made strong. The youth should get career guidance. They should be made aware of the challenges they may face in future. They should be taught to accept each failure as a challenge that ought to be overcome to achieve success.

Failure results when adequate preparation has not been made or the necessary amount of labour has not been put. At times, destiny may also play some role. Nevertheless, failure does not deter the brave or ruffle the lion-hearted. It provides the opportunity to assess oneself and prepare better to succeed. One cannot enjoy one's success unless one has tasted failure. Failure prepares the foundation for bigger things in life. Failures are thus the pillars of success.

Aid to Vocabulary

1. *Striving* — trying hard for a long time to achieve something
2. *Facets* — one side of a many-sided body
3. *Endeavour* — an attempt or effort
4. *Pessimism* — the tendency to be sad and anxious and to believe that the worst would happen
5. *Stumbling* — a problem or point that causes difficulty or prevents progress, an obstacle
6. *Optimist* — a person who is always hopeful and expects the best in all situations
7. *Spur* — incite, encourage
8. *Perturbed* — ruffled, distressed
9. *Sustained* — continued
10. *At our Disposal* — available for use

Points to Remember

1. Failures are a part of our life.
2. We learn a lot from failures.
3. A man who has not tasted failure does not know the value of success.
4. Fortune favours the brave.
5. The optimist sees opportunities in every difficulty.
6. The inventions and discoveries seen by the world have all been the results of hard work and sustained effort.
7. Our freedom fighters underwent various troubles and hardships to attain freedom.
8. The youth of today expect results overnight.
9. The youth in the educational curriculum should be given lessons on success and failure.
10. Failure prepares the foundation for bigger things in life.

Essay **79**

PREVENTION IS BETTER THAN CURE

SYNOPSIS

Prevention is the shield which protects mankind from many disasters, chaos and destruction. We must measure every step we take. A cure is a blessing, but prevention is better than cure. A wise act of a cautious mind can stop one from stepping into something wrong or dangerous. Prevention makes man escape dangers and difficulties. Cure is a solution for the suffering which has already engulfed him. Man can prevent himself from falling into bad habits. Prevention can be achieved by planning in advance. Vaccination has prevented many diseases from afflicting human beings. Likewise, preventive measures taken in other areas also lessen the intensity of suffering. One can lead a happy and healthy life by combining one's judgemental and preventive abilities.

Prevention implies 'to stop something from happening'. Cure means 'to find a solution'. Man is *prone*[1] to committing mistakes. Prevention is the shield which saves mankind from many disasters, chaos and destruction that could have happened. Man can *foresee*[2] the happenings of the future if he is alert and active. He has the capability to check himself from doing anything wrong.

We must measure every step we take. Cure involves much more effort and pain than what would be needed to prevent a problem from affecting us. A cure is a blessing, as it relieves one's suffering, but prevention is better than cure for it keeps suffering away A wise act of a cautious mind can check. one's stepping into something wrong or dangerous. The act of right living makes everything possible. Living the right way means living judiciously, wisely and cautiously.

Man has the knowledge of distinguishing between the right and the wrong, the good and the evil, the safe and the dangerous. He can sense dangers and difficulties and escape before they *engulf*[3] him. Those who fail to do so find themselves trapped. Then they seek a cure.

A man is judged by his character and manners. His character can be easily spoiled. Sometimes one happens to come in contact with bad people. This affects their life badly. They may become a slave to bad habits like smoking, drinking, gambling, etc. This may create problems in their family affairs, health and finances. They can lead a healthy and happy life if they avoid falling into bad company.

Prevention can be ensured by planning ahead. An unfortunate act can be avoided if planning is done well in advance. Everything usually goes systematically if we chalk out a proper plan for it. The planned programme of vaccinating children well ahead of time has led to the decrease of the *incidence*[4] of diseases like polio, measles, tetanus, etc. Thus, vaccination can prevent many diseases from *afflicting*[5] human beings. Prevention of these diseases in time helps in the eradication of the same.

At times, it is not unwise to take risks or pay heed to one's instincts. But education, health and finance are some areas where instincts and risk-taking may prove destructive to one's needs and aspirations and end in a disaster. So, it is better to take all necessary precautions beforehand.

A healthy, balanced diet and daily exercise can prevent one from falling prey to obesity. With *meticulous*[6] planning, one can keep a check on the obesity-related diseases like heart ailments, diabetes, blood pressure, etc., and ward off *fatality*[7].

Today, AIDS* is the most terrifying and deadly disease. AIDS may be incurable, but it is certainly preventable. Millions of people are suffering from this dreadful disease. A *negligent*[8] act can make one suffer from AIDS. The use of disposable needles, safe sex, tested donor's blood for a recipient and loyalty to one's spouse can prevent one from getting infected with HIV**.

Preventive measures taken in any area lessen the *intensity*[9] of suffering. Keeping an eye on market position can prevent a stockbroker and a shareholder from an economic fall or financial *catastrophe*[10]. Pollution control measures would lead to better living conditions. The world leaders have been meeting annually to devise measures like emission cuts to prevent global warming from reaching catastrophic dimensions.

Better educational system would result in well informed citizens taking right decisions. Dams can prevent the occurrence of flood. Weather forecasting helps people to take preventive measures against dangers like tsunami, cyclone, etc. The new technique of *seismology*[11] has been introduced to forecast earthquakes. It helps us to take preventive measures and gear ourselves with the *wherewithal*[12] to avert disaster.

---

*AIDS—Acquired Immune Deficiency Syndrome

**HIV—Human Immunodeficiency Virus

To know how to prevent, one needs to be alert. One should be very careful while doing something. We should start each task only after judging its *pros and cons*[13]. It is better to avoid doing certain things, the benefits of which are not significant. By combining one's judgemental abilities and by taking preventive measures, one can lead a joyous and healthy life.

Aid to Vocabulary

1. *Prone* — likely to do
2. *Foresee* — to know what is going to happen in the future
3. *Engulf* — surround
4. *Incidence* — the extent to which something happens
5. *Afflicting* — to cause trouble, pain or distress
6. *Meticulous* — careful and accurate
7. *Fatality* — death
8. *Negligent* — careless
9. *Intensity* — state of being severe or extreme
10. *Catastrophe* — a sudden event that causes many people to suffer
11. *Seismology* — the scientific study of earthquakes
12. *Wherewithal* — all that is required to do a certain thing
13. *Pros and Cons (idiom)* — arguments for and against something

Points to Remember

1. Prevention is the shield which saves mankind from many disasters.
2. A cure is a blessing, but prevention is more than a blessing.
3. Man can judge the dangers ahead of time and can escape from them before they engulf him.
4. Man can prevent himself from falling into bad habits.
5. Prevention can be achieved by planning ahead.
6. One can lead a healthy life by following a healthy and balanced diet.
7. AIDS is incurable, but it is preventable.
8. Preventive measures taken in other areas also lessen the intensity of suffering.
9. One needs to be alert and careful to check oneself from doing anything wrong.
10. One should judge the pros and cons of each task before starting it.

Essay 80

PRACTICE MAKES A MAN PERFECT

Synopsis

Practice is the constant use of one's intellectual and aesthetic abilities. Though perfection can never be reached; practice leads us very close to it. Perfection refers to achieving excellence in a particular subject or skill. Proper planning and practice promotes perfect performance. Practice is the bedrock on which all other qualities are cultivated. Practice enables one to avoid errors that were committed previously. Practice begins in the cradle and ends in the grave. Right from childhood, man practises various activities. Perfection is necessary in every sphere of life which includes arts, medicine, law, defence, etc. Perfection makes art and literature survive the test of time. A person cannot be perfect in every sphere of life. But repeated practice lessens one's deficiencies. One should also learn from one's failures. Failures are the stepping stones to success. Practice enables a person to reach the heights of success. It makes a man perfect.

Practice means constant use of one's intellectual and *aesthetic*[1] powers. Perfect means 'ideal, complete and excellent'. Proper planning and practice promote perfect performance. Practice depends on training and it means repeating an activity. Constant practice sharpens talent.

One has to *inculcate*[2] certain qualities to be perfect. These are hard work, strong willpower, faith, tolerance, positive approach, self-confidence and dedication. Practice forms the bedrock on which all these qualities are cultivated. One should not stop practising or be satisfied until one achieves perfection.

Perfection is pursuit of exellence; it can never be reached but repeated attempts to do a job in a nicer and better way lead us very close to it. Perennial movement of water over stones smoothens their rough edges and cleans them, enabling them to appear immaculate in all respects. Owing entirely to this fact, experienced persons who are supposed to have done the particular thing time and again are preferred in almost all walks of life. Needless to add, man while doing something for the first time faces difficulties of several kinds, but when he continues to do the same thing over a period of time, he overcomes those obstacles.

Practice is the best way by which one can achieve perfection. Practice makes one perceive and comprehend the same idea or thing again and again. The more one practises, the more *flawless*[3] one becomes. One does not repeat the errors that were committed previously.

Practice begins in the cradle and ends in the grave. Right from childhood, man practises various activities like talking, reading, writing, eating, cooking, etc. For learning an art or any activity, one needs constant practice. The child starts learning by imitating elders — practises their actions, then practises speaking, first by learning the alphabet, then words, sentences and finally the language. The child through repeated practice attains perfection in speaking. One cannot ride a bicycle or a motorbike, or drive a car at the very first instance. One needs practice till one achieves perfection in the same. The same theory applies in other areas also.

Perfection makes art survive the test of time. Such works of art give joy to generations. There is no end to practising while learning the fine arts, of music, dance, drama, painting, etc. Practice makes one better every time.

Writers put their imagination into words. They express their emotions, feelings and ideas in their writing. The perfection in their style of writing, to some extent, depends on practice. They never consider the popularity gained by one book as the end of their practice. They improve with every new project they undertake.

Practice or *riyaaz* plays an important role for a musician to become perfect. Every good musician takes proper education or *talim* from his master or guru. Only laborious practice can make one a perfect musician.

Dance is the expression of one's deep emotions using the movements of the body. To achieve perfection in this art, co-ordination between the body and the music matters the most. This co-ordination is achieved only by practice.

The painter expresses his thoughts and ideas on a canvas with the help of lines and colours. A single line, curve or shade can change the expression of the painting. Practice makes a painter perfect. There are some painters who have an inborn talent. Without much practice they can draw very well. Still, practice makes their work even better. The expertise of producing a masterpiece in casual or careless strokes is attained only after extensive practice of one's art and honing of one's talent.

Perfection is necessary in every sphere of life. Perfection in shooting is an essential quality that the defence personnel possess. Practice is essential in law and medicine too. Surgery can be mastered by practice for precision. Even the day to day cooking takes some practice to enable one to get the perfect taste one wants. Thus, from the kitchen to the workplace, practice is needed to gain perfection in every field.

A person cannot be perfect in every sphere of life. It is quite natural for anyone to have certain *deficiencies*[4]. But one can practice repeatedly to get rid of the deficiencies. One may face challenges during the course of practising but should not feel dejected in such a case. One should overcome them in order to achieve perfection.

Practice enables a person to reach the heights of success in all walks of life. Practice develops outstanding qualities in one's character. Practice not only brings perfection but also helps in building character. Thus, it is practice that makes a man perfect and enables him to face every challenge in his life.

Aid to Vocabulary

1. *Aesthetic* — artistic
2. *Inculcate* — learn by repeating again and again
3. *Flawless* — free from error or defect
4. *Deficiencies* — lack of necessary qualities

Points to Remember

1. Proper planning and practice promote perfect performance.
2. Practice is the bedrock on which all other qualities are cultivated.
3. Practice begins in the cradle and ends in the grave.
4. Perfection makes an art or a skill survive the test of time.
5. Writers, musicians, dancers, painters, lawyers, doctors, surgeons, defence personnel and others can achieve perfection only through repeated practice.
6. Practice helps to overcome the deficiencies in a person.
7. Practice enables a person to attain the heights of success.

GUIDED COMPOSITION

Develop the following paragraph into a full-fledged essay in 800-1000 words. The gist of the topic is provided in approximately 155 words for your help:

A LITTLE LEARNING IS A DANGEROUS THING

It is better to be ignorant and live in bliss than having a little learning and inviting danger to oneself and others. Imperfect knowledge of any subject is undesirable. An individual who has some knowledge about a subject, tends to believe that he has acquired expertise in it. A person, who makes tall claims of being an expert at a subject after acquiring elementary knowledge can certainly be very dangerous. An imperfect mechanic can spoil the machinery beyond repair. Similarly, a man who starts prescribing medicines, after reading a few books, can only cause more harm than good. Life becomes a burden for those miserable hypochondriacs who have a tendency to believe that they have symptoms of some or the other serious disease where there are none. All because, they happened to read an elementary book on human diseases. It is best to seek expert opinion whenever in need, than paying heed to the self-proclaimed experts. They themselves are ill equipped to swim ashore when in trouble. There is every possibility that little learning may one day endanger the lives of poor ignorant people who may have trusted such quacks. (155 words)

Essay
81

KNOWLEDGE IS POWER

SYNOPSIS

Knowledge is the awareness of a fact or a situation. It is the amassed thought and experience of countless human beings. At the dawn of civilisation, man was at the mercy of nature. Gradually, he started making progress in various fields. The successful discoveries and inventions encouraged man to contemplate and come up with new ideas. He used the forces of nature for his own benefit. Life became comfortable. Advancements in the field of medicine, surgery, agriculture, information technology, etc., are all fruits of man's quest for knowledge. Ignorance is a curse. Education and knowledge are desirable for a democracy. Sadly, man started misusing knowledge with the passage of time. He has created unfavourable conditions for himself. Knowledge should be used to further peace, progress and prosperity.

"It is not in skill but in the knowledge which can be communicated from one to another, that the civilised man shows his superiority to the savage."

—*Henry George*

Francis Bacon has famously, said, 'Knowledge is power'. It is the power of awareness, information, understanding and skill that is acquired with experience or education. It is a rich and a unique possession that cannot be stolen or *plundered*[1] by thieves. Human knowledge is the *amassed*[2] thought and experience of countless human beings. Knowledge in the words of JM Clark, is the only instrument of production that is not subject to diminishing returns.

The growth and survival of mankind depends upon knowledge. From the Stone Age till date, man has struggled to know the unknown. He has explored land, water and space by virtue of his knowledge. Man has made progress in all the fields from science and technology to arts, etc.

At the dawn of civilisation, man was at the mercy of nature. He lived the life of a *nomad*[3]. He invented tools and weapons for hunting. Verbal communication also developed. He discovered fire and the wheel. Man, then, started living in communities. He settled near rivers and took up agriculture. The settlements soon transformed into villages. Waterways and canals were constructed for irrigation purposes. *Surplus*[4] grains were stored in *granaries*[5] to be used later. Soon villages transformed into towns, then provinces and later into cities and countries. Man discovered new places and invented things for his own benefit. The gradual change and development from the Stone Age to the present Age has been made possible by knowledge.

The successful discoveries and inventions encouraged man to *contemplate*[6] and come up with new ideas. His ability to *rationalise*[7], analyse and store the events in his memory enabled him to achieve success. Knowledge gave him the power, confidence and courage to make life worth living. He began to harness the forces of nature for his own benefit and utilise his knowledge to improve life. Thus, life became comfortable.

Man has been able to *eradicate*[8] a number of diseases like small pox, plague, etc., from the face of the earth. The discovery of a number of antibiotics and drugs has reduced the suffering of mankind. Agriculture has also been developed. The use of high yielding variety of seeds, fertilisers, and improved methods of irrigation have increased crop yield. The invention of various devices of communication has transformed the world into a global village. The Computer has changed human life altogether. All these have been the fruits of man's *quest*[9] for knowledge.

Knowledge gave man strength and power. One can gain the highest position in society by dint of one's knowledge. While ignorance is a curse, incomplete knowledge can be harmful. Samuel Johnson writes that knowledge without integrity is dangerous and dreadful. Learned people are usually efficient, honest and sincere. Knowledge develops the mental *faculties*[10] of man. It leads to the achievement of excellence in the sphere of the mind. It enables one to make sound judgement. Only persons having knowledge of the wide world and human affairs can become statesmen.

It is true that intellectuals do not like the hustle and bustle of politics. But a political leader must have all-round education and extensive knowledge. This is desirable for a democracy. In his book *Republic*, the great philosopher Plato suggested the need of a 'philosopher king' for the betterment of society.

Education and knowledge are a prerequisite for democracy to flourish. Illiteracy and ignorance lead to its failure. We should endeavour to spread knowledge among the teeming millions of the country. Illiteracy is a curse and is directly responsible for many ills of society. Illiterate people are generally superstitious, narrow minded and poor. They fall prey to *fundamentalism*[11] *fanatacism*[12], *bigotry*[13] and *communalism*[14]. *Restraint*[15], tolerance, understanding, and capacity to manage affairs come with the attainment of knowledge. If knowledge is imparted to our rural children, youth, women and men, they will, emerge as a major social force.

There is no end to the process of gaining knowledge. It is only the foolish man who thinks he knows everything. Modern knowledge is very intricate and wide in scope. Thousands of researchers, all over the world are constantly at work to acquire more knowledge for further advancement of the human race. But the immense increase in the knowledge base of the world does not necessarily make us better human beings.

Sadly, with the passage of time, man has started misusing knowledge. He is using knowledge to destroy the very forces that provided him *sustenance*[16]. He has interfered with nature and disturbed the ecological balance. He has polluted the air, land and water. He has, thus, created unfavourable conditions for himself as well as for others species on earth. Man has developed destructive weapons that can completely destroy mankind. The bombing of Nagasaki and Hiroshima proves this fact. Man is posing a threat to the existence of flora and fauna.

Knowledge should not be misused. Nuclear power must be used for useful and peaceful purposes. Man should find solutions to control and check pollution. The conventional sources of energy are *depleting*[17] at a fast rate. Man should try to find out sources of economical power generation.

Knowledge must be acquired and shared. It should be a collective effort. Lack of knowledge leads to poverty and economic downturn. Knowledge should be utilised for the upliftment of the poor masses. It should be used to further peace, progress and prosperity.

Man has become egotistical, self-centred and claims that knowledge, of the world, is power which is only partially true. Our religious scriptures have preached from time immemorial that true knowledge is the knowledge of the self. It is self-knowledge which gives man moral and spiritual power to withstand the *vicissitudes*[18] of life, without getting discomposed. Knowledge gained is sometimes superficial and tends to create waves of dissatisfaction, arrogance greed and lust. Any person who has realised this, can claim with pride that true knowledge comes from self-realisation and it, in turn, generates in man the power to live life *stoically*[19] with all its joys and sorrows, ups and downs, pleasures and pains.

AID TO VOCABULARY

1. *Plundered* — robbed, stolen
2. *Amassed* — accumulated
3. *Nomad* — a person who does not stay at one place, a wanderer
4. *Surplus* — in excess of what is needed
5. *Granaries* — storehouses of grains
6. *Contemplate* — to anticipate, view mentally

7. *Rationalise* — explain by reason
8. *Eradicate* — remove, get rid of
9. *Quest* — search, seeking out
10. *Faculties* — mental powers
11. *Fundamentalism* — Strict adherence to religious beliefs
12. *Fanaticism* — obsessive devotion to certain beliefs
13. *Bigotry* — unjust hatred towards other people, ideas, etc.
14. *Communalism* — conflict with different racial or cultural group
15. *Restraint* — check, self-control
16. *Sustenance* — nourishment, support
17. *Depleting* — emptying out, exhausting
18. *Vicissitudes* — ups and downs, change of fortune
19. *Stoically* — suffer pain without complaining

Points to Remember

1. Man has struggled to know the unknown from the times of the Stone Age.
2. Man's growth and development has been made possible by knowledge.
3. The successful discoveries and inventions encouraged man to work on new ideas for further advancement of the human race.
4. There have been major developments in the field of medicine, surgery, agriculture, information technology, etc. All these have been the fruits of man's quest for knowledge.
5. Education and knowledge are desirable for democracy.
6. Illiteracy is directly responsible for many ills of society.
7. With the passage of time, man started misusing knowledge.
8. Knowledge should be used to further peace, progress, and prosperity.
9. True knowledge comes from self-realisation.

GUIDED COMPOSITION

Develop the following paragraph into a full-fledged essay in 800-1000 words. The gist of the topic is provided in approximately 150 words for your help:

EDUCATION SHOULD BE FOR LIFE AND NOT FOR JUST LIVELIHOOD

It has been universally acknowledged that the chief aim of education is to bring about all round development of human mind and body. It should prepare one for life, and not just to earn one's bread and butter. Education plays a very important role in the development of the intellect, refinement of the heart and discipline of the spirit of an individual. Education should not be equated with instruction for training the pupil to earn his livelihood. It should be considered an instrument of bringing about desirable changes in the pupil to enable him to adjust to self and society. True education equips an individual to face life, accept its challenges boldly and remain calm under all circumstances. Certainly, education should emphasize the practical aspect of life and train the individual to earn his livelihood. The means one adopts in life, to earn one's bread and butter are ultimately determined by the values one cherishes in life. Hence, education must help to inculcate the right values which will guide us in every sphere of life.

(150 words)

Essay 82

PATRIOTISM IS NOT ENOUGH

Synopsis

Patriotism is an inherent quality by virtue of which one loves one's country. It manifests itself in many forms. Serving the downtrodden is an appreciable form of patriotism but the desire to save one's country from enemies and happily laying down one's life for it, exhibits the most exalted form of patriotism. The revolutionary zeal of the social reformer is another noble form of patriotism. In modern times, it has degenerated into chauvinism, nationalism and jingoism. Many terrorist outfits, in the name of patriotism, train youngsters to kill. Nationalism is the attachment towards the nation state. Mere patriotism is not enough. We should develop spiritual unity among ourselves.

Patriotism is the love for one's own country accompanied with the sentiment to defend its honour. Patriotism is more than a mere sentiment. It can inspire a person to do heroic deeds in moments of crisis. A true patriot is respected everywhere.

Gladstone said, "Of the whole sum of human life one small part is that which consists of a man's relations to his country and his feelings concerning it." Patriotism is an *inherent*[1] quality by virtue of which one loves one's country and *zealously*[2] supports and defends it and its interests. People hold a true patriot in high regard. A mere sentiment does not suffice a sense of patriotism which can well inspire a person to lay down his life to safeguard the glory and honour of the nation. Joan of Arc, called the Maid of Orleans, was only nineteen when she protested against the English domination of France. She was captured by the British and burnt alive on the stake. She became a national hero and was *canonised*[3] in the 20th century.

Allegiance to one's motherland combined with a readiness to stake everything—property, siblings, progenies, job, conveniences, comforts etc.—to defend her honour and glory is true patriotism. It demands *altruism*[4] and *stoicism*[5] and a complete withdrawal from the rest of the world just for the sake of the country. It has two facets – 'Destructive and Constructive'. Laying down one's own life for the sake of the country and mass slaughter of the enemies of the motherland come under the destructive facet whereas actions like helping the poor, feeding the hungry, serving the downtrodden, eliminating social evils, assisting the old folk, looking after the patients, *galvanising*[6] support to do away with social vices etc., all refer to the constructive facet of patriotism.

Perceived from this perspective, everyone is a patriot. Teachers by shaping the future of students, engineers by building roads, dams and bridges, doctors by serving the patients, ministers by leading the country to the next higher level, so on and so forth, are serving the nation as per their will and talent, but what makes a patriot stand apart is that he serves the nation selflessly without harbouring the hope to get something in return.

Patriotism manifests itself in many forms but the desire to save one's country from enemies exhibits the most *exalted*[7] form of patriotism. In the event of a foreign invasion people are known to give up their narrow differences and emerge as a united force. In the epic, *The Odyssey*, Telemachus, though young, tries to save his country from his mother's suitors in the absence of his father, Odysseus. The Frenchmen, though much divided, rose unitedly against the British subjugation after they were inspired to do so by Joan of Arc. Similarly, all Englishmen were roused with patriotic *fervour*[8] to repel the Spanish Armada. When Gandhiji gave the *clarion*[9] call to the people of the country, they rose from their narrow bounds of distinctions based on caste, religion and creed and participated actively in the freedom struggle. Patriotism is, therefore, one of the noblest virtues because it unites the people of a country against a common enemy. It not only is responsible for the unification of the citizens but also inspires them for the noblest possible deeds.

The revolutionary zeal of the social reformer is another noble form of patriotism. Love for one's country means a regard for the country's welfare and its beings. The reformer *endeavours*[10] to eradicate the social evils faced by the society. He fights against vested interests and vicious traditions and customs. Swami Vivekanand believed that patriotism is something which is felt by the heart for one's people. He asked the citizens, "Do you feel that millions are starving today and millions have been starving for ages? Do you feel that ignorance has come over the land as a dark cloud? Does it make you sleepless?" A true patriot would not be content with making speeches on social reforms or inaugurating social reform movements but would also work to ameliorate the condition.

A *whistle-blower*[11] in a professional set-up is also a patriot for he/she brings into public notice something that is counter productive or harmful to the nation's interest. Such a person is often disliked because his allegations are often candid and blunt. Hence, instead of receiving praise, he is often condemned. But this, undoubtedly, is the truest form of patriotism.

A person who is settled abroad yearns for his homeland. This is another form of patriotism. Irish poet, Oliver Goldsmith, when in exile, wrote

The Traveller, wherein he said:

The patriots boast, wherever we roam,
His first best country ever is at home.

A person living in a foreign country can never forget his homeland. In his dreams, he roams in his native land. The commitment of the statesman, who serves his country without any selfish motives and seeks to uphold and enhance its glory at home as well as abroad, is another form of patriotism. The civic-minded and *conscientious*[12] citizen, who faithfully discharges his civic duties and obeys the law of the land is also a patriot. He is always on the path of righteousness and order. He gives strength to those who wish to improve the state of affairs.

In modern times, patriotism has degenerated into *chauvinism*[13] and *jingoism*[14]. The rise of Fascism in Italy and Nazism in Germany was essentially the result of patriotism being interpreted in the narrowest possible sense as jingoism.

Many terrorist outfits, in the name of patriotism, train youngsters to choose the wrong path of causing death and destruction. The Palestinian suicide bombings and Israeli retaliation in the Middle East is often attributed to patriotism. Terrorist outfits, across the globe, perpetuate the idea of killing for a common goal. In the hands of *unscrupulous*[15] and *callous*[16] politicians, the noble sentiment of patriotism has got buried under a cloak for passions and prejudices. It was the chauvinism and jingoism exhibited by the Nazis in erstwhile Germany that plunged the whole world into the Second World War. The jingoism displayed by the corridors of power in the USA led to the *annihilation*[17] of Hiroshima and Nagasaki in 1945.

Mere patriotism is not enough. Though the scientific inventions and discoveries have shrunk the world, the political walls erected by jingoism are still intact, and have become stronger than ever before. Man has failed miserably in achieving moral and spiritual unity which could have aided peaceful co-existence of all nations. When we identify ourselves as Hindus, Muslims, Indians, French or Germans, we do not cease to be human beings. The world today has turned into a global village. What we need today is global unity that can only be founded on a spiritual unity that binds people of diverse origins with the bonds of humanity. The United Nations commission on human rights promotes humanism which transcends the boundaries of nations. It helps people of diverse nations to foster close relations. It is hoped that the bond of humanity will be strengthened in times to come.

A patriot loves not only his country, but also the people of his country. In India, we have numerous examples of patriots like Mangal Pandey,

Bhagat Singh, Khudiram Bose, Surya Sen, etc., who sacrificed their lives for the country's freedom. In the global world of today, we need the same patriotic zeal in global citizens so that the world becomes one's country and humanity and human good one's true patriotism. Patriots all over the world want not only peace and prosperity for their nation but also the greater good of humanity.

Aid to Vocabulary

1. *Inherent* — forming an essential part of
2. *Zealously* — earnestly
3. *Canonised* — made a Saint by the Pope
4. *Altruism* — selfless service
5. *Stoicism* — self-control in adversity
6. *Galvanise* — stimulate or excite (to act)
7. *Exalted* — heightened
8. *Fervour* — zeal
9. *Clarion* — rousing sound
10. *Endeavours* — attempts
11. *Whistle-blower* — one who reveals to the public, police or press an in-house crime or dishonest activity
12. *Conscientious* — governed by a strict regard to the dictates of conscience
13. *Chauvinism* — absurdly exaggerated patriotism of considering one's own country superior
14. *Jingoism* — the policy of professed patriotism which advocates aggression
15. *Unscrupulous* — having no principles
16. *Callous* — not concerned about the sufferings or feelings of others
17. *Annihilation* — complete destruction

Points to Remember

1. Patriotism is an inherent quality by virtue of which man loves his country, and defends it and its interest.
2. There are many forms of patriotism but the most exalted form of it is to save one's country from enemies.
3. In modern times, patriotism has degenerated into chauvinism and jingoism.
4. Patriotism is being misinterpreted by many terrorist organisations.
5. In the hands of unscrupulous and callous politicians, patriotism has got buried under a cloak of passions and prejudices.
6. Mere patriotism is not enough, we have to be human in our thoughts and practices and become citizens of one world.

Essay
83

LEADERSHIP

SYNOPSIS

A leader is a person who leads or exercises dominion over a group of people. Great deeds make great men, whom others try to emulate. Great leaders have sacrificed their personal well-being and familial interests for the welfare of their nations. Apart from sharpening the innate qualities of leadership, proper grooming instils in a prospective leader the traits of courage, initiative, drive, a sense of responsibility and impartiality. Schools and colleges are the most appropriate places to train and groom the future leaders. The success of a leader lies in his ability to command respect from the whole community and to inspire them to act courageously. A leader lives for others. He should be prepared to sacrifice everything for the good of others. True leaders rise to prominence not through bloodshed or coups, but because of the acceptance and the trust put in them by the masses.

A leader is a person who leads or exercises *dominion*[1] over a group of people. Leadership is the personality trait which enables a person to command a mass following. In every society, community or nation, there is bound to be someone who stands out from others and acts as a guide or leader for them. A leader emerges from a crowd of people because the rest lack the *initiative*[2] of taking up the responsibility of the masses.

Great deeds make men great. Any person who excels in any sphere of activity sets an example for others to follow. He becomes a leader whom others try to *emulate*[3]. Mahatma Gandhi became the leader of the masses because of his exceptional appeal and leadership qualities. He initiated his struggle against the colonial rule in South Africa with his principles of Satyagraha and non-violence. When he returned to India, he launched his non-violent agitation against the British rule. By leading a life of self-denial and hardship, he was able to endear himself to the masses. They adored him and swore by his name. Thousands rose to his *clarion*[4] call of the Civil Disobedience, the Satyagraha and the Quit India movement. Indian history and the world history are replete with *anecdotes*[5] of great men who endured hardships and sufferings for the betterment of the society. Great leaders have sacrificed their personal well-being and *familial*[6] interests for the welfare of their nations.

William Shakespeare said, "Some are born great, some achieve greatness and some have greatness thrust upon them." Some people are born leaders with an inner compulsion or urge which drives them to accomplish great tasks. Some achieve greatness when their mental faculties are disciplined to acquire leadership qualities whereupon they may take up a leadership role. This is done by channelising their *innate*[7] qualities of leadership into the desired direction. To achieve desired goals training and grooming should begin at an early age. It is said, "train up a child to go the way he should and when he is grown up, he will not depart from it." Apart from sharpening the innate qualities of leadership, training *instils*[8] in one the traits of courage, initiative, drive, a sense of responsibility and impartiality, too. A leader should be intelligent and conscientious, have a liberal outlook and possess excellent communication skills to convey his ideas effectively.

School is the most appropriate place to train and groom future leaders. The *rigours*[9] of school life helps in fostering certain leadership qualities which make one *tower*[10] over others. One would exhibit all these qualities, when entrusted with responsibilities, for instance, while discharging duties as the monitor of the class or the captain of a team. Playfields in schools are, perhaps, the best places for developing leadership qualities among children. Sports not only inculcate a sense of fair play among the children but also help to develop qualities like team spirit, *endurance*[11], sportsmanship and discipline. The captain of a team takes decisions in consultation with his team members, maintains discipline on the field, wins the confidence of his team mates and inspires them to give their best to the game.

Every school and college conducts extra-curricular activities. Schools provide ample opportunities to students to choose the area of their interest. There are a number of societies for debating, organising tours, excursions, cultural programmes and other activities. By participating in such activities, students get training in organising and conducting these activities as well as in speaking to a large audience. It helps them shed their inhibitions and in this process they gain tremendous confidence, a leader's trait which may later prove useful in different fields of activity. Training imparted in the NCC* camps also makes the children disciplined and instils in them the quality of patriotism and the feeling of brotherhood. It teaches young men and women the skill to organise events and control groups.

The success of a leader lies in his ability to command respect from the

---

*NCC—National Cadet Corps

whole community and to inspire people to act in the desired manner. However, some leaders become *perverted*[12], once they acquire fame and power they start losing their interest in social welfare and end up losing their mass appeal. Some become so *obsessed*[13] with their power that they forget their humble beginnings and become dictators. They start looking down with *disdain*[14] on the very masses whose *adulation*[15] had in the first place enabled them to gain their stature and position. Hitler was the most notorious example of a dictator who was tyrannical and self-possessed. According to Lenin, "A true leader must submerge himself in the fountain of the people." A true leader does not allow himself to be *overwhelmed*[16] by his status. On the contrary, he becomes humble, tolerant and forgiving. He understands that everyone is not bestowed with wealth, power and prosperity and hence, he takes upon himself the responsibility of providing the deprived with their needs.

A leader lives for others. A leader should be prepared to sacrifice all for the good of others. Mahatma Gandhi was a living *testimony*[17] to this. He sacrificed his personal interests to serve his countrymen. He worked selflessly to draw the support of the masses for the freedom struggle. He worked for the upliftment of the backward classes and also tried to dispel the communal hatred between the Hindus and the Muslims. Similarly Pt. Jawaharlal Nehru, though born in a rich aristocratic family, gave up everything and plunged into the national struggle for freedom. Both, along with several other prominent leaders, were subjected to torture and had to spend many years in prison, sometimes even in solitary confinement. But these leaders had a fiery passion towards the realisation of their ideals and they worked *ceaselessly*[18] to make it a reality. Obstacles encountered on the way did not deter them from marching *steadfastly*[19] towards their goals.

True leaders rise to prominence not through bloodshed or *coups*[20], but because of the support and trust put in them by the masses. Any leader who tries to become an overreacher is likely to lead his country to ruin as it happened to Germany under Hitler. He misused his qualities of leadership and brought about his own downfall. A prudent leader never isolates himself from the masses. He does not live in an ivory tower away from public gaze. He rather makes constant efforts to understand the masses and works for their welfare. He has the ability to recognise a problem before it becomes insoluble. He *articulates*[21] his speech and ensures that the public sentiments are not hurt. A leader's path is paved with difficulties, yet he walks on *undauntedly*[22] with his eyes fixed on his goal.

Aid to Vocabulary

1. *Dominion* — sovereignty, control
2. *Initiative* — an introductory step
3. *Emulate* — admire somebody and try to be and do like them
4. *Clarion* — rousing sound
5. *Anecdotes* — biographical incidents
6. *Familial* — pertaining to a family
7. *Innate* — inborn
8. *Instils* — gradually causes (one) to have
9. *Rigours* — rigidity or strictness in principles
10. *Tower* — be superior
11. *Endurance* — ability to withstand strain
12. *Perverted* — corrupt
13. *Obsessed* — preoccupied
14. *Disdain* — contempt
15. *Adulation* — high compliment
16. *Overwhelmed* — overpowered or affected strongly
17. *Testimony* — evidence
18. *Ceaselessly* — without stopping
19. *Steadfastly* — with devotion and loyalty
20. *Coups* — acts of sudden, illegal and violent take over of government
21. *Articulates* — speak with ease and express clearly
22. *Undauntedly* — fearlessly

Points to Remember

1. Leadership is the personality trait of a person which enables him to become a leader.
2. Any person who excels in any sphere of activity and sets an example for others to follow, becomes a leader.
3. Some people are born leaders with an inner compulsion or urge which drives them to accomplish great tasks.
4. Apart from sharpening the innate qualities, training instils in a prospective leader courage, initiative, drive, a sense of responsibility and impartiality.
5. Schools are considered the most appropriate place to train and groom future leaders.
6. Some of the leaders become so obsessed with their power that they forget their humble beginnings and become dictators.
7. True leaders rise to prominence not through bloodshed or coups, but because of the support and trust put in them by the masses.

Essay
84

THE ROLE OF HUMOUR IN LIFE

Synopsis

Humour means 'the quality in speech, writing or action which tends to excite laughter.' In the absence of humour, life becomes dull. There are many sources of exploring humour like books, cinema, television, gossip, etc. In olden times, kings patronised wits and jesters for their amusement. Tenali Rama and Birbal were the most famous court wits in medieval India. Literature is a rich source of genial humour. Shakespeare created great humour through the character of the 'Fool' in his comedies as well as in his tragedies. Humour cuts the stress level down to half. A sense of humour is considered as the best survival skill. The true meaning of humour is to tickle, not to hurt the sentiments of anyone. Nowadays, people find relief in comedy shows and comedy movies. But there should always be genial humour which lightens the atmosphere and does not embarrass anyone. The value of humour in human life cannot be denied.

Samuel Johnson, the British *satirist*[1] and a prominent literary figure of the 18th century believed, "Human life is everywhere in a state in which much is to be endured, and little to be enjoyed." At the same time, George Santayana, the American philosopher, observed, "There is no cure for birth and death, save to enjoy the interval." While the former reflected his *pessimistic*[2] attitude in his statement, the latter, his *optimism*[3]. Life on earth is accompanied by its highs and lows and one should not get *bogged down*[4] by the lows—the miseries and pains. One should, rather, look to attain *poise*[5] and sail through the *vicissitudes*[6] of life by spicing it up with humour.

The Oxford Dictionary defines humour as the "*faculty*[7] to perceive and enjoy what is *ludicrous*[8] or amusing in a given situation." The New Webster's Dictionary defines humour as "that quality in speech, writing or action which tends to excite laughter; the capacity for perceiving the amusing or ludicrous." Total absence of humour renders life restless and dull. Humour is the soul of comedy. The elements of comedy are *wit*[9], *satire*[10] and *farce*[11]. All these three elements of comedy are related to the ability to combine clever words, ideas, situations, etc., to produce humour.

Humour helps us cope, conquer and carry on. It is needed by one and all.

People always try to find out something to laugh at for making their life less monotonous. Humour may be found in books, on television, cinema, etc. In olden times, people did not have many means of entertainment. Most of the kings' courts in medieval India were known to patronise court wits or jesters.

The wit or jester was attached to the court and had the licence to indulge in *gibes*[12] at the local people, the courtiers and even his own master, the king. He would utter words of wisdom and subtle criticism, which would rarely be challenged. The jester, through his gimmicks, could also make the king realise his follies without hurting his sentiments. Tenali Rama was such a jester in the court of Krishna Dev Raya. Birbal is also famous for his *witticisms*[13]. He was *anointed*[14] as one of the nine gems in the court of the Mughal Emperor Akbar. These were the wits whose jokes are still enjoyed by people. Today, certain elements of the court jesters of the past can be traced to the stand-up comics of today who perform live on stage before packed houses.

Many great literary figures created a lot of *genial*[15] humour. Geoffrey Chaucer, one of the greatest English writers, is considered to be the first great humorist of Europe. His humour was a combination of wit, fun, comedy and satire. The greatest English dramatist, William Shakespeare, also created a number of comedies which are still a great source of gentle humour. Shakespeare's comedies have a mix of wit, satire, humour and farce since they were meant for the *sophisticated*[16] and the *rustic*[17] alike. Oscar Wilde, the victorian playwright, has been rated as Britain's greatest wit. Once, stopped at the US airport to declare his assets, he quipped, 'I have nothing to declare but my genius.' When asked to make changes in one of his plays, Wilde protested: "who am I to tamper with a masterpiece"? There are many other literary figures who produced great and immortal humour.

Life in present times, compare actively, has become stressful, dull and monotonous. Acute scarcity of time keeps one away from entertainment, enjoyment and pursuance of hobbies which are active stress relievers in human life. Of all the medicines, laughter and happiness are said to be the best, for they not only enhance the healing power and give the muscles a good exercise, but also enable patients to recover speedily. Life devoid of humour is like a landscape bereft of vegetation. Humour is an oasis in the desert of monotony and gloom. But humour is humour till it causes smiles; the moment it begins to hurt, it becomes ridicule, a ploy to downsize somebody and ceases to be humour. There is a *fine line*[18] between humour and ridicule. While ridicule makes fun of someone in a cruel manner, humour is gentle and pure; it criticises but does not hurt; instead, it amuses and causes amendment of the flaw referred to therein. While ridicule can shatter one's self-respect, humour injects vigour to start afresh with new zeal towards one's goal. Shakespearean 'fool' created to provide comic relief is worth mentioning in this respect; he *castigates*[19] as well as offers wise counsel in times of need, but he never hurts.

Nature ensures that, 'One does not worry while one laughs'; and psychologists maintain that 'Humour cuts the stress level down to half.' Laughing helps people to stay happy and healthy. It helps people to recover from a state of illness. Research in the field of medicine has proved that patients have a better and speedy chance of recovery if initiated with humour therapy.

In the modern world, life is so hectic and fast that people do not get enough time to relax their mind. As a result, depression and frustration are common these days. Humour is one of the best solutions to these lifestyle diseases as it is believed that a sense of humour is the greatest survival skill. Maintaining a sense of humour helps even in the midst of *adversity*[20]. Acknowledging the role of humour in life, people have made laughter a serious business these days, from comedy shows on television to humour slots on FM stations, there is an abundance of mirth everywhere. Comedians and comedies are in great demand nowadays. A comedy movie attracts people more than an action movie, romance, thriller or tragedy does.

But humour should maintain a *benchmark*[21] and avoid *going overboard*[22]. It is often seen that people create laughter even at the cost of one who is stuck in an embarrassing situation. Humour, at times, ceases to be associated with the intellect, and *degenerates*[23] into *slapstick*[24] comedy. Often, to incite laughter, cheap gimmicks and mannerisms are portrayed on screen.

Our humour should not be fragmented; neither should we give humour a casteist or communal touch. We should know how to laugh at ourselves. We cannot deny the role of humour in human life. colette was right when he said, "Total absence of humour renders life impossible."

Aid to Vocabulary

1. *Satirist* — a writer who ridicules vice or folly through his composition in verse or prose
2. *Pessimistic* — expecting bad things to happen

3. *Optimism* — the tendency to expect the best in all things
4. *Bogged down* — submerged in
5. *Poise* — to have balance and confidence in manner
6. *Vicissitudes* — change of circumstances
7. *Faculty* — ability to do something particular
8. *Ludicrous* — ridiculous, very foolish
9. *Wit* — the quality of being clever and funny
10. *Satire* — comic highlighting of human weakness, folly or vice
11. *Farce* — funny presentation of ridiculous situation or event
12. *Gibes* — remarks which make someone look foolish
13. *Witticisms* — witty remarks
14. *Anointed* — designated, officially named
15. *Genial* — friendly in a cheerful way
16. *Sophisticated* — showing or having a knowledge of social life and behaviour
17. *Rustic* — simple and not refined, rural
18. *Fine line* — subtle difference
19. *Castigates* — criticises harshly
20. *Adversity* — difficulties, troubles
21. *Benchmark* — point of reference
22. *Going overboard* — behaving immoderately
23. *Degenerates* — passes into worse physical, moral or mental state
24. *Slapstick* — a type of broad comedy in which rough play and knock out method prevails

Points to Remember

1. Humour means a quality in speech, writing and action which tends to excite laughter.
2. People always search for different sources of humour.
3. In olden times, kings patronised wits and jesters to amuse them in their courts.
4. Tenali Rama in the court of Krishna Dev Raya and Birbal in the court of Akbar, were famous wits.
5. Many literary figures like Geoffrey Chaucer and William Shakespeare created a lot of genial and immortal humour.
6. Research in the medical field has proved that patients have a better and speedy recovery if initiated with humour therapy.
7. It always helps if we maintain a sense of humour in the midst of adversity.
8. Humour often degenerates into slapstick comedy.
9. Humour should not be casteist or communal in nature.

Essay
85

LEISURE

Synopsis

Leisure is the opportunity or time when one is free from one's regular occupation or duty. Occupation with a hobby at leisure helps one to get relaxation. One could join some classes to improve one's hobby or can also indulge in reading books. Acting and modelling are two avenues, which are being exploited by many. Gardening is known to relax one's strained mind. Stamp, coin and postal envelopes collection is a good pastime requiring skill and concentration. Pets also give a lot of relaxation when one is feeling blue. Social service could give one an inner satisfaction. One should not misuse leisure, rather one should make use of it by doing something constructive.

Leisure is the opportunity or time when one is free from one's regular occupation or duty. Some people try to define leisure as the period of doing nothing. To them, J.B. Priestly gives a befitting reply "Any fool can be fussy and rid himself of all energy all over the place but a man has to have something in him before he can settle down to do nothing". In this age of consumerism, man has become materialistic. His quest for materialistic pleasures is never satiated. With time, he finds himself stuck in a daily *grind*[1] and fails to spare time for his own self.

This often leads to frustration at the workplace and sometimes causes *irreparable*[2] damage to one's health. It is, therefore, necessary for every person to take some time off from one's daily routine and indulge in some activity, which pleases him. Engaging into a hobby at leisure is known to relax the strained muscles and soothen the nerves. It makes one feel relaxed and energised to resume one's occupation.

Many people these days are not satisfied or comfortable with their jobs due to various reasons. This often leads to stressful situations. Taking up an interesting hobby is a very effective way of relieving stress and *rejuvenating*[3] oneself for future endeavours. But one should be very careful regarding the utilisation of one's free time. Prudent utilisation of leisure time is as important as judicious economic management.

It is, important to identify the activity which one feels is close to one's heart. One can join some classes which would help improve particular skills. It could be driving, cooking, painting and sketching, etc. One can join a club to learn the *nuances*[4] of some sport. Swimming is said to relieve all the lethargy that creeps into one's system. Indulging in sports, like cricket, football, polo, golf or squash, is known to offer tremendous relaxation.

Reading books is also a good and useful pastime. One can indulge oneself in reading books across various genre and subjects . By enrolling oneself in a library, one could come across a variety of books. Novels by different authors are read by many during their leisure. Apart from these, magazines and newspapers that provide news to enhance one's knowledge are popular among many. Books are man's best friends and one never feels lonely in their company. An individual may have preference for a particular genre of books. One should identify one's preferences and go for those books which suit one's taste.

Acting and modelling are the two pursuits which are being explored by many, especially the youth. Sometimes, film and television actors perform on stage in their leisure time. It helps them to develop their acting skill as well as heighten their recognition and popularity. This also enables them to interact with the audience directly. So, some opt for stage performances as a hobby. Young professionals are venturing into modelling as a hobby for the glamour associated with this field.

Gardening is another hobby, which is known to relax the strained mind of those who possess *green fingers*[5]. For practising this hobby, one does not necessarily need a garden. As the saying goes, "A single rose can be my garden." The pleasure one derives on seeing a plant flourish, especially after one has taken care of it, is immeasurable. As a bud emerges from a plant, one is very excited to see it bloom and enjoy nature's benevolence. Gardening can be practised with a few pots in the initial stage. Plants require adequate care, along with sunlight, air, water and good manure. But it is better to take the advice of a good gardener or a person who has some idea about gardening.

With some, collection of coins dating back to ancient times, and of stamps of the present and previous era, is a passion. The activity, seemingly passive, not only enthuses the doer but also *effectuates*[6] learning about the past. Stamps of different shapes and sizes with splendid drawings on them offer relaxation, cause excitement and de-stress the burdened mind. Same is true for coins too. There are still some who collect flawed post cards, inland letters and postal envelops. Contrary to popular belief, the activity requires utmost concentration, imagination and dexterity to arrange and present them in the nicest possible manner. No doubt it involves a little investment but it can well become a considerable source of income later on. Collector's items are known to fetch millions in exhibitions.

Pets give a lot of relaxation. Having a pet in the house would benefit all. But one should *browse*[7] through a few good books to study pet behaviour, their needs and habits. This would give one an indepth knowledge about one's pet, its food habits, the diseases it could contract and the various vaccinations and medicines that would prevent those diseases. A pet in the house develops a sense of responsibility in the people living with it. However, pets like birds or fishes should not be kept in confinement. It is necessary that they have the freedom to thrive in their own habitat. Man should respect their freedom and not restrict their movement. Pets like cats, dogs and rabbits can be kept at home.

Some celebrities utilise their spare time in social service. They organise charity shows to collect money to help the poor and the needy. Their *charisma*[8] helps them raise funds. Ordinary citizens can also work for the poor and the underprivileged. This would give them an inner satisfaction of doing something worthwhile. It breathes into them a renewed *vigour*[9] towards life. With the break up of the joint family system in the wake of urbanisation, the aged are the worst hit. One can pass one's leisure time by visiting Old Age Homes run by NGOs. Giving a little love and affection to the aged people will mean a lot to them and will earn one their blessings.

It has been noticed that sometimes people indulge in extravagant parties only to gossip and make merry. Such indulgence amounts to sheer wastage of precious time and misuse of leisure. To drive away boredom and *ennui*[10] and to break the monotony of daily life, one should indulge in something constructive. Children should be encouraged to pursue hobbies. Love for reading, drawing, painting, or participating in cultural events should be *inculcated*[11] in them. This relieves the tension of studies and examinations. Cultivating a hobby in childhood would help them continue with the same when they are grown up and are in a profession. This would help them enjoy life and develop a zest for it.

Bertrand Russell said, "To be able to fill leisure intelligently is the last product of civilisation." He condemned the stupid hurry and overwork of modern life. We should choose a hobby which *recoups*[12] our energy and provides us recreation and relaxation.

Aid to Vocabulary

1. *Grind* — difficult and dull work
2. *Irreparable* — which cannot be rectified
3. *Rejuvenating* — restoring vigour or freshness
4. *Nuances* — delicate details

5. *Green fingers* — unusual skill in making plants grow
6. *Effectuates* — causes to happen
7. *Browse* — to leisurely look through
8. *Charisma* — a personal aura which endows its possessor with the capacity for inspiring popular enthusiasm
9. *Vigour* — physical energy
10. *Ennui* — feeling of weariness from lack of occupation, interest
11. *Inculcated* — caused to be learnt by repeating again and again
12. *Recoups* — regains, recovers

Points to Remember

1. Leisure is the opportunity or time when one is free from one's regular occupation or duty.
2. Taking up an interesting hobby is a very effective way of relieving stress and rejuvenating oneself for future endeavours.
3. Cooking, driving, painting, reading and gardening are some of the common leisure-time activities.
4. Some television and film actors perform on stage in their leisure time.
5. Some celebrities devote their spare time to social service.
6. Some people indulge in gossiping and partying. They should realise the value of time.
7. Leisure should not be misused, rather, it should be such that it helps us to enjoy life, and develops in us a zest for it.

GUIDED COMPOSITION

Develop the following paragraph into a full-fledged essay in 800-1000 words. The gist of the topic is provided in approximately 155 words for your help:

AN ADVENTURE IS AN INCONVENIENCE RIGHTLY UNDERSTOOD

Life is always springing surprises on people. No one can predetermine an incident in his life. Whenever something happens out of the blue, it causes a bit of inconvenience because of its sheer unexpectedness. The ability to take these unforeseen happenings in one's stride and even look upon them as the high points in one's life is a sign of maturity. We derive great pleasure by narrating incidents which, when they actually happened caused a lot of inconvenience, but in retrospect are not recounted as unpleasant. In fact, we often hear people talk of mishaps in life as adventures. That is because everything has a brighter side to it and a wise man never gets bogged down as to overlook it. To take an inconvenience in the spirit of adventure is the right approach to deal with it. In a foreign land, one often finds language a big barrier which makes him feel like a handicap, but it becomes very challenging to open lines of communication in spite of it. What begins as an inconvenience, turns out to be an adventure eventually. (155 words)

Essay
86

THE ART OF LIVING

SYNOPSIS

Living is an art, indeed the most complicated art. Life's path, not at all smooth, offers both pains and pleasures. The life of modern man has become so complex that even children and youth lead a hazardous life. The art of living has become the science of living. Scientific advancements have distorted man's mind and made him averse towards love of humanity. An optimist puts up a brave front, though. Many great men have followed the principle of simple living and high thinking. There are people who are able to achieve success not only for themselves but also for the nation. In modern times, living has become materialistic and one needs to learn the art of living right.

Living is the most complicated art as it is based on the scientific application of the good principles of living one's life span. Life has different interpretations for different people. For some it could be an unfulfilled dream and for some, pleasure. Others may live to perform their duties. Some live just for enjoyment. They like to enjoy life and make merry without caring for tomorrow. For some, life is a bed of roses while for others, it is full of thorns. For some, life is an adventure and they want to explore more in life. Nothing can deter them from their endeavours. But it is a fact that in one's lifetime, a person has to endure moments of agony, pain and *perpetual*[1] uncertainty along with brief moments of happiness. O. Henry said, "Life is made up of sobs, *sniffles*[2] and smiles, with sniffles *predominating*[3]." On the other hand, George Santayana felt, "There is no cure for birth and death, save to enjoy the interval."

Since time immemorial, all attempts to define life made by several thinkers, saints, recluses and other eminent personalities have proved to be largely futile, for no one could come out with a wholesome definition owing to its complexities and *vagaries*[4]. In Macbeth, one of the greatest Shakespearean tragedies, life has been compared to 'a tale told by an idiot' which again justifies the contention that life is undefinable. An interval between birth and death, life is to be taken as it comes. Harbouring resentment over the unpleasant gifts of life or arrogance over the pleasant, serves no purpose, because sooner or later, all of it has to go. The art of living, well said in the '*Bhagwad Geeta*', is to discharge one's duties honestly without aiming for the ultimate outcome or for the fruit your deeds bear. "Hope for the best, prepare for the worst and leave unto God the rest", is the basic principle of life. Since every happening on earth has a purpose of the *Providence*[5], and being a poor role player you can't alter the process, the best way is to accept what life offers. This must not mean that one should stay contented being at the receiving end always; instead, one should try to overcome the obstacles with whatever resources one has at one's disposal. Success or failure should not guide one's KARMA (deeds). Adjustments and compromises are part and parcel of life. Instead of cursing the darkness, one should light a candle. The simple rule of life is that one must strive to get what one likes or one will have to like what one gets.

The life of modern man has become highly complex and materialistic. Ancient man lived life as it came each day. He had to fend for himself and his community and hence, hunting expeditions and agriculture were carried out by the whole community. There was an element of unity in ancient man and this helped him sustain the vagaries of life. With scientific and technological advancements, life became complicated. Natural way of life gave way to artificiality. Man became selfish and began *shuttling*[6] from one place to another to fulfil his desires and those of his family. And in this endeavour, he forgot to live his life in an ideal, orderly way.

Modern life has become so complicated that even children do not have the opportunity to enjoy pure laughter. Right from infancy, the children are subjected to the *ordeal*[7] of getting into the grind of the education system. They are unable to enjoy their childhood because of the pressure of studies. Parental and peer pressure take their toll on the child. Because of lack of time in the morning to groom themselves and to take proper care of personal health and hygiene, they suffer from various maladies, such as dental cavities, abdominal pain, severe headaches. They may suffer from poor vision due to prolonged television viewing and may also experience bouts of depression. Breakfast and fruits are usually skipped, which adversely affects the performance of the child in school. Water and environment pollution, in addition, contribute to the woes of the child.

Once out of school and later, out of college, one embarks on an *odyssey*[8] to secure a job. His degrees and certificates are not enough to fetch him a job. The education system for want of modernisation, has not equipped one with the nuances of any trade, and hence, he finds it difficult to apply his theoretical knowledge to the practical front. *Nepotism*[9] and bribery enable the less competent people to secure jobs. As a result, the competent person becomes frustrated, dejected and disillusioned with life.

The art of living has become the science of living in modern life. Modern amenities of life have provided comfort and luxury to men. But the *cut-throat*[10] competition among human beings to avail themselves of these comforts, has snatched the natural pleasure from life. These amenities that make human life more and more comfortable have considerably reduced human interest in the beauty of Nature. No one has the time to 'stand and stare' at the birds and the flowers or to gaze at the stars or the moon at leisure. One prefers sitting comfortably in one's living room and watching a place of historical interest on television rather than braving the odds and visiting the place.

An optimist puts up a brave front in the battle of life. As William Hazlitt has said, "The art of life is to know how to enjoy a little and to endure much." The real art of living lies in looking at the bright side of things. Brave is the man who is able to sail smoothly through the *vicissitudes*[11] of life and take the shortcomings in his stride. In fact, this is the attitude of life which can bring maximum happiness to man. One should always remember the basic *tenet*[12] of the *Gita*, "Do your duty and leave the rest unto God." All great men have practised this doctrine and achieved great success. If one does one's duty regardless of rewards, even small successes can bring happiness, joy and satisfaction. The greatest wisdom lies in living life thoroughly and intensely in the present, deriving lessons from the past and keeping high ideals for the future.

While the past is history and the future, a mystery, today is a gift which is why, it is called the 'present'. So, one can well enjoy 'the present' in full measure.

Many great leaders of our country, like Mahatma Gandhi, S. Radhakrishnan, Rajendra Prasad, to name a few, have followed the principle of 'simple living and high thinking'. According to this principle, the art of living does not lie in acquiring wealth and struggling for the achievement of personal happiness in life but in pondering over the different aspects of life and deciphering their true meaning. Mother Teresa, a saint of the modern times, believed in selfless service towards the underprivileged and downtrodden. She led a simple and frugal life but she had noble ideas which guided her to provide *succour*[13] to the sick and the needy. Only by being noble and selfless, she was able to achieve her mission of compassion and charity.

For most of the people of the present age, living comprises dependence on modern scientific *amenities*[14]. Yet, there have been some who gave a new meaning to human life. They were able to achieve success not only for themselves, but also for the community and the nation they lived in. Jamshedji Tata worked with a messianic zeal for the upliftment of the community around his steel mill and established India's first steel city at Jamshedpur. Bill and Melinda Gates, the Microsoft couple, have undertaken the philanthropic mission of educating the world's underprivileged children.

The art of living consists in a healthy development of the body, mind and intellect. Modern life provides all the facilities for maintaining a lean physique, well-groomed personality and sharpened intellect. Besides education, modes of entertainment and information like cinema, television, radio, the Internet, etc., help people to keep themselves abreast with the times. To appear presentable, one should groom oneself and acquire the etiquettes of carrying oneself decently in the society. At the same time, each one of us must adopt the ideals of brotherhood, compassion and social responsibility.

The art of living, in modern times, has undergone a sea change. There is less appreciation for selfless service done in a silent way than for a self-serving charity done with a lot of publicity and fanfare. It is the recognition that matters these days, not the real intent and content of purpose. Even religious and spiritual endeavours seek publicity for being recognised. The art of living, therefore, demands that human beings live up to the expectations of their society and do their best in every way. They should strive to create an atmosphere of happiness, promote moral and spiritual values and prefer virtue to vice, unfailingly.

AID TO VOCABULARY

1. *Perpetual* — continuing
2. *Sniffles* — nasal congestion due to cold or repressing tearful emotion
3. *Predominating* — surpassing in numbers, size or power
4. *Vagaries* — changes that are unpredictable and difficult to control
5. *Providence* — God or protector of human beings
6. *Shuttling* — moving to and fro
7. *Ordeal* — trying experience
8. *Odyssey* — a long journey
9. *Nepotism* — favouritism
10. *Cut-throat* — intense and merciless
11. *Vicissitudes* — changes in circumstances

12. *Tenet* — doctrine
13. *Succour* — help, relief
14. *Amenities* — anything that adds to a person's comfort and convenience

Points to Remember

1. Living is an art, indeed, the most complicated art in modern times.
2. The life of modern man in comparison to that of the ancient man is highly complex.
3. Even the children and the youth lead complicated lives in modern times.
4. The art of living has become the science of living in modern life.
5. An optimist puts up a brave front in the battle of life.
6. Many great men follow the principle of 'simple living and high thinking'.
7. The art of living consists in a healthy development of the body, mind and intellect.
8. Life has become materialistic.
9. The art of living demands that human beings live up to the expectations of their society and do their best in every way.

Essay
87

SELF-RELIANCE

Synopsis

Self-reliance means the capacity to gratify and satisfy every want by oneself. While interdependence establishes relationship; self reliance builds self confidence and self respect. It is applicable to individuals as well as to nations. Man depends upon others for his physical needs. His ability to think independently, in the mature stages of life, enhances his self-respect. Our national leaders realised the importance of self-reliance. Since man is a social animal, he can never be totally self-reliant. There has been a serious erosion in man's moral and spiritual values. A self-reliant man is not guided by ulterior motives. Unless man understands the true meaning of the word self-reliance, there can be no moral and spiritual regeneration.

Self-reliance refers to the capacity to *gratify*[1] and satisfy every want by oneself without frequently depending upon others. The best place to find a helping hand is at the end of your own arm. However, in the nature's scheme of things, all living beings are interdependent and they sustain each other. Plants, animals and human beings cannot exist in isolation. Although man is dependent on others for his *subsistence*[2], he should strive to be self-reliant. The greatest achievement in the world, probably, is to know how to be self-sufficient. The concept of self-reliance is applicable to individuals as well as to nations.

Man depends on others for his physical needs. When a child is born into this world, he is totally helpless and depends upon his parents for the gratification of his physical needs, security and emotional *sustenance*[3]. Under the able guidance and loving care of his parents, he begins to grow. As they nurture him, he gradually learns to walk, hold himself and interpret the language of his parents. Gradually, he becomes less dependent upon his parents and is able to feed and clothe himself. The outside world, which initially seemed to him in a state of confusion, slowly unfolds before him. Venturing into the world helps him to build his self-confidence and a sense of self-worth. He gradually learns to take care of some of the needs for which he used to depend on his parents in the early phase of his life.

A child is sent to school and later to college to prepare him to face the *vicissitudes*[4] of life boldly. Usually when we talk of self-reliance we refer to economic independence. Self-reliance does not mean merely the ability to earn one's living. It is much more than this. A person can be called truly self-reliant if he has learnt not only to be self-supportive but also to have cultivated spiritual and moral values in his life. Such a person thinks without fear and works with devotion. He develops confidence in his abilities, so essential for success in life. He develops the power of thinking independently and taking decisions boldly which *enhances*[5] his self-respect. The famous Greek dramatist Aeschylus is right when he says, 'God loves to help him who strives to help himself.'

What is true for an individual is equally true, in a larger perspective, for nations. The importance of self-reliance was realised by our national leaders during the pre-Independence days. Gandhiji's *swadeshi* movement was started with the sole objective of making the nation self-reliant and the people proud of their own heritage. The colonial rule of the British for about 200 years destroyed our traditional handicrafts and cottage industries. They procured the raw materials from India at low prices and marketed their machine-made goods at a higher price in India. Gandhiji wanted to revive the traditional crafts to make the villages self-reliant. He *dissuaded*[6] the people from buying British goods and appealed to them to purchase the indigenous products. After more than sixty years of freedom, India can now boast of self-reliance in the fields of agriculture, industry, science and technology.

Aristotle said, "Man is a social animal." Indeed, it is impossible for any individual or nation to be totally self-reliant in all fields. Interdependence is a natural phenomenon. Just as an individual is dependent upon a number of people for his food, clothes and other necessities, nations are also dependent upon one another. With the progress of science and technology, the world has shrunk and there has been a growing interdependence between nations. Some countries are, by virtue of their geographical location, more suitable for the production of particular types of goods. Some have an abundance of natural resources which can be exported. This creates the need to develop trade and commerce among nations. Leaders of all countries should understand this and learn to live in peace and harmony.

Somewhere down the ages, self-reliance became *synonymous*[7] with economic independence. Mankind has made much progress as a result of the sustained efforts of scientists, doctors, engineers and others who shared their knowledge with the rest and worked for the benefit of humanity. Had they been guided by selfish motives they would not have *divulged*[8] their vast knowledge. A truly self-reliant person does not suffer from a sense of insecurity. He is not guided by fear and anxiety. He does not make calculated moves but acts in a natural way. He is not guided by *ulterior*[9] motives and works for the betterment of mankind. Such is the stuff, a truly self-reliant person is made of, be he an ordinary farmer, an unskilled worker or a highly educated scientist.

It is a pity that in the process of his evolution, man became selfish. Unless man understands the true meaning of the word self-reliance, there can be no moral and spiritual regeneration for him. It is a lesson that should be taught early in life, when the young minds are being trained for a vocation. It is education alone which can teach the impressionable young apprentice how to live life and not merely how to earn a living. Thus, a lesson in self-reliance should be initiated early in life so that no one grows up to be selfish, narrow-minded and parasitic. Such total self-reliance will bring about a dramatic change in human life and will help in promoting a spirit of mutual love, respect and faith. It will help usher in an era which Gandhiji had *envisaged*[10]. Self-reliance, which is fostered by peaceful co-existence among nations and the citizens, is the need of the hour in the strife-torn world today.

AID TO VOCABULARY

1. *Gratify* — to do or give whatever is wanted or demanded by somebody or something
2. *Subsistence* — food, money, etc., needed for staying alive
3. *Sustenance* — that which supports life
4. *Vicissitudes* — change of circumstances
5. *Enhances* — increases
6. *Dissuaded* — persuaded against
7. *Synonymous* — having the same or nearly the same meaning
8. *Divulged* — revealed
9. *Ulterior* — secret, beyond what is seen
10. *Envisaged* — seen in the mind as a future possibility

POINTS TO REMEMBER

1. Self-reliance means the capacity to gratify and satisfy every want by oneself.
2. At the time of birth, man is totally helpless and depends upon his parents for the gratification of his physical needs, security and emotional sustenance.
3. A person can be called truly self-reliant if he has learnt not only to be self-supportive but also to live with spiritual and moral values to guide him.
4. Self-reliance is needed not only by individuals but also, in a larger perspective, by nations.
5. As 'Man is a social animal', so, it is impossible for any individual or nation to be totally self-reliant in all fields.
6. Nowadays, people consider self-reliance as synonymous with economic independence.
7. Unless man understands the true meaning of the word self-reliance, there can be no moral and spiritual regeneration for him.

Essay **88**

MORAL & SPIRITUAL DEPRIVATION OF MODERN MAN

SYNOPSIS

Man has become excessively preoccupied with materialistic pursuits. The excessive urge for material possessions has made him oblivious to spiritual and moral needs. Abolition of joint family system coupled with 'spare the rod and spoil the child' theory have made children instinctual and immoral. Today, man is disillusioned because he is unable to find peace and happiness through the gratification of his senses. He feels lost. Unless there is a revival of spiritual and moral values, this sense of ennui and unhappiness will lead man further into the state of chaos.

Modern man has become highly materialistic and is preoccupied with the pursuit of material possessions. Acquisition of money has become the objective of every pursuit and the means do not matter. This excessive urge for materialistic gains has made him ignore the spiritual and moral aspects of his life. He considers them *obsolete*[1] and unproductive. Today, man is motivated to do something only when he is assured of reasonable profit. He has neither the time nor the inclination to pause and ask himself, where he is leading himself to. Such is the present social environment that even a child cannot remain unaffected by it. It is easy to quieten a child with a promise of a gift and, divert his mind from something the parents have no patience to deal with.

Life has become mechanical. A child is constantly under parental and peer pressure to excel in his studies and stay ahead of his companions. The ultimate goal of every student is to get an education which would fetch him/her a job with good remuneration which would be the object of envy for others. As a consequence, from a very tender age, young minds become *warped*[2] due to the obsessive preoccupation of the adults with financial security. It has been felt that the basic physical needs cannot be met without money, hence the need to prepare for a means of livelihood. But man is not merely a creature who will be content with getting food, shelter and clothing. He has a soul which also needs to be nurtured. It is, however, a pity that the spiritual aspect of the personality gets totally ignored in the mad rush for material gains.

With the abolition of the joint family system, many things have changed for the better but certain others, do pinch us time and again. In the lap of their grandparents, children of the previous generation heard the mythological stories of Gods and Goddesses; and, developed an inclination for righteousness and justice along with an indomitable courage to stand up against all odds and evils—all with a touch of love and care. In a sharp contrast, children of the present generation watch on internet and television indecent stuff with no parental guidance. In addition, in the name of child rights, the theory of 'spare the rod, and spoil the child' has altogether been done away with instilling in them fearlessness regarding any unpleasant consequence. This contributes to making them *instinctual*[3] and, at the same time, immoral. Indifferent teachers at school and preoccupied parents at home hardly find time to check this trend which deprives children of spirituality and morality.

No wonder that the young generation feels restless, demoralised and disillusioned. The young people of the western countries are turning towards the East for *solace*[4] and spiritual comfort. They experience a sense of *ennui*[5] and feel impatient with the preoccupation of their parents with work and money. It is largely due to such disillusionment of people that ordinary men who self-style themselves as godmen, promising salvation and spiritual regeneration, are able to have a large following.

In our country, the youth is influenced by the 'Western Culture' and it has led to an *erosion*[6] of moral and spiritual values. They mechanically ape their western counterparts in their dressing, thinking, mannerisms, interests and pursuits and look down upon their own rich cultural heritage. The educational system and the attitude of the parents are also largely responsible for this state of affairs. It is a fact, that today the educational system has failed to *inculcate*[7] in young people moral and spiritual values. Parents in urban areas are so preoccupied with their responsibility of catering to the material needs of the family that they fail to pay attention to the emotional needs of the growing children. Consequently, children feel directionless and may become addicted to drugs and other vices at an early age. Thus, millions of tender minds, who are the future citizens of the country, go astray and start following a path which can only lead to the ruin of the self.

A question has been haunting the modern man—where will the mindless pursuit of *transient*[8] things lead to? It has certainly not made man happier or peaceful. Today, everyone complains of degeneration of values and corruption in all walks of life, but nobody seems to be prepared to shatter them and make a fresh beginning. Corruption has become a chronic malady of our times, so much so that people have started treating it as a normal feature. They no longer show any *righteous*[9] indignation against corrupt practices, nor do they fight injustice or express any shock when cruel or inhuman acts are committed against their brethren. They either remain apathetic or give vent to impotent rage in the comfort of their drawing rooms. However, there can be no hope for humanity, if the present trend continues and man remains insensitive to the needs of others. Unless there is a revival of spiritual and moral values, this trend will continue making man morally and spiritually bankrupt.

In ancient India, education followed the *Guru-sishya parampara*. Children were sent to the Guru's ashram not only to take education which could equip them to earn their livelihood, but also to imbibe moral and spiritual values. Such values helped them to sustain themselves in their moments of confusion and anxiety. Hence, they were able to sail through the ups and downs of life with a reasonable sense of *equanimity*[10] which sadly the present generation has lost. Today, it has been completely overlooked that man exists on five planes—physical, emotional, intellectual, functional and existential. Only the physical part of the being is taken care of. In fact man has, in his folly, been trying to find peace and happiness through his senses.

The tremendous progress in the field of science and technology has made life comfortable. The various kinds of gadgets available today have taken away the drudgery from life. Instead of making science serve him, man himself has become its servant. He has become materialistic and has developed an insatiable desire to accumulate wealth and buy comforts. In the process, he has lost his conscience. The decision over whether he wants science to serve him or himself become *subservient*[11] to it, rests entirely upon him.

Modern man has dug his own grave by rejecting the moral and spiritual values upheld in the religious scriptures of the world. The *Bible*, the *Adigranth* (Guru Granth Sahib), the *Ramayana*, the *Upanishadas*, the *Bhagvad Gita,* the *Holy Quran* all contain words of wisdom which modern man has disdainfully rejected. Money has become God today, as man reserves for it, an *unwavering*[12] loyalty and his utmost devotion.

Today, there are many who will readily *bequeath*[13] their soul to the devil in exchange for pleasure and power like the famous literary character Dr Faustus, immortalised by Christopher Marlowe. Today, Faustus has a universal appeal. At this juncture, it would be prudent for modern man to ponder over the last moments of Faustus, which he had spent in great pain and agony. Modern man is confronted with temptation at every step. He yields to it, realising only later that the price he has had to pay for that was invaluable in terms of losing his peace and happiness. It is because of this inherent weakness of modern man that we find so much sin, evil and corruption in the society. It is indeed a tragedy that man has become a victim of his own greed and lust. The only way out is the spiritual and moral regeneration by listening to the inner voice, the conscience, which can never mislead man. The future of mankind is really in the hands of those who can bring about a reawakening in man's higher consciousness.

Aid to Vocabulary

1. *Obsolete* — outdated
2. *Warped* — become bent or twisted out of its natural shape
3. *Instinctual* — acting on instinct rather than intellect
4. *Solace* — comfort in grief or anxiety
5. *Ennui* — mental exhaustion due to lack of occupation or interest
6. *Erosion* — gradual wearing off, destruction
7. *Inculcate* — to fix ideas or principles in someone's mind
8. *Transient* — short-lived
9. *Righteous* — moral
10. *Equanimity* — composure, calm
11. *Subservient* — subordinate
12. *Unwavering* — steadfast, resolute
13. *Bequeath* — leave to a person by a will, gift

Points to Remember

1. Modern man has become excessively preoccupied in the pursuit of material things.
2. Life has become mechanical.
3. The spiritual aspect of the personality is totally ignored.
4. Consequently there is moral and spiritual degeneration.
5. The moral and spiritual values are no longer considered virtues which need to be inculcated from childhood.
6. The mindless pursuit of transitory things is leading man to his own grave.
7. Man has become a victim of his insatiable lust for wealth and comfort.
8. Unless there is a revival of moral and spiritual values, the future of mankind is very bleak.

GUIDED COMPOSITION

Develop the following paragraph into a full-fledged essay in 800-1000 words. The gist of the topic is provided in approximately 150 words for your help:

HEALING POWER OF PRAYER

Prayer is one of the simple necessities of life, as basic to the individual as sunshine, food and water. At times perhaps more so. Prayer is man's effort to get in touch with God for solace, peace and comfort. Experts in physical and mental health have also realised the importance of prayer in healing. It is remarkable how prayer restores the harmonious functioning of body and soul. Prayer releases energy in the system which normalises the function of the body. It is necessary to pray with faith in heart, to reap the benefits of prayer. Practice of prayer, daily in the morning or at any time of the day, freshens the mind and gives extra energy to the body to approach day's tasks with cheer and optimism. It removes negative thoughts from the mind, which alone cause more harm than any poison. A man who prays daily remains serene and poised even in most difficult times. His faith sustains him and helps him tide over the difficult times and also the difficulties in his path. Prayer heals a sick man, in agony, simply by teaching him to accept God's will without resentment. Prayer is a great healer indeed. (150 words)

Essay **89**

LOVE IS THE BASIS OF A HAPPY LIFE

Synopsis

Everyone wants to be happy in this world. People seek happiness in wealth, power, sex, fashion, drugs, drinks, etc. But these are temporary pleasures. It is love that makes man eternally happy. True love does not have any selfish motive. Hatred gives rise to unhappiness. It robs one of peace of mind. Love fills a person with noble feelings. A mother's love for her children is something very divine. Love between neighbours brings peace in the neighbourhood. Love between friends strengthens the bonds of friendship. There have been saints whose love was universal. Lack of love leads to divorce, quarrel, crime, aggression and war. Love can unite the people of the world into a common brotherhood.

"True love is the gift which God has given to man alone beneath the heaven."

—*Walter Scott*

Everyone wants to be happy in this world. But there are only a few people who are really happy. Some people believe that wealth gives happiness. They spend most of their time and energy in acquiring it. But wealth does not give happiness. It provides man with the basic amenities and materialistic comforts of life but cannot give the emotional and spiritual satisfaction.

There are some others who seek power to gain happiness. Different means may be adopted to attain power. One may attain power in the political sphere. Power corrupts and one may even try to become a dictator after gaining power. Some try to establish their supremacy in the world. But even such powers do not give happiness. With power one can force others to do certain things but there is a world of difference between a forced action and a spontaneous action.

In the present age, many people strive for happiness in sex, fashion, drinks and drugs. They wish to escape from the problem-ridden world into a world of dreams. They try to derive pleasure from these sources. But they do not realise that these are temporary and *illusory*[1] pleasures. These things may help people to forget their worries for a limited period of time but not forever. Most of them are harmful rather than helpful.

There is a difference between happiness and what we describe as joy and pleasure. On a warm day, what a glass of cold lemon juice gives you is pleasure because it is a momentary satisfaction. On the other hand, happiness is experienced in the mind and is therefore infinitely more powerful.

Few know the secret of true happiness. It is love that makes man happy. It is the love between children and parents, wife and husband, brother and sister, lover and beloved, teacher and student, and master and servant. It is the love between neighbours and between friends. It is the love between man and God. Love is the storehouse of happiness. True love does not have any selfish motive. Those who make others happy by loving also make themselves happy.

Hatred breeds enmity. It robs one of peace of mind. A person who does not have peace of mind cannot be happy. Hatred may result in physical violence. Crimes are often outcomes of hatred. Hatred gives rise to unhappiness. Jealousy and prolonged anger are agents of death. So, one should follow the path of love to achieve happiness.

Love fills a person with noble feelings: *compassion*[2], sympathy, sacrifice, understanding, welfare, etc. A mother's love for her children is something very divine. She is forever ready to suffer any hardship for the happiness of her children. Love between a child and its mother is the purest form of love. Love of a mother is so deep and eternal that she can understand even that which her child does not express. It is a divine and encompassing love that throws a protective ring around her child.

Love between neighbours brings peace and harmony in the neighbourhood. People willingly come forward to help one another. They share their joys and sorrows. They can never think of causing harm to one another. Love among neighbours fosters brotherhood. People of such a neighbourhood lead a happy life. Neighbours who love and respect one another refrain from doing anything which may displease or annoy others. They frequently get together on festive occasions. They jointly celebrate festivals and enjoy one another's company.

Love between friends strengthens the bond of friendship. They can never think of *betraying*[3] each other. A friendship based on love is never affected by selfish motives. Even differences of opinion do not *hamper*[4] the strong bond of friendship. We enjoy every moment we spend with our friends. We forget all worries and hardships of life when we are with them. Love between friends, thus, *generates*[5] happiness.

There have been saints who widened the horizon of their love. Their love was universal. They loved mankind and even animals and birds. Jesus Christ, Prophet Muhammad, Gautama Buddha, Mahavira, Guru Nanak

Dev and others worked for the welfare and happiness of all. Mother Teresa filled many a heart with happiness by her *dedicated*[6] service to the poor and the needy.

There will be no quarrels or divorces between married couples if love is adopted as the guiding principle of marriage. There will be no *friction*[7] between parents and children and no bitterness between friends; and there will be no *exploitation*[8] of man by man if all follow the path of love. Lack of love makes the life of a child bitter. It develops a sense of insecurity within. Lack of love may cause stress and depression in life. It leads to crime, aggression and unhappiness. It sows the seeds of hatred and triggers acts of terrorism. Another important drawback of a loveless life is a tendency to take to narcotics. A mechanical world, driven by a consumerist society leads the youth into these dark alleys.

Love alone can lessen many ills of the society. Love is the basis of a happy life. If nations of the world were to follow this principle, there would be no world wars, *massacres*[9] or widespread destruction. Love can unite the people of the world into a universal brotherhood.

Aid to Vocabulary

1. *Illusory* — unreal, imaginary
2. *Compassion* — pity
3. *Betraying* — being disloyal to
4. *Hamper* — obstruct
5. *Generates* — brings into existence, evolve
6. *Dedicated* — devoted to
7. *Friction* — clash of opinions
8. *Exploitation* — utilising someone for one's own ends unjustly
9. *Massacres* — killings of people in large numbers

Points to Remember

1. Wealth does not provide happiness to man.
2. Some people seek happiness in power.
3. Sex, fashion, drinks and drugs give only temporary happiness.
4. It is love that makes man happy.
5. Hatred breeds enmity.
6. Love fills a person with noble feelings.
7. Love between neighbours brings peace in the neighbourhood.
8. Love between friends strengthens the bond of friendship.
9. There have been saints whose love is universal.
10. Lack of love leads to crimes and aggression.
11. Love can unite the people of the world into universal brotherhood.

Essay
90

FREEDOM OF ART

SYNOPSIS

Freedom of expression is enshrined in our Constitution as a fundamental right under Article 19(1)(a). Intellectuals of all ages fight for freedom of expression. Various types of art are the means of aesthetical comprehension and portrayal of the world. The concept 'Art for Art's sake' leads to extreme individualism. Artistic freedom is vital for our society. But, there should be a clear distinction between private expression and public exhibition. One cannot hurt other's religious sentiments for the sake of 'art' only. Over the last few years, some extremist groups have become self-appointed guardians of morality in our country. This should not be tolerated. Freedom of expression is recognised as a basic human right. This right should be protected by the laws of our Constitution.

Freedom of expression is enshrined in the Constitution of India as a fundamental right under Article 19(1)(a). Freedom of expression means the freedom to express not only one's own views, but also the views of others. Freedom of expression is very important for a democratic set-up. In the Indian democratic system, the people have the fundamental right of expressing their ideas and to comment or criticise within constitutional framework.

Since ancient times, intellectuals, artists, writers, philosophers have been fighting for freedom of expression. Socrates, Jesus Christ, Galileo, Joan of Arc-all sacrificed their lives for the sake of this freedom. During the British rule in India, freedom fighters expressed their views openly against the *tyranny*[1] of foreign ruler. British liberal philosopher, J.S. Mill, in his book 'On Liberty' said that there should be no limitations on the freedom of expression of one's opinions and ideas. Karl Popper in his book, 'Open Society and its Enemies' criticised the concept of a closed society where we cannot express our views freely.

Freedom of Art is very important for a liberal society. Art is a specific form of social consciousness and human activity, which reflects reality in artistic images. It is one of the most important means of *aesthetical*[2] comprehension and portrayal of the world. It is for this reason that man, his social links and relations, the life and activity of people in concrete historical conditions are always in the centre of any work of art. The specific methods of reproducing reality and artistic tasks as well as the material means of portraying artistic images determine the specific types of art. Thus, in literature the aesthetic reproduction of the world is made through the word, in painting through the visual images of the colour, in sculpture through three-dimensional forms, in music through sound intonations, in theatre and cinema through the characterisation of the actors. Art should develop freely, enabling "a hundred flowers to bloom" and should not be influenced by some artistic dogmas of a particular political authority. 'High art' by exceptionally gifted individuals should be encouraged as a source of enjoyment.

In the nineteenth and twentieth centuries, idealist aestheticians advocated the absolute nature of art, which supposedly aims only at purely aesthetic pleasure, i.e., "Art for Art's sake". This leads to the claim that the artist is free of society and bears no responsibility to the people. This view leads to extreme *individualism*[3] and subjectivism.

Artistic freedom is vital to both the cultural and political health of our society. But, this freedom is threatened when art is challenged because of its content, message or viewpoint. A challenge may be raised by the disagreement with the perceived message. It is the result of negative public reaction. It may come from general public, representatives of organisations, government officials and also from within the arts community.

Salman Rushdie's The Satanic Verses, Rohinton Mistry's Such A Long Journey, A.K. Ramanujan's Three Hundred Ramayans, Joseph Lelyveld's Great Soul: Mahatma Gandhi and His Struggle with India are some of the important books, which are banned by our government. Books are mostly banned without reading them. The hurting of religious sensibilities creates problem, when someone expresses his own views and does not care about the sentiment of the particular religious groups. Naked Saraswati or a nude Bharat Mata painted by M.F. Hussain were banned on the ground that it hurt the religious sentiments the of Hindus. Pradip Dalvi's play Godse was banned on the ground that it hurt the image of Mahatma Gandhi and justified his assassination. UP Government banned the play 'My Sandal', clearly a satire on Chief Minister Mayawati by Mukesh Verma. The screening of 'Da Vinci Code' was prohibited in our country.

The audio-visual media, especially television and the cinema, are showing a growing number of films *depicting*[4] sex, violence, some of which are extremely gory. Though it is not easy to establish a direct correlation between cinema, TV viewing and violence, there can be no denying that such depiction have had ill effects on the immature, adolescent, the unemployed or school dropouts. Sometimes, censor board does not perform its duty properly.

Now-adays, it has become fashionable for artists, writers, claiming artistic 'license' to *brazenly*[5] insult Islam, Christianity and other religions. But, there is no such license. While an analytic critique of a religion is fine, *vilification*[6] and abuse of a religion is not.

The problem with the manner, in which the debate over intolerance and artistic expression is conducted in India, is that we confuse too many different components. It is easy enough to condemn violence, authoritarian overreaction or conservative definitions of obscenity. This is a debate that is as old as art itself. It is probably right to say that a man is free to paint or write whatever he likes. But, is he as free to exhibit it in public? If he is, then why do we have *obscenity*[7] laws? Why do we have a film censor board? Clearly, there is a distinction between private expression and public exhibition. Hindu temples are full of nude representations of gods and goddesses. But, it does not follow that there should be no limits to artistic expression of religious figures. Paintings of naked Saraswati or visual representation of Prophet Muhammad are cases of hurting religious sentiments. Hurting religious sentiments is strictly condemned.

However, it is also not justified that anybody destroys the works of art. It is a clear sign of growing intolerance. In a democracy, there are civilised ways of expressing one's dissent. There is a need to educate people on forms of protest that are consonant with a liberal society.

Our problem in India is that we have no standards, no barriers and no sense of what is acceptable and what is not. No principles are ever discussed. No guidelines are drawn up. Instead, each time a sensitive issue erupts, we engage in the same debate. Pakistan has *blasphemy*[8] law. Under the law, anyone who speaks ill of Islam or Prophet Muhammad faces the death penalty. Several liberal minded leaders in Pakistan want to change this blasphemy law, which is necessary for the protection of religious minorities.

In our country, a new phenomenon has developed. It is described as cultural policing, which is monitored not only by the party in power, but by communal or non-secular parties, who decide what is good or bad for our culture. Beating the girls in nightclub and disrupting the valentine's day celebration are some of the handiworks of communal parties.

In the last few years, some extremist groups or parties have become self-appointed guardians of morality in our country. They, want to dictate what people can or cannot read, which film or play is to be censored, which performer can or cannot appear on stage, and also what or what not or what an artist can exhibit.

This trend should not be tolerated. Fortunately, the judiciary in our country has been a source of protection of freedom of expression. Freedom of expression is recognised universally as a Human Right—a basic right of every human being irrespective of colour, race, gender or status. In a free society, which prides itself on democracy, it is the constitution that should be the supreme law, not fatwas or *edicts*[9] issued by cultural *vigilantes*[10]. Bowing to any other power would be a betrayal of the liberal, secular values we hold dear.

Aid to Vocabulary

1. *Tyranny* — cruel and unfair treatment by people with power over others
2. *Aesthetical* — of or relating to art or beauty
3. *Individualism* — the belief that the needs of each person are more important than the needs of the whole society or group
4. *Depicting* — to describe something using words, a story etc.
5. *Brazenly* — acting or done in a very open and shocking way without shame or embarrassment
6. *Vilification* — to say or write very harshly
7. *Obscenity* — obscene language or behaviour
8. *Blasphemy* — great disrespect shown to God or to something holy
9. *Edicts* — decrees
10. *Vigilante* — a person who is not a police officer, but who tries to catch and punish criminals

Points to Remember

1. Freedom of expression is enshrined in our Constitution as a fundamental right.
2. Since ancient times, intellectuals have been fighting for freedom of expression.
3. Art is the most important means of aesthetical comprehension and portrayal of the world.
4. The concept of 'Art for Art's sake' leads to extreme individualism.
5. The hurting of religious sensibilities creates problem in society.
6. Nowadays, it has become fashionable to criticise religion in the name of artistic license.
7. There should be a distinction between private expression and public exhibition.
8. Over the last few years, some extremist groups have become self-appointed guardians of morality in our country, which should not be acceptable.
9. We should follow the laws laid down by our Constitution.

Essay 91

THE LATEST TRENDS IN INDIAN ECONOMY

SYNOPSIS

The Indian economy is a dynamic and transforming economy. It has evolved as a mixed economy. A significant increase in the national income as well as the per capita income has been recorded since Independence. The annual economic growth is the indicator which reflects the performance of an economy. In the past few years, the growth rate had been close to 9 per cent per annum. However, because of unprecedented global economic crisis, it came down to 7 to 8 per cent during the years 2008-09 to 2011-12. The economy grew at 7.3 per cent in 2014-15 due to improvement in the performance of both services and manufacturing sectors. India is set to emerge as the world's fastest-growing major economy ahead of China, as per the World Bank. The improvement in India's economic fundamentals accelerated in the year 2015, with the combined impact of strong government reforms and the RBI's focus, on inflation supported by benign global commodity prices. The challenge before us is to make the growth process socially more inclusive and regionally more balanced. Hence, a pragmatic approach is required for balanced economic growth.

Indian economy is a *dynamic*[1] and *transforming*[2] economy. The United States Agency for International Development (USAID) now describes India as a "transforming" rather than a "developing" country. It indicates a new way of looking at India even as it acknowledges the unique position she occupies in the world.

For half a century before Independence, the Indian economy registered virtually no growth at all. A significant increase in the national income as well as in the per capita income has been recorded since Independence. In the first three decades after Independence, we grew at 3.5 per cent per annum. In the next three decades, the national growth rate went up to nearly 6 per cent. In the last few years, the growth rate was close to 9 per cent per annum. The annual economic growth rate is the indicator which reflects the performance of an economy. Economic growth is calculated on the basis of increase in the Gross Domestic Product (GDP) indicating the value of goods and services produced in an economy during a year and estimated either at current or constant prices.

As of now, the Indian economy is robust. This has been made possible by an increasing rate of investment. In the pre-British period, the Indian economy was *self reliant*[3]. The British East India Company ruled over India from 1757 to 1858 and transformed India into a 'profitable' colony for the Britishers. commercialisation of agriculture in addition to 'de-industrialisation' of India had strategically been done by the British throughout their reign. As a result, the Indian economy became impoverished. In 1905, the *Swadeshi Movement* encouraged the growth of Indian industries. After Independence, the first Five Year Plan described the Indian economy as an underdeveloped economy. A plan was formulated to check the imbalance created in the Indian economy in the wake of the Bengal Famine of 1943, and later, by the Partition of India, in 1947. A 'socialistic pattern of society' was adopted as the primary objective of the economic policy. The Indian economy *evolved*[4] as a mixed economy characterised by the co-existence of the private and the public sectors. The last few years have been very good for the Indian economy. There has been a considerable rise in productivity, labour and capital. If we can sustain these growth levels, and step up the productivity of land and labour, we should be able to achieve a double digit rate of growth very soon. India is definitely on a roll.

The Indian economy has witnessed its fastest growth in the last 20 years. However, benefits *bypassed*[5] agriculture while manufacturing and service sectors saw *robust*[6] growth. India's economic growth rate is second only to China among the major global economies.

"Indian Economy is on an unprecedented *trajectory*[7] of strong economic growth". *Vigorous*[8] growth in GDP, with a *resurgence*[9] in the industrial sector and continued dynamism in the services, has characterised the Indian economy since 2003-04. The economy recorded an annual growth of about 8.5 per cent during the last few years. However, because of the unprecedented global economic crisis, it came down to 7 to 8 per cent during the years 2008-09 to 2011-12. The economy grew at 7.3 per cent in 2014-15 due to improvement in the performance of services as well as manufacturing sectors. India is set to emerge as the world's fastest-growing major economy ahead of China, as per a report by the World Bank. The improvement in India's economic fundamentals accelerated. In the year 2015-16, the economy grew at 7.6 per cent with the combined impact of strong government reforms and the RBI's focus on inflation, supported by *benign*[10] global commodity prices.

The Indian growth experience is *novel*[11]. India's reforms have encompassed the real, monetary, financial, fiscal and external sectors. Structural reforms have transformed the industrial sector from a command and control structure to a liberal and competitive one. The fiscal environment has been marked by prudence and backed by fiscal responsibility legislations, *steep*[12] reductions in import duties and other tax rates, introduction of VAT, and a taxpayer friendly regime. The financial sector has been restructured with independent regulatory mechanisms in place. India has emerged as one of the strongest performers with respect to deals across the world in terms of *mergers*[13] and *acquisitions*[14] .

India's economy has grown rapidly over the past few years on the back of impressive performance in the manufacturing and service sectors. The data showed that while the manufacturing and the service sectors powered ahead, agriculture lagged behind. The economy has grown but the benefits have largely bypassed the farming community which make up for about 58 per cent of India's total population. Growth has also been socially uneven. Hence, the challenge before us is to make the growth process socially inclusive and regionally balanced. Numerous foreign companies are setting up their facilities in India on account of various government initiatives like Make in India and Digital India. The Make in India initiative with an aim to boost the manufacturing sector of Indian economy, is expected to increase the purchasing power of an average Indian consumer, which would further boost demand, and hence *spur*[15] development, in addition to benefiting investors. The Digital India initiative, focuses on three core components: creation of digital infrastructure, delivering services digitally and increasing the digital literacy.

Currently, the manufacturing sector in India contributes over 15 per cent to the GDP. The Government of India, under the Make in India initiative, is trying to give a boost to the contribution made by the manufacturing sector and aims to take it up to 25 per cent of the GDP. The Government of India has launched a digital employment exchange which will allow the industrial enterprises to find suitable workers and the job-seekers to find employment.

Under its Digital India vision, the government of India has launched Kendriya Vidyalaya Sangthan's (KVS) e-initiative 'KV ShaalaDarpan' aimed at providing information about students electronically on a single platform; and has announced that all the major tourist spots like Sarnath, Bodhgaya and Taj Mahal will have a Wi-Fi facility. Free Wi-Fi service at Varanasi ghats is already under way.

The Union Cabinet, chaired by the Prime Minister Mr Narendra Modi, has given its approval to enter into a MoU* for strengthening cooperation in the field of Micro, Small and Medium Enterprises (MSMEs), between India and Sweden.

The Government of India has launched an initiative to create 100 smart cities as well as Atal Mission for *Rejuvenation*[16] and Urban Transformation (AMRUT) for 500 cities. Smart cities are satellite towns

*MoU — Memorandum of Understanding

of larger cities which will consist of modern infrastructure and will be digitally connected. The first 20 cities. led by Bhubaneshwar, have already been shortlisted to be developed in the first stage.

While we rejoice in our success, we have to be aware of the challenges too, in order to sustain our impressive progress. We need to promote exports of goods and services in an ever so highly competitive global market. This would erect a strong *edifice*[17] of sustained economic growth and lead to the creation of gainful employment. These were the aims for which the Government of India mooted the Special Economic Zones (SEZs) policy in April 2000. This policy was intended to make the SEZs an engine for economic growth.

If India aims at a 10 per cent growth, its policies should be long term rather than reactive. A soft approach to currency management may be accompanied by fiscal incentives for exporters as well as domestic producers which is ideally required for balanced economic growth. The prospects are encouraging but the hurdles have to be cleared and not allowed to hamper the growth of the country. We have miles to go before we realise the full potential of our people.

As per the Global Economic Prospects report by World Bank, India is leading the World Bank's growth chart for major economies. According to Ministry of Finance, Indian economy would continue to grow at 7 to 9 per cent and would double in size to US$ 4–5 trillion in a decade, becoming the third largest economy in absolute terms. Furthermore, initiatives like Make in India and Digital India will play a *vital*[18] role in driving the Indian economy.

Aid to Vocabulary

1. *Dynamic* — forceful and having a lot of energy
2. *Transforming* — changing the appearance of something completely
3. *Self-reliant* — relying on self for all needs
4. *Evolved* — developed naturally and gradually
5. *Bypassed* — went around or avoided
6. *Robust* — strongly built
7. *Trajectory* — path of object developing under given forces
8. *Vigorous* — strong and active, forceful
9. *Resurgence* — rising or arising again
10. *Benign* — favourable or of a mild type or character
11. *Novel* — of new kind or nature
12. *steep* — sudden and very high
13. *Mergers* — combining of two things, especially companies, into one
14. *Acquisitions* — the act of acquiring or gaining possession
15. *Spur* — to encourage, stimulate something

16. *Rejuvenation* — restoration to an original or new state
17. *Edifice* — a building, especially a large imposing one
18. *Vital* — essential or important

POINTS TO REMEMBER

1. The USAID now describes India as a "transforming" rather than a "developing" country.
2. In the pre-British period, the Indian economy was self-reliant.
3. The British East India Company ruled over India from 1757 to 1858.
4. In 1905, the Swadeshi Movement encouraged the growth of Indian industries.
5. Mixed economy is characterised by the co-existence of the private and the public sectors.
6. Indian economy grew at 7.3 per cent in 2014-15 due to improvement in the performance of services as well as manufacturing sectors.
7. As per a report by the World Bank, India is set to emerge as the world's fastest-growing major economy ahead of China.
8. Numerous foreign companies are setting up their facilities in India on account of various government initiatives like Make in India and Digital India.
9. Currently, manufacturing sector contributes 15 per cent of the GDP. The Government aims at increasing its share up to 25 per cent of GDP.
10. The IMF forecasted India to grow at the rate of 7.5 per cent in 2016.

KNOW THE ECONOMIST

ADAM SMITH (1723-1790)

The Scotch economist and moral philosopher Adam Smith believed that in a laissez-faire economy the impulse of self-interest would work towards the public welfare. Smith's central notion in his work 'The Theory of Moral Sentiments' is that moral principles have social feeling or sympathy as their basis. Sympathy is a common or analogous feeling that an individual may have to the affections or feelings of another person. Adam Smith is regarded by most people as the father of economics due to his vision of capitalism as an economic system that makes everyone better off.

Adam Smith was born on June 5, 1723, at Kirkcaldy. In 1751, Smith became professor of logic at the University of Glasgow and the following year, professor of moral philosophy. Eight years later he published 'The Theory of Moral Sentiments', which was on human nature. In 1764, Smith resigned from his professorship to take up duties as a travelling tutor for the young Duke of Buccleuch and his brother. Carrying out this responsibility, he spent two years on the continent. Returning to Kirkcaldy in 1767, he spent much of the next nine years there and in London, working on 'The Wealth of Nations'. This work contained, among other things, Smith's famous exposition of the 'invisible hand' of competition as guiding an economic system based on individual self-interest. Smith then settled in Kirkcaldy with his mother. He continued to work on The Wealth of Nations, which was finally published in 1776. Smith assumes that if each person pursues his own interest, the general welfare of all, will be fostered. He objects to governmental control, although he acknowledges that some restrictions are required. He died in Edinburgh on July 17, 1790 after a painful illness. On his deathbed he demanded that most of his manuscript writings be destroyed. He had apparently devoted a considerable part of his income to numerous secret acts of charity.

Essay 92

ECONOMIC LIBERALISATION IN INDIA

SYNOPSIS

The process of liberalisation of the Indian economy began in true spirit in July-August 1991. Plans were formulated for effective economic development. Rapid economic growth gave rise to economic disparities. The economic liberalisation was aimed at augmenting exports. It linked imports with the availability of foreign exchange at market rate. It was meant to boost economic development. But it triggered an artificial share market boom and poor quality goods dampened the objectives of the policy. The new EXIM policy was formulated to accelerate India's economy towards becoming a global economic force. The development of the indigenous market, technology and infrastructure should be undertaken.

The development process in India till the beginning of 1990s was dominated by the public sector. The government had decided that all sectors of the economy should move strictly in accordance with the programmes and targets laid down in the Five-Year Plans. These plans imposed many physical controls, such as licences, quotas, permits, etc., on the private sector industries and foreign trade. Unfortunately, these policies did not produce the desired results. Public sector bred inefficiency and heaped huge losses on the government. Restrictions on foreign trade resulted in perpetual deficits in the balance of payments. Inflow of foreign capital reduced to a trickle. All these factors were responsible for the low growth of our economy.

The process of economic liberalisation was initiated in India way back in 1977-78 with the liberalisation of imports. Though it was carried on through the 1980s, the country moved towards liberal trade policy in true spirit only in July-August 1991. India ran out of foreign exchange in 1991, and was forced to mortgage its gold reserves. Structural change became imperative. 1991 was truly a turning point for the Indian economy, when P.V. Narasimha Rao became the Prime Minister and inducted Dr. Manmohan Singh as Finance Minister and together they engineered economic reforms. The government announced a series of packages that initiated reforms in trade, finance and industrial sectors. It marked the end of the protectionist attitude hitherto pursued by the government towards *indigenous*[1] industries. According to economist Rajesh Mehta, "While the objectives of self-reliance and self-sufficiency influenced the trade policy formulation in 1950s and 1960s, factors like export-led growth, improvement of efficiency and competitiveness of Indian industries prevailed upon the trade policy-making during the late 1970s and the early 1980s. The current trade policy reforms, on the other hand, seem to have been guided mainly by the concerns over globalisation of the Indian economy, improving the competitiveness of its industry and adverse balance of payments situation."

The economic liberalisation of the country incorporated in the trade policy, aimed at *augmenting*[2] exports of the country. Prior to introduction of the reforms, imports and exports were carried out by giving them a strong market orientation. Except in 1972-73 and 1976-77, foreign trade in India witnessed heavy trade deficit. The new policy was formulated to make the imports dependent upon the availability of the foreign exchange generated through exports. Though the country took loans from the International Monetary Fund (IMF) and the World Bank to tide over the balance of payment crisis, the expansion of exports was considered to be a durable solution against the suppression of imports. Apart from working towards the increase of the existing exports, the government identified new areas of exports. Export of agro-based products was encouraged, which helped generate employment as well as valuable foreign exchange. The new policy also identified the service industries, pertaining to architecture, consultancy, education and the medical services, as the prospective zones for foreign exchange generation. The devaluation of the rupee in July 1991 was undertaken to boost exports. The big change, which stood out, was the virtual abolition of industrial licensing and MRTP* clearance. Import duties which once exceeded 200% were gradually brought down to 10% over the next 15 years. Income and corporate tax rates came down steadily as did excise duties. Capital market reforms produced a booming stock market and resulted in substantial inflow of foreign portfolio investment, and India for the first time moved to a dual-exchange rate system and later to a market-determined exchange rate system.

The main components of the New Economic Policy are: reforms in industrial policy, reforms in trade policy, reforms in fiscal policy and financial sector reforms. This policy is set to make the economy more efficient, competitive and global in character.

The new policy linked imports with, and limited it to, the availability of foreign exchange at market rates. The changes in the foreign trade and exchange rate regime had helped to strengthen the balance of payments.

*MRTP — Monopolies and Restrictive Trade Practices

Provisions were made to curtail imports of non-essential items like cereals and cereal preparations. The new policy aimed at the production of import-substitutes of certain commodities like pulses and edible oils. During the pre-reforms period, the trade policy had several categories of importers, import licences and alternative ways of importing. The policy led to the elimination of a substantial volume of import licensing. With the passage of time, most of these industries have also been delicensed. As of now, licensing is compulsory for only five industries. These are alcohol and cigarettes; hazardous chemicals; electronics; aerospace and defence equipment; and industrial explosives. All industries, except for a short list of 18 industries, were permitted to establish, expand, renovate or set up new units without acquiring a licence for this purpose. Only essential commodities remain distributed through public sector undertakings, like petroleum and allied products by the Indian Oil Corporation. The move had been planned to end the *red-tapism*[3] prevalent in Indian bureaucracy. Actually, the New Economic Policy has tried to free the economy of the shackles of the licence-permit-quota Raj. The all-pervasive State that controlled most of the economic space and restricted free entrepreneurial play, suddenly assumed the role of a facilitator to steadily withdraw from the running of businesses.

The New Industrial Policy announced in July 1991, started the process of full scale liberalisation and intensified the process of integration of the Indian economy with the global economy. New sectors such as mining, banking, telecommunications, highways construction and management were thrown open to private, including foreign-owned, companies. Public Sector Undertakings (PSUs) banks have had to compete with the new breed of market-savvy private banks. The liberal industrial policy was meant to boost economic development. The quantitative restrictions on imports were reduced, and import duties on capital goods were brought down. The government also abolished subsidies in various sectors, allowed a partial tax exemption on export profits, removed certain roadblocks for foreign trading companies and liberalised interest rates.

Liberalisation brought, in its wake, dollops of opportunities for the entrepreneurial class. Scrapping of licensing and other policies opened up new vistas of opportunity for businesses. On the other hand, these developments posed a big challenge for traditional business houses. Developing a mindset of free competition was not easy after being under state control and licensing for decades. A vibrant stock market, however, created robust fund-raising opportunities for entrepreneurs.

The 1990s also witnessed the rise of India's software power in the form of IT and ITES* companies. The government played the role of a great facilitator by creating the right infrastructure in the form of software parks in addition to facilitating rapid expansion of technical education infrastructure.

Foreign Trade Policy of India 2015-20 (FTP 2015-20) aims at supporting manufacturers and service sectors with special emphasis on improving ease of doing business. This five year foreign trade policy introduces new schemes for exporters of India called, Merchandise Exports from India Scheme (MEIS) and Service Exports from India Scheme (SEIS). Special focus on trade facilitation also is one of the features of Foreign Trade Policy of India 2015-20.

Other Salient Features include, *Duty Credit Scrips*[4] to be freely transferable and usable for payment of custom duty, excise duty and service tax; boost to "MAKE IN INDIA"; reduced Export *Obligation*[5] (EO) for domestic procurement under Export Promotion Capital Goods(EPCG) scheme; higher level of rewards under MEIS for export items with high domestic content and value addition; online filing of documents/ applications and paperless trade in 24 × 7 environment; online inter-ministerial *consultations*[6]; simplification of procedures/ processes, digitisation and *e-Governance*[7]; forthcoming e-Governance Initiatives; new initiatives for Export Oriented Units (EOUs), Electronic Hardware Technology Parks (EHTPs) and Software Technology Parks (STPs); facilitating & encouraging export of dual use items, namely Special Chemicals, Organisms, Material, Equipment and Technologies (SCOMET) *e-Commerce*[8] exports; *Duty Exemption*[9]; additional ports allowed for export and import; Duty Free Tariff Preference (DFTP) Scheme; quality complaints and trade disputes; Vishakhapatnam and Bhimavaram added as Towns of Export Excellence.

The combined effect of all these efforts is likely to result in achieving the desired target in addition to creating favourable conditions for the development of the Indian economy in the world market. But the indigenous sector must be supported properly by the government so that it does not crumble under the pressure of competition from the multinational corporations (MNCs). The government must develop the infrastructure of the country and it must root out corruption from the bureaucracy so that the Indian economy can attain new heights. While the economic liberalisation has helped the upper and middle classes of India, the rural poor are yet to reap any benefit. The government should remain sensitive to the adverse impact of the neoliberal policies on the poor. Social security measures should not be abolished arbitrarily in the pursuit of higher economic growth.

---

*ITES — IT Enabled Services

Economic liberalisation, which seeks to *dismantle*[10] unnecessary regulations, controls and restrictions prevailing in various sectors of economic activity, continues to remain a subject of discussion and controversy. while some believe it to be a step in the right direction, others view it as an unnecessary interference by the IMF, the World Bank and the capitalist economies.

Aid to Vocabulary

1. *Indigenous* — native, local
2. *Augmenting* — increasing
3. *Red-tapism* — the state of following rigid or excessive routines and procedures causing delay or inaction
4. *Duty Credit Scrips* — an important export promotion incentive allowing holder to import by not paying a specified amount in import duties
5. *Obligation* — a duty or commitment
6. *Consultations* — the process of formally discussing
7. *e-Governance* — government process re-engineering using IT
8. *e-Commerce* — trading of goods and services using computer network
9. *Duty Exemption* — a scheme enabling duty free imports of inputs required for export production
10. *Dismantle* — to pull down a structure, organisation or system gradually

Points to Remember

1. Economic liberalisation was introduced in July-August 1991.
2. Economic liberalisation aimed at augmenting exports.
3. The New Economic Policy aimed to make the economy more efficient, competitive and global in character.
4. It linked imports with, and limited it to, the availability of foreign exchange at market rates.
5. The New Industrial Policy announced in July 1991 started the process of full scale liberalisation and intensified the process of integration of India with the global economy.
6. The EXIM Policy or Foreign Trade Policy of India 2015-20 aims at supporting manufacturers and service sectors with special emphasis to improve ease of doing business.
7. The formulation of the new EXIM policy also aims to accelerate India's economy towards becoming a global economic force.
8. Economic liberalisation has helped the upper and middle classes of India, but not the rural poor.
9. The New Economic Policy continues to be a subject of discussion and controversy.

Essay
93

PLANNING IN INDIA: A STORY OF SUCCESS OR FAILURE?

SYNOPSIS

Proper economic planning is very essential for the overall progress and prosperity of our country. Indian economy has made reasonably good progress under the Five-Year Plans. India has completed eleven Five-Year Plans and some intervening annual plans. These Plans have long-term as well as short-term objectives. The Eleventh Plan achieved a growth rate of 8 percent vis-a-vis the target growth rate of 9 percent. The Twelfth Plan in an attempt to achieve a 'faster, sustainable, and more inclusive growth' has targeted a growth rate of 8 percent over the five year period starting from 2012 to 2017. Now greater importance is being given to market mechanism, international trade and foreign investment with the implementation of the New Economic Policy of 1991. Indian economy has started moving steadily on the growth path. But the problems of poverty, unemployment, inequalities and defective social justice have yet to be resolved. Planning must be devised according to the emerging economic issues and problems.

Planning means formulation and implementation of a comprehensive programme of action to achieve certain pre-determined objectives within a given time period. The planning process involves making certain economic decisions regarding the goals to be attained and targets to be achieved within a given time period. Economic planning means utilisation of the country's resources for the developmental activities in accordance with national priorities. In a developing country like India, proper planning for the country's overall progress and prosperity, assumes great importance. Planning in India derives its objectives and spirit from the Directive Principles of State Policy *enshrined*[1] in the Constitution. The responsibility of formulating the national plans, after taking an overall view of the needs and resources of the country, and making assessments of the performance of these plans, lies with the Planning Commission.

The Planning Commission was set up in 1950 as a follow-up of a resolution taken by the Government of India. The Planning Commission formulated plans for medium-term developments which are called the Five-Year Plans. It also formed plans for long-term development (15 years or so) which are called Perspective Plans. Within the Five-year Plan, it drew Annual Plans for each year of the Five-Year Plan. The Planning

Commission was purely an advisory body. It only made the plans and advised the government on various economic policies that needed to be adopted for the achievement of the planned targets. The Planning Commission also made an assessment of the progress made during the plans. On January 1, 2015, the 65-year-old Planning Commission was replaced with a new body called *NITI* (National Institution for Transforming India) *Aayog* (Commission) that is mandated to provide "governments at the Central and state levels with relevant strategic and technical advice across the *spectrum*[2] of key elements of policy".

The Prime Minister will be the Chairperson of the *NITI Aayog* whose Governing Council will comprise all Chief Ministers and Lt. Governors (of UTs) in an exercise *envisaged*[3] by the Centre to involve states in working out and pushing the national development agenda. The key objective of the *Aayog* is to foster cooperative *federalism*[4]. Indeed, it is the states where reforms take root and have the *spillover effect*[5]. Every Five-Year Plan is conceived with high expectations, with the hope of avoiding past mistakes, and to implement new ideas in order to build a more prosperous India.

India, by now, has undergone about six decades of planned economic development. It has already completed eleven Five-Year Plans and has also run a number of intervening Annual Plans. The normal sequence of Five-Year Plans was interrupted in 1966 due to *drought*[6] conditions and the dislocation caused by the Indo-Pak war in 1965, the Fourth Plan was postponed to April, 1969. During 1966–69, three Annual Plans were launched while the regular Five-Year Plan was suspended. This period, called 'Plan Holiday', marks the discontinuity of Five-Year Plans after fifteen years of continual planned economic development under the first three Five-Year Plans. This discontinuity raised questions with regard to the *efficacy*[7] of planned development in India.

The Sixth Five-Year Plan which was to start in 1979, was postponed due to the fall of the Janata Government and the return of the Congress to power. The Sixth Five-Year Plan was, therefore launched in April, 1980. The gap year of 1979–80 was filled by an Annual Plan. Again, due to the electoral defeat of the congress government in late 1989, the Eighth Plan, scheduled to have been launched in April, 1990 was postponed to April, 1992 and the period of 1990–92 was filled by two Annual Plans. Thereafter, the Five Year Plans have had a smooth run with the Twelfth Plan (2012-2017) currently under way.

India struggles with the issues of low income, inequality, poverty, unemployment, etc., and eradication of these problems may take a very long time. These may be called the long term goals of development plans. There are also problems which may crop up from time to time during the course of development. price rise, inflation, food storage, etc., are some such problems. Tackling these problems may be listed as short-term objectives of some plans. In case of India's development plans, while short-term objectives have varied from one plan to another, the long-term objectives have continued to remain common to all the plans. The basic objectives of planning in India are to achieve a high rate of growth of GDP and national income, improve the standard of living, ensure sustainability of growth, modernise agriculture and industry, promote social justice and regional balance, alleviate poverty, reduce the rate of growth of population, stabilise prices, etc. All these objectives are sought to be achieved through democratic policy framework.

With the implementation of the New Economic Policy in July, 1991, the role of planning and state participation in the development process has undergone a quantitative as well as qualitative change. In the new development strategy, the Five-Year Plan has become merely indicative in nature wherein the indicated targets are to be achieved through largely private initiative and market forces. Now, greater importance is being given to market mechanism, international trade and foreign investment.

The Indian economy has made reasonably good progress under the Five-Year Plans. An economy which had been stagnating in the pre-Independence era, started moving steadily on the growth path. The growth rate between 1951 to 1981 was only around 3.5 per cent. The Tenth Plan recorded an annual growth rate of 7.7 per cent. The focus of the Five-Year Plans is still on growth with equity and social justice.

High and *sustainable*[8] growth rate and inclusive growth which included poverty reduction, unemployment removal and social justice were the major objectives of the Eleventh Five-Year Plan, which aimed at achieving an average annual growth rate of 9 per cent. However, due to worldwide economic recession, which affected the Indian economy as well, the growth rate of 9 per cent could not be maintainable. The anticipated figure of 8.2 per cent towards the end of the period matched the estimated growth. The nation saved and invested nearly one-third of its income as against a less than 10 per cent share in 1951.

The Twelfth Five-Year Plan (2012-17) is expected to be different from all the earlier plans. This is basically because of the differences in the economic environment in which the plan has to be operationalised. The

Draft Approach to the 12th Five-Year Plan (2012-2017), approved by the National Development Council showcased the theme "faster, sustainable and more *inclusive*[9] growth". It proposed a growth target of 8 percent. Considering the uncertainties in the global economy, and challenges in the domestic economy, achieving the growth rate of 9 percent may not be feasible unless difficult decisions are taken. Some other major targets of the Twelfth Plan are: Increasing green cover by one million hectare every year; adding 30,000 MW of renewable energy generation capacity in the Plan period; reducing emission intensity of the GDP in line with the target of 20-25 reduction by 2020 over 2005 levels; raising agriculture output to 4 per cent for the full Plan; manufacturing sector growth to 10 per cent for the full Plan; and adding over 88,000 MW of power generation capacity in the plan period. It also wants all the states to set higher targets of growth than what was achieved in the 11th Five-Year Plan.

The process of planned economic development in India brought in a lot of good things for the people and the country. But the plans have left many unfulfilled promises and many weak spots in our economy as well. The problems of poverty, unemployment, inequalities and social justice have not been solved yet. Quality of life, though better, is still low as compared to that of developed countries.

Economic planning in India cannot be described either as a great success or as all-round dismal failure. The country owes its development to planning. The gigantic irrigation, industrial and infrastructural projects bear a testimony to the vision and efforts of the policy makers. Our country owes its socio-economic development to the Plans and it also has a lot to learn from their mistakes and failures. Our economic planning has not been an unmixed blessing. It has a lot of things on its credit as well as debit sides. We can overlook neither our shortcomings nor the challenges that lie ahead of us. Actually some of our Plans were dictated by the ideological considerations and political motives rather than by their economic value and development potential. Economic strategy is not a static concept but a dynamic one. With the change of time, economic planning should be changed accordingly to face the challenges of the emerging economic issues and problems. The policies of our planning are aimed at making India a self-reliant and strong nation and establishing an *egalitarian*[10] society, where inequalities of income and wealth are minimised, where all regions grow in tandem and where benefits of growth *percolate*[11] to the poorest of the poor.

Aid to Vocabulary

1. *Enshrined* — stated in an important document
2. *Spectrum* — a broad range of similar things or qualities
3. *Envisaged* — formed a mental image of something that is not present
4. *Federalism* — a system of government in which power is divided between the Central authority and the constituent political units
5. *Spillover effect* — a secondary effect following a primary event
6. *Drought* — long spell of dry weather
7. *Efficacy* — the power to produce the desired result
8. *Sustainable* — which conserves an ecological balance by avoiding depletion of natural resources
9. *Inclusive* — including the limits specified
10. *Egalitarian* — holding the principles of equal rights for all
11. *Percolate* — filter, especially through small holes

Points to Remember

1. Proper planning is very essential for the overall progress and prosperity of our country.
2. 65-year old Planning Commission has been replaced with a new body called *NITI* Aayog.
3. *NITI* Aayog will ensure a genuine and continuing partnership of the Centre and states in the planning process.
4. India has completed eleven Five-Year Plans and some intervening Annual Plans.
5. In our country, planning has long-term as well as short-term objectives.
6. The Twelfth Five-Year Plan (2012-17) aims at "faster, sustainable and more inclusive growth". It proposes a growth target of 8 per cent.
7. The objectives of planning are sought to be achieved through democratic policy framework.
8. With the implementation of the New Economic Policy, planning has undergone a quantitative as well as qualitative change.
9. Indian economy has made reasonably good progress under the Five-Year Plans.
10. The problems of poverty, unemployment, inequalities and social justice have not been fully resolved yet.
11. Economic planning must be changed according to the emerging economic issues and problems.

Essay 94

THE EMERGENCE OF THE SERVICE SECTOR IN INDIA

SYNOPSIS

With economic development, the share of agriculture in GDP declines and that of industry and service sector rises. The service sector becomes the largest contributor to the GDP. Various sectors like Trade, Hotel, Railways, etc., combine together to constitute the service industry. According to the Economic Survey 2014-15, India's service sector remains the major driver of economic growth contributing 72.4% of GDP growth in 2014-15. Service-sector growth has increased from 8.0% in 2012-13 to 9.1% in 2013-14 and further to 10.6% in 2014-15. The service sector can be categorised into three segments, viz., consumer services, producer's services and government services. The service sector in India has also witnessed a remarkable rise in its share of the global market apart from the Indian market.

The process of economic development is *accompanied*[1] by structural changes in the economy. With economic development, the dominance of agriculture and primary sector declines and that of industrial and service sectors rises in national income. The service sector then gradually picks up and becomes the largest contributor to the GDP (Gross Domestic Product). In India, there has been a marked increase in the share of service sector in GDP with economic development, while the share of agriculture declined substantially and the industrial sector remained more or less *stagnant*[2].

The service or 'tertiary sector' of the economy covers a wide gamut of activities like trading, banking and finance, infotainment, real estate, transportation, security, management and technical consultancy among several others. The various sectors that combine together to constitute the service industry in India are: Trade, Hotels and Restaurants, Railways, Other modes of transport and storage, Communication (Post and Telecom), Banking, Insurance, Real Estate, Business Services, Public Administration, Personal Services, Community Services, etc.

In the 1950s, India launched its programme of planned economic development. At that time, the country's economy was dominated by the agricultural sector which itself was backward and primitive in nature. In the first decade of development, agriculture contributed more than half the share of the national income, while industry provided for less than one-sixth share. During the following two decades, i.e., 1960-61 to 1979-80, there was a slow and gradual improvement in the service sector's share in the national income. It increased to over 34 per cent during the decade 1970-71 to 1979-80. During the last decade of the twentieth century, viz., 1989-90 to 1999-2000, the average share of the service sector was over 44 per cent, while the share of the industry sector was 27 per cent. Unlike many other developing countries, India showed resilience to the global economic crisis of 2008 on the back of one of the main drivers, i.e., the service sector. It accounted for about 88 per cent of the growth rate in real GDP in 2008-09, even as agriculture and industry recorded a steep decline in growth. As per the Advance Estimates (AE), growth of the services sector accelerated further mainly due to growth acceleration in financial, real estate, professional services, public administration, defence, and other services. There was also good growth in trade, hotels, transport, communication, and related services.

The factors contributing to rapid growth of the service sector are: rapid industrial growth that has led to larger demand for trade, transport, storage, etc; growth of financial services due to liberalisation and greater private participation; private sector entry into infrastructural area; huge external demand for India's software services; increase in general services due to expanding incomes; and expansion and increased expenditure on public administration and defence services.

For a meaningful analysis of the service sector's growth, services can be categorised into three segments, viz., consumer services, producer's services and government services.

The consumer services include hotels, restaurants, domestic services, etc. This segment has grown under the impact of increase in income levels. Growth in producer's services is a consequence of rapid growth in manufacturing industry and larger export demand for banking, finance, insurance and software services. It has the largest share in the service sector. Government services include defence and public administration. This segment is an important factor in high growth rate of the service sector. The Seventh Pay Commission report has proposed a *substantial*[3] increase in salaries and allowances of the Central Government employees, while seeking to *streamline*[4] allowances, pension and medical insurance.

The service sector in India has remained the most vibrant sector in terms of contribution to national and state incomes, trade flows, FDI inflows, and employment. According to the Economic Survey 2015-16 tabled in Parliament on February 26, 2016, the service sector contributed almost 66.1% of its gross value added growth in 2015-16, becoming the important net foreign exchange earner and the most attractive sector for FDI (Foreign Direct Investment) inflows. As per the ILO (International Labour Organisation) report on 'Global Employment and Social Outlook : Trends 2015' job creation in the coming years will be mainly in the service sector. As per the 'World Economic Outlook', April 2016, by the IMF, India ranked 7th in terms of overall GDP at current prices in the year 2015, with US topping the list followed by China. Data for FY 2015 indicates that the increase in the FDI inflows was primarily driven by investments in infrastructure and service sector. Within Infrastructure, Oil & Gas, Mining and Telecom witnessed higher FDI inflows, whereas IT services and trading (wholesale, cash & carry) drove the services inflows.

According to Department of Industrial Policy and Promotion (DIPP), the total FDI investments India received in FY 2015-16 (April 2015-March 2016) was US$ 40 billion, indicating that government's effort to improve ease of doing business and relaxation in FDI norms is yielding results. Services sector attracted the highest FDI equity inflow of US$ 6.9 billion, followed by the computer hardware and software sector (US$ 5.9 billion).Healthy inflow of foreign investments into the country helped India's Balance of Payments (BoPs) situation and stabilised the value of rupee. FDI in India witnessed an increase of 29 per cent and reached US$ 40 billion during April 2015-March, 2016 as compared to US$ 30.93 billion in the same period April 2013-March 2014. India has also overtaken China as world's top foreign direct investment (FDI) destination with US$ 63 billion of FDI announced in 2015 including high-value project announcements across the coal, oil and natural gas, and renewable energy sectors.

The Government of India recognises the importance of promoting growth in the service sector and provides several incentives in a wide variety of sectors such as health care, tourism, education, engineering, communications, transportation, information technology, banking, finance and management, among others.

The Government of India has taken quite a few initiatives to boost the services sector. It is considering a two-rate structure for the Goods and Service Tax (GST), under which key services will be taxed at a lower rate compared to the standard rate, which will help to minimise the impact on consumers due to increase in service tax. The Government of India plans to take mobile network to nearly 10 per cent of Indian villages that are still unconnected. The Government of India has proposed to provide tax benefits for transactions made electronically through credit/debit cards, mobile wallets, net banking and other means, as part of a broader strategy to reduce use of cash and, thereby, constrain the parallel economy operating outside *legitimate*[7] financial system. The Reserve Bank of India (RBI) has allowed third-party white label automated teller machines (ATM) to accept international cards, including international prepaid cards, and has also allowed white label ATMs to tie up with any commercial bank for cash supply.

It is a healthy and encouraging sign that the global economic crisis could have only a marginal effect on the Indian economy. The better than expected performance of 'trade, hotels, transport and communication' as well as the strong showing of 'financing, insurance, real estate and business services' indicate *entrenched*[8] growth.

However, there is no room for *complacency*[9]. Inflation is a real risk and hardening commodity prices can hurt growth without adequate policy intervention. Therefore, 'Cautious optimism' is the principle that governs the state of Indian economy.

Aid to Vocabulary

1. *Accompanied* — go with, escort
2. *Stagnant* — motionless, having no current
3. *Substantial* — of real importance, of large size or amount
4. *Streamline* — make simple or more efficient or better organised
5. *Fragility* — quality of being delicate or vulnerable
6. *Corroborated* — conformed or supported
7. *Legitimate* — conforming to the law or to rules
8. *Entrenched* — placed (something) in a very strong position and cannot easily be changed
9. *Complacency* — smugness, self-satisfaction

Points to Remember

1. The process of economic development is accompanied by structural changes in the economy.
2. There are various sectors that combine together to constitute the service sector in India.
3. In the 1950s, India launched its programme of planned economic development. There was a slow and gradual improvement in the service sector's share in the national economy.
4. In spite of global economic crisis of 2008, the service sector, being one of the main drivers of growth, accounted for about 88 per cent of the growth rate in real GDP.

5. Many factors like rapid industrial growth and growth of financial services due to liberalisation, etc., contribute to rapid growth of the service sector.
6. India's service sector remains the major driver of economic growth contributing 66.1% of GDP growth in 2015-16.
7. For a meaningful analysis of the service sector's growth, services can be categorised into three segments, viz., consumer services, producer's services and government services.
8. Apart from the Indian market, the service sector of India has witnessed a remarkable rise in the global market also.
9. The government of India has taken initiatives to boost the service sector.

Essay
95

SPECIAL ECONOMIC ZONES

SYNOPSIS

A Special Economic Zone (SEZ) is a free trade enclave which has economic and labour laws more liberal than those in the rest of the country. It is not a new concept. Today, India hopes to replicate the Chinese success story of SEZs by creating its own brand of SEZs. There is a clear difference between Export Processing Zones (EPZs) and Special Economic Zones (SEZs). SEZs attract global manufacturing companies and Foreign Direct Investment (FDI). SEZs create lakhs of new jobs for both skilled and unskilled labour. The main disadvantage of SEZs is that it causes revenue loss to the government. Again, the problem of rehabilitation of the farmer is a significant challenge for the government. SEZs are responsible for environmental pollution. Besides all these disadvantages, SEZs can bring about a great deal of transformation in developing countries by implementing liberal market economy.

A Special Economic Zone (SEZ) is a designated free trade *enclave*[1] that is *deemed*[2] as a 'foreign territory' only for trade operations, duties and *tariffs*[3]. It has economic and labour laws more liberal than those in the rest of the country and hence has the capacity to attract foreign investments, help promote exports and create a level-playing field for domestic enterprises and manufacturers to compete in the global market. In March 2000, a scheme for setting up of SEZs in India was announced in the Export and Import (Exim) Policy. India passed the SEZ Act in February 2005. The SEZ Policy supported by the SEZ Act 2005 and SEZ Rules 2006 intends to make SEZs an engine for economic growth supported by quality infrastructure, and complemented by an attractive fiscal package, both at the central and state levels.

Special Economic Zone is not a new concept. Since the end of World War II, SEZs, Export Processing Zones (EPZs) and Free Trade Zones (FTZs) have been *bandied about*[4] as a solution for economic development in the developing countries. In 1980, a nondescript town Shenzhen, in the Guangdong province in Southern China, was designated Special Economic Zone (SEZ) by the authorities. Today, Shenzhen is a modern, sprawling metropolis with a population of more than 10.5 million and home to some elite global brands and Fortune 500 companies. China's other three highly successful SEZs are located at Zhuhai, Shantou and Xiamen. Today, India hopes to replicate the Chinese success story by creating its own brand of SEZs.

India has a long history of *dabbling in*[5] export promotion schemes. Asia's first EPZ was set up in Kandla in 1965. It was followed by the Santa Cruz EPZ in 1973. There were, in all, eight EPZs set up in the country, but there was not much to talk about their performance. These were eventually converted into SEZs.

While EPZs are just industrial estates, SEZs are industrial townships that provide supportive infrastructure such as housing, roads, ports and telecommunication. EPZs have little protection from *cumbersome*[6] procedures and paperwork while SEZs have easy clearances that reduce transaction costs and procedural hassles. Again, while EPZs enjoy no benefits in terms of relaxation in labour laws, the SEZ Act allows state governments to liberalise the labour laws in SEZs falling within their jurisdiction. The incentives and facilities offered to the units in SEZs for attracting investments into the SEZs, include, Duty free import/domestic procurement of goods for development, operation and maintenance of SEZ units; 100% Income Tax exemption on export income for SEZ units for first 5 years; 50% for next 5 years thereafter and 50% of the ploughed back export profit for next 5 years; Exemption from minimum alternate tax; External commercial borrowing by SEZ units upto US $ 500 million in a year without any maturity restriction through recognised banking channels; Exemption from Central Sales Tax; Exemption from Service Tax; Single window clearance for Central and state level approvals; Exemption from state sales tax and other levies as extended by the respective state governments; and Exemption from Service Tax (Section 7, 26 and Second Schedule of the SEZ Act).

The SEZs have been an issue of intense debate. Arguments have been advanced both for and against SEZs. If we consider the benefits of setting up SEZs, we can say that they are a boon. SEZs attract global manufacturing companies to set up their base as well as create world-class infrastructure, and thus eliminate the problems of attracting Foreign Direct Investment (FDI). Foreign investors are attracted towards India's low-cost labour and strong domestic market. But they are apprehensive about the poor conditions of roads, airports, and ports. SEZ developers must create necessary infrastructure to reassure foreign investors. Only then can SEZs attract foreign investment, technology and managerial talent.

Not only foreign companies, but also the big players in the private sector like Reliance, Tata, Infosys, Wipro, etc., participate actively in setting up as well as operating the SEZs.

In order to impart stability to the SEZ regime and to achieve generation of greater economic activity and employment through the establishment of SEZs, the Special Economic Zones Act, 2005 has been enacted in February 2006 supported by SEZ Rules, 2006.

Since the SEZ Act and Rules were notified in February 2006, formal approvals have been granted for setting up of 415 SEZs, of which 329 have been notified. As per report released on December 31, 2015, exports from SEZ in 2015-16 is ₹ 3,41,685 crore. Of the total employment of 15,56,537 persons in SEZs as a whole, 14,21,833 persons were in incremental employment generated. The total investment in SEZ is ₹ 3,73,445.83 crore.

The spin-off effects of SEZs, particularly the new generation ones, are creation of employment, development of infrastructure and additional economic activity in the hinterland. It makes units competitive through flexible labour laws. It also makes the balance of payment favourable for India by giving tremendous impetus to export. Thus, SEZs can earn valuable foreign exchange, with which the country can import modern technology, and machinery in various sectors including services, transportation, healthcare and heavy industries. It has also been proposed to convert the Agricultural Export Zones (AEZs) into SEZs. That way, the agricultural sector would benefit from concessions in export.

One of the most important advantages of an SEZ is that it creates lakhs of new jobs, both for skilled and unskilled labour. The Information Technology Parks, Computer Software as well as Hardware Parks create lots of job opportunities for professionals. Even during the economic meltdown of 2008-09, SEZs registered impressive growth in exports, besides investment and employment generation.

However, there are several disadvantages of setting up of the SEZs. In fact, the policy has received severe criticism from various quarters across many states; SEZs tend to result in significant revenue losses for governments. This is because the SEZ units get 100 per cent tax holiday for the first five years and 50 per cent tax break for five more years thereafter. But, sometimes, the benefits in terms of growth and increase in exports become greater than what is needed to compensate the revenue loss, if any.

The most important issue with SEZs is the acquisition of land for the purpose of establishing the SEZs. Since agriculture is the only sector in the country which has not been doing well for the last few years, the agricultural lands could potentially be converted into SEZs. However, in the current scenario, acquiring fertile agricultural land for setting up of industries only aggravates the problems of the farmers whose lands are acquired. They lose their livelihood for good. Sometimes, they are not offered adequate amount of compensation. On the other hand, it is not possible to absorb this unskilled labour in the new technologically advanced industries. The problem of *rehabilitation*[7] of the farmers becomes a major challenge for the government. The central as well as the state governments have been talking about rehabilitation of the uprooted families. Past experience, in cases of various projects, wherein people were promised adequate compensation and rehabilitation package, has not been positive.

The SEZs, which are the hubs of manufacturing units, are responsible for acute environmental pollution. The chemicals released from the SEZs pollute nearby water resources, creating shortage of clean water, and their emissions pollute the air of the surrounding areas. SEZs cause both air and water pollution. The spectre of such environmental hazards has become a reality in China. Thus, necessary steps should be taken to handle this problem associated with SEZs.

SEZs can bring about great *transformation*[8] in developing countries. This particular aspect can be a ground for implementation of liberal market economy. Considering the great success of SEZs in China, one can expect that the SEZs model will be successful in India, too. But before implementing it, Government of India should take the necessary corrective steps to *mitigate*[9] the sufferings of, and adequately compensate, farmers whose lands may be acquired. The tragedies of Nandigram (West Bengal) and Dantewada (Chhattisgarh), where exploited farmers revolted are examples of a developmental process gone horribly wrong. Therefore, there is a need for an improved vision of development.

Aid to Vocabulary

1. *Enclave* — a portion of territory
2. *Deemed* — regarded
3. *Tariffs* — a table of fixed charges
4. *Bandied about* — discussed casually or informally
5. *Dabbling in* — taking superficial interest in
6. *Cumbersome* — bulky, large, long or slow and hence inconvenient
7. *Rehabilitation* — restoration to effectiveness or normal life by training, etc.

8. *Transformation* — a thorough or dramatic change in the form, character, etc.
9. *Mitigate* — make less severe, harmful, etc.

Points to Remember

1. Special Economic Zone is a free trade enclave with more liberal laws.
2. India hopes to replicate the Chinese success story of SEZs.
3. There is a clear difference between EPZs and SEZs.
4. SEZs attract global manufacturing companies and foreign direct investment.
5. Not only foreign companies, but also big players in the domestic private sector participate in setting up of SEZs.
6. SEZs have both advantages and disadvantages.
7. SEZs can bring great transformation in the economy of developing countries.
8. For the implementation of SEZ model of development, the government must take necessary steps to compensate the farmers whose lands may be acquired.

EXPORTS FROM THE OPERATIONAL SEZS DURING THE LAST DECADE

Years	Exports		Growth over previous year
	Value in ₹ crores	Billion USD	
2005-2006	22,840	5.08	-
2006-2007	34,615	7.69	52.00%
2007-2008	66,638	14.81	93.00%
2008-2009	99,689	22.15	50.00%
2009-2010	2,20,711	49.05	121.00%
2010-2011	3,15,868	70.19	43.11%
2011-2012	3,64,478	81.00	15.39%
2012-2013	4,76,156	88.18	31.00%
2013-2014	4,94,077	82.35	4.00%

KNOW THE ECONOMIST

KARL MARX (1818-1883)

Karl Heinrich Marx, a revolutionary, sociologist, historian, and economist, was the author (with Fredrich Engels) of Manifest der Kommunistischen Partei (1848), commonly known as Communist Manifesto, the most celebrated pamphlet in the history of the socialist movement, as well as of its most important book, Das Kapital. These and other writings by Marx and Engels form the basis of the body of thought and belief known as Marxism.

Karl Marx was born on May 5, 1818 in Trier, Prussia (now in Germany), of Jewish parents, but later his father was converted to Protestantism. In 1841 Marx received a Ph.D. in Philosophy, and in 1843 got married to Jenny Von Westphallen and started to work as a journalist, but his paper was closed down because of his radical controversial articles on social conditions. Marx was first expelled from Germany and then from France, for expounding his revolutionary philosophy. Finally Marx settled in London with his family in 1849. The philosophy of Karl Marx has had the single, greatest influence on the political institutions of the twentieth century. Till the disintegration of the Soviet Union, the world was polarised into communist and capitalist blocs.

Marx studied very closely the functioning of the capitalist society in 19th century Europe and from it, he derived the conclusion that capitalism thrived on the exploitation of the poor workers, and also that seeds of destruction of capitalism were inherent in itself. He also concluded that communism was a natural outcome of capitalism, but today's capitalism does not justify Marx's belief that class conflict is essentially revolutionary in character and that structural changes are always the product of violent upheavals.

His major work Communist Manifesto, was published in 1848 in collaboration with Engels, in which he had advocated the violent overthrow of the capitalist social order and gave the famous call to the world's workers—"Workers of all countries unite". In 1867, Marx's epoch making work in social philosophy, the Das Kapital was published. Marx, the founder of the theory of Marxism had profoundly influenced western thought—sociological, political and economic. Marx's influence on contemporary sociological theory is growing and Marxist sociology has already become an established branch of the discipline.

Essay
96

INDIA'S FOREIGN TRADE

SYNOPSIS

The evolution of India's foreign trade can be traced back to its colonial past when exports exceeded imports and India had trade surplus. But the partition of India strained the balance of payments. Trade deficit in Five-Year Plans resulted in acute foreign exchange crisis and consequently, India had to devalue its currency. The composition of India's foreign trade is diverse, with exports comprising agro-based products, handicrafts, etc., and imports comprising of foodgrains, electrical and non-electrical equipments, etc. Except during 1972-73 and 1976-77, Indian imports have always exceeded its exports. Liberalisation of the Indian economy helped in the expansion of India's foreign trade.

Foreign trade, in general terms, can be defined as the trade among different countries. It refers to the exchange of goods and services between two countries. It is also known as 'international' trade. Since India was a British colony, the pattern of its foreign trade before 1947 was typically colonial. It served as a supplier of foodstuffs and raw materials to the industrialised nations particularly England and as an importer of manufactured goods. The volume of exports was high and imports took a backseat. This led to the exploitation of India as a country in two ways: the raw material from India was procured at low prices and finished goods were sold back at exorbitant prices. This practice also gave a severe blow to the indigenous Indian handicrafts.

Prior to independence, India's foreign trade was moulded to suit the *unilateral*[1] interests of the colonial rulers. But with the dawn of independence, the colonial pattern of trade was changed to suit the needs of a developing economy. During the early years of development, imports increased at a fast rate resulting in heavy trade deficit. In 1950-51, the Indian exports stood at ₹606 crore and imports at ₹608 crore. The excess of imports over exports was largely due to the shortage of food and basic raw materials like jute and cotton, which was a fallout of the Partition. Thereafter, import of heavy machinery and equipment was also undertaken to industrialise the country. Thus, the First Five-Year Plan (1951-56) witnessed trade deficit mainly due to the programmes of industrialisation which required import of capital goods. In the Second Five-Year Plan (1957-61), along with capital goods, foodgrains were also imported to meet the internal shortages. The trade deficit at the end of the Second Plan was ₹467 crore. During the Third Five-Year Plan period (1962-67), the increase in the volume of imports leading to trade deficit was mainly because of the additional defence needs following aggression by China and Pakistan, rapid industrialisation and extensive failure of crops. *Persistent*[2] adverse balance of trade since 1951 and consequent adverse balance of payment, acute shortage of foreign exchange, extensive borrowing from foreign countries and international institutions like International Monetary Fund (IMF), induced India to devalue the rupee. Devaluation was resorted to in order to reduce the volume of imports, boost exports and create a favourable balance of trade and balance of payment. Green revolution in the late 1960's, helped India become self-sufficient in foodgrain production. Export promotion was launched and import policies were restricted. As a result, for the first time since independence, favourable trade balance was achieved in 1972-73. However, in 1973-74, due to price *hike*[3] of petroleum products, steel and non-ferrous metals, fertilisers and newsprint in international market, imports created a trade deficit. But overall trade deficit during the Fourth Plan was of much lower magnitude as compared to the Second, the Third and the Annual Plans. In the Fifth Five-Year Plan (1974-79), exports exceeded imports.

Indian exports are broadly classified into four categories: (i) Agriculture and Allied products which include coffee, tea, oilcakes, tobacco, cashew, kernels, spices, sugar, raw cotton, rice, fish and fish preparations, meat and meat preparations, vegetable oils, fruits, vegetables and pulses; (ii) Ores and Minerals which include manganese ore, mica and iron-ore; (iii) Manufactured goods which include textiles and readymade garments, jute manufactures, leather and footwear, handicrafts including pearls and precious stones, chemicals, engineering goods, iron and steel; and (iv) Mineral Fuels and Lubricants. Over the years, exports have shown diversification and have been increasing.

Imports are made to meet the essential requirements of domestic consumption, investment, production and inputs for exports. Import in India consists of bulk and non-bulk imports. Bulk imports include petroleum, oil and lubricants (POL) and non-POL items like fertilisers, iron and steel; non-bulk imports include gems, pearls, electrical and non-electrical goods. The other principal imports consist of precious and semi-precious stones, machinery, project goods, medicinal and pharmaceutical products, organic and inorganic chemicals, coal, artificial resins, etc.

The Government of India has initiated a number of measures to 'open up' the foreign trade sector since July 1991. Rupee was devalued. To give further boost to exports, there was a substantial reduction in customs tariff rates, decentralisation of many items of trade was undertaken and the convertibility of the rupee, first on trade account and then for all current account transactions, was introduced. In 1993-94, tariff cuts and liberalisation boosted exports, and gradually a cut in the imports led to a decline in the trade deficit. India's trade increased from 15% during the 1980s to around 20% in 1995-98. To sustain a high growth rate in an increasingly competitive export market, Market Access Initiative (MAI) was launched in September 2001 to give more thrust for marketing our products in the global markets.

The global economic environment appears *poised*[4] for a change for the better with the recent sharp fall in the international prices of crude petroleum, which is expected to boost global aggregate demand, and the sharp recovery in the US economy in the face of gradual withdrawal from monetary accommodation. In the case of emerging market and developing economies (EMDEs), which continue to struggle with *tepid*[5] domestic demand and *headwinds*[6] from structural *impediments*[7], the IMF Update projected growth to moderate to 4.7 per cent in 2016.

India's total merchandise trade increased from US$ 467 billion in FY* 2010 to US $757 billion in FY 2015. Indian exports have increased at a CAGR (compound annual growth rate) of 11.6% taking its export to GDP ratio from 13.3% to 15.6% in the same period. In 2014, India ranked 19th in world merchandise export with its share at 1.7%. Indian Foreign Trade Policy 2015-2020 aims at increasing India's merchandise and service exports to US$ 900 billion by FY 2020.

The commodity composition of India's trade has undergone many changes since liberalisation and has been driven by trade policy,movements in international prices, and the changing pattern of domestic demand. Manufactured goods constitute the bulk of exports, followed by crude and petroleum products (including coal) with a 20 per cent share, and agriculture and *allied*[8] products.

Growth in exports of petroleum and agriculture and allied products; gems and jewellery; and electronic goods, continued to register a declining trend during 2014-15 (April-January), even as some sectors like transport equipment; machinery, chemicals and related products, textile and allied products; base metals and marine products and leather and leather manufactures registered positive growth in exports.

There has been significant market diversification in India's trade in recent years –a process that has helped in coping with the *sluggish*[9] global

*Financial Year

demand, which owes to a great extent to the weakness in the euro zone. Region-wise, India's export shares to Europe and America have declined over the years. Conversly, the shares of India's exports to Asia, Africa and LDC (Less Developed Countries) regions have increased sharply; of this, share of Asia region rose from 48% to 50% during this period.

The robust external-sector outcome of moderate trade and current account deficits, abundant financial flows, a build-up of foreign exchange reserves and broadly stable exchange rate movement points to a return to the path of strength and *resilience*[10] that was in evidence before the global financial crisis of 2008. The correction in the international prices of crude petroleum in the second half of the current fiscal has helped in the decontrol of diesel prices. The overall trade performance signalled an *opportune*[11] time for withdrawal of restrictions on gold imports. The resilience also owed in part to the trade diversification process. While trade and current account deficits are on even *keel*[12], the *copious*[13] financial inflows in excess of the financing requirement has helped shore up foreign exchange reserves. The global economic outlook remains somewhat uncertain but stable and likely to gain strength if lower global crude petroleum prices drive the demand recovery process in key emerging market economies.

Over the years, significant changes in the EXIM (Export Import) policy have helped to strengthen the export production base, remove procedural irritants besides focussing on quality and technological upgradation and improving competitiveness. The Exim Policy, 2009-14, aimed at arresting and reversing the declining trend of exports; doubling India's exports of goods and services by 2014; doubling India's share in global merchandise trade by 2020 - its long term aim; simplifying application procedure for availing various benefits; to encourage exports through a mix of measures including fiscal incentives, institutional changes, procedural rationalisation and efforts for enhancing market access across the world and diversification of export markets.

Foreign Trade Policy 2015-20 (FTP 2015-20) aims at supporting manufacturers and service sectors with special emphasis to improve ease of doing business. This five year foreign trade policy introduces new schemes for exporters of India called MEIS, (Merchandise Exports from India Scheme) and SEIS, (Service Exports from India Scheme). Special focus on trade facilitation is one of the key features of Foreign Trade Policy of India 2015-20.

Other Salient Features include, Duty Credit Scrips to be freely transferable and usable for payment of custom duty, excise duty and service tax; Boost to "MAKE IN INDIA"; Reduced Export Obligation (EO) for domestic *procurement*[14] under Export Promotion Capital Goods(EPCG) scheme; Higher level of rewards under MEIS for export items with high domestic content and value addition; Online filing of documents/applications and paperless trade in 24 × 7 environment; Simplification of procedures/ processes, digitisation and e-governance; New initiatives for Export Oriented Units (EOUs), Electronic Hardware Technology Park (EHTPs) and Software Technology Park (STPs); e-Commerce Exports; Duty Exemption; Additional Ports allowed for export and import; Duty Free Tariff Preference (DFTP) Scheme; Vishakhapatnam and Bhimavaram added as Towns of Export Excellence.

Thus, one can safely conclude that before Independence, the pattern of trade in India was largely colonial and agricultural in nature with bulk of foreign trade confined to Britain and other Commonwealth countries. But after Independence, there has been an impressive industrial development in the country and India's foreign trade has undergone a vast change. Various measures have been taken and policies have been drafted by the government to increase India's exports and all this has been seen as an encouraging sign for India's foreign trade.

Aid to Vocabulary

1. *Unilateral* — one-sided
2. *Persistent* — continuing without interruption
3. *Hike* — a sharp rise in prices, costs, etc.
4. *Poised* — in a state of balance or equilibrium
5. *Tepid* — showing little enthusiasm
6. *Headwinds* — a wind opposed to the course of a moving object
7. *Impediments* — hindrances or obstructions in doing something
8. *Allied* — of a similar nature or related
9. *Sluggish* — slow moving or inactive
10. *Resilience* — capacity to recover quickly from difficulties
11. *Opportune* — convenient or suitable for a particular occurrence
12. *Keel* — base
13. *Copious* — abundant in supply or quantity
14. *Procurement* — action of obtaining something

Points to Remember

1. Foreign trade refers to the exchange of goods and services between one country and another.
2. Since India was a British colony, the pattern of its foreign trade before 1947 was typically colonial. But after Independence, the colonial pattern of trade had to be changed to suit the needs of a developing economy.

3. The First Five-Year Plan (1951-56) witnessed trade deficit mainly due to the programmes of industrialisation which required import of capital goods.
4. Indian exports are broadly classified into four categories
   (i) Agriculture and allied products. (ii) Ores and minerals.
   (iii) Manufactured goods. (iv) Mineral fuels and lubricants.
5. India has trade relations with almost all the major trading blocks and all the geographical regions of the world.
6. Foreign Trade Policy 2015-2020, aims at increasing India's merchandise and service exports to US$ 900 billion by FY 2020.
7. Direction of exports is moving towards developing countries away from developed nations.

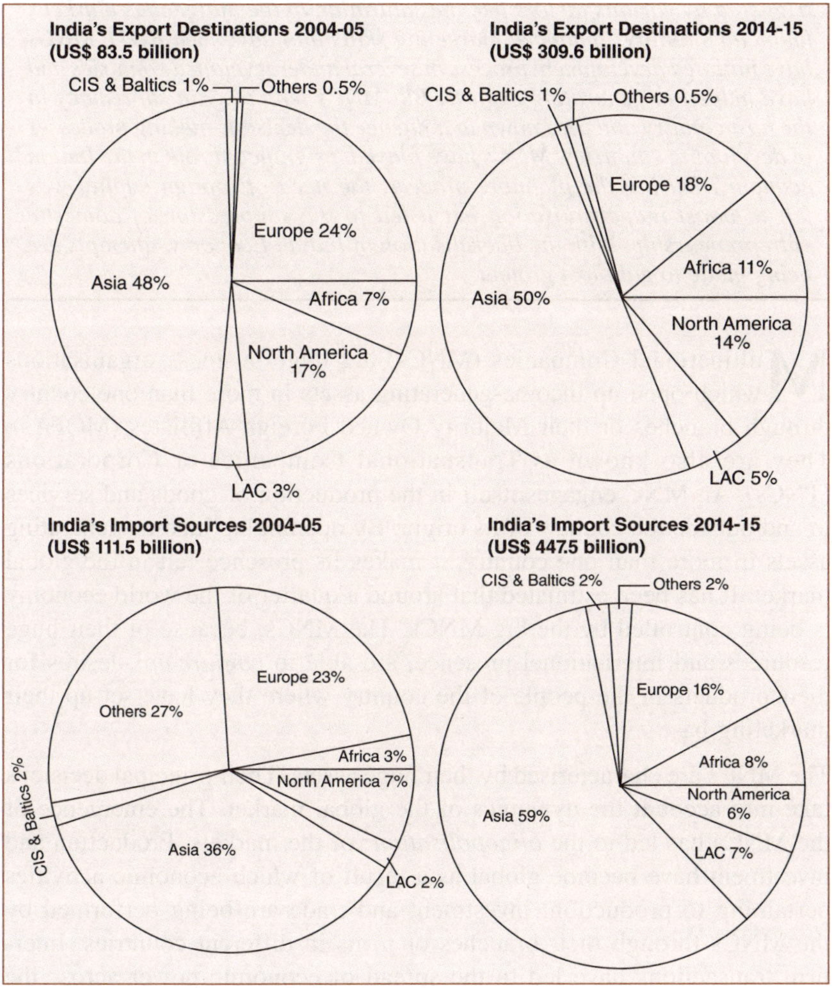

Source: Ministry of Commerce & Industry, Government of India

Essay 97

THE ROLE OF MULTINATIONAL COMPANIES

SYNOPSIS

MNCs are huge business organisations which open up income-generating assets in more than one country. These organisations engage in the production of goods and services in many countries, in and outside the country of their origin. These are characterised by their huge assets and their objective of profit maximisation. The expansion of the MNCs is triggered by various factors like the saturation of the indigenous markets, financial stability, enhanced marketing skills and advanced R&D. MNCs have initiated development process in several underdeveloped countries and have helped in generating exports. But MNCs tend to gain supremacy in the host country and are known to influence the decision-making processes in developing countries. MNCs have played a significant role in the Indian economy. During the planning process, the need of foreign capital was felt to boost industrialisation but it led to the suppression of domestic entrepreneurship. With the liberalisation of Indian Economy, attempts are being made to gain lost ground.

Multinational Companies (MNCs) are huge business organisations which open up income-generating assets in more than one country through branches or their Majority Owned Foreign Affiliates (MOFAs). They are also known as Transnational Companies or Corporations (TNCs). An MNC engages itself in the production of goods and services in and outside the country of its origin. By opening up income generating assets in more than one country, it makes its presence felt in the global market. It has been estimated that around a quarter of the world economy is being controlled by the big MNCs. The MNCs, because of their huge resources and international presence, are able to *conjure up*[1] desires for their products in the people of the country where they have set up their marketing base.

The MNCs are characterised by their huge assets. Their principal decisions take into account the dynamics of the global market. The emergence of the MNCs has led to the *oligopolisation*[2] of the markets. Production and investment have become global as a result of which economic activities pertaining to production, investment and trade are being performed by the MNCs through their branches or firms in different countries. Inter-firm transactions have led to the spread of economic power across the countries.

Initially, the development of the MNCs was effected by means of what has been termed as 'creeping *increment*[3]'. Slowly, but steadily, the MNCs established their *subsidiaries*[4] beyond their country of origin, in developed and under-developed countries. The MNCs also aid in the transfer of resources from the host country to the country where their operations are based. Resources transferred by MNCs include technical expertise, equipment, managerial and marketing skills, among others.

The reasons for the growth of multinational companies are manifold. Saturation of the indigenous markets for their products necessitated the MNCs to look out for additional alternatives. It triggered the need to expand the area of operations beyond the physical limitations of their country. Enhanced marketing skills helped them to study the various aspects required to operate in foreign countries. Through advertising and sales promotion skills, they were able to market their products which were not necessarily superior to the indigenous products. As they gained acceptance, they spread their net over different countries and made their presence felt. The Research and Development (R&D) departments of the MNCs worked to evolve new products or improve the existing products to cater to the tastes of the people in the countries of their operation.

The MNCs help to initiate development processes in several underdeveloped countries through the transfer of capital and technology. To establish a proper base in a foreign country, the MNCs invest in labour, raw materials, advertising and marketing; help in the development of human resources; generate further employment; and also help to transfer sophisticated western technologies to the underdeveloped countries. The technological expertise, advanced production skills and use of local labour in foreign shores facilitate transfer of technology to those countries. Through R&D, the MNCs develop products which are superior in all respects to those which are indigenously produced by the less developed host countries. This induces the indigenous industries to *brace up*[5] for competition and then to develop superior products themselves.

The operations of the multinationals cause several harmful effects impacting the host country. The primary objective of the MNCs is profit maximisation. They believe in developing an oligopoly and, therefore, indulge in unfair means to further their interests. They set up technology intensive branches of manufacturing to gain supremacy in the host country. Because of their huge capital reserves, they have the capacity to bear initial losses. But through advanced marketing skills, advertisement and promotions, they gain access and acceptance in the host countries and suppress domestic entrepreneurship. Because of their economic reserves and technical expertise, the MNCs are known to influence the decision-making processes in developing countries. The profits earned by the MNCs are diverted to the country of their origin or to expand their markets globally. Because of their international goodwill, the MNCs are able to establish themselves in new countries. Transfer of technology often accompanies 'transfer pricing', which is usually in the form of royalties, technical fees, management service fees, etc.

The Industrial Policy Regulation (IPR), 1948, had emphasised the need to carefully regulate foreign investment. The Five-Year Plans were broadly formulated keeping this principle in mind. The first phase from 1951-65, was marked by a liberal attitude towards foreign capital to boost industrialisation and promote, thereby, the development of the country. The second phase, which began from the mid-60's to late 70's was characterised by strict control over the area of operation of the foreign capital. The third phase, from late 70's to early 90's, saw the MNCs' participating in the domestic market through collaboration with Indian industries. These were the early signs of liberalisation of the Indian economy. The fourth phase began with the adoption of the economic liberalisation policy announced in July 1991. It was aimed at attracting a free flow of foreign investment.

The MNCs have been quite successful in India. In the post-liberalisation era, as the licence regime has more or less been abolished, the MNCs are thriving in India. They are present in almost every sector of the Indian economy, especially in the consumer durable market and automobiles. Automobile manufacturers like General Motors, Ford, Toyota and Hyundai are making good profits. Korean companies LG and Samsung have become market leaders in electronic goods. The softdrink market of India has almost been monopolised by US multinational Pepsi Co.

Control over the MNCs rests with the Ministry of Company Affairs, the Reserve Bank of India (RBI), the Ministry of Industrial Development and the Ministry of Finance. The Foreign Exchange Regulation Act (FERA) was enforced in January 1974 to regulate the operations of MNCs in India. The Foreign Exchange Management Bill was introduced in August 1998, to consolidate and amend the law relating to foreign exchange. The Bill was proposed to replace FERA. With FEMA (Foreign Exchange Management Act), the emphasis has been shifted from regulation of foreign exchange to its management. It also specifies that the RBI will be the sole administrator for the permissible capital account transactions. With the relaxation of foreign exchange controls and the move towards convertibility, the Indian economy is bound to recover lost ground. India has already marked its presence as one of the fastest growing economies of the world. It has been ranked among the top 3 attractive destinations for inbound investments. Since 1991, the regulatory environment in terms of foreign investment has been consistently eased to make it investor-friendly.

As of now, MNCs in India can increase foreign equity up to 51 percent by *remittances*[6] in foreign exchange in specified high priority areas. Subsequently, MNCs are free to own a majority share in equity in most products; borrow money or accept deposit without the permission of Reserve Bank of India; transfer shares from one non-resident to another disinvest equity at market rates on stock exchanges; go for 100 percent foreign equity through the automatic route in specified sectors; deal in immovable properties in India; carry on in India any activity of trading, commercial or industrial, except a very small negative list.

Thus, MNCs have been placed at par with Indian Companies and would not be subjected to any special restrictions under FERA.

Capital inflows from other countries, particularly of an investment nature, which add to domestic investment, have, therefore, been important. Equity inflows are more stable and bring in new management practices and technology together with the investment. To encourage Foreign Direct Investment (FDI) inflows, the policy has continued to be fine tuned and liberalised progressively allowing investment in more industries under the automatic route. In the new policy regime, all the activities have been put on an automatic route on a negative listing basis except for those that attract industrial licencing. Technology collaboration has also been brought under automatic route and royalty ceilings have been removed.

The FDI policy has been gradually simplified and rationalised and more sectors have been opened up for foreign investment. Some of the recent FDI decisions are: 100% in medical devices; 49% in insurance & sub-activities, the pension sector, and defence sector; 24% in foreign portfolio investment; beyond 49% on a case to case basis with the approval of Cabinet Committee on Security, 100% in white label ATM operations, and 100% in construction, operation and maintenance of specified activities of Railway sector. FDI policy on construction development sector has been liberalised by relaxing the norms pertaining to minimum area, minimum capitalisation and *repatriation*[7] of funds or exit from the project. To encourage investment in affordable housing, projects committing 30 percent of the total project cost for low cost affordable housing have been exempted from minimum area and capitalisation norms.

Government relaxed foreign investment rules in 15 sectors such as civil aviation, banking, defence, retail and news broadcasting and eased the process for foreign direct investment (FDI) approval, putting more sectors on the automatic route, introducing *fungibility*[8] between FDI and Foreign Institutional Investors (FII) and having a single reference document for all FDI related guidelines to boost investor confidence.

While 100 per cent foreign direct investment (FDI) has been allowed in DTH (direct-to-home), cable network and plantation crop, overseas investment limit in uplinking of news and current affairs, TV channels has been raised to 49 per cent from 26 per cent. The government relaxed conditions for FDI in single-brand retail and allowed 100 per cent FDI under automatic route in duty-free shops and Limited Liability Partnerships (LLP).

In order to harness its potential as an attractive FDI destination, the Government of India has taken steps for improving infrastructure. Introduction of Value Added Tax (VAT) from April 2005 is a major step towards addressing the need of uniform taxation. The regulatory framework is under periodical review and steps have been taken to rationalise and simplify, to a substantial extent, procedures dealing with FDI at the central level. Government is also making efforts to bring about such procedural simplification and transparency in the FDI framework at the state level.

India ranked at 130 among 189 nations in the World Bank's Doing Business 2016 study. According to Department of Industrial Policy and Promotion (DIPP), the total FDI investments India received in FY 2015-16 was US$ 40 billion, indicating government's effort to improve ease of doing business and relaxation in FDI norms is yielding results. According to World Economic Forum's Global Competitiveness Report 2015-16, India has jumped 16 places to rank 55 out of 140 countries. The Government of India has already embarked on an ambitious agenda to further improve India's Doing Business rank.

The World Bank released a state-wise Ease of Doing Business report for India, in 2015, according to which, Gujarat, Andhra Pradesh, Jharkhand, Chhattisgarh and Madhya Pradesh emerged as top 5 states in ease of doing business which is basically an assessment of business reforms sponsored by the Department of Industry Policy and Promotion (DIPP). In the 1970's, MNCs were characterised as objects of harm, not instruments for good. Today, they constitute a powerful force in the world economy. A recent study on the subject concluded that in today's world of global capitalism, foreign investments, i.e., multinational corporations are the only instrument that can reduce the inequalities among nations.

Aid to Vocabulary

1. *Conjure up* — evoke, bring into existence
2. *Oligopolisation* — ushering in the state of a market which is controlled by a few producers in relation to many buyers

3. *Increment* — rise, increase
4. *Subsidiaries* — companies controlled by another company by virtue of ownership of the controlling stock
5. *Brace up* — prepare for effort
6. *Remittances* — sum of money sent in payment or as a gift
7. *Repatriation* — process of sending foreign money back to one's own country
8. *Fungibility* — interchangeability

Points to Remember

1. MNCs are huge business organisations, which open up income-generating assets in more than one country.
2. These are characterised by:
   (a) huge assets; (b) maximisation of profits; and
   (c) oligopolisation of the markets.
3. Through advertising and sales promotion skills, MNCs expand their business.
4. MNCs help to initiate developmental process in underdeveloped countries.
5. The profits earned by the MNCs are diverted to expand their market globally.
6. India ranked at 130 among 189 nations in World Bank's Doing Business 2015 study.
7. As per World Economic Forum's Global Competitiveness Report 2015 -16, India has jumped 16 places in the global competitiveness ranking.
8. The Government of India aims to further improve India's Doing Business rank.
9. Today, MNCs constitute a powerful force in the world economy.

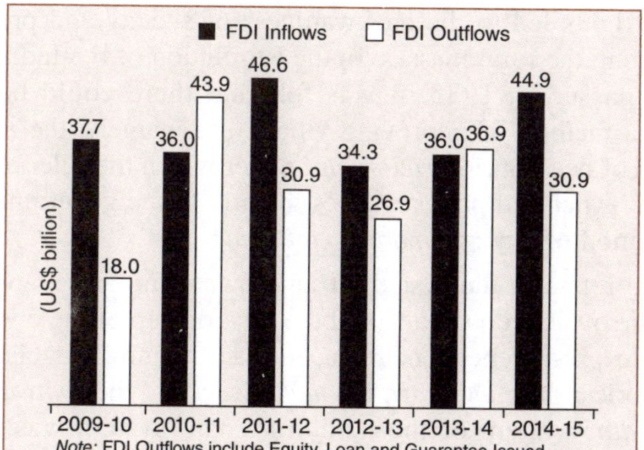

Note: FDI Outflows include Equity, Loan and Guarantee Issued

Source: Reserve Bank of India (RBI)

Essay 98

LAND REFORMS IN INDIA

SYNOPSIS

The agrarian society in pre-Independent India was governed by semi-feudal principles. The land tenure was classified into three categories, viz., zamindari, mahalwari and ryotwari. These systems gave rise to social injustice. Independent India felt the need for evolving a congenial agrarian structure to accelerate the process of development. A series of steps were taken for effecting land reforms. The zamindari system was abolished, surplus land was distributed among the landless but the objectives of the reforms were not met. There was a lack of political will; the laws were full of loopholes and there was an absence of updated land records. In some of the states, like Kerala, political will and resultant intervention have led to successful land reforms. The Five-Year Plans propose to ameliorate the sufferings of the landless.

Agriculture is the mainstay of the Indian economy. Prior to India gaining Independence, our agrarian society was governed by *semi-feudal*[1] principles. The society was broadly divided into four classes—the cultivating holders, the intermediaries-cum-cultivating holders, tenants-at-will and agricultural labourers. The agricultural labourers constituted the unemployed, under employed and seasonal employed class of the agrarian sector. The intermediaries were large land owners, while the other two constituted the small and marginal land owners. The feudal structure of society, the small size of farms, high land rents and lack of tenancy rights led to the backwardness of society and prevalence of poverty among the rural masses. In the Resolution of the Indian National Congress, passed in 1935, it was felt that there could be only one fundamental method of improving village life, namely, the introduction of a system of peasant *proprietorship*[2] under which the tiller of the soil is himself the owner and pays revenues directly to the government without the intervention of any *zamindar* or *taluqdar*.

Land tenure refers to the system of land ownership and management. It identifies the ownership of land and the relationship of the owner and the cultivator. In pre-Independent India, the land tenure was classified into three categories: the *zamindari*, the *mahalwari* and the *ryotwari* systems. The *zamindari* system or the landlord-tenant system was introduced by Lord Cornwallis in 1793 in Bengal. During the British rule, this system prevailed over around 40 per cent of the land under cultivation. The *zamindar* or the landlord acted as an intermediary between the cultivators and the State. Under this system, two distinct classes emerged, one of the landlords and the other of the cultivators. The system was introduced to create a loyal class of landlords who were assigned the task of collecting land revenue for which they received a commission. The revenue collectors were raised to the status of landowners thereby creating a permanent interest on land. This system prevailed in Bengal, North Madras and Banaras. The *zamindari* villages were divided into two agricultural classes—the absentee owners and the non-owner cultivators. The absentee owners or landlords exploited the actual tillers and became the symbol of oppression and tyranny.

Under the *mahalwari* system, the land was held under the joint ownership of the entire village community. The community was responsible for the payment of the land revenue to the government. This system was first introduced in Agra and Oudh and later on in Punjab. This system was the product of Muslim tradition which had developed particularly in Punjab.

Under the *ryotwari* system, the cultivator held single independent land holding and was solely responsible to the State for the payment of land revenue. Under this system, there was no intermediary between the cultivator and the State. The *ryotwari* system was the product of Hindu tradition. This form of tenure was prevalent in Bombay and Central India. The *ryot* is at liberty to sublet his land and enjoys a permanent right of tenancy so long as he pays the assessed land revenue. Some elements of *zamindari* tenure did appear in this system too because the peasants in ryotwari areas could sublet their land.

These systems of land tenure gave rise to social injustice. The cultivators did not get a fair share of the agricultural produce. They were constantly under the threat of eviction from the land. This degraded their position to that of the *serfs*[3]. The economic disparities between the landlords and the agricultural labourers widened. Under the *zamindari* system, the landlord was only interested in extracting the maximum revenue from his tenants. During the British rule, famines and starvation deaths became common. The *catastrophes*[4] arose mainly because of the low purchasing power of the tiller.

In the post-Independence period, it was felt that a congenial agrarian structure had to be evolved to accelerate the process of development. The land reforms programme was formulated to break the feudal socio-economic structure of rural India. It was basically intended to stop the exploitation of the actual tillers of the soil and pass on the ownership of land to them. The main aim of the reforms was to get maximum advantage of the available land resources. The Planning Commission sums up the objectives of the land reforms in two comprehensive steps to be taken. The first is to remove such impediments to increase in agricultural production as have arisen from the agrarian structure inherited from the past. This should help to create conditions for evolving, as speedily as possible, an agricultural economy with a high level of efficiency. The second, which is closely related to the first, is to eliminate all elements of exploitation and social injustice within the agrarian system to provide security for the tiller of the soil and assure equality of status and opportunity to all the sections of the rural population. And towards this endeavour, the first step taken was the abolition of the *zamindari* system.

With the removal of the intermediaries, the cultivators came in direct contact with the government. An area of considerable size of cultivable wasteland and private forest-land, which fell under the possession of the government, was distributed among the landless agricultural labourers. One of the most important events in the history of land reforms is the 'Bhoodan Movement', although it was not a part of land reform policy. This movement was started by Acharya Vinobha Bhave. About 54.60 lakh acres of land was donated under this movement. After Independence, the need to enact legislation for the regulation of rents was felt. In the First and the Second Plan, it was proposed that rents should not exceed one-fourth or one-fifth of the farm yield.

The objectives of the land reforms were to bring down economic disparity and bring about social justice. Agricultural production increased after the mid-60s with the adoption of the new agricultural strategy. The feudal-oriented social structure gave way to market-oriented commercialised farming. The *zamindars* gave way to modern entrepreneurial farmers who were landholders and employed hired labourers to cultivate their lands. The agrarian society got restructured into three distinct groups, the first being the modern entrepreneurial farmers, the second, the small and marginal farmers and the last, the landless agricultural labourers. States like Bihar witnessed a number of massacres involving landless peasants and wealthy landlords because of the failure of the government to implement land reforms.

Land reforms programme was started with great enthusiasm, which was soon lost and the implementation of land reforms became a rather tame affair. There is no doubt that land reforms were conceived comprehensively in the right perspective but being riddled with loopholes, failed to meet the ends of justice. The principal reasons for poor implementation of land reforms are: lack of political will; absence of pressure from below because the poor peasants and agricultural workers are passive, unorganised and inarticulate; lukewarm and often *apathetic*[5] attitude of the bureaucracy; absence of up-to-date land records; and legal hurdles hindering implementation of land reforms.

In the subsequent Five-Year Plans after the initial few, there was no separate allocation of funds for financing land reforms. Some states like West Bengal and Kerala took steps to better the fate of the agricultural labourers by providing security of employment to them, ensuring prompt payment of wages to the workers and also by regulating the working hours. In the Ninth Plan (1997-2002), it was pointed out that rural poverty exists largely among the landless and the marginal farmers. So, access to land remains a key element of the anti-poverty strategy in rural areas. The Plan proposed the detection and redistribution of surplus land. The Tenth Five-Year Plan (2002-2007) furthered the reforms in the agricultural sector which were earlier neglected.

The Eleventh Five-Year Plan period (2007-2012) had identified the farm sector as a high-priority area and had set an average agricultural growth target of 4 per cent to 'ensure a broader spread of benefits' to the agrarian community. One of the main objectives of the Twelfth Five-Year Plan is to move Indian agriculture from a low-productivity-staple-producing system to a rising-productivity- commercially-oriented sector.

The Twelfth Plan Working Group on Disadvantaged Farmers, including women has provided evidence-based assessment of the ground situation. New insecurities of tenure from urbanisation and industrialisation are impacting small farms which are efficient but lack adequate access. Its main recommendation is that a collective approach should be promoted in agriculture for small and women farmers at all points of the value chain. Since land access was the most difficult part in all the above efforts, the Working Group has suggested that, except distribution of *homesteads*[6] to the homeless which should have the highest priority, future government land distribution should be to groups of landless and women farmers rather than to individuals. This could take the form of long-term lease which would expire if the group broke down, for which it would be necessary to legalise tenancy at least for this purpose.

Moreover, an innovative suggestion of both this Working Group and the Working Group on Marketing is to set up Public Land Banks (PLB) at Panchayat level. Landowners could 'deposit' uncultivated land and receive regular payments from the PLB varying by period of deposit and rents actually obtained with the guarantee that this 'deposit' can be withdrawn with suitable notice. The PLB could then lease out to small and women farmers or their collectives. A form of 'limited' tenancy aimed at fuller agricultural use of available farm land and to slow down *speculation*[7] in such land for future non-agricultural use, this idea excludes leasing to corporate entities.

Access to finance, especially by small holders, is crucial for improved agricultural performance. Small and marginal farmers face problems not only with shrinking land assets and with credit; they have difficulty in accessing critical inputs for agriculture such as quality seeds and timely technical assistance. In this situation, Farmer Producer Organisations (FPOs) offer a form of aggregation that leaves land titles with individual producers and uses the strength of collective planning for production, procurement and marketing to add value to members' produce through pooled resources of land and labour, shared storage space, transportation and marketing facilities. These factors also improve the bargaining power of small formers and, most, importantly, reduce transaction costs of banks as well as buyers. Investing in such group efforts has strong externalities.

Aid to Vocabulary

1. *Semi-feudal* — pertaining to the system of landlords and the landless peasants
2. *Proprietorship* — ownership
3. *Serfs* — persons bound in the service of a landowner
4. *Catastrophes* — sudden or widespread disasters
5. *Apathetic* — having no emotion or interest
6. *Homesteads* — a house, especially a farm house
7. *Speculation* — investment in property, stocks, etc., in the hope of gain but with the risk of loss

Points to Remember

1. At the time of Independence, the society was broadly divided into four classes—the cultivating holders, the intermediaries-cum-cultivating holders, tenants-at-will and agricultural labourers.
2. The land tenure, in pre-Independent India was classified into three categories—the *zamindari,* the *mahalwari* and the *ryotwari* system.
3. Due to these three systems, the economic disparity between the landlords and the peasants came to be widened.
4. After Independence, a congenial agrarian structure had to be evolved to accelerate the process of development.
5. The objectives of the land reforms were to bring about economic efficiency and social justice.
6. Lack of political will is one of the main reasons for poor implementation of land reforms.
7. Agriculture was the core element of the Tenth Plan.
8. The Planning Commission had set a target of average 4 per cent growth of agriculture in the Eleventh Five-Year Plan.
9. Main recommendation of the Twelfth Plan Working Group on Disadvantaged Farmers, including women is that a collective approach should be promoted in agriculture for small and women farmers at all points of the value chain.
10. Access to finance, especially by small holders, is crucial for improved agricultural performance.

Essay **99**

AGRICULTURE: THE BACKBONE OF THE INDIAN ECONOMY

SYNOPSIS

Agriculture is the most important sector in our economy. Agricultural production has primarily, two components, food grains and non-food grains. Food crops and non-food crops have shown tremendous increase in production since Independence. After the Green Revolution, India achieved self-sufficiency in food grain production. The Green Revolution generated self-confidence in our agricultural capability. The first Five-Year Plan accorded the highest priority to the increase of agricultural production. The share of agriculture in total employment was 54.6 per cent as per 2011 Census. Efforts were made to improve the facilities in all respects and make the system more approachable, accessible and farmer friendly. The Indian countryside needs a revolutionary tranformation to march on the path of an evergreen revolution in agriculture.

Agriculture includes the cultivation of crops, rearing of livestock, fishing and forestry. It is the most basic and the most widespread form of human activity.

Agriculture is the most important sector in our economy. Basically, agriculture forms the backbone of the Indian economy. Agriculture provides raw materials to many industries. It plays a significant role in the economic development of our country. However, there has been a decline in the absolute number of cultivators, from 127.3 million (Census 2001) to 118.7 million (Census 2011) and it is indicative of a shift from farm to non-farm employment.

Over 58 per cent of the rural households depend on agriculture as their principal means of livelihood. Agriculture, along with fisheries and forestry, is one of the largest contributors to the GDP.

As per the first revised estimates released by the Central Statistics Office (CSO) on January 29, 2016, the share of agriculture and allied sectors (including agriculture, livestock, forestry and fishery) was approximately 17.0 per cent of the India's Gross Value Added (GVA) during 2014–15 at 2011–12 prices. The country is the largest producer, consumer and exporter of spices and spice products. It ranks third in farm and agriculture outputs. Agricultural export constitutes 10 per cent of the country's exports and is the fourth-largest exported principal commodity.

The agro industry in India is divided into several subsegments such as canned, dairy, processed, frozen food to fisheries, meat, poultry, and food grains.

The Department of Agriculture and Cooperation under the Ministry of Agriculture is responsible for the development of the agriculture sector in India. It manages several other bodies, such as the National Dairy Development Board (NDDB), to develop other allied agricultural sectors.

Agricultural production has two components, food grains and non-food grains. Food grains like rice and wheat have made India self-sufficient. In the non-food grains category, products like tea, coffee, cocoa, oil cakes, fruits and vegetables, spices, sugar, cotton and jute form the basis of the country's exports. Food crops and non-food crops have shown tremendous increase in production after Independence. There has been a considerable increase in dairy, poultry, and the agricultural wealth of the country. India is the largest producer of cashew nuts, spices, tea and the second largest producer of fruits and vegetables. Along with this, it is also the largest producer of milk and has the largest *bovine*[1] population. India is the largest producer and importer of pulses. It is the second-largest producer of sugar, and the sixth-largest exporter of sugar.

We have come a long way since Independence. India has achieved self-sufficiency in food grain production and has made significant progress in agricultural sciences and technologies. Agricultural production increased sharply because of the improved *infrastructure*[2]. Semidwarf and high yielding varieties of wheat (Sona Moti) and rice (1036) were introduced. Irrigation facilities were improved. Fertilisers and pesticides were provided to the farmers at subsidised rates. Considerable attention was paid to conservation, cultivation, and commerce. The National Bank for Agriculture and Rural Development (NABARD) was also set up to provide easy finance to the farmers in the rural sector.

All these steps led to a *quantum*[3] jump in the productivity and production of crops such as wheat and rice. After that in 1968, the Green Revolution *ushered*[4] in a new era and helped India to become self-reliant. It generated self-confidence in our agricultural capability.

Agriculture has occupied a pivotal place in India's Five-Year Plans. The allocation of funds to this sector has been very high. The First Five-Year Plan *accorded*[5] the highest priority to the increase of agricultural production and the development of irrigation, power and transport. The goal of the Third Plan was to establish a self-reliant and self-generating economy, which helped in further development of agriculture. The subsequent plans initiated programmes for agricultural development and the generation of productive employment.

The resilience of Indian agriculture is evident in this sector last posted negative growth in 2002-03 and has registered a remarkable average growth rate of 4.1 per cent during the Eleventh Five-Year Plan (2007-08 to 2011-12).

The role of the agriculture sector, however, remains critical as it accounts for about 54.6 per cent of employment in the country (as per 2011 Census). Moreover, this sector is a supplier of food, fodder, and raw materials for a vast segment of industry. Hence the growth of Indian agriculture can be considered a necessary condition for 'inclusive growth'.

Agriculture being a state subject, the primary responsibility for increasing agricultural production and productivity, exploiting untapped potential, and enhancing incomes of the farming community, rests with state governments. Their efforts are supplemented by many centrally sponsored and central sector schemes. The NSSO 70th round survey indicates that about 59% of farmers do not get much technical assistance and know-how from government-funded farm research institutes or extension services.

The Budget 2014-15 allocated ₹ 100 crore to Kisan TV for *disseminating*[6] realtime information to farmers regarding new farming techniques, water conservation, organic farming, etc., to partly make up for the adverse ratio of one extension worker for every 800 to 1000 farmers and to provide farmers a direct interface with agricultural experts. Around 5300 crore rupees has been allocated to support micro-irrigation, watershed development and the 'Pradhan Mantri Krishi Sinchai Yojana'.

Strategies and programmes have been directed towards the replacement of traditional and inefficient implements by the improved ones. Efforts are being made to improve the facilities in all respects and make the system more approachable and farmer friendly. Focus is on cropping systems and on small and marginal farmers through development of Farmer Producer Organisations (FPOs) and creating value chain and providing market linkages. The Technology Mission on Oilseeds and Oil Palm (TMO & OP), introduced in the Twelfth Plan, aims to increase domestic production of edible oilseeds/oil. Several players have invested in the agricultural sector in India, mainly driven by the government's initiatives and schemes.

According to the Department of Industrial Policy and Promotion (DIPP), the Indian agricultural services and agricultural machinery sectors have cumulatively attracted foreign direct investment (FDI) equity inflow of about US$ 2,182 million from April, 2000 to May, 2015.

Some major investments and developments in agriculture in the recent past are, Belgium-based Univeg recently collaborated with Mahindra & Mahindra to develop a fresh fruit supply chain. Companies from the US, Canada, Australia, Israel, the Netherlands and other European countries have shown strong interest to transfer the best practices, linkages between scientific institutes, agriculture storage, cold-chain management, market access, and productivity enhancement such as the introduction of new technology in seed and plant biotech. Canada-based International Food Security Research Fund has major investments in food security research in several Indian universities. These strengthen food-processing and sustainable agricultural techniques.

The Government of India has taken steps to address two major factors (soil and water) critical to improve agriculture production. Steps have been taken to improve soil fertility on a sustainable basis through the soil health card scheme and to support the organic farming scheme 'Paramparagat Krishi Vikas Yojana'. Other steps include improved access to irrigation through 'Pradhanmantri Gram Sinchai Yojana'; enhanced water efficiency through ₹ Per Drop More Crop'; continued support to MGNREGA and the creation of a unified national agriculture market to boost the incomes of farmers.

The central government recognises the importance of micro-irrigation, watershed development and 'Pradhan Mantri Krishi Sinchai Yojana'; thus, it allocated a sum of ₹ 5,300 crore (US$ 830 million) for it. It urged the states to focus on this key sector. The state governments are *compelled*[7] to allocate adequate funds to develop the agriculture sector, take measures to achieve the targeted agricultural growth rate and address the problems of farmers.

The Department of Agriculture and Cooperation under the Ministry of Agriculture has inked MOUs/agreements with 52 countries including the US. In addition, the Department of Agriculture Research & Education (DARE) and the Department of Animal Husbandry, Dairying & Fisheries (DAHD&F) under the Ministry of Agriculture have signed MOUs/ agreements with other countries, taking the number of partnerships with other countries to 63.

The agriculture sector needs special attention to drive growth, employment and economic prosperity in rural areas of the country. The Indian countryside needs a revolutionary change. There should be an *agrarian*[8] transformation that targets landlordism, moneylenders, exploitation by merchants and caste and gender oppression. We can achieve an *inclusive*[9] economic growth only through accelerated agricultural progress. Higher growth in agriculture production and the prosperity of the farmer would be a great asset to the country. A holistic approach is required to march on the path of an evergreen revolution in agriculture.

The agriculture sector in India is expected to generate better momentum in the next few years due to increased investments in agricultural infrastructure such as irrigation facilities, warehousing and cold storage. Factors such as reduced transaction costs and time, improved port gate management and better fiscal incentives would contribute to the sector's growth. Furthermore, the growing use of genetically modified crops is likely to improve the yield for Indian farmers. Also, a 4 per cent growth would help restructure the agriculture sector in India in the next few years.

AID TO VOCABULARY

1. *Bovine* — relating to or affecting cattle
2. *Infrastructure* — basic installations and components
3. *Quantum* — sudden, and of a considerable quantity
4. *Ushered* — brought
5. *Accorded* — granted
6. *Disseminating* — spreading widely
7. *Compelled* — forced or obliged to do something
8. *Agrarian* — agriculture based
9. *Inclusive* — including much or all

POINTS TO REMEMBER

1. Agriculture is the backbone of the Indian economy, with over 58 percent of the rural households depending on agriculture as their principal means of livelihood.
2. However, the decline in absolute number of cultivators is indicative of a shift from farm to non-farm employment.
3. The Agro industry is divided into subsegment such as canned, dairy, processed, frozen food to fisheries, meat, poultry and food grains.
4. India is the largest producer of cashew nuts, spices, tea, pulses, milk and the second largest producer of sugar, fruits and vegetables.
5. The National Bank for Agriculture and Rural Development (NABARD) was set up to extend finance to the farmers in the rural sector.
6. The Green Revolution helped India to become self-reliant.
7. New and advanced targets have been set under the NFSM.

8. The TMO & OP aims to increase domestic production of edible oilseeds/ oil.
9. Several players have invested in the agricultural sector in India, mainly driven by the government's initiatives and schemes.
10. There should be an agrarian transformation that targets the eradication of landlordism, moneylenders, exploitation by merchants, and caste and gender oppression. debt and death

DEBT AND DEATH

The More a Farmer Owes, The Higher His Chances of Suicide

Data on rural indebtedness in the recently released NSSO and the National Crime Records Bureau's statistics on farmer suicides for 2013, the year in which survey samples were collected, show a strong correlation between debt and farmer suicides. For instance, more than 31% of rural households in Maharashtra had big liabilities in 2013 and the state saw over 3,000 farmer suicides that year, highest in the country.

Suicides by People Self-employed in Agriculture

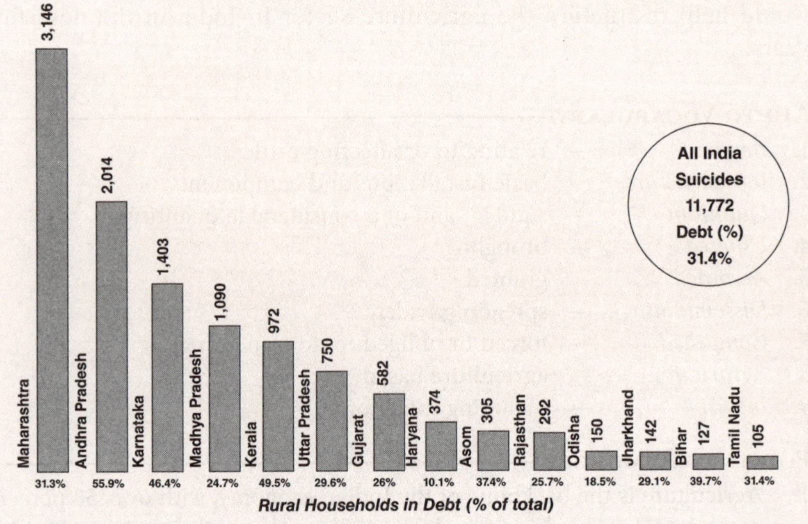

Essay

100 FOODGRAINS MANAGEMENT IN INDIA

SYNOPSIS

The famine of Bengal in 1943 exposed the acute shortage of food supplies in India. The second Foodgrains Policy Commitee (FPC) felt that Indian food problem can be solved only when the internal food production is increased. The First Five Year Plan was formulated keeping in mind a certain objective—the 'most effective and balanced utilisation of the country's resources'. The food situation eventually improved. But in the late 50's, food shortage re-emerged along with the rise in prices. The government entered into an agreement with the US in 1956 for the import of wheat and rice for the subsequent three years. For a decade after 1956, Indian food policy was based on imports from the US. At the end of the Third Plan, again there was a severe food shortage which led to rise in food prices. The three instruments of food policy are production and supply, consumption and the distribution of foodgrains. The food policy of the country could not live up to the expectations. The PDS was accused of being biased. The RPDS was launched to benefit the people in the rural areas. With the joint efforts of scientists and biotechnologists, India has achieved self-sufficiency in the production of foodgrains.

The famine of Bengal, in 1943 i.e., during the second world war, in which millions died due to starvation, exposed the acute shortage of food supplies in India. The first Foodgrains Policy Committee (FPC) was appointed in the same year to examine the food situation which advised the Government to introduce *rationing*[1] in the country. In September 1947, the Government appointed the second FPC to study the food situation in Independent India. Under the prevailing circumstances, it was felt that the country could not continue the extension of the rationing system started by the British. It recommended stopping the import of foodgrains and decided that the Indian food problem could be resolved only if the internal food production was increased *substantially*[2], in the least possible time. The Committee recommended decontrol, which was immediately introduced, and which expectedly resulted in price increase. Thereafter, the Foodgrains Procurement Committee, appointed in 1950, recommended a system of control. It proposed abolition of the free market, monopoly in procurement of foodgrains by the government at the village level and complete rationing of foodgrains. The Government, however, rejected the proposal because it was impracticable.

The Indian planners, right from the beginning, acknowledged that the need to attain self-sufficiency in foodgrains must be one of the important goals of planning. The government realised that food surplus countries used their position of being food-surplus as a weapon to force several countries to submit to their dictates. Realising this, Prime Minister Pt. Jawaharlal Nehru said: "It is only when we obtain self-sufficiency in food that we can progress and develop ourselves. otherwise, there is the continuous pressure of circumstances, there is trouble and misery and there is sometimes shame and humiliation."

The First Five-Year Plan accorded the highest priority to agriculture and more than 40 per cent of the Plan's outlay on agriculture was devoted to minor irrigation. This was done, keeping in view the large-scale imports of foodgrains in 1951 to supplement the domestic production and to limit the inflationary impact of the imports on the economy. The food situation during the First Plan improved because of a series of good harvests in the country.

But in 1955, the problem of food shortage re-emerged along with the rise in prices. Natural calamities like drought, floods and cyclone in certain parts of Rajasthan, Bihar, Odisha and Tamil Nadu contributed to the situation. The problem of food-shortage *aggravated*[3] and developed into a 'food crisis'. In 1956, the Government entered into an agreement with the US, which was known as the PL-480 Agreement, for the import of wheat and rice for the subsequent three years. It helped to stabilise food prices. The Foodgrains Enquiry Committee appointed in 1957 felt that the 'food problem was likely to remain for a long time to come.' For the decade that followed, Indian food policy was based on imports from the US.

At the end of the Third Plan, internal foodgrain production *slackened*[4] and traders and middlemen resorted to *hoarding*[5] and selling in the blackmarketing. This resulted in severe food shortages leading to rise in food prices; and at the same time, many parts of the country witnessed famines which further worsened the situation. To counter these challenges, the Government resorted to importing huge quantities of foodgrains. The Government afterwards realised that an assured supply of imports was unable to sustain the food policy and that a policy of proper distribution of foodgrains, produced in the country, had to be formulated to *alleviate*[6] the food crisis. Another FPC was set up in 1966 to study the food crisis and it concluded that future payments towards the imports would have to be made in dollars. It also pointed out that the food aid to India by the US was used to influence the internal economic and foreign affairs policies of the country. The Committee recommended the preparation and implementation of a National Food Budget for the distribution of foodgrains. The Government accepted the recommendations of the Committee and it led to the increase in food production and a gradual reduction in imports. Procurement of foodgrains was done to ensure essential supplies, *buffer*[7] stocks of foodgrains were built up and a system of public distribution was introduced. In the free market, the prices of foodgrains increased and it led to the take-over of the wholesale trade in wheat by the Government.

In 1967, the Government of India, under the leadership of Prime Minister Indira Gandhi introduced Seed-Water-Fertiliser Policy popularly known as the Green Revolution, which transformed the situation from food scarcity to food self-sufficiency. It led to manifold increase in India's farm production and productivity. India succeeded in raising its foodgrains production from 51 million tonnes in 1950-51 to a record 213 million tonnes, in 2003-04. India had achieved self-sufficiency in foodgrains by the year 1976 and since then, imports of cereals have remained negligible. According to the Ninth Five-Year Plan, 'one of the first efforts of the country was to build up a food security system to ensure that the threat of famine no longer stalks the country'. Although India has been able to avert famines and acute food scarcities, yet it has not been able to provide food 'needed for an active and healthy life', to its population. In other words, the goal of a balanced diet is still a distant dream.

India was forced to import 6 million tonnes of food grains in 2006-07, after which the government launched the National Food Security Mission (NFSM) in 2007 to raise food production by 20 million tonnes over the next five years. Today, the government is the single largest procurer and *hoarder*[8] of grain.

The distribution of foodgrains has been an important aspect of the food policy in the country. In 1967-68, the fair price system was renamed the 'Public Distribution System' (PDS). The system was created to benefit both the producers and the consumers. The foodgrains are procured from the producers at minimum support prices and distributed among the consumers, at uniform prices, all over the country. The PDS has been able to check hoarding of essential foodgrains to sell in the black market. The Government has built up buffer stocks to maintain the supply of foodgrains throughout the year and also to maintain the supply in the event of unforeseen circumstances. Another objective of maintaining buffer stocks is to stabilise prices. The country is divided into a number of zones. Movement of foodgrains within a zone is not restricted but inter-zonal movements are checked to ensure self-sufficiency within each zone.

The Commission for Agricultural Costs and Prices (CACP) is *entrusted*[9] with the task of recommending the minimum support prices (MSP), for 23 crops. In the case of sugarcane, it is the fair and remunerative price (FRP). The Food Corporation of India (FCI) and its nominated state agencies undertake procurement operations in the case of major cereals, The National Agricultural Co-operative Marketing Federation of India Limited (NAFED) provides price support for oilseeds and pulses, the Cotton Corporation of India (CCI) for cotton and the Jute Corporation of India (JCI) for jute, whenever the need arises, at least in theory. In reality, even for paddy and wheat, market prices often go below MSPs in several markets in the absence of any effective procurement machinery to provide price support. Other crops too suffer from this from time to time, as the procurement machinery remains weak.

The National Food Security Act, 2013 (NFSA), was notified on September 10, 2013, and by March 2014, 11 states had implemented the act. The act marks a fundamental change in the country's food policy in that it makes people's right to a basic amount of food a legal entitlement. Interestingly, the entitlement has been delinked from poverty levels. The act aims to provide a legal entitlement to subsidised food grains to at least 75 per cent people in rural areas and 50 per cent in urban areas.

The Food Safety and Standard Act 2006, which came into force in India in 2011 ensures improved quality of food for the consumers and brings India on par with international standard. It also prevents of unfair trade practices that eventually harm the consumer through unsafe, contaminated or substandard food.

The Food Safety and Standards Authority of India (FSSAI), established under the overarching legislation, will lay down science-based standards for food items and regulate their manufacture, storage, distribution, sale and import to ensure availability of safe and wholesome food for human consumption. The FSSAI will collect and *collate*[10] data regarding food consumption, incidence and prevalence of biological risk, residues of various contaminants in food products, identification of emerging risks and introduction of a rapid alert system. According to Economic Survey 2014-15, the price instruments used for food management are MSP and central issue price (CIP). Since 2012-13, the growth of MSPs of various crops has been the moderate. To enhance efficiency of procurement and public distribution, and to extend the benefits of MSP to local farmers, the Decentralised Procurement (DCP) scheme has been adopted by some state governments. The central government is urging all state governments to adopt the DCP scheme so that costs of distribution can be saved and outreach of price support mechanism to the farmers in hitherto weaker areas can be improved. To overcome the problem of gaps in the flow of information about procurement operations on day-to-day basis, an Online Procurement Monitoring System (OPMS) has been evolved for reporting and monitoring on a daily basis, procurement operations for wheat, paddy, and coarse grains in the country.

The FCI on behalf of the government has been undertaking sale of wheat at predetermined prices/reserve price in the open market from time to time to enhance market supply of foodgrains; to exercise a moderating influence on open market prices and to offload surplus stocks. Almost 100% (99.9%) ration cards have been digitised across the country. The food policy of the country despite all odds, has been quite satisfactory. To benefit people in the tribal regions, desert areas, hilly regions and drought-prone areas, the Revamped Public Distribution Scheme (RPDS) was launched. The Storage and Research Division is responsible for the procurement of foodgrains for the buffer stock. The Central Grain Analysis Laboratory, with its branches in New Delhi, Kolkata and Hyderabad, monitors the quality of foodgrains at the time of procurement, its storage and later, distribution.

The Government decided to distribute foodgrains to people below poverty line at 50% subsidised rates, and freely to the poorest of the poor through various schemes like, *Antyodaya Anna Yojana, Mid-day Meal Scheme, Annapurna Scheme, Targeted Public Distribution System*, etc. A scheme *Save Grain Campaign* is being implemented in collaboration with the State Governments, NGOs, Corporate Houses, etc. The main objective of this scheme is to transfer the technical know-how developed by the IGMRI to the farmers for minimising the post harvest losses in foodgrain. Efforts are being made to provide a package insurance policy for the farmers, right from sowing of the crops to post-harvest operations, including market fluctuations in the prices of agricultural produce. The National Agricultural Policy envisages National Agriculture Insurance Scheme covering all farmers and all crops throughout the country.

Hence, it can be safely concluded that the foodgrains production as well as distribution in India has been managed satisfactorily with the country having achieved a comfortable food security and self-sufficiency level.

Aid to Vocabulary

1. *Rationing* — distribution of foodgrains, etc., in quotas or fixed quantities
2. *Substantially* — considerably
3. *Aggravated* — worsened
4. *Slackened* — became less
5. *Hoarding* — overstocking secretly with food, etc., in times of scarcity
6. *Alleviate* — reduce, mitigate
7. *Buffer* — reserve
8. *Hoarder* — one who collects or stores something for future use
9. *Entrusted* — assign the responsibility for doing something to
10. *Collate* — to gather information from different sources in order to study it carefully

Points to Remember

1. There was food crisis in the early 40s and 50s in India.
2. The system of rationing was introduced in India during the second world War.
3. The First Five Year Plan helped in the increase of agricultural production.
4. In the late 50s, due to a food crisis, India had to import wheat and rice from the US.
5. In 1966, Foodgrains Policy Committee was set up to study the food crisis and formulate a policy of proper distribution of foodgrains.
6. By introducing Seed-Water-Fertiliser Policy that ushered in the Green Revolution, India achieved self-sufficiency in foodgrains.
7. In 1967-68, the fair price system was renamed as the public Distribution System (PDS).
8. The Commission for Agricultural Cost and Prices (CACP) is entrusted with the task of recommending the MSP for 23 crops.
9. The National Food Security Act, 2013 was notified on September 10, 2013 marking a fundamental change in the country's food policy.
10. The Government has introduced many important schemes like Antyodaya Anna Yojana, Mid-Day Meal Scheme, etc., to feed the poorest of the poor. The present state of foodgrains management is quite satisfactory.

INDIA RANKED 97TH AMONG 118 IN HUNGER INDEX

India is ranked a lowly 97th among 118 developing nations for which the Global Hunger Index (GHI) was calculated in 2016. Countries worse than India include extremely poor African countries such as Niger, Chad, Ethiopia and Sierra Leone, besides two of India's neighbours: Afghanistan and Pakistan. Other neighbours Sri Lanka, Bangladesh, Nepal and China are all ranked above India.

International Food Policy Research Institute (IFPRI) makes the annual calculations of GHI. Basing its readings on the most recent data, the 2016 GHI for India was derived from the fact that an estimated 15% of its population is undernourished-lacking in adequate food intake, both in quantity and quality.

215 million Indians, roughly 15.2% of the country's population, are undernourished.

Hunger Still Haunts India

India has improved its hunger level from alarming to serious, according to the International Food-policy Research Institute Global Hunger, Index, 2016. Yet, it's likely to miss its target of zero hunger by 2030 if it doesn't quicken its progress.

Where India Stands

A 'serious' hunger score means some sections of the populations may face dire situations of hunger-nutrition. Improvement in South Asia's hunger score hinges on India.

India's Overall Hunger Rank — 97

Hunger Scorecard: India's Progress Over The Years

Year	Hunger Score
1992	46.4
2000	38.2
2008	36.0
2016	28.5

There Countries Do Better Than Us In South Asia

Rank	Country	Score
72	Nepal	21.9
84	Sri Lanka	25.5
90	Bangladesh	27.1
97	India	28.5
107	Pakistan	33.4
111	Afghanistan	34.8

Essay **101**

INDUSTRY—ITS ROLE IN ECONOMIC DEVELOPMENT

SYNOPSIS

Industry is intrinsic to a country's economic prosperity. Industry is a commercial activity. The British rulers did not encourage industrialisation during their rule. After Independence, there was an urgent need for increasing the national wealth. The government favoured the policy of mixed economy. Some industries were set in the public sector; others were left to the private sector. The industrial growth had been slow over the years. India has been facing industrial sickness intermittently since the early 70's. The government is undertaking steps through the Five-Year Plans to speed up the process of industrialisation. The New Industrial Policy of 1991 liberalised the economy. Planners have envisioned India as a developed nation by 2020.

India started her quest for industrial development after Independence in 1947. The Industrial Policy Resolution of 1948 marked the beginning of the evolution of the Indian Industrial Policy.

Industry is *intrinsic*[1] to a country's economic prosperity. Industry is the making or producing of goods in factories. It is a *commercial*[2] activity. India is an agriculture based economy. The British rulers, during their rule, did not encourage industrialisation in India. After Independence, there was an urgent need of increasing the national wealth. The process of industrialisation started with the Industrial Policy Resolution of 1948.

In the earlier stages, industry included textiles, sugar, etc. Gradually, importance was laid on basic and capital goods industries. The Government favoured the policy of mixed economy. Some industries were put in the public sector; others were left to the private sector. Industries like coal, iron, textile, jute, sugar, tea, cement, leather goods, mineral oil, etc., were left to private enterprises. These were subject to certain regulations and control by the government. The industries like arms and ammunitions, atomic energy, river valley projects, railways, steel, aircraft manufacture, ship building, telephone and telegraph were kept under the state control, i.e., the public sector. This policy was, later on, changed.

Industry in India is divided into large-scale and small-scale industries. Among India's major large-scale industries are cotton textile industry with over a thousand textile mills; iron and steel industry with six integrated steel plants and over 216 mini steel plants. Other major industries are aluminium, automobiles, cement, cycles, copper smelting, fertilisers, glass, heavy electricals, jute, leather goods, machine tools, paper, pesticides, pharmaceuticals, railway equipments, ship building, silk textiles, woollen textiles, sugar, tractors, etc. The large-scale industrial sector is a source of employment to millions of people.

Cottage industries are generally associated with agriculture and part-time and whole-time occupation in rural and semi-urban areas. The Khadi and Village Industries Commission (KVIC) defines a village industry as one with a capital investment of up to ₹ 1 lakh. Agro-based industries are based on the processing of agricultural produce, or they cater to the input needs of the agriculturist. Agro-based industries may be organised on a cottage scale, small scale or large scale. We can distinguish between two types of small industries, viz., modern small-scale manufacturing enterprises and intermediate group of small enterprises.

The industrial growth in India had been slow over the years. The main causes of this slow progress were narrowness of the market, increase in capital-output ratio, import substitution, technological incapacity and decline in public investment. Other factors included inefficiency of public sector projects, controls and administrative inefficiency, declining investment growth rate, administered prices, etc. As per the Index of Industrial Production (IIP), the industrial sector is recovering slowly led by the infrastructure sectors, viz. electricity, coal, and cement. Mining sector growth has turned positive while manufacturing growth continues to remain tepid. Infrastructure growth in terms of eight core industries has been higher than industrial growth since 2011-12 and this trend is expected to continue.

Developing economies like India have limited resources. Since the early 70's, India has faced industrial sickness intermittently. Industrial sickness is a universal *phenomenon*[3]. It is a situation when productive assets become non-operational. It causes serious concern to the Government, the Reserve Bank, the commercial banks and other financial institutions. An industrial unit can become sick due to internal and external factors. The internal factors arise due to disorders in an industrial unit. This can be controlled if the management is effective. The external factors arise from changes in the environment. This is beyond the control of the management. The Industrial Reconstruction Corporation of India is the principal agency for reconstruction and rehabilitation of the sick units.

The Five-Year Plans were launched to secure the balanced growth of public and private sectors as well as of large-scale and small-scale industries. The large investment plans made for infrastructure during the Eleventh Five-Year Plan and beyond are expected to ease the infrastructural constraints that bind the industry. Such investments in infrastructural projects not only alleviate supply side constraints, but also stimulate additional domestic demand required for industrial growth. Foreign capital was invited to speed up industrialisation. The government is undertaking steps for a proper use of the country's resources. It has also planned for the *equitable*[4] distribution of various industries among the states.

The New Industrial Policy of the government in 1991 liberalised the economy and the industry. It *did away with*[5] industrial licensing except for 18 cases (further reduced to 15) and removed restrictions on MRTPC*. It removed registration formalities and redefined the role of the public sector. The domestic liberalisation and the globalisation of the Indian economy have greatly increased the opportunities as well as challenges for industries. The emphasis has been on rapidly improving ease of doing business and launching fresh initiatives like Make in India and Digital India; creating a National Industrial Corridors Authority, *streamlining*[6] environment and forest clearances and introducing labour reforms. To overcome critical constraints holding up use of land and natural resources, action has been taken to remove regulatory uncertainty by passing *ordinances*[7] to streamline land acquisition, e-auction of coal blocks for private companies, and auction of iron ore and other new coal mines. In infrastructure, the focus has been on resolving long-pending issues like pricing of gas, establishing processes and procedures for transparent auction of coal and minerals, and improving power generation and distribution. In railways, there are several policy announcements, such as 100 per cent foreign direct investment (FDI) to build a variety of rail infrastructure; new initiatives like bullet/semi-high speed trains and modernisation of stations; and timely completion of major projects like Dedicated Freight Corridors, which are being monitored closely. In the road sector, efforts have been undertaken to resolve problems associated with projects which are yet to be completed; and, the National Highways and Infrastructure Development Corporation Ltd. has been set up for speedy implementation of highway projects in the north-east.

To bring about complete industrial revolution and enjoy the fruits of industrial growth, India should be self-sufficient in raw materials, technical knowledge, machines, skilled labour and technicians rather than relying much on foreign aid.

---

*MRTPC—Monopolies and Restrictive Trade Practices Commission.

Private investment is the engine of long-run growth. There has been emphasis on reviving targeted public investment as an engine of growth in the short run to *complement*[8] and *augment*[9] private investment. India accounts for 1.8 per cent of the world's manufacturing output. Growth rates in manufacturing are uniformly low worldwide because industrialised economies are experiencing slow growth and emerging economies are finding it difficult to sustain as they are facing low demand in the global market as well as in their domestic economies. India needs to be part of the global manufacturing chain to *partake of*[10] the benefits of growth in these items, and the electronics industry needs to be incentivised to set up domestic production facilities.

The world wide economic slowdown means demand for industrial goods may be further reduced. But it is not good news for industries. Since wage costs are among the easiest to cut, deflationary situations often lead to wage cuts and job loss, adding to the problem of declining demand. Necessary measures are being taken by RBI and the government to tackle this situation, as a result of which the Indian Industry may bounce back. Economic planners *envision*[11] India as a developed nation by 2020.

Aid to Vocabulary

1. *Intrinsic* — essential, fundamental
2. *Commercial* — concerned with commerce, of making profit
3. *Phenomenon* — a fact or an event
4. *Equitable* — fair and just
5. *Did away with* — put an end to
6. *Streamlining* — to improve efficiency of a process by simplifying or eliminating unneccessary steps
7. *Ordinances* — authoritative orders
8. *Complement* — contribute to complete something
9. *Augment* — increase
10. *Partake of* — to take part in or experience something along with others
11. *Envision* — imagine as a future possibility

Points to Remember

1. Industry is a commercial activity that provides services.
2. Initially, the Government favoured the policy of mixed economy.
3. Industry in India is divided into large-scale and small-scale industries.
4. There are various factors that caused slow industrial growth in India.
5. The Government is undertaking steps through the Five-Year Plans to speed up industrialisation.
6. The New Industrial Policy of 1991 liberalised the Indian economy.

7. India should not depend much on foreign aid.
8. Measures are being taken by RBI and the new Government to tackle the economic slowdown and boost up the industrial sector.
9. India accounts for 1.8 per cent of the world's manufacturing output.
10. Planners envision India as a developed nation by 2020.

MAKE IN INDIA*

'Make in India' initiative, which is based on four pillars—new processes, new infrastructure, new sectors and new mindset—has been taken by the government, with the objective of making India a global hub of manufacturing, design, and innovation. As envisaged by the National Manufacturing Policy 2011, 'Make in India' seeks to create 100 million additional jobs in manufacturing by 2022.

INDUSTRY SECTOR REFORMS*

- The list of industries that can be considered as defence industries requiring industrial licence has been reduced.
- FDI policy has been amended allowing FDI in defence up to 49 per cent, in railway infrastructure up to 100 per cent and in the insurance and pension sector up to 49 per cent.
- The investment limit requiring prior permission from the Foreign Investment Promotion Board (FIPB)/Cabinet Committee on Economic Affairs has been increased from ₹ 1200 crore to ₹ 3000 crore.
- The definition of investment by Non Resident Indians (NRI), Persons of Indian Origin (PIO) and Overseas Citizens of India (OCI) in the FDI policy has been revised.
- Several programmes/initiatives such as ease of doing business, Make in India, Invest India, and e-biz Mission Mode Project under the National e-Governance Plan have been launched.
- A pentagon of corridors has been built across the country to boost manufacturing and to project India as a global manufacturing destination.
- The National Investment and Infrastructure Fund (NIIF) has been approved to extend equity support to infrastructure Non-Bank Financial Companies (NBFC).
- Issue of tax-free infrastructure bonds has been allowed for rail, roads and irrigation programmes.
- The system for coal block auctions has been streamlined so that these are now granted in a transparent framework.
- To improve financial viability of the State Electricity Distribution Companies, a comprehensive financial restructuring of these bodies has been taken up through the Ujwal DISCOM Assurance Yojana (UDAY) programme.

MICRO, SMALL AND MEDIUM ENTERPRISES SECTOR*

Micro, Small and Medium Enterprises (MSME) have a contribution of 37.5 per cent to the country's GDP, with 3.6 crore units spread across the country, employing 8.05 crore people.

*Economic Survey 2015-16

FDI REFORMS*

Foreign Direct Investment (FDI) is a major source of non-debt financial resources and employment generation, and thus is critical for sustaining a high growth rate.

Government has introduced the following reforms with a view to liberalise and simplify the FDI policy to provide ease of doing business climate in the country:

- A number of sectors including defence, construction, broadcasting, civil aviation, plantation, trading, private sector banking, satellite establishment and operation, and credit information companies, have been liberalised.
- During 2015-16, FDI policy in the pension sector was revised to permit foreign investment up to 49 per cent, with 26 per cent under automatic route.
- Manufacturing of medical devices and white label ATM operations have been opened up to 100 per cent FDI under automatic route.

The various reforms in the FDI sector have led to a significant increase in FDI inflows into India.

In the World Bank's ***Ease of Doing Business Report***, India's position is stated as: for the year 2015 – rank 142, for 2016 – rank 131, and for 2017 – rank 130.

*Economic Survey 2015-16

Essay
102 PUBLIC SECTOR UNDERTAKINGS

Synopsis

The PSUs were intended to bring about rapid growth of the economy. In the Second Plan, emphasis was laid on industrialisation. The PSUs were promoted to foster a balanced development of the different parts of the country. The public sector was based on the lines of evolving a socialistic pattern of society. It was set up to protect the workers from exploitation, to stimulate exports, to substitute imports and promote self-reliance. The PSUs intend to protect the workers from exploitation by the private monopolists. The New Industrial Policy of 1991, proposed to grant greater autonomy to the managements. The government is working towards the disinvestment of its shareholding. Implementation of the proposals of the Disinvestment Committee could restore the viability of the PSUs.

The public sector consists of all the industrial and commercial enterprises which are owned by the government and managed either by the government itself or by some other agency on behalf of the government. The public sector was assigned the following roles: (i) to ensure rapid economic development; (ii) to promote redistribution of income and wealth; (iii) to develop industries requiring huge financial resources; (iv) to achieve balanced regional growth; (v) to prevent the concentration of economic power; (vi) to generate resources for development; (vii) to promote import substitution; (viii) to generate employment; (ix) to help in the development of small-scale industries; and (x) to accord commanding heights to the economy.

The public sector has played a pivotal role in the planned economic and industrial development of the country. For the purpose of planning and national accounting, all activities of the public sector in India are funded out of the Government's budget. The objectives of the industrial policy were derived from the Directive Principles of State Policy in the Constitution of India. It states that the objectives of the state are to promote the welfare of the people by the creation of a social order based on social, economic and political justice. One of the fundamental decisions that Jawaharlal Nehru took after he became the Prime Minister was structuring the economy on the lines of a mixed pattern in which both the public and private sectors participated and had their roles *demarcated.*[1]

The Public Sector Undertakings (PSUs) evolved in India after the attainment of Independence in 1947. The Railways, the Post and Telegraph Department, the Port Trusts, the Ordnance and Aircraft Factories and a few other state-managed undertakings, like the government salt factories, quinine factories, etc., are some of the first public sector undertakings. At the time of independence, India had an *agrarian*[2] economy with a weak industrial base, low level of saving and investment and near absence of infrastructure facilities. To improve the situation, nationalisation of some of the industrial, banking and insurance units was undertaken. The expansion of the public sector was undertaken as an integral part of the industrial policy in 1956. The Industrial Policy Resolution stated that the State will progressively assume *predominance*[3] and direct responsibility for setting up of new industrial undertakings and for developing transport facilities.

The essential characteristics of development are—social justice with a view to *eradicate*[4] poverty and reduce income inequalities, self-reliance to avoid the dictates of the developed countries, planned utilisation of the limited resources of the country and devising a mechanism to carry out the plans, irrespective of profit considerations. To ensure this, in March 1950, the Planning Commission was set up by the Government to formulate a plan so as to make the most effective and balanced utilisation of the country's resources. The Second Five-Year Plan *envisaged*[5] the adoption of the socialistic pattern of society as the national objective, as well as the need for planned and rapid development, requiring that all industries of basic and strategic importance, or in the nature of public utility services, be in the public sector. There has been an appreciable growth in investment in the public sector over the years. The public sector has immensely helped in the development of the private sector industries by supplying cheap inputs like steel, cement, power, etc. It directly employs about 17.8 million persons, besides indirectly providing employment to millions of persons. It has made significant contribution towards achieving balanced regional growth. It intends to protect workers from exploitation by private monopolists. The PSUs were also set up to stimulate exports, substitute imports and promote self-reliance.

Different types of Public Enterprises are as follows: CPSEs (Central Public Sector Enterprises)—companies where the direct holding of the Central Government or of other CPSEs is 51% or more; PSBs (Public Sector Banks)—banks where the direct holding of the Central/State Government or other PSBs is 51% or more; and SLPEs (State Level Public Enterprises)—companies where the direct holding of the State Government or other SLPEs is 51% or more.

Central Public Sector Enterprises (CPSEs), spanning industries and infrastructure, continue to play a key role in the development of the economy. According to Public Enterprises Survey 2014-2015, there were only five Central Public Sector Enterprises (CPSEs) with a total investment of ₹ 29 crore. At the time of the First Five-Year Plan, there were 298 CPSEs with a total investment of ₹ 10,96,057 crore as on March 31, 2015. Out of which 235 were operational and 63 under construction. During the year 2014-15, the number of profit making CPSEs have decreased to 157 from 164 CPSEs in previous year and the number of loss making CPSEs have increased from 70 to 77 during the same period.

Public sector enterprises offer a wide range of products and services which include: manufacturing of steel, heavy machinery, machine tools, heavy machine building equipment, heavy electrical equipment for thermal and hydel stations, transportation equipment, telecommunication equipment, ships and sub-marines, fertilisers, drugs and pharmaceuticals, petrochemicals, cement, textile, mining of coal and minerals, extraction and refining of crude oil, operation of air, sea, river and road transport, national and international trade, consultancy, contract and construction services, inland and overseas telecommunication services, financial services, consumer items such as newsprint, paper and contraceptives, hotel and tourism services.

In 1997, the Government identified 11 PSUs as *Navratnas* and decided to give enhanced powers to the Board of Directors of these PSUs to facilitate their becoming global players. The other profit making enterprises were recognised as *Miniratnas* and granted a package of financial, operational and managerial autonomy. The *Maharatna* scheme was introduced in December, 2009, and some *Navratnas* were upgraded with greater powers and autonomy. As of October, 2014, there are 7 Central Public Sector Enterprises (CPSEs) identified as *Maharatnas* and 17 as *Navratnas* while 73 CPSEs have been recognised as *Miniratnas* (Category I-56, Category II-17).

One of the major initiatives undertaken in the public sector as outlined in the New Industrial Policy of July, 1991 pertained to bringing all public sector enterprises under the system of Memorandum of Understanding (MoU). MoU system in CPSEs was introduced in 1986. Its main purpose is to ensure a level playing field to public sector enterprises vis-a-vis the private corporate sector. An MoU is a mutually negotiated agreement between the management of the CPSE and the concerned administrative Ministry/Department of Government of India. Under this agreement, the performance of the enterprise is evaluated based on the targets set out at the beginning of the year. The targets comprise both financial and non-financial parameters having equal weightage (50 per cent each).

Based on the recommendations of the second Pay Revision Committee, the Performance Related Pay (PRP) payable to executives in CPSEs, in case of profit making CPSEs, is linked to the performance of the CPSEs as evaluated under the MoU system.

The public sector's performance in terms of ensuring adequate return on investment has been rather poor. The gross profit PBIT* has continued to remain between 13 and 15 per cent though lately it has gone up to 20 per cent in some cases. What is worse is that for many years these enterprises had been making huge losses. But profitability is not the only criterion for judging the efficiency of the PSUs. Some losses are inevitable due to heavy social responsibility placed on these enterprises in the form of providing cheaper goods to the common people and helping development of other industrial sectors.

The issues relating to disinvestment and privatisation have emerged as a direct offshoot of the public sector's failure. The Government has drawn up a plan for the disinvestment of various PSUs as part of its privatisation programme. As strategic sales under the disinvestment policy, the Government's stake in many important companies was sold (wholly or partly). As of March 31, 2011 the total employment in the public sector was about 175.48 lakh persons. A negative growth of employment was recorded in public sector while private sector showed an increasing trend.

The Government of India constituted the National Investment Fund (NIF) on November 3, 2005 into which the proceeds from disinvestment of Central Public Sector Enterprises (CPSEs) were to be channelised.

The public sector still remains the biggest employer in the organised sector and has a better track record with regard to having smooth industrial relations than the private sector. Board for Reconstruction of Public Sector Enterprises (BRPSE) was established in December 2004 as an advisory body to advise the Government on the strategies, measures and schemes for strengthening, modernising, reviving and restructuring of public sector enterprises. BRPSE has not been able to deliver the desired results because of various external factors, which include political pressures. The government has considered a proposal to dissolve the Board for Reconstruction of Public Sector Enterprises (BRPSE) and replace it with a new panel to speed up decisions related to revival of

*Profit Before Interest and Tax

ailing[6] state-owned units which have become a burden on taxpayers, i.e., strategic sale of its stake in most of the 65 sick central public sector companies, or closure of *unviable*[7] units.

Once the panel comes into being, a loss-making PSU will be considered for revival only if it is operational in a strategic area or if banks are willing to lend it money without a government guarantee. In case a PSU has a market share of at least 10%, then the government may continue its efforts to revive it. If a company's return on capital employed is lower than the rate it pays lenders, it may be considered as a case for strategic sale.

Strong views were expressed against disinvestment by some economists who believed that it is a clear move towards privatisation that would result in establishing a free economy and capitalist society. However, vehement opposition to privatisation and disinvestment has come largely from political parties and leaders having leftist leanings. The issue of disinvestment and privatisation is presented as an anti-people, anti-poor and anti-labour policy measure that is against the common good and larger social welfare. But the baggage of inefficiency associated with the public sector also cannot be ignored. Even the best possible management policies have failed to make most of the CPSEs efficient or economically viable.

Aid to Vocabulary

1. *Demarcated* — fixed the limits
2. *Agrarian* — relating to agriculture
3. *Predominance* — the state of being in a leading or controlling position
4. *Eradicate* — to put an end to
5. *Envisaged* — imagined as a future possibility
6. *Ailing* — in poor health
7. *Unviable* — not feasible or not capable of working successfully

Points to Remember

1. The PSUs were intended to bring about rapid growth of the economy.
2. The emphasis, in the Second Plan, was laid on industrialisation.
3. The growth of public sector came through nationalisation of private sector and direct investment in new industrial units.
4. The PSUs were established to reduce social inequalities.
5. The new Industrial Policy of July, 1991 was to bring all CPSEs under the system of Memorandum of Understanding (MoU).
6. Public sector's performance, in terms of profitability is poor but the PSUs do meet heavy social responsibilities.

7. Disinvestment means reducing the government's share in the equity stock of the PSUs by selling a part of its stockholding to private sector investors.
8. The Government of India constituted the NIF to channelise the proceeds from disinvestment.
9. BRPSE, established in December 2004 as an advisory body to advise the Government on the strategies, measures and schemes supporting PSEs, has not been able to deliver the desired results because of external factors.

List of Maharatna and Navratna CPSEs	
Maharatna	
Bharat Heavy Electricals Ltd. (BHEL)	National Thermal Power Corp. Ltd. (NTPC)
Coal India Ltd. (CIL)	Oil & Natural Gas Corp. Ltd. (ONGC)
Gas Authority of India Ltd. (GAIL)	Steel Authority of India Ltd. (SAIL)
Indian Oil Corp. Ltd. (IOCL)	
Navratna	
Bharat Electronics Ltd.	National Mineral Development Corp. Ltd.
Bharat Petroleum Corp. Ltd.	Neyveli Lignite Corp. Ltd.
Container Corporation of India Ltd.	Oil India Ltd.
Engineers India Ltd.	Power Finance Corp. Ltd.
Hindustan Aeronautics Ltd.	Power Grid Corp. of India Ltd.
Hindustan Petroleum Corp. Ltd.	Rashtriya Ispat Nigam Ltd.
Mahanagar Telephone Nigam Ltd.	Rural Electrification Corp. Ltd.
National Aluminium Company Ltd.	Shipping Corp. of India Ltd.
National Buildings Construction	

Essay

103 SMALL AND MEDIUM ENTERPRISES

SYNOPSIS

The Micro, Small and Medium Enterprises (MSMEs) play a vital role in the growth of the Indian economy. They have been classified broadly into two categories, viz.; manufacturing, and providing/rendering of services. The Industrial Policy Resolution of 1956 favoured the SSIs on the basis of four points, viz., employment generation, equitable distribution of national income, use of latent resources and decentralisation. Despite aiding foreign exchange generation and preservation of ancient and traditional skills, these MSMEs face many problems like non-availability of credit and finance, marketing problems, difficulty in procuring raw-materials, transportation, communication, etc. To boost this sector, the government announced Small-Sector Industrial Policy in 1991, and since then a number of steps have been taken to strengthen this sector in view of the evolving, liberalised and competitive economic environment.

Government of India enacted the Micro Small and Medium Enterprises Development (MSMD) Act 2006. The Micro, Small and Medium Enterprises (MSME) sector has emerged as a highly vibrant and dynamic sector of the Indian economy over the last five decades. MSMEs called SSIs (Small Scale Industries) earlier, not only play crucial role in providing large employment opportunities at comparatively lower capital cost than large industries but also help in industrialisation of rural areas. MSMEs are complementary to large industries as *ancillary*[1] units and this sector contributes *enormously*[2] to the socio-economic development of the country. The sector consisting of 36 million units, as of today, provides employment to over 80 million People, creating one million jobs every year. The sector through producing more than 8,000 quality products for the Indian and international markets, contributes around 15 to 16 per cent to India's GDP and is expected to touch a figure of 22 per cent in the next 3 years, besides 45% to the total manufacturing output and 43% to the exports from the country, which is anticipated to go up to at least 47-48 per cent by 2018. The MSME sector has the potential to spread industrial growth across the country and can be a major partner in the process of inclusive growth.

MSMEs also play a significant role in nation development through high contribution to domestic production, significant export earnings, low investment requirements, operational flexibility, location wise mobility, low intensive imports, capacities to develop appropriate *indigenous*[3] technology, import substitution, contribution towards defence production, technology – oriented industries, competitiveness in domestic and export markets thereby generating new entrepreneurs by providing knowledge and training.

After the liberalisation of the Indian economy, the products of MSMEs have had to face tough competition from the imported ones. To help them, the Government announced on 6th August 1991, an industrial policy which was aimed at providing MSMEs access to the capital market and encouraging their modernisation and technical sophistication. The industrial policy allowed equity participation by other industrial undertakings in the MSMEs. It proposed to introduce factoring services through Small Industries Development Bank of India (SIDBI), so as to solve the problems of delayed payments to the sector. Marketing of the products was proposed to be undertaken through co-operatives and priority was given to this sector for the allocation of raw materials. To revitalise the MSME sector, the government decided to improve their credit availability and introduce schemes to address the problems of *collaterals*[4], and encourage technology upgradation. The excise exemption limit and investment limit have been enhanced. The Government has made policies to protect the products of small-scale industrial sector from unequal competition by the large-scale industrial sector. It has reserved a large number of items which can be produced exclusively in the small scale industries.

While the MSME sector was largely protected through tariff walls and reservation policy, with the lowering of tariffs the sector has been subjected to foreign competition by way of cheap imports. The ongoing process of economic reforms and the changes in the international economic scene including the emergence of the World Trade Organisation (WTO), have thrown up several challenges as well as new opportunities for the SME sector. In fact, under the policy of reservations and concessions, the SME sector has neither been able to grow much nor create the desired impact on employment.

In India, the Micro, Small & Medium Enterprises have been classified broadly into two categories: (i) Manufacturing; and (ii) Those engaged in providing/rendering of services. Both categories of enterprises have been further classified into micro, small and medium enterprises based on their investment in plant and machinery (for manufacturing enterprises) or on equipments (in case of enterprises providing or rendering services). The Government of India in October 2006 enacted Micro, Small and Medium Enterprises Development Act 2006. Under the Act, Micro, Small and Medium Enterprises are classified as under:

(a) in the case of the enterprises engaged in the manufacture or production of goods pertaining to any industry specified in the First Schedule to the Industries (Development and Regulation) Act, 1951, as—(i) a micro enterprise, where the investment in plant and machinery does not exceed twenty-five lakh rupees;(ii) a small enterprise, where the investment in plant and machinery is more than twenty-five lakh rupees but does not exceed five crore rupees; or (iii) a medium enterprise, where the investment in plant and machinery is more than five crore rupees but does not exceed ten crore rupees; (b) in the case of the enterprises engaged in providing or rendering of services, as— (i) a micro enterprise, where the investment in equipment does not exceed ten lakh rupees; (ii) a small enterprise, where the investment in equipment is more than ten lakh rupees but does not exceed two crore rupees; or (iii) a medium enterprise, where the investment in equipment is more than two crore rupees but does not exceed five crore rupees.

District Industries Centers in all the districts of the State and the institutions have been instrumental in accelerating the pace of development of MSSIs. On the other hand, MSMEs have also played an important role in dispersal of industries.

Following the enactment of the MSME Development Act from October 2, 2006, registrations of all the MSMEs came within the *purview*[5] of the Industries *Commissionerate*[6]. Over a period of time, Gujarat has registered a sizeable growth of MSME sector. As many as 2,61,760 MSMEs were registered in Gujarat till March 2014. Surat district leads the state with the highest number of MSME units followed by Ahmedabad, Rajkot and other districts.

According to "MSME at a Glance, 2016", released by the Ministry of Micro, Small and Medium Enterprises—the MSMEs sector, consisting of 36 million units, provides employment to over 80 million persons. The Sector through more than 6,000 products contributes about 8% to GDP, has a critical role in boosting industrial growth and ensuring the success of the Make in India programme. Despite their high enthusiasm and inherent capabilities to grow, MSMEs in India are facing a number of problems like sub-optimal scale of operation, not getting the required support from the concerned government departments, banks, financial institutions and corporate as the loans that they get are not on preferential rates but are available around 15-18 per cent rate of interest which adds to their cost of operation, technological *obsolescence*[7], supply chain inefficiencies, increasing domestic & global competition, working capital shortages due to delayed payments, not getting trade receivables from large multinational companies on time, insufficient skilled manpower, change in manufacturing strategies and, *turbulent*[8] and uncertain market scenario. Excise duty is another issue faced by the MSME sector. While the cost of raw materials has gone up to 100 per cent, the excise limit is not increasing accordingly. It is very difficult for the small and tiny units to compete with the large units, because the large units are getting discounts on their purchase, given that they buy in bulk. To survive with such issues and compete with large global enterprises, MSMEs need to adopt innovative approaches in their operations. Nearly 60 per cent of the MSMEs in India fall in the unorganised sector. MSMEs that are innovative, inventive, international in their business outlook; and have a strong technological base, competitive spirit and willingness to restructure themselves, can withstand the present challenges and come out successfully to contribute 22% to GDP. Indian MSMEs are always ready to accept and acquire new technologies, new business ideas and automation in industrial and allied sectors. Once this untapped potential becomes the source of growth of these units, the size of Indian GDP can surpass that of developed nations.

Promoting growth of MSMEs is critical from the perspective of job creation which has been recognised as a prime mover of the development agenda in India. A number of schemes are being implemented for the growth and development of existing ones and for the establishment of new MSMEs. These include: (a) the Prime Minister's Employment Generation Programme, (b) Micro and Small Enterprises- Cluster Development Programme, (c) Credit Guarantee Fund Scheme for Micro and Small Enterprises, (d) Performance and Credit Rating Scheme, (e) Assistance to Training Institutions, and (f) Scheme of Fund for Regeneration of Traditional Industries. The Apprentice Protsahan Yojana was launched to support MSMEs in the manufacturing sector in engaging apprentices. The government is working to bring a single uniform law for the MSME sector to ensure operational efficiency and improve productivity while ensuring job creation on a large scale. The government is also taking several steps to boost manufacturing sector growth as it would lead to job creation and boost the country's economy. The government has already announced a National Manufacturing Policy

(NMP) that aims at raising the share of manufacturing to 25 per cent of GDP by 2022. The NMP *envisages*[9] setting up of national investment and manufacturing zones, which are industrial townships, benchmarked to the best manufacturing hubs in the world. The Central Government on its part has also set up National Manufacturing Competitiveness Council to suggest ways to enhance competitiveness in the manufacturing sector. The government is taking measures to promote exports by small and medium pharmaceutical manufacturers by providing technology up-gradation in the pharma sector. Ministry of Micro, Small and Medium Enterprises is running Credit Linked Capital Subsidy Scheme (CLCSS) under which Micro and Small Enterprises are entitled to take loan up to ₹ 1 crore with 15 per cent subsidy. Other initiatives to increase MSMEs, share in exports include providing financial assistance through export promotion councils, facilitating trade delegation meets and organising international exhibitions among others.

Small Industries Development Bank of India (SIDBI) offers loans to SMEs without collateral to the tune of around ₹ 1 crore. However, many are of the opinion that this limit needs to be increased to ₹ 2.5 crore.

The MSME Business Development Chamber of India is the leading National premier Chamber, working for the growth of MSMEs from Manufacturing and Service Sectors for the last 20 years. The Chamber supports export promotion, channelises bank finance and investment, joint ventures, technology transfers, exchange of know-how, setting up industries, marketing, distribution and connectivity with buyers, importers, investors and strategic business partners from abroad. The Chamber has presence in various countries and supports MSMEs in identifying emerging business and collaboration opportunities in Gulf Countries, Africa, North and South America, Japan and European countries. The Chamber is in the forefront to resolve the issues and problems of MSMEs and Industry; it provides recommendations and suggestions for policy change and emphasises on its implementation.

India has the longest history of small enterprise development policy in Asia as well as in the world at large. India has built up one of the most elaborate small enterprise development programmes in the world for providing assistance to individuals and institutions for setting up small scale enterprises, both in the urban and rural areas over the last six decades. In order to give more impetus to MSMEs, a number of central and state-level institutions have been set up to look after different aspects of the development programmes. At the central level, the different organisations are Small Industries Development Organisation (SIDO), National Small Industries Corporation (NSIC) and Small Industries Development Bank of India (SIDBI) while at the State level, the different organisations are Directorate of Industries, Small Industries Development Corporation (SIDC) and Small Industries Marketing Corporation (SIMC), etc. Not only institutions, but various assistance programmes Concessional Finance, Priority Sector Lending, Fiscal Incentives, Price Preference, etc., have been introduced.

AID TO VOCABULARY

1. *Ancillary* — providing necessary support to primary activities
2. *Enormously* — to very large extent or considerably
3. *Indigenous* — originating or occuring naturally in a particular place
4. *Collaterals* — security pledged as guarantee for repayment of loan
5. *Purview* — scope of influence or the extent local of activity
6. *Commissionerate* — a government-al official in charge of a department
7. *Obsolescence* — obsolete status.
8. *Turbulent* — not stable or clam
9. *Envisages* — conceive of as a possibility or a desirable future event

POINTS TO REMEMBER

1. The MSMEs sector plays a crucial role in providing large employment opportunities. It leads to industrialisation of rural areas.
2. Government of India, in October, 2006, enacted Micro, Small and Medium Enterprises Development Act 2006.
3. According to Economic Survey 2014-15, the 3.61 crore MSMEs sector contributed 37.5 per cent to the country's GDP.
4. Promoting MSMEs is critical for job creation perspective and thus is recognised as a prime mover of development agenda in India.
5. The MSME Business Development Chamber of India works for the growth of MSMEs form Manufcuturing and Service sectors.
6. The scarcity of finance and credit is the main obstacle in the development of MSME units.
7. There are some other constraints like the availability of power, transportation and communication.
8. Several measures have been taken by the government to boost the MSME sector.

KNOW THE ECONOMIST

AMARTYA SEN (B. 1933)

Amartya Sen is, inarguably, the most distinguished economist, India has ever produced. Prof. Sen is the recipient of the Nobel Prize for Economics for the year 1998, the sixth Indian Nobel Laureate to have been honoured with the award. The Bengal famine of 1943, marks the beginning of his life-time commitment to the study of deprivation and disparity. Sen has been a proponent of welfare economics and a bold critic of the Malthusian theory of population growth and assorted problems. According to him, apart from the shortage of food materials, there are also other relevant factors that cause famines.

Born in Shantiniketan, in the year 1933, Prof. Sen completed his Ph.D. in 1959 from Trinity College, Cambridge. This Shantiniketan-born economist, is a pioneer in Welfare Economics, and has to his credit several books and papers on aspects of welfare and development. He has broadened economists' notion of human 'well-being' so that it encompasses not just additional consumption but also developing human potential. Sen has also studied how underdevelopment adversely affects women and has argued that economists who study economic development need to focus more on developing opportunities for people. An economist with a difference, Prof. Sen is also a humanist. He has distinguished himself with his outstanding writings on poverty, famine, democracy, gender and social issues. The 'impossibility theorem' suggested earlier by Kenneth Arrow, states that it was not possible to aggregate individual choices into a satisfactory choice for society as a whole. Prof. Sen showed mathematically that societies could find ways to alleviate such a poor outcome. He was honoured with Bharat Ratna in 1999. The work of Amartya Sen has attempted to broaden the horizon of economic analysis. He has pointed out that the goal of a well-performing economic system is not just more goods and services, but improving the lives of most people. He has seen the development of human abilities as the real end of economic growth and the real reason to be an economist.

Essay
104 BANKING IN INDIA

SYNOPSIS

Banking in one form or the other has been prevalent in India since ancient times. The British government established the Presidency Banks in India. The need to regulate and control commercial banks was felt in the wake of the banking crisis. The Reserve Bank of India (RBI), the central bank of the country was established to bring the indigenous bankers together. Nationalisation was undertaken with a view to bring commercial banks into the mainstream of economic development. The banking sector has diversified its areas of operation. The Narasimham Committee felt the need to revamp the system. Based on its recommendations, reforms were introduced in the banking system. The government of India and RBI have set up the Bharatiya Mahila Bank Ltd—an all women bank; granted 'in principle' clearance to eleven entities for setting up 'Payment Bank' and shortlisted 10 microlenders for establishing 'Micro financing Institutions'.

Banking is an age-old phenomenon. It has been prevalent in India since ancient times. References to the money-lending business are found in the 'Manu Smriti' as well. *Indigenous*[1] banks operating in India used to grant loans against securities like jewellery, land and, *promissory*[2] notes or against personal credit of the borrowers. However, such bankers or moneylenders charged heavy rates of interest and thus, exploited the needy even as they took advantage of the latter's illiteracy and desperate need of money. The General Bank of India was the first joint stock bank which was established in the year 1786. The others which followed were the Bank of Hindustan and the Bengal Bank. The Bank of Hindustan had reportedly continued its operations till 1906 while the other two failed.

In 1809, when the Government realised the need for banks, the first Presidency Bank, called the Bank of Calcutta—later, the Bank of Bengal was opened in erstwhile Calcutta. The other two Presidency Banks, the Bank of Bombay and the Bank of Madras were established in 1840 and 1843, respectively. The Government had subscribed ₹ 3 lakh to their share capital. These Presidency Banks exercised monopoly in government banking. The East India Company had established these three banks. These banks were also given the authority of currency issue in 1823, which was, however, revoked in 1862. In 1921, they were *amalgamated*[3] into the Imperial Bank of India. The Oudh Commercial Bank, founded in 1881 was the first bank of limited liability which was managed by Indians. In the wake of the Swadeshi Movement, a number of banks with Indian management were established in the country namely, Punjab National Bank Ltd., Canara Bank Ltd., Indian Bank Ltd., Bank of Baroda Ltd., and Central Bank of India Ltd. The banking crisis during 1913-1917 and the failure of about 588 banks in different states created an urgent need for regulating and controlling commercial banks.

The Reserve Bank of India (RBI) was established under the Reserve Bank of India Act, 1934 on April 1, 1935 and afterwards nationalised on January 1, 1949. The RBI is the sole authority for the issue of currency other than one-rupee coins and subsidiary coins in India. As the agent of the Central Government, the Reserve Bank undertakes the distribution of one-rupee coins as well as other small-value coins which are issued by the Government. The Bank acts as a banker to the Central Government and state governments by virtue of the agreements entered into, with them. It also handles the borrowing programme of the Central and state governments. It formulates and administers monetary policy with a view to ensure price stability while promoting higher production in the real sector through deployment of credit. The RBI plays an important role in maintaining orderly conditions in the foreign exchange market and acts as an agent of the Government with respect to India's membership in the International Monetary Fund. It performs a variety of developmental and promotional functions. It also regulates and supervises the commercial banking system, urban co-operative banks and non-banking financial sector.

The Indian banking system faced many crises and failures, which caused its slow progress in the first half of the 20th century. However, in the latter half, it witnessed rapid progress. India had proceeded towards establishing public sector banking through the progressive nationalisation of commercial banks. On July 1, 1955, the Government of India nationalised the Imperial Bank of India to form the State Bank of India and thereafter its seven associate banks were nationalised in 1959-60. On July 19, 1969, fourteen major banks were nationalised by the Government with a view to bring them into the mainstream of economic development with definite social objectives and obligations. The Government acquired the ownership and control of these banks having deposits of over ₹ 50 crore each. Six more commercial banks were nationalised on April 15, 1980. In 1993, the New Bank of India merged with Punjab National Bank.

The Regional Rural Banks (RRBs) have been set up in different parts of the country in order to meet the credit requirements of the weaker sections, farmers, landless labourers, artisans and small entrepreneurs. The National Bank for Agriculture and Rural Development (NABARD) was established on July 12, 1982 as an apex body with the responsibility for overall development, policy, planning and financial support for agriculture and rural development. It provides credit to the rural sector through co-operative banks, commercial banks, RRBs and other financial institutions set up to finance rural development.

Though the State Bank of India was established as a commercial bank, with its efforts, it ushered in a new era of mixed banking system in the country. Apart from commercial banking, State Bank of India is also involved in the financing of agriculture and other priority sectors. Section 6 of the Banking Regulation Act 1949 issued guidelines of the banks permitting them to diversify their areas of operation with the nationalisation of banks, the banking companies felt the need to venture into new and progressive area.

With the policy of *liberalisation*[4], many foreign banks ventured into India with prompt, efficient and round-the-clock services, thus creating tough competition for the Indian banks. With the passage of time, the concept of banking has widened. Currently, overall, banking in India is considered fairly mature in terms of supply, product range and reach. Even in terms of quality of assets and capital adequacy, Indian banks are considered to have clean, strong and transparent balance sheets as compared to other banks in comparable economies in its region.

As capital is a key measure of a bank's capacity for generating loan assets and is essential for balance sheet expansion, the government has regularly been investing additional capital in the Public Sector Banks (PSBs) to support their growth and keep them financially sound and healthy so as to ensure that the growing credit needs of the economy are adequately met. Banks have also financed Small Scale Industries (SSIs) and the agricultural sector. The banking sector has diversified its areas of operation. The Integrated Rural Development Programme (IRDP) was launched to provide self-employment opportunities to the rural poor, and it was aided by the banking system.

To review the progress in the banking sector, a committee under the chairmanship of the former RBI Governor, M. Narasimham was constituted on August 14, 1991. Based on the recommendations of the Committee, a comprehensive set of reforms of the banking system was introduced in 1992-93. The reform process aimed at improving the productivity, efficiency and profitability of the banking system. Banking Ombudsman Scheme has been in operation since 1995. The scheme works under the control and supervision of RBI. Banking Ombudsman is an independent body with legal powers to settle disputes quickly and inexpensively. RBI has appointed Banking Ombudsmen all over the country. The system is designated to ensure, in normal course, satisfactory resolution of complaints as early as possible. Any customer whose grievance has not been resolved by banks to his satisfaction can approach the concerned Banking Ombudsman. The Banking Ombudsman Scheme 2006 was further amended in consultation with the government in February, 2009.

There are currently 27 public sector banks in India out of which 19 are nationlised banks, 6 are SBI and its associate banks, and rest two are IDBI Bank and Bharatiaya Mahila Bank, which are categorised as other public sector banks. As of March 31, 2014, there were 32 State Co-operative Banks and 50 Scheduled Urban Co-operative Banks in all, and 57 RRBs (Regional Rural Banks) operated with a network of 19, 081 branches in the country. There are, in all, 149 commercial banks including 25 private banks in India. As of December 31, 2015, 325 foreign banks have a branch form of presence, while 39 have a representative office form of presence in India.

The Reserve Bank of India on August 19, 2015 'in principle' cleared 11 entities—including department of posts, top conglomerates such as Reliance Industries and Aditya Birla Group, Telecom giants like Airtel and Vodafone, and a number of tech and finance companies—to set up 'payments banks'. Unlike 'universal banks'—as the regular banks are called—payments banks can accept deposits up to only ₹ 1 lakh and cannot grant loans. They can only deposit their money in government bonds. They can issue debit cards, but not credit cards. Other than this, they can provide all the services of a universal bank.

Ever since the first round of bank nationalisation in 1969, only two private business groups have been allowed to promote a bank. Although most corporate houses had applied for a universal bank licence, they all drew a blank, with only IDFC and Bandhan Microfinance being granted licences in 2015. Payments banks will largely depend on mobile and ATM infrastructure to provide banking services. Analysts expect tough competition to drive down charges for fund transfers and other transactions.

The Reserve Bank of India on September 16, 2015 shortlisted 10 micro lenders to set up 'small banks' to advance loans primarily to the unbanked, small businesses and farmers, micro and small industries and unorganised sector entities which do not have access to finance from the larger banks. The 10 entities were granted in principle approval to transform into banks, Small finance banks are similar to regular commercial banks except that their scale of services will be much smaller. These new type of banks should generate at least 75% of their business from the priority sector (largely agriculture) and mainly from areas where large banks are not present. Besides, 50% of their loans should be of ticket sizes under ₹ 25 lakh. Payments banks, on the other hand, are those specialised small banks which can only receive deposits and offer remittance services, but cannot give loans. The payments banks are also not allowed to hold a balance of more than ₹ 1 lakh per customer in their bank accounts.

With the new technological developments, banking has become easier and more convenient. Electronic Fund Transfer (EFT) facilitates transfer of funds electronically within and across cities and between branches of a bank and across banks. The government has introduced Direct Benefit Transfer (DBT) to transfer cash benefits like pension, scholarship, etc., directly to the bank or post office accounts of identified beneficiaries, using their unique identity (AADHAR) number issued by UIDAI*. Most of the banks in urban areas are computerised. With an ATM card, a person can withdraw money anytime. Debit card, credit card, petrocard, etc., facilitate transactions.

As in any other business, technology has completely transformed the landscape of the financial services sector. While the customers have been benefited immensely from the changes, there is still a long way to go for the banking sector to tap its full potential.

Aid to Vocabulary

1. *Indigenous* — local
2. *Promissory* — pertaining to a binding declaration of something to be done in the future
3. *Amalgamated* — joined or clubbed together
4. *Liberalisation* — free from political, religious, legal or moral restrictions

Points to Remember

1. The General Bank of India was the first joint-stock bank to be established in the year 1786.

*UIDAI — Unique Identification Authority of India

2. The Reserve Bank of India (RBI) was established under the Reserve Bank of India Act 1934, on April 1, 1935.
3. In the latter half of the 20th century, public sector banks were established and commercial banks were nationalised.
4. The National Bank for Agriculture and Rural Development was established in 1982 as an apex body for rural development.
5. With the passage of time, the concept of banking widened and it concerned itself not only with accepting deposits and loaning fund but also with development-oriented banking.
6. Banking Ombudsman is an independent body with legal powers to settle disputes quickly and inexpensively.
7. An all-women bank—Bhartiya Mahila Bank Ltd.—has been set up.
8. The RBI has cleared 11 entities to set up 'payments banks' that can accept deposits only to ₹ 1 lakh.
9. The RBI has shortlisted 10 micro-lenders to set up 'small banks' to advance loans to those without access to larger banks.
10. With the new technological developments, banking has become easier and more convenient.

WOMEN'S BANK—BHARATIYA MAHILA BANK LIMITED

With a view to promote gender equality and economic empowerment of women, the Government took a decision to set-up India's first Women's Bank, to address the gender related aspects of financial access to all sections of women, empowerment of women, and financial inclusion.

This would help promote both asset ownership by women (control over resources) and entrepreneurship, which would increase employment opportunities for them.

Government has infused an initial capital of ₹1,000 crore in the Bharatiya Mahila Bank Limited.

The Bank became functional on November 19, 2013.

PRADHAN MANTRI JAN DHAN YOJNA

Prime Minister Narendra Modi launched Pradhan Mantri Jan Dhan Yojana (PMJDY) on 28th August 2014 as a National Mission for Financial Inclusion to ensure access to financial services, namely, banking/savings & deposit accounts, remittance, credit, insurance, pension in an affordable manner. The scheme is aimed at ensuring that every family has at least one bank account.

The Programme is being implemented by the Ministry of Finance.

PAYMENT BANKS: FOCUS WILL BE ON TRANSACTIONS

1. Aditya Birla Nuvo	7. Reliance Industries
2. Airtel M Commerce Services	8. Dilip Shantilal Shanghvi
3. Cholamandalam Distribution Services	9. Vijay Shekhar Sharma
4. Department of Posts	10. Tech Mahindra
5. Fino Pay Tech	11. Vodafone M-Pesa
6. National Securities Depository	

WHAT ARE PAYMENTS BANKS?

Payments banks have differentiated licences with limitations on what they can do

- RBI norms limit demand deposits to a maximum of ₹ 1 lakh
- They cannot provide loans or accept term deposits
- The deposits raised by them will have to be invested in government bonds and a maximum of 25% can be invested in an account with another bank

BENEFITS FOR CUSTOMERS?

- Service charges will come down
- The requirement of minimum monthly quarterly balance is unlikely to be applied
- Competition from these new entities will force existing banks to offer low-cost (or low balance) basic accounts

MICRO FINANCING INSTITUTIONS: MICRO LENDERS

AU FINANCIERS | 1996
Rajasthan-based NBFC offers auto and SME loans

CAPITAL LOCAL AREA BANKS | 2000
Punjab-based local area bank

DISHA MICROFIN | 2009
Based in Ahmedabad, provides microfinance products and services to rural, semi urban and urban women in Gujarat, Rajasthan, MP and Karnataka

EQUITAS HOLDINGS | 2007
The Chennai-based MFI for the una banked is into financing vehicles and homes, also operates retail stores, schools, etc in rural areas

ESAF MICRO FINANCE & INVESTMENTS | 1992
Chennai-based organisation is into microcredit, insurance and business services like skill development for economically backward sector in Kerala

JL FINANCIAL SERVICES | 1999
MFI-turned-NBFC is based in Bengaluru and has presence in 15 states: is into loans to people and SMEs; backed by Morgan Stanley, Tata Capital, TPG

RGVN (NORTH EAST) MICRO FINANCE | 2008
Guwahati-based NGO-turned-MFI offers loans and savings products and has presence in Asom, Meghalaya, Arunachal, Nagaland and Sikkim

SURYODAY MICRO FINANCE | 2008
Navi Mumbai-based NBFC provides individual and group loans to low-income customers in Maharashtra, Odisha, Gujarat, Tamil Nadu, Karnataka, Rajasthan and MP; backed by IFC-World Bank, HDFC

UJJIVAN FINANCIAL SERVICES | 2005
One of the largest MFIs in India with over 400 branches; provides a full range of financial services to the economically active poor to build better lives

UTKARSH MICRO FINANCE | 2009
Varanasi-based MFI offers group, micro-enterprise and home loans; present in UP, Bihar, MP, Uttarakhand, Delhi, HP, Haryana and Maharashtra; backed by Norwegian Microfin Initiative, Commonwealth Development Corp

Essay **105**

ENERGY SCENE IN INDIA

SYNOPSIS

'Energy' refers to the capacity to make something happen. Energy is an essential input for economic and social development. There are two sources of energy—conventional and non-conventional. Conventional sources include coal, petroleum and firewood. These pollute the atmosphere. Non-conventional sources include water, wind, sun, organic wastes and biogas. The conventional sources of energy are estimated to last for a limited period only. There can be no industrial progress without energy. Power development started in India in 1897. Energy crisis occurred in 1973. This crisis in India pertains to scarcity of coal and electricity. Effective steps have been undertaken to tackle the energy crisis. India is one of the largest producers of solar equipments. India will soon become one of the leading centres of the energy system.

Energy refers to the capacity to make something happen. Forms of energy include heat and chemical energy. It is also associated with the transmission of light, sound and electricity. Energy is an essential *input*[1] for economic development and for improving the quality of life. Social development owes a lot to the development of energy resources of a particular country. India has an agriculture-based economy. But for ensuring India's prosperity, the industrial sector must also be developed. There can be no industrial progress without energy.

The first source of energy known to man was fire. Then he discovered *asphalt*[2], *peat*[3] and coal in the earth's crust. After the discovery of natural gas, man learnt to convert energy from one form into another. He learnt to *harness*[4] wind and water to run machines.

The sources of energy can be broadly classified into conventional and non-conventional sources. The conventional sources of energy consist of coal, petroleum and firewood, while the non-conventional sources consist of water, wind, sun, organic wastes and biomass. The latter do not pollute the environment, are available free of cost and are *replenishable*[5] unlike the conventional sources of energy. Among the primary resources of conventional energy, coal and oil are the most dominant while electricity generated from coal and oil is the principal secondary source of conventional energy in India. Hydel power has also gained importance. Besides, solar energy is an important renewable non-polluting source of energy which can be harnessed most economically.

Power development in India commenced at the end of the 19th century. Electric supply was commissioned in Darjeeling in 1897. This was followed by the setting up of a hydroelectric (hydel) power station at Sivasamudram in Karnataka in 1902. In the pre-Independence era, the power supply was mainly in the hands of the private sector and was restricted to the urban areas. With the formation of the State Electricity Boards during the formulation of Five-Year Plans, a significant step was taken in bringing about systematic growth of power supply all over the country. A number of multi-purpose projects came into being and with the setting up of thermal, hydel and nuclear power stations, power generation increased significantly.

The total installed capacity of power utilities in the country increased from 124, 287 MW in March 31, 2006 to 245, 259 MW as on March 31, 2014, with a compound annual growth rate of 7.84% over the period. The capacity as on 30.09.2016 was 306, 358 MW. At the end of September 2016, thermal power plants accounted for an overwhelming 69.60% of the total installed capacity in the country, whereas, the share of Nuclear energy was only 1.9% (5,780 MW). Hydro power plants come next with an installed capacity accounting for 14.5% of the total installed capacity.

Coal is one of the main source of energy in the country. Coal and Lignite were the major sources of energy production, accounting for about 73.48% of the total production during 2013-14. Crude Petroleum was second (11.81%), while Natural Gas (10.18%) was third. Coal deposits are mainly confined to eastern and south central parts of the country. The states of Jharkhand, Odisha, Chhattisgarh, West Bengal, Madhya Pradesh, Andhra Pradesh and Maharashtra account for more than 99% of the total coal reserves in the country. The State of Jharkhand had the maximum share in the overall reserves of coal in the country as on March 31, 2014 followed by Odisha.

The estimated reserves of crude oil in India as on March 31, 2014 stood at 762.74 million tons (MT), with maximum reserves in the western offshore whereas the estimated reserves of natural gas in India as on March 31, 2014 stood at 1427.15 billion cubic meters (BCM). India was the fourth largest consumer of crude oil in the world and the third largest crude oil consumer in the Asia-Pacific region after China and Japan. India's share in the total world production of natural gas during 2013-14 was only 1% (30.3 MTOE*). India's consumption of 46.3 Mtoe accounted for only 1.53% of total world consumption of natural gas. Electricity generation, followed by steel industries, is the biggest consumer of coal, The maximum use of Natural Gas is in fertilisers

*MTOE — Million Tonnes of Oil Equivalent

industry, followed by power generation. Of the total consumption of electricity in 2013-14, industry sector accounted for the largest share, followed by domestic, agriculture and commercial sectors.

The importance of increasing the use of renewable energy sources was recognised in the country in the wake of the two oil shocks 1970s. India has developed a very large programme for renewable energy. It covers almost all major renewable energy sources such as biogas, solar energy, wind energy, small hydel power and other emerging technologies. At the Government level, political commitment to renewable energy *manifested*[6] itself in the establishment of the first Department of Non-Conventional Energy Sources in 1982, which was then upgraded to a full-fledged Ministry of Non-Conventional Energy Sources (MNES) in 1992 and was subsequently renamed as Ministry of New and Renewable Energy (MNRE). MNRE is the *nodal*[7] ministry of the Government of India at the Federal level for all matters relating to new and renewable energy. MNRE has prepared a strategic plan for the period 2011-17 (covering the last year of the Eleventh plan and the next 5 years period of the Twelfth plan) and perspective till 2022. The mission of MNRE is to increase the contribution of 'Renewable Energy' in the total energy mix of the country to 6 per cent by 2022. Under the 50,000 MW* initiative launched by the Government in 2003-04, 162 hydro-electric projects spread across 16 states, with an installation of 47,930 MW, were taken up. To meet the requirement of additional capacity during the Twelfth Plan (2012-17), a shelf of 83 candid hydel projects having an aggregate capacity of 22,011 MW (excluding slippages from Eleventh Plan) have been prepared. India has added highest ever power generation capacity during the Twelfth Five-Year Plan. It has added cumulative power capacity of 61, 014 MW upto March 2015, an achievement of 469% of the targeted capacity addition of 88, 537 MW during the plan. Solar energy is being *tapped*[8] for a variety of applications like cooking, water-heating, drying of farm produce, water-pumping at home and street-lighting, power generation for meeting decentralised requirements in villages, schools and hospitals, etc.

There is high potential for generation of renewable energy from various sources—wind, solar, biomass, small hydro and cogeneration *bagasse*[9]. The total potential for renewable power generation in the country as on March 31, 2014 is estimated at 147615 MW. This includes wind power potential of 1,02,772 MW (69.6%), SHP (small-hydro power) potential of 19749 MW (13.38%), Biomass power potential of 17,538 MW (11.88%) and 5000 MW (3.39%) from bagasse-based cogeneration in sugar mills. The geographic distribution of the estimated potential of renewable

*MW — Mega Watt

power as on March 31, 2014 reveals that Gujarat has the highest share of about 25.04% (36,956 MW), followed by Karnataka with 13.08% share (19,315 MW) and Tamil Nadu with 11.17% share (16,483 MW), mainly on account of wind power potential.

Out of the total installed generation capacity of renewable power as on March 31, 2014, wind power accounted for about 66.69%, followed by biomass power (12.66%) and small hydro power (12%). Tamil Nadu had the highest installed capacity of grid connected renewable power (8070.26 MW) followed by Maharashtra (5630.20 MW) and Gujarat (4430.20 MW), mainly on account of wind power.

The national companies Oil and Natural Gas Corporation (ONGC, 1956), Oil India Limited (OIL, 1959), and Gas Authority of India Limited (GAIL, 1989) and a few private and joint venture companies are engaged in the exploration and production of crude oil and natural gas in the country. However, India has had to *resort*[10] to the import of oil to meet its energy requirements. As oil was cheap at that time, the imports *accelerated*[11] India's industrial development. But in 1973, a major crisis developed in India. The organisation of Petroleum Exporting Countries (OPEC) *hiked*[12] the oil prices by 400 per cent. As a result, expenditures on oil imports in India rose from 12 per cent to 76 per cent. This led to a wide gap between exports and imports and resulted in an adverse balance of trade. To pay off the import bill, India had to take loans from the International Monetary Fund (IMF).

The average quality of Indian coal is not very high and this necessitates the import of high quality coal to meet the requirements of steel plants. There has been an increasing trend in the import of coal. Net import of coal has steadily increased from 36.60 MTs* during 2005-06 to 199.88 MTs during 2015-16 (Provisional). India is highly dependent on import of crude oil. Net import of crude oil have increased from 99.41MTs during 2005-06 to 189.24 MTs during 2013-14.

The energy crisis compounded for India in the wake of global oil shortage as it *pertained*[13] to coal and electricity shortages, too. Oil shortage affects the transport sector. Coal shortage affects the generation of electricity. Power shortage affects industrialisation, agriculture and domestic supply. By way of recognising the need of efficient use of energy and its conservation as well as to meet the increasing energy demand, the Government of India enacted the Energy conservation Act-2001 and established the Bureau of Energy Efficiency (BEE) under the Ministry of Power in March, 2002. The Act provides for the institutionalisation, and

*MTs — Metric Tonnes

strengthening of the delivery mechanism for energy efficiency services in the country, in addition to facilitating the much-needed co-ordination between the various entities.

In the last few years, the Government has undertaken concerted efforts for enhancing 'Energy Security', with a view to increase the outreach of renewable energy technologies in a big way for *augmenting*[14] the energy needs of cooking, lighting, etc.

Oil and Gas companies have increased their exploratory drilling operations for crude oil and natural gas. India has purchased oil fields in Sudan. the discovery of oil at the Bombay High has already given a *boost*[15] to oil exploration in India. Natural gas reserves have been identified in the Krishna-Godavari basin in Andhra Pradesh. Nuclear Energy has been harnessed as an alternative source of energy. Nuclear power from 20 reactors that have a combined installed capacity of 4,780 MW accounts for a little less than 3% of electricity generated in India. Plans are in place to increase the capacity to 20,000 MW by 2020 and touch 60,000 MW by early 2030's, with 40,000 MW to be generated from reactors imported from France, US and Russia. Announced in November 2009, the Government of India proposed to launch its Jawaharlal Nehru National Solar Mission under the National Action Plan on Climate Change with plans to generate up to 20,000 MW grid-based solar power and 2,000 MW of off-grid solar power; and cover 20 million sq metres with collectors by the end of the final phase of the mission in 2020.

India's Annual Solar installations are estimated to grow over four times by 2017. 10.86 GW* of utility-scale solar and grid connected rooftop solar capacity will be added by 2016-17. Wind energy accounts for nearly 70% (23.44 GW) of installed capacity, thereby making India the world's fifth largest wind energy producer. The Government of India has set targets which will take the total renewable capacity to almost 175 GW by the end of 2022. To reduce the dependence on non-renewable energy resources, new technologies have been developed like hydrogen energy, geothermal energy, ocean energy, biofuels, fuel cells, battery operated vehicles, etc. To *tackle*[16] the energy crisis further, solar energy is being tapped to electrify houses, streets, etc. Sea waves and wind are also being tapped to provide energy. India is one of the largest producers of solar cells and photovoltaic modules in the world.

Modern life cannot be contemplated without the different sources of energy that make our life liveable. Washington-based world Watch Institute predicted that India, along with China, is especially positioned

---

*GW — Giga Watt

to become a leading centre of the next energy system. Our government has taken some important steps (like Special Area Demonstration Programme) to create greater awareness on new and renewable energy in order to facilitate greater acceptability, both in rural and urban areas, and in industrial and commercial sectors.

Aid to Vocabulary

1. *Input* — that which is put in
2. *Asphalt* — black substance derived from petroleum and used to surface roads
3. Peat — dark substance made up of decaying vegetable matter and used as fuel or garden soil
4. *Harness* — to control and use a natural force to produce electric power
5. *Replenishable* — able to build up again
6. *Manifested* — revealed or made apparent
7. *Nodal* — serving as intersecting
8. *Tapped* — extracted
9. *Bagasse* — residue left after the extraction of juice from sugar cane
10. *Resort* — to make use of, as a means of achieving something
11. *Accelerated* — made (something) happen faster, sped up
12. *Hiked* — raised sharply
13. *Pertained* — belonged, related (to)
14. *Augmenting* — increasing
15. *Boost* — an increase
16. *Tackle* — to deal with

Points to Remember

1. Energy plays a very important role in economic and social development.
2. The first source of energy known to man was fire.
3. There are two categories of sources of energy — conventional and non-conventional.
4. Electric supply was commissioned in Darjeeling in 1897.
5. India's first hydel power station was set up at Sivasamudram in Karnataka in 1902.
6. Total installed capacity of power utilities increased with a compound annual growth rate of 7.84% over the period from March, 2006 to March, 2014.
7. The use of renewable sources of energy is gaining importance.
8. Electricity generation, followed by steel industries, is the biggest consumer of coal.
9. India was faced with power crisis due to the global rise in oil prices.
10. MNRE – the only such ministry in the world, is for all the matters relating to new and renewable energy.
11. Solar energy is being tapped to tackle the energy crisis.

INDIA'S N-POWERMENT	
1948	Atomic Energy Commission constituted.
1951	Uranium Deposit at Jaduguda discovered; drilling begins.
1956	APSARA, first research reactor in Asia, goes critical at Trombay, Mumbai.
1957	Atomic Energy Establishment (AEET) inaugurated. Renamed Bhabha Atomic Research Centre (BARC)in 1967.
1960	Canadian Indian Reactor Uranium System (CIRUS), the 40 MW research reactor, goes critical.
1965	Plutonium plant inaugurated at Trombay.
1968	Nuclear fuel complex set up at Hyderabad, AP.
1969	Reactor Research Centre (RRC) starts at Kalpakkam, Tamil Nadu.Renamed Indira Gandhi Centre for Atomic Research (IGCAR) in 1985.
1969	Heavy Water Project constituted at Mumbai. Later renamed Heavy Water Board.
1969	Tarapur Atomic Power Station starts commercial operation.
1970	Uranium-233 is separated from irradiated Thorium.
1974	Underground nuclear test conducted at Pokhran, Rajasthan.
1983	Fast Breeder Test Reactor attains first criticality.
1984	Uranium-233 fuelled reactor PURNIMA-II goes critical.
1985	Fast Breeder Test Reactor at IGCAR goes critical.
1987	Nuclear Power Corp of India Ltd. formed.
1993	BARC supplies one millionth radioisotope consignment.
1996	Uranium-233 fuelled Kalpakkam Mini Reactor (KAMINI) goes critical.
1998	Five underground nuclear tests conducted at Pokhran Range, Rajasthan.
2005	India's first 540MW Nuclear Power Reactor Tarapur Unit 4 goes critical.
2006	India joins International Thermo-nuclear Experimental Reactor project.
2008	**Nuclear Deal Sealed**—On October 11, 2008, in Washington, India's then External Affairs Minister Pranab Mukherjee and U.S. Secretary of State Condoleeza Rice signed and sealed the Nuclear deal.
2011	Locals protested against the Kudankulam plant in Tamil Nadu and the Jaitapur plant in Maharashtra; the Fukushima disaster in Japan gave a serious blow on a global scale to the public's confidence in the safety of nuclear plants.
2012	The Atomic Energy Regulatory Board (AERB) gave its nod for the second heat up (all systems of the entire nuclear power plant at Kudankulam put to test to demonstrate its operability and safety).
2013	The first 1000 MW unit of the much delayed Kudankulam project was commissioned.
2014	North eastern power system improvement project got approval.
2015	India added highest ever power generation capacity during the Twelfth Five Year plan. It added cumlative power capacity of 61, 014 MW upto March 2015.

Essay
106

TOURISM IN INDIA

SYNOPSIS

Tourism plays a vital role in the economic development of a country. Tourism is the second largest foreign exchange earner in India. The tourism industry employs a large number of people, both skilled and unskilled. It promotes national integration and international brotherhood. India has always fascinated people from all over the world with her secularism and the diversity of her culture. There are historical monuments, beaches, places of religious interest, hill resorts, etc., that attract tourists. Every region is identified with its handicraft, fairs, folk dances, music and its people. The Department of Tourism promotes international and domestic tourism in the country. The Tourism Advisory Board recommends measures for promotion of tourist traffic in India. Indian tourism is adversely affected by terrorism, touts and pollution. Sincere efforts could help to further develop the Indian tourism industry.

Tourism is one of the fastest growing industries of the world. It plays a *vital*[1] role in the economic development of a country. India is one of the popular tourist destinations in Asia. Bounded by the Himalayan ranges in the north and surrounded on three sides by water (Arabian sea, Bay of Bengal and Indian Ocean), India offers a wide array of places to see and things to do. The enchanting backwaters, hill stations and landscapes make India a beautiful country. Historical monuments, forts, etc., add to the *grandeur*[2] of the country. They attract tourists from all over the world.

Tourism is the second largest foreign exchange earner in India. The tourism industry employs a large number of people, both skilled and unskilled. As compared to other modern service sectors, a higher proportion of tourism benefits accrue to women. Hotels, travel agencies, transport including airlines benefit a lot from this industry. Tourism promotes national integration and international understanding. It promotes cultural exchange. Tourism also promotes the traditional handicrafts sector. The tourist gets an *insight*[3] into the rich and diverse cultural heritage of India.

India has a composite culture wherein, there is a harmonious blend of art, religion and philosophy. Though India has been subjected to a series of invasions, she has *retained*[4] her originality despite absorbing the best of the external influences. Religions like Christianity, Buddhism, Islam, Hinduism, Jainism, Sikhism and Zoroastrianism have co-existed in India. India has fascinated people from all over the world with her secularism and the diversity of her culture.

The diverse geographical *locales*[5] of India delight the tourists. The monuments, museums, forts, sanctuaries, places of religious interest, palaces, etc., offer a *treat*[6] to the eyes. Every region is identified with its handicrafts, fairs, folk dances, music and its people.

Some of the places that attract a huge number of tourists are Agra, Jaipur, Jhansi, Hyderabad, Nalanda, Mysore, Delhi, Mahabaleshwar, Aurangabad, etc. Haridwar, Ujjain, Shirdi, Varanasi, Allahabad, Puri, Ajmer, Amritsar, Vaishno Devi, Badrinath, Kedarnath, Rameshwaram, etc., are places of religious importance. Srinagar, Kullu, Manali, Dehradun, Mussoorie, Nainital, Darjeeling, Ooty, etc., are famous hill resorts.

The Department of Tourism has been formed to promote international and domestic tourism in the country. It provides infrastructure and carries out publicity campaigns. It provides information aimed at the promotion of tourist sites in the world market. It *formulates*[7] policies and programmes for the promotion of tourism in India. It has offices in India and abroad. The Indian Institute of Tourism and Travel Management, The National Council for Hotel Management and Catering Technology, etc., provide professionally trained personnel to the industry.

The Tourism Advisory Board recommends measures for promotion of tourist traffic in India. It reviews the tourist *trends*[8] and suggests appropriate measures. Some of the palaces, *havelis* and castles have been converted into heritage hotels. In these hotels, the tourists get to experience the *exotic*[9] lifestyle of a *bygone era*[10]. The magnificent 'palace on wheels', a tourist train which travels through Rajasthan, attracts a lot of foreign tourists. The Indian Tourism Development Corporation (ITDC) organises entertainment programmes like folk dances and songs and provides shopping facilities for tourists. Today, many private companies like Make my Trip, Sterling Holidays, Club Mahindra, etc., arrange domestic as well as foreign tours.

With the growth of the urban professional middle class, tourism in India is flourishing. Many states have taken necessary steps to promote tourism. Goa promotes water sports like sailing, scuba diving and surfing. Jammu & Kashmir and Himachal Pradesh, offer the pleasure of winter sports like skiing and mountaineering. Kerala, following Kashmir, has introduced the concept of houseboats in its lagoons. Highlighting monuments, as venues for cultural events, is becoming a popular means of attracting tourists these days.

Since the year 2005, the Indian Tourism Development Corporation (ITDC) has been running a campaign called 'Incredible India' to encourage tourism in India. The slogan of this campaign is 'Atithi Devo Bhavah'. For better growth, ITDC categorised different places under different sections like 'spiritual tourism', 'spa tourism', 'ecotourism' and 'adventure tourism'. Things have now started looking bright for the Indian tourism industry.

Initiatives of Ministries of Tourism and Culture include—*Swachh Bharat Swachh Smarak e-poster*, a special poster with Prime Minister's message requesting the tourists and the people of the nation to wholeheartedly engage themselves in the cleanliness of their surroundings and help create a *Swachh Bharat, Swachh Smarak*; *Welcome Cards*, that will be handed to all the tourists, landing at 9 international airports where Tourist Visa on Arrival (TVoA) enabled with Electronic Travel Authorisation (ETA) facility is operational. This card will carry the information of the local India Tourism office along with online and offline contact information which the tourists can use in case of any queries; *Swachh Bharat Swachh Pakwan (Hunar Zaika)*, a program aimed at upgrading the skills and hygiene standards of Street Food Vendors, so that they become a distinctive aspect of Indian tourism; *Incredible India Helpline*, to address and guide tourists during any emergency which may include medical, crime, natural calamities or being stranded; *Mega Project-Destination Development of Gwalior,* for development of tourism in Gwalior – which is least developed.

On the other hand, some other initiatives taken by Ministry of Culture include – *Launching of Web based e-Ticketing*, to facilitate visitors to the monuments in getting better access; *25 Model Monuments (Adarsh Smarak)*, under which 25 identified monuments will be provided necessary tourist facilities including wi-fi, security, signages, *encroachment*[11] free area, interpretation centres showing short films about the importance of monuments and signboards of *Swachh Bharat Abhiyan* mentioning the slogan *'Swachh Smarak: Swachh Bharat'*.

Union Home Minister and Tourism Minister launched landmark Tourist Visa on Arrival (TVOA), enabled with Electronic Travel Authorization (ETA) scheme to facilitate nationals of 43 countries to travel to India for tourism for a short stay of 30 days.

Several steps that have been taken to ease the Visa regime include, abolishing the restriction of two months' gap between two consecutive visits of a foreigner, introduction of Visa fees payment through debit and credit cards, increasing the number of airports for TVoA from four to nine, simplification of Visa form, introduction of local language to help foreigners in filling online visa application form, removing the requirement of filling of Departure (Embarkation) card by outgoing foreigners and Arrival (Disembarkation) card by incoming Indians and the simplification of Embarkation/Disembarkation Cards, besides the introduction of Collective Landing Permit (CLP).

'Tourism and Hospitality' has been identified as one of the important sectors, which have the potential to generate significant employment opportunities for the skilled population of India. Making the job seekers employable in this sector in order to bridge the skill gap is the key objective of THSC (Tourism and Hospitality-sector Skill Council).

Tourism is the largest service industry in the country and has the potential to stimulate economic growth of the country.

The tourism ministry has set an ambitious target of creating 24.9 million jobs during the Twelfth Five-Year Plan to increase the sector's growth from 9 per cent to 12 per cent. However, the Indian tourism industry has certain problems to deal with, the major among these being that of pollution. *Emission*[12] from the Mathura Refinery has led to the discolouration of the Taj Mahal in Agra. The condition of many other monuments is also deteriorating due to the negligence of the authorities concerned. On the other hand, beaches have become the dumping grounds of garbage littered by tourists. This nuisance needs to be checked.

Terrorism is a major global problem today. Our country is no exception. The terrorist attacks, agitations and separatist movements hinder the growth of tourism. Kashmir is paradise for domestic and international tourists. However, *incessant*[13] terrorism in this valley hampers the growth of tourism, which is very important for the economy of the state. Necessary steps should be taken by state governments as well as the Central Government to curb terrorism and insurgency, and bring about peace.

The government has set a holistic agenda for tourism development among various government departments at the national level. To achieve its target, the tourism infrastructure in India should be strengthened. Airports and railway stations should provide information about the tourist destinations. The Government should also make the maintenance of tourist destinations a *priority*[14]. Steps should be taken to restore the ancient *splendour*[15] of the monuments. Sincere efforts could help to further develop the Indian tourism industry. In fact, this high potential sector, which has multiple effects on income and employment generation, is still relatively untapped.

Aid to Vocabulary

1. *Vital* — important
2. *Grandeur* — magnificence
3. *Insight* — deep understanding
4. *Retained* — continued to have
5. *Locales* — scenes
6. *Treat* — thing that gives great pleasure
7. *Formulates* — creates or prepares something carefully
8. *Trends* — general tendencies
9. *Exotic* — unusual and striking
10. *Bygone era* — past period
11. *Encroachment* — entry to another's property without right or permission
12. *Emission* — releasing of harmful substances in the air
13. *Incessant* — continuing without stopping
14. *Priority* — more important and urgent than other things
15. *Splendour* — grand, magnificent

Points to Remember

1. India attracts tourists from all over the world.
2. Tourism generates foreign exchange.
3. India has a composite culture.
4. There are historical monuments, beaches, places of religious interest, hill resorts, etc., that attract tourists.
5. The Department of Tourism promotes domestic and international tourism.
6. The Tourism Advisory Board recommends measures for promotion of tourist traffic in India.
7. The tourism industry is affected by terrorism and pollution.
8. Several initiatives have been taken by Ministries of Tourism and Culture in order to strengthen the tourism industry.
9. The key objective of THSC is to generate significant employment opportunities for the skilled population of India.

MONTH-WISE FOREIGN ARRIVALS IN INDIA, 2013-2015			
Month	**Foreign Tourist Arrivals (FTAs) in India**		
	2013	**2014**	**2015 (P)**
January	720321	757786	790100
February	688569	755678	761487
March	639530	690441	729636
April	450580	535321	539748
May	417453	465043	510736
June	451223	502028	513427
July	506427	568871	633347
August	486338	575750	589098
September	453561	509142	NA
October	598095	668398	NA
November	733923	765497	NA
December	821581	885144	NA
Total	6967601	7679099	NA
Sub total (Jan-August)	4360441	4850918	5067579

Source: (i) Bureau of Immigration, Govt. of India, Total arrivals for 2013 (6967601) & for 2014 (7679099)

(ii) Ministry of Toursim, Govt. of India for 2015

Essay
107

POVERTY IN INDIA

SYNOPSIS

India was once known for her prosperity as she had abundant resources. Foreign rule made India a poor country. Poverty is the state of being poor. A substantial percentage of the total population of India lives below the poverty line. According to the United Nations Development Programme's Global Human Development Index, 2015, India is ranked 130th among 188 countries. People living below the poverty line are deprived of the basic requirements of life. The chief causes of poverty are over-population, unemployment, uneven distribution of resources, slow industrial growth, rise in the cost of living, etc. Poverty leads to many social and economic problems. Several anti-poverty programmes have been launched over the years. The programmes of the Five-Year Plans need to be carried out more effectively.

India was once known for its prosperity. Its abundance in riches and resources had earned it the sobriquet of 'the golden bird'. However, successive invasions by foreign powers made India a poor country. The Turks, the Mughals and the British exploited the resources to a great extent and bound India with the shackles of poverty. Poverty is a *grim*[1] reality in India today.

Poverty is the state of being poor. It can be defined as a social phenomenon in which a section of the society is in the state of not having the minimum income to fulfil the basic requirements of life. These include food, clothing, shelter, education and health. Poverty leads to misery. It lowers the standard of living and breeds diseases.

According to the United Nations Development Programme's (UNDP) Global Human Development Index-2015, India is ranked 130th among 188 countries. The report says that India fails dramatically on the income measure. The annual income per person (measured in purchasing power parity terms) for India is $5.150, slightly more than our neighbours, but lowest among the BRICS countries, and less than half the global average of $13,723. The average for developed countries, is way ahead at $40,046.

In addition, according to the global Multidimensional Poverty Index (MPI), 2015, an international measure of acute poverty covering over

100 developing countries, analysed at the University of Oxford, there are 1.6 billion people living in multidimensional poverty across the world and nearly 440 million of them are in eight large Indian states.

The eight Indian states that have similar number of poor as in 25 African countries are Bihar, Jharkhand, Madhya Pradesh, Uttar Pradesh, Chattisgarh, Odisha, Rajasthan and West Bengal. The poorest region in South Asia is Bihar, the analysis states.

The least poor Indian states according to the global Multidimensional Poverty Index (MPI) in 2015 remained the same as in the 2010 analysis, they are: Kerala, Tamil Nadu, Himachal Pradesh, Punjab, Mizoram, Goa and Delhi.

According to the Millennium Development Goals India Country Report 2015, during the last two decades, India has liberated more than 100 million of its citizens from extreme poverty; i.e, the proportion of people whose income is less than one dollar a day stands halved, between 1990 and 2015; still, it is home to a very large number of people living in abject poverty. The *erstwhile*[2] Planning Commission of India had periodically released poverty estimates on the basis of large sample surveys on household consumer expenditure by National Sample Survey Office under the Ministry of Statistics & Programme implementation. The methodology for poverty estimation has been reviewed frequently by the central government and revised accordingly. During this period, poverty declined by 16.10 percentage points in rural areas and by 12 percentage points in urban areas and that resulted in decline of total poverty by 15.3 percentage points.

The Socio-Economic Caste Census (SECC) 2011 released on July 3, 2015 was the first *comprehensive*[3] exercise to estimate India's rural poverty level. It was conducted across 640 districts and 17.91 crore households, excluding households having motorised 2/3/4-wheelers or fishing boats, Kisan Credit Card with ₹ 50,000 credit limit, a member with a government job or earning ₹ 10,000 a month, etc.

With more than half (over 9 crore) of all rural households living by doing casual manual labour, the much *heralded*[4] non-agricultural enterprises were providing livelihood to just 29 lakh households, a meagre 1.6% of the total. Cultivators were reported as making up about 30%. On the other hand, the service class—government, public and private sector—constitutes just 14%.

The Census says that a *staggering*[5] 92% of rural households reported their maximum income below ₹ 10,000 per month. Nearly three quarters of all rural households said that the income of the highest earning member was ₹ 5,000 or less.

The main cause of poverty is over-population. The national income has failed to *keep pace with*[6] the growing population. In rural areas, poverty is due to inadequate land base as well as low level of productivity. The uneven distribution of resources and improper *sectoral investment*[7] are other significant causes of poverty.

Poverty gives rise to many problems in the society, child labour being the most glaring of those. The total number of child labour in the country has reduced by 65 per cent as per the Census 2011. The total number of working children in the country has declined from 1.26 crore as per the Census 2001 to 43.53 lakh as per Census 2011 which shows 65 per cent reduction.

Poverty also leads to illiteracy, crime, corruption, prostitution, etc. In Odisha, extreme poverty has forced parents to sell their children for money. There are reports of farmers committing suicide on not being able to repay loans. They are not able to repay loans even after selling off their lands. Seeking a better source of living, people often migrate to towns and cities. In fact, people below poverty line create slum areas in cities. Slums are characterised by very unhygienic conditions and are breeding grounds of various epidemics.

Several anti-poverty programmes have been launched over the years. These programmes generate additional employment and create productive *assets*[8]. They impart technical and business skills and raise the income level of the poor. But the rate of success remains low because of over-population.

Poverty reduction has been an important goal of development policy since the inception of planning in India. Alleviation of poverty attained top-most priority for the plan panel.

The Swarnajayanti Gram Swarozgar Yojana (SGSY) was formed in 1999. The objective of the scheme is to bring the poor families above the poverty line. The Jawahar Gram Samridhi Yojana, the Sampoorna Gramin Rozgar Yojana, the Swarnajayanti Shahari Rozgar Yojana, the Annapurna Scheme, the Samagra Awaas Yojana, the Pradhan Mantri Gram Sadak Yojana, the Indira Awas Yojana, etc., are other important schemes. These schemes were launched to provide shelter, sanitation and drinking water to the poor.

The National Rural Employment Guarantee Act 2005 was implemented, as of February, 2006, in 200 backward districts. During 2009-10, it was rechristened as Mahatma Gandhi National Rural Employment Guarantee Act (MGNREGA). The Act aims at enhancing livelihood security of households in rural areas of the country by providing at least one hundred days of guaranteed wage employment, in a financial year, to every household whose adult members volunteer to do unskilled manual work.

The Mahatma Gandhi National Rural Employment Guarantee Act (MGNREGA) is the largest public employment programme in the World providing work to 5 crore rural households or 10 crore workers. One in every 3 rural households is a worker under the programme. It addressed 41% of the problem of underemployment in the rural areas. Studies have shown that this programme yields an income while there is no other means of livelihood; and it, therefore, has smoothened the rural consumption in the lean periods and drought periods.

Though the government has been successful to some extent, *eradication*[9] of poverty is not an easy task. Many other related factors need to be looked into, if we are to accomplish the goals. The alarming rate of increase of population should be checked. The government should undertake effective steps to make India a fully literate country. The vast tracts of land which are lying barren should be fertilised and utilised for cultivation. The various programmes launched by the government should be carried out more effectively.

A lot remains to be done before we can match the standards of the developed countries of the world.

Aid to Vocabulary

1. *Grim* — very serious, depressing
2. *Erstwhile* — former
3. *Comprehensive* — including all or nearly all elements of something
4. *Heralded* — much talked about before happening or becoming available
5. *Staggering* — astonishing or overwhelming
6. *Keep pace with* — match the level of
7. *Sectoral investment* — use of money in a branch of a particular area of a country's economy
8. *Assets* — valuable properties
9. *Eradication* — elimination, putting an end to something

Points to Remember

1. Foreign rule had changed India into a poor country.

2. According to the Global MPI, 2015, among the 1.6 billion people living in multidimensional poverty across the world, nearly 440 million are in eight large Indian states.
3. Proportion of people with income less than one dollar a day stands halved between 1990 and 2015, as per Millennium Development Goals India Country Report 2015.
4. First comprehensive exercise to estimate India's rural poverty levels is the Socio-Economic Caste Census (SECC) 2011.
5. There are several causes of poverty. The main cause is over-population.
6. Poverty leads to many problems like child labour, illiteracy, crimes, etc.
7. Since the Fifth Plan steps have been taken by the government through various programmes to eradicate poverty.
8. A lot remains to be done before we can match the standards of the developed countries.

GUIDED COMPOSITION

Develop the following paragraph into a full-fledged essay in 800-1000 words. The gist of the topic is provided in approximately 155 words for your help:

POVERTY IS THE MOTHER OF ILL HEALTH

Poverty is a curse on man. It is the mother of all human weaknesses. It breeds ignorance, corruption, disease and superstition. A poor man cannot afford to provide even the basic amenities to his family. He leads a most undignified life. Forced by circumstances, he adopts means of livelihood which do not meet the society's approval. Thus, homeless, jobless, ill-fed and ill-clad he becomes a victim of ill health. A never ending vicious cycle holds him in its grip, from which there is no freedom. Society shuns the poor like plague and considers them parasites. Nobody waits to ponder over their sorry plight and restore some dignity to their lives. Hence, poor continue to grapple with their poverty, while the rich enjoy their riches totally oblivious of the miserable condition of their brethren. Undoubtedly, poverty is the biggest curse. It robs man of everything human. He loses his dignity, health and the will to live.

(155 words)

Essay 108

RISING PRICES—IMPACT ON THE COMMON MAN

SYNOPSIS

India is a developing country. Rise in prices is inevitable in a developing economy. Limited inflation contributes to economic growth. But for some time now, the level of inflation has gone far beyond reasonable limits. This has caused harassment to the common man, especially the poorer sections of the society. Over population is the major factor for rise in prices. Steps should be taken to increase production in all sectors. Continuous price-hikes may lead to anarchy—a complete failure of all government and official systems. Effective steps must be taken to check rise in prices and to maintain a stable economy.

India is a developing economy. Rise in prices is *inevitable*[1] in a developing economy. The programmes of economic development generate large employment and income. These increase the demand for *consumer*[2] goods and services. There has been a sharp increase in the prices of essential commodities in the past few years. Retail inflation has really been a matter of great concern.

Inflation refers to a rise in prices and wages caused by an increase in the money supply and demand for goods and services resulting in a fall in the value of money. Limited inflation contributes to economic growth. The standard of living of the common people is closely linked to the nation's economic situation.

In 2013, the Consumer Price Index (CPI) replaced the Wholesale Price Index (WPI) as the main measure of inflation. The Indian consumer price index is a measure of the average price which consumers spend on a market-based "basket" of goods and services. In India, the most important category in the consumer price index is Food and beverages (45.86 per cent of the total). Housing accounts for 10 per cent; Transport and communication for 8.6 per cent; Fuel and light for 6.84 per cent; Clothing and footwear for 6.5 per cent; Medical care for 5.9 per cent; and Education for 4.5 per cent. Inflation Rate in India is reported by the Ministry of Statistics and Programme Implementation (MOSPI), India.

Blackmarket and scarcity of essential commodities are both causes and effects of rising prices. Corrupt traders try to earn money by indulging in malpractices. They, sometimes, by *hoarding*[3], create artificial shortage in ration shops as well as in free market, and deny the consumers their due. Corruption, in all its forms, *fuels*[4] price rise.

The alarming rise in population is another factor for the rise in prices. India is the second most populated country in the world with a population of more than one billion. In spite of the considerable development in all sectors since Independence, conditions of scarcity still prevail mainly due to overpopulation.

The majority of the people of India are poor. The Government should take measures to tackle the *menace*[5] of price rise on a priority. The consumers should be guided with regard to their rights and privileges. They should be made aware of the prevalent corrupt practices. The public distribution system should be strengthened. Corrupt officials should be *brought to book*[6]. Effective steps should be taken to increase production in all sectors. The rise in population should be checked to reduce the demand and pressure on our limited resources.

Rise in prices gives rise to economic *disparities*[7]. It widens the gulf between the rich and the poor. Due to *soaring*[8] prices, even food items are going beyond the reach of the poor. A democracy cannot flourish or function in such a condition. However, some steps taken by the Central Government have given some relief to the common people. Implementation of Mahatma Gandhi National Rural Employment Guarantee Act (MGNREGA) is one of them.

There is *testimony*[9] to the fact that price rise leaves a great impact on the common man's mind. In the 1990's, the sudden and steep increase in the price of onions brought about the downfall of one state government. A similar rise in the price of sugar brought down another. Continuous price-hike may lead to anarchy—a complete failure of all government and official systems. Effective steps must be taken to solve the problem of price hike. The government's *mounting*[10] administrative expenditure must be *curtailed*[11].

In May, 2007 the Government launched a mammoth scheme to double the growth rate in agriculture to 4 per cent over the Eleventh Plan period. The Centre provided ₹ 25,000 crore for new initiatives launched by states. It also announced a time-bound Food Security Mission to counter rising prices of food products by enhancing production of wheat, rice, pulses, and edible oil to ensure visible changes in their availability over three years.

Rising prices spare neither the rich nor the poor. Rising prices have given rise to widespread distress among the fixed income groups, viz., wage earners and the salaried classes. The Central and state governments often blame each other for the rise in prices. The drop in agricultural production results in the shortage and non-availability of food items, which hit the economically weaker sections of the society the most.

The National Food Security Act, 2013 (NFSA 2013) (also Right to Food Act) is an Act of the Parliament of India which aims to provide *subsidised*[12] foodgrains to approximately two thirds of India's 1.2 billion people. It was signed into law on September 12, 2013.

The Act converts into legal entitlements the existing food security programmes of the Government of India. It includes the Mid Day Meal Scheme, Integrated Child Development Services (ICDS) scheme and the Public Distribution System (PDS). Further, the NFSA 2013 recognises maternity entitlements. The Midday Meal Scheme and the Integrated Child Development Services Scheme are universal in nature whereas the PDS reaches about two-thirds of the population (75% in rural areas and 50% in urban areas). Ushering in a new era in the domain of food safety, the food safety and Standards Act of 2006 came into force in India on August 5, 2011. This Act will ensure prevention of fraudulent, deceptive or unfair trade practices which harm the customer through the provision of sub-standard grains.

Food prices are cyclical in nature. A sharp increase in food prices has been a cause for concern. A significant part of this inflation is due to supply bottlenecks in some of the essential commodities, precipitated by the delayed monsoon and drought conditions in some parts of the country. India cannot be immune to global price situations, of crude oil in particular, especially when a significant proportion of the country's requirement of oil is met through imports.

India's average inflation was more than 9 per cent between 2006 and 2013. Inflation Rate in India averaged 8.14 per cent from 2012 until 2015, reaching an all time high of 11.16 per cent in November of 2013 and a record low of 3.66 per cent in August of 2015. After remaining high for a *prolonged*[13] period, inflation finally trend down. Prices of the major commodity groups contributing to high inflation, namely 'eggs, meat, and fish', fruits and vegetables, and fuel, all softened.

The major developments driving the *stubborn*[14] inflation down were falling global commodity prices, especially of crude oil; softness in the global prices of tradables, particularly edible oils and even coal; decline in the growth rate of rural wages triggered by substantial increase in minimum support prices (MSP) and the launch of MGNREGA; reducing of the demand pressures on protein-based items. The tight monetary policy helped contain demand pressures, creating a *buffer*[15] against any external shock and keeping *volatility*[16] in the value of the rupee under check. Though it was high food inflation that contributed to elevated headline inflation, for sustainability of low inflation the policy focus should be on enhancing the *resilience*[17] of the agriculture sector; and eliminating leakages, inclusion and exclusion errors, as well as various *distortions*[18] created by the present food policy. The upside risk to inflation outlook also *emanates*[19] from uncertainties surrounding the monsoon, international crude oil prices, and the stability in the value of the rupee, particularly in the event of monetary tightening by the Federal Reserve Bank of the US.

The decline in inflation is found to be substantial in commodities where the government had taken effective measures. The government took a series of measures to improve availability of foodgrains and *de-clog*[20] the distribution channel. Some of the major steps taken recently in this regard includes: Moderation in increases in the MSPs; Advisory to the states to allow free movement of fruits and vegetables by delisting them from the Agricultural Produce Marketing Committee (APMC) Act; Bringing onions and potatoes under the purview of the Essential Commodities Act 1955, thereby allowing state governments to impose stock limits to deal with *cartelisation*[21] and hoarding, and making violation of stock limits a non-bailable offence; Imposing a minimum export price (MEP) for potatoes and onions.

For keeping food inflation low in a sustainable manner, more radical measures will have to be taken to revamp agriculture, and food sector production, storage, marketing, and distribution – including the public distribution system (PDS) and NFSA. The upside risk to this outlook emanates from the fact that crude oil prices will have to *bottom out*[22] from these levels, though it is unlikely that they will flare up in a short space of time. Also, the lower *acreage*[23] in oilseeds and pulses could create supply pressures. Given the capacity constraints in warehousing and cold storage, seasonal commodities may also add to the inflation risk.

For food prices to stabilise or to be brought down, agriculture production would have to be given top priority. Incentives for the farmer, subsidies on fertiliser and seeds (it may be reviewed on year to year, crop to crop basis) and remunerative rates for farm produce may help to increase the yield. Availability of easy loans to help mechanise the farming may also help to increase food production.

The middleman, who makes hay, while the farmer suffers, may either be removed or his role minimised. Prices of food items multiply many a time, between the field and the common consumer. Severe action against hoarders, who pile stocks while the common man suffers, must also be taken. Forward trading in food items must be banned. If these steps are taken sincerely by the Central and state governments, the common man may be spared the pangs of rising prices.

Aid to Vocabulary

1. *Inevitable* — certain to happen, impossible to avoid
2. *Consumer* — a person who buys goods or uses services
3. *Hoarding* — collecting and hiding to sell at a premium later
4. *Fuels* — increases the intensity
5. *Menace* — threat, danger
6. *Brought to book* — forced to give an explanation for having done something wrong
7. *Disparities* — differences
8. *Soaring* — rising
9. *Testimony* — evidence
10. *Mounting* — increasing
11. *Curtailed* — reduced
12. *Subsidised* — supported financially
13. *Prolonged* — continuing for a long time
14. *Stubborn* — difficult to move, remove or cure
15. *Buffer* — something that lessens or absorbs the shock of an impact
16. *Volatility* — the trait of being unpredictable
17. *Resilience* — capacity to recover quickly from difficulties
18. *Distortions* — misleading impressions; inaccurate figure.
19. *Emanates* — originates from
20. *De-clog* — remove blockages
21. *Cartelisation* — to organise into a business cartel
22. *Bottom out* — reach lowest level before rising again
23. *Acreage* — extent or area in acres

Points to Remember

1. Rise in prices is inevitable in a developing economy.
2. Rise in prices is mainly due to over population and non-availability of goods, etc.
3. Steps should be taken to increase production in all sectors.
4. Price hikes pose a threat to the existence of democracy.
5. There are examples of downfall of governments due to rise in prices of certain essential commodities.

6. Consumer Price Index (CPI) replaced the Wholesale Price Index (WPI) as a main measure of inflation in 2013.
7. The NFSA 2013 aims to provide subsidised food grains to approximately two thirds of India's 1.2 billion people.
8. Inflation touched a record low of 3.66 per cent in August 2015.
9. For sustainable low inflation, agriculture should be revamped, and hoarders and middle men removed.
10. If some important steps are taken sincerely by the Central and state governments, the common man may be spared the pangs of rising prices

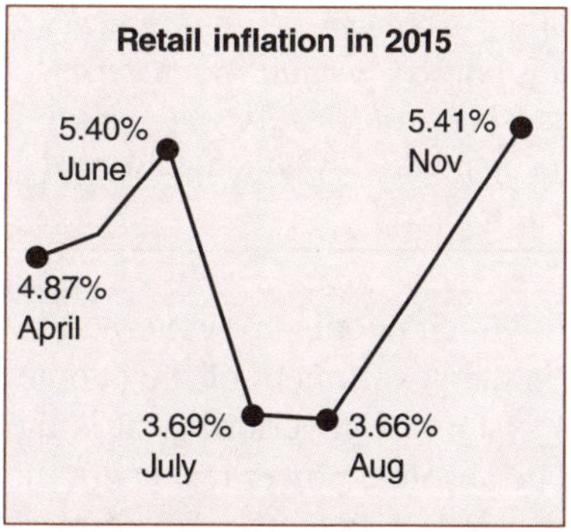

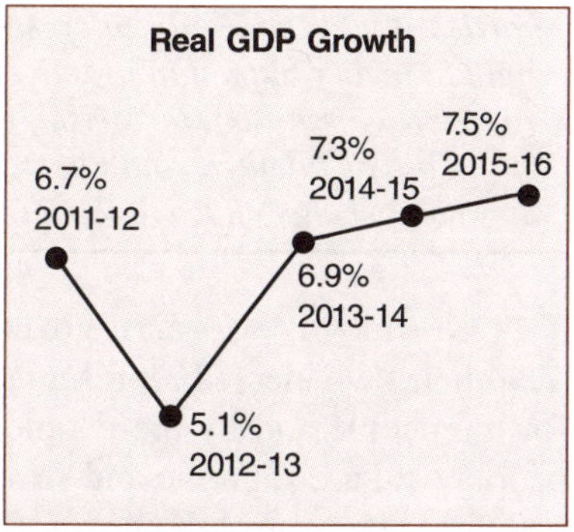

4% INFLATION TARGET IS SET FOR 2021

RBI governor Urjit Patel has been seen as a reticent central banker — he spoke little as deputy governor and his thoughts on policy were not well known.

While he spoke even less in his maiden policy conference, he has made his stance clear and has come out with an unambiguous action plan. Besides the reduction in the policy rate, a key announcement in Patel's first policy was the decision to target domestic real rates in the range of 1.25-1.5% from 1.5-2.0% earlier. Patel also clarified that the inflation target was 4% (plus/minus 2%) over five years.

The central bank indicated its resolve to contain inflation through self-imposed targets and a framework agreement with the government.

Source: The Times of India

Essay
109

DEMOCRACY IN INDIA

Synopsis

Democracy is the government of the people, for the people and by the people. Democracy has been in existence since ancient times, but it reached its golden era in the twentieth century. India is the largest democracy in the world. The Indian political system is a multiparty system. Most political parties, today, are only interested in coming to power. We enjoy every right in theory but not in practice. Illiteracy, poverty, inequality, casteism, violence, corruption, terrorism, etc., are posing problems for democracy in India. The talented youth of today should be politically educated so that they can become effective leaders of tomorrow.

Democracy is a form of government in which people are governed by their own elected representatives. It is the government of the people, for the people and by the people. In this system of government, it is the people who are supreme and sovereign. The absolute power rests with the people. They control the government. They are free to elect a government of their own choice. Freedom of choice is the *core*[1] of democracy.

Democracy existed in ancient Greek and Roman republics but with limited success. It had very little scope in ancient India. Democracy entered its golden stage in the twentieth century. Many countries in the world today follow the democratic form of government. Democracy depends on certain prerequisites like co-existence of different ideas and of parties, the right to free discussion, universal adult suffrage and periodical elections.

India is the largest democracy in the world. The Constitution of India was *enforced*[2] on 26th January, 1950. It *ushered*[3] in the age of democracy. India became a democratic republic *infused*[4] with the spirit of justice, liberty, equality and fraternity. The Preamble to the Constitution, the Directive Principles of State Policy and the Fundamental Rights reflect the Indian ideology as well as the democratic ideals. All citizens above the age of 18 irrespective of colour, caste, creed, religion, property or gender have the right to cast their vote. After an election, the majority party or a *coalition*[5] of parties forms the government and its leader becomes the Prime Minister.

Political parties are the vehicles of ideas and ideologies on governance. Parties act as the bridge between the social thought and political decision in democracy. The Indian political system is a multiparty system and over the years, politics has become a game of *opportunism*[6] and *corruption*[7] in India. Most political parties are only interested in coming to power. Every party adopts different means to come to power. Some try to influence the people through caste politics. Ideology today, has been replaced by caste and religious considerations. More than thirty-five parties are represented in our Parliament. This has made Parliament more diverse and often leads to chaos, particularly when regional issues are raised and debated. Another flaw that has spread its tentacles in Indian democracy is 'dynasty rule'.

The Constitution of India gives all its citizens above 18 years of age the right to vote but due to illiteracy, inequality and criminalisation of politics, only 60 to 65% of people cast their votes and the rest keep away. As a result, the representative of only 30-33 per cent of the people is declared victorious and sent to occupy a seat in parliament or state legislature. In democracy, the vote of an illiterate is at par with that of an intellectual while it is universally established that the, decision of an intellectual is far more informed, thoughtful and sensible than that of the former. Democracy, thus, reflects a number game wherein quality is superseded by quantity. Majority has to be granted to a candidate or a party regardless of the absence of democratic values in them.

We enjoy every right in theory, but not in practice. Real democracy will come into being only when the *masses*[8] are awakened and they take active part in the economic and political processes of the country. There is inequality in every sphere—social, economic and political. Illiteracy is the main cause of inequality. The illiterate masses cannot choose the right leaders. A large section of the population in India is illiterate. Election is always a costly affair. The illiterate masses are lured by money and various consumables during such an event. Also, many of our legislators have criminal records against them. The people who make laws are often the ones who break them.

Even after more than seventy years of Independence, one-fourth of the population today lives below the poverty line; goes to bed with an empty stomach; and, struggles without *access*[9] to safe and clean drinking water, sanitation or proper health facilities. Governments have come and gone, policies have been framed and *implemented*[10], crores of rupees claimed to have been spent, yet many people are still struggling to reach *subsistence level*[11].

Casteism is more pronounced today than ever. Untouchability remains abolished only in theory. There are frequent newspaper reports of Dalits being denied entry to temples or other public places. Violence has taken a serious turn in the country. Bandhs, strikes and terrorist activities have become a common affair. No sphere of national life is free from corruption. Indian society is largely capitalistic. The rich exploit the poor, who have no voice or share in the democratic structure. For a successful democracy, all these need to be changed.

Copious[12] use of unconstitutional and unparliamentary words for rival parties is common during election. Instead of furthering their ideas and ideologies, the political parties stoop to play blame-game which not only causes the civilised people to refrain from voting but also hampers the process of election by damaging law and order in the area. To add fuel to the fire, most sensitive issues concerning particularly caste or religion are excavated to arouse sentiments in their favour. All this is done with scant regard for decency, decorum and discipline.

Despite blemishes, India, as a democratic country, has progressed in many spheres. It has achieved self-sufficiency in foodgrains as a result of the green revolution. People vote for change whenever a government fails to live up to their expectations. India has been a successful democratic country mainly because the people are *law-abiding*[13], self-disciplined and socially and morally responsible.

For a democracy to be fully successful, the *electorate*[14] should be literate and politically conscious. The people should be fully aware of their rights and privileges. The illiterate masses of India should be given education so that they can sensibly vote for the right candidates. The U.S.A., Britain, Germany and Japan are successful democratic countries and have progressed in every sphere because the masses are literate.

To be a political leader in India, it is *flummoxing*[15] to find, no academic qualification whatsoever is required. A matriculate, or a college drop-out, as a result, becomes the education minister. Such a person guides and rules the process of, and provisions in, education; he/she formulates laws to be followed by the highly qualified persons of eminence. No wonder then, the standard of education in India has reached a *nadir*[16]. Needless to add, a definite academic qualification must be made mandatory to become a leader.

There should be equality in every sphere of life. The politicians should also respect the true spirit of democracy. They should *refrain*[17] from corruption, caste and communal politics. The citizens should elect leaders having good moral values and integrity. Poor and uneducated people should be guided to choose their representatives. They should not be influenced by anyone in this respect. Individuals should learn tolerance and understand that freedom is not *unbridled*[18] but dependent on right action safeguarding the other individual's rights along with one's own.

Democracy demands from the common man a rational conduct and an intelligent understanding of public affairs. People should not allow communalism, separatism, casteism, terrorism, etc., to raise their ugly heads. These are a threat to democracy. The government, the NGOs and the people should work collectively for the economic development of the nation. Changes should come through peaceful, democratic and constitutional means. The talented youth of today should be politically educated so that they can become effective leaders of tomorrow.

Aid to Vocabulary

1. *Core* — the most important or basic part
2. *Enforced* — made effective
3. *Ushered* — marked the start of something
4. *Infuse* — to cause (a person or thing) to be filled with something (such as a quality)
5. *Coalition* — a union of different political parties to form a government
6. *Opportunism* — using opportunities to gain advantage for oneself
7. *Corruption* — dishonest or illegal behaviour
8. *Masses* — people
9. *Access* — a way in
10. *Implemented* — carried out
11. *Subsistence level* — having enough to fulfil basic needs
12. *Copious* — abundant
13. *Law-abiding* — obeying the law
14. *Electorate* — all the electors considered as a group
15. *Flummoxing* — confusing, bewildering
16. *Nadir* — worst or lowest point
17. *Refrain* — to stop oneself from doing something
18. *Unbridled* — not controlled, extreme

Points to Remember

1. In a democracy, people elect the government.
2. Democracy originated in Greece and Rome.
3. India is the largest democracy in the world.
4. The Indian political system is a multiparty system.
5. We enjoy every right in theory, but not in practice.
6. India continues to struggle with several problems even after more than sixty years of Independence.
7. India has progressed as a democratic country.
8. Literacy and political consciousness along with social and economic development are a must for democracy to be fully successful.

Essay **110**

OPTING FOR A PRESIDENTIAL FORM OF GOVERNMENT

SYNOPSIS

Our national leaders chose the Parliamentary system of government for India to revitalise the society. During the formative years, the Congress provided political stability. The one party system eventually led to misrule and also, the rise of several regional parties. Parliamentary system is considered to be the better option for our country. Owing to the general belief, that coalition governments are unstable, adoption of the Presidential form of government has been suggested. This system is successful in the United States. It is not easy to amend the Constitution. Unless we make sincere efforts to root out dishonesty and corruption, no system will be effective.

When India attained independence, some forms of Parliamentary institutions were already functioning both at the Central as well as provincial levels. Our national leaders had chosen the Westminster model of Parliamentary system for India after weighing the merits and demerits of both the Presidential and Parliamentary forms of government. India had inherited a semi-feudal, caste-ridden society, which was ripped apart in the wake of Partition. At that time, our *pluralistic*[1] society lived in a stagnant economy. Our leaders felt that elections, i.e., adult suffrage would create awareness among the rural masses about their rights and would thus help to curb social backwardness.

The concept of a 'welfare state' within a democratic framework was approved for Independent India. During India's *formative*[2] years, Congress, under the leadership of Pt. Jawaharlal Nehru, provided political stability to the country. But the one-party dominance of the Congress eventually led to misrule. The concept of federalism was dropped in favour of a strong Centre. Till the mid-60's, the party enjoyed the support of the masses but it began to decline with the death of Pt. Nehru. During the period 1966 to 1975, Mrs. Indira Gandhi, as Prime Minister, strengthened the Centre. But during the last two decades Indian politics has witnessed the emergence of regional parties in almost all the states. Not only are they important for their respective states, but they also play a major role in deciding the ruling alliance at the Centre.

Traditionally, the Parliamentary system has been considered to be better suited than the Presidential form of government, for a diverse and huge country like India. By and large, our Parliamentary democracy has succeeded in protecting our rights and freedom. Despite the *blemish*[3] of the Emergency, Parliamentary democracy has not only survived but has also flourished in India.

Parliamentary democracy is not only transparent in governance but also highly educative for the people of the country. The problems of the country are thoroughly discussed in the legislature and the people take keen interest in these debates. The administration under this system comes under terrible criticism by the opposition parties which make it more responsive to public opinion. The legislature in this system is more representative and stands as an effective balance between the executive and the judiciary.

On the negative side, Parliamentary government is a violation of the theory of separation of powers, as the executive and the legislative functions are fused together with a bureaucracy functioning under various ministries. It is argued, that in the Parliamentary form of government, the Prime Minister has to go in for many populist measures. For fear of losing the elections, he/she has to surrender to the wishes of his/her own party as well as to those of the allied parties. In our country, Parliamentary system has given rise to unstable coalitions formed as a result of coming together of parties whose main concerns are their regional or state interests. Our political leaders always exploit the class and caste distinctions prevalent in the society. Another emerging trend witnessed in politics is the criminalisation of politics. It is the result of criminals entering politics. They manipulate the state machinery and introduce corruption in the bureaucracy. Thus, democracy in India, has failed in its endeavour to evolve as a two-way communication system, between the government and the masses. Moreover, some sociologists believe that Parliamentary government is rendered ineffective in times of war and emergency.

It has been observed that successive coalition governments in our country have failed to provide stability due to lack of a common ideology. This has prompted some sociologists to suggest that we should go for change and should adopt the Presidential form of government, in which the President is the executive head, independent of the legislature. Usually, he/she is elected directly by the people or by a college of electors.

While Britain, Canada and Australia have the Parliamentary form of government, Presidential form of government is practised in the USA and France. However, the French President enjoys limited powers.

The Presidential system of government, established in the United States, has been a source of inspiration for many countries. The system is based on a single executive structure which tends to be individualistic. The President is responsible to the Constitution rather than to the legislature. The powers of the Presidential executive *vis-à-vis*[4] the legislature and the judiciary are defined. Both the executive and the legislature are elected by the electorate. The members of the legislature cannot seek office in the administration and vice-versa. The legislature cannot be dismissed by the President. The executive and the legislature are independent arms of the government. The budget and other important measures require the assent of the legislature. The American President is the head of both the State and the government. The President, being the chief diplomat, formulates the foreign policy.

In India, the President is the Constitutional head of both the State and the executive. The Constitution of India provides for an indirectly elected President, who holds office for a term of five years. Article 54 of the Constitution states that the President is to be elected by an electoral college consisting of the elected members of both the houses of Parliament and the elected members of the Legislative Assemblies of the states. Under Article 53, the President is the supreme commander of the defence forces of the Union. But the exercise of power is regulated by law under the Constitution. Under the administrative powers, he has the authority to appoint or remove the Prime Minister, the Attorney-General, judges of the Supreme and High Courts and other judges.

If we were to adopt a Presidential form of government, it would cause a dramatic change in the political scene of the country. The small regional and local parties might in course of time disappear. They would either unite or be absorbed by the national parties. Presidential form of government would lead to a two-party system, beginning with the polarisation of like-minded parties into two broad *alliances*[5]. So, the President would take only such measures which would be beneficial for the country because the President would have a fixed tenure and therefore, would have no fear of losing office. Hence, the President will have to be a person with a clear vision, unlike those who care only for their castes, religion or areas. It is not possible to follow blindly the existing system of the United States in our country. We have our own problems and limitations. In the complex political scenario that we have, in terms of the multi-party system, coalition governments and criminalisation of politics, the President would need to keep a strict *vigil*[6] on the functioning of the democracy.

The Constitution of India states that, the 'executive power of the Union shall be vested in the President' (Article 53). The President of India is, thus, is the head of the 'executive power' of the Union; but he has certain Constitutional limitations within which he has to exercise the executive powers. He must exercise these powers, first, according to the Constitution and second, in accordance with the advice of his Council of Ministers.

Presidential form of government in India may not be feasible because passing an amendment of the Constitution, which is necessary for this purpose, may not be supported either by the Parliament or by the Supreme Court. There *inheres*[7] a *dogma*[8] among the political class that the Parliamentary system of government is the 'basic feature' of our Constitution.

Unless corruption is rooted out at the grassroots, a change over to Presidential system will merely result in the installation of irresponsibility and *autocracy*[9]. Power corrupts and absolute power corrupts absolutely. From where shall we get a 'clean' President and a nationally inspired electorate to keep him under control? In order to save our democracy, all of us should make a sincere and concerted effort to root out dishonesty and corruption. Unless there is sincerity and commitment towards the common good, no system will be effective.

Aid to Vocabulary

1. *Pluralistic* — the nature of society where diverse ethnic, social and cultural interests exist and develop together
2. *Formative* — having influence in forming and developing
3. *Blemish* — flaw, defect
4. *Vis-à-vis* — in relation to
5. *Alliances* — unions or agreements to co-operate
6. *Vigil* — watch
7. *Inheres* — is inherent
8. *Dogma* — principle, belief
9. *Autocracy* — absolute government by one person

Points to Remember

1. After Independence, our national leaders chose the Parliamentary form of government.
2. The one-party dominance of the congress led to misrule which, in turn, led to the rise of several regional parties.
3. Regional parties play a major role in forming a coalition government.
4. Due to the unstable nature of a coalition government, some suggest we should go for a Presidential form of government.
5. Presidential form of government in the United States is a source of inspiration for many countries.

6. Presidential form of government in our country may cause a dramatic change in the political scene.
7. The President of India has Constitutional limitations in the exercise of his power.
8. Unless we make a sincere effort to root out dishonesty and corruption, no system will be effective in our country.

SOME MORE POINTS TO ENRICH YOUR ESSAY

Given below are certain features which are associated with nearly all Presidential forms of government.

- *Veto Power*—The President does not propose bills, but has the power to veto acts of the legislature.
- *Fixed Tenure*—The President has a fixed term of office. Elections are held at scheduled times and cannot be triggered by a vote of confidence or other such parliamentary procedures.
- *Direct Election*—In a Presidential system, the President is often elected directly by the people.
- *Speed & Decisiveness*—President wields wide powers and can usually enact changes quickly.
- *Stability*—A President by virtue of a fixed term, provides more stability.
- *Tendency towards Authoritarianism*—Presidents often tend to become authoritarian.
- *Impediments to Leadership Change*—It is not easy to remove an unsuitable President from office before his or her term has expired.

GUIDED COMPOSITION

Develop the following paragraph into a full-fledged essay in 800-1000 words. The gist of the topic is provided in approximately 150 words for your help.

POLITICS IS THE ART OF COMPROMISE

A successful politician is the one who has mastered the art of making compromises and adjustments. He is quick to sense the mood of the masses and act in accordance with it. Politics, like any other game has to be played by keeping an eye on the weaknesses and strengths of the opposition. However, the rules and regulations and ethical codes of politics is different from that of other fields. In politics one has to assess the situation and then take action. One cannot afford to be idealistic, unyielding and unbending. One must be adaptable to survive and learn all the tricks to turn the tide in one's favour. A politician cannot isolate himself from the masses by stubbornly sticking to his ideals. He has to continually surrender his personality and individuality. The sooner he learns that compromise is the name of the game, the better are his chances of survival. Thus, success is sure to smile on a politician who has learnt to swim with the tide.

(150 words)

Essay
111

IS A REVIEW OF OUR CONSTITUTION NECESSARY?

SYNOPSIS

The question of the need for a review of our Constitution has often been raised. Eminent national leaders and experts were involved in the framing of the Constitution. The Constitution expressed the will of the people and the need of the hour. The procedure for amendments has been stated in the constitution itself. Delay in declaring punishment to the criminals and unbridled terrorism grew manifold. The National Commission, constituted to look into the working of the Constitution, has given a report on this issue. Certain reforms are necessary to keep abreast of the times. The debate would continue as politicians would use it to strengthen their hold on power.

We the people of India, have more than once pondered over the question, "Is the Constitution we gave ourselves in 1950 good enough, or does it need a serious review?" Responses to this question have been varied on each occasion and have been so *ambivalent*[1] and *ambiguous*[2] as to have initiated serious debate over the issue.

However, the truth is that neither are people reformed by merely making pious wishes nor is politics shaped by perfectly designed Constitutions. People, politics and Constitutions are formed, first of all, by historical and ideological legacies. They cannot reform themselves in any fundamental way unless they face the task of resolving the tensions and contradictions straining these legacies.

The Constitution of India was drawn up by a Constituent Assembly initially summoned on December 9, 1946 under the presidentship of Sachidananda sinha, for undivided India. On July 1, 1947 the British parliament passed the 'Indian Independence Act' to divide the country into India and Pakistan. On August 14, 1947, the Constituent Assembly met again as the sovereign Constituent Assembly for the dominion of India. With the demise of Sachidananda Sinha, Dr. Rajendra Prasad became the President of the Assembly. Other eminent leaders who framed the Constitution were Abul Kalam Azad, Vallabh Bhai Patel, Jagjivan Ram, Shyama Prasad Mukherjee, C. Subramaniam, and many others. Above all, B.R. Ambedkar, as the President of the Drafting Committee, played a leading role in the shaping of the Constitution. A draft Constitution was published in February, 1948. It came into effect on 26th January, 1950.

The Constitution of India is unique in many ways. It cannot be fitted into any particular mould or model. It is a blend of the rigid and the flexible, federal and unitary, and Presidential and parliamentary features. It attempts to strike a balance between the fundamental rights of the individual on the one hand, and the socio-economic interests of the people and security of the State on the other.

The nature of the amending process as envisaged by the makers of our Constitution can be best explained by referring to the observation of Pt. Jawaharlal Nehru. He observed that the Constitution should not be so *rigid*[3] that it cannot be adapted to the changing needs of national development and strength. A two-third majority in the Parliament would be required for making an amendment.

Our Constitution originally contained 395 Articles and 8 schedules. At present, it consists of more than 450 Articles and 12 Schedules. About one hundred amendments have been effected in the 61 years of its working. Thus, instead of being rigid, as some critics supposed during the early days of the Constitution, the procedure for amendment has proved to be rather flexible. The Indian Constitution strikes a good balance between extreme rigidity and too much flexibility. Jawaharlal Nehru had said, "...While we want this Constitution to be as solid and as permanent as we can make it, there can be no permanence in the Constitution. There should be a certain flexibility. If you make anything rigid and permanent, you stop the nation's growth, the growth of a living, vital, organic people... when the world is in turmoil and we are passing through a swift period of transition, what we may do today may not be wholly applicable tomorrow".

The world is indeed in a turmoil today. To keep abreast of the times, certain amendments to the existing laws have become necessary. Despite clear evidences against them, terrorists have appeared to be successful in deceiving the judiciary. Criminals accused of different offences too seem to have found a way out to be exempted from any kind of punishment. Ajmal Qasaab, the lone terrorist caught alive after the Mumbai terror attack in 2008, remained alive in an Indian jail for quite a long period of time due to prolonged delay in his sentencing, even after perpetrating a heinous crime of *genocide*[4]. Crimes and criminals, encouraged by such instances, have begun to increase manifold causing deep concern to the people in power. The whole nation is under the threat of the foreign terrorists. Review of the Constitution, therefore, looks necessary to nail them.

A National Commission was constituted in March, 2000, to look into the core issues of the working of the Constitution. Ten committees were set up to look into different aspects of its working and consider the necessity of rewriting the Constitution. The committees consisted of people from the judiciary, experts in various fields and politicians. Its recommendations have not been accepted by successive governments.

The point to be noted is that the rigidity or flexibility of the amending process essentially depends upon the complexity of the political *dispensation*[5] at the centre and in the states and also upon the attitude of the Supreme Court. In the absence of a single party that has garnered the support of the majority in both the houses of Parliament, no amendment can possibly be carried out. But if the party in power at the centre enjoys substantial majority in the Parliament as well as in most of the state legislatures then there is no difficulty in passing a bill for amendment.

An amendment to the Constitution may be initiated only when a Bill, for the same purpose, is introduced in either House of the Parliament, and is subsequently passed in each House by a majority (i.e. more than 50%) of the total membership of that House, with a majority of not less than two-thirds of the members of that House, present and voting.

With regard to the debate over a review of the Constitution, the late Prime Minister I.K. Gujral had recalled that the Indian Constitution was framed by a Constituent Assembly, whose members were elected representatives; and every individual or party had its own ideas, yet many provisions were adopted through *consensus*[6] instead of majority voting. A review of the Constitution through nominated members defeats the very spirit in which it was originally framed. He had also observed that the Constitution does not provide for a review, but only amendments because a review could look into anything, even the *Preamble*[7] or the basic structure.

Aid to Vocabulary

1. *Ambivalent* — opposite feelings towards the same situation
2. *Ambiguous* — obscure, having double meaning
3. *Rigid* — inflexible, strict
4. *Genocide* — mass murder
5. *Dispensation* — management or administration
6. *Consensus* — general agreement or opinion
7. *Preamble* — introductory statement (to the constitution)

Points to Remember

1. The question of the need to review our Constitution has been raised many times.
2. The Constitution of India came into effect on 26th January, 1950.

3. Our Constitution originally contained 395 Articles and 8 Schedules. As of now, it has 450 articles and 12 schedules.
4. Indian Constitution strikes a good balance between extreme rigidity and too much flexibility.
5. If the political party in power has substantial majority, then there will be no difficulty in carrying out an amendment to the Constitution.

THE PREAMBLE

The Constitution of India is preceded by a Preamble which outlines its aims and objectives. It reads:

"WE, THE PEOPLE OF INDIA, having solemnly resolved to constitute India into a SOVEREIGN SOCIALIST SECULAR DEMOCRATIC REPUBLIC and to secure to all its citizens:

JUSTICE, social, economic and political;

LIBERTY of thought, expression, belief, faith and worship;

EQUALITY of status and of opportunity;

and to promote among them all:

FRATERNITY assuring the dignity of the individual and the unity and integrity of the nation;

IN OUR CONSTITUENT ASSEMBLY this twenty-sixth day of November, 1949 do HEREBY ADOPT, ENACT AND GIVE TO OURSELVES THIS CONSTITUTION."

THE PROCEDURE FOR THE AMENDMENT OF THE CONSTITUTION

(a) Subject to the special procedure laid down in Article 368, our Constitution vests constituent power to amend the constitution upon the ordinary legislature of the Union, i.e., the Parliament (of course, acting by a special majority); there is no separate body for amending the Constitution, (e.g., a Constitutional Convention) as it exists in some other Constitutions.

(b) The State Legislatures cannot initiate any Bill or proposal for an amendment to the Constitution. The only mode of initiating a proposal for amendment is to introduce a Bill in either House of the Union Parliament.

(c) Subject to the provisions of Article 368, Constitution Amendment Bills are to be passed by the Parliament in the same way as ordinary Bills.

(d) Prior sanction of the President is not required for introducing in the Parliament any Bill for an amendment to the Constitution.

(e) The requirement relating to ratification by the State legislatures in India is more liberal than the corresponding provisions in the American Constitution. While the latter requires ratification by not less than three-fourths of the States, for the former, ratification by not less than half of them, suffices.

(f) In the case of an ordinary Bill, governed by Article 111, when the Bill, after being passed by both the Houses of the Parliament, is presented to the President, he may, instead of assenting to it, 'withhold assent therefrom'. In the latter case, the Bill cannot become an 'Act'. But an amendment to Article 368 in 1971 made it obligatory for the President to give his assent to a Bill for an amendment to the Constitution, when it is presented to him after its passage by the Legislature.

Essay
112

PANCHAYATI RAJ IN INDIA

SYNOPSIS

India is regarded as a land of villages. In order to awaken and empower the villagers, an elaborate system of local self-government called Panchayati Raj was introduced. Panchayati Raj is basically a three-tier structure of local self-government at the village, block and district level. A Panchayat consists of five or more public representatives. The tenure of the Panchayat in various states varies from three to five years. This council of five representatives is fully responsible for the administration and development of a village. To perform these functions, Panchayats have been given certain sources of revenue. The State Government has the power to delimit and alter its jurisdiction. Some remedial measures have been taken to remove the flaws that afflicted the Panchayati Raj. With this, a bright future for Panchayati Raj has been ensured in India.

Immediately after *emancipation*[1] from the British rule, India was reeling under acute shortage of food-grains; the *vandalism*[2] caused due to partition of the country had left a long trail of mass destruction; law and order had ceased to exist on account of riots between communities; and, the whole nation was groping in the dark, Every walk of life needed help from the government which itself was in the making. At this juncture, an urgent need for self governing bodies, with a view to delegate powers to the local bodies, for the upliftment of an area, was felt deeply, which in turn gave birth to Panchayati Raj. Although the confidence reposed in the system did not turn out to be true to expectations, due to faulty implementation, Panchayati Raj continues to exist.

India is rightly regarded as the land of villages. About 70 per cent of India's population *dwells*[3] in the villages. So, the importance of rural local self-government, known as Panchayati Raj, is self-evident.

Panchayats have been amongst the oldest political institutions of India. But Panchayati Raj, the form of local self-government in which it is constituted and made to work, is a modern *innovation*[4]. After Independence, Panchayati Raj was strengthened by the Central and state governments. In 1952, the Community Development Programmes (CDP) were initiated. The National Extension Service (NES) followed it. In 1957, a committee was set-up to study the working of CDP and NES. The committee, under the chairmanship of Balwant Rai Mehta, recommended a three-tier system of rural local government namely Village Panchayat at village level, Panchayat Samiti at block level and Zila Parishad at the district level. All the state governments except Meghalaya, Mizoram and Nagaland have passed the Panchayati Raj Legislation.

Prime Minister Jawaharlal Nehru inaugurated independent India's Panchayati Raj on October 2, 1959 at Nagaur, Rajasthan. Regarding Panchayati Raj, Article 40 of the Indian Constitution reads, "The state shall take steps to organise village Panchayats and *endow*[5] them with such powers and authority as may be necessary to enable them to function as units of self-government." Panchayati Raj is basically a three-tier structure of local self-government at village, block and district levels. Panchayati Raj is a complete process of governance and it refers to a system organically linking people from the Gram Sabha to the Lok Sabha.

A Panchayat consists of five or more public representatives. Members of the Panchayat are called the *Panchas*. They are elected by the *Gram Sabha*.

The presiding officer of the Panchayat is known by a variety of names. He is called 'President' 'Sarpanch', 'Pradhan', 'Mukhiya', 'Adhyaksh', etc. The mode of the president's election is also not the same in every state. In some states, he is elected by the *Panchas* and in some, by the *Gram Sabha.* The president can be removed from his office. There is a legislative *provision*[6] in all states for his/her removal. It is usually done by a majority of two-third votes of the members of the Panchayat.

The *tenure*[7] of the Panchayat in various states varies from three to five years. This council of five representatives is fully responsible for the administration and development of a village. The functions of a Panchayat are usually classified into two categories—*obligatory*[8] and *discretionary*[9]. Obligatory functions include—construction and maintenance of public wells and streets; *sanitation*[10]; development of agriculture and cottage industry; registration of birth, death and marriage; collection of land revenues; etc. The discretionary functions generally include planting and nursing of trees on the roadside; construction and maintenance of *dharamshalas, sarais* and resthouses; looking after public health and safety; etc.

To perform these functions, the Panchayat has been given certain sources of revenue. It is empowered to impose some compulsory taxes, such as tax on buildings, trade, private toilets, vehicles and animals, etc.

In addition, the Panchayat can also *levy*[11] some other taxes with the approval of *Zila Parishad.*

Panchayati Raj is an integral part of our democracy. But there are some *ailments*[12] the Panchayats suffer from. lack of *adequate*[13] finance comes in the way of effective functioning. In the absence of trained and full-time secretaries, the Panchayats fail to function properly. The *Sarpanch* as a member of the *Panchayat Samiti* has *assumed*[14] overriding importance and has over-shadowed the Panchayat.

In many places, the panchayats themselves are working as oppressive instruments. Absence of land reforms, low levels of literacy, especially among women, patriarchal system, etc., work against the weaker sections in the village. It also seriously affects women's position. The Asoka Mehta committee, constituted in 1978 to look into the flaws that were affecting the functioning of the Panchayati Raj, concluded that Panchayati Raj institutions had little resources and the State was not paying attention to them. The attitude of bureaucrats, red-tapism and corruption in the system stood in the way of the effective functioning of the Panchayats. The states of Karnataka, Andhra Pradesh and West Bengal passed legislation based on the recommendations of the Asoka Mehta Committee to spruce up the Panchayati Raj but political *impediments*[15] did not allow a proper implementation in any of these states.

The State Government has the power to delimit and alter the Panchayat's jurisdiction. It may suspend a *resolution*[16] of the Panchayat if it considers it a danger to public life. It may suspend or remove a *Panch* or a *Sarpanch* under certain conditions. The reservation of seats for women, Scheduled Castes and Scheduled Tribes is a welcome step. The Union Cabinet approved a proposal for a Constitutional Amendment Bill for enhancing reservation for women in Panchayats at all tiers from one-third to at least 50 per cent.

The proposal aims to amend Article 243 D of the Constitution that currently provides for 33 percent reservation for women in the Panchayats. Bihar, Uttarakhand, Himachal Pradesh, Chhattisgarh and Madhya Pradesh already have 50 per cent reservation for women at the local level. The Panchayat elections are conducted and supervised by the Election Commission to ensure free and for fair elections. All these measures ensure a bright future for Panchayati Raj in India. Stronger and abler governance at the grassroots level will make for a stronger state, and a more powerful nation.

Aid to Vocabulary

1. *Emancipation* — liberation
2. *Vandalism* — act of destroying property
3. *Dwell* — to live in or at a place
4. *Innovation* — a change, a new technique or idea
5. *Endow* — to provide with a good quality, ability or feature
6. *Provision* — a condition or arrangement in a legal document
7. *Tenure* — the period of holding an important political position
8. *Obligatory* — required by rule or law, compulsory
9. *Discretionary* — decided as per the judgement of a person in authority, not decided by rules
10. *Sanitation* — the process of keeping places free from dirt, infection and disease by removing garbage, cleaning streets, etc.
11. *Levy* — to demand or collect a payment or tax by authority or force
12. *Ailments* — illnesses
13. *Adequate* — sufficient
14. *Assumed* — accepted something as true
15. *Impediments* — hindrances, obstructions
16. *Resolution* — a formal statement

Points to Remember

1. In India, about 70 per cent of the population dwells in the villages.
2. Panchayats have been amongst the oldest political institutions of India.
3. Panchayati Raj is basically a three-tier structure of local self-government at village, block and district level.
4. A Panchayat consists of five or more public representatives.
5. Members of the Panchayat are called the 'Panchas'.
6. The tenure of the Panchayat in various states varies from three to five years.
7. The functions of the Panchayat are usually classified into two categories-Obligatory and Discretionary.
8. To perform these functions, the Panchayat has been given certain sources of revenue.
9. There are some ailments the Panchayats suffer from.
10. The State Government has the power to delimit and alter the Panchayat's jurisdiction. Some remedial measures have been taken by the government to ensure the bright future of Panchayati Raj in India.

Essay **113**

CASTE POLITICS AND COALITION GOVERNMENTS

SYNOPSIS

The division of the society into several castes and creeds has led to the disorientation of the society. A splintered society cannot rise against external aggression. In Independent India the one-party dominance of the Congress led to misrule and corruption. Corruption and Criminals creeped into politics in this era (1966-1977). In the absence of issue-based parties, caste-based parties burst on the Indian scene. 1977 elections saw a highly fragmented opposition, which could come to power by forming a coalition. But, the leadership aspirations of these individual groups hindered the smooth running of the coalition. Coalitions in 1977, 1989, 1996 and 1998 failed because of selfish aspirations, leading to instability in the country. NDA, a coalition under Atal Bihari Vajpayee; completed its full term from 1999-2004. Coalition governments should be formed by parties which share a common ideology.

The exact origin of the caste system is difficult to trace back. The records of the Indo-Aryan culture contain the first mention as well as a continual history of the factors that made up caste. *RigVeda* described the caste system for the first time. Brahman, Kshatriya, Vaishya and Shudra emerged as the four castes of society. The division of castes further into sub-castes and creeds led to the disorientation of the society. As a result, the society was never able to face external aggression unitedly and always remained under the threat of attacks. In the medieval period, India was constantly attacked and plundered by the Mongols, the Turks and the Mughals. A *splintered*[1] society could not rise as a united force against the enemies. The Mughal period had a great influence on the Indian populace for almost a quarter of the total population of India got converted to Islam.

Subsequently, the weak and divided Indian social structure helped the British in gaining control over the whole of the country. The theory of 'divide and rule' propounded by the British distanced the Hindus from the Muslims. After Independence, the Congress provided the much-needed stability to India during its *formative*[2] years. The party under the leadership of Pt. Jawaharlal Nehru did work for the upliftment of the minorities and the backward classes, but it did not benefit everyone. One-party dominance of the Congress gradually led to misrule, and corruption became the order of the day. This led to the decline of the party.

A coalition government or coalition cabinet is a government in which several parties co-operate in governance. A coalition government might also be created in a time of national difficulty or crisis. For example, during war time, a coalition government plays a role in diminishing internal political strife. Cabinets constituted by a single party are typically even more stable, provided their majority is sustainable.

Emergence of caste politics in the Indian political system severely hampered the rise of issue-based political parties. The election results of 1967 marked the decline of the one-party dominance of the Congress as it failed to secure majority in eight states whereby its majority at the Centre was also considerably reduced.

The Indira era (1966-1977) of Indian politics was marked by the indulgence of the ruling Congress party in *dubious*[3] means to achieve the desired end of reigning supreme. The Congress party distanced itself from the ideals on which it was raised.

Failure to achieve power and retain that on the basis of its ideas and ideologies forced the Congress party to find refuge in criminalisation of politics and politicisation of criminals. To be an accused or a criminal became the qualification to procure a ticket from the party to fight an election. Money and muscles marked the politics of that era (1966-1977).

In 1969, the Congress split into two—'new' Congress led by Indira Gandhi while the 'old' remained under Nijalingapa. Her slogan of 'Garibi Hatao', abolition of the zamindari system and the nationalisation of banks, helped her *augment*[4] public support and the 'new' Congress emerged as the winner in the 1971 elections. In 1975, the Allahabad High Court declared Indira Gandhi's election in the 1971 General Elections invalid on two corruption charges and hence, debarred her from holding the office of the Prime Minister. By then, Indira's Congress had already been trounced in the mid-term elections in Gujarat. Meanwhile, a countrywide revolution spearheaded by students, on the call of Jay Prakash Narayan, against price-rise, unemployment and corruption in government offices under Congress misrule was already under way. Facing Jay Prakash Narayan's demand to resign in the wake of the court ruling, and threatened by a political crisis looming large, Indira Gandhi declared a National Emergency in the country.

Socialist leaders like Dr. Ram Manohar Lohia had been working to create an anti-Congress alliance since the fifties. In 1975, opposition parties joined hands against the Congress to win the Gujarat elections. In the 1977 Lok Sabha elections, attempts were made by Jay Prakash Narayan to provide an alternative government with a non-Congress alliance. The movement was initially started as an opposition to the corrupt practices of the ruling party. However, it gradually broadbased its ideology on an all-India level by joining hands with the Jan Sangh, Socialists, Congress (O) and Bhartiya Lok Dal (BLD). To challenge the one-party dominance of the Congress, most of the non-Congress parties formed an alliance and contested the sixth Lok Sabha elections in March, 1977. The alliance of the Congress (O), the Jan Sangh, BLD, the Socialist Party, the Congress for democracy and the dissidents of the Congress who left in protest against the Emergency, formed the Janata Party in May, 1977. In March, 1977, the Janata Party came to power under the leadership of Morarji Desai and stood as an alternative to the Congress Party.

Differentiated social base and different interests of the members of the alliance caused the disintegration of the Janata Party in July, 1979, leading to the formation of the Lok Dal. The Lok Dal under Charan Singh gave priority to agriculture and cottage and small-scale industries while heavy industry was downgraded. On the social level, the party zealously worked for the emancipation of the backward castes. This made them unpopular with the other sections of the society and eventually led to the *debacle*[5] of the first coalition alliance at the Centre.

In the December 1980 mid-term polls, the Congress returned to power but efforts were undertaken to merge the various opposition parties under a single alliance. In October, 1984, the Dalit Mazdoor Kisan Party (DMKP) was formed, with the merger of the Lok Dal, the Democratic Socialist Party (DSP), the Rashtriya Congress and the dissidents of the Janata Party. In the 1980 elections, the Lok Dal-DMKP combine emerged as the largest opposition party but the alliance failed to secure seats in the 1984 elections. The sympathy wave for the Congress in the wake of the assassination of Indira Gandhi gave the Congress its biggest ever victory of 415 seats in the 1984 Lok Sabha elections.

The ‘clean’ government under Rajiv Gandhi was tarnished with corruption charges levelled against him. V. P. Singh resigned from the cabinet of Rajiv Gandhi and formed the Jan Morcha. In the latter half of 1987, efforts were made to build a foil to the Congress Party. The Janata Dal was launched in October 1988 with the merger of the Janata Party, the Lok Dal and the Jan Morcha. Failing to secure a majority, it came to power with the support of the BJP and the Left Front in 1989 under the leadership of VP Singh. In August 1990, the VP Singh government implemented the Mandal Commission recommendation of extending 27% job reservation to the Other Backward Classes (OBCs) along with the already existing 22.5% reservation for Scheduled Castes and Tribes. The move was launched to consolidate its vote bank on the strength of the backward classes.

The promise of reservation made the Muslims and the OBCs shift their support to the Janata Dal. It also created a rift between the OBCs and the SC/STs. Mulayam Singh Yadav's Samajwadi Party championed the cause of the OBCs. Kanshi Ram's Bahujan Samaj Party (BSP) now under the leadership of Mayawati in UP, was formed with an eye on the Dalit vote bank. In the 1991 elections, the Congress emerged as the winner, but there was growing dissent among the people. The mishandling of the Babri Masjid controversy led to the debacle of the Congress in the 1996 elections.

The Ayodhya issue brought to the forefront the Bharatiya Janata Party (BJP), which was founded in 1980 after the second split in the Janata Party. The BJP split the traditional vote bank of the Kshatriyas as it was considered the party of the upper and middle-class castes, Hindu urban traders, shopkeepers and middle-class Hindus. It emerged as the single largest party in the 1996 elections, but was unable to survive the no-confidence motion. Because of the pronounced anti-BJP attitude of the Congress and the United Front, Janata Dal's Deve Gowda became the Prime Minister of a coalition government. The Congress extended outside support. In April 1997, the Congress sought a change in leadership and I. K. Gujral took over as Prime Minister. In November 1997, the Congress sought the dismissal of the DMK from the United Front government, and their refusal to comply led the nation to a mid-term election.

In the 1998 elections, an alliance of 13 parties led by the BJP was forged to form the coalition government at the Centre. The AIADMK* led by Jayalalitha remained a threat to the working of the BJP-led coalition. The withdrawal of support by the AIADMK led to the fall of the 13-month old BJP-led coalition by a solitary vote and burdened the country with another mid-term poll. This time, the BJP-led National Democratic Alliance (NDA) managed to secure a working majority.

The NDA a coalition government under the leadership of Atal Bihari Vajpayee ruled the country from October, 1999 to May, 2004. The policies of the government were greatly regulated by the *Sangh Parivar*. In India, all the parties profess their faith in the same set of issues like

---

*AIADMK-All India Anna Dravida Munatantra Kazagham

socialism, secularism, mixed economy and non-alignment. The BJP was considered an exception for its obsession with *Hindutva* but in its attempts to broaden its base of support it has now begun to sound and behave, more or less, like other parties, except on the emotive issue of national identity.

India's last governing coalition, the United Progressive Alliance under the leadership of Dr. Manmohan Singh, comprised of many parties. It exposed how a coalition government at the national level, formed by political parties with varying national reach and limited sub-national appeal, suffers from limitations. Sometimes, the resolution of problems encounters an *imbroglio*[6] arising out of staunch political considerations, for example, the situation created by the opposition of Left parties to the Nuclear deal with the US that was being pursued by the UPA government. Such disputes can distort the national vision and sense of wider collective purpose.

In the absence of issue-based politics, caste-based parties have burst on the scene. Indulgence in caste-based politics has led to successive fractured verdicts by the electorate. All political parties exploit the issue of casteism prevalent in our society. They try to appease the Dalits, the impoverished class and the minority communities. But once they come to power, they are only concerned with serving their own interests. Even the government schemes are not implemented properly. Only 42% of the total money *allocated*[7] for the welfare of Dalits and other disadvantaged sections, was utilised in the Tenth Five-Year Plan.

Lack of *credibility*[8] and *accountability*[9] in all politicians, across different parties, has disillusioned the average voter. The political parties appear to have renounced their ideologies to pursue a dubious agenda in their quest of power. There is a dire need to check the growing number of regional and caste-based parties that only promote *factionalism*[10] in our country. Further, in a coalition the allies should stop making undue and unjustified demands.

After many decades, one single party BJP secured absolute majority on its own in 2014 Parliamentary elections and its leader Mr. Narendra Modi became the Prime Minister of the country. Though Mr. Modi still leads a coalition government—NDA—the leading coalition partner BJP is not dependent on other coalition partners, and as such may not succumb to their undue pressure or demands. Coalition governments should be formed by parties having a common ideology so as to facilitate a stable government.

Aid to Vocabulary

1. *Splintered* — separated from the main body
2. *Formative* — developmental
3. *Dubious* — doubtful
4. *Augment* — increase
5. *Debacle* — a sudden collapse
6. *Imbroglio* — complex dispute
7. *Allocated* — assigned or devoted
8. *Credibility* — the condition of being believable
9. *Accountability* — responsibility
10. *Factionalism* — dissent and intolerance of a small group within a larger one

Points to Remember

1. Congress provided the much-needed stability to India during its formative years.
2. One-party dominance of the Congress led to misrule.
3. In the absence of issue-based parties, caste-based parties emerged.
4. The Janata Party under the leadership of Morarji Desai emerged as an alternative to the Congress Party.
5. Coalitions in the Centre failed to provide a viable alternative to the Congress government until NDA, a coalition under Atal Bihari Vajpayee completed its full term.
6. NDA and UPA have been successful coalition governments.
7. Coalition should be formed by parties having a common ideology.

Essay 114

CENTRE-STATE RELATIONS IN INDIA

SYNOPSIS

The federal framework created by the Constituent Assembly provided for a strong Centre. The Constitution had formally divided the legislative, administrative and financial powers between the Centre and the states. But, these powers are biased towards the Centre. India has inherited the federal structure from the Government of India Act, 1935. The ruling elite of the post-Independence era were in favour of a strong Centre. Initially, the authority of the Centre was used by the party in power to prevent other parties from coming to power in the states. But the later decades have witnessed the emergence of regional parties in almost all states. There has been misuse of legislative, administrative and financial powers by the Centre. The Sarkaria Commission made certain recommendations to better Centre-state relations. After the virtual failure of the Sarkaria Commission, the Union Government appointed another commission, headed by Justice MM Punchhi. It is hoped that the commission would do justice to its job. The Centre must have the decision-making power and the states should have the power to implement the same.

The Constituent Assembly, on January 22, 1947 declared India as an Independent Sovereign Republic, wherein the states would possess and retain the status of autonomous units. By July 1947, the question of Partition was resolved with the fulfilment of the demand for Pakistan. Eventually, the provision for autonomy to the states was dropped in favour of a strong Centre.

While speaking in the Constituent Assembly on the issue related to federalism, Dr. Ambedkar said, "Though India was to be federal, the federation was not the result of an agreement by the states to join in a federation. Not being the result of an agreement, no state has a right to *secede*[1] from it". Thus, the federal framework created by the Constituent Assembly provided for a strong Centre. In the Constitution, India is proclaimed as a 'Union of states' rather than as a federal State. The distribution of powers between the Union and the states makes the latter subordinate to the Centre.

The Constitution had formally divided the legislative, administrative and financial powers between the Centre and the states. The legislative powers are distributed in three lists namely, the Union, State and Concurrent. The Union List gives the Centre the authority to act in matters of national importance which include defence, foreign affairs, currency, communication, banking services, income taxation and custom duties. The State List entrusts the states with matters which include law and order, local self government, public health, education, agriculture, economic and social planning among others. Laws passed by the Parliament prevail over those which are passed by the state legislatures in the Concurrent List. The residual powers lie with the Union and in case of a conflict between the Union and a state, the former prevails over the latter.

The administrative powers give preference to the Union over the states. The Constitution provides that the executive power of every state shall be so exercised as to ensure compliance with the laws made by the Parliament and the existing laws under Article 256 of the Constitution. Under Article 355, the Union has the duty to protect the states against internal disturbance and to ensure that the governance of every state is carried on in accordance with the provisions of the Constitution.

Over the years, the state governments have been *clamouring*[2] for more and more rights for themselves and lesser domination by the Union government. The provisions with regard to dismissal of a state government under Article 365 of the Constitution on account of non-compliance with the Union Government's direction, as well as the Emergency provisions under Article 352, have also come under the attack of various states and political parties from time to time. Other areas of conflict are the virtually total control of the Union Government over Central revenues and the subordinate position of the states in accessing those revenues. The distribution of revenue sources is especially critical in determining the nature of the state's relationship with the Centre.

The Planning Commission and the Finance Ministry monitor the transfer of finances to the states. Raising of loans through financial institutions like the LIC, the Provident Fund and the like are governed by the Central Government. A glance at the distribution of powers between the Centre and states indicates that the Centre is more powerful than the states. Article 275 of the Constitution also empowers the President to make grants-in-aid to the states as he/she may *deem*[3] it necessary. This provides the Union government with a lot of Constitutional authority to give grants-in-aid to the states by using its *discretion*[4].

India has inherited the federal structure from the Government of India

Act, 1935 which prescribed a federal type Union of autonomous provinces. The Act of 1935 was made to consolidate the position of the British in India and prolong the colonial rule. The Congress opposed the Act during its inception because the leaders felt that it was made to serve the vested interests of the British Empire. But, while framing the Constitution of free India, the Constituent Assembly liberally lifted almost all the provisions, which were related to the 'Crown–Autonomous Provinces Relations' and incorporated them in the Constitution.

Indian federalism was intended to work in a democratic way keeping in view the various segments of the society. But the ruling elite, which took over the reins of the government after Independence, was in favour of a strong Centre. Its members felt that the centralised powers were insufficient and hence, they started *augmenting*[5] their powers by *dubious*[6] means. Attempts were made to maintain the dominance of the ruling Centre at the state level too, and also to consolidate the central leadership's authority within the party. To achieve these *conceited*[7] aims, various constitutional methods were employed, which included the use of the Governor's office and Presidential powers.

The imposition of emergency in 1975 helped the Congress consolidate its position as the ruling party, check the growing dissidence within the party and replace non-Congress governments at state level. In the 1977 elections, the Congress was routed out of power, which led to the installation of the first non-congress government at the centre. With this, the one-party dominance of the Congress, at the Centre and the states, gave way.

The later decades witnessed the emergence of regional political parties in almost all states. Such regional parties are not only important for the effective governance of the states concerned, but they also play a major role in deciding the ruling alliance at the centre.

The federal system has not only survived in the country for more than six decades, but it has also shown signs of maturity. The small issues under Union-state relations which were blown out of proportion by the states earlier are now being ignored by most of the state governments. Solutions have been found within the existing Constitutional provisions to quite an extent though the centre never really desisted from trying to assume more and more financial and Constitutional powers. Nevertheless, it will not be correct to say that the interests of only the Union government have been pursued. Our federal system has indeed tried to address a few problems faced by the states as well.

There has been a growing demand for consensus and co-operation between the Centre and the states for the smooth functioning of democracy. In order to find a way to ease the tension between the two, the Sarkaria Commission was appointed in March, 1983, under the chairmanship of Justice (Retd.) R.S. Sarkaria. The Sarkaria Commission submitted its report in 1988. The Commission favoured a strong Centre to safeguard national unity and integrity but viewed the centralisation of power as dangerous for national integration.

Several recommendations were made by the Sarkaria Commission. The Commission recommended that Article 356 that provides for imposition of President's Rule in a state, should be used sparingly, as a last resort, when all other alternatives have failed. It recommended that Bills awaiting the President's assent should be disposed of within four months. Appointment of the Governors, as proposed, was recommended to be done with the consultation of the state Chief Ministers. The Commission observed that the concept of governors being agents of the Centre, in itself, compromises the federal principle, and converts the office into that of a party functionary which destroys not only the federal structure but also the Constitutional intent. It recommended that a governor should not belong to the party in power at the Centre, when the state is controlled by an opposition party. For the survival of democracy and the safeguard of the federal spirit of a multi-lingual, multi-religious and multi-racial country like India, the politicians should rise above their vested and *partisan*[8] interests and strive towards the welfare of the country.

After the virtual failure of the Sarkaria Commission to solve the problem of Centre-state relationship, the Union Government appointed another Commission, headed by Justice. M.M. Punchhi, the former Chief Justice of India, on April 27, 2007. The Commission was required to look into the powers, functions and responsibilities in all spheres, including legislative and administrative relations, the role of Governors, emergency provisions, financial relations, economic and social planning, Panchayati Raj Institutions, etc. The Commission was asked to look into the social and economic developments, that had taken place over the previous two decades. The Commission submitted its report on April 19, 2010. The recommendations are under consideration.

In our country, political parties with varying national reach and limited sub-national appeal, may form a coalition at the national level. Sometimes, the narrow political considerations based on regional ideologies can distort the national vision. So, the main issues of national import, like foreign policy and economy, must be controlled by the Centre. Now the centre has devolved upon the states power and responsibility in tax revenue, shares, grants, plans, special grants, loan, etc. In every one of these programmes, the Centre and the states are partners. Decision-making should be in the hands of the centre, but the implementation, in the hands of the states. If these plans are implemented smoothly regardless of political differences, it would be beneficial for the country. Only then can the true goals of federalism be achieved.

Aid to Vocabulary

1. *Secede* — withdraw formally from membership of a political federation
2. *Clamouring* — demanding strongly
3. *Deem* — consider, judge
4. *Discretion* — the freedom to act and think as one wishes
5. *Augmenting* — increasing
6. *Dubious* — causing doubt or suspicion
7. *Conceited* — vain, egotistic, self-important
8. *Partisan* — biased

Points to Remember

1. In the Constitution, India is proclaimed as a 'Union of states'.
2. The Constitution formally divides the legislative, administrative and financial powers between the Centre and the states.
3. Over the years, the state governments have been demanding more power.
4. India has inherited the federal structure from the Government of India Act, 1935.
5. The ruling elite of the post-Independence era were in favour of a strong Centre.
6. The later decades witnessed the emergence of regional parties in all states.
7. In order to find a way to ease tension between states and the Centre, the Sarkaria Commission was appointed.
8. The Union Government appointed another Commission, headed by Justice M.M. Punchhi, after the failure of the Sarkaria Commission.
9. The Centre must have the decision-making power and the states, the power to implement the same for the benefit of the nation.

AN UNFINISHED AGENDA OF FEDERALISM

Article 1 of the Constitution states, "India, that is Bharat, shall be a Union of States." While the Constitution doesn't mention the term "federal," it does provide for a governance structure primarily federal in nature. It provides for separate governments at the Union and in the states. Further, it specifies and demarcates the powers, functions and jurisdictions of the two governments. Last, it details the legislative, administrative and financial relations between the Union and the states.

The distribution of legislative powers has been broken down clearly into three lists: the Union List, the State List and the Concurrent List. The Union List, comprising the "vital interests of the State," is the longest, with 100 items. It includes defence, arms and ammunition, foreign affairs, foreign trade, atomic energy, treaties, war and peace, currency, and the Constitution. The State List (61 items) comprises of, among others, public order, police, trade and commerce within the state, agriculture, land revenue and various taxes. The Concurrent List (52 items) includes preventive detention, contracts, economic and social planning, social security, education, labour welfare and electricity.

On the Union List, Parliament has exclusive powers to legislate. While the State has exclusive powers to legislate on the State List, in certain situations, Parliament can also do so. As regards the Concurrent List, the issue is more complex. In case of a conflict between a state and a Central legislation, the parliamentary legislation shall prevail (Supreme Court, 2005). This, coupled with the fact that residuary powers of legislation are vested in the Union, gives a "unitary" tilt to federalism in India.

Efforts at co-operative federalism have commenced but need to be strengthened.

Co-operative and competitive federalism may be two sides of the same coin. Their complementarity is contingent on many affirmative steps. We have made significant progress. This is an unfinished agenda.

Source: The Indian Express, N K Singh

Essay **115**

INDIA'S RELATIONS WITH HER NEIGHBOURS

SYNOPSIS

India occupies a strategic position in Asia. She shares her political borders with Pakistan in the west; Bangladesh and Myanmar (Burma) in the east; China, Tibet, Nepal and Bhutan in the north; and Sri Lanka in the south. India has always been friendly with her neighbours. Jammu and Kashmir has been a bone of contention between India and Pakistan. Infiltration of Bangladeshis and the Ganga water-sharing issue have been a problem between India and Bangladesh. Ethnic clashes between the Tamilians and the Sinhalese had strained the relations between India and Sri Lanka. China illegally occupies a part of the Indian territory. Nepal and Bhutan have friendly ties with India except for smuggling of drugs and other valuables in the cross-border area. The SAARC and the SAFTA have been established to restore normalcy both politically and economically in the Asian region.

India occupies a *strategic*[1] position in Asia. Geographically, the Himalayan ranges keep the Indian subcontinent apart from the rest of Asia. India shares her political borders with Pakistan in the west and Bangladesh and Myanmar (Burma) in the east. The northern boundary is shared with China, Tibet, Nepal and Bhutan. India is separated from Sri Lanka by a narrow channel of sea formed by the Palk Strait and the Gulf of Mannar.

Since Independence, India has been trying to build and maintain good relations with her neighbouring countries. India's foreign policy has been *formulated*[2] to safeguard freedom, promote cooperation, and maintain international peace. This policy opposes racial discrimination and favours *non-alignment*[3] with any power bloc. However, over the years, relations with some of the neighbours have become *strained*[4]. India has sincerely worked towards building bridges of friendship with its neighbours.

The divide and rule policy of the British resulted in the partition of the country into India and Pakistan in 1947. Pakistan attacked India several times (1947-48, 1965, 1971 and the Kargil war of 1999) looking to *annex*[5] Jammu and Kashmir. Several agreements like the Ceasefire Agreement, Tashkent Summit, Shimla Agreement, etc., were signed between the two countries to end hostilities but to no avail. The two countries have acquired the status of nuclear powers which has further worsened the situation. The bus *diplomacy*[6] undertaken during the tenure of Prime Minister Atal Bihari Vajpayee proved a failure though the Lahore bus service was eventually *resumed*[7]. The Samjhauta Express international train service running between Lahore and Delhi since 1976 was bombed in 2007 by extremists who opposed normalisation of relations between the two neighbouring countries.

In October 2003, India made twelve offers to Pakistan which included resumption of air travel and cricket ties, and an offer for the treatment of Pakistani children in Indian hospitals. However, the state protection granted by Pakistan to the main accused of Mumbai terror attacks (November 26, 2008) has greatly strained bilateral relations between India and Pakistan. When the United States hunted down and killed the world's most wanted terrorist Osama bin Laden on May 2, 2011 in Abbottabad in Pakistan, it reaffirmed India's claim that Pakistan provides shelter to terrorists. The fact that Pakistan allows its soil to be used for nurturing terrorists is now amply clear to the entire world.

Bangladesh was created in December 1971 after Pakistan was defeated in the war by India. The sharing of the waters of Teesta, a tributary of the Brahmaputra, has remained one of the *core*[8] issues of conflict between the two countries. The *influx*[9] of *refugees*[10] from Bangladesh had led to an increase in tensions in bordering areas of north-east India but the cross border *infiltration*[11] problem has now been solved. India and Bangladesh, on August 1, 2015 exchanged 162 adversely held enclaves ending difficult border disputes that had kept fifty one thousand people of the two countries in a stateless limbo since the 1971 war.

Pacts on renewable energy, conservation of Sunderbans, overland transit traffic between Nepal and Bangladesh, and cooperation between Dhaka University and Jawaharlal Nehru University, Delhi are some of the other positive steps towards fostering friendly relations.

Sri Lanka and India, for several years, have remained traditional friends. A large number of Tamilians of Indian origin live in Sri Lanka. Ethnic clashes between the Tamilians and the Sinhalese had strained the relations between the two countries following which, many Tamilians migrated to India. India lost crores of rupees and thousands of lives by sending the Indian Peace Keeping Force (IPKF) to Sri Lanka. In May 2009, the three decade long bloody ethnic conflict ended with the killing of LTTE (Liberation Tigers of Tamil Eelam) leader Velupillai Prabhakaran and his cadres. The successful conclusion of the ethnic conflict ended all doubts in Sri Lanka about India's commitment to its neighbour's unity and territorial integrity. Sri Lanka is today India's largest trading partner in SAARC (South Asian Association for Regional Cooperation). Relations between the two countries have gradually improved. Economic ties between the two countries have also strengthened.

India's relations with China are, at best, *circumspect*[12]. China had proclaimed friendship through the slogan 'Hindi-Chini bhai bhai!' but had back-stabbed by invading India in 1962. As India was not prepared for a war and was caught off guard, China stealthily seized and occupied over 38,000 sq.km. of Indian territory. Furthermore, China is helping Pakistan, India's proclaimed adversary, in developing its nuclear programme. The visit of Prime Minister Atal Bihari Vajpayee to China in 2003 had helped in improving *bilateral*[13] relations. After the visit, the Chinese government had conceded that Sikkim is a part of India. Both sides celebrated the year 2006 as the "India-China Friendship Year". The visit of Prime Minister Dr. Manmohan singh in 2007 further improved the relations. In May 2015, China reiterated that it considered the McMahon line illegal, and deemed Arunachal Pradesh as part of Southern Tibet, but also said, that it was willing to resolve this dispute through friendly consultations.

On Tibetan spiritual leader, the Dalai Lama's visit to Arunachal Pradesh in 2009, Beijing fumed and the trip renewed the tensions between India and China. The Dalai Lama, for the first time said that Arunachal Pradesh is a part of India. But China claimed the region and rejected the McMahon Line—a border, drawn by the British, that gave Arunachal Pradesh to India. India lodged a protest with Beijing over the Chinese Embassy issuing to the residents of Kashmir stapled visas instead of stamping it on their passports. Former Chinese Prime Minister Wen Jiabao, on his visit to India had emphasised that India and China are friends, not rivals, but had declared at the same time, that the border issues are sensitive and not 'easy to resolve'. His successor Le Keqiang assured the visiting Prime Minister of India Narendra Modi in 2015 that China is committed to a 'fair resolution' of its border dispute with India.

President XI Jinping and Prime Minister Narendra Modi had four meetings in 2018. This has helped to further improve the bilateral ties to a great extent.

On October 13, 2015, China operationalised its largest dam – Zam hydropower station – on the Brahmaputra in Tibet raising serious concerns for India as its states of Asom and Arunachal Pradesh rely on this river and India's own hydropower projects on the Brahmaputra will get affected.

Nepal and Bhutan have had close cultural ties with India. India has helped both the countries in their development projects in the field of industry, telecommunications and education. But smuggling of drugs and valuables in the cross border area of the three countries has been a problem. Treaties have been signed and plans formulated to improve bilateral cooperation and trade, and to harness water resources between India and Nepal.

India-Nepal relations took a nosedive in the aftermath of mass protests against the new constitution in Nepal. Nepal blamed India's informal blockade for its fuel shortage and China jumped to take the fuel supplier's role that would later serve its strategic interests. Though India, through its large humanitarian aid to Nepal in the aftermath of the massive earthquake of April 25, 2015, managed to mitigate, to quite some extent, the anti-India sentiment prevailing in the Himalayan Kingdom.

The SAARC started operating from December 1985. It aims at promoting technical, cultural and economic co-operation in South Asia. The SAARC is trying to put in place a free trade area in the region. The South Asian Free Trade Area (SAFTA) has been established to promote trade in the least developed nations. India has always endeavoured to improve its relations with its neighbours. It is a strong advocate of peaceful co-existence and close co-operation.

Aid to Vocabulary

1. *Strategic* — that gives an advantage in a war
2. *Formulated* — created with attention to detail
3. *Non-alignment* — not supporting any major world power
4. *Strained* — not friendly or relaxed
5. *Annex* — to take possession or control of a territory by force
6. *Diplomacy* — the management of relations between countries
7. *Resumed* — continued again after having stopped for some time
8. *Core* — the most important part
9. *Influx* — arrival of people from elsewhere
10. *Refugees* — people who are forced to leave their country due to political or religious reasons or because of war, shortage of food, etc.
11. *Infiltration* — entering a place/country without being noticed
12. *Circumspect* — cautious, wary
13. *Bilateral* — affecting or involving two sides or countries

Points to Remember

1. The Himalayan ranges keep the Indian subcontinent apart from the rest of Asia.

2. India has always tried to have good relations with her neighbours.
3. India and Pakistan have been at war several times.
4. India made twelve offers to Pakistan in October, 2003 including treatment of Pakistani children in Indian hospitals which continues despite setbacks in bilateral relations.
5. Relations between India and Pakistan remain strained as Pakistan is shielding the main accused of Mumbai terror attacks of November 2008.
6. Infiltration of Bangladeshis into India, and Teesta water-sharing are the two major areas of conflict between India and Bangladesh.
7. The killing of LTTE leader Prabhakaran ended the ethnic conflict between the Tamilians and Sinhalese in Sri Lanka.
8. China illegally occupied parts of Indian territory in 1962.
9. India has friendly ties with Nepal and Bhutan.
10. The SAARC and SAFTA have been established to promote economic and political cooperation among the Asian countries.

INDIA-AFGHANISTAN: TIMELESS FRIENDSHIP

Prime Minister Narendra Modi on June 4, 2016, dedicated a ₹ 1,700 crore dam in strategically vital Herat province.

The dam, on river Harirud in Chist-e-Sharif neighbouring Iran, will irrigate 75,000 hectares of land and generate 42 MW of power. "This dam has not been built by bricks and mortar, but by the faith of our friendship and the valour of Afghans and Indians," Modi said.

MODI GETS AFGHANISTAN'S TOP CIVILIAN AWARD

President Ashraf Ghani on June 4, 2016 conferred Prime Minister Narendra Modi with Afghanistan's highest civilian honour, the Amir Amanullah Khan Award.

Essay
116

NATIONAL SECURITY

Synopsis

The world has become a 'global village' but it is still physically divided into 'Nation-States'. This division leads to occasional skirmishes which in turn affect the stability of the States. Thus, national security is a matter of utmost importance for any country. India has been attacked once by China and more than once by Pakistan since Independence. Insurgency and communalism are the major factors which have put the national security of our country to test. India's defence system comprises of a network of different intelligence agencies, the army and the government. Certain propositions for improving the overall defence system have been put forward. India's stand on nuclear weapons is one of 'no-first-use'. Economic resilience, political stability and a strong army can help us overcome any threat—internal or external.

The world today has become a 'global village', economically through globalisation, and socially through the Internet and other means of communication. But politically, it is far from obliterating all boundaries so as to become a single united entity. The world is still divided into nation-states by distinct, and in some cases, vague boundaries giving rise to occasional *skirmishes*[1] as well as *subtle*[2] and *sinister*[3] moves to alter the balance of power. India is bounded by 15106.7 km of land border running through 92 districts in 17 states and a coastline of 7516.6 km touching 13 states and union territories (UTs). In fact, barring Madhya Pradesh, Chhattisgarh, Jharkhand, Delhi and Haryana, all other states in the country either have a common border with other countries or have a coastline and, as such, can be regarded as frontline states from the point of view of border management. The Chinese proverb 'Those who sweat more in times of peace, lose less blood in times of war' seems to be the guiding principle with regard to devising the national security strategy of any country.

India, since Independence, has many a time faced a breach of its security system. The earliest instance when it was caught unaware, was in 1962. The Chinese attack alerted the country to the need of a vigilant security system. After the 1962 debacle, the then President Dr. S. Radhakrishnan, had warned the nation against being caught napping again. His *candid counsel*[4] and words of wisdom stood us in good stead and we were able to face the 1965 aggression (by Pakistan) with *dogged*[5] determination. This resulted in a decisive defeat of the enemy. However, this was not the end. Pakistan launched fresh offensives in 1971 (resulting in the creation of Bangladesh) and in 1999 (the Kargil war) though in both cases, India convincingly vanquished its hostile neighbour.

Besides this external threat, the internal danger from *insurgency*[6], and communalism is also of grave concern for our national security. Since Independence, Kashmir, Punjab, Asom and some other north-eastern states have passed through phases of violence. Insurgency has largely been brought under control, but *sporadic*[7] outbreaks of violence keep taking place in Kashmir. Another *scourge*[8], which has been causing grave concern and instability in the country, is communalism. It had raised its ugly head with the demolition of a religious structure at Ayodhya in December, 1992. The demolition triggered a series of communal riots, the worst being probably the Godhra riots targetting the major religious minority in 2002. Thus, both internal and external factors are responsible for putting our national security in *jeopardy*[9].

With religious fundamentalism having spread its tentacles across the country, the *contours*[10] and contents of national security have undergone a complete change during the past many years. The continual proxy war and acts of terrorism unleashed in different parts of the country also poses a grave threat to our national security.

There are seven central police forces under the Union Government, namely the Assam Rifles (AR), Border Security Force (BSF), Indo-Tibetan Border Police (ITBP) Central Reserve Police Force (CRPF), Central Industrial Security Force (CISF), Sashashtra Seema Bal (SSB) and National Security Guard (NSG). India's defence strategy is guided by information received from the intelligence agencies. These agencies include the Research and Analysis Wing (RAW), Director-General of Military Intelligence (DGMI), the Brigade Intelligence Team (BIT), Intelligence and Field Surveillance Unit (IFSU) and Intelligence Bureau (IB). These agencies should co-operate and co-ordinate with one another and keep the Government posted on the internal and external situation of the country. The Government should also set up a national centre on information systems security.

Incidents like the Kargil War have necessitated the reconsideration of our defence priorities. Less than 15 per cent of India's *armaments*[11] are contemporary as against a world average of thirty per cent. The army today spends around 85 per cent of its annual budget allocations just to maintain its existing forces, which leaves almost nothing for modernisation. Any increase in defence allocations would be a welcome relief for the 1.14 million-strong military. The Committee on Kargil intrusions found grave deficiencies in India's security management system. It proposed a thorough review by an independent body of credible experts. Some of their recommendations were quite timely and apt. The Government was to take steps to set up international-standard intelligence and *surveillance*[12] capability, particularly satellite imagery. Defence budget was to be increased for modernisation of armed forces. National security management and apex decision-making structure had to be reorganised and the Armed Forces Headquarters had to be located within the Government structure. The Committee also suggested that a full-time National Security Advisor be appointed and that border patrolling and surveillance be improved.

The DRDO* is the R&D** wing of the Ministry of Defence (MoD) working on a vision to empower India with cutting edge defence technologies. It evaluates defence equipments for military operational requirements; generates new technological know-how for development of state-of-the-art weapon systems; and advises the government to make technical assessment of international security threats and military capabilities of current and potential adversaries. The surface-to-surface missiles *Agni* and *Prithvi*, the nuclear powered submarine *Arihant*, the supersonic cruise missile *BrahMos*, and Light Combat Aircraft *Tejas* are some of the many achievements of the DRDO, towards strengthening national security.

Another important aspect of India's defence strategy is the stand of our Government on the use of nuclear weapons. India carried out nuclear tests in 1974 and later in 1998. India has reiterated its 'no-first-use' policy and also assured non-use against non-nuclear weapon States. It is widely acknowledged that nuclear war cannot be won for it incurs only losses on both sides and therefore, must never be fought. It is also accepted that nuclear weapons are more useful for gaining political *leverage*[13] and for coercion rather than for military purposes. India's 'no-first-use' doctrine further reinforces the stability factor because it acts as a strong deterrent against the use of these weapons by an adversary.

India's draft nuclear doctrine spells out minimum nuclear deterrent and robust command and control systems, in addition to the broad thrust on

---

*DRDO — Defence Research and Development Organisation

**R&D — Research and Development

nuclear forces, even as it reiterates strong adherence to the objective of 'no-first-use'. But India's adversaries must not *construe*[14] this as weakness. This is, rather, the policy that upholds and *manifests*[15] the country's culture of *ahimsa* or non-violence despite the country being capable of *trouncing*[16] any act of violence *perpetrated*[17] against it. With the cumulative might of the armed forces, furthered by economic resilience and political stability, India can overcome any threat—internal or external—with commendable conviction.

Aid to Vocabulary

1. *Skirmishes* — acts of irregular or unplanned fighting
2. *Subtle* — clever and not obvious
3. *Sinister* — suggestive of evil
4. *Candid counsel* — frank advice
5. *Dogged* — obstinate, persistent
6. *Insurgency* — rebellion against government
7. *Sporadic* — occasional
8. *Scourge* — a person or thing that causes trouble or suffering
9. *Jeopardy* — dangerous situation
10. *Contours* — form, shape
11. *Armaments* — military weapons and equipments
12. *Surveillance* — supervision, invigilation of suspected person
13. *Leverage* — influence, power or push to achieve a desired result
14. *Construe* — interpret
15. *Manifests* — shows clearly
16. *Trouncing* — defeating severely
17. *Perpetrated* — committed (something wrong or illegal)

Points to Remember

1. The security of a country is of utmost concern even in times of peace.
2. Foreign aggressions after Independence weakened our national security.
3. Insurgency and communalism are internal threats to national security.
4. India's defence strategy has been guided by information received from the intelligence agencies.
5. Incidents like kargil war necessitated the reconsideration of our defence priorities.
6. India carried out nuclear tests in 1974 and later, in 1998, and it has reiterated its 'no-first-use' policy.
7. India has emerged strong enough to overcome any threat to national security.

Essay

117 CRIMINALISATION OF POLITICS

SYNOPSIS

The term 'politics' is employed to designate political activity as well as the science that deals with that activity. Real politics is not possible under tyranny or oligarchy; it is only possible in a democratic form of government. Democratic form of government is by far the most preferred form of government. Democracy is based on three basic ideals—the individual, individual rights and liberty, and universal adult franchise. Democracy means majority rule. To win an election, politicians use money and muscle power. This leads to corruption and criminalisation of politics. Raising questions in the parliament in return for a bribe is a serious offence. Criminalisation gives rise to extra-constitutional power which threatens the very roots of democracy. Our judicial system is cumbersome, thus it is difficult to check the entry of criminals into politics. Some measures should be taken to tackle this problem. Only the educated and committed politicians can change the corrupt political scenario.

The meaning of the term 'politics' remains ambiguous to this day. Political thinkers from Aristotle to H.J. Laski have used the term 'politics' to designate political activity as well as the science that deals with that activity. Aristotle was the first thinker who recognised the distinctive quality of politics as one of the basic human activities. According to him, politics arises in organised communities, which permit the simultaneous existence of different groups, and which represent conflicting traditions and *divergent*[1] interests, within the same State. Politics represents at least a degree of tolerance for controversies and some understanding of the principle that government is best conducted amid the open propagation of antagonistic interests. Aristotle argues that real politics is not possible under tyranny or *oligarchy*[2]. Both these forms of government use coercion to suppress the expression of rival interests and this means elimination of all controversy and debate. It is believed that politics is only possible in a democratic form of government. It is not just another form of government, it is by far the most preferred form.

The word 'democracy' is derived from two Greek terms, *demos and kratia* and these together mean 'authority of the people'. More than a form of government, it is a way of life. The concept of democracy is based on three basic ideals, viz, individual, individual rights and liberty, and universal adult franchise. In order to ensure the protection of these ideals, democracy pleads for universal participation of people in the affairs of the government. The most direct form of participation is nothing but the adult franchise through which the leaders are elected by people irrespective of caste, creed or religion, and the government, constituted.

The system of adult franchise assigns importance to every individual in the society. Thus, it is imperative for the people to have a sense of discrimination between the 'desirable' and the 'undesirable'. J.S. Mill suggests that the capability of the people to have a democratic government and a sincere desire for the same, is essential for the success of democracy. The democratic government requires a higher level of consciousness among the people with regard to their rights and duties. At the time of election, people should be in a position to vote according to their own preferences.

Democracy follows majority rule in elections as well as in its working. To win an election, most of the politicians of our country use money and muscle power. Enormous power, *pelf*[3], privileges and patronage have become synonymous with public office. Candidates spend millions of rupees to get themselves elected. A good number of them get the major chunk of this money from mafia dons or criminals and big business houses. It is with this money that a network of muscle power is built. With this money the musclemen, and the gangs of criminals acquire social respectability and vital connections at all levels in the government machinery. From Panchayat level to the Cabinet-Ministerial level, they exercise their influence at every rung. This leads to criminalisation of politics as well as politicisation of criminals.

When political parties start accepting money from these sources, they become obligated to the fund-givers. Once the criminals obtain a hold on the leadership of political parties, they create pressure on law-enforcement agencies, dictate policies and start foisting their men as candidates for elections. With the strength of money and muscle power, their candidates easily win elections. A *pernicious*[4] linkage of politics with corruption is the real cause of criminalisation of politics.

More than ₹ 1,00,000 per hour is spent by the government to run a session of Parliament. No member, therefore, is supposed to raise questions of little value. Yet, representatives are reported to have raised questions of individual concern and that too in return for a bribe. Such corrupt practices need to be curbed without delay.

Owing to *pseudo-secularism*[5] or the policy of *appeasement*[6] and the people's loss of faith and hope reposed in the party, the Congress faced an ignominious defeat in the 1966 election which prompted it to field criminals to rig elections so as to bring it back to power. Failure of the government and its policies gave rise to discontentment among the masses. Voters are also responsible to an extent for this social degradation. It is sad that people often cast their vote for a criminal. This, however, does not mean that they have faith in the capabilities of the criminals. Most of the times, people do so out of fear, or because they want to earn some undue favour from these politicians, or else, it could be a case of caste consideration ahead of electing the right candidate.

The criminal-politician nexus ensures mutual benefits. To sustain this nexus, parliamentarians refrain from passing legislations which may stand to hit this association and, the criminals see to it that the former remain in power. In the process, politics continues to remain in the clutches of criminals. The situation becomes even more serious when the candidates having criminal background win elections and become parliamentarians or legislators themselves.

Gone are the days, when a candidate's personal goodwill and sacrifice were credentials to win an election. Earlier, politics was considered a *pious*[7] service to the society, but now it has become just another lucrative profession. Today, most of the politicians enter politics to make personal gains. They make easy money by means of corrupt practices through abuse of power.

Some thinkers believe that social inequality is the root cause of criminalisation of politics. In the social and economic spheres, inequality is the order of the day. A large section of the Indian population is illiterate and poverty-stricken. Therefore, the main focus of politics as well as governance is on quick fixes. It is easier to create jobs and educational quotas for backward castes and minorities than investing in basic education that would empower them to compete without *props*[8]. Actually, in our country, the politician-criminal nexus has been optimally used by the concerned parties to build an inaccessible empire of their own. This nexus has given rise to *proliferation*[9] of extra-constitutional power centres, which have rendered the constitutional arrangement literally irrelevant.

How to check the entry of criminals into political affairs is a serious question. Our judicial process is very *cumbersome*[10] and time consuming because of which there is *inordinate*[11] delay in the convinction of the accused. Some criminals, though confined behind bars, manage to win elections and even become Cabinet Ministers. Many a time, after a prolonged trial, it becomes difficult for the prosecution agency to bring these criminals to book.

Effective measures should be taken to tackle this problem. First, no political party, unless it is willing to maintain audited accounts of all its receipts and expenditure, should be recognised by the Election Commission; and, all politicians should be duly subjected to income-tax scrutiny. Secondly, minimum educational qualifications should be prescribed for the candidates. Former President Dr. A.P.J. Abdul Kalam made a point when he sought clarification on this vital issue: "How is it that while an applicant for even a peon's post is expected to be qualified, the elected representatives who influence the lives of more than 1000 million of our fellow men and women, are not required to have any education at all?"

It will not be easy to break the politician-criminal nexus. Corruption is a multifaceted problem and a well-planned strategy is needed to tackle it. It needs a comprehensive societal intervention to cleanse public life. Only the educated and committed politicians can change the disturbing scenario. It is the will power of the political parties which can help Indian democracy to get rid of this menace. Thus, the need of the hour is to break the evil nexus and save our democracy. Besides, the Constitution needs to be amended to prevent those having criminal records from being nominated and from contesting any election. Only a good and clean political practice based on ethics and morals can save our democracy.

Once the people's Representation Act is suitably amended so that convicted persons are disqualified; the judicial system is revamped to speed up criminal procedure in a just and fair manner; and the police and criminal investigative machinery acts with professional integrity to bring the culprits to book, true democracy will prevail in the country.

Aid to Vocabulary

1. *Divergent* — taking different courses
2. *Oligarchy* — government by a small group of people
3. *Pelf* — money, wealth
4. *Pernicious* — destructive, fatal
5. *Pseudo - secularism* — faking secular credentials
6. *Appeasement* — working towards pleasing others

7. *Pious* — religious
8. *Props* — supports
9. *Proliferation* — increase in number very quickly
10. *Cumbersome* — slow and not very efficient
11. *Inordinate* — endless

Points to Remember

1. The term politics is used to designate both political activity and the science that deals with that activity.
2. Politics is only possible in the democratic form of government.
3. Democracy is based on three basic ideals viz., individual, individual rights and liberty, and universal adult franchise.
4. Democracy means majority rule.
5. To win an election, politicians use money and muscle power, and this leads to corruption and criminalisation of politics. Criminals have acquired vital connections at all levels in government machinery.
6. Social inequality is the root cause of the criminalisation of politics.
7. Criminalisation of politics gives rise to extra-constitutional powers which threaten the very root of Indian democracy.
8. Lengthy process of judicial trial cannot check the entry of the criminals in our political system.
9. Some important measures should be taken to tackle this problem.
10. Only the educated and committed politicians can change the political scenario.

Essay
118

JUDICIAL ACTIVISM

SYNOPSIS

The unique feature of our constitution is the division of power among the three organs of the government—the legislature, the executive and the judiciary. India has an independent and strong judiciary. The system is in the form of a hierarchy with the supreme court being the apex court. Judicial activism has empowered citizens to fight for their own rights. Judges are like umpires and they are there to uphold laws, not create them. Judicial activism helps in fighting corruption, legislative malpractices and executive excesses. It is imperative in a democracy that the three organs of government work in close co-ordination to ensure the liberty and dignity of the citizens.

Since the time of Aristotle, it has been generally agreed that political power or government is divisible into three broad categories, viz., the legislature, the executive and the judiciary. The legislature formulates and expresses the will of the State. Being a representative organ, the legislature in a democratic country enacts the general rules of society in the form of laws. There must also be in a democracy some power to see that laws of the State are duly obeyed by all and there is no *infringement*[1]. This, precisely is the work of the executive. The judges determine whether the law is applicable in a particular case or not. The judiciary prescribes the manner in which the functions of the executive ought to be discharged. It sees that the exercise of executive authority conforms to the general rules laid down by the legislature.

Our Constitution empowers the judiciary to resolve the disputes which arise between the citizens and the State; between the states; or between the states and the Centre. The judiciary safeguards the Fundamental Rights of the citizens as enshrined in the Constitution. It *interprets*[2] the Constitution in order to determine the power assigned to the various wings of the State, the limits and *transgressions*[3] thereof, if any. The framers of the Constitution were *staunch*[4] advocates of an independent and strong judiciary as India evolved into a Parliamentary democracy with a written Constitution.

Just like the bureaucracy and the educational system, the judiciary also was inherited from the British. During the colonial rule, the judiciary was divided into two distinct systems: the English system of Royal Courts which followed the English law and procedure, and the Indian system of Adalats (Courts) which followed the Regulation laws and Personal laws. In 1861, under the High Courts Act, the two systems were merged and High Courts were established in the Presidency towns of Calcutta, Bombay and Madras.

The Indian Judiciary is in the form of a hierarchy with the Supreme Court being the apex national court. At the state level, the High Courts are the highest legal authority, followed by the subordinate courts, which deal with all disputes of civil or criminal nature as per the powers *conferred*[5] on them. The Supreme Court of India consists of a Chief Justice and not more than twenty-five other judges. The judges are appointed by the President after consultation with the Chief Justices of the Supreme Court and the High Courts of the states. Our Constitution says that there shall be one High Court for each state, but the Parliament has the power to establish a common High Court for two or more states. There are 24 High Courts in the country, of which six have jurisdiction over more than one state. Delhi has a High Court of its own, while the six Union Territories come under the jurisdiction of different state High Courts. A High Court consists of a Chief Justice and other judges, whose number varies from state to state. The structure and functions of the subordinate courts are almost uniform throughout the country. The High Court in a state possesses administrative control over the subordinate judiciary in the state in certain matters, besides its *appellate*[6] and supervisory jurisdictions.

The welfare of the citizens depends, in a way, upon speedy and impartial administration of justice. The judiciary is the guardian of the rights of a citizen and it protects these rights from all possible individual and public encroachments. The perception of an ordinary citizen that he/she can rely on the judiciary for a fair and prompt administration of justice, maximises his/her liberty. If there is no adequate provision for administration of justice, the liberty of the people stands *jeopardised*[7].

Our Constitution is federal in character. It has conferred the power of enacting laws on both the Parliament and the state Legislative Assemblies. It has also divided the executive powers between the Union and the states. Indian Constitution does not define the reach and content of judicial powers but does give power to the courts to strike down a legislation made by the country's elected Parliament. The Supreme Court is the ultimate *arbiter*[8] of constitutionality. But, since elections and elected representatives of people form the core of democracy, any action of the Court towards reversing a legislative proceeding is often resented and opposed by the members of Parliament. The fearless and active exercise of judicial review in the face of a *combative*[9] legislature has led to judicial activism.

Judicial activism involves innovative interpretations of the nuances of law. It pertains to the judiciary playing a pro-active role, rising to the need of the hour and employing the provisions of the Law to effect optimal deterrence from delinquent behaviour. It empowers the citizens to fight for their rights. Judicial intervention has to be invoked if the Government refuses to *comply*[10] with the Constitutional provisions in exercising legislative power. Judicial activism also becomes necessary to put a check on tyranny born out of a temporary political majority in legislature, which might otherwise seek to rewrite the Constitution in order to remain entrenched in power. Further, Judicial activism becomes inevitable when the executive and the legislature shirk their duties and responsibilities. Where the other organs of the Government, viz., the executive and the legislature, and the agencies under them fail to act as per the Constitutional provisions or any law pertaining to them, the court may intervene through writs and other means. This is nothing but judicial activism. Judicial activism is, in fact, an essential part of judicial review.

Judicial activism in India has its genesis in the provision for Public Interest Litigation (PIL). The concept of PIL has been derived from the American constitution, in line with which, Article 32 of our Constitution empowers the Supreme Court and High Courts to take action against any lower court, or against any government official. The common citizens find the administration so apathetic and non-performing, and corruption and criminality so widespread, that they have no option, other than moving the courts through writs and PILs which enlarges the scope for judicial intervention.

The *high watermark*[11] of judicial activism in India is the majority judgement in the Keshavananda Bharati case (the Fundamental Rights case). The Supreme Court unprecedentedly held that a Constitutional amendment duly passed by the legislature was invalid if it damaged or destroyed the basic structure of the Constitution. The Delhi High Court's intervention in cases like nursery admissions, free beds for the poor in hospitals, misuse of ambulances, begging in public, Blueline bus menace, demolition of unauthorised constructions, crime against women, etc., are important examples of judicial activism. The laws in a democracy postulate the importance of an individual's freedom and liberty. And freedom, if violated, can only be secured through courts, and not, the legislature or executive.

However, there always lurks the fear that the judiciary may overstep its authority. In the thick of judicial activism, courts sometimes intervene in matters which are solely within the domain of the executive. Democratic theory objects to such judicial activism. Our social and political processes should be kept separate from judicial litigation. So the limits of exercising judicial power need to be clearly mentioned and defined.

In an unprecedented confession, in the wake of a raging debate over judicial activism, the Supreme Court admitted that the judiciary had erred in usurping the powers of the executive. If the judiciary does not exercise restraint, and over-stretches its limits, there is bound to be a reaction from politicians as well as other stakeholders. The politicians will then, in retaliation, try to curtail the powers, or even the independence of the judiciary. Justices A.K. Mathur and Markandey Katju of the Supreme Court have gone on record thus, "In the name of judicial activism, judges cannot cross their limits and try to take over functions which belong to another organ of State ... They (judges) must remember that judicial activism is not an unguided missile, failure to bear this in mind would lead to chaos." Indeed, judges are like umpires and they are meant to uphold laws, not create them.

The Supreme Court added that in order to maintain the judiciary's independence, judges would have to exercise restraint and honour the separation of powers among the three wings of governance, as *mandated*[12] by the Constitution. Judges must restrain themselves from overreaching domains reserved for the other separate wings, i.e., the executive and the legislature.

In the words of Justice J.S. Verma, "Judicial activism and judicial restraint are two faces of the same coin. Self-discipline is to be practised strictly by the members of the judiciary, and judges must refrain from commenting on policy matters."

A former judge of the Supreme Court, Justice Krishna Aiyyar says that "judicial activism is only a passing phase. This passing phase has come as a timely device to meet the socio-political crisis which is the result of bureaucratic administrative inefficiency and legislative short-sightedness."

There is hardly any doubt about the fruitfulness of judicial activism. It helps in fighting corruption, curbing legislative malpractices, and checking executive excesses. The businessman-politician-bureaucrat nexus often comes to the fore and manipulates laws to meet their selfish ends. This, at times, sets the stage for confrontation between the executive and the judiciary. On a petition challenging the *Moratorium*[13] Act, the Supreme Court stayed the Government directions that were issued under that law to *evade*[14] the sealing drive in Delhi.

Judicial activism continues to be, with the judiciary retaining its power of review over the executive and the legislature, so as to rise to the occasion and deliver justice. The poor and underprivileged sections of society are the ones who benefit the most from judicial activism. Providing of healthcare and medical assistance, cleaning of the Yamuna river, reducing of pollution by making usage of CNG mandatory to run public transport and enforcing emission norms are clearly well-meaning public welfare measures which have become possible only due to judicial intervention. A slew of measures to safeguard the honour and safety of women are currently under way thanks only to judicial activism.

Above all, a working democracy requires an independent judiciary, an effective executive and a responsive legislature. It is necessary that these three organs of the Government work in close co-ordination to ensure the liberty and dignity of the citizens.

Aid to Vocabulary

1. *Infringement* — breach or violation
2. *Interprets* — explain the meaning of
3. *Transgressions* — going beyond the bounds of
4. *Staunch* — devoted and loyal
5. *Conferred* — granted, bestowed
6. *Appellate* — law concerned with appeals
7. *Jeopardised* — endangered
8. *Arbiter* — a person with authority, power, influence or expertise in a specific field
9. *Combative* — hostile
10. *Comply* — act in accordance with
11. *High Watermark* — height of success
12. *Mandated* — instructed on action
13. *Moratorium* — a temporary prohibition or suspension of an activity
14. *Evade* — escape from, avoid

Points to Remember

1. The three organs of Government are legislature, executive and judiciary.
2. Indian Constitution is in favour of an independent judiciary.
3. The Supreme Court is the highest authority in the Indian judicial system.
4. The fearless and active exercise of judicial review has led to judicial activism. It has empowered citizens to fight for their rights.
5. Judicial activism in India has its genesis in the provision for Public Interest Litigation.
6. Judges are like umpires and they are meant to uphold laws, not create them.
7. There is no doubt about the fruitfulness of judicial activism.
8. The three organs of the Government must work in close co-ordination to ensure the liberty and dignity of the citizens.

Essay
119

DO WE NEED A UNIFORM CIVIL CODE?

SYNOPSIS

The Constitution of India has included the provision of laying down a Uniform Civil Code in the Directive Principles of State Policy under Article 44. However, this is a non-enforceable right. Some argue that a Uniform Civil Code is against the spirit of secularism and that it leads to the involvement of religion in politics. To this day, India has not reached that genuine stage of secular democracy wherein a uniform code can be implemented. The society is still polarised. Minorities fear that a uniform code will be a violation of their rights. Therefore, the code should be implemented when the demand comes from the minorities themselves. It should be the result of consensus and accommodation, and not a unilateral imposition.

The need for a Uniform Civil Code in India has been discussed and debated several times, and it remains one of the most controversial clauses mentioned in our Constitution. The Indian Constitution includes laying down of a Uniform Civil Code for its citizens in Part IV—the Directive Principles of State Policy. The legal nature of the Directive Principles is such that it cannot be enforced by any court and, therefore, these are *non-justiciable*[1] rights. The Constitution further calls upon the State to apply these principles in making laws as these principles are fundamental in the governance of the country. Article 44, which deals with the Uniform Civil Code, states: "The State shall endeavour to secure for the citizens, a Uniform Civil Code throughout the territory of India."

The Uniform Civil Code is meant to constitute a legal framework of uniform secular laws which shall govern for one and all, regardless of their religions affiliation, activities like marriage, inheritance and divorce, presently controlled by the personal laws of various religions.

One of the fundamental problems emanating from the absence of a Uniform Civil Code, applicable throughout India, is that it goes against the concept of equality which is one of the basic *tenets*[2] of our Constitution. The people of India are affiliated with different religions and faiths. They are governed by different sets of personal laws with respect to matters relating to family affairs, i.e., marriage, divorce, succession, etc. Laws relating to marriage and/or divorce have been codified in different enactments applicable to people of different religions. These are: the Indian Christian Marriage Act, 1872, the Indian Succession Act, 1925, the Parsi Marriage and Divorce Act, 1936, the Hindu Marriage Act, 1955, and the Muslim Women (Protection of Rights on Divorce) Act, 1986, etc. The Special Marriage Act, 1954 extends to the whole of India barring the state of Jammu and Kashmir; it, however, applies to the citizens of other states of India domiciled in Jammu and kashmir. Persons governed by this Act can specifically register marriage under the said Act even though they may belong to different religious faiths. Arguably, by having different personal laws for different religions we are, in a sense, undermining the credibility of the secular ethos of India. Ideally, there should be uniformity in the governing of such activities and this should be ensured by the State.

We find that no serious efforts have been made by the Government to formulate a Uniform Civil Code for the citizens of India. Muslims, like some other communities, have their own personal law for marriage and divorce. The problem with the personal laws is that in most cases, women are at the receiving end owing to the biased nature of these laws. This became a matter of debate especially after the Supreme Court's verdict in the case filed by a Muslim woman, Shah Bano. The case pertained to her right to maintenance after divorce. According to the Muslim Personal Law, the husband was not *obligated*[3] to pay the wife any maintenance after divorce. This was challenged in the Court and the Court, citing Section 125 of the Criminal Procedure Code, ordered that a husband had to provide maintenance for a divorced wife with no means of income. The Court also observed that a Uniform Civil Code would remove the disparities that existed in different personal laws. The judgement created an uproar among the conservative sections of the Muslim community. However, the issue *pitchforked*[4] the Uniform Civil Code issue into prominence.

Discrimination against women is not found in Muslim personal law alone. Divorce in Christianity, governed by the Indian Christian Marriage Act of 1872 blatantly discriminates against women. For a Christian woman to get divorce, she has to prove against her husband charges of adultery along with *bigamy*[5], incest, cruelty, change of religion, etc. However, a husband is required to prove charges of adultery alone. Muslim men are allowed the liberty to divorce merely by uttering *talaq* three times. These discriminatory practices further *augment*[6] the need for introducing a Uniform Civil Code.

The Uniform Civil Code was made a non-justiciable right under the Directive Principles of State Policy by our founding fathers keeping in mind certain crucial factors. India's Independence in 1947 was followed by large-scale religious riots which was the result of the Partition. Consequently, the environment that prevailed in the country while the Constitution was being framed was not conducive enough for the State to take on the personal laws of various religions with respect to their objectionable clauses. Therefore, the provision of Uniform Civil Code was included in the Directive Principles leaving the task to the later generations to decide and implement, when the moment arrived.

Unfortunately, time is still not ripe for the implementation of the Uniform Civil Code. Polarisation in the society along religious lines is very much alive in our country. The demolition of the Babri Masjid in Ayodhya, and a number of communal riots like the Mumbai riots and the Gujarat riots, are clear pointers towards the fact that India is yet to achieve the level of a stable, tolerant, mature and secular democracy. If the Uniform Civil Code is introduced in the current society, it may lead to further complications. After the Supreme Court's reiteration of the importance of the Uniform Civil Code, Syed Shahabuddin, the President of the All India Muslim Majlis-e-Mushawarat (AIMMM) argued that since the Constitution puts together the freedom of conscience and freedom of religion, it is impossible to ignore religious faiths based on scriptures. Moreover, for Indians, religion is not just a casual part of their personal life. Here, religion plays a primary role in the lives of most of the people. Therefore, introduction of the Uniform Civil Code should be a well-thought out process, as Pt. Jawaharlal Nehru had rightly said.

Another argument against the Uniform Civil Code is that its imposition will be a violation of the Fundamental Rights as envisaged in the Constitution. Fundamental Rights are justiciable rights and are regarded as the most important rights guaranteed by the Constitution. Those who argue against the Uniform Civil Code are of the opinion that for believers, matters like marriage, divorce and inheritance are religious affairs and since the Constitution guarantees freedom of religion, the Uniform Civil Code will be a violation of that.

Religion is an extremely sensitive issue which would require the most delicate handling. Hence, Uniform Civil Code is an issue which would require extensive as well as exhaustive consultations among various religious groups, within the religions, and also between the State and the religious groups. The minorities should not feel that the government is imposing the Code on them.

Uniform Civil Code can be successfully introduced only after attaining improved levels of literacy, awareness on various socio-political issues and increased social mobility. A unilateral attempt towards the imposition of the Uniform Civil Code would encourage vested interests to whip up communal passions and thereby create further problems. There are political parties and leaders who are always ready to hijack such issues in order to expand and consolidate their vote banks. Apart from the religious minority groups, there are also communities belonging to the Scheduled Castes and Scheduled Tribes who oppose the Uniform Civil Code as they believe that it might dilute or *obliterate*[7] their age-old traditional practices.

First raised by the All India Women's Conference in the 1930s the UCC was once a simple demand for equal rights in marriage, divorce, adoption and succession for all women irrespective of religious laws. The common view, as voiced by historian Romila Thapar, is that India must gradually remove all religious considerations from the law to be strictly secular. "This would not be a cosmetic change; or mean uniformity only in personal law, but all the codes we conform to that are determined by religion or caste", she says. That kind of strict uniform secularisation would upset many vote banks, apart from Muslims — it would end the Hindu undivided family's tax benefits, it would extend reservations to eligible castes in all religions. Assume that Parliament irons out all the conflicts and designs a dream civil code — through what political scientist Narendra Subramanian calls an "amplification of the Special Marriage Act" — extending across all domains of family law, (many women's groups have indeed floated versions of such a code); Should this be obligatory or optional? If it is optional, it would give citizens a common set of rights, and also let them choose the sphere of personal law if they so prefer. This might prompt further reform of personal law, to keep women within the fold. And conversely, for those who hope for secularisation in the Western mode, this would make the advantages of civil law obvious enough for personal law to slowly wither away.

It is imperative that the demand for Uniform Civil Code comes from the minority communities themselves. The process can start with a revision of the personal laws by the respective minorities. If the Uniform Civil Code is to be introduced in India, it should be the result of proper consensus and enlightened discussion among concerned parties.

AID TO VOCABULARY

1. *Non-justiciable* — not subject to court jurisdiction
2. *Tenets* — principles or beliefs
3. *Obligated* — made to do (something) by (somebody)
4. *Pitchforked* — forced something suddenly
5. *Bigamy* — the crime of marrying again when one is legally married
6. *Augment* — to improve or make larger
7. *Obliterate* — destroy completely

Points to Remember

1. The Uniform Civil Code is mentioned in Article 44 of the Indian Constitution, under the Directive Principles of State Policy.
2. Advantages of the Uniform Civil Code over Personal Laws are—
   (a) It promotes secularism and equality.
   (b) It simplifies legal procedures.
   (c) It promises to be more gender-sensitive.
3. Arguments against the Uniform Civil Code are—
   (a) It may polarise social atmosphere and trigger communal riots.
   (b) Its imposition may be regarded as a violation of Fundamental Rights envisaged in the Constitution.
4. Demand for a Uniform Civil Code should come from the minority communities themselves.
5. The Uniform Civil Code should be the result of a proper consensus.

SINGLE CIVIL CODE: CHRISTIAN, HINDU WAYS ALSO UNDER LENS

Law Panel Seeks Public Opinion On Anti-Women Practices

The law commission's exercise to formulate a uniform civil code has reached a critical phase as it has asked the citizens to give their views on ending several religious practices and customs that have been branded anti-women in all the three major religions.

Some Key Questions

Law commission is asking whether to ban or regulate polygamy?

It wants to know whether similar practices, such as Maitri-Karar, seen among Hindus in Gujarat, be ended as well (Maitri-Karar is practice of a married Hindu man signing a friendship pact on stamp paper with another woman and bringing her home to live with him).

On triple talaq, which the commission is asking whether it should be abolished altogether, retained only in customs without legal sanctity or retained with suitable amendments.

Asking public for steps needed to 'ensure that Hindu women are better able to exercise their right to property, which is often bequeathed to sons under customary practices'.

Seeks citizens' response to desirability of a two-year waiting period for finalisation of divorce among Christians and whether it affects Christian women's right to equality.

MUSLIM WOMEN : AIMPLB USING SHARIA TO PERPETUATE PATRIARCHY

The All India Muslim Personal Law Board (AIMPLB)'s decision to boycott the law commission's questionnaire on triple talaq and polygamy drew sharp reactions from Muslim women across the country, with some activists even speakig out against the discriminatory laws in the sharia.

The Muslim Mahila Foundation president Nazneen Ansari condemned the AIMPLB for twisting sharia law to their advantage. "Why should the sharia be taken into account only when there's a debate on the freedom of Muslim women?" asked Nazneen. "Why don't these clerics press for sharial laws against Muslim men accused of rape and other such crimes?"

Essay
120

ILLEGAL MIGRATION OF BANGLADESHIS TO INDIA

SYNOPSIS

Migration is the change of residence of an individual or group. Migration can be internal or international, voluntary or forced, legal or illegal. Illegal migration is a problem in India especially in the form of infiltration from Bangladesh. Migration from Bangladesh started in 1947 and is still in progress. These migrants have become an inseparable part of the Indian population and some are even employed in sensitive security positions. This immigration has a socio-economic as well as political impact besides posing a security threat. There are many Indians who have illegally migrated to the USA and the Gulf countries. The exchange of adversely-held enclaves between India and Bangladesh has eased the situation. The Indian Government's approach for deportation of Bangladeshis should be humanitarian even when employing political acumen.

Migration is a change of residence, more or less permanent in nature, by an individual or a group. It excludes human movements like migrant labour flow, nomadism, tourism, etc., which are more or less transitory. People generally migrate in search of better living conditions. Migration can be classified into internal or international migration. The movement of individuals or groups from one area of a country to another is called internal migration while migration involving the crossing of national boundaries is called international migration. Migration can be forced or voluntary. It can be legal or illegal. Illegal migration involves migrating into a country in a *clandestine*[1] manner, without permission and without carrying relevant documents. Illegal migration can often adversely affect the socio-economic conditions of a country.

The issue of illegal migration has been a bone of *contention*[2] between India and its neighbour on the eastern side, Bangladesh. Migration occurs when individual rights and conditions of life in a country become endangered for some reason, or some other country holds promise of a better life. 'Push factors' are those factors that force one to leave one's native country. In Bangladesh, persecution of religious and ethnic minorities along with *pauperisation*[3] of landless rural masses constitute the push factors. On the other hand, 'pull factors' are the situations or conditions that attract one to a foreign country. Such pull factors in India include job opportunities, access to the public distribution system, social security benefits, free education, easy acquisition of immovable property, enrolment as voters and, above all, a *congenial*[4] socio-cultural atmosphere. All these attract Bangladeshi migrants to India.

Bangladeshi migration to India began prior to 1947. Job-seekers from erstwhile East Bengal or East Pakistan used to come to Kolkata, Asom and Tripura. After the partition of India in 1947, a pervasive sense of insecurity pushed the Hindus of East Pakistan (Bangladesh) to migrate to West Bengal and other border states in North-east India. In the aftermath of the 1974 famine in Bangladesh, Muslims migrating to India outnumbered Hindu immigrants. This has changed the demography and the communal balance of the border population. According to the Home Ministry, around 33 per cent of West Bengal's population comprises of illegal Bangladeshis.

In 1971, India helped to create Bangladesh. Now there are 10 million Bangladeshis in India while Hindus remain a persecuted lot in Bangladesh. Distressed Bangladeshis have flowed into India driven by poverty, hunger, natural disasters and diseases. Political parties use them as their vote bank. Labour contractors, *mafia*[5] kingpins, and even the salaried class make use of their services for lower wages. This indicates a total breakdown of border management and immigration control. This has imposed a crushing socio-economic burden on the country and is posing a serious threat to India's national security.

According to a Government report, these migrants have not only procured ration cards and driving licences but also PAN cards, voter identity cards and *Aadhar* numbers. Many have joined government services as well. These include the police and paramilitary organisations, armed forces and even other sensitive security agencies. A Parliamentary panel report pointed out that the *porous*[6] border was the main reason behind the influx of illegal Bangladeshi migrants. The Home Ministry has taken various measures like border fencing, flood lighting and construction of roads to enable more effective patrolling. The Indian Government's plan to identify, detect and deport all the immigrants is overambitious. A more pragmatic approach needs to be employed to prevent further infiltration.

A co-ordinated action plan centred around five immediate priorities needs to be devised. There should be a time-bound exhaustive census of the immigrant population and their locations. The next measure would be streamlining border management and using legal measures to *detain*[7] illegal entrants. The third measure should be to discipline the BSF and weed out its corrupt practices. The fourth measure should be to create a separate immigration service, and finally, there should be sustained diplomacy to garner international support for the programme as well as for public education campaigns.

A large immigrant population can pose difficulties for the country since a *burgeoning*[8] population is its biggest problem. Yet, the solution to this lies in seeing migrants as less of a legal than a humanitarian problem. The matter could easily be sorted out by *deporting*[9] illegally staying Bangladeshis. However, for this to work, economic conditions back home need to be made more attractive for them. Our own non-resident Indians would not have migrated to foreign shores had a strong pull factor not been at play. These pull factors were better jobs and a higher quality of life. The Indian diaspora boasts of a proud population of emigrants—NRIs and H-1B visa holders. Yet, there are thousands of young Indians roaming the world as illegal immigrants. Most of them manage to leave the country with the help of manpower exporters. However, that they retain strong emotional ties with their own country, as many stories in the media demonstrate, proves a point. Likewise, the people from Bangladesh cross over to India for they are attracted to jobs available across the border, but rarely do they sever their emotional ties with the country of their origin, and would any day prefer to return if conditions were to get favourable.

India is not the only country which treats certain categories of its people as *aliens*[10]. The US, which was once a *haven*[11] for immigrants, enforced severe restrictions on them, especially after the Gulf War of 1991 and made them even stricter after the terrorist attack on the World Trade Centre. This is quite evident from the plight of immigrants from Islamic countries. There is a strong possibility of US *paranoia*[12] extending to other immigrants as well.

The problem of illegal immigration from Bangladesh is deep-rooted. It would not be easy and practical to identify all of them and send them back to Bangladesh. The exchange of 102 adversely held enclaves between the two countries has somewhat eased the situation. Further, the only way to stop infiltration is to complete the process of border fencing. According to political commentator B.G. Verghese, immigrants should be given work permits and not voting rights. In the long run, attempts have to be made to bridge the economic gap between India and Bangladesh. Economic development of the border areas in West Bengal and better trade initiatives would also help the economy of Bangladesh. Above all, there should be a combination of humanitarian considerations and political *acumen*[13] to nurture a friendly neighbourhood.

Aid to Vocabulary

1. *Clandestine* — secret
2. *Contention* — dispute
3. *Pauperisation* — leaving people without means of livelihood
4. *Congenial* — pleasant and friendly
5. *Mafia* — organised body of criminals
6. *Porous* — full of pores, letting air, water, etc., through
7. *Detain* — keep a person in confinement against his/her will
8. *Burgeoning* — growing fast
9. *Deporting* — sending away to another country
10. *Aliens* — foreigners
11. *Haven* — refuge, shelter
12. *Paranoia* — unreasonable fear or suspicion of others
13. *Acumen* — keen insight

Points to Remember

1. People generally migrate in search of better living conditions.
2. Illegal migration has been a bone of contention between India and its neighbour, Bangladesh.
3. Distressed Bangladeshis have flowed into India driven out by poverty, hunger, natural disasters and diseases.
4. These people enjoy Indian citizenship and all the facilities that come with being Indian citizens.
5. A large immigrant population can pose difficulties for the country.
6. Attempts have to be made to bridge the economic gap between India and Bangladesh.
7. There should be a combination of humanitarian consideration and political acumen to solve the problem of illegal immigrants.

In many ways, Bangladesh is still fighting the battles of 1971. The domestic political tension between the two Begums – Prime Minister Sheikh Hasina and Opposition leader Khaleda Zia – itself emanates from a debate over 'who owns the narrative of 1971, and who secured freedom', as Salil Tripathi, the author of a book on Bangladesh's modern history, puts it.

India played a part in these events; it has been considered Delhi's most successful neighbourhood intervention. But the intervention did not create the kind of pliant state that Delhi would have hoped.

Essay 121

THE RETURN OF THE NATIVE: THE INDIAN DIASPORA

SYNOPSIS

Since ancient times, man has left his homeland and travelled far and wide in search of adventure or employment, or for a better standard of living. The origin of the Indian diaspora can be traced back to the colonial times. The Indian diaspora faces a dilemma — whether to be loyal to the homeland or to the adopted country. The Indian diaspora can contribute in improving the Indian economy and effecting an increase in FDI. Red tapism and corruption are the major demotivators for them. The Indian government is considering granting of dual citizenship to them.

Since ancient times, man has left his homeland and travelled far and wide either in search of livelihood or for adventure. The United States was born out of migration of people from different countries. In modern times, people migrate primarily for better employment opportunities and for better standard of living. Some do so for higher education and stay on after getting employment. However, the biggest challenge for every immigrant community pertains to integrating harmoniously into the political, economic and social *milieu*[1] of the host country, while preserving and cherishing its own civilisational heritage. Similar is the case with immigrant Indians. In this context, we may distinguish an NRI (Non-Resident Indian) from a PIO (Person of Indian Origin). An Indian citizen who stays abroad for employment or for business purpose or vocation for an uncertain period of time is an NRI. On the other hand, a foreign citizen (excluding a citizen of Pakistan or Bangladesh) is deemed to be a PIO if he/she, at any time, had held an Indian passport, or he/she or either of his/her parents or grandparents was a citizen of India by virtue of the Citizenship Act 1955.

On the 9th of January every year, *Pravasi Bhartiya Divas* is celebrated in New Delhi, owing to its symbolic significance. This occasion marks the ceremonial recognition of the *expatriates*[2] by the Indian Government. It was on this date in 1915 that Mahatma Gandhi, himself a Pravasi Bharatiya in South Africa, had returned to India. On his return, he had started the Freedom Struggle which ultimately gave India her Independence. The Pravasi Bharatiya Samman Award (PBSA) is the highest honour conferred on overseas Indians for their significant contributions in their respective fields. The Indian *diaspora*[3] is present in large numbers in many countries across the globe. In the Western countries like the United States, the UK and Canada, there are millions of NRIs and a majority of them are citizens in their host countries. In countries like Myanmar, Fiji, Mauritius, Malaysia, and in certain Caribbean islands there is a sizeable number of people of Indian origin whose forefathers had migrated to these countries centuries ago. A third category of the Indian diaspora is *conspicuous*[4] by its presence in the Gulf countries, especially Saudi Arabia. These people in the host countries are expatriate workers who continue to retain their Indian citizenship. The Indian diaspora represents India across the world, and it has made a mark in every sphere of life—politics, economics, literature, industry, music, and so on. Eminent among them are Mahendra Chaudhary (ex-Prime Minister of Fiji), Anerood Jugnauth (ex-Prime Minister of Mauritius) both PIOs, Dr. Amartya Sen, who won the Nobel Prize in Economics, renowned authors Salman Rushdie and Nobel laureate V.S. Naipaul, industrialists L.N. Mittal, Sir Swaraj Paul, Satya Nadella (CEO, Microsoft), Sunder Pichai (CEO, google Inc.) and many others. The music of Zubin Mehta, Zakir Hussain and the late Ravi Shankar enthralls audiences the world over.

The origin of the Indian diaspora dates back mainly to the times during the subjection of India by the erstwhile British Empire. Indians were taken as *indentured*[5] labour to the remote colonies of the empire in the 19th century. The Indian population in Fiji, Mauritius, Guyana, Trinidad, Surinam, Malaysia, South Africa and Sri Lanka owes its origin to migrations that had taken place during those times. The later stage of migration of Indian labour was to the Gulf region. The main countries of the Gulf region, where maximum migration has taken place are Bahrain, Kuwait, Libya, Oman, Qatar, Saudi Arabia and the United Arab Emirates. Kerala, Tamil Nadu and Andhra Pradesh are the three states which account for a big chunk of the total migrants. The latest outflow of migrants to the USA and Europe comprises of highly educated professionals, such as doctors and engineers, especially in the *software*[6] discipline. India is the second largest exporter of students to the USA, the first being China. After the completion of courses abroad, many students get lucrative job offers. They do not want to return to India. Nowadays, Indians mainly emigrate to the USA, the UK, Canada and Australia. A large number of Indians living abroad have taken up the citizenship of their countries of residence.

There are more than 28 million overseas Indians in the world. More than 90 per cent of these workers are in the Gulf countries and Southeast Asia.

As per the Ministry of Overseas Indian Affairs, there are 11,379,746 NRIs and 17,075,280 PIOs that makes a total of 28,455,026 overseas Indians across the globe. Uttar Pradesh, Kerala, Tamil Nadu and Andhra Pradesh are the leading sourcing states.

The expatriate is caught between the *nostalgia*[7] of home and better prospects abroad. The association with home and adopted country can be emotional, political or commercial, or a combination of all the three. The first generation immigrants want to be, in the words of Sir Swaraj Paul, "100 per cent Indian and 100 per cent British". The ethnic loyalties are stronger than national loyalties. Many Indians who had left the country to take up good jobs, went on to settle in England or in the USA, and attained prosperity by dint of their hard work and industry. Yet, they tend to be more concerned about their distant homeland than about the country they live in. In their countries of residence, they build temples, gurudwaras and mosques, where they go to worship and can meet people of their respective communities of descent. In this way, they forge the bonds that unite them in a land far away from their homeland. They observe Diwali, Holi, Durga Puja and the birthdays of the Gurus with great fervour.

NRIs are exercising tremendous influence on their home country. The green Revolution in Punjab and Haryana owes a great deal to the foreign *remittances*[8] which enabled the farmers to invest in modern implements of agriculture. It also helps Indian society at large, as foreign remittances improve the country's balance of payment besides promoting latest technology. On the political front, countries like the USA and the UK have recognised Indian expatriates as a critical vote bank in their political system. On the insistence of the Indian diaspora, Diwali was celebrated in the White House for the first time in 2003. India gains by attracting NRI investments, forming a powerful global lobby of NRI investors and by making use of their managerial and trading skills. The NRIs should be offered high-profit investment opportunities so that they are motivated to invest in the country of their origin. The PIOs and NRIs are also worried about the cultural identities of their children. This, they feel, could be addressed by having greater interaction and business relations with their roots.

Some of the NRIs have been so moved by the horrible conditions of social and economic services in India, that they have volunteered to return and serve the country. For instance, the renowned technocrat Sam Pitroda came to India and dedicated himself to the transformation of the inefficient telecommunication system in India, thus, bringing about a revolution in this field.

The economic clout of the Indian diaspora came to the fore after the Indian nuclear testing in 1998. Even as the Indian economy was threatened by the sanctions imposed by the developed countries, the Government of India came out with the Resurgent India Bonds. The overseas Indians responded enthusiastically to this venture by subscribing to the bonds and thereby raising billions of dollars. The NRIs in the United States form a significant component of the India *Caucus*[9] in the US administration and the Congress. They use their economic and political clout to influence policy decisions by the US government concerning Indian interests.

Sometimes, the newly acquired prosperity of the NRIs earns them warm reception and high regard back home. But their fellow citizens in their adopted countries sometimes do not treat them as equals both socially and professionally. This makes them consider the option of returning home for good. The second generation of NRIs may not experience such conflicts, as they are acclimatised to the country of their residence and tend to have an indifferent attitude towards their ancestral country.

The Parliamentary Committee on Empowerment of Women (EWC) (14th Lok Sabha) working on "Plight of Indian women deserted by NRI husbands" had recommended a well defined coordinated mechanism for dealing with the issue of problematic NRI marriages. The inter-ministerial meeting, convened in the Ministry of Overseas Indian Affairs, considered the recommendation of EWC and decided that The National Commission for Women (NCW) be made the coordinating agency at the national level to receive and process all the complaints related to Indian women deserted by their overseas husbands. The NCW runs an NRI Cell to deal with such problems and renders all possible assistance to victims of NRI marriages.

Like any other nation, India also expects loyalty from all Indians—Indians in India as well as Indians who have taken overseas citizenship. We need not go too far for inspiration. China's prosperity is largely a result of huge investment by non-resident Chinese. The NRIs form a huge pool of resources themselves. But the *archaic*[10] business laws, red tapism, inefficient bureaucracy and rampant corruption back home are major demotivators for the diaspora. A lot needs to be done to tap their potential and retain their ties with their country of origin. Provision for dual citizenship along with simplification of investment procedures, increase in accountability, and a more constructive role by the government would be able to attract more and more of the diaspora to give back to the motherland in ample measure.

Aid to Vocabulary

1. *Milieu* — environment or social surroundings
2. *Expatriates* — persons living abroad (away from their homeland)
3. *Diaspora* — any group of people living away from their homeland
4. *Conspicuous* — open to view, obvious
5. *Indentured* — bound by indenture to work, especially, as apprentice (indenture is a sealed contract)
6. *Software* — the programs, etc., used to operate a computer
7. *Nostalgia* — regretful or wistful memory of an earlier time
8. *Remittances* — money sent
9. *Caucus* — a group of people meeting to discuss a political issue or decision
10. *archaic* — primitive, no longer of any use

Points to Remember

1. Since ancient times, man has left his homeland in search of adventure or occupation.
2. *Pravasi Bhartiya Divas* is celebrated on 9th January. It marks the ceremonial recognition of the expatriates by the Indian Government.
3. Indian diaspora is present in large numbers in many countries across the globe.
4. Indians were taken as indentured labour to the remote colonies of the British empire in the 19th century.
5. The expatriate is caught between the nostalgia of home and better prospects abroad.
6. The NRIs are exercising tremendous influence on their homeland.
7. The archaic business laws, red tapism, inefficient bureaucracy and rampant corruption are major demotivators for the Indian diaspora.
8. Dual citizenship, simplification of investment procedures and a more constructive role by the Government would be able to attract the Indian diaspora to do more for their motherland.

UN : INDIAN DIASPORA IS WORLD'S LARGEST AT 16 MILLION

3.3% of Population Across Globe Live in a Country other than their Birthplace

According to the latest United Nations estimate, 244 million people, or 3.3% of the world's population, live in a country other than the one where they were born. Their ranks are growing at a faster pace than the world population as a whole, with enormous economic, social and demographic repercussions for their native and adopted countries. Indians make up the largest diaspora: 16 million Indians are scattered across the world, which partly reflects the country's demographic size (1.2 billion) and youth (median age is around 26).

Essay 122

IS RESERVATION NECESSARY FOR BETTERMENT OF SOCIETY?

SYNOPSIS

The principle of democratic equality can work only if the nation as a whole is brought up to a level wherein there are no socio-economic disparities. That is why the framers of our constitution had laid down the provision of reservation for a limited period. This limited period has been routinely extended by successive governments by way of employing vote bank politics. First, V.P. Singh announced 27% reservation in jobs for OBCs. Then, the UPA government announced 27% reservations in all central educational institutions. Caste-based reservation is very harmful for national integration as it creates an atmosphere of mistrust and victimization. The true essence of democracy lies in a society wherein people are not segregated by caste and creed. The successive agitations by various caste groups, namely Gujjars and the Patels in 2015 and the Jats in 2016 are a wake up call to review the national reservation policy. Justice in a democracy would pertain to fair treatment of the people. It is high time we created an egalitarian society wherein the sufferings of the poor and needy, irrespective of caste or creed are brought to an immediate stop.

Our Constitution is founded on the ideals of equality and justice in the social as well as the political spheres. It abolishes any *discrimination*[1] whether against or in favour of any class of persons on the grounds of religion, race or place of birth. In keeping with these ideals, the Constitution did away with communal representation or reservation of seats in the Legislature or in the offices on the basis of religion.

The principle of democratic equality can work only if the nation as a whole is brought up to a level wherein there are no socio-economic disparities. Therefore, the Constitution of India prescribed certain provisions to help the backward sections of the society come up the social ladder. It was a well-meaning plan on the part of the framers of the Constitution to create an institutional mechanism that would allow diverse people of India's pluralistic society to live in harmony as citizens of India. That is why, they had laid down the provision of reservation, which would in essence be a positive discrimination to ensure economic justice. However, it was clearly mentioned that all these provisions should be continued only for a limited period, that is, until the objective is achieved after which these should be discontinued.

The original pact on which the current reservation for Scheduled Castes and Scheduled Tribes is based is the 1932 Poona Pact between Dr. B.R. Ambedkar and Mahatma Gandhi. There is, however, no definition of Scheduled Castes and Scheduled Tribes in our Constitution itself, though the President is empowered to draw up a list in consultation with the Governor of each state, subject to revision by the Parliament. The Constitution provides for 15% and 7.5% of vacancies in government aided educational institutions and jobs in the government and the public sector to be the reserved quota for SC and ST candidates respectively, for a period of 15 years. This period has been routinely extended by successive governments and the Indian Parliament, and no revisions have been undertaken for fear of losing votes. The prescribed limited period of positive discrimination has become an abiding feature of our socio-political life.

In the 1989 general election, Janata Dal in their election manifesto first promised to implement the recommendations of the Mandal Commission. All the other political parties including the Congress were also committed to implementing these recommendations. No party dared to oppose it for the fear of losing the *Dalit* vote bank. On August 7, 1990, the then Prime Minister V.P. Singh announced the acceptance of Mandal Commission's recommendations of 27% reservation in jobs for the OBCs. Its repercussion was a large scale country-wide agitation by students of non-reserved classes.

A nine-judge bench of the Supreme Court in the Indira Sawhney's case, popularly known as Mandal Commission, laid down with regard to reservations that it should not exceed 50%.

The UPA government under Prime Minister Dr. Manmohan Singh again recommended 27% seats reservation for OBCs in educational institutions. The five-member Supreme Court Bench had upheld OBC quota in central educational institutions clearing the way for reservation of 27% seats for 'backward' castes over a period of three years from the academic year 2008-09. In a judgment, the Supreme Court allowed 27% quota for OBCs and consequently the overall reservation increased to 49.5%, although it had kept the 'creamy layer' out. This meant that children of those holding constitutional positions, Group A and B officers and their equivalents, military officers in the rank of colonel and above, children of professionals like doctors and lawyers, would be excluded. Most political parties opposed this exclusion of creamy layer but the Supreme Court rejected their demand. The five-judge Constitution Bench headed by former Chief Justice K.G. Balakrishnan unanimously decided to keep the 'creamy layer' out of the *purview*[2] of the quota and recommended review of the quota every five years. However, in spite of large scale criticism and agitation, the government maintains that the scheme must continue to bring the backward sections of society on par with the privileged sections.

Now, as it has turned out, reservation is no longer a positive discrimination or a way to ensure social justice and equality. It is more like a curtain to hide the failure of our political machinery to create a *conducive*[3] atmosphere for socio-economic development of all sections of society. It goes on to show that the democratic process employed could not, with all the measures and means, achieve the desired goal even after 65 years of independence. on the contrary, society has ended up being fragmented even more on caste lines which was never the objective of our Constitution makers. Reservations have strengthened and consolidated the already existing caste divisions within the society.

Caste based reservation has unfortunately established caste as the only determinant of social identity. Caste is being considered as an *indispensable*[4] trait of citizens. It is detrimental for the individuals who seek socio-economic justice through affirmative action and merit. This policy of caste based reservation is dividing society and creating an environment of mistrust and victimisation.

Democracy flourishes in that society wherein division on the basis of caste has no place, where people are not identified by their race or place of origin. It is ironical that in a democratic country, the government itself categorises people into caste-groups and metes out a differential treatment on various grounds. Caste-based reservation does nothing to eliminate caste system from the society. On the contrary it *perpetuates*[5] it, or makes caste-stratification 'more rigid'. As we can see, this policy is a major hindrance for national integration and an *antithesis*[6] to the Preamble of our Constitution which declares India to be a sovereign, socialist, secular, democratic and republican polity.

The Hardik Patel led agitation demanding inclusion of Patels in the OBC category for reservation in jobs, coming class on the heels of a similar demand by the Gujjars, that had eventually been met, and followed by another in February 2016 by the Jat Community, is a wakeup call to review the national reservation policy. On the other hand, whether or not the Indian political class is willing to refine the system while keeping social justice at the core is a big question to be answered. Justice Shiva Kirti Singh of the Supreme Court echoes the words of the RSS chief Mohan Bhagwat when he says— 'Positive action is needed to help the needy but time frame for reservation should be fixed; say 20-30 years'. "Reservation has to be," Prof. Rajinder Chaudhary opines, "an exception to be used to tackle *pervasive*[7] discrimination and not a common tool to be used to tackle backwardness of various kinds. Reservation is not meant to perpetually *segregate*[8] various communities and give proportionate representation to various groups. It is meant to overcome caste divisions".

With a view to secure vote-banks by means of caste-based reservations, the government doles out a host of facilities and privileges to particular castes, such that others feel cheated. People reportedly arrange fake certificates which substantiate their status as 'backward' to avail themselves of the opportunities provisioned for the backward sections of the society. At the same time, many people who are indeed educationally and economically backward may be deprived of government welfare schemes for the reason that they are not classified into a reserved category. The assumption of backwardness being limited to certain castes is wholly deceitful and should not be allowed to continue.

Justice in a democracy lies in the fair treatment of all sections of the society. By implementing reservation for OBCs, we risk becoming a fractured society; besides, the primary goal of being a casteless and classless society would never be accomplished in this manner. The need of the hour is to depart from 'group centric', and shift to 'individual centric' benefits. Benefits should uplift an individual and not a group. This is what has been indicated in Article 15(4) and 16(4) of the Constitution. Pandit Jawaharlal Nehru had said, "It is the backward individual citizen that we should help; why should we brand groups and classes as backward and forward?"

The time is ripe to end casteist politics and form an *egalitarian*[9] society wherein the sufferings of the poor and the needy irrespective of caste and creed, are brought to an immediate end.

AID TO VOCABULARY

1. *Discrimination* — the practice of treating a person or group of people unfairly differently from other people or groups of people
2. *Purview* — scope or range
3. *Conducive* — helping something to happen or making it likely
4. *Indispensable* — absolutely essential
5. *Perpetuates* — makes something continue
6. *Antithesis* — opposite, contradictory

7. *Pervasive* — existing in every part of something
8. *Segregate* — to separate groups of people because of their particular race, religion, etc.
9. *Egalitarian* — showing or holding equal rights, benefits and opportunities for everybody

Points to Remember

1. Our Constitution is founded on the ideals of equality and justice in the social as well as political spheres.
2. The Constitution had laid down 15% and 7.5% reservations for SCs and STs respectively, for a period of 15 years only.
3. This period was routinely extended by successive governments for fear of losing votes.
4. On August 7, 1990 the then Prime Minister V.P. Singh first announced 27% reservations in jobs for the OBCs on the basis of the Mandal Commission report.
5. A nine-judge bench of the Supreme Court laid down with regard to reservation that it should not exceed 50%.
6. The UPA government recommended 27% reservations for OBCs in all central educational institutions.
7. Society has fragmented even more on caste lines, which was never the intent of the Constitution makers.
8. Other classes feel cheated by the facilities provided to the reserved categories.
9. The time is ripe to end casteist politics and ensure an egalitarian society.

GUIDED COMPOSITION

Develop the following paragraph into a full-fledged essay in 800-1000 words. The gist of the topic is provided in approximately 150 words for your help:

ONE MAN'S MEAT IS ANOTHER MAN'S POISON

People differ from one another in taste, interests, attitudes and abilities. Even identical twins, who have vast similarity in their mental, physical and emotional make up, show differences in their behaviour. Thus, men differ greatly from one another. Hence, what is good for one may prove bad for the other. We respond to situations according to our own personalities. A man who is aggressive may not bow down to adverse circumstances and may ultimately conquer them. Whereas another man, who is less sure of himself may break down under extreme poverty, adversity and deprivation. Thus, it is very difficult to say that what is true for one will be true for another. One man's elixir of life can prove poison for another. Therefore, what is good for one may be bad for another. Hence, man should follow his own instincts tempered with reason and act in accordance with them. He should not blindly follow another out of envy and a feeling of discontent with himself. *(150 words)*

Essay 123

THE NEED OF RESERVATION FOR WOMEN

SYNOPSIS

Women, once considered fit only for domestic activities, are today thriving as professionals. Representation in the legislature can help to bring about some change in the position of women in India. Men show little interest in facilitating or extending opportunities to their female colleagues. Women's Reservation Bill was introduced in the Lok Sabha in 1999. The most important provision was reservation of one-third of the seats in the State legislatures as well as in the Union Parliament. No consensus could be reached on reservation for women with some parties demanding special quotas within quotas. The bill was again introduced in March 2010 in the Rajya Sabha, the upper house of the Indian Parliament. Reservation for women is necessary because our democracy will remain seriously flawed if it fails to yield adequate space to women.

Women, once considered fit only for shouldering domestic duties and rearing children, have expanded their horizon to thrive as professionals too. In India, they have made inroads into various male-dominated professions including the bureaucracy. Women who were educated and were given opportunities to acquire the necessary skills went on to prove themselves capable of holding their own, in the fields of business, medicine, engineering, law, art and culture. However, in spite of the fact that we have had a woman Prime Minister, several women Chief Ministers, even a woman President, women have not really been able to make their mark in politics. Even the best of female parliamentarians feel sidelined and powerless within their respective parties. Women are nearing equal political participation in only a handful of countries such as Sweden, Norway, Finland, Iceland and New Zealand.

India is ranked 130th among 188 countries as per the Gender Inequality Index in the Global Human Development Report 2015 released by UNDP (United Nations Development Programme). It is ahead of only Afghanistan in South Asia on an indicator which measures gender parity, in education, reproduction health (maternal mortality and adolescent fertility rate), etc. Even on the other two major components that drive gender equality—women's representation in national parliament and the participation of 25 years plus women in economic activities—India is far behind many even in South Asia. Nepal is the best in this category with 33.2 per cent women in the Parliament while China and Pakistan have 21.3 and

21 per cent women respectively—much better than India's 10.7 per cent.

The report makes a strong case for the need of reservation for women in all elected bodies. The same politicians who *scramble*[1] to declare their support for a special quota for women, show little willingness to include women in party decisions, or to help create a conducive atmosphere for women's participation in various matters. Women's *marginalisation*[2] is even more pronounced in the day-to-day functioning of almost all political parties. In areas of decision-making and policy implementation, representation of women is almost negligible. The exploitation of women is a 'reality' in India and gender justice a 'fragile myth' with the sad state of affairs generally attributed to social prejudices. Through law and policy provisions, women have over the years secured for themselves entitlements, but so far they have not been able to protect themselves from crimes committed against them. Therefore, it is imperative to take special measures to enhance women's political participation so that they get a say in formulating the kind of laws needed for their safety.

The Constitution provides for *affirmative*[3] action to redress social inequalities. Even today, we have only about 10 per cent women in the Parliament. The reason for this is not the lack of able and competent women. Rather, they have intentionally been kept out of the arena of politics by people with *vested interests*[4]. The 85th Constitutional Amendment Bill introduced in the Lok Sabha in December, 1999 includes the following key provisions for women:

- One-third of all seats in the Lok Sabha and the Vidhan Sabhas shall be reserved for women.
- Such reservation shall also apply in case of seats reserved for the Scheduled Castes (SCs) and Scheduled Tribes (STs).
- There shall be rotation of seats so reserved for women. (Such rotation shall be determined by draw of lots, in such a manner that a seat shall be reserved only once in a block of three general elections.

In December 2009, the parliamentary standing committee on Law and Justice, and Personnel recommended passage of the Women's Reservation Bill by the 108th Constitutional Amendment. The Bill was cleared by the Union Cabinet on February 25, 2010 and was introduced in March, 2010 in the Rajya Sabha, the upper house of the Indian Parliament, where it was passed by an overwhelming majority.

Till date the Lok Sabha has not passed the Bill owing to opposition from different quarters. It has been deferred many times due to lack of *consensus*[5] among the parties. One of the oppositions to this Bill is the apprehension that the high class or economically advanced women would secure all the reserved seats in the Parliament. If the Bill were to be approved by the Lok Sabha, it would then have to be passed by half of India's state legislatures and signed by the President.

Before this Bill was introduced, the 73rd and 74th amendments (1993) had provided for the reservation of seats for women in the local bodies of the Panchayats and the Municipalities. The reservation of 33% seats for women in Panchayat bodies, was approved by the Cabinet. In a move aimed at empowering women further at the grassroots level, the Centre on August 27, 2009 approved a proposal to amend Article 243D of the Constitution that provides for 33 per cent reservation for women in the Panchayats by increasing it to 50 per cent. The 'Women Only' seats in the Panchayats are to be rotated. This provision, if fully utilised, can offer them an enhanced role in village affairs and will add to their strength in fighting gender discrimination.

In an interesting development relating to reservations for women, the Law Ministry's Department of Company Affairs (DCA) proposed that all public limited and joint stock companies should reserve a fifth of their *Board*[6] for women. the DCA added that the presence of women would ensure that the issue of workers' welfare is appropriately addressed. Women would bring before the Board a more sensitive perspective to issues at hand. It is being widely acknowledged that the woman who manages both a family and a career is a professional asset. As Dilnavaz Shroff, the head of El Dorado Group commented, "increasingly, motherhood is being recognised as an excellent school for managers, demanding many of the new skills."

Reservation for women both in government jobs and democratic institutions—would amount to a positive discrimination. At the same time, it might foster an inferiority complex among women with regard to the impression that they had been, as it were, provided with crutches to walk while the rest had to struggle in the demanding world. Also, reservation for women, in case of the Scheduled Castes, Scheduled Tribes and Other Backward Classes, runs the risk of becoming a populist tool in the hands of politicians. Politicians only talk about reservation instead of hitting at the basic cause of such inequality between men and women. Instead of providing solutions to this problem, it may give rise to social, political as well as psychological tensions. It is debatable whether more women will attend school, college or office as a result of reservation. There are many complex reasons behind the low representation of women in the socio-political and economic sectors of the country. Reservation is not the complete solution.

Reservation in education and jobs may seem unfair as they may deprive the meritorious and deserving candidates who do not belong to a reserved category. But the 50 per cent reservation for women in Panchayats has definitely addressed, to some extent, the real issues at the grassroots. It has made development far more organic than a top-down approach ever could. Similarly, the proposed reservation for women in the Parliament may lead to ground-breaking legislations to improve the lot of women as well as the society as a whole.

Our democracy will remain seriously flawed if it fails to yield adequate space to women. Betterment of women is only possible with the betterment of society as a whole; reservation for women is an important step towards achieving this end.

AID TO VOCABULARY

1. *Scramble* — to move before someone else does
2. *Marginalisation* — treating as insignificant, and depriving one of opportunities
3. *Affirmative* — expressing approval
4. *Vested interests* — ulterior motives
5. *Consensus* — general agreement or opinion
6. *Board* — the group of directors of a company.

POINTS TO REMEMBER

1. Women, once considered fit only for carrying out domestic chores, have expanded their horizon to take up the role of professionals.
2. According to Gender Inequality Index report 2015, India ranks 130th among 188 countries.
3. It is imperative that we take special measures to enhance women's political participation.
4. The 85th Constitutional Amendment Bill provides for reservation of one-third seats for women in the Lok Sabha and the Vidhan Sabhas.
5. Reservation of 50% seats for women in Panchayat bodies has already been approved by the Cabinet.
6. Our democracy will remain seriously flawed if it fails to yield adequate space to women.

QUOTA FOR WOMEN

The 108th Constitutional Amendment Bill seeks quota for women not only in the Lok Sabha but also in all State Assemblies.

Lok Sabha		Assemblies	
Total	**: 543***	**Total**	**: 4,109**
SC/ST	: 122	SC/ST	: 1,167
Women	: 181	Women	: 1,370
Open	: 282	Open	: 2,942

**Note:* The Lok Sabha at present consists of 545 members. 543 members are directly elected from States (530) and Union Territories (13) and two are nominated by the President to represent Anglo-Indian community.

Essay

124 IMMORAL TRAFFICKING

SYNOPSIS

Human trafficking constitutes one of the gravest violations of human rights as well as dignity. Trafficking can be classified into three categories: (a) commercial sexual exploitation, (b) exploitative labour and (c) organ selling. The cause of trafficking is two dimensional—the demand factor and the vulnerability of the person trafficked. The Immoral Traffic Prevention Act (ITPA) of 1956 does not criminalise prostitution, but punishes those who are profited from this crime. Women and children are preferred for cheap labour. The Human Organ Transplant Act, 1994 has not been able to control organ selling in India. Kidney is the most preferred organ in trafficking business. Our Government adopted a National Plan of Action to combat immoral trafficking in 1998. UNODC has set up Anti-Human Trafficking Units AHTU in several states. All who are committed to safeguarding human rights must join hands in fighting human trafficking.

Exploitation of human beings through immoral means, especially of women and children within their own countries as well as across international borders, against their will, is called *human trafficking*. It is one of the *gravest*[1] violations of human dignity apart from being a serious violation of human rights. Trafficking has reached alarming proportions in the past two decades, globally. Trafficking of women and children for commercial sexual exploitation, and for other abusive purposes, is rampant in India. The incidence of intra-country trafficking is also very high.

The Constitution of India, under Article 23, prohibits trafficking in any form. There are special legislations in place like the Immoral Traffic Prevention Act (ITPA), Bonded Labour Abolition Act, Juvenile Justice Act, etc., in addition to the provisions in the Indian Penal Code (IPC). The Government of India has proposed amendments to the Immoral Traffic Prevention Act, 1956. The changes have been proposed as the existing framework is inadequate to counter trafficking.

Human trafficking can be classified into three categories: (a) commercial sexual exploitation, (b) exploitative labour like domestic work, work in carpet industry, camel jockeying, etc., and (c) organ selling. The first category, i.e. Commercial Sexual Exploitation (CSE) could take place in brothels, massage parlours, beer bars, etc. Even some of the 'marriage bureaus' are said to be trafficking women under the guise of forging marriage alliances, especially in places where the ratio of male to female population is unfavourable or *skewed*[2]. Trafficking of exploitative labour (EL) could take place in the form of labour in industries, agriculture, domestic service, entertainment industry, etc. This could victimise children, men and women. The third category pertains to organ trafficking.

The cause of trafficking is two dimensional in character. First, the demand factor and second, the *vulnerability*[3] of the person being trafficked or likely to be trafficked—both abet human trafficking. Where there is more demand, there is a higher incidence of human trafficking. Human trafficking in any form is demand-driven. In association with the demand factor, vulnerability of the victims makes it easier for the traffickers to commit the crime. However, vulnerability is not the outcome of poverty alone. It is a combination of several factors. These factors include illiteracy, lack of awareness of rights, disparities in income, scope of exploitation of the person, poor law enforcement, lack of public awareness, etc.

The Immoral Traffic Prevention Act, 1956 does not criminalise prostitution, but mostly punishes acts by third parties facilitating prostitution, for instance running a brothel, living off a sex-worker's earnings even though sex work has not been coerced, etc. The Government of India in the year 1950 ratified an international convention for repression of human trafficking and prevention of exploitation of the prostitute. The law was introduced in 1956 as SITA (Suppression of Immoral Traffic Act) and in 1986 it was amended to form the current ITPA, in which the legal framework is the same. Studies have shown that despite the noble intentions of Indian lawmakers, the police have used every means possible to harass sex workers. Sex workers marched along the streets of Delhi to draw public attention to the fact that the amendments would deny them their already *meagre*[4] earnings from their livelihood. Not only the sex workers, but also AIDS activists as well as peer educators are regularly harassed by the police. Now, the sex workers with moral as well as material support from celebrities and NGOs are saying with confidence: 'we are here because we prefer this lifestyle. Give us the right to openly practice our trade'. They want amendment of the existing law, which prescribes legal action against *the pimps*[5] as well as the clients of sex workers. They might have valid arguments with regard to their claim. Arrest and rescue operations by the police are mostly *orchestrated*[6] to keep the terror alive, so that the sex workers and pimps keep bribing them. Actually, almost all brothels and those who run the sex trade, function under the 'protection' of or with the *connivance*[7] of the police. The more sex trade flourishes, the more money the police make. Again, the police-pimp nexus makes it more dangerous for those women who are being coerced into this profession or those who try to get out of it. Amendment of the law alone cannot protect such destitutes.

Women in India are mostly tricked, forced and sold into this profession. However, not all Indian women become prostitutes through trafficking. Many enter the trade to earn a living in the absence of other means of livelihood. It is an outcome of their social as well as economical backwardness. But if this profession were to be legalised, several questions will arise. What does the term legalise actually mean? Does it mean that a sex worker can open a brothel anywhere she likes and advertise her services? How many, even among those who are empathetic towards the *plight*[8] of prostitutes, are willing to allow a brothel to run right next to their own house? How can renting a women's body for sex be considered a perfectly legitimate activity when this very concept is immoral? How can the law handle the high society call girls, who are there by choice, and with the help of influential pimps? Those who demand that sex work be given the same 'respect' as any other profession need to explain how to coerce or ensure respect. Even in those countries where sex work is legal, sex workers do not command social respect. So law can do little to purify the depraving implications of sex slavery.

The other known purposes of trafficking pertain to the entertainment industry, domestic work in the carpet and garment industries, fishing and brick industries, forced labour, camel jockeying, drug trafficking, begging, etc. Mainly, women and children are victimised in these activities. About seventy-three million children belonging to the age group of 10-14 years are engaged in child labour all over the world. Article 24 of the Constitution of India bans child labour below 14 years of age. More than 20 per cent child labourers aged 5-14, in India, are toiling in the fields or hunting in forests for a livelihood. Children work in farms, plantations, fisheries and cottage industries. They do not go to school as they have to work to add to the income of the family.

With globalisation and increasing competition, there is a growing demand from employers and enterprises for cheap labour of women and children. Many women and children are lured out of their homes by false promises of love, marriage or work. They may willingly accompany their friends or acquaintances only to find themselves trapped in a vulnerable situation. Camel race is a very popular game in some countries of the Middle East. Children are mostly preferred for camel jockeying. A report said that many children from Andhra Pradesh, Rajasthan, Maharashtra, West Bengal, Uttar Pradesh, etc., are trafficked for engagement in this inhuman profession. Their living conditions are *deplorable*[9] with facilities provided at the work place as well as in the living quarters being below acceptable standards. Wages paid are very low and sometimes they are not paid at all. These children have no access to health or medical facilities. The employer takes advantage of their *docility*[10] and their willingness to do monotonous jobs. Rescue of minors from prostitution or from any kind of illegal profession is primarily the state's responsibility. NGOs, however, have done a much better job by themselves throughout the country.

Organ trafficking is not new to the world and India is considered to be one of the biggest hubs of organ trafficking. The Human Organs Transplant Act was enacted in 1994. But it drew more attention in 1998 after the *exposè*[11] of organised rackets in Uttar Pradesh and Karnataka that year.

Kidney is a paired organ in the human body and one of the kidneys can be safely removed from a living person; and thus, it is the most preferred organ in the trafficking business. However, the number of transplants is almost static at 4000-5000 operations per year, against the demand of approximately 50,000 operations in our country. There is a yawning gap between the demand and supply of kidneys worldwide and this leads to trading of kidneys in the black market. The rich people are willing to pay huge sums of money to save their lives, and there is a set of donors who donate for the sake of earning money. The donors are mainly poor people, who are lured by very *lucrative*[12] offers in terms of money and jobs but end up being paid a meagre sum by brokers involved in the racket. The hefty financial gains are mainly enjoyed by the person running the racket. The kingpin of Gurgaon (Haryana) kidney racket, Dr. Amit Kumar, was arrested in Nepal.

The World Health Organisation (WHO) estimated that ten per cent of all transplants involved patients from developed countries going to poor countries to buy organs. The various policies and strategies adopted to boost organ donations have not yielded results. Till date, the main source of organs for transplantation has been *altruism*[13]. We need to facilitate enactment of a law pertaining to 'presumed consent' which would authorise the doctors to remove organs from a 'braindead' individual provided there are no objections from the family members. Several European countries like Austria, Belgium, France and Italy have legalised kidney transplants from the braindead, and these countries have witnessed an increase in the number of donations. Organ donation rate is the highest in countries like Mexico and Spain where more than 30 per million population (PMP) agree with regard to organ donation after death, against a dismal figure of about 0.1 PMP in India. Apart from religious beliefs, lack of public awareness about the usefulness of organ donation after death, and non-acceptance of 'brain death criteria' as cessation of life, are found to be the main reasons behind such a low rate of organ donation in our country. We may feel that buying and selling of organs is ethically wrong, but letting a patient suffer endless sessions of dialysis only to eventually die, when a donated organ can be transplanted to save his life, is not only unethical, but also criminal. However, the multiple-organ donation of a brain dead youth to thirty different beneficiaries, in New Delhi in 2012, may well mark a watershed in the Indian scene. Once we bridge the ever-widening gap between demand and supply, such rackets will cease to flourish.

The Government of India formulated a National Plan of Action to combat immoral trafficking in 1998. It was formulated by the Department of Women and Child Development and the Ministry of Human Resource Development. A committee was formed to look into the problems of trafficking with the help of NGOs and other organisations that are engaged in addressing this issue. Anti-human trafficking is an area which beckons all those who are concerned with human rights violations. The United Nations Office on Drugs and Crimes (UNODC), New Delhi, in partnership with the Government of India and the state Government agencies, has set up Anti-Human Trafficking Units (AHTU) in several states. All those who are committed to protecting human rights must join hands in this global initiative to fight human trafficking.

Aid to Vocabulary

1. *Gravest* — most serious
2. *Skewed* — slanting, unequal
3. *Vulnerability* — exposed to damage
4. *Meagre* — lacking in amount or quantity
5. *Pimps* — men who make money illegally by bringing customers for prostitutes
6. *Orchestrated* — planned and organised
7. *Connivance* — secret help for something illegal or dishonest
8. *Plight* — condition or state, especially an unfortunate one
9. *Deplorable* — exceedingly bad
10. *Docility* — trait of being controllable

11. *Exposè* — disclosure of a discreditable thing
12. *Lucrative* — profitable
13. *Altruism* — principle of selfless service or help

Points to Remember

1. Human trafficking constitutes one of the gravest violations of human rights.
2. Trafficking can be classified into three categories:
   (a) Commercial sexual exploitation
   (b) Exploitative labour
   (c) Organ selling
3. The cause of trafficking is two dimensional in character, i.e., demand factor and vulnerability of the person trafficked.
4. The Immoral Traffic Prevention Act of 1956 does not criminalise prostitution, but punishes the person who facilitates it or benefits from it.
5. Mainly women and children are victimised in exploitative labour as they are paid low by the employers.
6. The Human Organ Transplant Act of 1994 could not check organ trafficking.
7. The Government of India formulated a National Plan of Action in 1988 to combat immoral trafficking which involves NGOs and other organizations that are engaged in addressing this issue.

Essay
125

SHOULD EUTHANASIA BE LEGALISED?

Synopsis

There are many who, due to some fatal disease, are condemned to live a painful life devoid of any hope of recovery. In such cases, the concept of euthanasia or 'mercy killing' gains prominence. There are two kinds of euthanasia, active and passive. Some believe that active euthanasia may be immoral but passive is rather acceptable. The Supreme Court on March 7, 2011 legalised passive euthanasia. Many people consider euthanasia to be illegal as they believe that it is like interfering in God's work. They argue that life is a gift of God and it is presumptuous on the part of humans to throw it away. But there are several cases wherein a patient has to live in unbearable suffering, and the agony of the patient is difficult to put up with for his/her relatives. In such cases, the choice of euthanasia should be made available. Some thinkers feel that active euthanasia is preferable to passive one, for it gives immediate relief. The ultimate decision should be of the patient, and in extraordinary situations, the decision should be of the doctors and the patient's closest relatives.

Euthanasia basically means 'gentle and easy death to end suffering' or 'mercy killing'. It is a term which has long lost its connection with the Greek idea of good death, and it is often used in current debate with a totally different meaning. We often come across many heart-rending stories about the painful condition of people suffering from different kinds of fatal diseases and disabilities. There are cases wherein people slip into coma and never gain consciousness, yet they cannot be pronounced dead. Some people whose bodies have undergone *irreversible*[1] damage due to accidents live on but become totally dependant on others with no hope of recovery. At such moments, the idea of an easy death appears satisfactory. In the backdrop of such a scenario, the concept of euthanasia gains prominence.

The issue of euthanasia involves two aspects: passive and active. Passive euthanasia refers to the right to refuse or withdraw medical treatment, which merely prolongs life technically with no possibility in actual terms of a cure or *resumption*[2] of normal activity. Passive euthanasia results when there is an *abstention*[3] from interventions that may keep the subject alive. Active euthanasia, in literal terms, amounts to legalised suicide or legalised murder. In this case, a physician or someone else in authority, acts directly to cause the patient's death. Some believe that passive euthanasia is all right and may be accepted but active euthanasia is immoral.

In a landmark judgment, the Supreme Court on March 7, 2011 legalised passive euthanasia, giving thousands of patients living in a vegetative state all over the country, the right to have artificial life-support systems withdrawn so as to enable them to end a life of misery.

A bench comprising Justice Markandey Katju and Justice Gyan Sudha Mishra, however, said the right to permit a terminally ill patient to refuse medical treatment would be given under 'guarded conditions' so as to prevent its misuse. The bench ruled that active euthanasia, which involves giving terminally ill patients lethal drugs to end their lives, could not be allowed as it was not only immoral but also unconstitutional. The bench laid down a procedure to be followed in case a patient or his or her family opts for passive euthanasia. The guidelines include seeking a declaration from the High Court after having secured clearance from a medical board as well as the state government. The court rejected the Centre's contention that euthanasia should not be permitted in any form as India is still a 'backward and emotional country'. It referred to various international judgements on the subject and said that passive euthanasia should be allowed if a patient wished for it. In case of its non-voluntary application, the patient's close relative or friend should give his or her consent.

There is a deep-rooted belief in most people that life is a gift of God and it is *presumptuous*[4] on the part of humans to throw it away. As for taking it away from another human being, howsoever merciful the motive, many would frown upon it as coming dangerously close to playing God.

Moreover, it is a gross violation of an individual's rights. For instance, wherein a person has become totally *incapacitated*[5] physically and mentally, who will do the decision making for him? The vital question here pertains to the consent of the person. In fact, physician-assisted suicide is fundamentally inconsistent with the physician's professional role. As far as the issue of resources goes, euthanasia can contribute very insignificantly towards overcoming the paucity of medical funds and inadequacy of infrastructure globally. The whole issue is very individual as well as personal. Another strong objection with regard to legalisation of euthanasia is—whenever a patient is in misery, people would, on the pretext of ending that misery, put the patient to rest forever. At the same time, this practice will discourage research and development of new treatments. If physician-assisted suicide were made legal, insurance companies and family members unwilling to waste funds on costly medical bills would unethically use euthanasia with respect to their relatives or clients without bothering to obtain proper consent. Similarly, the possibility of greedy and *unscrupulous*[6] relations conspiring with an equally unscrupulous doctor to kill the patient from whose death they may draw material benefits, is indeed horrifying. This is of major concern to the disabled persons who worry about the possibility that eventually laws will be created to allow the authoritarian States to kill those citizens whom it deems to be worthless.

Advocates of euthanasia say that it is to be used only in cases of those who are 'terminally ill'. However, there are many definitions for the word 'terminal'. Some say that a terminal disease can be any disease which curtails life even for a day; some define terminal condition as one from which death will occur in a relatively short time. Others state that terminal means death which is expected within six months or less. At the same time, medical experts acknowledge that it is virtually impossible to predict the life expectancy of a particular patient. It is very much possible that a terminally ill person remains alive for years. There are many other phrases which have been used in place of 'terminally ill', such as hopelessly ill, incurably ill, meaningless condition, hopeless condition, etc.

Euthanasia is also inherently pitched against one of the basic principles of morality, that says 'killing is wrong'. It does not comply with religious beliefs, legal traditions or medical ethics. It is also a rejection of the importance and value of human life. There have been a number of cases which have exposed us to the dangers of euthanasia. This is the reason why there are only a few countries in the world today where it has been legalised. Active Euthanasia is permitted in countries like The Netherlands, Belgium and Switzerland. Passive Euthanasia is allowed in the UK, the USA and Canada.

Proponents[7] of active Euthanasia are of the strong opinion that passive Euthanasia—discontinuation of the medical treatment or withdrawal of life support—aggravates the pain of the patient instead of alleviating it. The patient may suffer too long and that too without the relieving effects of medicines, if death is not immediate. Although it appears immoral and against God's will, active Euthanasia, according to this school of thinkers, is far more soothing because it relieves the patient of their unbearable pain with immediate effect. Moreover, the close relatives too are saved from suffering with the patient and from a further drain on their financial resources.

Discontinuing painful medical treatment so as to facilitate the patient to attain natural death, and administering something to consciously induce death, are two different things. There are individuals who go through unbearable suffering and pain and whose agony becomes difficult to comprehend for those close to him, especially when death is *inevitable*[8] and there is not a ray of hope for improvement. In such situations, the choice of euthanasia should be made available. Advocates of euthanasia believe that death is preferable for people whose quality of life has gone down into an *abyss*[9] and who simply want to die with dignity.

This being a very personal issue, the person who is undergoing the pain directly or indirectly, should have the right to choose euthanasia. In extreme cases, it serves the interests of everyone concerned. Seeing someone close suffering in pain can spell severe mental distress. It is a mercy to the patient and it also relieves the emotional strain on family and friends. It conserves medical resources and finances. Preservation of human life may come naturally to anyone. However, in cases of impending death where further medical intervention would merely end up draining more resources without really having an impact in terms of ameliorating the pain, new emotions pertaining to the futility of fighting a lost battle may begin to surface. It may, arguably, be judicious to direct the same resources to an area of greater urgency, for instance, education of children.

Euthanasia is a very *controversial*[10] as well as debatable issue and there is no consensus on it in sight. Euthanasia should be considered only in cases of severe mental and physical suffering with no hope of relief. But the decision ought to rest with the patient . If the patient is not in a condition to take a call whether to continue the treatment that merely prolongs a meaningless existence, the decision should be a collective one, based on the consent of doctors and the patient's closest relatives. After all, the right to live would not be complete if the right to die with full dignity is not available to an individual.

Aid to Vocabulary

1. *Irreversible* — that cannot be changed to original state
2. *Resumption* — the action of beginning something again after an interruption
3. *Abstention* — practice of not doing or having a particular thing
4. *Presumptuous* — too bold or confident
5. *Incapacitated* — weak, unable
6. *Unscrupulous* — lacking moral principles
7. *Proponents* — advocates, supporters
8. *Inevitable* — impossible to avoid
9. *Abyss* — void, bottomless pit
10. *Controversial* — causing or likely to cause controversy

Points to Remember

1. Euthanasia basically means 'a gentle and easy death' or 'mercy killing.'
2. The issue of euthanasia involves two aspects, passive and active.
3. Some believe that passive euthanasia is all right and quite acceptable while active euthanasia is immoral.
4. The Supreme Court of India on March 7, 2011 legalised passive euthanasia.
5. Life is the gift of God and it is deemed presumptuous on the part of humans to throw it away.
6. Euthanasia is inherently pitched against the basic principles of morality, legal traditions, religious belief and medical ethics.
7. At times when there is not a ray of hope of improvement, the choice of euthanasia should be made available.
8. The decision should be a collective one after having taken into account the consent of the patient, the doctor(s) and the patient's closest relatives.

Essay
126 FREEDOM OF SPEECH

SYNOPSIS

Freedom of speech is recognised as a Right to Freedom under the Fundamental Rights guaranteed in our Constitution. It is the most precious feature of democracy which emerged during the European Enlightenment. After Independence, the members of our Drafting Committee included this as a Fundamental Right in our Constitution. Freedom of speech is a powerful instrument for all civilised and democratic nations of the world. Today, we are living in a world dominated by the mass media. Sometimes, the media becomes partial and coloured. A free press can help to remove the evils of the society. The impact of electronic media on our society is immense. NGOs are also playing a crucial role in spreading awareness of democratic rights. But this freedom of speech is not absolute, it is limited by our social duties and obligations.

The Constitution of India grants six Fundamental Rights to Indian citizens. These amount to basic human freedom which every Indian citizen has the right to enjoy for the proper development of the self. The right to freedom of speech is recognised as a Right to Freedom under Articles 19-22 of our Constitution. Freedom of speech guarantees the freedom to speak without censorship or limitation. But in practice, the right to freedom of speech is not absolute it has some limitations also. It is recognised as a human right under Article 19 of the Universal Declaration of Human Rights. Actually, the Right to Freedom of Expression is synonymous with the Right to Freedom of Speech. Freedom of Expression is sometimes used to indicate not only freedom of verbal speech, but any act of seeking, receiving and imparting information relating to ideas, regardless of the medium used.

Freedom of speech is the most *precious*[1] feature of democracy. This concept had emerged gradually during the European Enlightenment. England's Bill of Rights (1689) granted 'Freedom of Speech in Parliament'. This concept is also inspired by the Declaration of the Rights of Man and of the Citizen adopted during the French Revolution in 1789. In India, the Rowlatt Act in 1919 gave extensive powers to the British government and the police to control individual rights and freedoms like restrictions on public gatherings, censorship of the media and publications, etc. Public opposition to this Act eventually led to the non-violent Civil Disobedience Movement throughout the country under the leadership of Mahatma Gandhi. The main demands of this movement were guaranteed civil freedoms, and limitations on the powers enjoyed by the British government.

After India got independence, the Fundamental Rights were included in the Constitution by the Drafting Committee. The framers of the Constitution regarded democracy of no *avail*[2] if civil liberties, like freedom of speech and religion were not recognised and protected by the State. According to them, democracy is, in essence, a government by opinion and therefore, the means of formulating public opinion should be secured to the people of a democratic nation. For this purpose, our Constitution guaranteed to all citizens of India the freedom of speech and expression in the form of a Fundamental Right.

In democracy, empowerment of the common citizens not only to develop their personality and means but also to raise their voice against injustice and oppression is necessary, and hence, the right to freedom of speech stands indispensable. Since democracy is a form of government 'of the people, for the people and by the people,' it is the people who check, guide and control the system. In the absence of freedom of speech, no measure taken to strengthen the common man would bear fruit. Since every right is associated with a duty, it should be exercised with some restraint. A speech that outrages the religious, political or social sentiments of the common man should not, at any cost, be delivered.

Freedom of speech is a powerful instrument for all civilised and democratic nations of the world. In democracy, freedom of speech mainly pertains to freedom of the press. The phrase 'freedom of the press' has not been used in Article 19 of our Constitution but freedom of expression includes freedom of the press. By the press we mean all the media of mass communication. Free press generally means the right to publish, the right to confidentiality of sources, and the right to access. Not only is the press an integral part of the freedom of speech, but it is a part of a system of social control whereby relationships between individuals and institutions are adjusted. The press has the power to monitor all the important social institutions of society like family, religion, polity, law, etc.

Today, we are living in a world dominated by the mass media, which has moved steadily to take centre stage in our lives. It acts as an effective *catalyst*[3] for change in our society. The newspaper is a mirror of the times and has become an integral part of our life. The press in India has a very high tradition. Many newspapers like Bal Gangadhar Tilak's *Kesari* and *Maratha*, Gandhiji's *Harijan*, etc., roused the wave of nationalism in the country. The Indian press played a very crucial role during the freedom struggle. Today also, the press plays a very important role in our society. It serves the society by highlighting crime, nepotism and corruption in our country. It serves as a link between the people and the Government. It is the duty of the press to highlight the *grievances*[4] of the people. With changing times, the media is increasingly adopting a proactive role in curbing the ills of the society.

People often complain that the press is partial and unpatriotic. The editorials of the newspapers and news coverages on the television channels are often not objective and impartial, but coloured and motivated. Actually, the media is controlled and owned by media *barons*[5], corporate giants, industrial houses, etc. Often, the media lords use the power of the media to promote their own interests. The media men try to please their patrons and thus their coverages become biased and motivated. Common people think that their grievances and interests are ignored.

The electronic media, namely the television, the Internet and, to some extent, the radio, also play an important role. The radio had lost its popularity for a while, but a revolutionary transformation of FM Radio has brought it back in the reckoning. The power of the visual media, i.e., the television, is immense. The television coverage of an incident can instantly mould public opinion. It can reach every *nook and cranny*[6] of the globe to cover the extraordinary events like scenes of war, terrorist attacks, violence, natural *calamities*[7], sporting events, etc. To cover all these, the journalists and the photographers sometimes put their lives at stake. A free press can help to remove the evils of the society, like social inequality, child marriage, child labour, dowry, insecurity of women, criminalisation of politics, etc.

A free press can help the society by exposing and criticising the corrupt politicians and government officials. Thus, the press can play the role of a watchdog of the society. However, the media often does much harm to society due to its biased coverage.

The free press has played a very significant role in our democracy. Several newspapers came up with blank editorial pages at the time of Emergency declared by the then Prime Minister, Indira Gandhi. It was an unfortunate time, when the fundamental freedom of the press was curtailed. All the political activities of non-congress political parties were banned and no newspaper was allowed to report the factual position.

Organisations for protection of human rights have been set up in many countries. In India, many Non-Governmental Organisations (NGOs) are engaged in spreading awareness about civil liberties, and empowerment of women and other weaker sections of the society.

Freedom of speech is essential for our society. Without it, our literature, science, art, and music cannot *flourish*[8]. If there is no Freedom of Speech to be enjoyed as a right, how can an epic be written or an invention be recognised? Freedom of speech is necessary for the development of our civilisation. It has great value for both the individual and the society. Here arises the question of social responsibility. The individual should realise that he cannot publish anything that he may desire. Freedom of speech must be exercised with caution, keeping in mind others' sensitivities, or else, the freedom may be lost through its misuse and abuse. The right to freedom of speech is not absolute. It is bound by our social duty and moral obligation.

Aid to Vocabulary

1. *Precious* — very valuable or important
2. *Avail* — use
3. *Catalyst* — a person or thing that causes a change
4. *Grievances* — a feeling of having been treated unfairly
5. *Barons* — persons who own or control a large part of an industry
6. *Nook and Cranny* — every part or place
7. *Calamities* — disasters
8. *Flourish* — to be very successful

Points to Remember

1. The Right to Freedom of Speech is recognised as a 'Right to Freedom' under Articles 19-22 of the Indian Constitution.
2. It is a powerful instrument for all civilised and democratic nations of the world.
3. Indian media acts as an effective catalyst to effect social change.
4. Sometimes, the media becomes coloured and motivated.
5. The power of the electronic media, like the radio and the television is immense.
6. The press has played a very significant role in our democracy.
7. Many NGOs are engaged in spreading awareness of one's democratic rights.
8. The Right to Freedom of Speech is not absolute, it is bound by our social duty and moral obligation.

FREEDOM OF SPEECH

Freedom of speech and expression has never been absolute — neither in India nor anywhere in the world. The Indian Constitution guarantees it as a fundamental right and the Supreme Court has taken pains to give it a liberal and expansive interpretation through the years. The Supreme Court has zealously protected the right to free speech and expression through many landmark judgements. The SC never diluted any of the eight restrictions on free speech provided under Article 19(2), inserted through the first constitutional amendment in 1951 by the Jawaharlal Nehru government. At the same time, it never foresaw free speech acting as a catalyst for a clash of ideas or ideologies. It had hoped that free flow of ideas through free speech would make democracy more vibrant.

"But the freedom has to be guarded against becoming a licence for vilification and condemnation of the government established by law. A citizen has a right to say or write whatever he likes about the government, or its measures, by way of criticism or comment, so long as he does not incite people to violence against the government established by law or with the intention of creating public disorder," held the SC.

The debate on free speech will take us nowhere if we do not abandon the line, "If you don't agree with me, then you are wrong."

FREEDOM OF EXPRESSION : DUBIOUS DISTINCTION

- India ranks 133 among 180 countries in the latest annual World Press Freedom Index (2016)
- The rankings are an indicator of the independence afforded to scribes in different countries
- The report shows that Europe has the freest media
- Among India's neighbours, Pakistan ranks 147, Sri Lanka 141, Afghanistan 120, Bangladesh 144, Nepal 105 and Bhutan 94; China is ranked at 176 one of the worst in the world

Top Three Countries With Press Freedom	**Bottom Three Countries With Press Freedom**
• Finland	• Yemen
• Netherlands	• Cuba
• Norway	• Djibouti

GUIDED COMPOSITION

Develop the following paragraph into a full-fledged essay in 800-1000 words. The gist of the topic is provided in approximately 145 words for your help:

THE ART OF CONVERSATION

The manner in which a man converses sets him apart from others. The art of conversation is one of the most distinctive features of human personality. It is aptly said that a man reveals himself through his conversation. A man who has mastered the art, can make a great impact on people with the strength of his skill at making conversation. He can enliven a social gathering with his wit and gain popularity among friends and colleagues. Most of us pay scant attention to this important aspect of our personality. We try to be very meticulous in our dress, but neglect developing the ability to converse well. A person who speaks well, stands out in a crowd. He makes his presence felt. He exudes an extra confidence and poise, which by itself compels others to pay attention to him. Good conversation is undoubtedly an art and like all arts can be acquired with practice.

(145 words)

Essay
127

FEMALE FOETICIDE

SYNOPSIS

Female foeticide is common in many places in India. The socio-economic conditions, constant pressure on Indian women to bear a male child and the loopholes in the laws are factors that are responsible for this situation. The status of women in our society continues to be secondary and hence everybody prefers a son. The practice of prenatal sex determination has become popular. If the foetus is found to be female, the woman carrying it is forced to abort it. To stop this evil practice, the Government has introduced two laws: the Prenatal Diagnostic Techniques (PNDT) Act and the Medical Termination of Pregnancy Act. People are aware about female foeticide being an illegal activity, but are unaware of the PNDT Act. Many state governments have taken some important measures to curb this evil. Decrease in sex ratio is attributed to over the counter sale of MTP pills and unauthorised practice by midwives and quacks. Due to the skewed sex ratio, sometimes barter system takes place in marriages. The mindset of men needs to change and women should be empowered.

Female *foeticide*[1] is common in many places in India. The parents-to-be get the sex of their unborn child determined by ultrasonography, and if it is a girl, they go in for abortion. As a result, the decline in female child population has taken a turn for the worse. In India, the ratio of 0-6 years old female to male child declined from 976 : 1000 in 1991 to 927: 1000 in 2001. Ever since then, India has been losing about 9 lakh girls a year. According to the 2011 census, child sex ratio has worsened having declined from 927 in 2001 to 914 in 2011. An increasing trend in the child sex ratio (0-6) has been noted in Punjab, Haryana, Himachal Pradesh, Gujarat, Tamil Nadu, Mizoram and Andaman & Nicobar Islands. In the remainder 27 states/UTs, the child sex ratio shows a decline over Census 2001. Among the big states, Chhattisgarh has the highest ratio of 964 followed by Kerala with 959. Haryana is at the bottom (830) followed by Punjab (846).

The socio-economic conditions, constant pressure on Indian women to bear a male child and the *loopholes*[2] in the laws are the factors that have contributed towards making the situation alarming. Indian society is a patriarchal society; women's status continues to be secondary. Manu visualised a woman in various roles—as that of a daughter, a wife, a mother and a widow—but her true identity has always been dependent on a male member of her family. The scenario has not altogether changed in the 21st century.

The custom of organising lavish ceremonies at the time of marriage and of paying dowry to the groom's family is widely *prevalent*[3] in India. The daughter becomes a liability for her parents on account of this economic burden. Often, it is not possible for the bride's parents to meet the demands of the groom's family. In the event that the bride is thrown out of her husband's home, her parents have to take her back and also face the ire of the society; besides, the whole episode usually gives their daughter a bad name. Hence, the parents choose to fulfil all the unnecessary and unreasonable demands of the groom's family.

In India, socially, divorce is not really acceptable as a practice. It is not easy for a divorced woman to get remarried, to earn social respect, or to fend for her children herself and with dignity.

In India, very few women get vocational training. Most of them settle for low-skill and low-paying jobs. They are groomed, primarily, for the role of a mother and wife, and not for the role of an earning member of the family. Earning *potential*[4] of women is, therefore, low.

Women's status in the society is generally secondary to that of men's. In our traditional society, they are not allowed to take decisions or sometimes even to have a say in decisions concerning their own life. The treatment meted out to the male child is visibly different from how the female child is treated. While the boy is prized since he is viewed as an investment which will eventually pay off in the form of service and support to his old parents, the attitude towards the girl is biased right from her childhood. The perception that girls will go away to another family one day, and that they therefore do not form part of the lineage, seriously undermines their status. They face discrimination in every respect, be it food, clothing, education or medical attention.

Hence, to have a daughter or to be one is widely considered a curse in India. It is, therefore, not surprising that parents prefer to have a son.

It is regrettable that due to female infanticide as well as female foeticide, the female population is rapidly declining in the our country. Under an evil practice prevalent in some parts of ancient India, the unwanted girl child was put to death right after birth. She was either *strangulated*[5] or poisoned. Though the practice was not widespread then, female foeticide is being practised by the Indian masses today to avoid the burden of having a daughter. The technique of pre-natal test was brought to India in 1975 to investigate genetic abnormalities in the foetus. But this technique was reinvented as a popular means to identify the sex of the foetus. The wide availability of this technique and the fact that it came cheap helped in making it popular. After the test, if the foetus was found to be female then the woman carrying it was forced to abort it. Across the rich-poor and other social divides, an Indian seldom prefers a girl child.

Not surprisingly, female foeticide leads to an artificially *skewed*[6] sex ratio. In most regions of North India, the ratio of females to males has fallen below 900. In some towns, it is as low as 750. The 2001 and 2011 census figures for Delhi are 886 and 866 girls per 1000 boys respectively. In this context, the Government decided to implement two laws viz., the Prenatal Diagnostic Techniques Act, 1994 and the Medical Termination of Pregnancy Act. Due to the loopholes in the law, unfortunately, very few people have been convicted since the implementation of the PNDT Act in 1994. By section 3 of the Pre-natal Diagnostic Techniques Act 2002, the nomenclature stands revised to Pre-conception and Pre-natal Diagnostic Techniques Act.

The Centre has now decided to make the Pre-natal Diagnostic Techniques (PNDT) Act more stringent. Under the proposed amendments to the Act, clinics and doctors conducting sex determination tests would be *stripped*[7] of their licences, fined up to ₹ 7 lakh and be imprisoned up to three years.

Perturbed by the sharp fall in the boy-girl ratio, the government has launched the 'Save Girl Child Campaign'. In economically advanced states, such as Maharashtra, Delhi, Haryana, Punjab and Gujarat where access to ultrasound clinics is easily obtainable, the ratio has dropped to less than 900 girls per 1000 boys. Although doctors are aware of female foeticide taking place under their nose, no one is willing to go on record against this malpractice. Many pathology laboratories do not have consulting gynaecologists, though ultrasound facility is easily available there. The majority of sex-selective abortions are performed by doctors or nurses of private clinics or even by quacks.

Factors responsible for decrease in sex ratio, according to Dr. Amandeep Aggarwal, Human Rights cell, Punjab are over the counter sale of MTP pills and unauthorized practice by quacks and midwives. Since the mindset of the society towards a girl child is adverse, he further suggests, it should be made compulsory for all pregnant women to get a scan at the Government Hospital for sex determination of the foetus, and every female foetus thus detected must be followed up till delivery and one year thereafter to rule out both foeticide and infanticide. Smt. Maneka Gandhi, Union minister of women and child development stated that under the scheme,'Beti bachao, beti padhao' (BBBP), a media based campaign will be started to change the attitude of society. Along with this, some incentives will be granted to couples having daughters.

For no fault of hers, a girl child is killed in the womb prior to her birth. This malpractice is rooted in the social pattern and traditional beliefs which have made sons a preferred commodity and daughters a liability. In order to curb this social evil, the Government has to take strong measures. Dowry has already been made illegal but the law must be effectively enforced. Women must be empowered and free legal counsel must be made available to all citizens. Abortion should be allowed only in cases of medical emergency. Some state governments, including Himachal Pradesh, have taken important measures to popularise schemes that intend to spread awareness with regard to this.

Research conducted in connection with female foeticide reveals that criminalisation of sex selection has not reduced its incidence. Rather, this practice has turned covert. According to a survey, there have been many instances wherein young women were sent to their parents' home to get the sex determination test done and abort the foetus if it turned out to be female. Thus, the *onus*[8] is forced upon the girl's parents to commit the sin of female foeticide. Sometimes, it is the girls themselves who opt for it for they do not want their unborn babies to suffer all that they underwent as daughters.

Studies show that sex selection is done even for the first child in Punjab, Himachal Pradesh and Haryana. Driven by economic compulsions, many families are increasingly adopting the one-child norm; however, that one child must be a son.

In some regions, the sex ratio is so low that an exchange system or mutual marriage has come to gain popularity. Here the sole condition is: if there is a girl in the groom's family, she, irrespective of her age, is to be married off to the bride's brother. As a result, sometimes, child marriage takes place and consequently all the related social problems follow.

Girls need and expect equal access to education, nutrition, health, employment as well as productive resources. Boys as well as men should perceive girls not as *subservient*[9] beings but as empowered individuals who are equal partners in the course of life.

Female foeticide is a major social evil which must be fought with a firm resolve and must be eliminated. The mindset of the people needs to change, and women need to be empowered. Besides this, the unethical behaviour of doctors also needs to be exposed and checked. In this respect, the media can play a crucial role in sensitising the society with regard to the immorality of this evil practice. We all have some responsibilities towards eradicating this social evil.

The situation is changing for the better. Educated classes today bestow the same love and affection on their daughters, as on their sons. However, things are moving at a slow pace and this encouraging shift is limited to certain segments of the society only.

In this changed scenario, women constitute a larger proportion of the population of Indian towns and cities today than ever recorded in Indian history. This startling fact comes to light despite the child sex ratio having fallen alarmingly in recent decades; data from Census 2011 reveals that the population of urban women grew at a brisk 34% in the decade spanning 2001 to 2011. In the same period, their rural population grew by just over 12%. As a result, the sex ratio for urban areas jumped from 900 women per 1000 men in 2001 to 926 in 2011, the highest decadal increase since Independence. In rural areas, the sex ratio increased nominally from 946 to 947. Between 1981 and 2011, the child sex ratio fell from 959 to 902 in urban areas and from 963 to 919 in rural areas. Yet the female population is rising in urban areas. Had female foeticide not been so widespread, the female population would have been even higher. According to a research conducted by the Centre for Women's Development Studies, a Delhi-based research institution, the answer to the mystery may lie in the increased migration of women from rural to urban areas. Migration rates are higher among women belonging to highly educated as well as higher income group as compared to their less privileged counterparts, according to the same report.

In our society, a handful of successful women enjoy freedom on par with men. There is a huge majority of women who have not even dreamt of enjoying such freedom either at home or outside. The mindset of men needs to change to be able to acknowledge women as their equals and at the same time, women need to be empowered to take informed decisions. Only then can a social evil like female foeticide be curbed.

AID TO VOCABULARY

1. *Foeticide* — killing of a foetus (a child in the womb)
2. *Loopholes* — errors that enable legal evasion

3. *Prevalent* — generally existing or occurring
4. *Potential* — capable of coming into being or action, latent
5. *Strangulated* — killed by pressing at the throat
6. *Skewed* — slanted, unequal
7. *Stripped* — deprived.
8. *Onus* — responsibility, duty
9. *Subservient* — servile, subordinate

Points to Remember

1. In our country due to rampant female foeticide, the decline in female child population has worsened.
2. Indian society is a male-dominated society, wherein the status of women is secondary.
3. A daughter becomes an economic burden for her parents owing to the dowry system.
4. In most of the families, the respective treatments meted out to the male child and the female child, are visibly different.
5. Prenatal test has become popular as it serves the purpose of identifying the sex of the foetus. If it is a female foetus, the woman carrying it is forced to abort it.
6. To curb this social evil, the Government has introduced two Acts of laws—PNDT Act and MTP Act.
7. The Government has launched the 'Save Girl Child Campaign'.
8. Many state governments have taken some important measures to curb this social evil.
9. The mindset of men needs to change and women need to be empowered.
10. Data from Census 2011 reveals that the population of urban women grew despite the child sex ratio having fallen alarmingly.

Essay
128

INDIA TODAY: ITS DIFFERENT FACETS

SYNOPSIS

India has undergone many phases of development and growth. India has faced continual political degradation. India's relations with other countries have strengthened. Political instability, corruption and red tapism have affected the otherwise good performance of the Indian economy. The society is plagued by poverty, unemployment, illiteracy, population explosion, communalism, insensitiveness, crime and violence. Achievements in the fields of science and technology and space science have been commendable. However, India still has a long way to go before it can be called a truly developed nation.

During the period spanning more than six decades of Independence, India has undergone many phases of development and growth, transforming itself from being a state of deprivation and scarcity into one brimming with economic empowerment and abundance. After Independence, India had to struggle in every field be it economics, politics, social field, education, or any other. But with the concerted efforts of the devoted leaders coupled with the prudent planning of the policy-makers, India gained self-sufficiency in major areas in a relatively short span of time.

On its way to rapid development, however, India has faced continual political degradation. Frequent elections have brought forth the *rot*[1] in Indian politics under the garb of democratic principles. The politicians reveal their shameless selves when they engage in *mudslinging*[2], slandering, opponent-bashing and what not—all in the name of democracy! The imposition of mid-term elections with *unwavering*[3] regularity tries the patience of the voter. What has *conspicuously*[4] come to the fore is that every political party has to offer the same *agenda*[5] and all the political parties are founded on more or less identical ideologies, although their *manifestos*[6] are refashioned every time to suit the burning issues.

In the thirteenth Lok Sabha elections, a 24 party BJP-led alliance came to power. It was for the first time in the history of India that a multi-party alliance, contesting under different election symbols and in different constituencies, had managed to cobble together a simple majority in the Lok Sabha.

Thereafter, a multi-party alliance, the UPA, ran the Government for two Lok Sabha terms—the fourteenth and the fifteenth. Though the sixteenth Lok Sabha elections (2014) mandated a clear majority to the BJP, a national party, the party chose to retain its alliance (the NDA) with regional parties for all practical purposes. All this bears testimony to the fact that regional parties have come of age and have carved their *niche*[7] in Indian politics. The national parties can no longer ignore them. They forge alliances with regional parties to win Vidhan Sabha (state assembly) elections also.

India has always tried to maintain good relations with the other nations of the world including her neighbouring countries. India's foreign policy has been formulated with a view to promote co-operation and international peace, and to extend support to nations seeking freedom from foreign occupation. It is also true, however, that relations with some of the neighbouring countries were *strained*[8] owing to border conflicts, etc., but India has been trying her best to patch things up and she has, thus far, been partially successful too. Relations with Sri Lanka had got *embittered*[9] because of ethnic clashes between the Tamilians and the Sinhalese; assassination of former Prime Minister Rajiv Gandhi by an Liberation Tigers of Tamil Eelam (LTTE) suicide bomber also added to the tensions; fortunately things have improved gradually. In spite of having major problems with Pakistan, India has always tried to nurture peaceful relations with this volatile neighbour and is zealously pursuing its Aman ki Asha programme with respect to the same. Earlier, relations with China had also turned sour but things are now taking a turn for the better. Eventually, China has come to foster robust trade relations with India. Bangladesh, Nepal and Bhutan are also strengthening economic and cultural ties with India.

After liberalisation and initiation of economic reforms, the rate of growth of the Indian economy has been quite satisfactory, considering the fact that during the first three decades of economic development, the growth rate was *abysmally*[10] low. Owing mainly to the inflow of foreign capital in the form of Foreign Direct Investment, the Indian economy achieved reasonably good results and showed tremendous *resilience*[11] even as the fast track economies of South Korea, Malaysia and Indonesia experienced low growth rates due to economic slowdown in the world economy.

On the flip side, the World Economic Forum in a study found India to be among the most corrupt nations in Asia. The report stated with evidential backing that Foreign Direct Investment (FDI) was greatly hampered owing to *rampant*[12] corruption. Yet, according to the World Investment Report, UN Conference on trade and development (UNCTAD) released by India is the second largest recipient of FDI, China being at the top.

India's achievements in the fields of science and technology and space science have indeed been commendable. India is already a nuclear power. The country has demonstrated its capability after having entered the global satellite launch market with the successful launch of PSLV-C2 that placed three satellites into orbit—IRS-P4 (Oceansat) and two micro satellites belonging to Korea and Germany (Kitsat-3 and DLR-Tubsat). The images/data received from these satellites are used in various fields covering agriculture, water resources, mineral prospecting, environment, forestry, drought and flood forecasting, ocean resource management, etc. India's communication satellite GSAT-12 augments the availability of transponders for various communication services, including tele-medicine and tele-education. India has achieved major feats in missile capabilities after having successfully test fired the *Prithvi* and *Agni* surface missiles, the anti-tank guided missile *Nag* and the surface-to-air missile *Akash*.

In the field of medical science, India's progress has been remarkable. Doctors can now cure leprosy and several other dreadful diseases. India's biotechnological advancements have led to the creation of cloned buffaloes. In a major medical breakthrough in 2007, doctors of the All India Institute of Medical Sciences (AIIMS), New Delhi, used one cornea to provide sight to three patients. India's first geoscientific data centre has been set up at the Geological Survey of India, Kolkata. The hi-tech data centre significantly contributes to making the Indian mining policy more effective apart from helping to evolve national mineral exploration strategies.

In 1951, four years after Independence, the total literacy rate in India was only 18.33 per cent. But over the decades, literacy rates have shown considerable improvement. From 64.84 per cent recorded in Census 2001, it rose to 74.04 per cent as per Census 2011. While Kerala, as it held on to the top spot, improved from 90.92 per cent to 93.91 per cent, Bihar, that had the lowest literacy rate, also recorded an increase from 47.53 per cent to 63.82 per cent in this decade. Literacy rate for females showed a greater increase (65.46 per cent from 54 per cent) than that for males (82.14 per cent from 75 per cent).

Many government schemes aimed at removing illiteracy have been implemented successfully. Sarva Siksha Abhiyan (SSA), launched in

2001, aims to impart quality education to all children in the age group of 6-14 years. It also aims to provide computer education in rural areas so as to bridge the digital divide. Adult literacy programmes are also being run to provide basic education to illiterate adults. As female literacy still lags behind, many programmes have been implemented with a view to improve the education of girls.

Despite several developments, there are still certain areas wherein India needs improvement. India's burgeoning population is its biggest worry. According to Census 2011, the population of India is 1.21 billion, having added about 16 million people every year. The country accounts for 17% of the world population and to feed this population, it has only 2% of the world's arable land. Grain output has been stagnating for over a decade and as a result, there is now a growing gap between demand and supply. Some serious effort will have to be made to solve this problem. Besides this, India has to fight off many other problems like poverty, unemployment and gender inequality.

India still has a long way to go before it can be called a developed nation from all perspectives—political, economic, social and scientific. Efforts must be put in to regain the *regal*[13] status of the past—the 'Golden Period'. India has the youngest workforce in the world today. If this pool of talent is driven with honesty, sincerity, commitment, motivation and firmness, India can indeed aspire to become the next superpower of the world.

Aid to Vocabulary

1. *Rot* — decay
2. *Mudslinging* — saying disparaging or abusive things about others
3. *Unwavering* — steady
4. *Conspicuously* — very noticeably, glaringly
5. *Agenda* — things to be done
6. *Manifestos* — declaration of policies
7. *Niche* — a suitable place, position, etc.
8. *Strained* — mutually distrustful, tensed
9. *Embittered* — aroused bitter feelings
10. *Abysmally* — profoundly, infinitely
11. *Resilience* — ability to recover from difficulty, etc.
12. *Rampant* — widespread and difficult to control
13. *Regal* — very impressive, royal

Points to Remember

1. India has undergone many phases of development and growth.
2. Frequent elections have brought forth the rot in Indian politics.

3. The foreign policy of India aims to promote co-operation and international peace.
4. According to UNCTAD's World Investment Report, India is the second largest recipient of FDI.
5. Achievements of the country in the field of science and technology and space science have been commendable.
6. In 1951, Indian literacy rate was 18.33 per cent which rose to 64.84 per cent in 2001 and to 740.4 per cent in 2011.
7. India is adding about 16 million people to the world population every year.
8. India still has a long way to go before it can be called a developed nation.

Essay
129 THE CHANGING FACE OF INDIAN SOCIETY

SYNOPSIS

Indian society has had a glorious era in the past. Now the scenario has totally changed. Social change is a gradual process which is effected by demographic, technological, political, economic, cultural and legal factors. Family is the basic unit of the social structure. Today, nuclear family is replacing the traditional joint family system. Economic development gives rise to individualism. Woman's position as well as status is undergoing change. In the present day society, age-old values of tolerance, hospitality, warmth, attachment, politeness and patience are fast fading out. Technological innovations have changed even the common man's way of life. A great change has occured in the field of education too. In a dynamic society, change is inevitable, but it must be for the betterment of the society.

Indian society has had a glorious era in the past. We were one of the most advanced civilisations of the world. The Aryans, the West Asians and the Dravidians made economic and social progress. No other nation had as rich a cultural heritage as India had. We were highly respected for the richness of our culture and societal wisdom. But the past is gone and the future of Indian society beckons even as it paints a very complex picture. While being deeply rooted in spirituality, our society is equally inclined towards materialism. Untouchability has been constitutionally abolished as well as banned, yet casteism is the most common tool with respect to vote-bank politics in our country.

Social change is a broad term which implies change in infrastructural facilities, culture, traditions, behavioural attitude, norms of living, etc., in a society. Change is a natural as well as an inevitable process which takes place in every age and will continue to do so in the future. Social change is a gradual process which is effected by *demographic*[1], technological, political, economic, cultural, legal and other factors. Social change is basically a transformation that takes place in terms of behaviour, thought and action, and may lead the society towards progress or, *regression*[2].

Social conflict coupled with growth of knowledge gives rise to social change. Research leading to advancement in the field of science and technology brings about changes in the outlook of the society. Besides, the demographic factors also contribute to social change. For example, high population growth leads to poverty, illiteracy, housing and health problems—all of these affect our social climate. Economic development and urbanisation are usual outcomes of rapid industrialisation which also causes the growth of slums in urban areas.

Abolition of landlordism in India, brought in economic *upliftment*[3]. It reduced exploitation of the landless labourers. Cultural factors like *sanskritisation*—the process of upward mobility of a subcaste group in a caste system—brought about changes in the caste system, traditional attitudes and customs of the people. After Independence, introduction of new laws has played a prominent role with regard to social change. Numerous laws have been enacted so far that have changed the face of society after having removed the social ills, injustices, inequalities, discrimination, etc.

Family is the basic unit of the social structure and is universally regarded as the ideal and perfect living arrangement. In India, the joint family system has been in existence since ancient times. Today, for a number of reasons, the joint family system is not preferred in the cities. In search of jobs and better opportunities, people migrate to towns and cities. The overcrowded and congested living conditions, lack of space and high cost of living in the cities have given birth to the nuclear family system. The nuclear family comprises of a couple and their children. A nuclear family has advantages as well as disadvantages. However, it is the reality of the modern age. Very often, old parents and grandparents end up being deprived of the love and care of their near and dear ones. In the light of these changes, it can be said that the situation has become very complex, indeed.

As of today, economic and technological advancements have been taking place at a rapid pace. Economic independence has given rise to *individualism*[4]. It has affected both men and women, especially the latter. Modern Indian women have felt the need to assert themselves. Now they have two priorities: home and workplace. As both fronts are equally demanding, the modern husband helps his wife in the realignment of the traditional Indian structure of division of labour. He feels that it is imperative to share responsibilities whether at the homefront or at the work place. Social attitude towards women is changing, though the process has been slow.

Today, society is more liberal than before. In this age of individualism, authority is no longer unquestionably accepted even by children. In this age of information technology, children, in most cases, have greater awareness than their parents. Often, both the parents are professionals, and children are provided with material comforts in lieu of parental love and affection. Parents tend to become overly *indulgent*[5] under the misconception that providing the child with all the luxuries of life would help them earn, in return, the latter's respect and affection.

Parents, also become *meddlesome*[6] as they feel that in this fast-changing, self-centred and *hypocritical*[7] world, it is their duty to safeguard their children from going astray. Sometimes, it creates a rift in the family as the youngsters resent being treated as young and immature children, instead of being considered as grown ups who can take care of themselves. In today's society, age-old values of tolerance, hospitality, attachment, politeness and patience are fast fading out.

At the same time, some pleasant changes have also occurred in our society. Today, technological innovations have changed even the common man's way of life. Cable TV, mobile phones and other electronic gadgets, apart from the Internet, have effected a great change in the lifestyle of the people. Gas stove and biogas lighting have transformed village life. With the use of machines and *hybrid*[8] seeds, the *viability*[9] of the agriculture sector has been enhanced. With the development of roads and railway network, distances have been reduced. At the same time, the communication system has been revolutionised with satellites and consequently the general awareness of Indians has increased. Exposure to international culture has deeply influenced our minds. It has changed our dress code, food habits and outlook but the change has not always been beneficial.

In the field of education, drastic changes have occurred. Many important steps have been taken by the Government under the Five-Year Plans which have, consequently, improved the rate of literacy in the country. It has gone up from 65% (Census 2001) to 74% (Census 2011). A large number of central universities as well as private universities have come up and they offer many academic as well as professional courses. They render great service by way of augmenting the employability of the youth in the modern competitive world. In a dynamic society, change is inevitable. But it must be guided by principles which ensure a better future and help in building a progressive society—a society wherein people can enjoy their share in peace and prosperity. Thus, change can be the agent which would *herald*[10] a better life.

Aid to Vocabulary

1. *Demographic* — of the scientific study of the changing number of births, deaths, diseases, etc., in a community over a period of time
2. *Regression* — the process of going back to an earlier or less advanced form or state
3. *Upliftment* — raising or elevating of social condition, etc.
4. *Individualism* — the belief that every individual in the society should have the right to make their own decisions
5. *Indulgent* — willing to allow everything
6. *Meddlesome* — interfering, prying
7. *Hypocritical* — insincere, deceitful
8. *Hybrid* — an animal or plant that has parents of different species or varieties
9. *Viability* — workability, potential to succeed
10. *Herald* — be a sign of something to happen

Points to Remember

1. Indian society has had a glorious past but now it has become very complex.
2. Social change is a gradual process which is effected by demographic, technological, political, economic, cultural and legal factors.
3. It being the basic unit of the social structure, the concept of family has now changed. The age-old joint family has now been replaced by the nuclear family.
4. Economic development gives rise to individualism.
5. In this age of individualism, authority is no longer unquestionably accepted even by children.
6. Cable TV, mobile phones and the Internet have brought about a great change in the lifestyle of the people.
7. Massive changes have occurred in the field of education.
8. In a dynamic society, change is inevitable, but it should be for the betterment of society.

INDIAN DEMOCRACY HAS EMPOWERED BACKWARD CLASSES: VP ANSARI

The democratic process in India has brought about a shift in political power from the middle and higher castes and classes of urban society to the backward classes who are now politically the most influential ones in the country, Vice President Hamid Ansari said on October 17, 2016. "They (backward castes) have won reservations for themselves in legislatures and government services as were accorded to the Scheduled Castes and Scheduled Tribes after independence through Constitutional provisions," said Ansari. There are few examples in recent history of such a conspicuous shift of political power, involving such a huge mass of population, taking place in such a short period of time almost without any violence and in a democratic way. This is one more example of the miracles that democracy can create. "So there is much to celebrate, much to be proud of. At the same time, living societies also introspect from time to time, recall their foundational principles and assess the work still to be done," he said while addressing a seminar on 'Indian Democracy: Achievements and Challenges' at the Corvinus University in Budapest (Hungary).

He said, these, in India's case, are inscribed in the Preamble and the text of the Constitution. They were amplified in the concluding statement of Bhimrao Ambedkar, the man who chaired the drafting committee.

Ansari said the Indian Constitution stipulated Universal Adult Franchise and its basic principles were summed up in a brief and pithy form in the Preamble; its sections on Fundamental Rights and Directive Principles of State Policy made it a socio-economic manifesto.

Indian culture is syncretic in character and, as a historian puts it 'embraces in its orbit beliefs, customs, rites, institutions, arts, religions and philosophies belonging to different strata of societies in varying stages of development'. "It eternally seeks to find a unity for the heterogeneous elements which make up its totality. It is a veritable human laboratory where the cross breeding of ideas, beliefs and cultural traditions has been in progress for a few thousand years. The national movement recognised this cultural plurality and sought to base a national identity on it."

Source: Press Trust of India, Achinta Borah

Essay
130

HINDI AS THE LINGUA FRANCA OF INDIA

SYNOPSIS

The Indian languages have evolved through the ages and have produced a number of linguistic divisions within the country. Though the Constitution declares Hindi as the official language of the Union, it has not received its due status owing to lack of political will, prevalence of regional languages, especially in the southern states, and the apathy of the citizens towards the language itself. Not to have a language of one's own is tantamount to negating one's own existence. Hindi has a rich literary heritage. In spite of all odds, Hindi continues to thrive in India and other parts of the world.

Dr. Samuel Johnson, British *lexicographer*[1] and prominent literary figure of the 18th century, felt that "language is the dress of thought." According to British poet critic Samuel Taylor Coleridge, "Language is the *armoury*[2] of the human mind and it contains the trophies of its past and the weapons of its future conquest."

The same holds true for the language of a nation which embodies the nation's cultural ethos and depicts the evolution of its society in terms of its collective thought and aspirations. Pt. Jawaharlal Nehru said that a nation which has no language of its own is dumb and cannot make real progress.

By means of a random process through history, the Indian society has evolved into a *mosaic*[3] of diverse races, cultures and languages. Yet, it has been able to sustain unity in this diversity, thereby lending this very mosaic a unique character.

As of today, there are hundreds of languages and dialects that are spoken in India while many others have become *defunct*[4]. In the modern democratic context, a common communicative medium or *'lingua franca'*[5] is a necessity with regard to preserving the unity and integrity of the nation.

The Constitution of India recognises 22 official languages of the country. Article 343(1) of the Constitution recognises Hindi, in the Devanagari script, as the official language of the Union. The second clause of the Article provides for the simultaneous use of English, initially, for a period of 15 years from the day the Constitution came into force.

Accordingly, English was the principal official language till 1965.

Subsequent to 1965, Hindi was made the principal official language, but English continued to be the subsidiary official language. English has been the preferred language for the purpose of communication between the Union and those states which have not adopted Hindi as their official language.

Almost seven decades after Independence, Hindi is yet to acquire the status of the official language of India. There are many factors which have contributed to the decline of Hindi in India. Chief among them are—lack of political will, prevalence of regional languages, especially in the southern states, and people's apathy towards the language in the wake of the Westernisation of the society. Our policy makers have failed to promote Hindi effectively. Many people think that English and modernisation are synonymous. This perception is *corroborated*[6] by the media, since even the Hindi dailies and channels have adopted Hinglish—the combination of English and Hindi — to cater to a larger *clientele*[7]. The status of Hindi, even in the Hindi-speaking states, has deteriorated. Since Hindi does not get due recognition even in those states, it has been unable to attain the true status of an official language.

Most of the states in South India are unwilling to accept Hindi as the official language. These states use regional languages for official communication and English as the link language. When the use of Hindi was made compulsory, the southern states rejected it *outright*[8].

Multiple factors seem to act as impediments to the emergence of Hindi as the national language. Vote bank politics is a major impediment in this regard. In the modern political scenario, regionalism is a major factor at play in terms of deciding the polls. There are numerous regional parties that wield power at the Central as well as state levels. These parties strive to establish their regional identities partly through regional linguistic *chauvinism*[9]. In consequence, the growth of Hindi as a national language gets stunted.

Another hindrance to the growth of Hindi in the southern states is the practical preference of the people. As Hindi is not their mother tongue, most of the people have to learn it as a second language. In the wake of globalisation, English Language competence has become mandatory while knowledge of Hindi is not essential to carve a niche in the corporate world, whether in the Indian metros or overseas. So, if a student wants to be proficient in Hindi as well as in English, he/she is likely to find it too exacting to gain competence in both languages, being already over-burdened with the vast syllabus. Worried about his/her overall grade in the main subjects, he/she may naturally shun the less rewarding Hindi.

As their *colonial hangover*[10], the people of the country still have a tilt towards English. This is evident from the increasing number of English medium public schools coming up in India. Most parents want to send their children to convent schools or public schools. There has also been an increase in the number of institutes which promise to groom students in English conversation or communication skills. A convent or public school background is demanded by most of the employers not only abroad but also within the country.

Thus, we can say, that deterioration with regard to the use of Hindi has been brought about by the people themselves, who have failed to give the language its *entitlement*[11]. English, on the other hand, has been flourishing with every passing day. English is the preferred language of the elite, as well as those who can only manage Hinglish; and fluency in the language has become a status symbol.

Although, apart from Hindi, there is no other language which is spoken and understood all across the country, the diversity of India stands in the way of popularising Hindi as the national language. Since, not to have a language of one's own is tantamount to negating one's own existence, India, at the time of Independence, adopted Hindi as the official language and hoped to grant it the status of the national language within a span of 15 years thereafter. Unfortunately, despite several attempts, the dream has not been realised as yet. Reasons attributed to the failure of the mission are (a) it is not a powerful means of communication; (b) to a learner, it is difficult to read, understand or write; (c) it does not cater to all needs owing to a poor *lexicon*[12]; (d) since its grammar is complex, managing accurate and correct expression according to one's need is an uphill task (e) it is the informal language of a layman; and most importantly (f); it fails to get one a jab in today's global market.

Meanwhile, Hindi, as well as Hindi literature, continued to evolve at its own pace; its *Khariboli* dialect had become the chief literary medium by the 19th century. Kabir, Tulsidas and later, Munshi Premchand, Bhartendu Harishchandra, Maithili Sharan Gupt, Jayashankar Prasad, Suryakant Tripathi 'Nirala', Mahavir Prasad Dwivedi, and Agyeya enriched Hindi literature with their immortal contributions. It is rather unfortunate that despite this rich heritage, Hindi could never really take off.

Before colonial rule, the medium of instruction in India was the *vernacular*[13] language. During the colonial rule, people were so influenced by western education and its liberal views that they perceived English language as a sign of progress. English became the medium of instruction and soon, Trade and Administration also adopted English as a means of communication. Incidentally, it was for the first time in the history of India that the whole country had used a single language as the medium of instruction. After Independence, though it was believed that use of the foreign language would gradually be stopped in India, it continued to receive country-wide acceptance.

English, being an international language, is recognised as well as understood by majority of the people across the globe. After liberalisation, a number of multinational companies have set up their bases in India, and the knowledge of English alone has helped Indians to work with them. In the wake of scientific as well as technological progress, the world has shrunk. India being a developing country, endeavouring towards self-reliance, needs to endorse a language with international applicability. Were we to show apathy towards English, we would be hindering our own progress.

Some people believe, that however rich or useful, a foreign language can never be the official language of our country. However, for the sake national unity as well as cultural development, we do need a national language. We should respect all the languages spoken in India, but there must be one link language for the whole country. Since Hindi is spoken by majority of the Indian population, one would naturally expect it to be adopted as the national language.

Gradually, Hindi is beginning to find acceptance all over India. Hindi cinema has played a vital role in this regard. People in South India now enjoy watching Hindi serials and movies. Though English press in India boasts of its national presence, Hindi press, too, thrives and has made its presence felt in many parts of India. The Hindi literary scene is no less vibrant. In spite of all odds, Hindi continues to be alive and *resilient*[14]. Though the importance of English in India cannot be denied, Hindi will continue to hold its own in Hindustan. Both the languages, Hindi and English, therefore, should be allowed to flourish side by side.

Aid to Vocabulary

1. *Lexicographer* — a person who compiles a dictionary
2. *Armoury* — a place where arms are kept
3. *Mosaic* — diversified thing, a pattern made of various coloured pieces of glass, stone, etc.
4. *Defunct* — dead, no longer in existence
5. *Lingua Franca* — a language adopted as a common language between speakers whose native languages are different
6. *Corroborated* — supported with evidence

7. *Clientele* — regular customers at a particular business
8. *Outright* — altogether, entirely
9. *Chauvinism* — excessive or prejudiced support, or loyalty for something
10. *Colonial hangover* — after-effects of British colonial rule in India
11. *Entitlement* — due, what is rightfully deserved
12. *Lexicon* — dictionary, words in a language
13. *Vernacular* — native language
14. *Resilient* — ability to recover strength

Points to Remember

1. Indian languages have evolved through the ages.
2. But they have produced a number of linguistic divisions within the country.
3. The reasons for the slow acceptance of Hindi in India are:
   (a) Lack of political will.
   (b) North-South divide.
   (c) People's apathy towards the language.
4. Most of the South Indian states are not ready to accept Hindi as our national language.
5. Hindi literature was the chief literary medium in the 19th century.
6. English has been flourishing in India mainly because it happens to be the preferred medium of instruction.
7. English is recognised as well as understood by majority of the people across the globe.
8. Both English and Hindi should be allowed to flourish side by side.

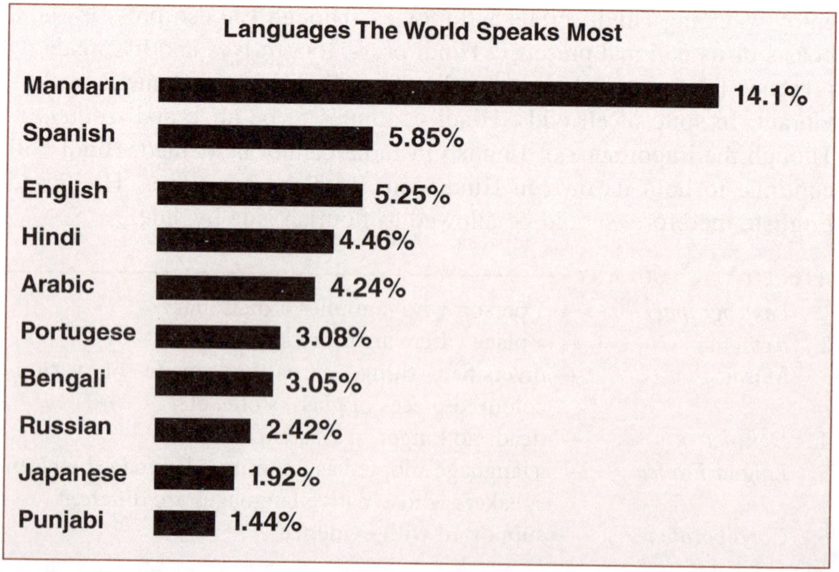

GUIDED COMPOSITION

Develop the following paragraph into a full-fledged essay in 800-1000 words. The gist of the topic is provided in approximately 155 words for your help:

THE BEST WAY TO LEARN A LANGUAGE IS TO SPEAK IT

Language is completely expressed in speech. Therefore, the best way to learn a language is to speak it. It is like a skill which can be perfected with use and practice. When a child learns its mother tongue, he first learns to speak it. Reading and writing come much later. But in order to develop correct speech habits, a proper environment is necessary. One cannot achieve proficiency in speaking a language if there is no opportunity to interact with people using the same language. Language learning is essentially, a matter of forming correct habits, these can be acquired only by speaking it without hesitation. Practice makes a man perfect. Once one has an active command over the spoken language, reading and writing will not pose much difficulty. Precisely because of this, the first lesson in a language course should be devoted to initiating the pupil into the world of sounds. Oral practice is the quickest way of learning a language.

(155 words)

Essay

131 YOUTH, MALL & BRAND CULTURE

Synopsis

Ten years ago nobody would have ever imagined the way mall culture has eventually come to spread. We were used to the traditional way of shopping wherein shops were small, with stocks of specific products only. But in malls, we can get everything under one roof. Mall culture has its genesis in metro cities but now even small towns are facing its onslaught. Malls cater to the various needs of the buyers. In malls, one can easily find coffee houses and food courts, in the event one wants a break from shopping. Malls often have movie theatres, gaming and riding parlours, etc. Malls have become a major hunting ground for the youth. Pleasant atmosphere and cool surroundings all contribute to making malls a much-sought-after hangout zone. Malls have proper parking spaces, clean washrooms and other basic amenities which traditional markets lack. However, malls have certain disadvantages also. In some, prices are extremely high. Parking charges are exorbitant. Nevertheless, malls are here to stay and in future malls are likely to redefine consumerism.

Ten years ago, nobody would have ever imagined the way mall culture has eventually come to spread. Creators of this new concept could have never visualised even in their wildest dreams that malls would start a social revolution in the shopping habits and trends of the people.

We were used to the traditional way of shopping wherein shops were small, with stocks of specific products only. One had to hop from one shop to another even to acquire the items of a small shopping list. But in malls, we can get everything from the smallest to the biggest items, under one roof. We can enjoy shopping without being troubled by bad weather, dust, etc. Not only shopping, one can also enjoy movies, dine, have coffee, play games, etc., all within the premises of a mall. For some, these malls are perfect places to hang out.

To begin with, malls had arrived in the metro cities only but eventually they spread like wild fire. Now even small towns are facing the *onslaught*[1] of mall culture. Electronic media has played a big role in this regard. Media has made people aware of different brands. Promotion of brands in the media is done in such a glamourised way that the young generation wants to use only those brands which their favourite actors *endorse*[2]. National and international brands of clothes, shoes, watches, accessories, etc., are readily available in malls. We can conveniently shop for every item we need like apparel, watches, shoes, furniture, etc., under one roof. Even travel agencies have set up their offices in malls.

While shopping, if one feels tired and needs a break for sometime or wants to have a cup of coffee, one can easily find a coffee house in the mall itself. There, food courts are also available which offer different kinds of food. One need not go outside the mall in search of a good restaurant—malls themselves offer great places for dining.

Some people are of the view that the items sold in malls are costlier than those sold in the traditional markets. But this notion of high price is also owing to cut-throat competition prevalent in the market. Now different kinds of sales strategies like discounts and offers are being adopted to attract customers. People are getting attracted to the malls as malls arguably offer a complete shopping experience.

Malls have become a major hunting ground for the youth. Whenever they are in a mood for an outing or in need for a break from their routine life, they can visit a mall; as malls are a *convenient*[3] place to hang around, to do window shopping and to stay abreast of the latest fashion. Pleasant atmosphere and cool surroundings contribute to making malls a much-sought-after hangout zone. Even for serious buyers, it is a godsend because they get everything in the comfort of a cool ambience in the mall.

Usually situated away from a city, a traditional market, unlike a mall, makes a poor show offering a shopping experience nothing short of exhausting. With dirt and filth scattered all around, bargaining and quarrelling taking place everywhere for lack of fixed price tag, shabbily dressed shopkeepers together with their wares spread all across their shops, no toilet nor any corner to relax, no eating joints etc., traditional marketplaces *repulse*[4] customers instead of beckoning them. With the rise in per capita income of the common people, *splurging*[5] has become a way of life.

The mall culture therefore, served the purpose not only of eliminating the health hazards but also of dignifying the shopping experience of people who want to spend. Moreover, since almost all the items with a price tag, needed in general, are kept in a systematic order and are available under one roof, and the atmosphere too corresponds to the taste of the buyers, the mall culture is a huge success.

Parking problems and lack of clean washrooms are the two major issues concerning almost all traditional markets. Even these have been taken care of in the malls. Malls have proper as well as planned parking space. One has easy access to parking there. In traditional markets, we rarely find washrooms and if there is one, it is neither clean nor maintained. In malls, there are a number of well maintained and clean washrooms. These are some of the main reasons why an educated and modern individual prefers malls to traditional markets.

Of late, malls which cater to specific needs of customers have come up. For example, there are some malls where nothing but jewellery and related items are sold. Some others specialise in items related to traditional Indian weddings. In these kinds of malls, people find it very convenient to shop, as they can avail themselves of a wide variety of choices with respect to a specific item, that too, at a single stop.

Every coin has two faces. Likewise, while malls have many benefits, they have certain disadvantages also. In most malls, prices are fairly high. As a result, the common people do not get to experience shopping in malls. Youngsters may want to go for brand value but not all would want to do the same. Some shoppers are also made to feel like misfits in the atmosphere of these malls. The general perception is that only people with money *throng*[6] these malls. Even the parking charges are *exorbitant*[7]. The cluster of pubs that has opened up in various malls attracts young crowd that feels freer in such environs. Some discotheques have also set up their shops in the vicinity of the malls. For getting entry into such a Disco, one has to pay through one's nose. At times, even the charges for food items are extremely high. As malls flourish, traditional business families lose their customers base and it is a big setback for them. Mall culture, in a way, is also against the traditional Indian *ethos*[8] of trade and commerce.

The point worth pondering whether malls would cause the demise of traditional markets. Well, old habits die hard. People still find it more convenient to go to neighbouring shops rather than going to shop in malls. Traditional markets will always have their rightful place with respect to the shopping needs of the customer. For petty things, one would not rather go to a mall as it involves a lot of expenses including that of transport. One may venture into malls for the purpose of shopping for major items or to spend one's leisure time. Malls are not a substitute for traditional markets—they either complement or supplement traditional markets. People who believe that traditional markets are on their way out, are mistaken.

All said and done, malls are here to stay and will eventually redefine consumerism. Their existence does not mean that the traditional markets will vanish completely. But they will certainly be affected; shop-keepers in these markets may not be able to make as much profit as they used to, earlier. Business will definitely suffer as far as traditional markets are concerned; and, malls, in times to come, will continue to hold their *sway*[9].

AID TO VOCABULARY

1. *Onslaught* — fierce attack
2. *Endorse* — approve or support something publicly

3. *Convenient* — suiting somebody's needs or plans
4. *Repulse* — disgust, repel
5. *Splurging* — excessive spending
6. *Throng* — to move as crowds do in a certain direction
7. *Exorbitant* — too high or great, unreasonable
8. *Ethos* — the guiding beliefs
9. *Sway* — rule or control

POINTS TO REMEMBER

1. Creators of the mall concept would have never visualised that it would eventually revolutionise the way people shop.
2. Earlier, people had to hop from one shop to another, but now they can buy all that they may need, under one roof.
3. Mall culture has had its genesis in big cities, but now malls are coming up in small towns as well.
4. One can easily find all national and international brands of almost everything in malls.
5. Malls are well-known not only for shopping options but also for entertainment and relaxation. They also have movie theatres, gaming zones, coffee houses, food courts, etc.
6. Malls have become a major hunting ground for the youth.
7. Malls have some disadvantages also.
8. In some malls, prices are fairly high. As a result, the common people are deprived of the experience of shopping in malls.
9. Although traditional markets will never go out of reckoning, malls will continue to hold their sway in times to come.

GUIDED COMPOSITION

Develop the following paragraph into a full-fledged essay in 800-1000 words. The gist of the topic is provided in approximately 155 words for your help:

A HIGHER STANDARD OF LIVING DOES NOT NECESSARILY MEAN A HAPPIER LIFE

A higher standard of living does not by any means guarantee happiness in life. It is a misconception of man that material comforts are a prerequisite to a peaceful and happy life. If it were so, then the very rich should have no reason to complain. Yet one observes that happiness is as elusive to them as to a less fortunate person. It is well known that human wants are never completely satiated. They tend to multiply. Every want that is satisfied gives rise to several others. So man finds himself caught in a vicious cycle, where he is endlessly trying to gratify his needs. This leads to overwork, tension, ill health and sometimes breakdown. So pursuit of sensual pleasures, wealth and luxuries cannot bring happiness. A man who earns barely enough to provide two square meals for his family may lead a more contented life than a rich man who in spite of all his wealth is miserable. Happiness is a state of mind. It is an attitude towards life. A man who is content with his lot is far happier than a man who is forever seeking happiness through worldly comforts. *(155 words)*

Essay

132

INDIAN JUDICIARY—A REVIEW

Synopsis

A modern democratic State like India functions through its three organs of government viz, the Legislature, the Executive and the Judiciary. The judiciary functions as the watchdog of democracy in India. Indian judiciary is passing through a problematic phase. Instances of corruption as well as reports of judicial overreach have come to light. Issues relating to transparency, disclosure of assets of judges and judicial backlog, which have been plaguing the judiciary, are no less serious. Lack of judicial accountability is a flagrant inadequacy of the Indian judicial system. The government has a number of constructive measures on the anvil and it is hoped that things will get better in the near future.

India, a modern democratic State, functions through its three organs of government viz, the Legislature, the Executive and the Judiciary. The legislature is the representative body. It expresses the will of the people through its elected members. It formulates policies and makes laws for the people. The executive, with its Council of Ministers and through its departments and officials, sees to it that the laws and rules as well as the policy decisions are enforced or implemented as required. The judiciary ensures the rule of law by upholding the constitutional as well as other laws; it also interprets law and decides upon the rights, duties and liabilities of individuals, entities and agencies of the state as well as those of others. The rule of law, supremacy of the constitution and an independent judiciary are among the most important pillars of our democratic edifice.

The constitutional provision for judicial review empowers the court to review any law or rule passed by the legislature, executive or any other body so as to determine whether it is valid as per constitutional provisions. If it deems the law or rule to be faulty, it can strike it down as unconstitutional. The judiciary safeguards the Fundamental Rights of the citizens enshrined in the constitution. By invoking the *writ*[1] provisions, the court can summon even the Prime Minister of India. The court can judge whether the election of the Head of the State i.e., the President of India, is lawful and if the court deems it otherwise, can declare the President disqualified to hold office. Such is the enormity and extent of the powers bestowed upon the Indian judiciary. The judiciary, indeed, functions as the watchdog of democracy in India.

A judiciary with great power inspires great hope in the underprivileged millions of India. In comparison with various agencies of the executive as well as the law enforcement departments, the judiciary and its officers appear less corrupt. So, the preceding fact on the one hand, and lack of reassurance from any other organ of the government on the other, make the average citizen repose absolute faith in the judicial system. Courts have been traditionally regarded as *hallowed*[2] *precincts*[3] of justice and humanity. Judges have been revered as unerring individuals of high nobility, professional *probity*[4] and intellectual sincerity. To many Indians, the judiciary is synonymous with trustworthiness. However, a number of adverse reports regarding the judiciary have come to light and they have left the ordinary citizen disillusioned.

Understandably, the Indian judiciary is passing through a phase ridden with problems. While there have been cases reeking of corruption as well as reports of judicial overreach, issues relating to transparency and disclosure of assets of judges have also come to light amidst mounting judicial backlog. Moreover, many High Court judges are facing charges of corruption. The cases involving Justice Soumitra Sen of the Calcutta High Court, Chief Justice P.D. Dinakaran of the Sikkim High Court (formerly of the Karnataka High Court) and Justice Nirmal Yadav of the Uttarakhand High Court (formerly of the Punjab and Haryana High Court) are all at various stages of progress. In fact, on earlier occasions also judges had come under the lens, but most escaped unscathed.

In the famous case involving Veeraswamy, the Chief Justice of Madras High Court, the accused judge, despite having judicial immunity, had to undergo impeachment proceedings, only to escape in the wake of the Congress party having abstained from voting. The West Bengal High Court judge, Soumitra Sen is another judge who had to face impeachment. He had submitted his resignation five days before his impeachment motion was taken up in the Lok Sabha.

On November 26, 2010 a Supreme Court Bench declared most of the judges of the Allahabad High Court (the largest High Court in the country with 160 judges) corrupt, in the backdrop of the ₹ 23 crore Ghaziabad PF scam involving one Supreme Court judge, seven Allahabad High Court judges, twelve judges of the subordinate courts and six retired High Court judges. Another blot of the land scam associated with the then Chief Justice of Karnataka, P.D. Dinakaran and the impropriety in assigning work to him, pending investigation, rocked the judicial as well as legal circles for quite some time.

Corruption is rampant not only in the higher *echelons*[5] of the Indian judiciary, but also at the lower rungs. There are stories of Metropolitan Magistrates issuing bailable arrest warrants against individuals of whose identities they had no clue, in return for an *inducement*[6]. A report alleging that a Metropolitan Magistrate in Ahmedabad had issued bailable arrest warrants against the President of India in return for an inducement of ₹ 40,000 had appeared in the press. Bribes are often paid in trial courts in order to speed up the process of judgements, receive favourable verdicts, obtain bails, manipulate witnesses, tamper with evidence and so on. Today, under the existing law, any citizen making any allegation of corruption against a sitting judge can be charged with as well as punished for contempt of court. It is a *retrograde*[7] law with *retrogressive*[8] effect and hence needs to be reviewed by the Law Commission as well as the Parliament.

Judicial overreach and judicial review are two aspects which draw *flak*[9] with regard to the functioning of the judiciary in India. Of these, judicial review has constitutional sanction. In an interview with newspaper editors, a former Prime Minister had observed that the Supreme Court should not get into matters relating to policy-making, which is the exclusive domain of the executive. The implied allegation was that of judicial overreach. In this case, the Court, while issuing a directive to the Centre to distribute food grains among the poor, was probably guided by the fact that it was its duty to protect the citizens' right to life as *mandated*[10] by the Constitution.

Lack of judicial *accountability*[11] is a *flagrant*[12] inadequacy of the Indian judicial system. As of now, an ordinary citizen cannot proceed against a judicial officer on charges of corruption or some other matter. Any such allegation or attempt to allege may result in the prosecution of the individual for contempt of court.

The higher judiciary, that is the High Court and the Supreme Court, as a matter of procedure, looks into the allegations and complaints against the judicial officers of the subordinate courts. However, as of now, there is no provision of law for proceeding against a judge of the higher judiciary on charges of corruption or some other matter. The only option available for the removal of a judge of the High Court or the Supreme Court comprises of a cumbersome procedure of impeachment in the Parliament. In the history of over six decades of democracy, the instances pertaining to *impeachment*[13] of a judge have been very rare. Hence, accountability on the part of the judiciary, especially the higher judiciary, unlike other domains of governance, has become a grave concern for the country.

The former Law Minister of the Indian Government, Veerappa Moily was keen on judicial reforms. As a sequel to a series of reformatory measures taken by Mr. Moily, the Judicial Standards and Accountability Bill was introduced in the Lok Sabha, though amid *din*[14] and interruption. The Bill seeks to provide for a mechanism to deal with complaints of the public against judges; to give legal shape to the Reinstatement of Values of Judicial Life adopted by the Supreme Court in 1977; to make it obligatory for judges to declare their assets and liabilities after assuming office and whenever new assets are acquired; and to replace the Judges Enquiry Act, 1968.

Justice delayed is justice denied, goes the saying. The *staggering*[15] pile of pending cases, called judicial backlog, is another concern facing the Indian judiciary. According to data available with the apex court, the number of cases pending with the Supreme Court as of December 1, 2014, was 64,919. The data available for the 24 High Courts and the lower courts up to the year ending 2013, showed pendency of 44.5 lakhs and a whopping 2.6 crores, respectively. Of the over 44 lakh cases pending in the 24 High Courts of the country, 34,32,493 were civil and 10,23,739 criminal. On May 31, 2016 the total cases pending in the country was 2.18 crores.

The Gram Nyayalaya Act envisages setting up of 5,000 village courts across the country. Former Chief Justice of India, Altamas Kabir, in a meeting of the National Court Management System (NCMS), had presented to the government a proposal to double the strength of the judiciary from the existing 18,871 to more than 30,000 within a period of five years. The NCMS was set up by the SC in 2012 and it was decided that the judicial system would be made five-plus free, i.e., free of cases which are more than five years old. The SC has estimated that the number of cases will swell to 15 crore in the next three decades requiring at least 75,000 courts/judges.

Lack of transparency as well as accountability is a major impediment that has afflicted the Indian judiciary since its establishment. Popular demand with regard to disclosure of assets of sitting judges of the higher judiciary, by invoking the provisions of the Right to Information (RTI) Act, was initially resisted even by the Chief Justice of India. However, Justice A.P. Shah of the Delhi High Court held that all courts including the court of the Chief Justice of India fall within the ambit of the RTI and are liable to disclose assets of the judges.

The judicial system is a mechanism for keeping a check on the other branches of governance, viz., the executive and the legislature. The US system is a model mechanism for such checks and balances wherein the *autonomy*[16] of the court is established in the constitution. In a TV interview, the former Chief Justice of India, Justice P.N. Bhagwati, had held the judges responsible for the fallen standards of Indian judiciary and had suggested revamping of the system. A number of constructive measures which the Government plans to implement are on the anvil and it is hoped that things will improve in near future.

Aid to Vocabulary

1. *Writ* — an order from a court of law (in India from the High Court or Supreme Court)
2. *Hallowed* — sacred and respected
3. *Precincts* — the area that is near or around a place
4. *Probity* — integrity, uprightness
5. *Echelons* — ranks or positions
6. *Inducement* — something given to somebody with a view to persuade to do something, bribe
7. *Retrograde* — directed backwards
8. *Retrogressive* — moving backwards, or deteriorating
9. *Flak* — harsh criticism
10. *Mandated* — required by law
11. *Accountability* — responsibility to explain one's actions
12. *Flagrant* — too bad to be ignored, blatant
13. *Impeachment* — charging an important public figure with a serious crime
14. *Din* — a loud confusing mixture of noises that lasts for a long time
15. *Staggering* — so great, shocking or surprising that it is difficult to believe
16. *Autonomy* — freedom to act or govern independently

Points to Remember

1. A modern democratic State like India functions through its three organs of government viz., the Legislature, the Executive and the Judiciary.
2. The Indian judiciary is passing through a phase ridden with problems.
3. There are instances pertaining to stinking stories of corruption.
4. Corruption is rampant in the Indian judiciary not only in the higher echelons of the judiciary, but also at the lower rungs.
5. Judicial overreach and judicial review are two aspects which draw flak as regards the functioning of the judiciary in India.
6. Lack of judicial accountability is a flagrant inadequacy of the Indian judicial system.
7. Lack of transparency along with accountability is a major impediment that has afflicted the Indian judiciary since its establishment.
8. A number of constructive measures are on the anvil and it is hoped that things will get better in the near future.

Essay
133

IS CAPITAL PUNISHMENT JUSTIFIED?

SYNOPSIS

Capital punishment is the highest degree of punishment as dispensed in the Indian judicial system. Extreme punishment is a matter of discretion. The President of India has been bestowed with the power to remit the penalty of death by accepting the convict's 'mercy plea'. Critics cite ethical, moral as well as humanitarian reasons with regard to abolishing death penalty. At the same time, the supporters of capital punishment demand a fair system and a just society which is cleansed of cold-blooded murderers. 140 member States of the UN have abolished death penalty either in law or in practice. India has witnessed a steep decline in the rate of administering death sentences as well as executions. The general perception is, that since it is against the law of natural justice, death penalty in India should be abolished altogether. If it is to stay, capital punishment should at least be awarded sparingly.

A punishment is a just reward with respect to a criminal act. This is what we expect the law-enforcers in any nation or State, to dispense, with a view to curb criminal acts. The severity of punishment increases in accordance with the brutality of the crime committed. According to the law, capital punishment is the highest degree of punishment.

In the Indian judicial system, extreme punishment is a matter of *discretion*[1] and not the norm or a mere *procedural*[2] act. The Indian Penal Code (IPC) awards capital punishment in cases of criminal conspiracy, waging war against the Indian Government, forging, manipulating or *counterfeiting*[3] evidences with respect to capital offences leading to the execution of an innocent person, abetment of suicide, murder in dacoity, grave sexual offence, and murder by a life convict. Except in the case of murder by a life convict, in all the other said offences, death penalty is not mandatory but discretionary. The judicial system observes leniency and avoids the death penalty except in cases of extremely gross and intolerable offences which it categorises as 'rarest of the rare'. The provisions in the IPC do not curtail the rights of the accused. The Indian law has a provision of remitting the death penalty by reverting to the 'mercy plea'. The President of India has the power to either accept or reject the mercy petition.

The critics, backed by humanitarian concerns, find the irrevocability of a death sentence regressive as well as extreme. Instead of putting an end to his life, a criminal should be awarded a fair chance to reform. Capital punishment is *reminiscent*[4] of the ancient barbaric practice of 'an eye for an eye' and, hence, it does not befit a civilised society. According to the critics, capital punishment has failed to serve as a deterrent. They argue that the claim, with regard to capital punishment helping in reducing the crime rate, is not based on facts and figures. Besides, on moral as well as ethical grounds, one has no right to take life for the reason that one cannot give life. It is against the law of nature. And, for a country which gave the world the greatest *apostle*[5] of non-violence in Mahatma Gandhi, abolition of death penalty from the Indian judicial system is the only rational and progressive way forward. This *creed*[6] hails the Gandhian *dictum*[7], that says—"An eye for an eye will make the whole world blind."

The arguments against the death penalty in some cases are socially pertinent. Critics argue that the vulnerable sections of the society may be implicated in criminal cases in various ways by oppressive forces including the police. Owing to financial and other constraints, they may not be able to defend themselves during the trial. Hence innocent people may become victims in a retrograde legal system. Thus, a robust legal system becomes necessary with a view to uphold the sovereignty of the state as well as to protect the citizens' Right to Life.

Another argument against capital punishment pertains to the traumatic wait on death row while appeals and retrials are under way; as a result, the accused may be subjected to mental agony for years. On the other hand, those in support of capital punishment assert that the safety, security and freedom of innocent people must be protected from anti-social criminal brutalities; and, strict punishment is a radical way to combat crime and establish peace and order. Capital punishment, some say, provides for a just way of cleansing the society of cold-blooded murderers. It is exemplary, and serves as a deterrent, too. Again, people argue that the law abiding taxpayers should not be burdened with the government's need of money with respect to the upkeep and rehabilitation of criminals. Execution of convicted murderers is just and fair, they say. The money thus saved can be used for the welfare of society.

Everyone has a right to live in a just and crime-free society. Administering due punishment to criminals deters crime, and helps in bringing down the crime rate in our society. The victim's family feels relieved and satisfied to know that the murderer has received apt punishment. Moreover, social history is witness to many *horrendous*[8] crimes; if the perpetrators of such crimes were to go scot-free, the conscience of the people shall be haunted.

The dispensation of just punishment not only reposes faith and belief in the judicial system but also enables the people to lead a life devoid of fear. This is the stand which the advocates of capital punishment adopt. A considerable number of countries around the globe have abolished death penalty. However, India, China, Pakistan, the United States of America, Russia, etc., have not done away with it as yet. With the adoption of the Universal Declaration of Human Rights by the United Nations, the first attempt at abolishing the death penalty was made. Since its adoption, 140 member states have abolished the death penalty, either in law or in practice. Also, the International Civil Code prohibits the imposition of a death sentence on a minor.

In the current context, the debate with regard to capital punishment needs to be taken up in a fresh light and discussed in an objective manner. An elaborate discussion did take place in July 2000, at the Conference Against death penalty, held in New Delhi. Retired judges and the Chief Justice of the Supreme Court participated in this conference, and *unanimously*[9] decided in favour of the abolition of death sentence in India. In December, however 2007, India voted against a United Nations General Assembly resolution that called for a moratorium on the death penalty.

As of today, the number of death sentences has seen a decline in the wake of the uproar against it in the society that began with the controversial execution of Afzal guru — the mastermind of December 13, 2001 terrorist attack on Parliament — on February 9, 2013 followed by that of Yakub Memon, the 1993 Mumbai serial blasts accused, on July 30, 2015. The execution on November 21, 2013 of Ajmal Kasab — the lone terrorist of November 26 - 29, 2008, caught alive — was, however, far from any controversy.

India's *persistence*[10], against the wave, to retain death penalty in its legal system comes as a big blow to the *philanthropic*[11] view of the society. That the apostles of non-violence Mahatma Gandhi, Mahavira and Gautam Buddha were all born and brought up in India stands a huge *paradox*[12] in this regard. But there is a point to ponder. All the cases of death penalty pending during Dr. Kalam's regime, a survey reveals, had a socio economic bias, and it substantiates that death penalty is mostly inflicted on the poor. At the same time, as eminent columnist Santosh Desai points out, "nothing is more vexing than the institutions of suicide bombers, for here the terrorist begins where the civilisation ends – by placing no value on his life." "A life spent in prison", observes Santosh Desai, "might actually be more of a punishment than death". The United

Nations Secretary General Ban Ki Moon has categorically stated that "the death penalty has no place in the 21st century".

The arguments both for and against the abolition of death penalty carry a lot of weight. In spite of anxious discussions, both at national and global platforms, whether or not, capital punishment should be abolished, remains an inconclusive debate.

Capital punishment should be awarded only after much deliberation; and, exercising a great degree of caution. It should be administered sparingly, in the 'rarest of the rare' cases. Convicts must have the right to appeal to a higher court, subsequently going up to the Supreme Court, apart from being able to file a mercy petition with the President of India. *Overhauling*[13] the present system of administering justice in India would not bear much fruit. However, constructive changes are always welcome in a democracy. Human rights must be taken into consideration while sentencing, even in cases of grave offences, and all efforts must be made to ensure justice to all citizens.

AID TO VOCABULARY

1. *Discretion* — ability to choose or decide with sound judgment as and when needed
2. *Procedural* — done in a certain or an accepted way or order
3. *Counterfeiting* — making an exact copy in order to cheat or trick
4. *Reminiscent* — that reminds of, or is similar to, something
5. *Apostle* — someone who believes in or supports an idea or belief or cause
6. *Creed* — an idea or a set of beliefs that guides a person or group
7. *Dictum* — a statement or a well-known remark
8. *Horrendous* — horrible, unpleasant
9. *Unanimously* — agreed to by everyone
10. *Persistence* — trying to do something even though it is difficult
11. *Philanthropic* — based on love for mankind
12. *Paradox* — two opposite view/things
13. *Overhauling* — examining every part of a machine or system and making necessary changes or repairs

POINTS TO REMEMBER

1. Capital punishment is the highest degree of punishment as administered in India.
2. In the Indian judicial system, extreme punishment is a matter of discretion.
3. The President of India has been bestowed with the power to remit the penalty of death by accepting the 'mercy plea'.

4. Critics of capital punishment cite moral, ethical as well as humanitarian reasons for abolishing it.
5. Supporters of death penalty are of the view that it is critical to secure a just and fair society.
6. 140 UN member States have abolished death penalty either in practice or in law.
7. Attempts to abolish it failed in India, however, the country has witnessed a sharp decline in awarding death sentences as well as executions.
8. Capital punishment should be awarded sparingly.
9. Overhauling the present system in India would not help much.

DEATH PENALTY IN INDIA

Death Sentence in India is a contentious topic for many reasons. According to the statistics available with the National Crime Records Bureau (NCRB), more than 2000 individuals were awarded the death sentence by the courts in the 16 year period from 1998 to 2013. Uttar Pradesh tops the chart with 506 death sentences in the 16 year period. The highest number of death sentences was awarded in 2007.

Number of Death Sentences Awarded each year (1998-2013)

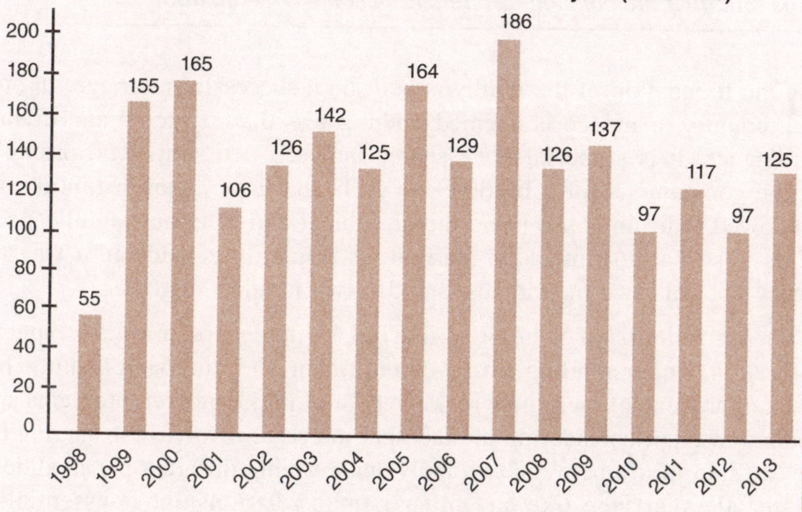

THE DEATH PENALTY WORLDWIDE

According to Amnesty International, as of July 2015, 101 countries have abolished the death penalty for all crimes in law, while 140 countries have abolished the death penalty in law or practice. At least 607 executions were carried out worldwide in 2014, a decrease of almost 22% compared to the figures recorded for 2013. Executions were recorded in 22 countries in 2014, the same number as 2013. This is a significant decrease from 20 years ago in 1995, when there were executions in 42 countries, highlighting the clear global trend of states moving away from the death penalty. Three countries have signed treaties to abolish the death penalty, but have not yet ratified them: Angola, Madagascar, Sao Tome and Principe.

Essay 134

THE RISING TREND OF DIVORCE IN INDIA

SYNOPSIS

In India, marriage as an institution is endowed with immense socio-moral, ethical as well as religious significance. Divorce is seen as an act of sacrilege against marriage which is considered a divine union of two people. With changing lifestyle and sensibilities and with the emergence of new attitudes, the number of divorce cases has also been on the rise. Apart from the avoidable and flippant reasons, there are also genuine grievances that people face which ultimately culminate in dissolution of marriage. The increasing number of divorce cases reported in India is perhaps a pointer to disintegration of the family as a social unit that is taking place. A balance needs to be struck between protecting the sanctity of marriage and safeguarding the individual interests of the aggrieved spouses. Another school of thought is that a marriage should be annulled the moment differences become irreconcilable.

The foundation of the family is built on a successful marriage. In our country, marriage is deemed nothing less than a sacred and divine ordinance. It is a special bond shared between two souls who promise to be companions for a lifetime. As such, marriage as an institution, is endowed with immense socio-moral, ethical and religious significance. This is so because in India, marriage is primarily considered a way to bring not only two individuals, but also two families, together.

The ingredients of a healthy marital alliance are mutual respect, affection, understanding, trust, commitment and companionship. The lack of any one of these may rock the boat of life. However, problems are bound to erupt considering the fact that marriage involves the sharing of everything in life between two individuals having different personalities. After all, marriage like any other human relationship, is essentially dynamic in nature. Mishandling of differences, especially with an impatient or immature attitude, can produce adverse consequences and may ultimately lead to divorce.

Between 1971 and 2015, five European countries legalised divorce. These countries are Italy, Spain, Portugal, the Republic of Ireland and Malta.

In our country, divorce is considered a *sacrilege*[1], for marriage is sacred; it is a divine union of two people. Divorce is indeed taboo in India. It brings dishonour to the cherished ideal of 'Marriages are made in heaven'.

The modern school of thought, despite the inherent tendency of the traditional mindset to resist change, is fast evolving new attitudes that have in turn redefined social conduct. Marriage too, has come to be influenced by *newfangled*[2] ideas. Marriage is fast becoming a pragmatic concern of the spouses, rather than being a responsibility of the kinship group. In metropolitan cities, the scene with regard to the concept of marriage among the professionals has undergone a drastic change. Usually, people prefer the nuclear family system, that affords freedom from interference from parents or in-laws. Modern society often also refuses to be bogged down by the obligations that its previous generation endorsed. As such, the trend that is springing out of this division is marked with an increase in the instances of marital breakdown. Therefore, in India, as is the case across the world in recent times, divorce rates have increased alarmingly. Thus, the family as a social unit on the back of which human civilisation has thrived thus far, is showing signs of disintegration.

With the changing lifestyle of the contemporary youth, the number of divorce cases has been on the rise. The youth of today has evolved in a more flexible as well as dynamic environment, yet their capacity for tolerance has not increased correspondingly. The ideals of compromise find no takers nowadays. The values that bind a family together are given little consideration. As such, disintegration of the family is the emerging trend.

The change that is taking place in the social system is mainly due to the change in the attitudes and sensibilities of the people. Increasing levels of education and economic independence have made the women of the present age more aware and assertive with regard to their choices. The youth take the acts of breaking up or forging a relationship as a passing ritual of life. A complex blending of abundant opportunities with a complicated modern way of life has made the youngsters restless. This restless spirit gets reflected in their preference for change and disregard for stability. A relationship, like many other constituents of life, is seen through this prism, and mainly forged or dissolved as a matter of convenience. A mere hint of being ill at ease, can trigger off a series of differences between the spouses who are not inclined to making sincere efforts to sort them out. Instead of charting the path of negotiation or compromise, they let things fall apart. The most convenient way for many is making an exit out of a souring relationship. The religiosity of relationships has been *desecrated*[3] in the modern age.

The urban youth are apparently addicted to surfing the Internet. They tend to turn to the Internet for virtually everything. Websites enable them to find a partner of their choice at the click of a Mouse. It is their restlessness that many a time blinds them to the dangers of *falsified*[4] information and fraudulent impostors that flourish on the Net. As a result, when people forge an alliance over the Internet, without proper background checks, it becomes imperative, in many cases, to ultimately dissolve the marriage. Annulling such marriages, however, is easy and hassle-free, more so because the kin on either side are generally not involved in such alliances. As such, no issues have to be tackled between the families of the estranged couple.

To avoid all the hassles, customs and regulations pertaining to a marriage and to get round the inconveniences of the lengthy, *convoluted*[5] as well as stressful procedures pertaining to a divorce, many youths today, are opting for live-in-relationships. Although it provides for a convenient substitute to the institution of marriage, it is devoid of any assurance or security that a marriage is known to provide. In this case, people are not bound by any commitment of lifelong togetherness and, therefore, can get separated without having to go through the stressful ordeal of procuring divorce. Live-in-relationships, arguably, do not conform to Indian culture.

Apart from avoidable as well as *flippant*[6] reasons that many couples are faced with, the issues that some couples face are genuine. In such cases, a growing sense of intolerance builds up and ultimately culminates in a dissolved marriage. Physical as well as sexual violence, mental torture, conflict with in-laws, extra-marital affairs, adultery, etc., have become a major source of conflict, abuse and mental trauma in relationships. When there is no cure in sight with regard to these *retardations*[7] in a marriage and the differences end up growing to an irreconcilable extent, the only viable solution which becomes apparent to the estranged couple is to stop dragging the carcass of a dead marriage and seek a divorce.

When we look further into the causes of the rising rate of divorce in India, there unfolds yet another dimension to this scenario. In spite of the professed civilisational advancement of the cyber generation, in reality, abusing one's wife is found to be a common practice among men in most regions of the country. As women's *emancipation*[8] and empowerment has emboldened many of them, eventually, to resist as well as react to such excesses, the cumulative effect has been the rising rates of divorce across Indian states. In a study conducted in the six Indian states of Bihar, Jharkhand, Rajasthan, Andhra Pradesh, Maharashtra and Tamil Nadu by the population council of India and the International Institute for Population Sciences, 18 to 30 per cent of married women aged between 15 and 24 have reported at least one instance of physical violence by their husbands.

The decision of a couple to get divorced is an emotionally difficult one especially when children are involved. Many children of single parent households are at risk of becoming delinquents. The children are not only deprived emotionally but also their performance at school may suffer.

As far as the divorce rate is concerned, it is very much lower in rural India when compared with urban India. This is so because, compared with urban women, rural women are much less emancipated or empowered. Illiteracy, economic dependence, social stigma, etc., force women to keep clinging on to the marital vow even in the face of *horrendous*[9] marital situations. Often, remarriage of a woman in most parts of rural India is either unacceptable or difficult. Divorce for them is equivalent to *destitution*[10]. Owing to these and other related reasons, the incidence of divorce in Indian villages is low.

The Indian society is passing through a phase of rapid *metamorphosis*[11]; as a result of which, social norms and conventions are gradually evolving. A number of marriages getting irreparably as well as *irretrievably*[12] difficult to salvage, could also be a consequence of this social evolution. Hence, as no one can help such estranged couples to get back to normal, healthy relationships, it becomes damaging for the individuals themselves as well as for the society at large to let them continue to be a couple. Divorce in such cases will only benefit the individuals as well as the society at large. But the Indian marriage laws, enacted in a less advanced socio-economic milieu of the 1950s are largely restrictive in their scope with regard to facilitating divorce. Hence, there has been a popular demand for quite some time for overhauling the marriage laws. As a salutary step in that direction, the Government introduced the Marriage Laws (Amendments) Bill, 2010. The Bill seeks to amend the Hindu Marriage Act (1955) and the Special Marriages Act (1954) so as to provide for "irretrievable breakdown" of marriage as a ground for divorce. In 2010, the Centre for the first time released the number of divorce cases i.e., 55,000 which have been pending in the country's courts.

Under the Muslim Personal Law, divorce is a much easier process. In the presence of witnesses, the word 'Talaq' is required to be pronounced thrice to end the marriage. However, in any religion, divorce is not the favoured choice. Divorce is granted only in cases where all steps to save the marriage have failed. Divorce is and should be considered only as the last resort, in the worst case scenario.

Despite everything, the fact remains—the growing trend of divorce is leading to the disintegration of family values. The concept of stability and security associated with healthy family life, has started to sink into *obscurity*[13]. Therefore, people need to foster a tolerant as well as mature attitude towards petty *quibbles*[14], in addition to not allowing differences, as much as possible, to disrupt married life. A balance needs to be struck between protecting the sanctity of the institution of marriage and safeguarding the individual interests of the aggrieved spouses. Divorce is a misplaced idea of modernity. *Emulation*[15] of western principles with respect to matrimonial matters is not accordance with our culture and is better avoided.

Another school of thought is that marriage like any other institution should be instrumental in adding peace and happiness to the lives of the couple concerned but if, on the contrary, it begins to cause disharmony and disruption, it had better break up, Children no doubt are the worst sufferers, but for them, this is far better than to be brought up in an atmosphere of hatred, jealousy and distrust. Breaking up of marriage is no more a sacrilege, rather it's a matter of convenience; both the parties falling apart feel rescued and it paves the path of individual progress and prosperity. The law of the land, or the society, needs to perceive things in the modern perspective; the views of the old generation hold no relevance any more.

It is quite paradoxical that we emulate western culture and principles on one hand and on the other, we want to keep our own intact too. How can the two co-exist? They are poles apart. So far as the values of the society are concerned, they too undergo change, universally, with passage of time; hence, they are simply irrelevant.

Aid to Vocabulary

1. *Sacrilege* — violation of what is sacred
2. *Newfangled* — recently invented or developed and hard to understand
3. *Desecrated* — treated with disrespect
4. *Falsified* — misrepresented
5. *Convoluted* — complicated and difficult to understand
6. *Flippant* — showing that you do not take something as seriously as other people think you should
7. *Retardations* — acts of slowing down the development or progress of something
8. *Emancipation* — freeing somebody from restrictions (legal, political or social)
9. *Horrendous* — extremely shocking, horrific, horrifying
10. *Destitution* — extreme poverty
11. *Metamorphosis* — the process of changing into a different form
12. *Irretrievably* — in a way something cannot be made right or got back again
13. *Obscurity* — the state in which something has been forgotten
14. *Quibbles* — argument on small matters
15. *Emulation* — imitating zealously

POINTS TO REMEMBER

1. In India, the institution of marriage is endowed with immense socio-moral, ethical and religious significance.
2. Divorce is considered as sacrilege against marriage, which is considered a divine union of two people.
3. With changing lifestyle and sensibilities and with the emergence of new attitudes, the number of divorce cases has also been on the rise.
4. Apart from the avoidable as well as flippant reasons, there are also genuine grievances that people face which ultimately culminate in the dissolution of marriage.
5. The decision of divorce is a difficult one, especially when children are involved.
6. The number of divorce cases in rural India is lower in comparison with that in the metropolitan cities.
7. The growing trend of divorce is leading to disintegration of the family as a social unit.
8. A balance needs to be struck between protecting the sanctity of marriage and safeguarding the individual interests of the aggrieved couple.

WHAT DIVORCE TELLS US ABOUT MODERN INDIA

The landmark Hindu Code Bill passed in the parliament in the mid-1950s gave women property rights, outlawed polygamy and allowed partners to file for divorce. The laws were further tweaked in 1976 to allow divorce by mutual consent. Over time, the traditional joint family has given way to nuclear families in cities and towns; and more and more women are going to work or setting up their own businesses. Many urban women no longer have to depend on their spouses for financial security, men are sharing household chores; and gender equations are slowly changing.

Now a significant study by economist Suraj Jacob and anthropologist Sreeparna Chattopadhyay has examined data from India's census to offer — possibly for the first time –some insights into divorce and separation in India.

— 1.36 million people in India are divorced. That is equivalent to 0.24% of the married population, and 0.11% of the total population.

— More strikingly, the number of people separated is almost thrice the number of people divorced – 0.61% of the married population and 0.29% of the total population.

— More women are divorced and separated than men.

— Divorce rates in north-east states are relatively higher than elsewhere in India: Mizoram has the highest divorce rate (4.08%), more than four times that of Nagaland, the state with the second highest rate (0.88%).

— Gujarat reports the maximum number of divorce cases among bigger states – with a population of more than 10 million – followed by Asom, Maharashtra, West Bengal and Jammu and Kashmir.

— Meghalaya has the most number of cases of separation, followed by Mizoram, Sikkim, Kerala and Chhattisgarh. Three of these five states are in north-eastern India.

Figures may vary depending on reports/data used and the period when the research was conducted.

Source: International New York Times

Essay
135

THE UNITED NATIONS AND WORLD PEACE

Synopsis

On October 24, 1945, fifty-one nations came together and ratified the UN charter and thus the United Nations Organisation came into being. Currently, the number of UN member States hovers around 200. The UN tries to maintain world peace through conflict resolution. It undertakes socio-economic initiatives with a view to establish a better world order. The United Nations implements its initiatives through its numerous specialised agencies as well as other organisations, namely UNESCO, UNICEF, WHO, ILO, FAO, IMF, IBRD, IDA, WMO, UNFPA, UNDP, UNHCR, etc. In many cases, the UN peacekeeping initiatives could not bring about any tangible results. However, through socio-economic initiatives, this world organisation has been helpful in the evolution of a new world order.*

More than three *score*[1] years ago, before the gloom cast by World War II had subsided, prominent world leaders of the time got together and vowed to join hands to maintain world peace and, thereby, avert the possibility of a third world war. On October 24, 1945, fifty-one nations came together and ratified the UN Charter and thus the United Nations Organisation came into being in place of its ineffective *predecessor*[2], the League of Nations. As many as 9 million human lives—around 25 per cent of the combined male population of France and Germany—were lost during World War I. During World War II, 55 million people had died, including 6 million Jews imprisoned in the Nazi concentration camps. The world community did not want a third *catastrophe*[3] and hence many more nations eventually joined the UN. Currently, the number of UN member States *hovers*[4] around 200.

The activities of the UN are focused on two areas, which are, maintaining world peace through conflict resolution, and undertaking socio-economic initiatives with a view to establish a better world order. As part of its role in maintaining world peace, the UN undertakes activities such as resolving conflicts between nations and also between groups, and takes peacemaking as well as peacekeeping initiatives. The United Nations Organisation implements its initiatives through its numerous specialised agencies as well as other organisations, namely UNESCO, UNICEF, WHO, ILO, FAO, IMF, IBRD, IDA, WMO, UNFPA, UNDP, UNHCR, etc.

The United Nations through its agencies, undertakes initiatives to resolve conflicts as well as to promote peace. There are many types of conflicts, that have diverse origins and dissimilar consequences. Conflicts can occur between States or within a State. International conflicts arise from disputes over land or natural resources such as water, oil, diamonds (e.g. Sierra Leone), valuable minerals, etc. International conflicts may also stem from other types of discord prevailing among the diverse groups within a territory or between some group and the State administration. The reasons behind domestic conflicts may be ethnic, religious or environmental in nature or may pertain to illiteracy, *sectarianism*[5] or unequal distribution of resources. Poverty, *depletion*[6] of natural or economic resources of the State, weakness of political institutions, and human rights violations are some of the other causes of internal conflicts.

Under the supervision of the United Nations' Economic and Social Council (ECOSOC), several programmes have been rolled out, and specialised agencies have been actively engaged to implement measures to prevent deadly conflicts. These initiatives aim at conflict resolution at the roots and not just at addressing the acts or outcomes of violence—as these are just the symptoms of conflicts. The UN programmes and agencies that are being engaged to prevent conflicts include the United Nations Development Programme (UNDP), the United Nations Educational, Scientific and Cultural Organisation (UNESCO), the United Nations Environment Programme (UNEP), the United Nations High Commission for Human Rights (UNHCHR), the United Nations Institute for Disarmament Research (UNIDR) and others.

The UN aims at resolving anything that could be the source of conflicts and hence the approach with regard to prevention of conflicts as well as promotion of peace could vary. In the post World War II era, the weapons have become more deadly. In addition, although the world is now economically better off, disparity in terms of distribution of wealth, both within as well as between nations, especially between the 'Northern' and the 'Southern' nations, has become greater. This has turned out to be a major cause of conflict among nations and the UNDP aims at reducing this disparity so as to *eliminate*[7] the possibility of such conflicts taking place. Illiteracy is another important cause of conflict since there exists a wide gulf between the educated and the illiterate; the former is usually in a position of power and hence keeps the latter *relegated*[8] and at a disadvantage. The UNESCO aims at eliminating illiteracy and thereby tries to check this sort of conflicts at its source.

Disputes arising out of mismanagement of natural resources constitute another major cause of conflict among nations. Many a time, pollution caused by the industrial activities of one nation affects other nations also—this could also be a cause of conflict. Oil spills in oceans, acid rains, chemical effluents flowing into international rivers, etc., are the fallout of mismanagement of resources—all of these, too, pose a threat to peace. *Ecological*[9] catastrophes can be averted to a great extent by sensitizing the concerned parties to the harm being done to the ecology. The UNEP works the world over to create greater awareness on these matters. Protection of human rights is a *sine qua non*[10] for maintenance of peace in the world. In this regard, the role of UNHCHR pertains to promotion of, or respect for, human rights. Through *affirmative*[11] action, the commission demonstrates the will and determination of the international community to safeguard human rights. International Federation of Human Rights (IFHR) and Amnesty International are two of the agencies of the UN which work towards achieving this objective.

The facilitator of all conflicts is the availability of arms. The UNIDIR is engaged in research activities with a view to formulate a mechanism which would facilitate nations to arrive at a general *consensus*[12] on disarmament. Certain agencies and organisations under the UN work to promote a culture of peace. The United Nations Children's Emergency Fund (UNICEF) helps to protect the rights of children. The World Health Organisation (WHO) promotes scientific cooperation in health matters. Hunger and poverty are two important factors that are directly connected with the outbreak of conflicts. With this in mind, the World Food Programme (WFP) works to promote better nutrition, gives food aid and promotes socio-economic development of nations. The Food and Agriculture Organisation (FAO) works towards achieving greater agricultural productivity.

Through the aforementioned agencies, organisations and programmes, the United Nations works to prevent conflicts, foster peace and to build a new world order. Along with this, the UN also works to pacify *belligerent*[13] nations by intervening through peacekeeping missions. The Security Council is the main organ of the UN dedicated to the resolution of conflicts and to peacekeeping. Until the end of the Cold War, the UN intervened, in majority of the cases, only in case of conflicts that involved two or more States, in keeping with the principle of non-interference. The first UN mission began in 1948 in Palestine and it was named United Nations Truce Supervision Organisation (UNTSO).

In its Cambodian mission, the UN successfully supervised the elections in that country and subsequently helped in the establishment of a democratic government. The Arab-Israeli peace accords and the establishment of a multi-racial democratic constitution in South Africa owe much to the UN efforts. However, in many cases, the UN peacekeeping initiatives could not bring about tangible results, though the efforts could ease the mounting tensions. In Yugoslavia (erstwhile) and Somalia, the UN initiatives did not bring any success. In Angola, the UN-observed elections were soon annulled and fighting resumed. There was little participation on the part of the UN with the peacekeeping operations that were intended to end the Liberian Civil War. In the Afghan crisis, the mediatory participation of the UN could not make any headway with regard to the clashes between rival Mujahideen groups.

In its *inception*[14], the United Nations was meant to work for world peace mainly through resolution of conflicts among nations. Conflict resolution within a State in civil war situations was not its intended objective. However, with time, the UN found itself involved in peacekeeping operations to resolve internal conflicts within nations. In the case of NATO's assault on Kosovo, which was backed by the US, the attacks were carried out *unabated*[15] despite UN protests. In the case of Cyprus, Turkish troops continued to remain stationed in the northern part of the country and during the period that spanned two decades, the UN could do little to resolve the issue. These and similar other failed attempts to resolve conflicts have raised questions with regard to the relevance of the UN in today's crisis-ridden world scenario.

Countering the persistent threat to world peace posed by the ISIS is the biggest challenge faced by the UN today. Calling on all United Nations member States to act to suppress the flow of foreign fighters, the financing and other support to Islamist extremist groups in Iraq and Syria, the Security Council has put six persons affiliated to those groups on its terrorist sanctions list. Through the unanimous adoption of resolution 2170 (2014), under the binding Chapter VII of the United Nations Charter, the Council has condemned in the strongest terms what it called "gross, systematic and widespread abuse" of human rights by the Islamist State in Iraq and the Levant (ISIL, also known as ISIS) and Al-Nusra Front. It has called on member States to take national measures to prevent fighters from their soil to join the groups, reiterating obligations under previous counter-terrorism resolutions to prevent the movement of terrorists, as well as their supply of arms or financial suppport. Through the resolution, the Council has demanded that ISIL, Al-Nusra Front and all other entities associated with Al-Qaida cease all violence and terrorist acts, and immediately disarm and disband. Acknowledging that their attacks against civilians on the basis of ethnic or religious identity might constitute crimes against humanity, it has stressed the need to bring those perpetrators including foreign fighters, to justice. The Council has directed the sanctions monitoring team to report on the continuing threat posed by ISIL and the Front, and their sources of arms, funding recruitment and demographics, so as to further address the threat.

The critics of the effectiveness of the UN in crisis-resolution need to realise that the organisation cannot exercise any binding authority on the member countries which are sovereign States. However, through socio-economic initiatives, the UN has been helpful in evolving a new world order. Though, in some cases, efforts of the UN towards conflict resolution did not bear tangible results, its initiatives could definitely reduce the extent of the damage. Also, in several other cases, the UN could restore normalcy and establish peaceful living conditions in the affected regions.

Aid to Vocabulary

1. *Score* — a set of twenty
2. *Predecessor* — a person or thing coming before another
3. *Catastrophe* — an event which causes widespread suffering, a disaster
4. *Hovers* — stays around in the air like a bird, to stay close to
5. *Sectarianism* — disliking/hating the followers of any other religion or sect
6. *Depletion* — reduction in large amount leading to scarcity
7. *Eliminate* — remove
8. *Relegated* — consigned to inferior status
9. *Ecological* — pertaining to the relation of living creatures with the environment
10. *Sine qua non* — absolutely necessary thing/situation/condition
11. *Affirmative* — positive
12. *Consensus* — agreement
13. *Belligerent* — individual, group or nation seeking or engaging in a fight, war, etc.
14. *Inception* — the start of an organisation, etc.
15. *Unabated* — continued in full force without weakening

Points to Remember

1. On October 24, 1945 fifty-one nations came together and ratified the UN Charter and thus the United Nations Organisation came into being.
2. Currently, the number of UN member States hovers around 200.
3. The United Nations implements its initiatives through its numerous specialised agencies as well as other organisations.
4. The UN aims at resolving anything that could be the source of conflicts.
5. In many cases, the UN peacekeeping initiatives could not bring about tangible results.
6. The UN organisation cannot exercise any binding authority on the member countries which are sovereign States.
7. Through its socio-economic initiatives, the UN has been helpful in evolving a new world order.

GUIDED COMPOSITION

A GREAT LEARNING EXPERIENCE

Gist of the Essays is given in approximately 150 words. Full-Fledged Essays may be developed in 800-1000 words. For the topics listed below (1-13) refer to the page number written against each topic.

14. BAD WORKMEN COMPLAIN OF THEIR TOOLS

Human nature is such that though we are all quick to find fault in others, none is prepared to accept his drawbacks, shortcomings and weaknesses. We are used to finding fault with everyone except ourselves. Students put the blame on the teachers for their poor performance in the examination; teachers hold poor incentives, government apathy and students' attitude responsible for their lackadaisical performance. Nobody is ready to admit that they are also responsible for the system to a certain extent. Thus, it becomes a vicious cycle. A good, conscientious worker tries to make the most of the prevailing conditions. He is more productive than his counterparts who merely sit and find fault in everything. Everyone likes to work under perfect conditions, but if those can't be created then one should learn to adapt and adjust with ease to ensure that the work is not affected. However, people who shirk work are too ready to pick up any reason to strike work. They are bad workmen who become a liability instead of an asset to the organisation they work for, simply, due to their difficult attitude and poor performance. *(150 words)*

15. BEGGARS CANNOT BE CHOOSERS

A beggar who lives on the mercy of others has no right to complain about what is given to him. The donor usually decides what is to be given and how much. The beggar or borrower does not have much option to demand something specific or pick and choose. Similarly, if one is in real need he should readily accept whatever help he gets. The terms and conditions of extending such a help or favour will always be dictated by the donor. This is true for an ordinary person and even for a nation. Extreme deprivation and poverty means total helplessness and the inability to opt for something of one's choice. However, it is unethical to exploit the helplessness of someone who is needy. Adverse circumstances may force a person or sometimes even a nation to pick up the begging bowl, but it should be done only as a last resort. *(150 words)*

16. CHARACTER IS DESTINY

Man is the maker of his own destiny. Some people believe fate is pre-determined and they are mere puppets in the hand of fate. Such people never make any effort to improve their lot. They convince themselves that it is God's will that they suffer. But a man of character carves out his own path to attain his objectives in life. His determination, perseverance and moral strength enable him to overcome the most difficult obstacles. He follows the dictates of his conscience and remains calm under all circumstances. He never wavers in his mind. His strength of character and moral discipline enables him to realise his dreams. He has tremendous capacity to bear stress, difficulties and setbacks because of his convictions. While others wait for a miracle to transform their lives, he relentlessly goes ahead to pursue his goal to shape his destiny. *(155 words)*

17. EASY COME, EASY GO

The proverb 'easy come, easy go' implies that, what is not hard-earned is lost easily. Sons of rich parents squander away their parents' wealth, in gambling, drinks, horse-racing and so on, without a thought, for the simple reason, that, it is not their hard-earned money. Many people earn money by gambling. Money won from gambling never lasts long. A person may lose all that he has at a go in gambling. Property or wealth, inherited or gained by illegal means never has the same significance as the wealth earned through sweat and blood. We value things only when we have worked hard for them. The proverb is a wholesome warning to those who are always on the look-out for short-cuts to success, fame and wealth. *(140 words)*

18. ERRORS, LIKE STRAW, UPON THE SURFACE FLOW; HE THAT WOULD SEARCH FOR PEARLS MUST DIVE BELOW

A superficial study of anything will not yield very revealing results. A seaman knows too well that he cannot get the best of pearls sitting by the seashore. The best pearls lie embedded in the dark caverns of the ocean. Only the worthless shells are washed ashore by the tides. One must be ready to take risks to gain something worthwhile in life. It is true in every sphere of life. We can never learn anything significant by making a cursory examination. The superficial study of a book does not yield much. In fact, all that is of value may escape you if you just read it carelessly. It is only when one tries to read between the lines, ponders over the thought expressed by the writer, then one can discern the pearls of wisdom. We often make the mistake of judging a thing, object or a person from appearances, without bothering to study, investigate or observe and find their true essence. Therefore, if we are really in search of truth, then we must be ready to plunge deep and explore, rather than be misled by the external manifestations. *(155 words)*

19. EVERY CLOUD HAS A SILVER LINING

Joys and sorrows are inextricably mingled in the texture of life. Man often feels overwhelmed when things do not turn out according to his expectations. All of us have a tendency to indulge in self pity. Hence, we become so preoccupied with our miseries and sufferings, that we fail to take note of even a ray of hope. However, a balanced person never allows himself to get too distressed in the face of tragedy and misfortune. He looks at calamities as blessings in disguise. He learns from his suffering and faces life with greater effort. A man who drives himself too hard may fall sick and discover that if he does not lead a moderate life, he may die sooner than his time. So in a way, sickness awakens him from his slumber and he is forced to review his priorities. Therefore, every setback teaches us a lesson. It is for man to recognise it in the midst of his sorrow. *(150 words)*

20. HE WHO NEVER CHANGES HIS MIND HAS NO MIND TO CHANGE

Change is the law of nature. A man who resists change is denying this essential quality of human nature. Life is forever demanding compromise, adjustment and adaptability. A wise man changes his attitudes, ideas, decisions and priorities when circumstances change. It is foolishness to cling to the past in the hope of some miraculous revival of the same situation. Life is full of ups and downs. If we continue to live in the past and refuse to face the challenge of the present out of sheer obstinacy, to resist change, then we can never grow and develop as human beings. A person who is stubborn and unchangeable is very difficult to live with, because he refuses to look at reality, objectively. On the contrary, a man with an open mind is forever willing to listen to another point of view and think afresh in the light of it. It is only thoughtless and self-centered individuals who lack the ability to adapt. Thoughtful people have flexibility in their ideas and are willing to change. *(150 words)*

SUBSTANTIAL, AUTHORITATIVE & LATEST MATERIAL ON G.K. & CURRENT TOPICS TO HELP YOU WRITE ESSAYS ON HUNDREDS OF TOPICS

Some Basic Facts, Relevant Figures, Important Data and Reports*

Why this Section ?

Dear Reader, a natural question which ought to come to your mind is, "Why has this section been included?" Understandably so, as no book on Essay Writing contains such a section as this one.

But should there never be a FIRST or the FIRST TIME ?

Is DHILLON GROUP not known for innovations ?

Is DHILLON GROUP not an acknowledged trend-setter ?

Arya-DGP Essay Books were — THE FIRST EVER — to contain *Synopsis, Aid to Vocabulary* and *Points to Remember*.

There is no dearth of imitators, and imitation itself is a tribute to originality. Mona Lisa has been copied the world over, again and again, and yet people make a beeline to have a glimpse of the original.

But the basic question remains unanswered, why this section?

This Section is Aimed at Helping You to Write Essays on a Variety of Subjects and to Add More Punch to Your Essays

---

**Source :* Leading National News Papers, National and International Agencies Reports, and Internet

'Arya-DGP Latest Probable Essays' has one hundred and thirty five full-fledged Essays besides a small section–Know the Economists and 20 topics under the head–Guided Composition. However, no claim can be made that the Examination Question Paper will not contain a topic, outside the topics covered in the book. If such a situation arises, you, Dear Reader, may find yourself trapped. We do not want you to feel helpless. We want you to sail through successfully even against the tides, currents and cross-currents.

This section will arm and equip you. It will provide you with plenty of ammunition to fire, bang on target. Read this section carefully and memorise the facts and important data to use the same effectively, as per the need of the essay at hand.

Finally, we seek your valuable opinion on this section as well as on the book itself. Do give us your considered opinion. We value it and will give due consideration to it when we come out with the new edition.

If you are a Student,

or a candidate taking up a competitive examination, please inform us as to how did you find the book.

Do you believe the topics covered in the book are adequate? If not, what are the other topics, which you will want us to include?

Give your opinion on the language, presentation of facts, development of the essays and any other aspect you might find relevant and useful.

If you are a Teacher,

we seek your expert opinion on all the above aspects and your suggestions for further improvement of the book.

If you have ever come across a better book on Essays, please intimate us, We value your opinion.

Can Arya-DGP rightfully claim that

LATEST PROBABLE ESSAYS

is the

BEST ESSAY BOOK

You evaluate and judge, we respect your judgement. ????

CONTENTS

Latest Material on G.K. & Current Topics to Help You Write Essays on Hundreds of Topics

The World—At A Glance

India—At A Glance

Indian Economy

Economic Scenario

SOCIAL ISSUES

Health Issues

Educational Issues

Environment Issues

DEFENCE AFFAIRS

SPACE SCIENCE

DEMOGRAPHICS

SPORTS WORLD

THE WORLD—AT A GLANCE

Seventy-one per cent of the earth's surface is covered with water. There are seven continents and Asia is the largest among these. The Pacific, the Atlantic and the Indian are the three great oceans. The Arctic and the Antarctic Oceans around the Poles, remain frozen for a major part of the year.

CONTINENTS OF THE WORLD

S. No.	Continent	Area (in sq.km.)	Highest Elevation	Other Features
1.	Asia	43,998,000	Mt. Everest	Asia is the largest continent. It occupies 29.5 per cent of the land area of the world.
2.	Africa	29,800,000	Mt. Kilimanjaro	Second largest continent. River Nile in Africa is the longest river in the world.
3.	North America	21,510,000	Mt. McKinley	Occupies 16.3 per cent of the total area of the world. It is rich in forest and mineral resources.
4.	South America	17,598,000	Aconcagua Peak	The continent has 1500 species of birds, and deposits of mineral oil also.
5.	Antarctica	13,600,000	Vinson Massif	It is the fifth largest continent and remains permanently covered with ice.
6.	Europe	9,699,550	Mt. Elbrus	Europe has a variety of natural resources. The continent is both populous and prosperous.
7.	Oceania including Australia	7,699,000	Puncak Jaya	It is the only country in the world that covers the entire continent.

About 9 per cent of Antarctica remains covered permanently with ice. About 70 per cent of the world's supply of fresh water is stored in the ice caps and ice sheets of this continent. The land surface is almost barren. Penguins, sea-birds and seals are abundant.

Did You Know? *We have numerous smaller islands, as in the South Pacific, which are located separately. The Oceans, apart from shifting the continents, also took their toll on the edges of these land masses which explains their shapes today. This activity of shifting is still continuing at the rate of one to ten centimeters a year and is one of the reasons why we have earthquakes.*

OCEANS OF THE WORLD

The Oceans are huge bodies of water, which are generally separated by continents. There are four major oceans.

Name	Area (in sq. km.)	Greatest Depth — Location	Greatest Depth (in metres)	Other Features
Pacific Ocean	166,241,000	Mariana Trench	10,920	The Pacific Ocean is bounded by Asia and Australia on the one side and North and South Americas on the other.
Atlantic Ocean	86,557,000	Puerto Rico Trench	8,605	The Atlantic Ocean is bounded by North and South Americas on one side and Europe and Africa on the other.
Indian Ocean	73,427,000	Java Trench	7,125	The Indian Ocean is bounded by land on three sides—Africa in the West, Asia in the North and Australia in the East.
Arctic Ocean	9,485,000	Arctic Basin	5,122	The Arctic Ocean is smallest and shallowest of the world's four major oceans. It is bounded by Greenland, Canada, Alaska, Russia and Norway.

WORLD ORGANISATIONS

The League of Nations

The League of Nations was formed in 1919. The primary objective of the league was the promotion of 'international co-operation, peace and security'. It had 44 members at the time of its inception.

The League of Nations proved to be a failure because the big powers could not settle their disputes amicably. The League of Nations was replaced by the United Nations Organisation (UNO) in 1945.

The United Nations Organisation (UNO)

The United Nations Organisation (UNO), also called the United Nations (UN), came into existence on 24th October, 1945. It was the idea of President F.D. Roosevelt of America and Prime Minister Winston Churchill of Great Britain to create an agency that would work for world peace. Delegates from the USA, Great Britain, former USSR and China met to make a draft proposal in Washington D.C., USA, in October, 1944. They prepared the Charter of the United Nations. Initially 51 nations joined the United Nations. Now it has 193 members. The headquarters of the United Nations is in New York.

Aims of the United Nations are:

- To be a centre for guiding and helping nations,
- To keep peace throughout the world and
- To eliminate poverty, disease and illiteracy from the world.

The principles of the United Nations are:

1. All members must have sovereign equality.
2. All members must obey the charter.
3. Countries must avoid using force or even threatening to use force.

The Organs of the United Nations

The United Nations has six main organs:

1. ***The General Assembly:*** The General Assembly comprises of the representatives of all the member nations. It is like a world parliament. It elects its own President and Vice President every year.
2. ***The Security Council:*** This is the most important organ of the UN. It has 15 members—5 permanent and 10 non-permanent. The five permanent members are: the USA, the UK, France, the People's Republic of China and the Russian Federation. They have the right to Veto, which means that if any of them votes against a popularly passed resolution, it becomes ineffective. The non-permanent members are elected for 2 years only. The Security Council has the primary responsibility to maintain international peace and security.

3. ***The International Court of Justice:*** It is the main judicial organ of the UN and is situated at The Hague in The Netherlands. It has 15 Judges from different countries who are elected for a period of 9 years. They examine the disputes among the member nations and resolve them. They also provide legal advice to the other organs.
4. ***The Secretariat:*** The duties carried out by the Secretariat are as varied as the problems they may encounter. The headquarters of the Secretariat is in New York. The Secretary-General is the administrative head and is appointed by the General Assembly on the recommendation of the Security Council.
5. ***The Economic and Social Council (ECOSOC):*** The Economic and Social Council takes care of the economic and social activities of the UN. The specialised agencies of the UN like the WHO and the UNICEF work under its supervision. The ECOSOC has 54 members. The General Assembly elects 18 members every year for a term of three years.
6. ***The Trusteeship Council:*** The Trusteeship Council was formed to help countries under foreign rule to gain independence. All the trust territories are now independent. The Council will now meet only when it is required.

The United Nations has succeeded in achieving its primary objective. It has prevented large scale wars in many areas. It received the Nobel Peace Prize in 2001 for its achievements in maintaining world peace.

The specialised agencies of the UN have made tremendous contributions to the economic and social development of many member countries.

Some of the other specialised agencies of the UN are: The UN Fund for Population Activities, The UN Environment Programme, The United Nations High Commissioner for Refugees, The International Atomic Energy Agency, The United Nations Industrial Development Organisation, The World Meteorological Organisation and The International Maritime Organisation.

UN SECRETARY-GENERALS

Year	Name	Nation
1946	Trygv Lie	Norway
1953	Dag Hammarskjold	Sweden
1961	U Thant	Burma
1972	Kurt Waldheim	Austria
1982	Javier Peres De Cuellar	Peru
1992	Dr Boutros Boutros Ghali	Egypt
1997	Kofi Annan	Ghana
2007	Ban Ki-Moon	South Korea
2017	Antorio Guterres	Portugal

SPECIALISED AGENCIES OF THE UN				
	Name of the Agency	**Set up in**	**Head-quarters**	**Objectives**
1.	United Nations Educational, Scientific and Cultural Organisation (UNESCO)	1946	Paris	Promotes education, science, culture and communication.
2.	World Health Organisation (WHO)	1948	Geneva	Improves facilities for healthcare throughout the world.
3.	International Labour Organisation (ILO)*	1919	Geneva	Promotes social justice to workers and ensures decent working and living conditions.
4.	Food and Agriculture Organisation (FAO)	1945	Rome	Fights hunger and malnutrition by improving agricultural output across the world.
5.	International Monetary Fund (IMF)	1945	Washington, D.C.	Promotes international monetary co-operation and expansion of international trade.
6.	United Nations Development Programme (UNDP)	1965	New York	Helps developing countries, by training local people to utilise resources and increase wealth.
7.	United Nations International Children's Emergency Fund (UNICEF)	1946	New York	Helps to improve the quality of life of the children all over the world.
8.	World Trade Organisation (WTO) (replaced GATT)	1995	Geneva	International trade body.
9.	International Bank for Reconstruction and Development (IBRD). The International Development Association (IDA)	1946 1960	Washington, D.C.	Collectively known as World Bank, provides a vital source of financial and technical assistance to developing countries around the world.

**ILO, established in 1919 as an autonomous part of the League of Nations, is an inter-governmental agency with a tripartite structure, in which representatives of governments, employers and workers participate.*

YEARS OBSERVED BY THE UNO

1973	:	Copernicus Year
1974	:	World Population Year
1975	:	International Women's Year
1979	:	International Year of the Child
1981	:	International Year of the Disabled
1983	:	World Communication Year
1985	:	International Youth Year
1986	:	International Year of Peace
1987	:	International Year of Shelter for the Homeless
1990	:	International Literacy Year
1992	:	International Space Year
1993	:	International Year for World's Indigenous People
1994	:	International Year of the Family
1995	:	International Year of Tolerance
1996	:	International Year for Eradication of Poverty
1998	:	Human Rights Year
1999	:	Year of Older Persons
2000	:	Year of the Culture of Peace
2001	:	International Year of the Volunteer
2002	:	International Year of Eco-tourism
2003	:	International Year of Fresh Water
2004	:	International Rice Year
2005	:	International Year of Sports and Physical Education
2006	:	International Year of Deserts and Desertification
2007	:	International Year of Dolphins
2008	:	International Year of Sanitation, Planet Earth, Potato, and Sustainable Tourism for Peace and Poverty Eradication
2009	:	International Year of Natural Fibres
2010	:	International Year of Biodiversity and Youth
2011	:	International Year of Forests and Chemistry
2012	:	International Year of Cooperatives
2013	:	International Year of Water Co-operation
2014	:	International Year of Family Farming
2015	:	International Year of Light and Light based Technology
2016	:	International Year of Pulses
2017	:	International Year of Sustainable Tourism for Development
2019	:	International Year of Indigenous Languages

THE WORLD'S FAMOUS OFFICIAL DOCUMENTS

Documents	Countries
Blue Book	Britain
Green Book	Italy and Iran
Grey Book	Japan and Belgium
Orange Book	The Netherlands
White Book	Portugal, China and Germany
White Paper	India
Yellow Book	France

OTHER WORLD ORGANISATIONS

1. **Asian Development Bank (ADB):** The Asian Development Bank started functioning in 1966. Its main aim is to provide concessional credits to needy members. It has 67 members and its headquarters is in Manila, Philippines.
2. **Association of South East Asian Nations (ASEAN):** This is a regional organisation formed by the South East Asian Nations in August, 1967. The main aim is to promote active mutual assistance in economic, cultural, technical, scientific and other fields. It has 10 members and its headquarters is in Jakarta, Indonesia. The members are: Indonesia, Malaysia, the Philippines, Singapore, Thailand, Bruńei, Cambodia, Laos, Myanmar and Vietnam.
3. **BRICS:** BRICS is an association of leading emerging economies, arising out of the inclusion of South Africa into the BRIC group in 2010. The group's five members are Brazil, Russia, India, China and South Africa.
4. **Group of Eight (G-8):** G-8, previously known as G-7 consists of industrially developed and most prosperous countries of the world. It was established in 1975 and its members are Canada, France, Germany, Italy, Japan, The United Kingdom, The United States of America and Russia. They meet periodically to discuss economic and other issues of the world.
5. **Non-Aligned Movement (NAM):** The Non-Aligned Movement is a group of 120 developing nations. It has 17 observer countries. The movement was initiated by Jawaharlal Nehru of India, Josip Broz Tito of Yugoslavia and Gamel Abdel Nasser of Egypt in Bandung (Indonesia). The basic approach of the movement is to favour peace, disarmament, development, eradication of poverty and illiteracy.
6. **Organisation of Petroleum Exporting Countries (OPEC):** The OPEC was created in September, 1960. The OPEC controls oil production to stabilise oil prices. It has 12 members. Its headquarters is in Vienna, Austria.
7. **South Asian Association for Regional Cooperation (SAARC):** The SAARC was formed in December, 1985. The member countries are India, Maldives, Pakistan, Bangladesh, Sri Lanka, Bhutan, Nepal and Afghanistan. It has been formed for the purpose of peace, stability and economic progress in the region through mutual co-operation. Its headquarters is in Kathmandu, Nepal.
8. **North Atlantic Treaty Organisation (NATO):** Formed in 1949 to counter the threat of post-war Communist expansion as the Soviet Union sought to extend its influence in Europe, NATO is the world's most powerful regional defence alliance. Originally, it had twelve members. Now, there are twenty eight members. Its headquarters is in Brussels, Belgium.

9. **International Monetary Fund (IMF):** The International Monetary Fund was established on December 27, 1945 as an independent international organisation and began operations on March 1, 1947. The IMF aims to preserve economic stability and to tackle, or ideally prevent, financial crisis. Over time, its focus has switched to the developing world. Its headquarters is in Washington, D.C.
10. **Interpol:** Interpol is the world's largest international police organisation, with 190 member countries. Created in 1923, it facilitates cross-border police co-operation, and supports and assists all organisations, authorities and services whose mission is to prevent or combat international crime. Its headquarters is in Lyon, France.
11. **International Bank for Reconstruction and Development (IBRD):** Conceived at the Bretton Woods Conference, July 1944, the 'World Bank' began its operations in June 1946. The World Bank is a vital source of financial and technical assistance to developing countries around the world. The World Bank is made up of two unique development institutions owned by 188 member countries—The International Bank for Reconstruction and Development (IBRD) and the International Development Association (IDA). Its headquarters is in Washington, D.C.
12. **Organisation of Arab Petroleum Exporting Countries (OAPEC):** The organisation has 11 members including Egypt which was re-admitted in 1989. Other members are: Algeria, Bahrain, Egypt, Qatar, Libya, Iraq, Kuwait, UAE, Syria, Saudi Arabia, Tunisia.

EURO-ZONE AND BREXIT

The European Union (EU)

The European Union is a politico-economic union of 28 member states that are located primarily in Europe. The EU has developed a single market through a standardised system of laws that apply in all member states. EU policies aim to ensure the free movement of people, goods, services, and capital.

Brexit

The people of Britain voted for a British exit, or Brexit, from the EU in a historic referendum on June 23, 2016. The free movement of citizens is a basic tenet of EU law, as such leaving the bloc was the only sure way for the country to stem a larger-than-expected influx of immigrants.

The Euro

The Euro (€), the official currency of most of the nations of the EU, binds them into a single currency zone (Euro zone) watched over by the European Central Bank (ECB). It leaves budget and tax policy to each member country.

INDIA—AT A GLANCE

THE COUNTRY

India measures 3,214 km from north to south and 2,933 km from east to west with a total land area of 32,87,263 sq. km. It has a land frontier of 15,200 km and a coastline of 7,516.5 km. Andaman and Nicobar Islands in the Bay of Bengal and Lakshadweep in the Arabian Sea, are parts of India. Countries having a common border with India are Afghanistan and Pakistan to the north-west, China, Bhutan and Nepal to the north, Myanmar to the far east and Bangladesh to the east. Sri Lanka is separated from India by a narrow channel of sea formed by the Palk Strait and the Gulf of Mannar.

Official Name	:	Republic of India, Bharat
Form of Government	:	Multiparty Federal Republic
Head of State	:	President
Head of Government	:	Prime Minister
Capital	:	New Delhi
Official Languages	:	English, Hindi and 22 officially recognised languages
Total Area	:	32,87,263 sq. km.*
Extent	:	8°4' to 37°6' North latitudes 68°7' to 97°25' East longitudes
Length from North to South	:	3,214 km
Width from East to West	:	2,933 km
Total Length of Coastline	:	7,516.6 km
Total Population	:	1,210,854,977 million
Population Density	:	382 per sq. km.
Sex Ratio	:	940
Literacy Rate	:	74.04%

NATIONAL SYMBOLS

National Flag

It is, horizontal tricolour having deep saffron (*kesaria*) at the top, white in the middle and dark green at the bottom, in equal proportion. In the centre of the white band is a navy-blue wheel which represents the *chakra*. It has 24 spokes. This Emblem on the flag is an exact reproduction of the *Dharma Chakra* on the Lion Capital of Ashoka's pillar at Sarnath. The ratio of the

**Provisional Figures*
Figures and percentages relating to population are based on Census 2011

width of the flag to its length is two to three. The design of the National Flag was adopted by the Constituent Assembly of India on July 22, 1947.

National Emblem

It is an adaptation from the Sarnath Lion Capital of Ashoka, adopted by the GoI on January 26, 1950. In the original, there are four lions, standing back to back, mounted on an abacus with a frieze carrying sculptures in high relief of an elephant, a galloping horse, a bull and a lion separated by intervening wheels over a bell-shaped lotus. Carved out of a single block of polished sandstone, the Capital is crowned by the Wheel of the Law (*Dharma Chakra*). In the State emblem only three lions are visible, the fourth being hidden from view. There is a *Dharma Chakra* in the centre of the base plate, on the right of which stands a bull and on the left, a horse and the outlines of other wheels on extreme right and left. The bell-shaped lotus has been omitted. The words '*Satyameva Jayate*' from the *Mundaka Upanishad,* meaning 'Truth Alone Triumphs' are inscribed below the abacus in *Devanagari* script.

National Anthem

The song *Jana-gana-mana*, composed originally in Bengali by Rabindranath Tagore, was adopted in its Hindi version by the Constituent Assembly as the National Anthem of India on January 24, 1950. The complete song consists of five stanzas of which, the first stanza contains the full version of the *National Anthem.* Playing time of the full version of the *National Anthem* is approximately 52 seconds.

National Song

The song *Vande Mataram*, composed in Sanskrit by Bankimchandra Chatterji is the National Song of India. It was first sung at the 1896 session of the Indian National Congress. It has an equal status with *Jana-gana-mana.*

National Calendar

The National Calendar based on the *Saka Era,* with *Chaitra* as its first month and a normal year of 365 days, was adopted from March 22, 1957. *Phalguna* is the last month of the year. Dates of the national calendar have a permanent correspondence with the dates of the Gregorian calendar.

National Animal

The magnificent Tiger is the National Animal of India. It has a thick yellow coat of fur with dark stripes. It exhibits a combination of grace, strength, agility and enormous power.

National Bird

The Indian Peacock is the National Bird of India. It is a colourful, swan-sized bird, with a glistening blue breast and neck and a spectacular bronze-green tail of around 200 elongated feathers.

National Flower

The Lotus is the National Flower of India. It is a sacred flower, an auspicious symbol of Indian culture and occupies a unique place in the art and mythology of ancient India.

National Tree

The Banyan Tree is the National Tree of India. This huge tree towers over its neighbours and has the widest reaching roots of all known trees, easily covering several acres. It sends out new shoots from its roots, such that one tree is practically a tangle of branches, roots, and trunks.

National Fruit

Mango is the National Fruit of India. Mango is one of the most widely grown fruits of the tropical countries. In India, mango is cultivated almost in all parts, with the exception of hilly areas. Mango is a rich source of Vitamins A, C and D. In India, we have hundreds of varieties of mangoes. They are of different sizes, shapes and colours. Mangoes have been cultivated in India since time immemorial.

National Sports

Hockey is India's national game. India had won the first Olympic hockey gold in 1928, in Amsterdam, defeating The Netherlands 3-0.

National Heritage Animal

The Elephant has been declared the national heritage animal by the Government with the aim to step up measures for its protection. A notification in this regard was issued by the Environment Ministry on October 22, 2010. According to the task force, there are over 25,000 elephants in the country, including 3,500 in captivity in zoos and temples—particularly in southern and north-eastern parts of the country.

National Currency

The symbol, '₹', is a combination of both Devanagiri letter 'Ra' and Roman letter 'R' with a stripe cutting at the middle to represent the tricolour. It also means equality.

National Monument

India Gate, one of the largest war memorials, situated in the heart of New Delhi, is the national monument of India. It was erected in memory of 90,000 soldiers who lost their lives fighting in the World War I and Afghan War for the British Army. It was designed by Sir Edwin Lutyens. Earlier it was called All India War Memorial.

National River

The Ganga or Ganges is the longest river of India flowing over 2,510 kms of mountains, valleys and plains. It originates in the snowfields of the Gangotri Glacier in the Himalayas as the 'Bhagirathi River'. It is later joined by other rivers such as the Alaknanda, Yamuna, Son, Gumti, Kosi and Ghagra. The Ganga river basin is one of the most fertile and densely populated areas of the world and covers an area of 1,000,000 sq. kms. The Ganga is revered by Hindus as the most sacred river on earth.

INDIAN LANGUAGES

Languages offered a special problem to the makers of the Constitution simply because of the plurality of languages used by the vast population. India is believed to have 1,652 spoken languages, including 63 non-Indian languages.

The makers of the Constitution had, therefore, to select some of these languages as the recognised medium of official communication. Fortunately for them, the number of people speaking each of these 1,652 languages was not anything like proportionate and some 18 languages (included in the 8th Schedule of the Constitution) could easily be picked up as the major languages of India, used by 91 per cent of the total population of the country. Out of these, Hindi, including Urdu and Hindustani, is spoken by 46 per cent. Hindi is accordingly prescribed as the official language of India (subject to the continuance of English for the same purpose for the limited period of 15 years), and, for the development of Hindi language as a medium of expression for all the elements of the composite culture of India, the assimilation of the expressions used in the other languages specified in the Eighth Schedule was recommended [Article 351].

8th Schedule Languages

The 8th Schedule was added to the Constitution to indicate all regional languages statutorily recognised. The Schedule contains 22 languages as follows:

(1)	Assamese	(12)	Tamil
(2)	Bengali	(13)	Telugu
(3)	Gujarati	(14)	Urdu
(4)	Hindi	(15)	Sindhi*
(5)	Kannada	(16)	Konkani**
(6)	Kashmiri	(17)	Manipuri**
(7)	Malayalam	(18)	Nepali**
(8)	Marathi	(19)	Bodo***
(9)	Oriya	(20)	Dogri***
(10)	Punjabi	(21)	Maithili***
(11)	Sanskrit	(22)	Santhali***

*Added by the Constitution (21st Amendment) Act, 1967

**Added by the Constitution (71st Amendment) Act, 1992

***Added by the Constitution (92nd Amendment) Act, 2003

INDIA: A UNION OF STATES

India, a Union of States, is a Sovereign Socialist Secular Democratic Republic with a parliamentary system of government. The Republic is governed in terms of the Constitution, which was adopted by the Constituent Assembly on November 26, 1949 and came into force on January 26, 1950.

The Constitution, which envisages parliamentary form of government, is federal in structure with unitary features. The President of India is the constitutional head of the Executive of the Union. Article 74 (1) of the Constitution provides that there shall be a Council of Ministers with the Prime Minister as the head to aid and advise the President who shall, in the exercise of his functions, act in accordance with such advice. Real executive power thus vests in the Council of Ministers with the Prime Minister as the head. The Council of Ministers is collectively responsible to the House of the People (Lok Sabha). Similarly, in the states, the Governor is head of the executive, but it is the Council of Ministers with the Chief Minister as the head in whom the real executive power is vested. The Council of Ministers of a state is collectively responsible to the Legislative Assembly.

The Constitution distributes legislative power between the Parliament and the state legislatures and provides for vesting of residual powers in the Parliament. The power to amend the Constitution also vests in the Parliament. The Constitution has provision for the independence of the Judiciary, the Comptroller and Auditor-General, the Public Service Commissions and the Chief Election Commissioner.

The Union of India comprises of 29 States and 7 Union Territories.

The States are:

Andhra Pradesh	Jharkhand	Punjab
Asom	Karnataka	Rajasthan
Arunachal Pradesh	Kerala	Sikkim
Bihar	Madhya Pradesh	Tamil Nadu
Chhattisgarh	Maharashtra	Telangana
Goa	Manipur	Tripura
Gujarat	Meghalaya	Uttarakhand
Haryana	Mizoram	Uttar Pradesh
Himachal Pradesh	Nagaland	West Bengal
Jammu and Kashmir	Odisha	

The Union Territories are:

Andaman and Nicobar Islands	National Capital Territory of Delhi
Chandigarh	Lakshadweep
Dadra and Nagar Haveli	Puducherry
Daman and Diu	

INDIA—BASIC DATA*

States	Capital	Area (sq. km.)	Population** (2011)	Density per km^2	Sex Ratio	Literacy (%)
Andhra Pradesh@	Hyderabad	2,75,069	84,665,533	308	992	67.00
Arunachal Pradesh	Itanagar	83,743	1,382,611	17	920	65.04
Asom	Dispur	78,438	31,169,272	398	954	72.02
Bihar	Patna	94,163	103,804,637	1,102	916	61.08
Chhattisgarh	Raipur	1,35,192	25,540,196	189	991	70.03
Goa	Panaji	3,702	1,457,723	394	968	88.07
Gujarat	Gandhinagar	1,96,024	60,383,628	308	918	78.00
Haryana	Chandigarh	44,212	25,353,081	573	877	75.06
Himachal Pradesh	Shimla	55,673	6,856,509	123	974	82.08
Jammu & Kashmir	Srinagar (Summer), Jammu (Winter)	2,22,236	12,548,926	124	883	67.02
Jharkhand	Ranchi	79,716	32,966,238	414	947	66.04
Karnataka	Bengaluru	1,91,791	61,130,704	319	968	75.04
Kerala	Thiruvananthapuram	38,852	33,387,677	860	1,084	94.00
Madhya Pradesh	Bhopal	3,08,252	72,597,565	236	930	69.03
Maharashtra	Mumbai	3,07,713	112,372,972	365	925	82.03
Manipur	Imphal	22,327	2,721,756	115	987	79.02
Meghalaya	Shillong	22,429	2,964,007	132	986	74.04
Mizoram	Aizawl	21,081	1,091,014	52	975	91.03
Nagaland	Kohima	16,579	1,980,602	119	931	79.06
Odisha	Bhubaneswar	1,55,707	41,947,358	270	978	72.09
Punjab	Chandigarh	50,362	27,704,236	551	893	75.08
Rajasthan	Jaipur	3,42,239	68,621,012	200	926	66.01
Sikkim	Gangtok	7,096	607,688	86	889	81.04
Tamil Nadu	Chennai	1,30,060	72,138,958	555	995	80.01
Tripura	Agartala	10,486	3,671,032	350	961	87.02
Uttarakhand	Dehradun	53,483	10,116,752	189	963	78.08
Uttar Pradesh	Lucknow	2,36,286	199,581,477	829	908	67.07
West Bengal	Kolkata	88,752	91,347,736	1,028	947	76.03
Union Territories						
NCT of Delhi	Delhi	1,483	16,753,235	11,297	866	86.02
Andaman & Nicobar	Port Blair	8,249	379,944	46	878	86.06
Chandigarh	Chandigarh	114	1,054,686	9,252	818	86.00
Dadra & Nagar Haveli	Silvassa	491	342,853	698	775	76.02
Daman & Diu	Daman	111	242,911	2,169	618	87.01
Lakshadweep	Kavaratti	30	64,429	2,013	946	91.08
Puducherry	Puducherry	490	1,244,464	2,598	1,038	85.08
India	New Delhi	32,87,263#	1,210,854,977	382	940	74.04

@On June 2, 2014, the new state of Telangana was created out of Andhra Pradesh. The basic data for the two states is as follows:

State	Capital	Area (sq. km.)	Population
Andhra Pradesh	Amravati (Hyderabad till 2024)	1,60,200	49,386,799
Telangana	Hyderabad	1,14,840	35,193,978

Source: *Census 2011, **India 2016
#Provisional Figures

SPECIAL STATUS OF JAMMU & KASHMIR AND ARTICLE 370

Provisions Under the Article

- It was a temporary provision included in the Constitution of India, granting special status to J&K. The provision was introduced after Maharaja Hari Singh signed the Instrument of Accession with the Indian Union in 1947.
- Dr BR Ambedkar, the architect of Indian Constitution and the first Law Minister of India, refused to draft Article 370. It was drafted by Gopalaswami Ayyangar, former 'dewan' of Maharaja Hari Singh along with Sheikh Mohammad Abdullah, the National Conference founder. Ayyangar was a minister in the Cabinet of then Prime Minister Jawaharlal Nehru.
- According to the Article, except for defence, foreign affairs and communications, Indian Parliament needs the consent of the state's legislature to implement laws of the Indian Union in the State.
- J&K has a separate constitution and flag. The Article imposes limits on the legislative power of Indian Parliament over the State. Special measures are required to extend any ordinary legislation to the State.
- Citizens of other states of India cannot purchase land or property in the State. Further, the Centre has no power to declare financial emergency in J&K. It can declare emergency only in case of war and external aggression.
- Residents of J&K live under a separate set of laws, They enjoy dual citizenship. They would lose their J&K citizenship if they marry residents of other states. However, the women of the State can retain their citizenship rights if they marry non-permanent residents of the state because of the High Court judgment in 2003. But her husband and children cannot enjoy the same rights.
- The term of the State legislature is six years, unlike other elected bodies which have a five-year period. The State Assembly had a five-year term but was extended to six years during the emergency on the pattern of Parliament in 1976. But it did not revert because of the special status.
- A Pakistani woman gains citizenship if she marries a citizen of J&K. However, lakhs of West Pakistan refugees living in the state for over six decades have been denied citizenship as they migrated from Sialkote and West Punjab (Pakistan), which was not part of J&K. The Article prevents them from enjoying their fundamental rights.

Source: A leading national daily

TELANGANA—THE COUNTRY'S 29TH STATE

Some Facts and Figures

Location:	Falls between two rivers—Krishna and Godavari
Neighbours:	Shares boundaries with Andhra Pradesh, Maharashtra, Karnataka, Chhattisgarh and Odisha
Size:	India's 12th largest in terms of area (1.14 lakh sq km) and population (3.52 crore)
Assembly seats:	119; **Lok Sabha Seats**: 17; **Founded:** June 2, 2014
Districts:	Adilabad, Nizamabad, Karimnagar, Medak, Khammam, Mahaboobnagar, Warangal, Ranga Ready, Nalgonda and Hyderabad
Capital:	Hyderabad (Will also be capital of Andhra Pradesh for 10 years)
Religions:	Hindus (86%), Muslims (12.4%), Christians (1.2%)
Languages:	Telugu (76%), Urdu (12%), Others (12%)
Literacy:	67.2% (Male 75.2%, Female 58.77%)

NATIONAL JUDICIAL APPOINTMENT COMMISSION

Both Judiciary and Executive to Get Equal Say and Veto Power

The Union Cabinet on August 6, 2014 cleared a constitutional amendment bill to provide for National Judicial Appointment Commission (NJAC) which proposes to radically change the process of appointment of judges by giving both the judiciary and the executive equal say and veto power.

The six-member NJAC will comprise—the Chief Justice of India (CJI), the two senior-most judges of the Supreme Court, law and justice minister and two eminent persons. The choice of 'eminent persons' will be made by a high-powered committee comprising the Prime Minister, CJI and leader of opposition or the leader of the largest party in opposition.

The two eminent persons will have a tenure of three years and one of them would be from one of the following categories: Scheduled Castes, Scheduled Tribes, women or minority community.

INDIAN ECONOMY

PLANNING COMMISSION

In 1950, the government of India set up the planning Commission with the Prime Minister as the Chairman. It had a few Central Ministers and a few non-official experts as Members. There were no state representatives as such on the commission which could thus be regarded as a purely central organ. The role of the commission was advisory.

NITI AAYOG

The Narendra Modi government on January 1, 2015 replaced the 65-year-old Planning Commission with a new body called *NITI* (National Institution for Transforming India) *Aayog* (Commission) that is mandated to provide "governments at the Central and state levels with relevant strategic and technical advice on key elements of policy."

The Prime Minister will be the Chairperson of the NITI Aayog whose Governing Council will comprise all Chief Ministers and Lt. Governors (of UTs) in an exercise envisaged by the Centre to involve states in working out and pushing national development agenda and priorities in a spirit of 'co-operative federalism'.

It will have five full-time members. The noted economist Arvind Panagariya has been appointed by the PM as the NITI Aayog's first Vice Chairman. The Aayog would have four Union Ministers as ex-officio Members and three Union Ministers as special invitees.

FIVE-YEAR PLANS/ANNUAL PLANS AT A GLANCE

Plan and Period	Main Objectives
First Plan *(1951-56)*	• To restore the economy which had run down. • Priority was given to agriculture and irrigation.
Second Plan *(1956-61)*	• Rapid industrialisation with emphasis on the production of iron and steel. • Reduction in inequalities in income and wealth.
Third Plan *(1961-66)*	• To increase agricultural production and achieve self-sufficiency in foodgrains. • To expand basic and key industries. • To make optimum use of the manpower resources.
Annual Plans	• 1966-67 to 1968-69.
Fourth Plan *(1969-74)*	• To achieve self-reliance. • To pay special attention to agricultural activities which have been neglected.
Fifth Plan *(1974-79)*	• Removal of poverty and achievement of self-reliance.
Annual Plans *(1979-80)*	• The Annual Plans were made by the Janata Government.

Sixth Plan *(1980-85)*	• Reduction in poverty, unemployment and regional inequalities. • Population control.
Seventh Plan *(1985-90)*	• Rapid growth in food production, employment opportunities and productivity.
Annual Plans *(1990-92)*	• The Eighth Plan could not take off due to political instability at the Centre. Therefore, these two years were assessed by Annual Plans.
Eighth Plan *(1992-97)*	• To achieve full employment by the turn of the century. • Strengthening of infrastructure.
Ninth Plan *(1997-2002)*	• Priority to agriculture and rural development. • Accelerating the growth rate of the economy with stable prices. • Ensuring basic facilities to the vulnerable sections of the society. • Empowerment of women and backward class people.
Tenth Plan *(2002-07)*	• Reduction of poverty ratio by 5 percentage points by 2007 and by 15 percentage points by 2012. • Providing gainful and high quality employment at least in addition to the labour force over the Plan period. • All children in school by 2003; all children to complete 5 years of schooling by 2007. • Reduction in gender gaps in literacy and wage rates by at least 50 per cent by 2007. • Reduction in the decadal rate of population growth between 2001 and 2011 to 16.2 per cent. • Reduction of infant mortality rate to 45 per 1000 live births by 2007 and to 28 by 2012.
Eleventh Plan *(2007-12)*	• To accelerate GDP growth from 8 per cent to 9 per cent. • To create 70 million new work opportunities. • To reduce educated unemployment to below 5 per cent. • To raise real wage rate of unskilled workers by 20 per cent. • To reduce infant mortality rate to 28 and maternal mortality rate to 1 per 1000 live births. • To ensure electricity connections to all villages and BPL households by 2009.
Twelfth Plan *(2012-17)*	• Connecting slow growth regions and remote areas (e.g., the tribal belt, the North-east, the Gangetic Plain and Kashmir) to the fast-growing mainstream economy. • Providing top-quality vocational training for young workers. • Reconstructing the plethora of anti-poverty and affirmative action programmes as a structured social security system. • Moving Indian agriculture from a low-productivity, staple producing system to a rising productivity, commercially oriented sector. • Reinventing the process and management of urbanisation. • Building much stronger economic links with China and East Asia. • Managing emerging stresses in the water economy. • Coping with the risk of climate change.

FINANCE COMMISSION

Article 280 provides for the appointment, by the President, of a Finance Commission consisting of a Chairman and four Members, every five years. The Commission shall make recommendations to the President in regard to the distribution of proceeds between the Union and the states and to suggest principles which should govern the grants-in-aid to the states from the Consolidated Fund of India.

CHRONOLOGY OF FINANCE COMMISSIONS				
Finance Commission	**Year of Establishment**	**Year of Reporting**	**Period of Award**	**Name of the Chairman**
First	November 1951	December 1952	1952-1957	K. C. Neogy
Second	June 1956	September 1957	1957-1962	K. Santhanam
Third	December 1960	December 1961	1962-1966	A. K. Chanda
Fourth	May 1964	August 1965	1966-1969	P. V. Rahamannar
Fifth	February 1968	July 1969	1969-1974	Mahavir Tyagi
Sixth	June 1972	October 1973	1974-1979	K. Brahmananda Reddy
Seventh	June 1977	October 1978	1979-1984	Justice J. M. Shelat
Eighth	June 1982	April 1984	1984-1989	Y. B. Chavan
Ninth	June 1987	July 1988	1989-1995	N. K. P. Salve
Tenth	June 1992	November 1994	1995-2000	K. C. Pant
Eleventh	June 1997	July 2000	2000-2005	A. M. Khusro
Twelfth	November 2002	November 2004	2005-2010	Dr C. Rangarajan
Thirteenth	November 2007	October 2009	2010-2015	Dr Vijay L. Kelkar
Fourteenth	January 2013	October 2014	2015-2020	Y. V. Reddy

14TH FINANCE COMMISSION

The government on January 2, 2013 constituted the 14th Finance Commission under the chairmanship of former RBI governor Y V Reddy, which, *inter alia*, will suggest steps for pricing of public utilities like electricity and water in an independent manner. The Commission, will look into issues like disinvestment, GST compensation, sale of non-priority PSUs and subsidies.

The recommendations of the Commission, set up under the provisions of the Constitution on sharing of tax proceeds between the Union and states, will apply for the period beginning from April 1, 2015.

Among other things, the Commission would look into the "need for insulating the pricing of public utility services like drinking water, irrigation, power and public transport from policy fluctuations through statutory provisions."

Finance Commission is set up every five years to suggest principles, governing the distribution of tax proceeds among Centre, states and local bodies.

MAJOR PROBLEMS OF INDIAN ECONOMY

1. ***Population*** : India is passing through the phase of population explosion. India's landscape constitutes just 2.4 per cent of the total world area, whereas its population is nearly 16.85 per cent of the world population.
2. ***Poverty*** : It is a social phenomenon in which a section of the society is unable to fulfil even its basic necessities of life. In India, the number of the poor is very large and they have very low productivity. Causes of poverty are rising population, lack of employment opportunities, illiteracy and inadequacy of anti-poverty programmes.
3. ***Unemployment*** : Unemployment means idleness of manpower. Backwardness of the Indian economy and increasing population are mainly responsible for this problem.
4. ***Fiscal Deficit*** : Fiscal deficit is the excess of total expenditure over revenue receipts and grants. It measures the additional liabilities of the Government of India.
5. ***Inflation*** : The price rise that has prevailed for many years and continues to do so, at present, is harmful for the country.

AGRICULTURE AND INDIAN FARMERS' PLIGHT

Indian agriculture and rural society have been passing through a phase of transition since the introduction of the neo liberal policy in 1991. This transition is reflected not only in the sharp decline in the share of agriculture in the GDP from 30 per cent in 1990-91 to 14 per cent in 2014-15, but also in the high level of agrarian stress on the peasantry, especially the small, marginal and tenant cultivators and agricultural labourers.

More than 3 lakh cultivators have committed suicide since 1997. There is decline in the absolute number of the workforce engaged in agriculture, which is caused by the fast rate of mechanisation, such as tractors for ploughing and harvester combines for harvesting.

It is high time that the magnitude of this crisis is understood and suitable policies are devised. India must plan this structural change by investing in agricultural infrastructure, and support to research and extension. Much more needs to be done to resurrect rural education and healthcare. Serious thought is also needed for the introduction of co-operative farming, as suggested by the Expert Committee on Agriculture, and the generation of rural non-farm employment.

RESERVE BANK OF INDIA

The primary duty of central banks is to regulate the flow of money. The RBI (the Central Bank of India) however, has a few associate roles, making the job of its chief more difficult. Here's a low-down.

MONETARY POLICY

- The central bank uses monetary tools to influence demand and prices.
- In times of weak growth and low prices, it is usual for the RBI to cut interest rates to goad companies to invest, add capacities, hire more, and prompt people to spend on houses, cars and other goods.
- When inflation is high, it raises interest rates to temper demand and cool prices.
- The government and the RBI have agreed on a new monetary policy framework that makes containing inflation the central bank's topmost duty.
- A six-member panel headed by the RBI governor will decide on interest rate decisions to keep inflation between 2% to 6% in the next five years.

BANK AND WATCHDOG

- Banks have to fulfil customers' cash requirements as billions move around every day.
- Banks need a mechanism to transfer money and settle transactions. As the banker to banks, the RBI oversees this system.
- The RBI is also the 'lender of last resort' to stay solvent, the RBI can come to its rescue to protect the depositors' interests.

GOVERNMENT'S BANKER

- Managing the Central and state government's banking transactions is a key role of the RBI.
- This sometimes brings it in conflict with its other major task of controlling inflation.
- The RBI also has to ensure that the money borrowed by the government's does not "crowd out" private investment.
- The RBI is a regulator and trader of government securities.

CURRENCY CUSTODIAN

- As the currency administrator, it prints money, and as the custodian of foreign exchange reserves, it is responsible for preventing volatility in currency markets.
- Banks, corporations, brokers, individuals and governments buy and sell currencies every day. That explains the daily fluctuations in the currency prices.
- The RBI has a responsibility to protect the economy from currency shocks.
- Central banks world over intervene through buying or selling of currencies through banks. To prop up a weak rupee, the RBI sells dollars and vice versa.

ECONOMIC SCENARIO

INDIA'S HDI RANKING AMONG G20 ECONOMIES

Among G20 economies, India is ranked lowest in Human Development Index ranking. India might be the third largest and the fastest growing economy among G20 countries, but it has miles to go to match the living standard of the other member states. By the yardstick of Human Development Index—a composite index that measures quality of life in a country by taking into account parameters like life expectancy, education, per capita income and so on—India is ranked the last.

VARIOUS INDICATORS FOR G20 ECONOMIES FOR 2016

Country	Population in Million	HDI Ranking in 2014	GDP per capita (PPP 1,000$)	GDP % of the World
Australia	24	2	48.2	1.0
Germany	83	6	47.5	3.3
United States	324	8	57.2	15.4
Canada	36	9	46.2	1.4
United Kingdom	66	14	42.0	2.3
Korea	51	17	37.7	1.6
Japan	127	20	38.7	4.1
France	65	22	41.9	2.2
Italy	61	27	36.2	1.8
EU (non G20)	236	30	34.6	6.8
Saudi Arabia	32	39	53.7	1.4
Argentina	44	40	22.3	0.8
Russia	146	50	25.2	3.1
Turkey	79	72	21.2	1.4
Mexico	129	74	17.9	1.9
Brazil	206	75	15.0	2.6
China	1,381	90	15.1	17.4
Indonesia	259	110	11.6	2.5
South Africa	56	116	13.2	0.6
India	**1,310**	**130**	**6.6**	**7.2**

Source: IMF, HDR Report 2015

JAM TRINITY—JAN DHAN, AADHAAR, MOBILE

Large-scale, technology-enabled, real-time Direct Benefit Transfers can improve the economic lives of India's poor, and the JAM Trinity — Jan Dhan, Aadhaar, Mobile — can help government implement them.

Important Facts Related to the Programme are:

- *Aadhaar:* 210 million Aadhaar cards were created in 2015, at the rate of over 4 million cards per week. 980 million individuals hold an Aadhaar card as of March 2, 2016.
- *Mobile:* Innovative use of mobile technology in e-governance. It seeks to ensure a mobile phone in every hand and provide in-hand access to government schemes.
- *Pradhan Mantri Jan Dhan Yojana:* Under it, nearly 120 million accounts were created in the year 2014-15 alone — at a pace of over 3 lakh accounts per day.
- *JAM scale and Distribution:* JAM was involved in distributing benefits across a range of government programmes—from education and labour schemes (scholarships and MGNREGS) to subsidies and pensions (National Social Assistance Programme).
- Only 27 per cent of villages have a bank within a radius of 5 km. To address this problem, the RBI in 2015 licensed 23 new banks — 2 universal banks, 11 payment banks and 10 small finance banks.

Direct Benefit Transfer (DBT) in LPG—The First Type of JAM

Government launched the 'Pahal Scheme'—which directly transfers LPG subsidies into customers' bank accounts, in the late 2014 and early 2015. With DBT in place, the government identifies beneficiaries by linking households' LPG customer numbers with Aadhaar numbers to eliminate 'ghost' and duplicate households from beneficiary rolls. Households buy at market prices, and have the subsidy credited into their bank account within 3 days. Pahal resulted in a 27 per cent reduction in sale of subsidised cylinders, with the maximum exclusion being of those ghost households. Thus, JAM in LPG has succeeded in reducing leakages. The Pahal scheme has been a big success. The use of Aadhaar has almost eliminated the black market. At present, the most promising targets for JAM are fertiliser subsidies and intra-government fund transfers.

GST COUNCIL

Cabinet Nod to GST Council

Moving on fast track to roll out the Goods and Services Tax (GST) regime from April 1, 2017, the Union Cabinet on September 12, 2016 approved setting up of the all-powerful GST Council, which will decide on the tax rate, exempted goods and the threshold.

The GST Council will consist of the Union Finance Minister, Minister of

State in charge of Revenue Department and State Finance Ministers. The Union Revenue Secretary will be the ex-officio secretary, but will have no voting rights. As per Article 279A of the amended Constitution, the GST Council will be a joint forum of the Centre and states.

All-powerful Body

- GST Council will make recommendations to the Union and states on important issues like goods and services that may be subjected to tax or exempted, principles governing place of supply, thresholds GST rates, etc.
- The Cabinet decided to provide for adequate funds for meeting the recurring and non-recurring expenses of GST Council Secretariat. It shall be manned by officers on deputation from Central and state governments.

GST EXEMPTION LIMIT AT ₹ 20 LAKH

No Tax For Businesses With Annual Turnover Below Threshold

Striking political consensus,the GST Council on September 23, 2016 said business, with an annual turnover of less ₹20 lakh will be exempted from the goods and services tax (GST). The threshold will be ₹10 lakh in the north-eastern and hill states.

The council headed by finance minister Arun Jaitley also decided that state authorities will have jurisdiction over assessees with annual turnover of less than ₹1.5 crore. For those with turnover of over ₹1.5 crore, there would be cross examination by officers from either states or the Centre to avoid dual control.

However, the power for assessment of 11 lakh service tax assesses, who are currently assessed by the Centre, would remain with it. New assessees would be divided between the Centre and states.

All state finance ministers are members of the GST Council.

The Council has also decided to keep financial year 2015-2016 as the base year for compensating in case of any revenue loss to states following GST's implementation.

GREAT JOB PROSPECTS

5-10 Million Jobs Set to Come up in 3-4 Years

Headhunters, are estimating that 5 to 10 million jobs are likely to be thrown up over the next three to four years.

With foreign direct investment limits being raised in several sectors, insurance, defence, infrastructure, construction and agriculture are likely to emerge as hotspots for hiring and employment seekers.

Further, FDI in manufacturing sector will also boost job creation in a major way. The new budget will help in the creation of 5 to 8 million jobs across sectors in the next 3 to 4 years, Increasing the FDI in the insurance sector will help create entry-level jobs.

With the GDP growth expected to reach 7-8%, in coming 3 to 4 years, about 10 million jobs would be created, primarily in manufacturing, infrastructure and insurance sectors.

The proposed investment of ₹500 crore to set up IITs and IIMs is expected to meet the huge demand for skilled workforce in India.

LIGHTING UP THE JOB MARKET

Provisions to increase foreign investment in several sectors, has created a stir in the human resource community

WHERE THE JOBS ARE GOING	MOOD SWINGERS
• Insurance • Defence • Infrastructure • Construction • Manufacturing • Agriculture	• Government viewed as pro-business, pro-investment • Foreign investors upbeat on relaxed FDI norms in insurance, infrastructure • Big push for start-up companies

SIGNALS
• GDP growth prospects to improve to 7-8% in short term, from 5.8%. • National multi-skill plan to empower youth with employability and entrepreneurial skills. • ₹ 500 crore proposal to set up new IITs and IIMs. • ₹10,000 crore proposed venture capital fund for seeding micro and small enterprises. • Emphasis on manufacturing and labour-intensive sectors with liberal imports of components that aid local manufacture in India.

SOCIAL ISSUES

RAPE—THE FASTEST GROWING CRIME

Rape is a notoriously under-reported crime, thanks to its social stigma. Yet, of all the major crimes, the incidence of rape has registered the highest growth in the country in the last four decades.

The case of the brutal gangrape on the night of 16th December, 2012 stirred the collective conscience of the country and resulted in the uprising of the younger generation, with unprecedented numbers out on the streets, forced the government to announce a slew of measures to ensure the safety of the fairer sex and safeguard their honour. The complete system was put under the scanner and a committee under Justice J S Verma was set up to suggest improvement in the existing laws to effect deterrence from sexual offences.

One Rape Every 30 Minutes in India

Even as an increasing number of violent crimes against women, especially rape, continue to be reported across the country, a 13-year analysis of crime data reveals that a little more than 57 rapes were reported every day. These averages at over two rapes every hour, every day during the last 13 years. A total of 2,72,844 cases were reported across 28 states and seven UTs in this period.

ALARMING INCREASE

- MP reported 40,422 cases, highest in 13-year period
- West Bengal next with 22,472 cases, but the only state to see a drop in 2013 figures compared to 2012

8,060
no. of rapes in Delhi despite state being smaller in size compared to Tamil Nadu (7,875), Karnataka (6,204), and Gujarat (4,981)

- UP followed with 22,108 rapes; Maharashtra next with 21,049 cases
- 1,14,785 rape cases were under trial in 2013—a 12% rise over 2012

Cases under Protection of Children from Sexual Offences Act (POCSO)

Rape Cases

63% increase in rape cases in 2015 against 2014

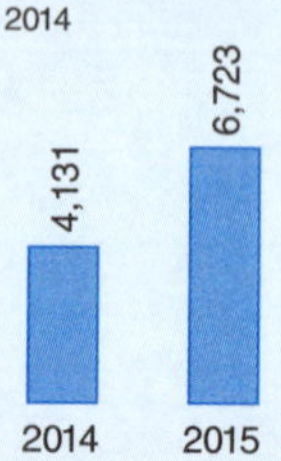

Molestation Cases

75% increase in cases of molestation in 2015 against 2014

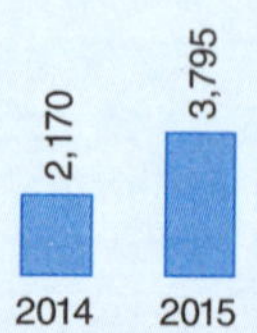

Poor legal support and social pressure has resulted in a uniformly high acquittal rate

RAPE CASES		
Year	Acquitted	Convicted
2014	185	51
2015	522	361

MOLESTATION CASES		
Year	Acquitted	Convicted
2014	48	17
2015	260	241

FOUR MINORS ARE RAPED EVERY DAY

UNSAFE FOR KIDS

Fewer children were brutalised in 2015 than 2014. Yet, 451 girls were raped before they could celebrate their sixth birthday, and another 1,151, before their twelfth.

- 11,393, children were raped in 2015
- 8,341, of attackers knew the victim's family
- 8,800, rape cases where POCSO was invoked

SEXUAL ASSAULT CASES

Total : 8,833

A girl, not old enough to begin primary school, and three others yet to enter their teens, were raped every day in 2015

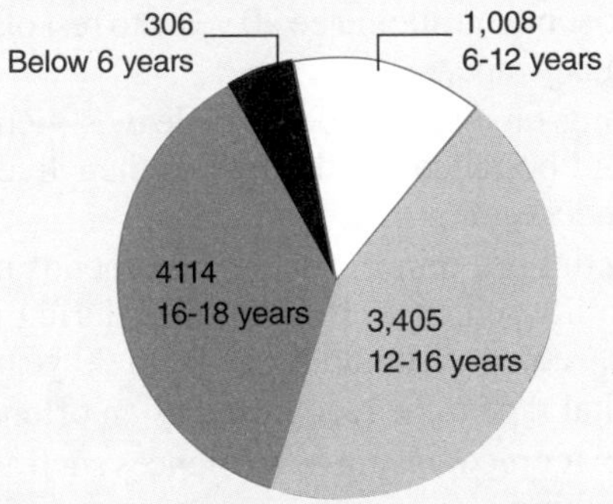

AGE OF CULPRITS

Total Arrested: 18,651

Age	Male	Female	Total
Below 18	492	2	494
18-30 years	11,768	71	11,839
30-45 years	5,044	113	5,157
45-60 years	1,067	19	1,086
Above 60	72	3	75

PROFILE OF CRIMINALS

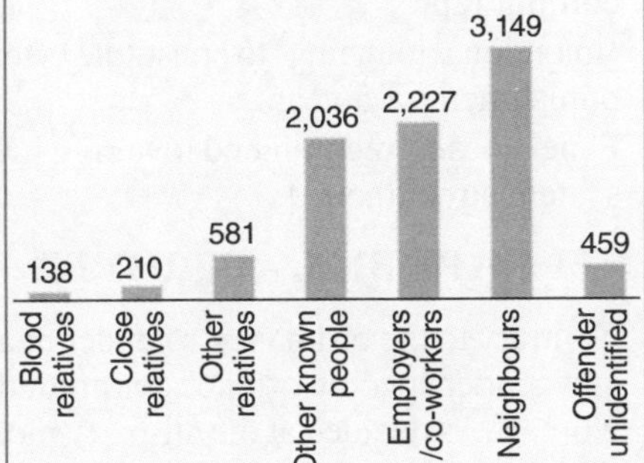

Source: National Crime Records Bureau Report : Crime in India 2015

"I know I can beat a molester to pulp and that might help me fight the deep sense of being defiled but why should it even come to that ? Desire is beautiful when it is reciprocal. We have often heard the explanation 'boys will be boys'. Let's build a society where girls can be safe, secure and respected."

— Mary Com, MP& Boxer

VERMA COMMITTEE REPORT

Harsher Punishment Suggested for Sexual Crimes

Justice J S Verma Committee set up after the December 16, 2012 incident, released its eagerly awaited report on January 23, 2013. It has raised the bar of punishment for a wide range of existing and proposed sexual offences even as it rejected the demand for introducing death for rape.

- Justice Verma panel rejects death penalty for rape, retains existing punishment of 7 years to life sentence (in which convict may be released after 14 years at government's discretion).
- But if rape causes death or leaves the victim in a vegetative state, imprisonment should be 20 years to rest of convict's life. Same punishment for gang-rape.
- If gang-rape causes death or leaves victim in vegetative state, convicts should be jailed for the rest of their lives. Same punishment for repeat offenders.
- If victim is a minor, panel recommends minimum of 10 years jail, going up to life sentence. If minor dies during rape or is reduced to vegetative state, sentence should range from 20 years to the rest of convict's life.
- Marital rape to be recognised as an offence for women of all ages.
- Panel for recognising new offences such as disrobing a woman, trafficking & stalking.
- Introduces offence of 'breach of command responsibility', making a senior officer of security forces liable to jail of 7–10 years if subordinates commit rape.
- 'Intentional touching' to constitute offence of sexual assault with maximum punishment of 5 years.
- Panel doesn't recommend lowering juvenile age but wants juvenile justice system strengthened.

ANTI-RAPE BILL APPROVED BY PARLIAMENT

- Contrary to the ordinance's gender neutral definition, the Bill regards rape as a gender specific offence committed by a man and where the victim is a woman. As decided at the all-party meeting, the age of consent is 18 years.
- Though the ordinance increased the maximum age for marital rape to 16, the Bill retains the existing limit of 15.
- Molestation will still be about the archaic notion of outraging the modesty of the woman but the punishment has been raised from two years to five years.
- Going beyond the "whole life sentence proposed by the Verma Committee", the Bill prescribes death penalty for rape leading to death or persistent vegetative state of the victim of gang rape.

New Offences Introduced on the Basis of the Verma Committee Report

- Sexual harassment carries imprisonment up to three years.
- Stalking is punishable with imprisonment up to five years.
- Voyeurism is punishable with imprisonment up to three years and in the case of a repeat offender, it goes up to seven years.
- Disrobing a woman in a public place is punishable with a maximum term of seven years.
- Acid throwing may attract life sentence.
- Trafficking of a person is punishable with life imprisonment, especially if the offender is a public servant.

The Fair Sex May Not Always Be Fair

- Rape is undeniably a heinous crime. But when women accuse men with whom they have shared intimate relations of the despicable act, it's not only society but even the judiciary that looks askance with scepticism and disapproval. No wonder the courts are asking pertinent questions.
- One judgement rules—even if you keep your hand on the shoulder of a woman, it is for the lady to comment on the nature of the touch, whether it was friendly, brotherly or fatherly (Bombay High Court, Justice Naresh Patil, 2014).
- Even in the West, where we assume there is greater equality and understanding of women's rights, date rape was believed to be a product of feminist hysteria.
- A Delhi HC Bench comprising the Justice Kailash Gambhir and Justice Sunita Gupta, observed that one of the major reasons contributing to increase in the rape cases is the failure of live-in relationships.
- The apex court has held that there is no straitjacket formula for determining whether consent given by the girl is voluntary or given under a misconception of facts, as it has to be decided on the basis of the circumstances and surrounding factors, which lead to the alleged consensual sex.

RAPE SCENE—THE WORLD OVER

If we were to go only by numbers, Australia and Sweden would seem to be the rape capitals of the world, with women being most unsafe in these countries. Of course the definition of rape differs from country to country and that, coupled with how well the crime is reported and recorded, determines what the numbers are finally going to look like.

WORKPLACE HARASSMENT

India: 17 per cent of urban working women admitted to sexual harassment. (Oxfam 2012). In 2014, 57 incidents were reported to police and 336 complaints made to National Commission for Women. (NCRB, MWCD, GoI)

Australia: 22 per cent of women and 5 per cent of men aged 18-64 experienced sexual harassment. (Australian human Rights Commission 2008)

Japan: 56 per cent female workers and 5 percent male workers had sexual consultations at the equal employment offices 2013. (Japan Gender Equality Bureau Cabinet Office, 2015)

Singapore: 54 per cent females had experienced some form of workplace sexual harassment. (AWARE)

China: 70 per cent of female employees are sexually harassed according to research at Guangzhou Industrial Zone; China. (Sunflower Women Worker Centre, 2013)

SIKKIM BEST, DELHI WORST PLACE FOR WOMEN TO WORK

The northeastern state of Sikkim has the best working conditions for women, while the Capital fares the lowest, says a report by the Centre for Strategic and International Studies — a top American think tank — and Nathan Associates.

State	Points Scored Out of 40
Sikkim	29.9
Telangana	28.5
Puducherry	25.6
Karnataka	24.7
Himachal Pradesh	24.2
Andhra Pradesh	24.0
Kerala	22.2
Maharashtra	21.4
Tamil Nadu	21.1
Chhattisgarh	21.1

How The Index Works

States were ranked on four main factors:

1. Legal restrictions on women's working hours in factories, retail, and the IT industry.
2. Responsiveness of the state's criminal justice system towards crimes affecting working women.
3. Number of women workers in the state as a percentage of total workers.
4. Incentives the state's start-up and industrial policies offer women entrepreneurs.

Scoring

All categories scored from 1-10. The 'justice' score is the average of the percentage of FIRs that are charge-sheeted and trials that end in conviction. for the 'freedom to work' score, states received 3 points for every sector where women were able to work at night.

Source: Press Trust of India

MARRIAGE OF UNDERAGE GIRLS AND MARITAL VIOLENCE

Adolescent marriage and domestic violence are two widely prevalent but unacknowledged practices. Studies on the married life of adolescent girls reveal a chilling link between the two. Adolescent marriage appears to be directly correlated with increased violence at home: emotional, physical and sexual, practiced both by the husband and the in-laws. It is unabated even during pregnancy and motherhood. Female children born to underage mothers also suffer from higher risks of dying before they reach their fifth birthday.

The study showed that 43 per cent of underage married women said, they had been subject to marital violence while 24 per cent of adult-married women have reported with regard to the same. Severe, life-threatening violence was experienced by 16 per cent of underage married women compared to 6 per cent of adult-married women. A study by Jay Silverman of Harvard School of Public Health, Anita Raj and others has shown that underage marriage led to higher infant and child mortality rates of daughters and not sons compared to women who were married in adulthood.

Another study showed that underage married women got less autonomy and were less likely to express opinions on domestic issues. Importantly, underage mothers were significantly less likely to have had their first delivery in a health facility.

Although the proportion of girls married off in the 15 to 19 years age group has declined from 56 per cent in 1971 to about 27 per cent in 2006, it still means that over 1.5 crore girls are thus married, and that 16 per cent of the age group, that is about 2.4 lakh women had already become mothers or were pregnant, according to the National Family & Health Survey-3.

INDIAN SCENARIO			
Experience Marital Violence		**Sexual Marital Violence**	
• Women married before 18	43%	• Women married before 18	13%
• Women married after 18	24%	• Women married after 18	7%
Source: Int Journal of Gynecology & Obstetrics, 2010			
Female Infant Mortality*		**Under 5 Girl Child Mortality***	
• Those experiencing domestic violence	77	• Those experiencing domestic violence	105
• Those not experiencing domestic violence	55	• Those not experiencing domestic violence	73
*Per 1000 live birth; *Source:* Arch Pediatr Adolesc Med. 2011			

INDIA'S FERTILITY RATE AND TEENAGE CHILD BEARING

India's fertility rates have declined, however the decline has not been uniform in all states.

Fertility decline has been the slowest in Bihar, which is the third-most populated state with a population of 110 million. Bihar is the only state in the country where couples on average continue to have more than three children, which had led the state's total fertility rate (TFR)—the average number of births a woman has in her lifetime–stay at a high 3.4, acording to National Family Health Survery-4, 2016. India's TFR is 2.2, with the urban India and 18 states having fertility rates below the replacement level of 2.1, which is when the population stops growing.

Teenage Childbearing by State/U.T.

• Adolescent (15–19 years) has halved in India over the past decade from 16% in 2005–06 to 8% in 2015–16

States With Higher Percentage

Women aged 15–19 years who began childbearing in 2015–16.

Tripura 19, West Bengal 18, Assam 14, Bihar 12, Andhra Pradesh 12

States With Lower Percentage

Lakshwadeep 0, Chandigarh 2.1, Himachal Pradesh 2.6, Punjab 2.6

DOMESTIC VIOLENCE

Women—Major Victims, Harassed Husbands—New Reality

A considerable improvement is witnessed in the reporting of crimes against women like rape and molestation. But, a majority of Indian women still prefer to exercise silence over issues of domestic violence. Domestic violence is a reality which one in three women globally experience—from an ordinary homemaker to celebrities. Women across social divide put up with violence as a way of life that comes from hyper-masculinity of their men. But when educated, empowered women continue to take violence passively, at home and even in a public space—it baffles social scientists.

Domestic violence works both ways. When it is physical, its victims bear the testimony on their bodies; broken limbs, burn marks, bleeding nose, etc. But, the other kind of violence that plagues millions of Indian homes is psychological in nature and the victims of this violence burn at both ends. The verbal and psychological violence involves the educated middle class women. The second kind of violence does not get reported either in a police station or in a hospital—reporting psychological disorders is still a taboo in our society. Not only in India, domestic violence is grossly under reported globally—in surveys as well as in filing a report to the police.

• Source: National Family Health Survey (2005–06) and NFHS (2015–16)

A Crime Has to Have a Proof

Domestic violence is also a violation of human rights, but it rarely gets reported as a crime. It is a manifestation of inequality within the home that refuses to come to terms with changing social reality of gender equality. Contrary to the general belief, violence faced by women in intimate relationships is neither restricted to certain social sections nor is it manifested only in its physical form. It can be physical, emotional, sexual, economic and verbal.

While men can subject their women to violence for their ever stretchable demands—that may begin with desire to have unlimited consumer goods in dowry, to good looks of the bride, to her ability to beget sons only and to be obedient, etc., a woman on her part is not supposed to raise her voice even when her rights are violated.

A strange mix of social, psycho-social and economic issues are involved in such situations. Indian men grow up internalising traditional views of male superiority. When they fail to acquire the desired status or prominence in social life, career, etc., they try to compensate it by trying to control their domestic life. Another situation occurs when this man enjoys a high status at work along with the sycophancy that accompanies it. He wants to be treated as a 'boss' at home, unable to leave behind the 'halo' and 'aura' of the workplace. As a result, he tortures his wife finding a sadistic pleasure in crushing her personality.

Retribution of Violence

Domestic violence is a serious social issue, and it validates gender inequality. It calls for a deeper understanding of the institution of family that is facing never-seen-before kind of structural changes with disintegration of values, changing gender roles, migration and an aggressive intervention of consumerism in private spheres. Because violence is treated as a male prerogative in a super-macho society like ours, when women acquire the role of the tormentor and men become the tormented, it invites ridicule. Though society is maturing to accept the existence of battered men and 'Harassed Husbands', it is still not accepting the gravity of the growing problem. Violence is a disease and it should be treated clinically, like a disease, without ostracising men and pitying women.

Laws and Some Glaring Facts About Domestic Violence

- Protection of Women from Domestic Violence Act 2005 (PWDVA)—it entitles women facing violence in intimate relationships to access the courts of law for civil relief in the form of "Stop Violence" orders.
- The new WHO report finds that violence against women is a global problem of epidemic proportions.
- 37.7 per cent of Asian women are abuse victims—the highest in the world.
- 30 per cent women across the world face beatings or rape, most often by their own partners.
- 1 in 3 women globally is a victim of sexual or physical attack.
- 38 per cent of female murder victims are killed by husbands or boyfriends.

THREE TIMES MORE WOMEN WIDOWED/DIVORCED/ SEPARATED THAN MEN

4.1% of India's population is widowed or divorced/separated. Among larger states, Kerala has the highest proportion of such people, Haryana has the lowest. The Sample Registration System (SRS)-2014 data reveals a much higher proportion of women in this category. Experts explain this could be because of women's higher life-expectancy as well as social factors that make remarriage more difficult for women.

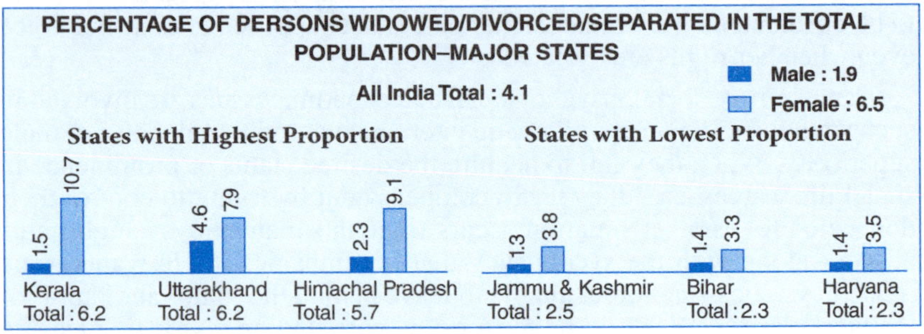

The Single Ladies: 73 Million and Growing

Unmarried, divorced, separated or widowed, the single woman now constitutes 21% of India's female population. Her spending power has even caught the attention of businesses. Travel companies customise vacations for her, and online rental services focus on her safety. Society too has started viewing her in a whole new light.

The Indian woman without a cohort was once considered a social anomaly. Now, she's in the company of around 73 million others — unmarried, divorced, widowed, separated — who constitute 21% of India's 353 million women above the age of 20. But the statistics that's striking is 40% — that's how much the population of single women has grown between 2001 and 2011, according to the latest census data. Number-crunching by India—Spend shows that single women in the age-group of 20 to 29 have clocked the sharpest rise — 68% suggesting that more of them are either separated or divorced or delaying marriage, perhaps to pursue education and careers, which in itself is a promising sign of independence and choice. Unlike China, which denigrates its unmarried women over 27 with the term 'Shengnu' — a disparaging reference to 'leftovers's — India has no such slur, and even cultural associations of misfortune or secret aberration linked with the unmarried, are waning.

INDIA	
No. of Single Women (2011) (in million)	**72.6**
Change since 2001 (for women above 20 years) • Single Women • Total Women	 40% 28%

RURAL INDIA	
No. of Single Women (2011) (in million)	**45.1**
Change since 2001 (for women above 20 years) • Single Women • Total Women	 30% 20%

GENDER DISCRIMINATION

SABARIMALA SHRINE

—Ban on Entry of Women Violates Article 25

The Supreme Court on April 11, 2016, frowned upon the practice of barring women between the ages of 10 and 50 years from the Sabarimala Shrine in Kerala, asserting that religious practice and tradition could not be allowed to dent constitutional principles and values.

Questioning the validity of tradition which has been under attack from feminists and others, a bench of Justices Dipak Misra, V Gopala Gowda and Kurian Joseph said a temple was a public religious place and it must observe the constitutional values of gender equality.

The judges said the issue involved the question whether tradition could override the Constitution which prohibited gender discrimination. "Why this kind of classification for devotees to visit the temple? We are on constitutional principles. Gender discrimination in such matters is untenable. You cannot create corrosion or erosion in constitutional values," the bench said.

Counsels of Kerala government and the temple board vehemently supported the ban on entry of women into the shrine revered by millions. However, the bench made it clear that the judiciary would decide such issues only on the basis of constitutional provisions and would not be swayed by tradition.

The bench pointed out that women had always been at a higher pedestal in society since time immemorial and it was part of the country's ancient tradition.

SHANI SHINGNAPUR TEMPLE

After a long crusade by women activists demanding entry to the inner sanctum of the Shani temple in Shingnapur, the temple trust finally granted women devotees passage on April 8, 2016.

This will be the first time in 60 years that women will be allowed to enter the garbhagriha after a decades-long tradition that barred women from entering it, and conditionally restricted men too.

"This is a big day for women today. We have managed to break a century old regressive tradition which had prevented women from entering the temple," said Desai.

The fight against gender inequality at places of worshipping in Maharashtra was started in 2000 by Narendra Dabholkar, who was assassinated in 2013 allegedly by those opposed to his rationalist ideology.

The temple's decision to allow entry follows a Bombay court order that states it is a woman's fundamental right to enter a temple.

HAJI ALI DARGAH

The Bombay high court struck down on August 26, 2016 a ban on women's entry into the inner sanctum of Mumbai's iconic Haji Ali Dargah. A bench of justices VM Kanade and Revati Mohite-Dere said the ban violated women's fundamental rights and asked the state to ensure protection for female devotees.

Though the 600-year-old mausoleum's history is undocumented, it is believed to be the tomb of an Islamic preacher from Iran. Located on a rocky islet a few hundred metres from the Mumbai shore, the complex is accessible through a narrow causeway during low tide.

The ban on the entry of women was imposed in 2012 with the trust saying that women's presence near the tomb of a revered saint is "a grievous sin" in Islam. A Muslim women's foundation petitioned the court seeking restoration of pre-2012 rules.

WOMEN EMPOWERMENT

Is It a Pipe Dream?

Women's empowerment happens to be the most discussed and yet least understood of major issues. Basically a woman is empowered when she is able to take decisions regarding herself, her family, community and society at large.

The fact is—even after almost 70 years of independence, women's empowerment still appears to be a mirage. Girls are performing better academically, are winning medals and scholarships; more women are entering as professionals, but they are unable to reach positions, where decisions are being made.

Crucial to Growth

Kofi Annan, former Secretary General of the United Nations has asserted that gender equality is a "pre-requisite" for achieving the 'Millennium Development Goals'. Amartya Sen has referred to the phenomenon of 'missing women' to capture the point that the proportion of women is much lower than what it should have been, had girls been allowed to take birth just like boys, and then to survive thereafter.

World Development Report of 2012 says that around 6 million women are missing every year, out of which 23 per cent are never born, 10 per cent go missing in early childhood, 21 per cent in the reproductive years and 38 per cent above the age of 60 years. These figures however do not include lakhs of women who are never able to access the resources, jobs and opportunities. In short, even in the 21st century, it matters a lot whether one is born a man or a woman.

The slow pace of women's empowerment reflected through increased incidents of honour killings, domestic violence, rape and molestation, trafficking in women, is often blamed on the mindset that refuses to change.

It is strange that we could so easily fight our religious beliefs for adopting abortion, at least easier than it was in the West; we threw away joint families to enjoy the independence of conjugal families; we prefer working daughters-in-law because they bring money; we rush to send our daughters to beauty pageants and film industry the moment they get an offer; why is it then the mindset refuses to see women as decision makers? Is it sufficient for the State to frame statutes, policies and then wait for the patriarchal mindset to change? Does the State care enough that the thoughtfully drafted policies get implemented with firmness and sincerity?

ROAD TO NOWHERE

- In patriarchal India, marriage is considered to be the only road for women to attain social security.
- The National Council for Applied Economic Research, conducted a survey with over 30,000 married women in 2011 and 2012 aged between 16 and 49, living in over 1,500 villages and 971 urban neighbourhoods.
- The study shows two in five Indian women didn't get to choose their spouse.
- About one in two was married before the legal age of 18.
- 54 per cent women said they would be beaten up for going out of the house without permission, 35 per cent for not cooking properly, and 36 per cent for inadequate dowry payments.
- India does not have a mechanism for maintaining official statistics of dowry payments.

It is women who shall have to break through the glass ceiling and claim the space where decisions are made. If women are not prepared to stand for themselves, no one else would, neither the State, nor men, nor the civic society.

FEMALE LITERACY

—A Dismal Picture

Literacy is still a distant dream for vulnerable young women. Going at the present pace of development, India will take at least another 56 years to achieve female youth literacy. A serious gender imbalance in global education has left over 100 million young women in low and lower middle income countries unable to read a single sentence, and will prevent half of the 31 million girls out of school from ever enrolling. These are among the main findings of the gender summary, which analyses data from the UNESCO Education for All Global Monitoring Report.

As per the South-West Asia factsheet of the report, young people who have spent just a few years in school do not develop literacy skills and in some cases even completing primary school is not always a guarantee for literacy. The report cited the example of India where after completing up to four years of school, 90% emerge illiterate and after five to six years in school, around 30% still emerge illiterate.

Poor women are the most vulnerable, with two out of three of them in South and West Asia who cannot read are from this category. While poorest young females in Bhutan are not projected to achieve universal literacy until 2083, Pakistan will not reach the target until the 22nd century. India is no better, projected to meet the target between 2070 and 2080.

WELL-EDUCATED MOMS HAVE HALF THE NO. OF KIDS THAT ILLITERATES DO: CENSUS DATA

With more girls reaching higher levels of education, the average number of children born to them after they get married is falling, Census 2011 data released on April 29, 2016 shows. India had nearly 340 million married women and the average number of children was 3.3, down from 3.8 in 2001 and 4.3 in 1991.

But hidden in this average figure is a wide range between an illiterate mother and well-educated one. Mothers who were deprived of education in their early life and have remained illiterate had 3.8 children on an average. At the other extreme, mothers with a graduate degree or above had just 1.9 children. That's half the number of children compared to illiterate mothers.

EDUCATION LEVEL OF MOMS	AVERAGE NUMBER OF CHILDREN	
	2011	2001
Illiterate	3.8	4.2
Below primary	3.2	3.3
Primary	3.0	3.7
Middle	2.8	3.3
Matric or secondary	2.3	2.7
Graduate and above	1.9	2.1
Total	**3.3**	**3.8**

JUVENILE JUSTICE ACT

Cabinet Clears Bill to Lower Juvenile Age

The cabinet on August 6, 2014 cleared a historic, all new juvenile justice law under which 16 to 18 year old who commit heinous offences such as rapes and robberies can be tried as adults. Heinous offence has been defined as "an offence for which the minimum punishment under the IPC or any other law is imprisonment for seven years or more."

The draft law says that 16 to 18 year old even if convicted for heinous offences can't be jailed and would have to be kept in places of safety, to be provided by state governments, until they turn 21. The Juvenile Justice Care and Protection Bill-2014 replaces the Juvenile Justice Act-2000, in which everyone below the age of 18 was treated as a child and tried by the Juvenile Justice Board for all offences. The maximum punishment under the old law was three years in a correction home. Children's courts are special sessions courts which were created to try cases involving minor victims of crimes under the National Commission for Protection of Children's Act 2005.

Trial by Children's Court

- 16 to18 year old can now be tried as adults for heinous crimes.
- Trial only by children's court, not adult courts as planned earlier.
- No jail for 16 to 18-year-old convicts until they turn 21.

CRIMES INVOLVING JUVENILES UP

Mainly Involved In Thefts, Rapes And Assaults

Cases of cognizable crimes involving juveniles have jumped by 50.6% between 2005 and 2014, the government informed the Lok Sabha.

"As per data collected from states and Union territories, an increase of 50.6% — from 25,601 cases in 2005 to 38,586 cases in 2014 —in cases under total cognizable crimes registered against juveniles in conflict with law, was reported." The cases registered were both under IPC and Special and Local Laws.

The major crime-heads against juveniles during 2014 were theft (20%), rape (5.9%), grievous hurt (4.7%) and assault on a woman with intent to outrage her modesty (4.7%). A look at state/UT-wise figures of crimes against juveniles shows Madhya Pradesh at the top of the table in 2014, followed by Maharashtra, Bihar, Rajasthan and Delhi.

HOW OTHER COUNTRIES DEAL WITH CRIMES COMMITTED BY JUVENILES?

UNITED KINGDOM

- Anybody who has attained the age of 17 is treated as an adult.
- Special youth courts try cases involving those under 18.
- If a juvenile under 17 is involved in heinous offences like sexual assault, he/she can be tried as an adult.
- Death penalty is not allowed.
- If a youth offender is jointly charged with an adult, the charge is heard and tried by a regular court.

FRANCE

- Only special juvenile courts to try those under 18.
- Tougher punishment but no death penalty.
- Heinous offences committed by juveniles between 16-18 tried by Juvenile Assize courts.

USA

- About 20 states allow juveniles to be tried as adults and if found guilty to be sentenced to life imprisonment.
- Special juvenile courts deal with under-18 delinquents.
- Minors can't be given the death penalty.

GENERATION GAP

Are You Accepting Your Teenager?

A teenager rebels and behaves in the most non-comprehensible manner. Well, that is a common and hackneyed opinion of a hapless parent who is just not being able to understand the sudden and bizarre changes in behaviourisms. Ironically, the contrary might just be true!

More often than not, what parents see as a rebellion is actually their own inability to accept that every age brings its own challenges and transformations. What any well-meaning parent fails to see is that the mould has broken and the child, as a person, is changing. We need to understand that adolescence is not always a period of emotional turmoil and not every teenager rebels. At times, there is just too much of hype around the whole concept. Instead, what you see could be an outcome of faulty child rearing practices or wrong peer pressures. Young adolescents have to go through a tumultuous phase to emerge as confident adults. This internal conflict emerges as a rebellion. Instead of repulsion, parents' acceptance and empathy is what they seek.

Communication Channels

Experts believe that the onus of a happy teenage period definitely lies on the parents. Parents who don't spend quality time with their children in the growing up years are unable to comprehend this transition. As a result, most teenagers have almost negligible communication with their parents, which often causes them to follow unethical ways like resorting to substance abuse.

So what really could be going wrong? To begin with, somewhere along the line, parents may have lost communication with the child. With parents' anxieties being fuelled by various teenager tales doing the rounds, they are too apprehensive of their teen flying off the handle. Owing to the concern for your child coupled with a gross lack of faith, you fail to keep the communication channel open, which is a must at this age. Well, parents, who try to swim along the tide, also have a point to make. The adolescents and teenagers of the present generation have a firm head on their shoulders.

They are not diplomatic at all and have a high level of emotional maturity. From academic struggles to peer pressure and hormonal changes, they have scores of battles to fight. It is the parents, who need to adapt and change conventional mindsets.

'Buying' Love

The case of a busy parent trying to buy love is in fact a bit too common! Loaded with worldly ambitions, parents make the disastrous mistake of replacing their love and attention with possessions. Sumita Ummat, director, learning expert and coach at 'Let Us Talk', a Delhi-based outfit, offers a word of caution against the practice, "As a parent, how involved are we in a child's life? All we are doing today is to load them with multiple aspirations of being an all-rounder. The disaster occurs when the adolescent or teenager realises that his dreams are different than his parents." It is then that a rebellion happens.

Critical Approach

Being constantly critical of someone will eventually drive the other person to behave likewise. It is indeed intriguing how children absorb whatever you say and actually begin to live your words. This phenomenon is, unfortunately, at its strongest in the tender teenage years when the mind, body and soul are at the zenith of sensitivity.

Realistic Expectations

With every well-meaning friend, relative and acquaintance doling out words of wisdom on the parenting rules for teenagers, a parent's mind could actually get into a whirlwind.

Instead of jumping to criticise at the first possible instance, make an effort to understand, appreciate, accept and acknowledge. Be realistic in your expectations from your child as he is bound to take risks and venture out on his own. Steer clear of hearsay and keep your own communication channel with him always open. Every person should be free to live his/her own life, even your teenager. As a parent, all you can do is to gently help them shape their goals and guide them through their journey.

Source: Article By Jasmin Pannu —The Tribune

FILMMAKERS CORRUPTING YOUTH : MADRAS HC

On September 3, 2016, the Madras High Court expressed displeasure over filmmakers "corrupting the minds of the youth" by using vulgar words in songs and by projecting more violence in films instead of inculcating moral values.

"Media is a powerful teacher whose teachings are never forgotten by people. Therefore, the filmmakers should realise their responsibility to imbibe good thoughts in the minds of the youth, who are the pillars of the future society and should act upon to bring up a good society," the judge said.

COMMUNAL VIOLENCE

Communal violence witnessed a 17% rise in 2015, with 751 incidents recorded across the country as against 644 in 2014. According to data put out by the Centre in reply to a Lok Sabha question on February 24, 2016, casualties from communal unrest also increased in 2015, with dead and injured up at 97 and 2,264 from 95 and 1,921 in 2014, respectively.

Though 2015 saw a rise in communal violence compared to 2014, it was lower than the 823 incidents, 133 deaths and 2,269 injured reported in 2013, largely on account of the Muzaffarnagar riots. States which saw the maximum communal incidents were UP (155), Karnataka (105), Maharashtra (105), MP (92), Bihar (71), Rajasthan (65), and Gujarat (55). While incidents in MP saw a sharp increase from 56 in 2014 to 92 in 2015, they declined in both Rajasthan and Gujarat.

ATTACKS ON CHRISTIANS RISE : NGO

'85 Major Incidents, One Crime A Day on an Average'

Citing 85 major incidents of alleged persecution of Christians across 20 states in 2015, a report by a minority and human rights NGO says 2015 saw an unprecedented spike in "intolerance" against the community. The report says on an average, India saw one such incident of hate crime against Christians a day in 2015.

While the report terms Madhya Pradesh as the worst state, followed by Telangana and Uttar Pradesh for such attacks, it calls Maharashtra 'the Hindutva capital'. Delhi too, the report says, is among the top 10 states that saw such incidents, with five Catholic churches vandalised and assaults on priests and community members.

The Catholic Secular Forum (CSF) in its report claims that at least seven pastors were killed and 8,000 Christians (including 6,000 women and children) targeted in 2015. There was at least a 20% increase in the incidents in terms of the number of people victimised as against 2014.

Catholic Secular Forum's Report

- On an average one incident reported per day until the year end. 2015
- Maharashtra is 'the Hindutva capital'.
- Chrisitans facing atrocities: Among top 10 states are TN, Jharkhand, Chhattisgarh, Haryana, Odisha, Rajasthan, MP, Telangana, UP and Delhi
- Minimum seven pastors killed, 8,000 victims of other atrocities.
- Over 500 clergy and community leaders targeted.

UNITE AGAINST VIOLENT EXTREMISM

UN's Five-point Plan of Action to Fight Terror

Violent extremism is a direct assault on the United Nations Charter and a grave threat to international peace and security. Terrorist groups have brazenly kidnapped young girls, systematically denied women's rights, destroyed cultural institutions, warped the peaceful values of religions, and brutally murdered thousands of innocents around the world. The threat of violent extremism is not limited to any one religion, nationality or ethnic group. On January 15, 2016, the Secretary General, Ban-ki-Moon presented to the United Nations General Assembly a 5-point Plan of Action to Prevent Violent Extremism, which takes a practical and comprehensive approach to address the drivers of this menace. The Plan puts forward more than 70 recommendations for concerted action at the global, regional and national levels, based on five inter-related points.

INDIAN JUDICIAL SYSTEM: SORRY STATE OF AFFAIRS

Known for the colossal pile-up of pending cases, the Indian judicial system is also marred by one of the world's lowest judge-to-population ratio. On the top of it the vacancies in all courts (sanctioned bench strength) are constantly rising. The following table provides the necessary data and shows the sorry state of affairs in the judiciary.

Court(s)	Sanctioned Strength	Actual Strength	Vacancies*
Supreme Court	31	25	5
High Courts	1079	615	464
Subordinate Courts	21303	16192	5111

*It may vary from day to day

Need 70, 000 Judges to Clear Pending Cases: CJI

"Access to justice is a fundamental right and the government cannot afford to deny the people their right" ***TS Thakur***

Chief Justice of India

While the Law Commission of India in 1987 had suggested for having 44,000 judges to effectively tackle the then number of pending cases, the country today has only 18,000 judges. "Thirty years down the line we continue to work with depleted strength. If you go by the number of people that have been added to the population, we may now require more than 70,000 judges to clear the pending cases," T.S. Thakur, former Chief Justice of India.

23 LAKH CASES STUCK FOR MORE THAN 10 YEARS

Reasons may be many, from inadequate number of trial judges to lack of infrastructure, but the snail-paced judicial system continues to carry a large chunk of cases that have been on its back for more than a decade. According to the statistics released by the Supreme Court as on May 31, 2016, courts across the country recorded a pendency of 2.18 crore cases, of which 27% or 59.3 lakh cases have been pending for more than five years entailing litigants to visit the courts several times. The Committee conceded that the national average of disposing of very old cases has come down. The

National Judicial Data Grid statistics revealed that at the end of April 30, 2016, there were 27.4 lakh undated cases pending in various courts and it increased to 36.1 lakh cases by September 23, 2016. Of the 66.6 lakh cases pending for more than five years, as many as 23.0 lakh cases have been on board of courts for more than 10 years, the statistics revealed. The states which reported the largest number of more than 10-year-old cases are: Uttar Pradesh—6.9 lakh; Gujarat—5.1 lakh; Maharashtra—2.6 lakh; Bihar—2.4 lakh; Odisha—1.8 lakh and West Bengal 1.9 lakh. Among the larger states, Punjab recorded the least number of more than 10-year-old cases with 1,241 of them are pending.

From time to time, the Chief Justice of India on behalf of the judiciary and the governments have been resolving to expeditiously dispose of old cases and cases filed by senior citizens and women. But, the message does not appear to have had the desired effect at the ground level. As many as 7.8 lakh cases filed by senior citizens and 22.3 lakh cases filed by women are pending in trial courts. Karnataka, which had done reasonably well in disposing of over 10-year-old cases, lags in attending to cases filed by senior citizens. States with large pendency of cases filed by senior citizens are: Maharashtra—2.2 lakh; Karnataka—1.2 lakh; Tamil Nadu 65,793; UP—72,960; Gujarat 51,890 cases. Highest pendency of cases filed by women has been reported from UP, which has 4.7 lakh such cases. Other states where large pendency of cases initiated by women are: Maharashtra—2.9 lakh, Bihar—2.3 lakh; West Bengal—1.7 lakh; Karnataka—1.6 lakh; Tamil Nadu—1.3 lakh.

TOTAL PENDING CASES

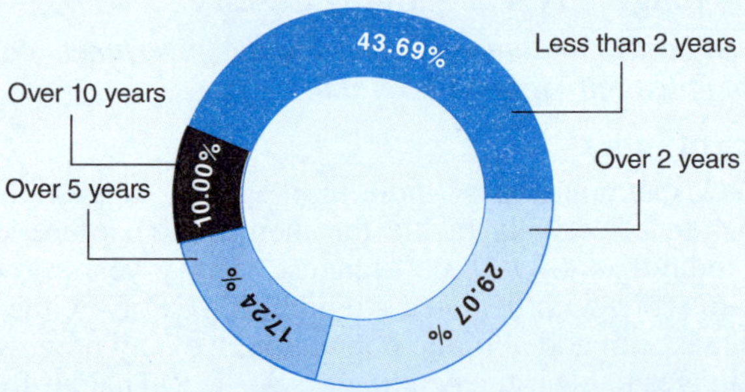

Pending Cases (Registered) over 10 years as on September 23, 2016		
State	**Cases**	**Percentage**
UP	693496	30.14 %
Gujarat	513244	22.31 %
Maharashtra	257237	11.18 %
Bihar	237294	10.31 %
Odisha	182084	7.91 %
West Bengal	178438	7.76 %
All India	**2300757**	**89.61 %**

DOES ONE HAVE RIGHT TO DIE PEACEFULLY

—The Debate is On

Can a terminally ill person be allowed to execute a living will authorising withdrawal of life support system if he/she reaches a vegetative state with no hope of revival? Acting on a petition filed by Common Cause, an NGO, the Supreme Court on July 16, 2014 issued notices to all states asking them to respond in eight weeks. A five-judge constitution, the bench headed by Chief Justice of India RM Lodha, said, permitting voluntary passive euthanasia would amount to abetment to suicide and attempt to commit suicide—which are criminal offences. The question of passive euthanasia needed to be examined comprehensively as there was no authoritative judicial pronouncement on the issue. It appointed former solicitor general TR Andhyarujina as *amicus curiae* to assist it.

The End-of-Life Dictionary

1. ***Suicide*** **:** Impulsive act under severe emotional stress where a person takes his own life.
2. ***Physician-assisted Suicide*** **:** Where a doctor knowingly and intentionally provides a person with the knowledge or means or both required to commit suicide.
3. ***Voluntary Death*** **:** Well considered decision by a person if he or she is still able to make medical decisions on how and when he or she would like to die.
4. ***Passive Euthanasia*** **:** Causing death of a person in a permanent vegetative state with no chance of recovery by withdrawing artificial life support.
5. ***Active Euthanasia*** **:** Administering patient a lethal drug to cause his or her death.

Attempts to pass laws decriminalising euthanasia have been rejected in many countries including Scotland, Canada, states of Western and Southern Australia, Israel and France.

A Look at The Assisted Death Atlas

- ***Dutch*** issued rules for passive or involuntary euthanasia called Groningen guidelines in 2004. Rules expanded in 2006 after reports that doctors were killing newborns if found ill.
- In ***Switzerland***, article 115 of the penal code does not consider assisting in suicide for an honorable motive illegal. Lethal drugs can be taken with assistance.
- The ***German*** federal court in June 2010 allowed passive euthanasia with applicant's consent.
- In ***UK***, bill on euthanasia in the Commons rejected in 2004, another rejected by House of Lords in 2007.

- In ***France***, under the 'end of life' law of 2009, doctors are advised not to take extreme measures to keep dying or brain dead patients alive.
- In ***Albania***, passive euthanasia allowed under 1995 law if 3 or more members agree to withdraw life support systems.

Dignified End

- Dignitas, a Zurich-based organisation that helps people end their lives has faced severe criticism.
- It's been blamed for making Switzerland the destination for suicide tourism
- Has about 7,000 members from across the world.
- Founded in 1998, till date it's helped 1,800 people from different countries end their lives peacefully.
- A death by Dignitas costs about 10,500 Swiss Franc (over ₹ 7 lakh).
- The countries with the steepest drops are Libya, which slipped 27 places and Syria, which fell 15 places. A new entry in 2016 is South Sudan.

India is up five places from last year, and now ranks at 130th in the index.

The Top 20 are — 1. Norway 2. Australia 3. Switzerland 4. Denmark 5. Netherlands 6. Germany & Ireland 8. US 9. Canada & New Zealand 11. Singapore 12. Hong Kong & China (SAR) 13. Liechtenstein 14. Sweden & UK 16. Iceland 17. South Korea 18. Israel 19. Luxembourg 20. Japan.

- The worst countries are Niger, Central African Republic, Eritrea, Chad and Burundi.

DENMARK WORLD'S HAPPIEST NATION

Denmark overtook Switzerland as the world's happiest place, as per a report that urged nations regardless of wealth to tackle inequality and the environment. India is at 118th rank.

The report, prepared by the Sustainable Development Solutions Network (SDSN) and the Earth Institute at Columbia University, showed Syria, Afghanistan and eight sub-Saharan countries as the 10 least-happy places on earth to live.

Aiming to "survey the scientific underpinnings of measuring and understanding subjective well-being," the report, now in its fourth edition, ranks 157 countries by happiness levels using factors such as per capita gross domestic product (GDP) and healthy years of life expectancy.

It also rates "having someone to count on in times of trouble" and freedom from corruption in government and business.

Happiest 10 are – Denmark, Switzerland, Iceland, Norway, Finland, Canada, Netherlands, New Zealand, Australia, Sweden.

Saddest 10 are – Madagascar, Tanzania, Liberia, Guinea, Rwanda, Benin, Afghanistan, Togo, Syria, Burundi.

India Fails to Improve Its Happiness Quotient

- India did not make any improvement in its happiness quotient, ranking 118th out of 156 countries, down one slot from 2015 and behind China (83), Pakistan (92) and Bangladesh (110).
- The report said India was among the group of 10 nations witnessing the largest happiness declines along with Venezuela, Saudi Arabia, Egypt, Yemen and Botswana.

Money Does Buy Happiness

Data suggests direct correlation between income of people and the state of their happiness.

	Most Happy	Per Capita GDP Ranking
1	Denmark	20
2	Switzerland	7
3	Iceland	19
4	Norway	5
5	Finland	25

Per Capita GDP Ranking	Least Happy	
135	Benin	153
139	Afghanistan	154
146	Togo	155
113	Syria	156
152	Burandi	157

Compared with Switzerland (2nd in happiness and 7th in per capita GDP) India is sadder and poorer (118th in happiness and 107th in per capita GDP).

MAJOR ECONOMIES			
Happiness Rank	Country	Per Capita GDP Ranking	GDP (PPP) Per Capita - 2015
13	US	9	55,805
16	Germany	17	46,893
56	Russia	46	25,411
83	China	76	14,107
118	**India**	**107**	**6,162**

Source: World happiness report 2016, IMF

INDIA SECOND FASTEST GROWING TOURIST DESTINATION

Analysing data on international tourist arrivals on World Tourism Day shows that among the top eight on this count are the world's largest economics. This perhaps indicates that business travel comprises a significant chunk of international tourism. And though India and Japan are both missing from the top 10 list, they have withnessed the fastest growth in the tourism segment in the past 19 years.

Annual Growth Rate of Tourism in Major Economies (1995 to 2014)	
Country	**Growth Rate (%)**
Japan	7.6%
India	**7.0%**
Brazil	6.4%
Russia	6.2%
China	5.5%
Germany	4.3%
Spain	3.3%
US	2.9%
Italy	2.4%
UK	2.2%

Top Five Countries by International Tourist Arrivals (in millions) (2014)		
Country	**1995**	**2014**
France	60	84
United States	43	75
Spain	35	65
China	20	56
Italy	31	49
India (4 times in 20 years)	**2**	**8**
World (2 times in 20 years)	541	1,161

Source: World Bank

INDIANS HAVE CELL PHONES BUT NO TOILETS

—*A Sad Reflection on Our Society*

A 2010 United Nations (UN) report found more people in India have access to a cell phone than to a toilet and improved sanitation. Research in India showed that roughly 366 million people (31 per cent of the population) had access to improved sanitation in 2008. Data, meanwhile, showed 545 million cell phones were connected to service in India. The publishing of the UN report and the Census 2011 revealed a similar situation.

According to UN estimates, India is home to 594 million people defecating in the open. This constitutes the major cause of microbial contamination of water, that causes diarrhoea. According to the UNICEF, in 2007, 386,600 children died of diarrhoea in India, the highest in the world. A recent World Bank study by Dean Spears also relates open defecation to stunting in children.

According to Census 2011, 53.1 per cent of households in India did not have toilets. The figure is 69.3 per cent for rural India. The National Human Rights Commission (NHRC) has been consistently emphasising upon provisions of wet latrines which in a way emphasises the need for having proper toilets for every household. The places where these women go to relieve themselves is often at a distance from their houses. Apart from that there are many health hazards of defecating in the open and it is also against basic human dignity.

Access to toilets, however, is a basic human need, that many would not want to relate to the threat of sexual violence against women.

HOUSEHOLDS WITHOUT TOILETS (%)

ALL INDIA: 53.1 **RURAL INDIA: 69.3**

Worst States		Worst States in Rural Areas		Schools Without Functional Girls' Toilets	
Jharkhand	78.0%	Jharkhand	92.4%	All-India	8.4 %
Odisha	78.0%	MP	86.9%	Arunachal	35.0 %
Bihar	76.9%	Odisha	85.9%	AP	28.0 %
Chhattisgarh	75.4%	Chhattisgarh	85.5%	Meghalaya	27.7 %
MP	71.2%	Bihar	82.4%	Odisha	25.0 %
Rajasthan	65.0%	Rajasthan	80.4%	Bihar	18.0 %
UP	64.4%	UP	78.2%	Mizoram	17.0 %
TN	51.7%	TN	76.8%	WB	15.0 %
AP	50.4%			J&K	14.6 %
				Manipur	14.0 %
				Asom	11.0 %

Source: Census 2011

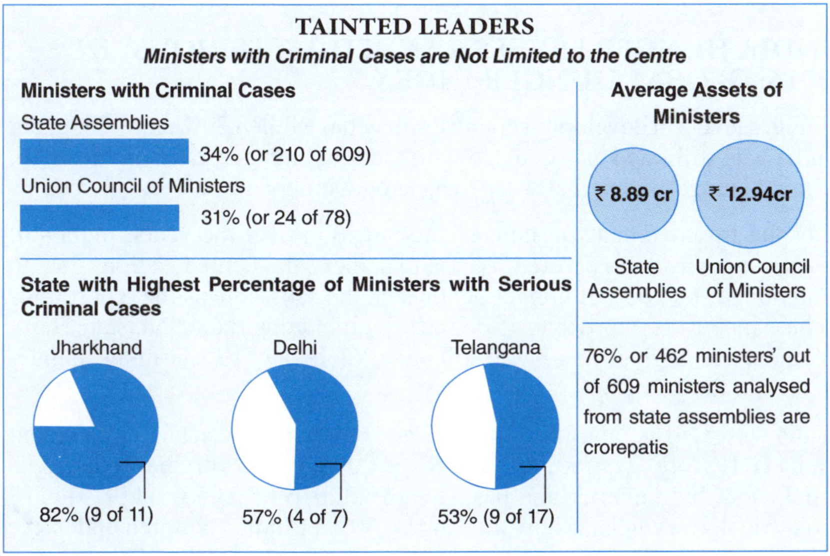

Source: ADR

CROREs IN INDIA DEPRIVED OF SAFE DRINKING WATER: STUDY

—The Figure Highest in World; Overuse of Ground Water to Blame

India has the world's largest number of people without access to safe drinking water, according to a report released to mark World Water Day on March 22, 2016. China, Bangladesh and Pakistan are also among the top 10 countries where maximum number of people are living without uncontaminated drinking water.

According to the report "Water: At what cost?" released by WaterAid, about 7.6 crore people, which is 5% of India's total population, are deprived of safe drinking water and the country registers around 1.4 lakh child deaths annually due to diarrhoea, a mainly water-borne disease.

WORST PERFORMERS IN SAFE WATER ACCESS			
Maximum number of people living without safe water		**Maximum percentage of people living without safe water**	
India	75, 777, 997	Papua New Guinea	60
China	63, 166, 533	Equatorial Guinea	52
Nigeria	57, 757, 141	Angola	51
Ethiopia	42, 251, 031	Chad	49
Congo	33, 906, 771	Mozambique	49
Diarrhoea caused by unsafe water & poor sanitation claims 3,15,000 children's lives annually			

Source: Water Aid Global Report

INDIA HUNGER LEVELS RANKED AS "SERIOUS" IN 2016: GLOBAL HUNGER INDEX

Hunger levels in developing countries may have fallen 29% since 2000, but India was still rated as a country with 'serious' hunger levels in the 2016, Global Hunger Index that was released on October 11, 2016.

Despite improvements in hunger and nutrition over the years, India still has a long way to go before it is able to achieve the United Nations goal to end hunger by 2030. If hunger declines at the same rate as the report finds it has since 1992, more than 45 countries—including India, Pakistan, Haiti, Yemen, and Afghanistan—will still have "moderate" to "alarming" hunger scores in the year 2030.

India was rated as "alarming" in 2013 and has experienced an improvement in its GHI score over recent years. Since 2000, the country has reduced its GHI score by a quarter and has a score in 2016 of 28.5 (rank 97 of 118 countries). Recent data show that almost 40% of Indian children under five years of age are stunted compared to over 60% in the early 1990s.

Stunting is an indicator for chronic under-nutrition and means the affected children are too short for their age. India currently has the fifth highest GHI score in Asia— better than only Afghanistan, Timor-Leste, Pakistan, and North Korea. "India is slated to become the world's most populous nation in just six years, and it's crucial that we meet this milestone with a record of ensuring that the expected 1.4 billion Indians have enough nutritious food to lead healthy and successful lives," said PK Joshi, International Food

Source: Hindustan Times

Policy Research Institute (IFPRI) Director for South Asia.

Director General, IFPRI, Shenggen Fan, says, "Simply put, countries must accelerate the pace at which they are reducing hunger or we will fail to achieve the second Sustainable Development Goal."

"Ending global hunger is certainly possible, but it's up to all of us that we set the priorities right to ensure that governments, the private sector and civil society devote the time and resources necessary to meet this important goal."

Globally, the Central African Republic, Chad, and Zambia had the highest levels of hunger in the report.

Rounding out the top 10 countries with the highest levels of hunger after Central African Republic, Chad, and Zambia are: Haiti, Madagascar, Yemen, Sierra Leone, Afghanistan, Timor-Leste, and Niger.

The GHI ranks countries based on four key indicators: undernourishment, child mortality, child wasting and child stunting. The 2016 report ranked 118 countries in the developing world, almost half of which have "serious" or "alarming" hunger levels.

PRINT MEDIA GROWING IN INDIA : UNION IB MINISTER

Bucking the international trend of print media losing steam, the sector in India is recording a growth with the latest data suggesting 6 per cent increase in publications and a jump in circulation by six crore.

MOST DEATHS

The fast changing technology presented a challenge to the print media across the world, India remained an exception where this sector registered growth both on account of increase in demand and subscriber base for regional newspapers.

The report said the print media registered a growth of 5.8 per cent over the previous year as a total of 5,817 new publications were registered during 2014-15 and 34 publications ceased their operation. Out of the total 1,05,443 publications registered as on March 31, 2015, 14,984 were dailies and bi/tri-week-lies while the remaining 90,459 were other periodicals. Of these, the largest number of newspapers and periodicals registered in any Indian language was 42,493 for Hindi, followed by 13,661 English periodicals. Total circulation claimed by the registered publications stood at 51.05 crore, as against 45.05 crore in 2014.

India––Asia's Deadliest Nation for Journalists

- Nine Indian reporters were among 110 journalists killed around the world in 2015, according to media watchdog group Reporters Without Borders (RSF).
- It dubbed India as 'Asia's deadliest country' for media personnel, ahead of both Pakistan and Afghanistan.
- Of the nine Indian media personnel killed, five journalists were done to death in the course of their work and four for undetermined reasons.

HEALTH ISSUES

PUBLIC HEALTH SYSTEM—INDIA

1.58% of GDP used for public health against 20% by the US.

Percentage of the GDP Spent on Public Health	
INDIA	
11th Five Year Plan	1.00%
Proposed under 12th Five Year Plan	1.58%
Suggested by Planning Commission's high-level expert group and the Steering Committee on Drafting the Plan	2.50%
UNITED STATES OF AMERICA	20.00%

Uneven Distribution

The required physical infrastructure available is unevenly spread across the country. In states like Tamil Nadu, Kerala, Odisha, J&K, Himachal Pradesh and many states in the northeast, there is no shortfall of CHCs (Community Health Centres). But in States like Asom, Bihar, Karnataka, Madhya Pradesh, Maharashtra, Uttar Pradesh and Bengal, the shortfall ranges between 33% and 91%. This clearly shows that as much as finances, political will at the state government level is also a key determining factor vis-a-vis the state of public healthcare.

INDIA IN HEALTHCARE HALL OF SHAME

Worst Ranked Among Peers, Neighbours

Among peers and neighbours, India is performing the worst when it comes to the health of its citizens. Whether it is life expectancy, mortality due to all causes, under-five mortality or mortality among men and women between 15 and 49 years, on most counts, India ranks way below China, Brazil and Sri Lanka, just below Bangladesh and Nepal and in some cases even Pakistan.

This was revealed in the Global Burden of Diseases, Injuries, and Risk Factors 2010 Study (GBD 2010), a collaborative project led by the Institute for Health Metrics and Evaluation (IHME) at the University of Washington. The study details the causes of death and disability across age groups and gender—for 187 countries around the world. In India, the top killer in 1990, diarrhoeal diseases, was replaced by ischemic heart disease (IHD) by 2010. Chronic Obstructive Pulmonary Disease (COPD) held second position through the two decades. However, lower respiratory infections were displaced by stroke by 2010 as the third most common cause of mortality. Diarrhoeal diseases moved to the fourth place followed by TB which continued at fifth place. In India, road injury is the leading killer of men in the 15–49 age group while suicides are the biggest cause of death among women in this age group. Among children in the under-five age group, pre-term birth complications was the leading cause of death in India in 2010 replacing diarrhoeal disease, the top killer of 1990. Pre-term complications are the biggest killers in most of the developed world too along with congenital anomalies.

Country	Rank by Mortality Rate	Top Mortality Cause		Life Expectancy (Years)
		All Ages	15 – 49 Years	
Sri Lanka	68	IHD	Self-harm	75.46
Brazil	80	IHD	Violence	74.08
Nepal	108	COPD	Self-harm	69.20
Bangladesh	113	COPD	Tuberculosis	69.00
Russia	125	IHD	HIV/AIDS	68.86
Pakistan	127	IHD	Tuberculosis	65.73
India	**139**	**IHD**	**Self-harm**	**65.21**
South Africa	154	HIV/AIDS	HIV/AIDS	59.90

INDIA—SELECTED HEALTH INDICATORS

S. No.	Parameter	1981	1991	Current Level
1.	Crude Birth Rate (CBR) (per 1000 population)	33.9	29.5	21.8 (2011*)
2.	Crude Death Rate (CDR) (per 1000 population)	12.5	9.8	7.1 (2011*)
3.	Total Fertility Rate (TFR) (per woman)	4.5	3.6	2.5 (2010*)
4.	Maternal Mortality Rate (MMR) (per 100,000 live births)	NA	NA	212.0 (2007–09*)
5.	IMR (per 1000 live births)	110.0	80.0	44.0 (2011*)
	Rural			48.0
	Urban			29.0
6.	Child (0 – 4 years) Mortality Rate (per 100 children)	41.2	26.5	13.3 (2010*)
7.	Life Expectancy at Birth	(1981–85)	(1989–93)	(2006–10)**
	Total	55.1	59.4	66.1
	Male	55.4	59.0	64.6
	Female	55.7	59.7	67.7

Source: Ministry of Health and Family Welfare, *Sample Registration Survey (SRS), RGI (Registrar General of India), **Abridged Life Table 2003–07 to 2006–10, RGI

COMMON DISEASES AND SOME SUGGESTIONS TO CHECK THEM

Heart Disease

Heart disease and stroke, clubbed together as cardiovascular disease because they involve the heart and blood vessels, account for 31% of all global deaths and one in four deaths in India. Heart disease in India is marked by early age of onset, accelerated build up and high death rate, with changing diets, obesity and low activity putting an increasing number of young people at risk.

Heart disease can be reversed. A healthy diet, regular physical activity and not using tobacco products, along with controlling risk factors such as high blood pressure, high cholesterol, weight and high blood sugar (diabetes) can prevent 80% of premature heart attacks and strokes, says the world Health Organisation.

Respiratory Diseases

Chronic respiratory diseases such as asthma, pulmonary hypertension, occupational lung disease, and interstitial lung disease damage the airways and other structures of the lungs, and lower breathing capacity, causing close to 8% of all deaths in India. Lung disease are not curable, but can be managed using treatments that dilate major air passages and alleviate shortness of breath.

In addition to tobacco smoke, factors that aggravate respiratory illnesses are air pollution, occupational chemicals and dusts, and frequent lower respiratory infections during childhood. Pulmonary fibrosis (scary issue in the lungs) is irreversible, with lung transplantation being the only option.

Cancers

More people are dying of cancer in India than ever before, with the disease accounting for 15% of all deaths in 2013, up from 12% in 1990.

They are projected to kill close to 736,000 people in 2016, mostly because only 12.5% of people are diagnosed and treated in the early stages. Breast cancer takes the most female lives, while lung cancer is the biggest cause of deaths in men in India and among men women around the world.

If treatment is hard, prevention is not. About one-third of cancer deaths are due to the five behavioural and dietary risks that are common to all lifestyle-related diseases: overweight, low intake of fruit and vegetables, lack of physical activity, tobacco use, and alcohol use.

Perinatal Conditions

More babies die in the womb, at birth or in the first week of life in India than anywhere else in the world.

Prematurity and low birth weight, neonatal infections such as septicaemia, birth asphyxia and birth trauma are the leading causes of perinatal deaths, defined as deaths between 22 completed weeks (154 days) of gestation and seven days after birth, and comprise 27.7 deaths per 1,000 live births in India compared to the world's average of 19.2 deaths per 1,000 live births.

CARE FOR YOUR HEART

Vascular disease is a major health problem in India. One in 20 people over 50 years of age have it. The total number of cases are over 42 million. More than half of those affected may not even know about the disease till it is too late.

Vascular disease is not just 'poor circulation'. It comes in various forms: peripheral arterial disease affects the arteries taking blood to the arms and the legs, carotid artery disease affects the arteries taking blood to the brain, and renal artery disease limits the blood flow to the kidneys causing high blood pressure or renal failure.

Risk Factors

Cigarette smoking is the No.1 risk factor for developing vascular disease.

- Obesity
- High cholesterol and lipids
- High-stress lifestyle
- Sedentary lifestyle
- Diabetes mellitus
- Heart disease
- Older than age 50
- High blood pressure

India's Heart is at Risk

Indians get their first heart attack at the average age of 53—six years earlier than the world average of 59 years. And the number of people over 65 years has jumped from 4.4% in 2000 to 7.6% in 2005.

INDIA STILL ACCOUNTS FOR 15% OF MATERNAL DEATHS GLOBALLY

Despite maternal mortality rate coming down to half worldwide since 1990, India accounts for 15% of such casualties during pregnancy and childbirth with 45,000 maternal deaths in 2015, according to a global report by Lancet which points out international as well as national disparities in maternal healthcare services.

Despite making significant progress in reducing its maternal mortality by 69% since 1990, India along with Nigeria accounted for one-third of the global maternal deaths in 2015, the report says while attributing it to a yawning gap in maternal healthcare between urban and rural areas. The report also highlights global inequalities by pointing at varying maternal mortality across countries. It shows that the gap between the group of countries with the lowest and highest rates of maternal mortality has doubled between 1990 and 2013.

Globally, the annual number of maternal deaths per 100,000 live births dropped by 44% between 1990 and 2015, from 385 to 216. The sub-Saharan African region accounted for an estimated 66% (201, 000) of global maternal deaths, followed by southern Asia at 22% (66, 000 deaths). In fact, only 5% of the world's countries accounted for 59% of the total maternal deaths globally."However, alongside the increasing gaps between different countries, the potential for growing inequities within countries also exists, spatially in terms of rural and urban areas or remote districts and between population subgroups," the report further says.

Despite improvement in coverage of institutional deliveries and skilled birth attendants, India has twice missed its Millennium Development Goals to reduce maternal mortality rate by three quarters. Currently, India's maternal mortality rate stands at 174 and to achieve its next target, it needs to reduce it to 103.

Experts say that coverage of life saving interventions and inequity are two of the biggest hindrances in India for improving maternal healthcare. The health ministry has introduced as well as expanded coverage of various schemes to address these challenges, with its main focus on remote areas. It has also started some new schemes to provide care to the pregnant women at different stages of pregnancy.

MORTALITY DIPPED BY 69%

India and Nigeria Account for One-third of Total Global Maternal Deaths

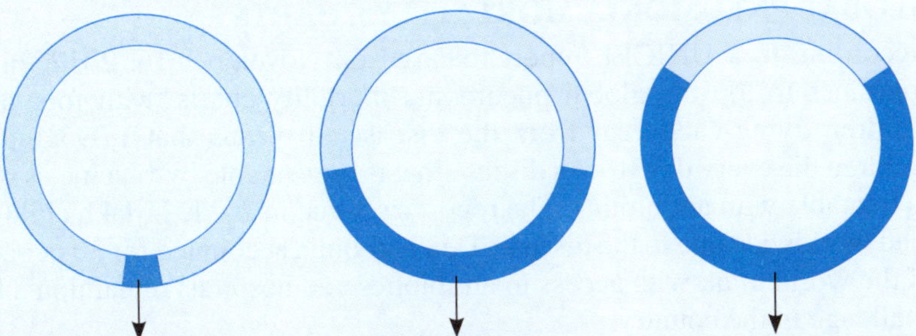

5% of the world's countries account for 59% of world's maternal deaths

Globally, annual maternal deaths declined by 44% between 1990 and 2015

In India, maternal mortality has declined by 69% since 1990

- Globally, births in the presence of skilled birth attendants rose from 57% to 74% between 1990 and 2013

PRETERM BIRTH, NEONATAL INFECTIONS BEHIND 57% OF TOTAL UNDER-FIVE DEATHS

Around 1.26 million children under five years of age die in India every year with prematurity and neonatal infections being the major causes accounting for almost 57% of total deaths, the government informed Rajya Sabha on April 26, 2016. 57% of under-five deaths occur within the first 28 days of life. In the post-neonatal period, pneumonia and diarrhoea are found to be the major reasons for under-five mortality. With over 3.8 lakh new cases of pneumonia annually, India tops the list in terms of total under-five deaths due to the disease. The government of India will provide free vaccination of pneumococcal conjugate (PCV) to children in three doses. It has also identified 184 districts for implementation of Reproductive Maternal Newborn Child Health + Adolescent (RMNCH+A) interventions for achieving improved maternal and child health outcomes. The government has also initiated an SMS-based electronic vaccine intelligence network (e-VIN) to monitor vaccine stocks in real-time in three states.

INDIA BIDS GOODBYE TO POLIO

On January 13, 2014, India was officially declared polio-free, three years after the last case was reported. Before a country is certified polio-free, it should have at least three years of zero polio cases. Since the launch of the 1988 Global Polio Eradication initiative to eradicate polio, 5 million people, mainly in the developing world, who would have otherwise been paralysed, will be free of polio. India's removal from the polio-endemic nation list follows a year of zero infections. The last case, detected on January 13, 2011, involved Rukhsar Khatoon of West Bengal's Howrah district. The child had never received polio drops.

GLOBAL PNEUMONIA MORTALITY CHARTS

According to a UNICEF report released on November 16, 2012, India continues to top the global pneumonia mortality charts, with four lakh children dying each year from the disease. It means that 1,095 Indian children die every day from a disease that is preventable by vaccine as well as treatable with antibiotics. The report says that in 2011, 11 lakh children died worldwide due to the disease. Death in India accounted for 30 per cent of the world total, with access to antibiotics and hospitals remaining a big challenge in the country.

The UNICEF report points out that India must accelerate its anti-pneumonia measures if it wants to meet the Millennium Development Goal 4 of reducing under-5 child mortality by two-thirds between 1990 and 2015.

47% OF GLOBAL MEASLES DEATHS IN INDIA

WHO-Spearheaded Study

Nearly half of all deaths worldwide due to measles occurred in India in 2010. While mortality due to measles dipped from 5.35 lakh in 2000 to 1.39 lakh globally in 2010, India recorded 47% of those deaths in comparison to 16% of global deaths in 2000. New research by the World Health Organisation (WHO), Penn State University and the US Centres for Disease Control and Prevention (CDC) has found that while globally, measles mortality fell by 74% between 2000 and 2010 that is still short of the 90% target; in India the numbers reduced by 26% during the same period.

HEALTH SCARE: ZIKA

Understanding the Disease

What is Zika and why is it so serious?

The Zika virus is a flavivirus, part of the same family as yellow fever, chikungunya and dengue. Zika is commanding worldwide attention because of an alarming connection between the virus and microcephaly, a neurological disorder that results in babies being born with abnormally small heads. The most common symptoms of Zika are fever, rash, joint pain, and conjunctivitis.

How is it transmitted?

Zika is primarily transmitted through the bite of infected Aedes mosquitoes. It can also be transmitted from a pregnant mother to her baby during pregnancy or around the time of birth. We do not know how often Zika is transmitted from mother to baby during pregnancy or around the time of birth.

Who is at risk of being infected?

Anyone who is living in or travelling to an area where Zika virus is found, who has not already been infected with Zika virus is at risk of infection, including pregnant women.

What is the treatment?

There is no vaccine or specific medicine to treat Zika virus infections. The best way to prevent diseases spread by mosquitoes is to avoid being bitten, i.e., to protect yourself and your family from mosquito bites.

How is it diagnosed?

See your healthcare provider if you develop symptoms (fever, rash, joint pain, red eyes). If you have recently traveled, tell your healthcare provider. Your healthcare provider may order blood tests to look for Zika or other similar viral diseases like dengue or chikungunya.

Is this a new virus?

No. Outbreaks of Zika previously have been reported in tropical Africa, Southeast Asia, and the Pacific Islands. Zika virus likely will continue to spread to new areas. In May 2015, the Pan American Health Organisation (PAHO) issued an alert regarding the first confirmed Zika virus infection in Brazil.

MALARIA ENDGAME

India's Target is to be 'Malaria Free' by 2030

Sharp Decline in Malaria Cases in India in 2017

India reported almost three million fewer malaria cases in 2017, a 24% decrease over the previous year (2016) while cases increased worldwide from 217 million to 219 million, after registering a steady decline since 2010, according to the World Malaria Report 2018.

India's reduction, the sharpest within a year, means now the country accounts for 4% of the world's total malaria cases, and is no longer among the world's top three countries in terms of number of cases (around 8.7 million in 2017). Around 70% of the world's malaria cases are found in India and 10 countries in sub-Saharan Africa. "There were 3.5 million more malaria cases reported in these 10 African countries in 2017 compared to the previous year, while

India showed progress in reducing its disease burden.

- 219 million Malaria cases in 2017 worldwide up from 217 million in 2016.
- 80% of the world's malaria cases occur in India and 15 countries in Africa.
  Malaria cases in 2017

Nigeria 25%	Drcongo 11%	Mozambique 5%	India 4%
Uganda 4%	Burkina Faso 4%	Ghana 4%	Nijer 4%,
Cameroon 3%	Mali 3%	Tanzania 3%	Rowanda 3%
Angola 2%	Malawi 2%	Guinea 2%	Benin 2%
others 19%.			

Pan-India Footprint

In India, 80% of malaria cases occur among 20% of its population living in the 200 high-risk districts of Andhra Pradesh, Chhattisgarh, Gujarat, Jharkhand, Karnataka, Madhya Pradesh, Maharashtra, Odisha, West Bengal and the seven north-eastern states. Frequent infections cause chronic malnutrition, anaemia, abortions and low birthweight babies, which raise the socio-economic burden of malaria to more than ₹ 11,000 crore ($1.94 billion), estimates the World Health Organisation.

Fever? It Could Be Malaria!

You are likely to have malaria if you have high fever with periodic chills followed by profuse sweating at intervals of 48 to 72 hours.

Malaria cases and Deaths in India in 2015

Many cases are undiagnosed and many more go unreported

	Ministry of Healths Family Welfare	WHO Estimates
Cases	1.13 million	18 million
Deaths	287.0	30,000

How to Prevent Infection

- Biological control using sterile insect technique (SIT), where male mosquitoes are exposed to radiation to make them sterile.
- Putting gummy fish (Gambusia) in ponds and ditches to feed on mosquito larvae.
- Insecticides such as aerosol sprays with allethrin, resmethrin, malathion or carbaryl methoprene.
- Repellents such as DEET (N,N-diethyl-3-methylbenzamide), permethrin and citronella.
- Mechanical mosquito zappers
- Environmental control by removing potential breeding sites such as old tyres, birdbaths, pots, etc.
- Mechanical barriers such as bednets and window- and door-screens.

SRI LANKA MALARIA-FREE, BUT INDIA TO TAKE MUCH LONGER

The spotlight has turned on India after successful elimination of malaria in Sri Lanka, which was certified by the World Health Organisation in September, 2016. Despite a sharp reduction in its malaria statistics, India is still at risk of the disease and may take a few more years before achieving malaria-free status.

The good news is that India is on the right track with an effective surveillance system and vector control programme and is likely to achieve its malaria eradication target well before the 2030 deadline, the UN agency's assessment shows.

Disease Elimination by 2030?

- Till July 1, 2016 more than 47,000 malaria cases and 119 deaths have been recorded in India.
- In 2015, 287 people died of malaria in India, less than half of 562 deaths recorded in 2014.
- Government has identified 40 endemic districts where 80% of malaria cases happen.
- India is likely to eliminate malaria before 2030.
- Currently, about 3.2 billion people are at risk of malaria globally.
- In 2015, there were 214 million cases of malaria and over 4 lakh deaths worldwide.

Sri Lanka brought down malaria from 264,549 cases in 1999 to zero in November 2012.

LEPROSY—STILL A CHALLENGE

With over one lakh new annual infections being reported for the last three years, leprosy continues to challenge India's public health system making the goal of complete eradication more elusive with time.

The latest Health Ministry data show that India recorded a whopping 1.25 lakh new leprosy infections in 2015 making it the highest contributor to the global burden of the chronic disease.

Leprosy is caused by the slows multiplying bacillus Mycobacterium leprae and mainly affects the skin, peripheral nerves, mucosa of the upper respiratory tract and also the eyes.

The biggest problem with leprosy management is its five-year incubation period and the fact that symptoms can take as long as 20 years to appear. In the meantime, the untreated, undetected leprosy patient can transmit the disease to others, thus adding to the burden.

Dr SK Noordeen, former director, Global Leprosy Programme, WHO, says "Leprosy treatment is very effective. But the challenge is detection. Once you start treatment you prevent the patient from further transmitting the disease. But patients are unaware of symptoms. Even if they know, they don't show up for treatment on account of stigma. Sustained detection is the key."

Contagious Syndrome

- A chronic infection, leprosy is caused by Mycobacterium leprae, an acid-fast, rod-shaped bacillus.
- It mainly affects the skin, the peripheral nerves, mucosa of the upper respiratory tract and also the eyes.
- It is curable and treatment in early stages averts disability.
- Multidrug-therapy treatment made available by WHO free of charge to all patients worldwide since 1995.
- WHO's elimination target was in 2000. India declared elimination in 2005, but 150 districts still remain endemic.

TUBERCULOSIS

India has the highest number of tuberculosis (TB) cases in the world. Each year in India, more than 2 million new cases of TB are diagnosed. Approximately 5,00,000 persons die of the disease.

During the last decade, multidrug-resistant TB has burgeoned in India resulting in an extremely large number of multidrug-resistant TB cases, second only to the number of cases noted in Latvia. Since 1993, in response to this epidemic, the government of India has implemented the Revised National Tuberculosis Control Programme based on Directly Observed Treatment Short-term (DOTS).

INDIA REPORTS 26% OF GLOBAL TB DEATHS: WHO

India continues to bear the brunt of tuberculosis (TB). More than one in every four TB deaths worldwide are reported from India. The World Health Organisation, in its "Global Tuberculosis Report 2016" released on October 13, 2016 said, while efforts to address TB saved more than 3 million lives in 2015, the TB burden is today higher than previously estimated. "In 2015, there were an estimated 10.4 million new TB cases worldwide. Six countries accounted for 60% of the burden, with India bearing the major brunt, followed by Indonesia, China, Nigeria, Pakistan and South Africa," the WHO says. India reported 16,67,136 new TB cases in 2015, making up 16% of new cases worldwide. Likewise, of the 18 lakh people who died from TB in 2015, over 4 lakh died in India alone, making up 26% of global TB mortality. "Though global TB deaths fell by 22% between 2000 and 2015, the disease was one of the top 10 causes of death worldwide in 2015, responsible for more deaths than HIV and malaria," the WHO said.

TOBACCO

A Giant Killer of Economy and Health

India loses more to tobacco than it spends on health. India is annually losing more in terms of economic costs of tobacco use than it is spending on health. A new research on the financial consequences of tobacco use has revealed that economic costs of tobacco use, which causes serious diseases, was ₹1,04,500 crore in 2011 for users aged between 35 and 69 years.

This burden translates into 1.16 per cent of the GDP— 0.12 per cent more than the combined central and state expenditure on health in 2011-2012, the year of study selected by the Public Health Foundation of India (PHFI), which says a comprehensive taxation policy is a must to prevent tobacco use. Of the total economic cost, 16 per cent was direct cost of treatment and 84 per cent was indirect cost in terms of morbidity. The non-communicable diseases (NCDs) account for 53 per cent of all deaths in India and over 80 per cent NCD deaths are attributed to four diseases—cardiovascular diseases (CVDs), cancers, chronic respiratory diseases and diabetes. Tobacco consumption is a major risk factor for all these NCDs.

The Research Says

- It translates into 1.16% of the GDP—0.12% more than the combined Central and State expenditure on health in 2011-2012.
- Men share 91% of the economic burden related to tobacco while women's contribution is higher (29%) for smokeless tobacco.

INDIA FACES DIABETES EXPLOSION

Number of Diabetics Projected to Cross 10 Crore in 15 Years

India has done well in curbing stunting over the last decade, but the growing number of overweight people, particularly those prone to diabetes, may be a cause of concern according to the Global Nutrition Report, 2016.

Though still home to one-third of the world's 159 million stunted children aged below five years, India has witnessed a sharp decline in the prevalence of stunting, from 48% in 2006 to 38.7% in 2014.

Stunting, defined by UNICEF as the most prevalent form of under-nutrition, develops as a result of sustained poor dietary intake or repeated infections or both. "There is real hope that India can become a major part of the solution (to malnutrition). It almost doubled the rate of stunting reduction in the past 10 years compared with the previous decade," the report says.

However, it also calls for urgent attention to tackle the rising percentage of the overweight in India, in particular the high rate of diabetes among them. It points out that the prevalence of adult diabetes in India was recorded at 9.5% in 2015, against a global average of 9%. According to the latest estimates of the World Health Organisation, the number of Indians with diabetes doubled from 32 million in 2000 to 63 million in 2013, and is projected to balloon to 101.2 million in the next 15 years.

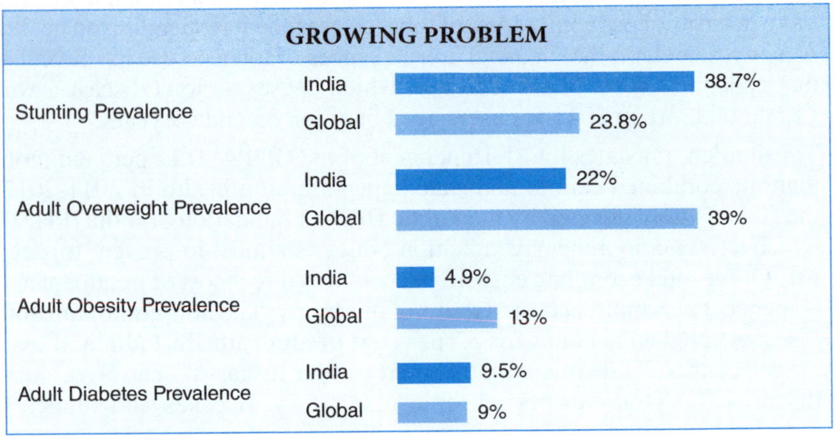

Source: Global Nutrition Report, 2016

EYEING VISION LOSS

Half the World's Population to be Myopic by 2050. One-Fifth of Them at Increased Risk of Blindness; Experts Blame it on All Work and No Outdoor Activities

Half the world's population — nearly five billion — will be short-sighted or myopic by 2050, with up to one-fifth of them at a significantly increased risk of blindness if the current trends continue, researchers, including those of Indian-origin, have claimed.

The number with vision loss from high myopia is expected to increase seven-fold from 2000 to 2050, with myopia to become a leading cause of permanent blindness worldwide, researchers said. The rapid increase in the prevalence of myopia globally is attributed to "environmental factors, principally lifestyle changes, resulting from a combination of decreased time outdoors and increased near work activities, among other factors," said researchers from Brien Holden Vision Institute, University of New South Wales Australia and Singapore Eye Research Institute.

STROKES STRIKE HARD

3 Adults Hit By It Every Minute in India

Three adults suffer from a stoke every minute in India and around 5 million people are disabled worldwide due to a brain attack each year.

A stroke occurs when a blood vessel bringing blood and oxygen to the brain gets blocked or ruptured. When this happens, brain cells don't get the required blood. Deprived of oxygen, nerve cells stop working and die within minutes, so the part of the body they control can't function either.

1 IN 6 DIES OF STROKE IN LIFETIME	
World	**India**
• 20 million people suffer from stroke every year. It causes five million deaths. • 5 million people are rendered disabled because of stroke. • One in six persons gets a stroke in his/her lifetime.	• 1.5 million people suffer from strokes every year. • 3,000-4,000 Indians suffer from stroke every day. • Strokes cause more deaths in the country than Malaria, Tuberculosis and HIV combined.

CASES OF CANCER RISE BY 3% EVERY YEAR

40% of Patients Die Annually in the Country

Cases of cancer, considered the worst of all maladies, have been rising 2-3% across the country annually, show data and estimates from the India Council of Medical Research (ICMR).

The figures, extrapolated from cancer registries across the country, show that if 10.28 lakh Indians were diagnosed with cancer in 2011, the number swelled by roughly 9% to 11.18 lakh in 2014. Correspondingly, the number of deaths increased from 4.52 lakh in 2011 to 4.92 lakh in 2014. Every year, about four out of 10 cancer patients (or 40%) die. The rate can be as high as 70% for some types of cancer.

Breast Cancer the Deadliest of All Types

Incidence of breast cancer (14%) tops in the country among both sexes, followed by cervical and oral cancers. Breast cancer seen as an urban woman's bane — claimed one life every 10 minutes.

Now, Globocan 2012, a software prepared by WHO's International Agency for Research on Cancer, has used data from the Census in 2011 to show that breast cancer has upstaged cervical cancer as the most common cancer among Indian women. In fact, Globocan 2012 shows that breast cancer affects 25 out of every 1,00,000 women in India; cervical cancer affects 22.

Preventive Aspects—Need of the Hour

According to a World Health Organisation (WHO) assessment, an estimated 60% of all deaths in India are due to non-communicable diseases. Cardiovascular diseases alone account for 26% of the total mortality, while chronic respiratory diseases lead to 13% of deaths. Cancer and diabetes, incidences of which are rapidly increasing in India, accounted for 7% and 2% of mortality respectively in 2014.

Besides, mental health conditions in India, including depression and schizophrenia, also contribute heavily to NCD (Non-Communicable Disease) burden. Estimates suggest that over 20 million or two crore Indians suffer from mental health conditions.

There is an urgent need for paying attention to the 'preventive aspects' of NCDs. Emphasising the need for creating wide awareness among people regarding healthy living, the union health minister J.P. Nadda recommended yoga as an integral intervention for prevention and management of such diseases. He said yoga and knowledge in AYUSH system of medicine can be of great help not only in preventing but also in controlling non-communicable diseases.

The health ministry has also drawn an overarching National Multi-Sectoral Action Plan with an aim to reduce premature deaths from cancer, diabetes and heart diseases by 25% by 2025.

- Over 10 lakh new cases of cancer are diagnosed every year in India.
- Prevalence of diabetes doubled to 63 million in 2013 from 32 million in 2000.

THE TICKING 'AIDS' TIME BOMB

In India, the first case of AIDS was reported in 1986 from Chennai. Since then, there has been an increase in the number of HIV infections over the years. In July 2003, India with the world's second highest population had at least 4 million HIV positive people. HIV sentinel surveillance data showed Maharashtra as the most affected state followed by Tamil Nadu, Andhra Pradesh, Karnataka and Manipur.

AIDS: Mapping the Disease

- Two in three people with HIV—23.5 million of 35 million—live in sub-Saharan Africa.
- At 5.6 million, South Africa has the largest HIV-infected population in the world, followed by Nigeria's 3.5 million and India's 2.39 million.

HIV in India

- 1.48 lakh people died of AIDS-related causes in 2011, 7% of them were children.
- 29% reduction in estimated annual AIDS deaths in 2007–11 due to wider access to ART (Anti-Retroviral Therapy).
- 39% was the coverage of ART for HIV+ kids in 2011.

Hope for AIDS Cure

In a breakthrough, Australian researchers claim to have discovered how to modify a protein in Human Immunodeficiency Virus (HIV) which could lead to a potential cure for Acquired Immuno Deficiency Syndrome (AIDS).

According to researcher David Harrich from Queensland Institute of Medical Research, the protein can be modified so that, instead of replicating, it protects against the deadly infection.

Breakthrough Treatment

American researchers claimed to have cured an infant of HIV infection in a medical breakthrough that raises hopes for thousands of babies across the world who contract the deadly virus in their mothers' wombs.

- Tests showed virus steadily decreasing in infant's blood till it became undetectable, 29 days after birth.
- Infant received antivirals till 18 months of age.
- 10 months later, repeated blood tests found no sign of HIV.

This is the first child—and only the second HIV-infected person—to have been cured of the disease, if the claim announced on March 3, 2013 by a research team from John Hopkins Children's Centre (JHCC) and the University of Massachusetts Medical School is found to be true.

India Winning AIDS War, New Infection Down 57%

India is winning the battle against HIV/AIDS, latest statistics have revealed. According to the UN AIDS Report-2013, the country reduced new HIV infections by as much as 57% among adults since 2001.

AIDS CONTROL SCHEME

Gets ₹ 300 Crore Boost, to Offer Relief to 21 Lakh Patients

In a move likely to bring relief to over 21 lakh HIV patients across the country, the health ministry has ramped up the national AIDS control programme with an additional investment of over ₹ 300 crore.

The new plan includes introduction of third-line treatment for over one lakh patients, increasing the benchmark for those eligible for free anti-retroviral therapy (ART) as well as ensuring more supplies of contraceptives.

This assumes significance as the AIDS control programme, which is on the verge of maturing from receiving international funding, suffered a huge cut in budgetary allocation 2015-16. This led to shortage of condoms, medicines and testing kits across the country. However, 2016-17 budget has proposed an allocation of ₹ 1615 crore for the programme, as compared to ₹ 1300 crore in 2015-16.

ACTION PLAN

In 2015, the total number of people living with HIV (PLHIV) in India: 21.17 lakh

National adult (15-49 years) HIV Prevalence: 0.26%

New HIV cases in India in 2015: 86,000 — showing 66% decline in new infections from 2000

WHAT GOVERNMENT PLANS TO DO

- Provide free anti-retroviral therapy (ART) to anyone below 500 CD4 cell count
- Provide free third-line anti-retroviral medicines
- Increase supply of condoms

HUGE SHORTAGE OF MEDICAL PROFESSIONALS IN RURAL INDIA

Only one-third of India's government doctors work in villages where almost 70% of the population lives, according to data obtained from a government health report released in July, 2014. The Central Bureau of Health Profile (NHP), 2013 shows only 29,562 of India's 1,06,613 government doctors work in villages, and the number of specialists in rural areas is even lower. Only 5,805 specialists work in villages. India has 9,18,303 doctors in the government and private sector for its 1.21 billion people, but most private practitioners and specialists choose to work in urban areas.

WORLD'S TOP 5 MEDICAL TOURISM HOT SPOTS

India is one among the top five medical tourist spots in the world having hosted nearly 1,66,000 medical tourists from across the globe in 2012, according to a PHD Chamber's Medical and Wellness Tourism Report released on July 25, 2014.

The medical tourism industry in India is expected to reach an estimated value of $6 billion (₹ 36,060 crore) by 2018. The growth of medical tourism in India has led to the enhancement of better and advanced medical facilities in the country. More tourists are coming to India because cost of treatment is much less compared to the US and the European countries. The report further mentions that highly-skilled doctors coupled with improvement in medical infrastructure are attracting medical tourists.

THERAPY FOR GROWTH

Government mulls enhancing facilities, promoting alternative treatments like Ayurveda and yoga to cash in on sector's growth

FROM WHERE

Asia-Pacific	47.8%
West Asia and north Africa	40.5%
Europe	8.6%
North and South America	2.6%

FOR WHAT

Cardiology, Cardiothoracic, Orthopaedic, Dentistry, Gastroenterology, Bariatric, Ophthalmology and Urology

GLOBE TROTTERS

Medical tourism as a proportion of overall tourism

Country	Percentage
Thailand	10 – 11%
Singapore	7 – 8%
Mexico	4 – 5%
India	2 – 3%

EDUCATIONAL ISSUES

GROWTH OF LITERACY IN INDIA

A Matter of Satisfaction or A Cause of Concern?

The 2011 Census showed that literacy in the country is up from 65% in 2001 to 74.04% in 2011. Many have hailed it as good news: the right direction, a substantial increase.

The truth is that the news is not so good, and the increase is not enough. In fact, the rate of growth of literacy has slowed down from the last decade to this decade, and this has serious implications on how we need to go forward. First, our education expenditure has shot up, indicating a worsening return on the same. Second, when the rate of literacy growth slows, it almost certainly has an impact on our overall economic growth in the following decade. Third, the deceleration in the trend is too early and, if continued, will lead us to reaching the universal literacy levels far more slowly than we should be prepared to accept.

In fact, 1991–2001 was the best decade in terms of literacy growth this country has seen. We must remember that we started at Independence with a level of just 18%—less than one in five Indians could read or write. Post-1947, as we started lifting ourselves by our bootstraps in education, the numbers started going up, slowly first, then more rapidly. In the last decade of the last century, literacy grew a full 12 percentage points, from 53% to 65%—truly a huge leap for a 10-year period. Many states saw double-digit literacy growth, with Rajasthan increasing literacy by 21 percentage points, from 39% to 60%. The larger states—Uttar Pradesh, Maharashtra, Andhra Pradesh, Tamil Nadu and Bihar—all grew in double digits, and that contributed to the overall trend. In terms of expenditure, clearly, we had just started increasing our expenditure on education, and the results were already showing—it was a very-high-return decade for us.

The impact on economic growth in the decade that followed, was significant with the economy accelerating to 6–8% per annum growth levels in the previous few years, despite global recession. While one could argue that the correlation between literacy and GDP growth (with a lag) is tenuous, it makes intuitive sense. It also helps explain how countries such as China, who have relentlessly pursued growth in literacy, have succeeded in sustaining rapid GDP growth in the past 30 years.

The increase in literacy in the decade 1991–2001 should have set us up for a faster move to universal literacy. With nearly 65% literacy by 2001, we should have been targeting 76–80% literacy by 2011. This would have suggested true rapid growth and success of all our literacy missions and strong return on our educational expenditure.

Instead, we see that the literacy level in 2011 was just 74.04%. The decade-on-decade growth rate dropped from 12 percentage points in the previous decade to 9 percentage points in this decade. The slowdown was significant in most large states, which were in the single digits. The exceptions were most of the north-eastern states and Bihar, which saw a growth from 47% to 64%, an increase of 17 percentage points.

The implications of this decrease in literacy growth rate were many. It pointed to a worsening productivity of the State's expenditure on education, which had gone up rapidly from 3% of GDP to 4–5% in the past 10 years. While the money spent had gone up substantially, we need to understand why it was not leading to acceleration, but deceleration, in literacy growth.

The deceleration means that we run the risk of reaching 80–85% literacy and then growing very slowly, leaving a huge 15–20% of the country's population out of the education ambit. This may have serious implications for inclusive growth, for equity and for our aim of universal literacy.

Clearly, the deceleration in literacy growth rate in the past 10 years should alarm us. We need to ask ourselves how we are, as a country, spending the increasingly larger amounts of money on education and what we are getting in return. We need far more accountability in the system. We need to understand the root causes of the decline and address them in qualitatively different ways. We need to be relentless in our drive to see everyone literate. In Kerala—which already had high level of literacy—the effort to introduce a universal literacy programme in the late 1980s in some districts is an example of ensuring that there is no slowdown till the last person is literate. There must be more such efforts if we are to achieve total literacy and, thereby, also ensure that we develop our human capital at a far more rapid rate than we have done in the last 10 years.

RIGHT TO EDUCATION ACT

India on April 1, 2010 took the historic step of providing the right to free and compulsory education—a revolution that aims to put nearly one crore children in school and involve a budget of ₹1,71,484 crore over five years.

The Constitution (Eighty-sixth Amendment) Act, 2002 inserted Article 21-A to provide free and compulsory education as a fundamental right to all children in India in the age group of six to 14 years. The Right of Children to Free and Compulsory Education (RTE) Act, 2009, means every child has a right to full time elementary education of satisfactory and equitable quality in a formal school which satisfies certain essential norms and standards. Article 21-A and the RTE Act came into effect on 1 April 2010.

Whereby it became incumbent upon the State to provide children in the age group of 6 to 14 years not only free schooling but also quality education. Schools running out of tents and under trees were no longer be allowed.

The Act marks the fulfilment of India's dream to join other powerhouses in the continent—Japan, South Korea, Singapore and Hong Kong—that have near-total literacy.

India is a late entrant to the group of countries that have legislated for compulsory education. Most countries in the West enacted laws long ago making elementary education a responsibility of the State.

HOW OTHERS DID IT?

- UK was among the last in Europe to enact laws making elementary education the State's responsibility in 1870. It was after this that Gopal Krishna Gokhale in 1911, urged the Imperial Legislative Assembly to confer on the Indian people, the Right to Education.
- In Asia, Japan, China, Korea, Malaysia and Mauritius have similar laws.
- In Japan, education is compulsory at the elementary and lower secondary levels. Around 97 per cent of its elementary education is funded by the government.
- South Korea was the first country to provide Internet access to all primary, junior, and high schools.
- In China, 91 per cent of the country has compulsory primary education.

KEY FEATURES OF THE RIGHT TO EDUCATION ACT

- All children in 6–14 age group must get free and compulsory education.
- No child shall be held back, expelled or required to pass a board examination till Class VIII.
- There must be 25 per cent reservation for poor children even in private and minority schools.
- There must be one teacher for every 30 students.
- No direct (school fees) or indirect cost (uniforms, textbooks, mid-day-meals, transportation) need be borne by the child or parents to obtain elementary education.
- Schools shall constitute School Management Committees comprising local officials, parents, guardians and teachers. The SMCs will monitor utilisation of government grants and the school environment. RTE mandates inclusion of 50 per cent women and parents of children from disadvantaged groups in SMCs.

To achieve the goal of providing elementary education to every child, the country also introduced the Sarva Shiksha Abhiyan in 2000-2001.

The aim was to boost universal access to education, to retain students in school, to bridge gender and social category gaps in elementary education and to improve the quality of learning. Sarva Shiksha Abhiyaan interventions include the opening of new schools and alternate schooling facilities, the construction of schools and additional classrooms, providing toilets and drinking water facility in schools, provisioning for teachers, periodic teacher training and academic resource support, textbooks and support for learning achievement.

To boost enrolment, retention and attendance, while also improving nutritional levels in children, India introduced the National Programme of Nutritional Support to Primary Education as a centrally sponsored scheme on August 15, 1995, which became the cooked Mid Day Meal Scheme in 2001.

OBC QUOTA IN EDUCATIONAL INSTITUTIONS

The Supreme Court on 10th April, 2008, upheld OBC quota in central educational institutions clearing the way for reservation of 27 per cent seats for 'backward' castes over a period of three years from the academic year 2008–09. This landmark verdict was given by the five-judge Constitution Bench headed by former Chief Justice K.G. Balakrishnan. They unanimously decided to keep the 'creamy layer' out of the purview of the quota and recommended review of the quota every five years. The 'creamy layer' must be excluded from the socially and educationally backward classes as per a 1993 government order. The government order excludes children of Constitutional functionaries from the President downwards, of class I and II services, PSU officers, officers in the three defence services and professionals ranging from doctors and engineers to sportspersons and authors, as belonging to the 'creamy layer'. The judges asked the government to exclude the children of former and present MPs and MLAs from the purview of OBC reservation. They however clarified that the 'creamy layer' concept was not applicable to Scheduled Castes and Scheduled Tribes.

THE GRIM REALITY : HIGH DROPOUT RATE

The dropout rates for children of 6-14 age group from SC and ST are 51 per cent and 58 per cent, respectively, much higher than the 37 per cent rate for non-SC/ST children. UNICEF reports 80 million Indian children are dropping out of school before completing elementary education. While the government reports may boast of a high net enrolment (in primary schools to be nearly 100 per cent), retention, desired learning outcomes and regular attendance is a challenge within the disadvantaged groups.

Top 5 Nations with Highest Number of Out-of-school Children in Primary Level (in millions)

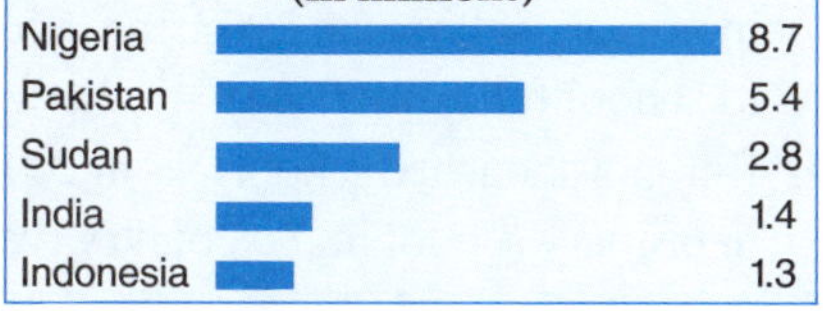

GDP PERCENTAGE IN EDUCATION

India (with a drop of 1%)

Year	Percentage
1994	4.34%
2010	3.35%

• 20%of total public spending should be on education according to the international recommendations.

Percentage of Total Public Spending Spent on Education

Country	Percentage
India	11.0%
Pakistan	10.1%
Sri Lanka	12.9%
Bangladesh	14.1%

Source: UN

OUT OF SCHOOL—THE BIG PICTURE

Unpleasant Truth

- Globally there were 99.8 million children who were out of the school in 2000 at primary level.
- By 2012, there were still 57.8 million children who were out of school at primary level.
- There were 30.6 million female children out of school in 2012 at primary level.
- Bid to reach out to out-of-school children since 2007 has stagnated at 9% at primary level.
- In 2012, 63 million young adolescents around the world were not enrolled at primary or secondary school, compared with 97 million in 2000.

Policies That Have Brought About Success

- 24% of children of primary school age were out of school in Nepal in 2000; by 2013, the rate had fallen to just 1% with the out-of-school population falling by 6,60,000.
- Vietnam, which introduced a new curriculum that paid particular attention to disadvantaged learners, managed to more than halve the percentage of children who had never been to school between 2000 and 2010.
- Ghana doubled education spending and saw the number of children enrolled in school rise from 2.4 million in 1999 to 4.1 million in 2013.
- In Morocco, which introduced the teaching of Amazigh (a local language) in primary schools in 2003, the percentage of children who had never been to school fell from 9% to 4% between 2003 and 2009.
- Burundi abolished school fees in 2005 and the percentage of children enrolled in primary school in the country rose from 54% to 94% in six years.

THE EDUCATION SYSTEM

System today pays little attention to creativity. The focus is on reproducing textbook knowledge rather than applying it. As a result, organisations spend a huge amount of money and time to re-educate fresh graduates before assigning them work. Generally, they are given an option of choosing between commerce, science and arts right after completing secondary school. Choosing a field at such a young age can lead to a wrong choice. Hence, students must be given a chance to switch streams easily and choose their career. The system must make it easy for students to realign their choices at a later stage.

Also, teachers should be provided regular training to update their knowledge about new trends in technology, industry and research. Medical education in India should not only focus on theory. Instead, it should synchronise theory with clinical practice to help students gain work experience before they graduate.

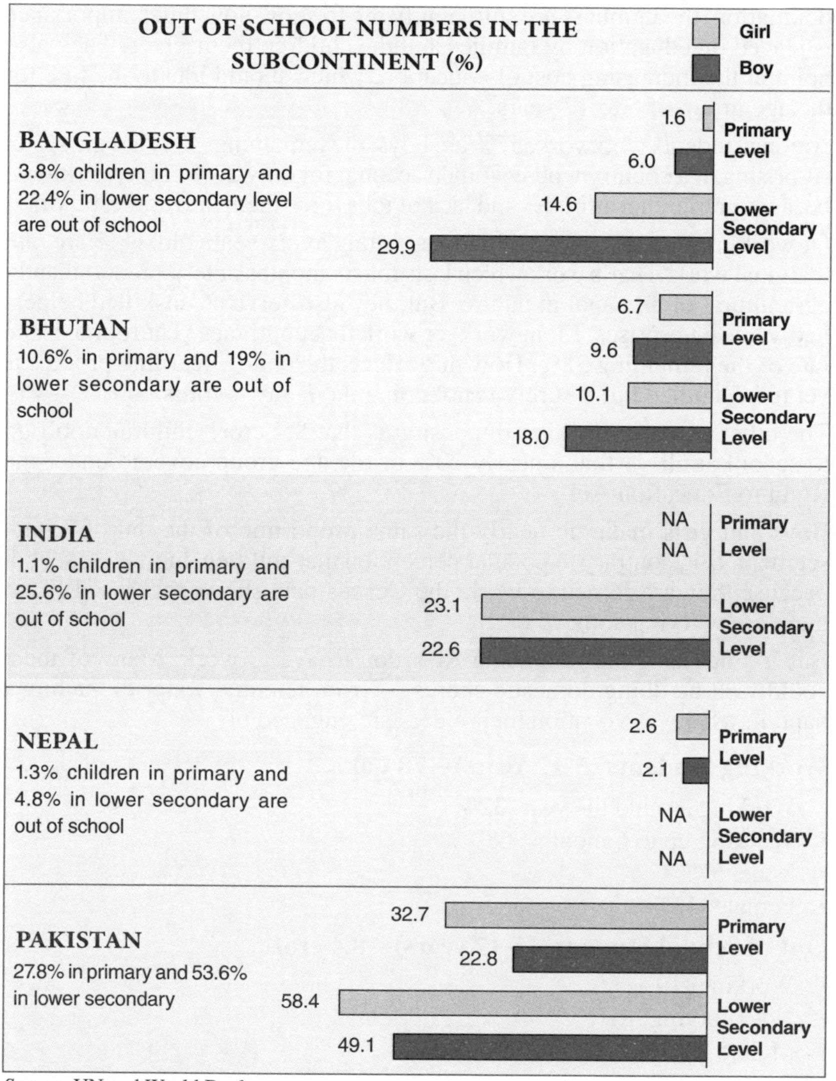

Source: UN and World Bank

8.4 CRORE INDIAN CHILDREN DON'T ATTEND SCHOOL: 2011 CENSUS

78 Lakh Forced To Earn While They Learn

Census 2011 data has revealed two alarming facts. As many as 78 lakh Indian children are forced to earn a livelihood even as they attend schools while 8.4 crore children don't go to school at all.

Although the share of working students is low compared to the whole student population, the numbers are sufficiently big to show how much importance is placed on education by families and the children themselves. They also point at the increasing cost of education, which should ideally be free for the age group of 5 to 17 years.

Among students who work, 57% are boys, the remaining, 43% are girls. Not surprising in a country where women account for only 27% of the workforce because patriarchal attitudes and lack of jobs force them into domestic work.

Of working students, some of them as young as six years old, 68% are into marginal work. That's work which lasts for six months or less-predominantly agricultural or artisanal in nature. But they also serve as unskilled helpers in diverse enterprises. Main work, or work that continues year round, is the fate of the remaining 32%. How this affects the child's learning process is yet to be studied but it surely is not doing them any favours.

The other equally shocking dimension is that 8.4 crore children don't go to school at all — that's nearly 20% of the age group covered under the Right to Education Act.

Boys and girls make up nearly the same proportion of the out-of-school segment. But, contrary to popular perception that children don't go to school because they are forced to work, the Census data shows that just 19% of them are working somewhere.

But it's not as if the remaining 81% don't have to work. Many of them could well be doing domestic chores — from fetching water to lending a hand in whatever vocation their elders are engaged in.

Working Students (5-17 Years)—78 Lakh

- Working around the year: 32%
- Working up to 6 months: 68%
- Male: 57%
- Female: 43%

Out of School Students (5-17 years)—8.4 crore

- Working: 19%
- Not Working: 81%
- Male:51%
- Female: 49%

Source: Census 2011

UN: INDIA 50 YEARS BEHIND EDUCATION GOALS

India isn't expected to achieve its global education commitments of providing universal upper secondary education until 2085 (55 years later than the 2030 deadline)

- India has the second highest number of children out of school of primary school age (2.9 million) & the highest number of out of school adolescents of lower secondary school age (11.1 million) & upper secondary education (46.8 million).

- 26% of primary school-age children in India attended private schools in 2009-10.
- Less than 5% of adults in India have ever participated in a literacy programme.

India will be half a century late in achieving its universal education goals, according to a UNESCO report released on September 5, 2016. This means the country will achieve universal primary education by 2050, universal lower secondary education in 2060 and universal upper secondary education in 2085. The 2030 deadline for achieving sustainable development goals will be possible only if India introduces fundamental changes in the education sector, according to the Global Education Monitoring (GEM) report.

The report says over 60 million children in India receive little or no formal education and the country has over 11.1 million out-of-school students in the lower secondary level, the highest in the world. At the upper secondary level, 46.8 million are out of school, while 2.9 million students do not even attend primary school. The report says that by 2020 there will be a shortage of 40 million workers with tertiary education.

IMPORTANT EDUCATIONAL POLICIES

Sarva Shiksha Abhiyan (SSA)

The Scheme of Sarva Shiksha Abhiyan (SSA) a national flagship programme, is being implemented in all districts of the country. The scheme of Sarva Shiksha Abhiyan (SSA) was launched in 2001.

Female literacy is one of the most potent weapons to fight 'Gender Bias' and Sarva Shiksha Abhiyan can accomplish this mission.

The Sarva Shiksha Abhiyan, a government scheme for universalisation of education for all, has been beneficial in its efforts towards girls' education. One of the largest education initiatives in the world, the targeted provisions for girls under Sarva Shiksha Abhiyan include:

- Free textbooks to be given to all girls upto class VIII.
- Separate toilets for girls.
- Back to school camps for out-of-school girls.
- Bridge courses for older girls.
- Recruitment of 50 per cent women teachers.
- Early childhood care and Education centres in/near schools; convergence with related programmes.
- Teachers' sensitisation programmes to promote equitable learning opportunities.

- Gender-sensitive teaching-learning materials including textbooks.
- Intensive community mobilisation efforts.
- 'Innovation fund' per district for need-based interventions for ensuring girls' attendance and retention.

Education Guarantee Scheme and Alternative and Innovative Education

Education Guarantee Scheme and Alternative and Innovative Education (EGS and AIE) are important components of Sarva Shiksha Abhiyan (SSA) aiming to bring out-of-school children in the fold of Elementary Education.

EGS addresses the inaccessible habitation where there is no formal school within the radius of one km and at least 15–25 children of 6–14 years age group, who are not going to school, are available. In exceptional cases, an EGS school can be opened even for 10 children in remote habitations and hilly areas. Alternative Education interventions for specific categories of very deprived children, e.g., child labour, street children, migrating children, working children, children living in difficult circumstances and older children in the 9+ age group, especially adolescent girls, are being supported under EGS and AIE all over the country.

Mid-Day Meal Scheme (MDMS)

In a country where an estimated 41 per cent of children are underweight or malnourished due to poverty, the provision of hot, cooked meals at schools has been a particularly popular programme. Initiated in typical half-hearted fashion in the 1990s, MDMS actually got traction after a landmark direction from the Supreme Court in 2001 making it mandatory for schools to provide cooked meals. Huge investments are required every year, but the benefits derived out of it make it worthwhile.

National Literacy Mission (NLM)

The National Literacy Mission, set up in May 1988, aimed to attain a sustainable threshold level of 75 per cent literacy by 2007 by imparting functional literacy to non-literates in the age group of 15–35 years—the productive as well as reproductive age group which constitutes a major segment of the work force.

The Total Literacy Campaign is the principal strategy of NLM for eradication of illiteracy. These are implemented through Zila Saksharata Samitis (district level literacy committees).

NLM fully recognises the vast potential of NGOs in furthering its objectives and has taken measures to strengthen its partnership with NGOs and has assigned them an active promotional role in the literacy movement. Apart from imparting literacy, the NGOs provide academic and technical resource support through experimental and innovative programmes.

ENVIRONMENT ISSUES

ASIA FACES SEVERE WATER CRISIS BY 2050

Rising Economic Activity, Population Boom and Climate Change to Blame: MIT

Countries in Asia, including India, may face severe water shortage by 2050 due to rising economic activity, growing populations and climate change, MIT scientists have warned. There is a high risk of severe water stress in much of an area that is home to roughly half the world's population. Having run a large number of simulations of future scenarios, the researchers found that the median amounts of projected growth and climate change in the next 35 years in Asia would lead to about 1 billion more people becoming water-stressed compared to today.

While climate change is expected to have serious effects on the water supply in many parts of the world, the study underscores the extent to which industrial expansion and population growth may by themselves exacerbate water-access problems. "It's not just a climate change issue," said Adam Schlosser, from the Massachusetts Institute of Technology (MIT) in US.

"We simply cannot ignore that economic and population growth in society can have a very strong influence on our demand for resources and how we manage them. And climate, on top of that, can lead to substantial magnifications to those stresses," said Scholsser. To conduct the study, the scientists built upon an existing model developed previously at MIT, the Integrated Global Systems Model (IGSM), which contains probabilistic projections of population growth, economic expansion, climate, and carbon emissions from human activity.

POLLUTION

Delhi has got rid of the 'world's most polluted city' tag. The World Health Organisation urban air quality database released on May 11, 2016, ranked the capital 11th among 3,000 cities in 103 countries on PM2.5 (fine, particulate pollution) levels and 25th in terms of PM10 (coarse pollution particles) levels.

Delhi had emerged as the most polluted city in WHO's 2014 database. In the latest database, Zabol in Iran is the most polluted city in the world.

Gwalior and Allahabad are a close second and third in terms of PM2.5 levels, associated with more serious health impacts than PM10. Patna and Raipur rank sixth and seventh respectively.

WORLD'S MOST POLLUTED CITIES

10 Indian Cities in Worst 20

City	Country	PM 2.5 Level
Zabol	Iran	216.7
Gwalior	India	176.1
Allahabad	India	169.7
Riyadh	Saudi Arabia	155.5
Al Jubail	Saudi Arabia	151.7
Patna	India	148.9
Raipur	India	143.7
Bamenda	Cameroon	132.0
Xingtai	China	128.0
Baoding	China	126.0
Delhi	India	122.1
Ludhiana	India	121.9
Dammam	Saudi Arabia	120.9
Shijiazhuang	China	120.6
Kanpur	India	114.9
Khanna	India	113.8
Firozabad	India	113.3
Lucknow	India	112.9
Handan	China	111.8
Peshawar	Pakistan	111.0

Source: WHO; PM2.5 in micrograms per cubic meter

WHO data showed that air pollution in smaller cities such as Gwalior, Allahabad, Kanpur, Jodhpur, Ludhiana and Bhopal has been rising at a much faster pace than in the big metros.

Air pollution is a national crisis and demands a concerted national action plan in response.

90% PEOPLE ARE BREATHING BAD AIR: WHO

According to a report released by World Health Organisation on September 27, 2016 nine out of ten person are breathing poor quality air. It has called for dramatic action against pollution that is responsible for more than six million deaths a year.

The UN body has urged governments to cut the number of vehicles on the road, improve waste management and promote clean cooking fuel. The report, based on data collected from more than 3,000 sites across the globe, found that "92 per cent of the world's population lives in places where air quality levels exceed WHO limits."

The Problem is most acute in cities, but air in rural areas is worse than many think, WHO experts said. Poorer countries have much dirtier air than the development world, according to the report, but pollution "affects practically all countries in the world."

The data focuses on dangerous particulate matter with a diameter of less than 2.5 micrometres, or PM2.5 that includes toxins like sulfate and black carbon, which can penetrate deep into the lungs or the cardiovascular system. Air with more than 10 microgrammes per cubic metre of PM2.5 on an annual average basis is considered substandard.

Alarming pollution

- The problem is most acute in cities, but air in rural areas is worse than many think.
- Poorer countries have much dirtier air than the developed world.
- Pollution affecting all countries in the world and all parts of society.
- Cutting number of vehicles, improving waste management and clean cooking fuel is must.

INDIA CUT CARBON EMISSION INTENSITY BY 12% IN 5 YEARS

On Course to Meet Target, Government Reports to UN Body

India, on January 22, 2016 submitted its first Biennial Update Report (BUR) to a UN climate body highlighting that the country is well on course to fulfil its global commitment by voluntarily cutting its carbon emission intensity (emission per unit of GDP) by about 12% between 2005 and 2010.

The result appears encouraging as it shows that the country is in line to reach its 20-25% reduction target by 2020 and subsequently the 33-35% emission intensity reduction goal by 2030 as promised by it in the country's climate action plan to the UN body. The BUR was submitted by India under its obligation to inform the United Nations Framework Convention on Climate Change (UNFCCC) about its action on the ground to deal with the challenges of climate change. As per the provisions of the conventions, countries need to periodically provide information in the form of their

'National Communication'.

The Paris climate agreement, reached by 195 countries on December 13, 2015 had called for developing countries to submit their first biennial update reports as soon as possible.

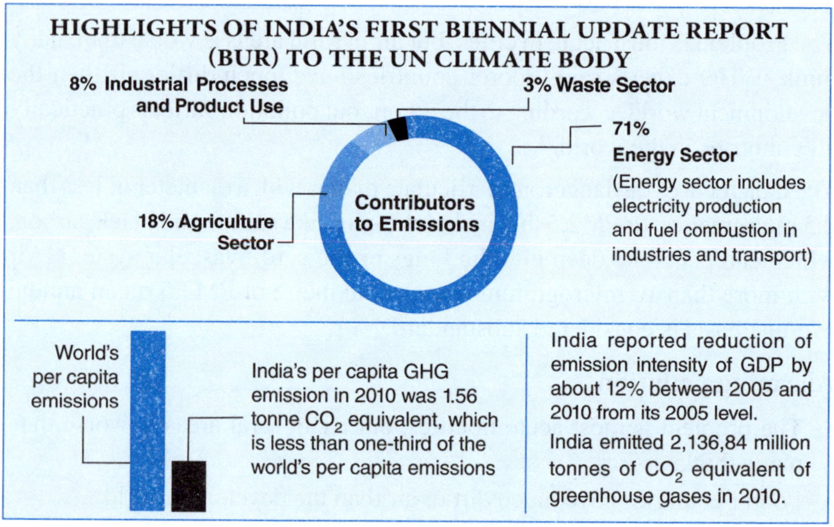

DEFENCE AFFAIRS

DEFENCE DEALS WITH RUSSIA & THE U.S.

Now, India Turns to Russia For Mega Defence Deals

After a pronounced tilt towards the US in terms of defence deals and military-to-military ties over the last decade, further reinforced by the recent inking of the bilateral logistics pact, India has reassured Russia that their traditional strategic partnership will continue on its upward trajectory.

Defence ministry sources said negotiations for mega defence projects with Russia like joint development of the futuristic fifth-generation fighter aircraft (FGFA) and Kamov Ka-226T light utility helicopters were "well on track" after being stalled for some time.

RUSSIA	THE US
Backdrop: Russia has been India's biggest arms supplier for decades, Sales worth over \$45 billion since early 1960s.	**Deals:** US has overtaken Russia in bagging Indian arms deals over last 4 years. Sales worth over \$15 billion since 2007.
Inductions: ranges from MiG fighters & Sukhoi-30MKI jets to Kiloclassubmarines & Talwar-frigates.	**Equipment:** ranges from C-17 Globemaster- III strategic airlifters & P-81 maritime patrol planes to Apache attack & Chinook heavy-lift helicopters.
Problems: India unhappy with Russia for not sticking to delivery schedules, jacking up costs midway, hurdles in tech transfer & unreliable spares support. But India knows only Russia will help with 'strategic projects' like nuclear-powered submarines.	**Problems:** India unhappy with the US for stringent technology export licencing regime. But hopes designation of India as a 'Major Defence Partner' will make tech transfer smoother & faster.
Some future Projects • Lease of 2nd nuclear-powered submarine for over \$1.5 billion. • Acquisition of 5 S-400 triumf air defence systems for ₹ 39,000 crore. • Joint production of 5th-Gen fighter based on Sukhoi T-50 (PAK-FA) in India. If IAF inducts 127 fighters, overall cost would be about \$25billion. • Joint production of 200 Kamov Ka-226T light utility helicopters in India for \$1 billion.	**Some Future Projects:** • \$750 million deal for 145 M-777 ultra-light howitzers for Army. • US push for F/A-18 'Super Hornet' or F-16 fighter production line under 'Make in India' policy. • Joint working groups under Defence Technology & Trade Initiative on aircraft carrier technologies; naval systems; air systems; intelligence, surveillance & reconnaissance; chemical & biological protection.

INDIA-FRANCE DEAL FOR NEXT GENERATION FIGHTER JETS

First Major Buy for IAF in 20years — French Company to Start Delivery in 3 years

India and France on September 23, 2016 signed a Euro 7.87 billion (₹ 59,000 crore) deal for the Rafale figher jets, equipped with the latest missile weaponry besides multiple India-specific modifications, that will give the Indian Air Force (IAF) a greater 'potency' over its adversaries.

India will buy 36 Rafale fighter jets. Importantly, 36 per cent of the deal value will comprise of India-made parts.

The deal was signed by Defence Minister Manohar Parrikar and his French counterpart Jean-Yves Le Drain — the first major deal for the IAF in nearly two decades. The IAF has not pro-cured any frontline fighter jet since the start of this century— the last one being Sukhoi 30-MKI from Russia (first ordered in the mid-1990s).

The first of the Rafale jets from Dassault Aviation, France, is to be delivered in 36 months — by September 2019 — and the entire lot over the next 31 months (by April 2022). The French company will make India-specific changes, such as equipping the aircraft with the next generation missiles Meteor and Scalp, which will add capability much beyond India's immediate adversaries, as well as with radar jammers, synthetic aperture radars and helmet-mounted displays.

36 Rafale Jets

Meteor, a BVR (Beyond Visual Range) air-to-missile with a range of more than 150 km, will allow the IAF to hit targets inside Pakistan and Tibet from within its own territory. Scalp is a long-range air-to-cruise missiles with a range of 300 km.

Signing the deal, Parrikar observed, "Rafale is a potent aircraft which will add to IAFs capability." Under the latter, Dassault will ensure at least 75 per cent of the fleet remains operational/airworthy at any give time. In other words, 27 of the 36-plane fleet will always be war-ready. Welcoming the deal, Eric Trappier, Dassault Aviation CEO, said, "I am certain that Rafale and its performance will hold high the colours of the Indian Air Force." He added that the company was open to manufacturing Rafale in India if bigger orders come through.

'Best Fighter in the World'

- The Omnirole fighter plane can simultaneously perform air defence and ground attack missions; its combat range is between 780 and 1,500 km.
- Can carry 9.3 tonne weapons, including nuclear ones. Has air-to-air and air-to-ground missiles (70-300 km range).

- First Rafale to be delivered by late 2019 and all 36 by 2022. But there's no 'Make in India' tag or tech transfer.
- ₹ 12,780 crore needed for India-specific tweaks in all 36 planes, pushing up the price per jet to ₹ 1,640 crore

"Rafale is the best fighter jet in the world. With it, you can conduct all kinds of missions." —Jean Yves Le Drian (French defence minister)

THERE ARE AN ESTIMATED 230 NUCLEAR WEAPONS IN THE INDIAN SUBCONTINENT

The world is sitting on a stockpile of more than 15,000 nuclear weapons located in nine countries. This nuclear capability is large enough to destroy the entire world. All the nuclear-weapon countries have also developed sophisticated missiles to deliver these warheads. Any conventional war among these nations could descend into a nuclear disaster with immense loss of human lives.

Country	Missile Range (km)	Estimated Nuclear Warhead Inventories
Russia	11,000 – 15,000	7,300
USA	9,650 – 13,000	7,100
France	6,000	300
China	13, 000	260
UK	7,400 +	215
Pakistan	1,300	120
India*	**2,000**	**110**
Israel	1,500 – 1,800	80
North Korea	1,300	8

Source: Arms Control Association

*India has successfully test-fired Agni III, IV and V with a range of over 3,000, 4000 and over 5000 km, respectively.

PERMANENT COMMISSION FOR WOMEN IN ARMED FORCES

A landmark ruling of the Delhi High Court has now allowed women Permanent Commission in the armed forces.

Under the existing policy, women are allowed only as officers in the Short Service Commission (SSC) for a maximum period of 14 years. While all male SSC officers are eligible for Permanent Commission (PC), women have only now been allowed, and that, too, only in a few branches.

The High Court on March 12, 2010 directed that PC be offered within two months to SSC women officers of the Air Force and the Army on a par with their male SSC officers. The first batch of women SSC officers joined in 1992. Permanent Commission will be open to only those who were recruited after March 2009, i.e., the first PC will be offered only in 2019.

INDIA GETS FIRST WOMEN FIGHTER PILOTS

Flying officers Avani Chaturvedi, Bhawana Kanth and Mohana Singh were commissioned as India's first three women fighter pilots.

Avani Chaturvedi, who was born in Satna, Madhya Pradesh, paints and plays the violin. She chose to join IAF as she was inspired by the lives of Army officers in her family.

Bhawana Kanth, who is from Darbhanga, Bihar, loves playing badminton and volleyball. It was her childhood dream to "fly like a free bird" which inspired her to join IAF.

Mohana Singh, who is from Jhunjunu, Rajasthan, likes to sing, sketch abstracts and read. Born in a family of IAF officers, Mohana wanted to carry forward their legacy.

Air Force Recruits More Women Officers Than Army and Navy

Recently, the Indian Air Force inducted three women fighter pilots. An analysis of data on female personnel in the armed forces also shows that the IAF that leads when it comes to recruiting women.

Overall, women personnel constitute a tiny fraction of the armed forces, whose strength is estimated at 1.3 million personnel.

Number of Women in the Armed Forces

Army : 1,514	Navy : 439	Air Forces : 1,584

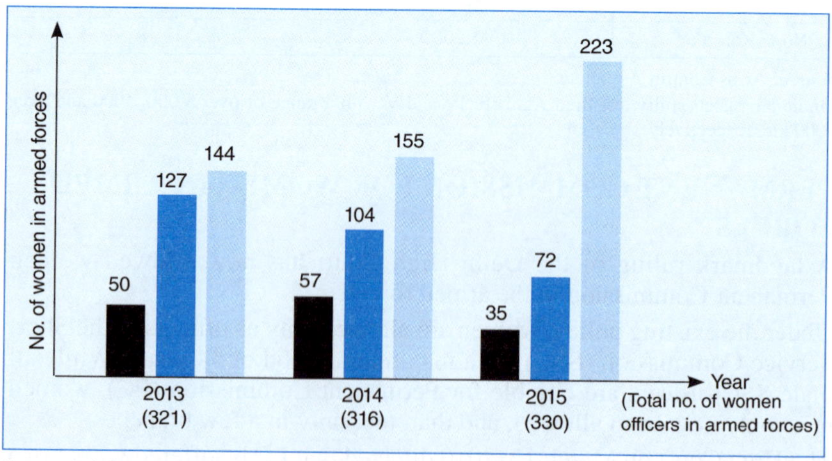

Source: Ministry of Defence, Data doesn't include the medical and dental branch, as of latest available data.

Army, Navy to Follow?

Pressure may now grow on the Army and the Navy to allow women in combat roles. Warships, tanks and combat positions in infantry are still no-go zones for women, who were allowed to join the armed forces outside the medical stream for the fist time in 1992.

NATIONAL DEFENCE ACADEMY

The National Defence Academy (NDA) is a premier Tri-Service institution which trains cadets of all three Services before inducting them into their respective pre-commissioning training academies. The three years course at the NDA is covered in six semesters and cadets are awarded with B.A/ B.Sc Degree. Thereafter, on conclusion of this training, the cadets proceed to their respective Service Academies for further training before being commissioned as officer in the Armed Forces.

COMMISSIONED RANKS IN DEFENCE SERVICES		
Army	**Navy**	**Air Force**
General	Admiral	Air Chief Marshal
Lieutenant General	Vice Admiral	Air Marshal
Major General	Rear Admiral	Air Vice Marshal
Brigadier	Commodore	Air Commodore
Colonel	Captain	Group Captain
Lieutenant Colonel	Commander	Wing Commander
Major	Lieutenant Commander	Squadron Leader
Captain	Lieutenant	Flight Lieutenant
Lieutenant	Sub Lieutenant	Flying Officer

India's Surgical Strikes: Response to Stun & Shock Pakistan

Indian Army on September 29, 2016 announced it had neutralised terrorists waiting to infiltrate. The brave military manoeuvre was hailed across the country.

The 'surgical strikes' was a resolute action by India 11 days after 18 soldiers were killed in the Uri sector in an attack by Jaish terrorists from across the border. The action came days after Prime Minister Narendra Modi promised that the blood of the jawans will not go in vain and the Army, asserting it will act at a place and time of its choosing, did so from midnight to dawn at five places and six launch pads.

"Based on specific and credible inputs that some terrorist teams had positioned themselves at launch pads along the LoC to carry out infiltration and conduct terrorist strikes inside J & K and in various metros, the Indian Army conducted surgical strikes at several of these launch pads. The operations were focussed on ensuring that these terrorists do not succeed in their design to endanger the lives of our citizens," the Director General of Military Operations, Lt. Gen Ranbir Singh, said at a joint briefing with the Ministry of External Affairs.

WHAT IS THE INDUS WATERS TREATY ABOUT?

When was the treaty signed ?

On September 19, 1960, Prime Minister Jawaharlal Nehru and Pakistan president Ayub Khan signed an agreement to share water of Beas, Ravi, sutlej, Indus, Chenab and Jhelum. As Indus was the biggest of them, the treaty was named the "Indus Waters Treaty'.

What Led to It ?

After Partition, Pakistan and India locked horns over the share of water in the Indus Basin as its source remained in India. In the early years after Partition, an Inter-Dominion Accord of 1948 apportioned the share. Pakistan was keen on a permanent solution. As both sides could not compromise, the World Bank negotiated a deal between them.

What Role did the World Bank Play?

In 1954, the World Bank offered a proposal to the two nations under which India retains control over the three eastern tributaries while Pakistan controls the three rivers in the west. While India was eager to seal this deal, Pakistan turned hostile, even threatening to walk out. After deliberations, talks gained momentum again in 1954. The Bank also helped to fund the construction of canals for Pakistan.

What are the Treaty's Main Provisions?

Waters of the eastern rivers were allocated to India; New Delhi is under obligation to let waters of the western rivers flow, except for certain consumptive use, with Pakistan getting 80% of it. The treaty gives lower riparian more "than four times" the water available to India.

Western rivers: Chenab, Jhelum, Indus

India's rights over these rivers are limited—can set up certain irrigation, run-of-the-river power plants, very limited storage, domestic and non-consumptive use, all subject to conditions.

Eastern rivers : Sutlej, Beas, Ravi

All exclusive rights over these rivers lie with India.

Indus Waters Commission—a success story

- Once every five years, conducts a general inspection of all rivers in parts. Total inspection tours so far; Over 100.
- Regularly meets once a year. Total meetings thus far, including those for taking up Pak objections; Over 100.

Pakistan's gains under the treaty

Financial assistance of £ 62 million to compensate for construction of new canals in lieu of eastern river waters that existing canals were getting. As a result of the IWT, Pakistan today has among the world's largest contiguous irrigation systems. All major reservoirs are post-IWT.

India's options if it walks out of the treaty

Block waters of the Indus
Challenge: Back up will inundate Ladakhi farmland and villages on the banks. Military camps may have to be relocated.

Build more dams on the Jhelum & Chenab to starve rural Pakistan during one-time filling and releasing water during monsoon to inundate land.

Challenge: Too far in future. Baglihar dam took 25 years to operationalise. A string of dams will take three decades.

Stop the flow of water from Punjab rivers from going to Pakistan.

Challenge: Massive acquisition of prime farmland will lead to unrest.

SPACE SCIENCE

ISRO SCRIPTS HISTORY, PUTS 8 SATELLITES IN TWO ORBITS

Two of the Satellites Were Made by Students of Indian Universities

India on September 26, 2016 achieved yet another space milestone when it successfully launched multiple satellites —including two made by students — from one rocket into two different orbits.

The mission was the longest for the polar satellite launch vehicle (PSLV C-35) that lifted off from Sriharikota at 9.12 am carrying eight satellites –three from India, including weather satellite SCATSAT-1, three from Algeria, and one each from Canada and the US.

The 371-kg SCATSAT-1, launched within 17 minutes of takeoff, will study oceans and help in weather forecast, including cyclone detection.

"Our space scientists keep scripting history. Their innovative zeal has touched the lives of 125 crore Indians and made India proud worldwide," Prime Minister Narendra Modi tweeted. Two of the Indian satellites were student-made.

Pratham, a 10kg satellite developed by students of Indian Institute of Technology. Bombay, will study the electron count in space which will help improve accuracy of the Global Positioning System in India, and also predict tsunamis.

The 5.25kg PISAT made by students of Bengaluru's PES University will take pictures of earth.

The PSLV has launched 39 remote-sensing satellites for ISRO, including the Mars mission of 2013-14. 'Pratham', or 'first' in English—has been designed to fit into a 30 cm cube.

Conceptualised in 2008, Pratham has been worked on by students across ITT-B engineering departments and spread over seven batches. It was pioneered by then students Saptarshi Bandyopadhyay and Shashank Tamaskar, under the guidance of then head of aerospace engineering professor K Sudhakar.

Bandyopadhyay, now a postdoctoral researcher at California Institute of Technology's Nasa Jet Propulsion Laboratory, and Tamaskar, a technical specialist with Advanced Dynamic Systems & Controls Group at Cummins Inc, USA - formed a small sixmember team.

It was 2007 and the trend of student satellites was growing all over the world, recalls Bandyopadhyay.

"Studying in the best institute in the country, we wanted to build something. That was really the motivation," Bandyopadhyay said. Pratham took eight years and seven graduating batches to finish.

In 2008, IIT-B was the first educational institute to approach ISRO with the idea of launching a student satellite– evident from the name given to the mission.

Previous Space Landmarks

Indian Regional Navigation Satellite System, 2016

The seven–satellite system created India's very own satellite navigation system e-terrestrial and will provide services in a host of fields, including marine navigation and disaster management.

Launching 20 Satellites, 2016

In June, ISRO launched 20 satellites in one mission, a record for the space agency. Apart from ISRO's own satellites and those built by students, the mission carried satellites from the US, Canada and Germany.

Reusable Launch Vehicle, 2016

In May, ISRO successfully tested the Reusable Launch Vehicle–Technology Demonstrator (RLV-TD) built at ₹ 95 crore. The vehicle was seen as the future of low cost and on-demand space access.

Mangalyan, 2014

India joined an elite global club when it successfully launched the Mars Orbiter Mission. The project collected data on Mar's atmosphere and mineral composition.

Chandrayaan, 2008

India's first unmanned lunar probe was a landmark event. ISRO joined a list of just six space organisations to send an orbiter to the moon.

Polar Satellite Launch Vehicle, 1993

Developed in the 1990s, it has become the Indian space mission's most reliable workhorse.

Indian National Satellite system, 1983

Better known as INSAT the system is a network of satellites that facilitates communication across the south Asian region.

Aryabhatta, 1975

It was India's first satellite and was completely designed in the country.

India has launched satellites for Austria, Canada, Denmark, France, Germany, Indonesia, Singapore, UK, USA, Algeria.

Who are the biggies in this business?

US, EU and Russia account for 80% of global space market.

What's the market worth?

Roughly $300 billion

What's the business outlook?

The demand now is for launching smaller satellites. Between 2014 and 2023, 200 such satellites are supposed to lift off.

NOW, INDIA HAS THE 7TH LARGEST SATELLITE FLEET

The launch of the latest satellite in the INSAT series on September 8, 2016 has once again put India cryogenic rocket technology in focus. India has the seventh largest constellation of satellites, the newest being the 42nd in the fleet. The US leads the world with about 600 satellites. The majority of these satellites are operated for commercial purpose and are located in low-earth orbit.

There are 1,420 satellites in space at the moment...

Country	Sole Operator	Jointly Operated	Total
US	561	28	589
China	180	1	181
Russia	136	5	141
Multinational	67	NA	67
Japan	57	7	64
UK	41	2	43
India	38	3	41
European Space Agency	33	3	36
Canada	28	4	32
Germany	24	3	27

DEMOGRAPHICS

CENSUS 2011—AT A GLANCE

Welcome Slowdown: Population Growth Declines

For the first time since Independence, India added fewer people to its population in the decade 2001–11 than in the previous one. While decadal population growth rates have consistently been declining since the 1960s, the absolute addition in each decade was always higher than in the previous decade. That has now changed.

According to Census 2001–2011, India's population has grown at 17.64 per cent as against 21.5 per cent in the previous decade. The country's population at present is 1.21 billion, an increase of 181.9 million since 2001.

What is even more comforting for the country's planners is the fact that female growth rate has been better than male growth rate. The male population is 623.7 million; and female population is 587.4 million as per *India 2014*.

A significant drop in the population growth of India's most backward states is driving the sharpest ever decline in the country's population growth rates. For the last 30 years, India's eight most backward states—Uttar Pradesh, Uttarakhand, Bihar, Jharkhand, Madhya Pradesh, Chhattisgarh, Rajasthan and Odisha—have grown at a constant rate, increasing their populations by a fourth percentage every ten years.

For the first time, growth rates have sharply dropped by over 4% in these states. In fact, population growth has dropped faster in these eight states than in better off states. This has contributed to an all-India population growth rate of less than 18% over the last ten years.

While there has been a 3.8 per cent drop in the overall growth rate, there is still scope for improvement as 14 States and Union Territories have registered over 20 per cent growth in population figures. Among the major states, Bihar has recorded the highest decadal growth in population (25.07 per cent) surpassing West Bengal, that had held the first position in 1991–2001.

More than two-thirds of the country's population lives in rural areas. As per Census 2011, 83.4 million people live in rural areas, while 377 million people live in urban centres. Delhi has highest proportion of urban population at 97.5 per cent.

RURAL AND URBAN POPULATION: 1901–2011				
Census Year	Population (Million)		Percentage of total population	
	Rural	Urban	Rural	Urban
1901	213	26	89.20	10.80
1911	226	26	89.70	10.30
1921	223	28	88.80	11.20
1931	246	33	88.00	12.00
1941	275	44	86.10	13.90
1951	299	62	82.70	17.30
1961	360	79	82.00	18.00
1971	439	109	80.10	19.90
1981	524	159	76.70	23.30
1991	629	218	74.30	25.70
2001	743	286	72.20	27.80
2011	834	377	68.85	31.15

Notes: 1. The population figures of India and Manipur Figures includes estimated figures of the three sub-divisions, viz., Mao Maram, Paomata and Purul of Senapati district of Manipur for Census of 2001 and 2011 due to administrative reasons.

2. The 1991 Census could not be held owing to disturbed conditions prevailing in Jammu and Kashmir. Hence, the population figures for 1991 of Jammu and Kashmir have been worked out by interpolation.

3. The 1981 Census could not be held in Asom. The figures for 1981 for Asom have been worked out by interpolation.

LITERACY RATE IN INDIA: 1951–2011				
Census Year	Persons	Males	Females	Male-Female gap in literacy rate
1951	18.33	21.16	8.86	12.30
1961	28.03	40.04	15.35	24.69
1971	34.45	45.96	21.97	23.99
1981	43.57	56.38	29.76	26.62
1991	52.21	64.13	39.29	24.84
2001	64.83	75.26	53.67	21.59
2011	74.04	82.14	65.46	16.68

Notes: 1. Literacy rates for 1951, 1961 and 1971 Censuses relates to population aged five years and above. The rates for the 1981, 1991, 2001 and 2011 Census relates to the population aged seven years and above.

2. The 1981 literacy rates exclude Asom where the 1981 Census could not be conducted. The 1991 Census Literacy rates exclude Jammu & Kashmir.

SEX RATIO: 1901–2011	
Census Year	**Sex Ratio (Females per 1,000 males)**
1901	972
1911	964
1921	955
1931	950
1941	945
1951	946
1961	941
1971	930
1981	934
1991	927
2001	933
2011	940

Notes: 1. For 1981, interpolated figures for Asom have been used.

2. For 1991, interpolated figures for Jammu and Kashmir have been used.

3. The population figures of India and Manipur, include estimated figures of three sub-divisions, viz., Mao Maram, Paomata and Purul of Senapati district of Manipur state for Census 2001 and 2011 due to administrative reasons.

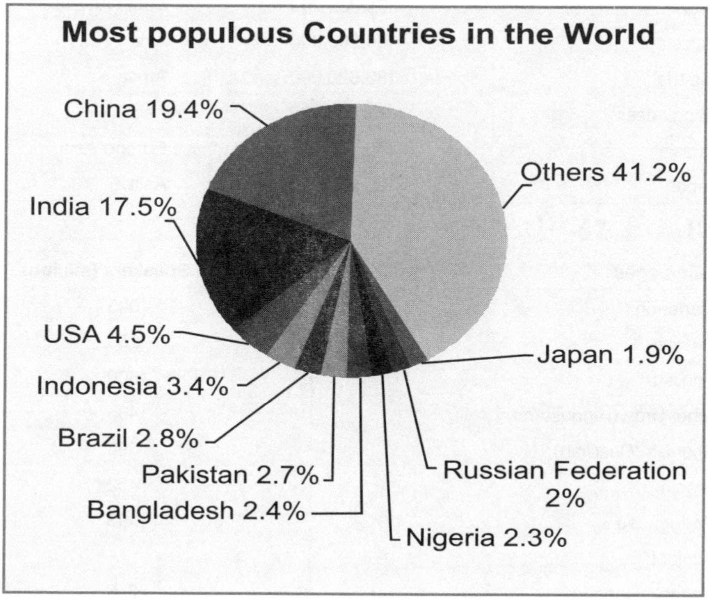

WORLD RANKING : THE BIGGEST STATES—

In Area

State	Area (Sq km)	Location
Russia	17,075,000	Europe-Asia
Canada	9,976,139	North America
China	9,561,000	Asia
USA	9,372,614	North America
Brazil	8,511,965	South America
Australia	7,682,300	South Pacific
India	3,287,263	Asia
Argentina	2,776,654	South America
Kazakhstan	2,717,300	Asia
Algeria	2,381,741	Africa

In Population

State	Population	Location
China	1,368,800,000	Asia
India	1,268,460,000	Asia
USA	320,616,000	North America
Indonesia	255,461,700	Asia
Brazil	204,038,000	South America
Pakistan	189,269,000	Asia
Nigeria	183,523,000	Africa
Bangladesh	158,014,000	Asia
Russia	146,270,033	Europe-Asia
Japan	126,970,000	Asia

WORLD LANGUAGES

Languages	Total Speakers (million)
Mandarin	1025
Russian	250
English	1500
Hindi-Urdu (Hindustani)	405
Spanish (Castilian)	390
Arabic	452
Portuguese	193
Punjabi	–
Bengali (Bangla)	250
Japanese	123

SPORTS WORLD

RIO DE JANEIRO – OLYMPICS –2016

FINAL MEDALS TALLY

	Country	Gold	Silver	Bronze	Total
1.	United States	46	37	38	121
2.	Great Britain	27	23	17	67
3.	China	26	18	26	70
4.	Russia	19	18	19	56
5.	Germany	17	10	15	42
6.	Japan	12	8	21	41
7.	France	10	18	14	42
8.	South Korea	9	3	9	21
9.	Italy	8	12	8	28
10.	Australia	8	11	10	29
67.	**India**	**0**	**1**	**1**	**2**

USAIN BOLT

Jamaican Runner Completes Third Successive Sweep of Sprint Titles—'Greatest' Track & Field Athlete Ever

- Usain Bolt drew down the curtain on his brilliant Olympic career by securing a sweep of the sprint titles for a third successive games when Jamaica successfully defended the 4×100 metres relay crown in Rio.
- Bolt anchored his country to victory in 37.27 seconds, adding the relay crown to the 100 and 200 metres titles he has owned since exploding onto the Olympic stage in Beijing in 2008.
- The Jamaican sprinter has never tasted defeat in Olympic finals, winning nine gold medals over three games and sharing record in athletics with Finnish distance runner Paavo Nurmi and American sprinter and long jumper Carl Lewis.
- The 11-times world champion has become one of the best known sportsmen on the planet and with the 'triple-triple' has a legitimate claim to the title of 'greatest Olympic track and field athlete' ever.

INDIA AT THE RIO DE JANEIRO OLYMPICS-2016

Indian athletes punched below their weight

India did have high hopes from a few events — chiefly, the hope lay in shooting, archery, tennis, wrestling, boxing. However some of our athletics could not perform upto their full potential.

Shooting

Shooting caused the biggest discontent in Indians. India had won medals in shooting in three straight Olympics — a silver in 2004, a gold in 2008, and silver and bronze in 2012. This time around, India placed its hopes in the gun of Jitu Rai, the 10m and 50m pistol specialist.

On the second day of competition, Rai came close in the 10m pistol event — he got to the eight-man final but was the first shooter to be eliminated, finishing eighth. In his favourite event, 50m pistol, Rai's hopes were blown away by the wind at the venue. He ended up twelfth.

Abhinav Bindra, competing in his fifth and final Olympics, missed a medal after a shoot-off with Serhiy Kulish, after the two were tied at 163.8 points after 16 shots in the final. To win bronze, Kulish shot a 10.5, Bindra shot 10 and his hope of a medal ended.

Tennis

Tennis also engendered hope, and the best chance was the mixed-doubles event, in which Rohan Bopanna and Sania Mirza teamed up. The men's team of a Leander Paes and Bopanna had made a first-round exit, but Bopanna and Sania zoomed to the semis. There they met Venus Williams and Rajeev Ram of the US and took the first set comfortably. At least a silver seemed within their reach. Then Venus started firing and India lost through the Super Tie breaker.

Archery

Deepika Kumari didn't win the medal but everyone believed she could win at the Olympics. The ace archer crashed out in the pre-quarterfinals, suffering a big loss to Chinese Taipei's Tan Ya-Ting. Deepika was beaten 28-27 29-26 30-27 by Tan and this, added to her first-round loss at the London Olympics, raised questions about her ability to handle pressure.

Wrestling

There was horrible news from wrestling — Narsingh Pancham Yadav thrown out of the Games Village because of his doping violation, Yogeshwar Dutt was knocked out on the final day.

3 Top Stars

There young women saved India the blushes. Dipa Karmakar's fourth position in vault felt like a medal-winning performance — an Indian in the Olympics gymnastics final was something no one thought possible. But India still seemed in the danger of returning home without a medal. It was then that Sakshi Malik and PV Sindhu rose to the challenge, getting two medals in two days.

PV Sindhu

PV Sindhu's sensational silver winning effort was the best ever show by an Indian shuttler since badminton made it to the Olympics in 1992. Sindhu started in style against Michelle Li in the group stage, losing the first game before winning the next two.

The 21-year-old raised her game from the prequarters. She was at her dominant best against Tai Tzu Ying. In the quarterfinals, Sindhu faced stiff resistance from Wang Yihan but prevailed with a superior display of grit and aggression. In the semifinals against Nozomi Okuhara, the Indian played like a champion. Sindhu, however, faltered in the final.

Sakshi Malik

The 24-year-old grappler won the bronze medal in the 58-kg category, becoming the first Indian female wrestler to win a medal at the Olympics and the fourth female Olympic medallist from the country.

Dipa Karmakar

The first Indian female gymnast to compete in the Olympics and the first Indian gymnast to do so in 52 years, the 23-year-old stood 4th in women's vault gymnastics event and wowed all with her death-defying Produnova vault.

INDIA AT THE LONDON 2012 OLYMPIC GAMES

Sushil Kumar had won silver, making it the best performance by an Indian in Olympic Wrestling. He had won bronze in Beijing, making him the first Indian to win medals in individual events in back-to-back Olympics.

OTHER WINNERS		
Name	**Medals**	**Game**
Vijay Kumar	Silver	25 m rapid fire pistol
Gagan Narang	Bronze	10 m air rifle
Saina Nehwal	Bronze	Badminton singles
MC Mary Kom	Bronze	Boxing, 51 kg
Yogeshwar Dutt	Bronze	Wrestling, 60 kg freestyle

2012 OLYMPICS FINAL TALLY					
S.N.	**Country**	**Gold**	**Silver**	**Bronze**	**Total**
1.	USA	46	29	29	104
2.	China	38	27	22	87
3.	GBR	29	17	19	65
4.	Russia	24	25	33	82
5.	S Korea	13	8	7	28
6.	Germany	11	19	14	44
7.	France	11	11	12	34
8.	Italy	8	9	11	28
9.	Hungary	8	4	5	17
10.	Australia	7	16	12	35
55.	**India**	**0**	**2**	**4**	**6**

INDIAN HEROES IN OLYMPIC GAMES (1928–2008)

The following are some of the memorable achievements:

- The hockey team had won eight gold medals, six in a row from 1928 to 1956 and again in 1964 and 1980.
- The first individual medal won by a sportsman from Independent India at the Olympics was at Helsinki in 1952 when khashaba Jadhov had won the bronze medal in 52 kg freestyle wrestling competition.
- Leander Adrian Paes was the first Indian Tennis Player to win an individual medal at Olympics. He had won bronze in 1996 at Atlanta in Lawn Tennis.
- Karnam Malleshwari became the first Indian woman to win an Olympic medal at Sydney in 2000. She had won the bronze in the women's 69 kg weightlifting event.
- Lt. colonel Rajyavardhan Singh Rathore became the first Olympic silver medallist from India in Athens in 2004. He had won this silver medal in shooting.
- India's performance at the Beijing Olympics (2008) was its best ever performance at any Olympics. Shooter Abhinav Bindra bagged the first individual gold for our country in the 10m air rifle event, while Sushil Kumar and Vijender Singh earned a bronze each in wrestling and boxing. India finished 50th at the Beijing Olympics.

Indian performances at the Olympics would be incomplete without a mention of the efforts of Milkha Singh at Rome in 1960 and PT Usha's run at Los Angeles in 1984, even though they missed the medals by a whisker.

PARAGRAPH WRITING

A paragraph occupies an important position in any literary work and hence has its own importance. A paragraph consists of a series of sentences grouped together and relating to one subject. All the sentences are connected with one another in various ways by unity of purpose. Usually, the main thought is stated in the opening sentence and then amplified in the body of the paragraph.

APPEARANCES ARE DECEPTIVE

Things are not what they appear to be on the surface. We are often misled by the external appearance of a person. An immaculately dressed man with perfect manners does not by any means prove from his sartorial sense and polished behaviour that he is a gentleman. He could very well be a cheat. Therefore, one should not be hasty in forming an opinion about people. It takes sometime to get to know the real person behind the facade put up for the world. A housewife, who got impressed with the innocent looks of a prospective servant, got a surprise after hiring him, when he decamped in broad daylight with the precious things of the house. Hence, it is necessary to use discretion, judgement and patience before arriving at any conclusion about a person. Nobody can be judged in the first meeting. Once you get to know a person, he may turn out to be a totally different person from what you had presumed him to be. There's more to people than what meets the eye.

(150 words)

A HIGHER STANDARD OF LIVING DOES NOT NECESSARILY MEAN A HAPPIER LIFE

A higher standard of living does not by any means guarantee happiness in life. It is a misconception of man that material comforts are a prerequisite to a peaceful and happy life. If it were so, then the very rich should have no reason to complain. Yet one observes that happiness is as elusive to them as to a less fortunate person. It is well known that human wants are never completely satiated. They tend to multiply. Every want that is satisfied gives rise to several others. So man finds himself caught in a vicious cycle, where he is endlessly trying to gratify his needs. This leads to overwork, tension, ill health and sometimes breakdown. So pursuit of sensual pleasures, wealth and luxuries cannot bring happiness. A man who earns barely enough to provide two square meals for his family may lead a more contented life than a rich man who in spite of all his wealth is miserable. Happiness is a state of mind. It is an attitude towards life. A man who is content with his lot is far happier than a man who is forever seeking happiness through worldly comforts. *(155 words)*

A LITTLE LEARNING IS A DANGEROUS THING

It is better to be ignorant and live in bliss than having a little learning and inviting danger to oneself and others. Imperfect knowledge of any subject is undesirable. An individual who has some knowledge about a subject, tends to believe that he has acquired expertise in it. A person, who makes tall claims of being an expert at a subject after acquiring elementary knowledge can certainly be very dangerous. An imperfect mechanic can spoil the machinery beyond repair. Similarly, a man who starts prescribing medicines, after reading a few books, can only cause more harm than good. Life becomes a burden for those miserable hypochondriacs who have a tendency to believe that they have symptoms of some or the other serious disease where there are none. All because, they happened to read an elementary book on human diseases. It is best to seek expert opinion whenever in need, than paying heed to the self-proclaimed experts. They themselves are ill equipped to swim ashore when in trouble. There is every possibility that their little learning may one day prove to be very expensive and dangerous to such people.

(155 words)

AS YOU SOW SO SHALL YOU REAP

Committing sins throughout life, one cannot expect to attain salvation. It is often believed that what one is going to receive at the end is commensurate with what he has done. However, in today's world, when we look around we find that the proverb 'as you sow so shall you reap' is not exactly right. Though sowing and reaping are two sides of the same job, in today's world we will find that each is done by separate group of people. While the rich businessmen and the wheeler dealers of the high society are enjoying the comforts of life without putting in any hardwork, the poor peasants, labourers and industrial workers are trying their best to make their ends meet. Going by the logic of the proverb this should not have been possible. Similarly, all the young men who sacrificed their life for the nation were not rewarded equally. Therefore, it is not necessary that you will be able to reap whatever you have sowed. All of it depends on the circumstances. *(130 words)*

BEAUTY IS NOT SKIN DEEP

Just as a book is not judged by its cover, similarly an attractive face is no guarantee of a beautiful heart. We often get tempted by the external appearance of a person. But gradually with familiarity we soon become aware of the ugly thought harboured by the person in his heart. Man reveals himself through his words and actions. Beauty of face cannot hide the dark, evil and selfish designs of a person. On the other hand, an ordinary, plain looking person is transformed by his inner beauty which is reflected in the glow on his face. It lends a special charm to his face. People feel attracted to such a person and get much comfort in his company. A serene, selfless and balanced approach to life lends a special aura to personality. This inner beauty of the soul is the real beauty, rest is an illusion which is deceptive and treacherous. *(145 words)*

A ROLLING STONE GATHERS NO MOSS

The key to success is to have a definite purpose in life. People who are wavering, irresolute and indecisive never come to much in life. They change their field of study or occupation very frequently. As a result, though they acquire a little knowledge about various fields, they are unable to achieve proficiency in even one field. Besides, a man shifting from trade to trade, is never able to utilize his past knowledge and experience. He always has to start from the lowest rung of the ladder. He never applies himself to anything seriously. It takes time to establish one's credibility in any organization one sets out to work for. If one is important and capricious by nature, then he does not wait to gain people's confidence and establishes one's reputation. One is forever moving on to greener pastures. Consequently, one remains a non-entity and never achieves a steady position in life. *(140 words)*

BAD WORKMEN COMPLAIN OF THEIR TOOLS

Human nature is such that though we are all quick to find fault in others, none is prepared to accept his drawbacks, shortcomings and weaknesses. We are used to finding fault with everyone except ourselves. Students put the blame on the teachers for their poor performance in the examination; teachers hold poor incentives, government apathy and students' attitude responsible for their lackadaisical performance. Nobody is ready to admit that they are also responsible for the system to a certain extent. Thus, it becomes a vicious cycle. A good, conscientious worker tries to make the most of the prevailing conditions. He is more productive than his counterparts who merely sit and find fault in everything. Everyone likes to work under perfect conditions, but if those can't be created then one should learn to adopt and adjust with ease to ensure that the work is not affected. However, people who shirk work are too ready to pick up any reason to strike work. They are bad workmen who become a liability instead of an asset to the organization they work for, simply, due to their difficult attitude and poor performance.

(150 words)

CHARACTER IS DESTINY

Man is the maker of his own destiny. Some people believe fate is pre-determined and they are mere puppets in the hand of fate. Such people never make any effort to improve their lot. They convince themselves that it is God's will that they suffer. But a man of character carves out his own path to attain his objectives in life. His determination, perseverance and moral strength enable him to scale the most difficult obstacles. He follows the dictates of his conscience and remains calm under all circumstances. He never wavers in his mind. His strength of character and moral discipline enables him to realise his dreams. He has tremendous capacity to bear stress, difficulties and setbacks because of his convictions. While others wait for a miracle to transform their lives, he relentlessly goes ahead to pursue his goal to shape his destiny. *(155 words)*

GOD HELPS THOSE WHO HELP THEMSELVES

Man's efforts and endeavours are always rewarded by God with success. It is only men who make sustained effort, have initiative, drive and determination combined with faith in God who attain their goals. Nobody can hope to reach anywhere in life with just faith. Sheer fatalism is a curse to man. A man with a fatalistic attitude to life, leaves everything to the will of God. He does not see much good in stirring or action. Such a man goes through life clinging to his hope of being rewarded by God for his prayers. Gandhiji was a great believer in God, but he was also a man of action. He never lost his faith in God even in the hours of his struggle. Success comes only when genuine effort is combined with faith. God certainly helps those who carry on their journey towards their goal with faith in their hearts and do not shirk hard work or feel dismayed at the initial setbacks. *(150 words)*

HAPPINESS IS A STATE OF MIND

The ultimate aim of human life is happiness. We are all seeking happiness. But it is a most elusive thing. The reason lies in people's wrong values, interests and pursuits. They equate happiness with acquisition of worldly goods. But happiness does not come from outside. It is a state of mind. It comes when a person learns to live in harmony with himself, accepts his weakness and strengths, adapts to his environment and remains calm in the face of difficulties. Thus, comes a state of inner calm and acceptance of the reality of life. This state of inner satisfaction cannot be achieved by winning a lottery or getting a windfall. This is why, sometimes even the most wealthy people are unhappy, whereas a poor worker who gets his wages in the evening after the day long hard work, may be able to snatch moments of happiness out of temporary relief from day to day anxieties. He may remain cheerful and enjoy the small things he can buy with his wages. *(155 words)*

QUOTABLE QUOTES

Faith is the voice in the back of your head that tells you to listen to the voice in the back of your head.

—Dennis Miller

A bone to the dog is not charity, charity is the bone shared with the dog, when you are as hungry as the dog.

—Jack London

A pessimist sees difficulty in an opportunity and on optimist sees opportunity in a difficulty.

—Anonymous

When the going gets tough, the tough gets going.

—Anonymous

Do not follow where the path may lead. Go instead where there is no path and leave a trail.

—Ralph Waldo Emerson

Everyone has weaknesses and faults. No one is perfect. Courage lies in overcoming your weaknesses.

—Anonymous

A bend in the road does not mean the end of the road.

—Anonymous

Our greatest glory is not in never falling, but in rising every time we fall.

—Confucius

Prosperity doth best discover vice, but adversity doth best discover virtue.

—Francis Bacon

One who is not wise himself cannot be well advised.

—Niccolo Machiavelli

Ah, but a man's reach should exceed his grasp. Or what's heaven for?

—Robert Browning

A journey of a thousand leagues begins with a single step.

—Chinese Proverb

If a man will begin with certainties, he shall end up in doubts, but if he will be content to begin with doubts, he shall end in certainties.

—Francis Bacon

Civilisation begins with order, grows with liberty and dies with chaos.

—Will Durant

The force that rules the world is conduct, whether it be moral or immoral.

—Nicholas Murray

Knowledge without conscience, is but the ruin of the soul.

—Francois Rabelais

What lies behind us and what lies before us are tiny matters compared to what lies within us.

—Anonymous

Courage stands halfway between cowardice and rashness, one of which is a lack, the other an excess, of courage.

—Plutarch

Success is not final, failure is not fatal: it is the courage to continue that counts.

—Winston Churchill

Curiosity is one of the most permanent and certain characteristics of a vigorous intellect.

—Samuel Johnson

It's always darkest just before the day dawneth.

—Thomas Fuller

A consistent man believes in destiny, a capricious man in chance.

—Benjamin Disraeli

It's choice—not chance—that determines your destiny.

—Jean Nidetch

To believe with certainty we must begin with doubting.

—Stanislaus

Reading maketh a full man, conference a ready man, and writing an exact man.

—Francis Bacon

Nothing great was ever achieved without enthusiasm.

—Ralph Waldo Emerson

Excellence is never granted to man but as the reward of labour.

—Sir John Reynolds

A moment's insight is sometimes worth a life's experience.

—Oliver Wendell Holmes

A man may fall many times, but he won't be a failure until he says that someone pushed him.

—Elmer G Letterman

'Tis better to have fought and lost.
Than never to have fought at all.

—Arthur Hugh Clough

A free man is he who does not fear to go to the end of his to thought.

—Leon Blum

When firmness is sufficient, rashness is unnecessary.

—Napoleon Bonaparte

The power of fortune is confessed only by the miserable; for the happy impute all their success to prudence and merit.

—Jonathan Swift

No pessimist ever discovered the secrets of the stars, or sailed to an uncharted land or opened a new heaven to the human spirit.

—Helen Keller

The wise are instructed by reason; ordinary minds, by experience; the stupid, by necessity; and brutes by instinct.

—M.T. Cicero

It is impossible for a man to learn what he thinks he already knows.

—Epictetus

It is only when we forget all our learning that we begin to know.

—H.D. Thoreau

Newspapers are the world's mirrors.

—James Ellis

A good newspaper, I suppose, is a nation talking to itself.

—Arthur Miller

Politicians are the same everywhere. They promise to build bridges even where there are no rivers.

—Nikita Khrushchev

The truths of religion are never so well understood as by those who have lost the power of reasoning.

—Voltaire

Science without religion is lame, religion without science is blind.

—Albert Einstein

Science without conscience is the death of the soul.

—Francois Rabelais

Science and art belong to the whole world, and before them vanish the barriers of nationality.

—J.W. Goethe

Science is the key which unlocks for mankind the storehouses of nature.

—V. Samuel

Success varies according to the strength of the effort expended to attain it — mild, moderate or intense.

—Patanjali

All they that take the sword shall perish with the sword.

—The Bible

Only such persons are fit to undertake the work of teaching as are thoroughly educated and virtuous.

—Swami Dayanand

Television is actually closer to reality than anything in books. The madness of TV is the madness of human life.

—Camille Paglia

Man must not check reason by tradition, but contrariwise, must check tradition by reason.

—Leo Tolstory

War should belong to the tragic past, to history; it should find no place on humanity's agenda for the future.

—John Paul II

Since wars begin in the minds of men, it is in the minds of men that the defences of peace must be constructed.

—Anonymous

If you have great talents, industry will improve them; if you have but moderate abilities, industry will supply their deficiency.

—Joshua Reynolds

Youth is a period of missed opportunities.

—Cyril Connolly